Technology and the Proliferation of Nuclear Weapons

Stockholm International Peace Research Institute

SIPRI is an independent international institute for research into problems of peace and conflict, especially those of arms control and disarmament. It was established in 1966 to commemorate Sweden's 150 years of unbroken peace.

The Institute is financed mainly by the Swedish Parliament. The staff and the Governing Board are international. The Institute also has an Advisory Committee as an international consultative body.

The Governing Board is not responsible for the views expressed in the publications of the Institute.

Stockholm International Peace Research Institute
Frösunda, S-171 53 Solna Sweden
Cable: SIPRI
Telephone: 46 8/655 97 00
Telefax: 46 8/655 97 33
E-mail: sipri@sipri.se
Internet URL: http://www.sipri.se

Technology and the Proliferation of Nuclear Weapons

Richard Kokoski

sipri

OXFORD UNIVERSITY PRESS
1995

Oxford University Press, Walton Street, Oxford OX2 6DP
Oxford New York
Athens Auckland Bangkok Bombay
Calcutta Cape Town Dar es Salaam Delhi
Florence Hong Kong Istanbul Karachi
Kuala Lumpur Madras Madrid Melbourne
Mexico City Nairobi Paris Singapore
Taipei Tokyo Toronto
and associated companies in
Berlin Ibadan

Oxford is a trade mark of Oxford University Press

Published in the United States
by Oxford University Press Inc., New York

British Library Cataloguing in Publication Data
Data available

Library of Congress Cataloging in Publication Data

Kokoski, Richard, 1952–
Technology and the proliferation of nuclear weapons /
Richard Kokoski

"Sipri, Stockholm International Peace Research Institute"
Includes index.
1. Nuclear weapons 2. Nuclear arms control. 3. Nuclear weapons–Iraq
4. Nuclear weapons–Korea (North)
I. Title II. Series
U264.K65 1995 327.1'74—dc20 95–4197
ISBN 0–19–829170–1

Typeset and originated by Stockholm International Peace Research Institute
Printed and bound in Great Britain on acid-free paper by
Biddles Ltd., Guildford and King's Lynn

Contents

Tables and figures

Preface

The decision to extend indefinitely the Treaty on the Non-Proliferation of Nuclear Weapons at the 1995 NPT Review and Extension Conference was an important milestone in the 25-year history of the Treaty and a most positive development for the entire nuclear non-proliferation regime. However, the pace of advancement, and the spread of the technology that can be used for nuclear weapon construction, make it more important than ever that the states parties reaffirm their NPT obligations and that the overall goals of the non-proliferation regime are maintained.

In this book Richard Kokoski describes the key areas in which technological progress has been made as well as the potential for future advances in technology that could enable nations or groups of individuals to produce materials which can be used in nuclear explosive devices. He also examines and assesses the regulatory regimes now in place and recommends areas in which these controls may need to be strengthened in the years ahead. In particular, reference is made to lessons learned from the revelations about the extensive nuclear weapon programme undertaken by Iraq prior to the 1991 Persian Gulf War.

The spread of technology and know-how may make it easier for nations wishing to do so to acquire the wherewithal to produce nuclear weapons, but rapid progress is also being made in other areas which will help keep track of proliferation-related activities. More sophisticated surveillance and reconnaissance platforms and increasingly efficient information-gathering and -processing systems allow data relevant to the spread of nuclear technology to be collated and more accurately assessed. The author describes developments in these areas and reviews the uses and potential future impact of enhanced verification capabilities.

Halting and reversing the spread of nuclear weapons must ultimately rest on politically agreed measures that provide sufficient transparency to assure long-term security. It remains vital, however, to be ever more aware of the dangers posed by the spread of nuclear technology. This vigilance will require increased knowledge of the means that could be employed to develop or obtain such technology and the methods which are and can be used to prevent its use for nuclear weapons, a goal towards which this book is dedicated.

I would like to thank Richard Kokoski for this volume, which reflects his imaginative and innovative approach to research work. My thanks also go to Billie Bielckus, who both edited and illustrated the book.

Adam Daniel Rotfeld
Director of SIPRI
August 1995

Acknowledgements

It is a pleasure to thank Billie Bielckus, without whom this volume could not have been completed. As in our previous collaboration she provided innumerable suggestions and improvements to the text, prepared the many illustrations and helped to make the research involved a pleasurable undertaking.

I am indebted to Ragnhild Ferm, who contributed appendix B on the status of implementation of the NPT, as well as to the SIPRI library staff—Christer Berggren, Nenne Bodell, Gunnie Boman, Olga Hardardóttir, Olle Persson and Sten Wiksten—for their tireless and good-humoured assistance in tracking down much difficult-to-locate source material.

A large part of the research for this book was carried out at the Center for Energy and Environmental Studies, Princeton University. I would like to thank Professor Frank von Hippel for his invitation to spend 1992 as Visiting Fellow at the Center and for the many interesting discussions that we had. I also owe thanks to Ron Cleminson and Alan Crawford of the Arms Control and Disarmament Division, Foreign Affairs and International Trade, Canada; as well as to the former Canadian Institute for International Peace and Security for providing partial funding for the research on which this volume is based.

Allan Krass, Professor of Physics and Science Policy at Hampshire College in Amherst, Mass. and a William C. Foster Fellow at the US Arms Control and Disarmament Agency, and Eric Arnett, Leader of the SIPRI Project on Military Technology and International Security, provided many valuable insights and comments on the manuscript. Further helpful comments on specific chapters were made by David Albright of the Institute for Science and International Security, Washington, DC, and by Maurizio Zifferero, Leader of the UNSC 687 Action Team, and Richard Hooper, Director of the Division of Concepts and Planning, Department of Safeguards, both of the IAEA.

My thanks are also due to many other past and present members of the SIPRI staff, including in particular Cathy Söderquist for her cheerful assistance with the manuscript, and Joan Allison and Marianne Lyons for their efficient secretarial assistance. I would also like to thank SIPRI's receptionist, Ingvor Wallin, whose considerable language skills were a constant asset.

Last but by no means least I would like to thank two SIPRI Directors. It was at the suggestion of the former Director, Dr Walther Stützle, that I undertook to write this book, and I am very grateful for his initial advice and confidence. The constant support and encouragement of the present Director, Dr Adam Daniel Rotfeld, has been invaluable in seeing the project to completion.

Richard Kokoski
SIPRI, 1995

Glossary

Aerodynamic enrichment method	A process of uranium enrichment based on the centrifugal effects of a fast-moving uranium hexafluoride (UF_6) gas in very small curved-wall chambers.
Alpha particle	A charged particle emitted from the nucleus of an atom, having a mass and charge equal in magnitude to a helium nucleus.
Americium (Am)	Transuranic element with atomic number 95. Americium-241, an alpha and gamma emitter, is a decay product of plutonium-241 (^{241}Pu).
Atomic bomb	A bomb whose energy comes from the fission of uranium or plutonium.
Burnup	The percentage of heavy metal atoms fissioned or the thermal energy produced per mass of fuel (usually measured in megawatt days per tonne, MWd/t).
Calutron	(California University Cyclotron*)*. A calutron is an electromagnetic uranium enrichment machine. Calutrons were used in the Manhattan Project to produce highly enriched uranium (HEU) for the Hiroshima bomb and also developed in the Iraqi bomb programme. Alpha machines are the first stage, producing low-enriched uranium (LEU) from natural uranium; beta machines are the second stage, producing HEU from the output of the alpha machines.
CANDU	Canadian deuterium–uranium reactor, the most widely used type of heavy water reactor, fuelled with natural uranium and cooled and moderated by heavy water.
Cascade	A connected series of enrichment machines, material from one being passed to another for further enrichment.
Centrifuge	In the nuclear context, this means a rotating vessel used to enrich uranium. The UF_6 gas molecules containing heavier isotopes of uranium concentrate at the walls of the rotating centrifuge and are drawn off.
Chemical enrichment	A method of uranium isotope separation that depends on the slight tendency of uranium-235 (^{235}U) and uranium-238 (^{238}U) to concentrate in different molecules when uranium compounds are continuously brought into contact. Catalysts are used to speed up the chemical exchange.
Cladding	Cladding is the material that encases the nuclear fuel in a reactor, reducing the risk of radioactive materials leaking from the fuel.

Containment and surveillance	Containment is the use of the physical features of a plant or store to restrict access to it (e.g., by sealing it off) and thus prevent the clandestine movement of nuclear material into or out of it. Surveillance means chiefly the use of instruments to detect any unreported movement of or tampering with safeguarded items.
Coolant	A substance circulated through a nuclear reactor to remove or transfer heat. The most common coolants are carbon dioxide, water and heavy water.
Critical mass	The minimum mass required to sustain a chain reaction. The exact mass varies with many factors, such as the particular isotopes present, their concentration and chemical form, the geometrical arrangement of the material and its density. When fissile materials are compressed by high explosives in implosion-type atomic weapons, the critical mass needed for a nuclear explosion is reduced.
Depleted uranium	Uranium with a smaller percentage of ^{235}U than the 0.7 per cent found in natural uranium. It is a by-product of the uranium enrichment process, during which ^{235}U is culled from one batch of uranium, thereby depleting it, and added to another batch to increase its concentration of ^{235}U.
Deuterium	*See* Heavy water.
Enrichment	The process of increasing the concentration of one isotope of a given element (in the case of uranium, increasing the concentration of ^{235}U).
Enriched uranium	Natural uranium, as found in nature, contains 0.7 per cent of the fissile isotope ^{235}U; the remainder is composed of the fertile (i.e., convertible into plutonium) isotope ^{238}U and traces of other isotopes. By various means (e.g., by passing it in gaseous form through the membranes of a gaseous diffusion plant or rotating it in a gas ultracentrifuge) the proportion of ^{235}U to ^{238}U is increased. When the percentage of ^{235}U reaches 20 per cent, the material is termed 'highly enriched uranium', although the charge of a nuclear explosive is much more highly enriched (90 per cent). HEU was used in the bomb dropped on Hiroshima; that dropped on Nagasaki used plutonium.
EURATOM	The European Atomic Energy Community, established in 1957 by the Treaty of Rome as the nuclear branch of the European Community.
Facilities list	The list of nuclear facilities declared by states parties to the NPT to the IAEA that may be subject to safeguards. In non-nuclear weapon states this includes all nuclear facilities; in nuclear weapon states it includes only facilities designated by the state.

Facility attachment	The detailed plan for applying safeguards at a particular plant. This usually defines the material balance areas, and indicates the strategic points to which the IAEA inspector may have access during inspections and at which safeguards instruments may be installed.
Fast breeder reactor (FBR)	A nuclear reactor that produces more fissile material than it consumes, normally by converting a 'blanket' of fertile ^{238}U into fissile plutonium; in the process it 'burns up' less of its fuel than the plutonium that it 'breeds' in the blanket.
Fast reactor	*See* Neutron.
Feed	Material introduced into a facility at the start of the process, such as uranium hexafluoride (UF_6) in an enrichment plant.
Fertile material	Material composed of atoms which readily absorb neutrons to produce fissionable materials. One such element is ^{238}U, which becomes ^{239}Pu after it absorbs a neutron. Fertile material alone cannot sustain a chain reaction.
Fission	The process by which a neutron strikes a nucleus and splits it into fragments or 'fission products'. During the process of nuclear fission, several neutrons are emitted at high speed and radiation is released.
Fissionable material	Material whose nuclei can be induced to fission by a neutron.
Fissile material	Material composed of atoms which *fission* (such as ^{235}U and ^{239}Pu) when struck either by a slow (thermal) or a fast neutron.
Fuel pin	A single rod of basic chain-reacting material, including both fissile and fertile materials.
Full-scope safeguards (FSS)	Complete IAEA safeguards which apply to all peaceful nuclear activities (i.e., both materials and facilities) of a country. Safeguards may be either *de facto* or *de jure* full-scope safeguards: *de facto* safeguards cover all nuclear activities currently in operation in the non-NPT countries, and *de jure* safeguards guarantee that future facilities, both those imported and those indigenously built, will also be safeguarded. *See also* Safeguards agreement pursuant to the NPT.
Fusion	The formation of a heavier nucleus from two lighter ones (usually hydrogen isotopes), with the attendant release of energy (as in a hydrogen bomb).
Gamma radiation	High-energy electromagnetic radiation emitted from nuclei as a result of nuclear reactions and decay.
Gas-centrifuge process	A method of isotope separation in which heavy gaseous atoms or molecules are separated from light ones by centrifugal force and an induced countercurrent flow in the swirling gas.

Gas-cooled reactor	A nuclear reactor employing a gas (usually carbon dioxide, CO_2) as a coolant, rather than water or liquid metal.
Gaseous diffusion	A method of isotope separation based on the fact that gas atoms or molecules with different masses will diffuse through a porous barrier (or membrane) at different rates. The method is used to separate ^{235}U from ^{238}U. It requires large plants and significant amounts of electric power.
Gas-graphite reactor	A nuclear reactor in which a gas is the coolant and graphite is the moderator.
Graphite	One of the two elemental forms of carbon, used as a moderator in some thermal reactor types.
Heavy water (D_2O)	Water containing significantly more than the natural proportion (1 in 6500) of heavy hydrogen (deuterium) atoms to ordinary hydrogen atoms. (Hydrogen atoms have one proton; deuterium atoms have one proton and one neutron.) Heavy water is used as a moderator in some reactors because it slows down neutrons more effectively and absorbs them less (than light, or normal, water) making it possible to fission natural uranium and sustain a chain reaction.
Heavy water reactor (HWR)	A reactor that uses heavy water as a moderator. Other moderators are ordinary (light) water and graphite. The moderator slows down the neutrons emitted by ^{235}U, plutonium or by the nuclei of other fissioning atoms. This permits the fertile ^{238}U to 'capture' the neutrons and through subsequent decay to be transformed into ^{239}Pu. Heavy water (and also graphite) is a more effective moderator than light water and makes it possible to produce a self-sustaining chain reaction with natural uranium; with light water as a moderator it is necessary to use enriched uranium to produce a chain reaction. *See also* CANDU.
Highly enriched uranium (HEU)	Uranium in which the percentage of ^{235}U nuclei has been increased from the natural level of 0.7 per cent to some level greater than 20 per cent, usually around 90 per cent.
Hot cells	Lead-shielded rooms with remote handling equipment for examining and processing radioactive materials. In particular, hot cells are used for examining spent reactor fuel.
Hydrogen bomb	A nuclear weapon that derives its energy largely from fusion. Also known as a thermonuclear bomb.
IAEA	The International Atomic Energy Agency (headquarters in Vienna). Its Statute, which came into force in July 1957, endows the Agency with the twin purposes of promoting the peaceful uses of atomic energy and ensuring that nuclear activities with which the IAEA is associated are not used to further any military purpose.

Irradiation	Exposure to a radioactive source; usually in the case of materials being placed in an operating nuclear reactor.
Isotopes	Nuclides with the same atomic number but different mass numbers. For example, ^{235}U (atomic number 92, mass number 235) and ^{238}U (atomic number 92, mass number 238) are the principal isotopes occurring in natural uranium. Two isotopes of the same atom are chemically similar and are therefore difficult to separate by ordinary chemical means. Isotopes can have very different nuclear properties, however.
Kilogram	A metric weight equivalent to 2.2 pounds.
Kiloton	The energy of a nuclear explosion that is equivalent to an explosion of 1000 tonnes of trinitrotoluene (TNT).
Laser enrichment	A process of uranium enrichment in which lasers are used to separate uranium isotopes.
Light water	Ordinary water (H_2O), as distinguished from heavy water (D_2O).
Light water reactor (LWR)	The most common type of power and research reactor, moderated and cooled by light water. *See also* Heavy water reactor.
Light water-cooled, graphite-moderated reactor	Russian Chernobyl-type reactor cooled by light water and moderated with graphite.
London Guidelines for Nuclear Transfers	*See* Nuclear Suppliers Group.
Low-enriched uranium (LEU)	Uranium in which the percentage of ^{235}U nuclei has been increased from the natural level of 0.7 per cent up to 20 per cent, usually 3 to 5 per cent. With the increased level of fissile material, low-enriched uranium can sustain a chain reaction when immersed in light water and is used as fuel in light water reactors.
Magnox fuel	Uranium metal fuel clad with magnesium oxide (magnox).
Magnox reactor	Gas-cooled, graphite-moderated reactor built principally in the UK and France.
Man-day	A day during which a single inspector has access to a facility at any time for a total of no more than eight hours (as defined in the NPT Model Safeguards Agreement).
Manhattan Project	The US Army's Manhattan Engineer District or 'Manhattan Project' was formed in September 1942 and developed the first nuclear bombs.
Maraging steel	Special hardened steel used in the fabrication of centrifuge rotors and rocket engines.

Mass number	The number of protons and neutrons in the atomic nucleus. Elements may occur in forms (isotopes) displaying a range of mass numbers—i.e., ^{238}Pu, ^{239}Pu, ^{240}Pu, ^{241}Pu and ^{242}Pu.
Material balance area (MBA)	An area inside or outside a nuclear plant which is constructed or laid out in such a manner that it is possible to measure, count or otherwise determine every transfer of nuclear material into or out of it as well as all nuclear material in it (i.e., its 'physical inventory' of nuclear material). A typical MBA is a store of fresh fuel, the bay in which spent fuel is stored or the core of a reactor.
MWe	Megawatt electric or 1 million (electric) watts. The unit used to indicate the electrical power that a power plant generates.
MWth	Megawatt thermal or 1 million (thermal) watts. The unit used to indicate the total power that a reactor generates.
Megaton (Mt)	Measure of the explosive yield of a nuclear weapon equivalent to 1 million tonnes of TNT.
Metric tonne (t)	1000 kilograms. A metric weight equivalent to 2200 pounds or 1.1 tons.
Mixed-oxide fuel	Nuclear fuel containing both uranium and plutonium. Most fissions in the fuel will be of plutonium nuclei.
Moderator	A component (usually water, heavy water or graphite) of some nuclear reactor types that slows neutrons, thereby increasing their chances of fissioning fertile material.
Missile Technology Control Regime (MTCR)	An informal association of governments, established in 1987, which produced the Guidelines for Sensitive Missile-Relevant Transfers. The goal is to limit the spread of weapons of mass destruction by controlling delivery systems. The regime consists of the Guidelines, revised 1992, and an Equipment and Technology Annex, revised 1993.
National technical means (NTM)	National technical means of verification are those methods making use of various sensing techniques and which are independent of the cooperation of the country being monitored. They range from satellites in a wide variety of earth orbits to submarines used to tap into undersea communications cables. The two broadest categories of NTM are usually referred to as image intelligence (IMINT) and signals intelligence (SIGINT).
Natural uranium	Uranium as found in nature, containing 0.7 per cent of ^{235}U, 99.3 per cent of ^{238}U and a trace of ^{234}U.

Neutron	An uncharged elementary particle, with a mass slightly greater than that of a proton, found in the nucleus of every atom heavier than hydrogen. Nuclear fission is caused when a nucleus is irradiated with neutrons. Fissions may be caused by relatively low energy (thermal) neutrons, or by high energy (fast) neutrons. Fission reactors are therefore classed as either 'fast reactors' or 'thermal reactors'.
NPT	The Treaty on the Non-Proliferation of Nuclear Weapons entered into force on 5 March 1970 and established a regime to prevent the proliferation of nuclear weapons while guaranteeing the peaceful uses of nuclear energy. Under the NPT, non-nuclear weapon states parties undertake to conclude safeguards agreements with the IAEA to prevent the diversion of nuclear energy from peaceful to weapon use. It was decided in 1995 that the Treaty should remain in force indefinitely.
Nuclear energy	The energy liberated by a nuclear reaction (fission or fusion) or by spontaneous radioactivity.
Nuclear fuel	Basic chain-reacting material, including both fissile and fertile materials. Commonly used nuclear fuels are natural uranium and LEU; HEU and plutonium are used in some reactors.
Nuclear fuel cycle	The set of chemical and physical operations needed to prepare nuclear material for use in reactors and to dispose of or recycle the material after its removal from the reactor. Existing fuel cycles begin with uranium as the natural resource and create plutonium as a by-product. Some future fuel cycles may rely on thorium and produce the fissionable isotope ^{233}U.
Nuclear fuel element	A rod, tube, plate or other mechanical shape or form into which nuclear fuel is fabricated for use in a reactor.
Nuclear power plant	Any device that converts nuclear energy into useful power. In a nuclear electric power plant, heat produced by a reactor is used to produce steam to drive a turbine that in turn drives an electricity generator.
Nuclear reactor	A device configured to sustain a controlled nuclear chain reaction when fuelled with fissile material. Reactors are of three general types: power reactors, plutonium production reactors and research reactors.

Nuclear Suppliers Group (NSG)	Also known as the London Club. In 1977 the NSG agreed on the Guidelines for Nuclear Transfers (London Guidelines). In 1978 the NSG member states sent letters to the IAEA promising to abide by the Guidelines. The London Guidelines were revised in 1993. The Warsaw Guidelines for Transfers of Nuclear-Related Dual-Use Equipment, Material and Related Technology were agreed by the NSG in 1992.
Nuclear weapons	A collective term for atomic bombs and hydrogen bombs. Weapons based on a nuclear explosion.
Nucleus	The part of an atom containing protons and neutrons.
Nuclear weapon state (NWS)	Article IX, para. 3 of the NPT defines a NWS as a state 'which has manufactured and exploded a nuclear weapon or other nuclear explosive device prior to 1 January, 1967'.
Pit	The shaped core of a nuclear weapon containing fissile material, a tamper and a reflector.
Plutonium (Pu)	An element which is artificially manufactured (it hardly exists in nature). Although there are other ways of manufacturing plutonium, almost all is produced in nuclear reactors. When the nucleus of an atom of ^{238}U captures an extra neutron (usually emitted by the fissioning of another nucleus in a nuclear chain reaction) it is eventually transformed into ^{239}Pu. ^{240}Pu is produced when ^{239}Pu captures a neutron instead of fissioning under the impact of the neutron. ^{239}Pu is the preferred isotope for making nuclear explosives or weapons; ^{240}Pu complicates the construction of a nuclear explosive because of its high rate of spontaneous fission. Generally speaking, the longer nuclear fuel is irradiated (i.e., the higher the 'burnup') the more ^{240}Pu will be produced.
Plutonium recycle	Use of plutonium as part of the fuel for a nuclear reactor. The plutonium may replace or partly replace ^{235}U and thus 'enrich' the fuel. The commercial alternative to recycling is to use the plutonium in a fast breeder reactor or to store it for later use.
Power reactor	A reactor designed to produce electricity as distinguished from reactors used primarily for research or for producing radiation or fissionable materials.
Primary	The fission explosive detonated first in a thermonuclear warhead containing two or more stages.
Production reactor	A reactor designed primarily for large-scale production of ^{239}Pu by neutron irradiation of ^{238}U.
Proton	A positively charged nuclear particle, one of the two principal components of nuclei, with a mass similar to a neutron.

Radioactivity	The spontaneous disintegration of an unstable atomic nucleus resulting in the emission of sub-atomic particles.
Radioisotope	A radioactive isotope.
Reprocessing	Chemical treatment of spent fuels so as to separate the plutonium and remaining uranium from the unwanted waste products.
Research reactor	A reactor primarily designed to supply neutrons for experimental purposes. It may also be used for training, materials testing and production of radioisotopes.
Safeguards	Technical and inspection measures for verifying that nuclear materials are not being diverted from civil to other uses.
Safeguards agreement pursuant to the NPT	A bilateral agreement between a state and the IAEA for the application of safeguards. Article III of the Non-Proliferation Treaty gives the IAEA the task of applying safeguards on 'all source or special fissionable material in all peaceful nuclear activities within the territory of such State, under its jurisdiction, or carried out under its control anywhere'. NNWS parties to the NPT are to conclude safeguards agreements with the IAEA within 18 months of the initiation of negotiations. NWS parties to the NPT are not obliged to apply IAEA safeguards to their peaceful nuclear activities, although some have voluntarily agreed to place part of their nuclear facilities under IAEA safeguards (UK, USA and France).
Separative work	A measure of the effort required in an enrichment facility to separate uranium of a given ^{235}U content into two fractions, one with a higher and one with a lower percentage of ^{235}U. The unit of separative work is the kilogram separative work unit (kg SWU), or SWU for short. The initial material is called the 'feed'. The fraction with a higher proportion of ^{235}U is called the 'product', the other is called the 'tails'.
Significant quantity (SQ)	The approximate amount of nuclear material (not just fissile material) which the IAEA considers a state would need to manufacture its first nuclear explosive. Eight kilograms of plutonium are considered significant and 25 kg of weapon-grade uranium are significant.
Spent fuel	Fuel removed from a reactor after use. It is usually removed when it contains too little fissile and fertile material and too high a proportion of fission by-products to sustain economical operation of the reactor.

START I Treaty	The 1991 Treaty on the Reduction and Limitation of Strategic Offensive Arms reduces US and Russian offensive strategic nuclear weapons to equal aggregate levels over a seven-year period. It sets numerical limits on deployed strategic nuclear delivery vehicles—ICBMs, SLBMs and heavy bombers—and the nuclear warheads they carry. In the 1992 Protocol to Facilitate the Implementation of the START Treaty (the Lisbon Protocol), Belarus, Kazakhstan and Ukraine pledge to accede to the START I Treaty, to eliminate all strategic weapons on their territories within the seven-year reduction period and to join the NPT as NNWS in the shortest possible time. In separate formal letters addressed to the US President, the leaders of Belarus, Kazakhstan and Ukraine pledge to 'guarantee' the elimination of all nuclear weapons located on their territories. The three states had all joined the NPT before the START I Treaty entered into force on 5 Dec. 1994.
START II Treaty	The 1993 Treaty on Further Reduction and Limitation of Strategic Offensive Arms requires the USA and Russia to eliminate their MIRVed ICBMs and sharply reduce their strategic nuclear warheads to no more than 3000–3500 each (of which no more than 1750 may be deployed on SLBMs) by 1 Jan. 2003 or no later than 31 Dec. 2000 if the USA and Russia reach a formal agreement committing the USA to help finance the elimination of strategic nuclear weapons in Russia. The Treaty was not in force by 1 Apr. 1995.
Tails	The waste stream of an enrichment facility that contains depleted uranium. It is expressed as a percentage of the ^{235}U content and called 'tails assay'.
Thermal reactor	*See* Neutron.
Thermonuclear bomb	*See* Hydrogen bomb.
Thorium (Th)	A radioactive element with atomic number 90. Naturally occurring thorium consists only of the fertile isotope ^{232}Th which through transmutation becomes the fissionable ^{233}U which is of safeguards relevance.
Trigger list	A list of the materials (besides source and fissile material), plant components and equipment the export of which to a NNWS requires the application of safeguards on the plant in which it is used or on the material which it uses, processes, etc. This list is only relevant to exports to non-NPT NNWS since in these countries virtually all nuclear material is required to be safeguarded. The original Trigger List was agreed by the Zangger Committee in 1974 and in its revised form it is part of the Guidelines for Nuclear Transfers. *See also* Nuclear Suppliers Group.

Tritium — The heaviest hydrogen isotope, containing one proton and two neutrons in the nucleus, produced typically by bombarding lithium-6 with neutrons. In a fission weapon, tritium is used with deuterium in a fusion process known as 'boosting' to produce excess neutrons, which set off additional fissions in the core. In this way, tritium can either reduce the amount of fissile material required, or multiply (i.e., boost) the weapon's destructive power many times. In fusion reactions, tritium and deuterium unite at very high temperatures, releasing a neutron with 14 million electron-volts of energy.

Uranium (U) — A radioactive element with the atomic number 92 and, as found in natural ores, an average atomic weight of 238. The two principal natural isotopes are ^{235}U (0.7 per cent of natural uranium), which is fissionable, and ^{238}U (99.3 per cent of natural uranium), which is fertile.

Uranium-233 (^{233}U) — A fissionable isotope bred in fertile thorium-232. Like ^{239}Pu it is theoretically an excellent material for nuclear weapons, but is not known to have been used for this purpose except in research programmes. Can be used as reactor fuel.

Uranium-235 (^{235}U) — The only naturally occurring fissionable isotope. Natural uranium contains 0.7 per cent ^{235}U; light water reactors use about 3 to 5 per cent and weapon-grade uranium usually has more than 90 per cent ^{235}U.

Uranium-238 (^{238}U) — A fertile material. Natural uranium is composed of approximately 99.3 per cent ^{238}U.

Uranium dioxide (UO_2) — Purified uranium. The form of natural uranium used in heavy water reactors. Also the form of uranium used to fabricate enriched uranium fuel elements.

Uranium enrichment plant — An installation for increasing the abundance of ^{235}U in uranium, through isotope separation processes such as gaseous diffusion, gas centrifuge, gas nozzle, chemical diffusion or laser excitation.

Uranium oxide (U_3O_8) — The most common oxide of uranium found in typical ores. U_3O_8 is extracted from the ore during the milling process. The ore typically contains only 0.1 per cent U_3O_8; yellowcake, the product of the milling process, contains about 80 per cent U_3O_8.

Uranium hexafluoride (UF_6) — A volatile compound of uranium and fluorine, UF_6 is a solid at atmospheric pressure and room temperature, but can be transformed into gas by heating. UF_6 gas (alone, or in combination with hydrogen or helium) is the feed in most uranium enrichment processes and is sometimes produced as an intermediate product in the process of purifying yellowcake to produce uranium oxide.

Urenco	The Uranium Enrichment Company, created in 1970 by the signing of the Treaty of Almelo by the FRG, the UK and the Netherlands.
Warsaw Guidelines	*See* Nuclear Suppliers Group.
Weapon-grade material	Nuclear material of the type most suitable for nuclear weapons, i.e., uranium enriched to over 90 per cent ^{235}U or plutonium that is primarily ^{239}Pu.
Yellowcake	*See* uranium oxide
Yield	The total energy released in a nuclear explosion. It is usually expressed in equivalent tons of TNT (the quantity of TNT required to produce a corresponding amount of energy).
Zirconium	A greyish-white lustrous metal which is commonly used in an alloy form (i.e., zircalloy) to encase fuel rods in nuclear reactors.

Sources: Albright, D., Berkhout, F. and Walker, W., SIPRI, *World Inventory of Plutonium and Highly Enriched Uranium, 1992* (Oxford University Press: Oxford, 1993); Cochran, T. B., Arkin, W. M., Norris, R. S. and Hoenig, M. M., NRDC, *Nuclear Weapons Databook, Vol. II, U.S. Nuclear Warhead Production* (Ballinger: Cambridge, Mass., 1987); Fischer, D. and Szasz, P., ed. J. Goldblat, SIPRI, *Safeguarding the Atom: A Critical Appraisal* (Taylor & Francis: London, 1985); Müller, H. and Kokoski, R., *The Non-Proliferation Treaty: Political and Technological Prospects and Dangers in 1990*, SIPRI Research Report no. 2, SIPRI, Stockholm, 1990; and SIPRI, *SIPRI Yearbook 1995: Armaments, Disarmament and International Security* (Oxford University Press: Oxford, 1995).

Acronyms and conventions

ABACC	Argentine–Brazilian Agency for Accounting and Control of Nuclear Materials
ABM	Anti-ballistic missile
AEC	Atomic Energy Commission (USA)
AEC	Atomic Energy Corporation (South Africa)
AECL	Atomic Energy Canada Ltd
AGR	Advanced gas-cooled reactor
ALOS	Advanced Land Observation Satellite
ASEAN	Association of South-East Asian Nations
AVLIS	Atomic Vapor Laser Isotope Separation
BDA	Battle damage assessment
BMVC	Baghdad Monitoring and Verification Center
BNFL	British Nuclear Fuels plc
BWR	Boiling water reactor
CALIOPE	Chemical Analysis by Laser Interrogation of Proliferation Effluents
CANDU	Canadian deuterium–uranium reactor
CC&D	Camouflage, concealment and deception
CD	Conference on Disarmament
CEA	Commissariat à l'Energie Atomique (France)
CFE	Conventional Armed Forces in Europe
CIA	Central Intelligence Agency (USA)
CIS	Commonwealth of Independent States
CNC	Computer numerical controlled
COCOM	Co-ordinating Committee on Multilateral Export Controls
COMINT	Communications intelligence
CRIEPI	Central Research Institute of the Electrical Power Industry (Japan)
CRISLA	Chemical Reaction by Isotope Selective Laser Activation
CTA	Aerospace Technology Center (Brazil)
CTB	Comprehensive test ban
CWC	Chemical Weapons Convention
DARO	Defense Airborne Reconnaissance Office (USA)
DOE	Department of Energy (USA)
DPRK	Democratic People's Republic of Korea
EC	European Community
ECU	European Currency Unit
EMIS	Electromagnetic isotope separation
ERFFL	Experimental Reactor Fuel Fabrication Laboratory (Iraq)
ERS	Earth Remote Sensing Satellite
ESA	European Space Agency
EU	European Union
EURATOM	European Atomic Energy Community

FSS	Full-scope safeguards
FSU	Former Soviet Union
FY	Fiscal year
GAO	General Accounting Office (USA)
GCFR	Gas-cooled fast breeder reactor
GCHQ	Government Communications Headquarters (UK)
HEU	Highly enriched uranium
HLW	High-level radioactive waste
HTGR	High temperature gas-cooled reactor
HWR	Heavy water reactor
IAEA	International Atomic Energy Agency
IAEC	Iraq Atomic Energy Commission
ICBM	Intercontinental ballistic missile
INF	Intermediate-range nuclear forces
INFCE	International Fuel Cycle Evaluation
INFCIRC	Information Circular
IPCR	Institute of Physical & Chemical Research (Japan)
IPEN	Institute for Energy and Nuclear Research (Brazil)
IRI	Industrial Research Institute (Japan)
IT	Isotopes Technologies
JAERI	Japan Atomic Energy Research Institute
JAPCO	Japan Atomic Power Company
JERS	Japan Earth Resources Satellite
JNAI	Jersey Nuclear-Avco Isotopes
JNFI	Japan Nuclear Fuel Industries Company
JSTARS	Joint Surveillance Target Attack System
LASER-J	Laser Atomic Separation Engineering Research Association of Japan
LEU	Low-enriched uranium
Lidar	Laser imaging detection and ranging
LLNL	Lawrence Livermore National Laboratory (USA)
LMFBR	Liquid metal fast breeder reactor
LWR	Light water reactor
MASINT	Measurements and signals intelligence
MBA	Material balance area
MIRV	Multiple independently targetable re-entry vehicle
MLIS	Molecular Laser Isotope Separation
MOX	Mixed-oxide (uranium and plutonium)
MTCR	Missile Technology Control Regime
MUF	Material unaccounted for
NAS	National Academy of Sciences (USA)
NIM	National intelligence measures
NMD	National Monitoring Directorate (Iraq)
NNWS	Non-nuclear weapon state
NPA	New Partnership Approach (EURATOM–IAEA)
NPC	Non-Proliferation Center (USA)
NPT	Treaty on the Non-Proliferation of Nuclear Weapons
NRC	Nuclear Regulatory Commission (USA)

NRDC	Natural Resources Defense Council (USA)
NRO	National Reconnaissance Office (USA)
NSA	National Security Agency (USA)
NSG	Nuclear Suppliers Group
NTM	National technical means
NWS	Nuclear weapon state
OMV	Ongoing monitoring and verification plan
OSCE	Organization for Security and Co-operation in Europe
OSCINT	Open source intelligence
OSI	On-site inspection
OTA	Office of Technology Assessment (USA)
PHW	Pressurized heavy water (reactor)
Purex	Plutonium–uranium extraction
PWR	Pressurized water reactor
R&D	Research and development
SAGSI	Standing Advisory Group on Safeguards Implementation
SAR	Synthetic-aperture radar
SEHEE	State Establishment for Heavy Engineering Equipment (Iraq)
SGHWR	Steam-generating heavy water reactor
SIGINT	Signals intelligence
SILVA	Séparation Isotopique par Laser de la Vapeur Atomique d'uranium
SIR	Safeguards implementation report
SIS	Special Isotope Separation
SLBM	Submarine-launched ballistic missile
SLCM	Submarine-launched cruise missile
SNF	Short-range nuclear forces
SOSUS	Sound-surveillance system
SQ	Significant quantity
SSACs	State Systems of Accounting and Control
START	Strategic Arms Reductions Treaties
SWU	Separative work unit
TAISIR	Temperature and Imaging System Infrared
TBP	Tributyl phosphate
UAV	Unmanned aerial vehicle
UCOR	Uranium Enrichment Corporation (South Africa)
UGS	Unattended ground sensor
UKAEA	United Kingdom Atomic Energy Authority
UN	United Nations
UNSCOM	United Nations Special Commission on Iraq
Urenco	Uranium Enrichment Company (UK, Germany, Netherlands)
USEC	US Enrichment Corporation
WEU	Western European Union

Conventions

kg	kilogram
kV	kilovolt
kW	kilowatt
kWh	kilowatt-hour
μg	microgram
μm	micrometre (micron)
m	metre
mA	milliampere
MW	megawatt
MWe	megawatt-electric
MWth	megawatt-thermal
MWd/t	megawatt days of energy per tonne of fuel
s	second
SWU	separative work unit
t	tonne
. .	data not available or not applicable

1. Introduction

I. Overview

A secure long-term halt to and reversal of the proliferation of nuclear weapons will require political solutions to long-held security concerns as well as the institution of transparency measures which are recognized as sufficient to maintain stability. With agreement in May 1995 to extend the 1968 Treaty on the Non-Proliferation of Nuclear Weapons (the NPT) indefinitely, the 179 states parties to the Treaty[1] took an important step by establishing a permanent base from which lasting solutions to the problem of nuclear non-proliferation can hope to be established.

As the Commonwealth of Independent States (CIS) and the USA finally begin the long process of reducing their nuclear weapon capabilities, there is renewed hope that they will achieve the necessary cooperation with the other nuclear powers to halt the horizontal spread of nuclear weapons as well. This can be achieved first and foremost by attacking the root causes of insecurity and instability, which are the prime factors underlying nuclear ambitions. However, since the NPT entered into force technological change and advancement have been rapid. The impact this has and will have on the overall effectiveness of the Treaty calls for particularly thorough assessment, not only of the NPT but also of the entire nuclear non-proliferation regime. Therefore, while difficult political questions are being addressed more concrete measures which may be more readily identified and acted upon include widening the scope of nuclear safeguards and strengthening the enforcement of export controls on nuclear materials.

Disposing of the plutonium from retired weapons and securing and safeguarding fissile materials and nuclear weapons, especially in the former Soviet Union, represent difficult and costly problems that are only now beginning to receive the attention they deserve. As the scope of the Iraqi nuclear programme uncovered after the 1991 Persian Gulf War has demonstrated, however, many aspects of the spread of nuclear technology, both through external acquisitions and through development of indigenous capabilities, are not sufficiently well understood. This book sets out to shed some light on these and other problems connected with the technology involved in nuclear weapon development as well as to point towards near- and longer-term solutions.

[1] Although Taiwan is not recognized as a state by the United Nations, it ratified the NPT in 1970 and is therefore included by SIPRI in the number of states parties to the Treaty. For a report on the status of implementation of the Treaty as of 15 Apr. 1995, see appendix B.

II. The proliferation of technology

Revelations in the wake of the Persian Gulf War about the technological capabilities of Iraq have made amply clear that it is necessary to be aware of all of the potential methods by which a nuclear weapon option may be pursued. Every possible effort should be taken to avoid another 'surprise' such as that experienced by the international community at the extent of the development of the Iraqi nuclear weapon programme. The revelations have spurred and will continue to influence political decisions to ensure the application of controls on the key technologies that have been identified as important for nuclear weapon development. They might also spur fresh attempts to identify new specific control measures or information-gathering capabilities which may prove useful and necessary to prevent such occurrences in the future.

In order to implement such measures effectively and to optimal advantage, it is of course important that the technologies involved in nuclear weapon development be well understood. A knowledge of the infrastructure and equipment required for the operation of the various technologies is essential in order to assess the capabilities of an individual country. For example, acquisition of specialized equipment such as a calutron, or components thereof, may signal an incipient nuclear weapon programme. Clearly the technologies that can be used for the production of nuclear weapons are here to stay, and a serious approach to limiting nuclear proliferation should be built upon a firm technological knowledge base.

It may be argued that there is a danger in discussing some details of the technology involved in nuclear weapon production and that it is desirable to keep as tight a lid on all of this information as possible. However, as has been succinctly noted elsewhere, 'the only thing more dangerous than discussing this subject is not discussing it'.[2] In addition, it should be stressed that only open materials related to these technologies have been used in the discussions contained in this volume.

It is also important to realize that, although new technologies such as laser isotope separation may be part of the *problem* in connection with the proliferation of nuclear weapons, as is demonstrated in chapter 7 on verification, new technological developments in other areas, such as those enhancing capabilities to monitor proliferation activity, will constitute a rather large part of the *solution,* as newer and more effective means of acquiring and processing relevant information become available.

While this book concentrates on nuclear technology and political issues directly related to this technology it must be borne in mind that often a decision by a state to pursue the development of nuclear weapons, or for that matter its success in the endeavour, will depend predominantly on non-technical considerations. Such factors will vary considerably from one country to another,

[2] Lovins, A. B., 'Nuclear weapons and power-reactor plutonium', *Nature*, vol. 283 (28 Feb. 1980), p. 818.

and will depend upon the capabilities of organization and management associated with the complex, long-term commitment of scientific and technological expertise and infrastructure, the ability to keep the operations covert, the type and extent of foreign trade and business contacts, hard currency supply, as well as the costs, both domestic and international, of the effort being uncovered at some stage.[3] While an analysis of these factors on a country-by-country basis is beyond the scope of this book, such considerations are assessed especially in discussions of nuclear programmes in countries of particular proliferation concern, such as Iraq and North Korea.

III. Causes for optimism and reasons for concern

Shortly after the dawn of the nuclear age there was widespread pessimism that substantial numbers of countries would proceed to develop nuclear weapons in a relatively short period of time. Even 50 years after the first atomic explosion, however, the number of states which have acquired a nuclear weapon capability remains relatively small. In the mid-1990s, with the accession of all of the declared nuclear weapon states (NWS) to the NPT[4] and the new impetus to pursue potential Treaty violators—in no small part a result of the revelations about the programme to develop nuclear weapons in Iraq—there is reason for continued hope that the number of states with such a capability can be kept low. In fact, with the dismantling of the South African nuclear arsenal and with the successfully negotiated freeze on the North Korean nuclear weapon programme in its early stages, there is considerable reason for optimism.

None the less, vigilance will be necessary to ensure that events such as those in Iraq and North Korea are not allowed to be repeated. Many seasoned observers, including some in the US intelligence community, for example, are concerned that the spread of nuclear (as well as chemical and biological) weapons will in fact be more likely now that the cold war has ended.[5] Nuclear ambitions, perhaps now less influenced by the kind of pressure formerly exerted by the superpowers, may be pursued with new fervour. Pent-up ethnic and other unsettled grievances may cause many countries to seek to acquire these much more lethal elements for their arsenals. The self-restraint shown by many client states that was one of the hallmarks of the era of superpower confrontation may not prevail to the same extent in many countries with respect to their interest in acquiring nuclear weapons.

In addition, the nuclear non-proliferation regime does not exist in isolation, and one of the most pressing reasons to ensure its effective continuance is that it is apparent to most observers that its effectiveness will to a large extent deter-

[3] Office of Technology Assessment (OTA), *Proliferation of Weapons of Mass Destruction: Assessing the Risks*, OTA-ISC-599 (US Government Printing Office: Washington, DC, Aug. 1993), pp. 119–21.

[4] Article IX, para. 3 of the NPT defines a nuclear weapon state as one 'which has manufactured and exploded a nuclear weapon or other nuclear explosive device prior to 1 Jan. 1967'. The text of the Treaty on the Non-Proliferation of Nuclear Weapons is reproduced in appendix A.

[5] Smith, J. R., 'Spread of atomic arms more likely now, U.S. fears', *International Herald Tribune*, 4 Oct. 1993, p. 1.

mine that of the other major arms control regimes, including those that seek to control the proliferation of chemical and biological weapons and missiles.[6]

With an increasing number of countries possessing the technological capabilities for nuclear weapon production the technical barrier at least to the acquisition of nuclear weapons has steadily eroded. For many countries the decision to acquire them is therefore entirely political. As barriers to the acquisition and development of nuclear-related technologies continue to fall it becomes steadily more necessary to ensure that the political and legal commitments to non-proliferation are reinforced and upheld.[7] In this context, and as the events in Iraq and North Korea have shown, it is crucial that sufficient *information* on nuclear weapon development be acquired to confirm that non-proliferation obligations are being adhered to and to enable the detection of any nascent nuclear weapon programme as early in its development as possible. As much of this information as feasible should be made available—through the International Atomic Energy Agency (IAEA), for example—to provide the increased transparency necessary for the success of the non-proliferation regime.

IV. The aims and scope of this book

This book highlights the prominent technological developments which may be endangering the nuclear non-proliferation regime—especially in the light of developments in the early 1990s regarding the nuclear programmes in Iraq and North Korea and of events surrounding the breakup of the former Soviet Union.

It focuses on three main elements: an explication of the crucial technologies of relevance to the proliferation of nuclear weapons; a description of the potential ramifications of the existence, spread and further development of these technologies for the non-proliferation regime as a whole; and an analysis of potential policy options which could ameliorate or perhaps eliminate the dangers resulting from the spread of these technologies. In addition the technological capabilities associated with various modes of relevant information collection, including intelligence capabilities, and the possibilities of dissemination of appropriate information to help prevent proliferation are discussed.

The primary focus on technology follows from the belief that it is crucial in a discussion of issues concerned with non-proliferation and the NPT that the technology involved be well understood. An exploration of current technological developments is of course most meaningful and useful when discussed in the setting of current political developments and problems. This philosophy forms the basic approach.

[6] Davis, Z. S., 'Nonproliferation regimes: policies to control the spread of nuclear, chemical, and biological weapons and missiles', CRS Report for Congress, 93-237 ENR, Library of Congress, Congressional Research Service, Washington, DC, 18 Feb. 1993, p. 7.

[7] Fischer, D., *Stopping the Spread of Nuclear Weapons: The Past and the Prospects* (Routledge: London, 1992), pp. 18, 26.

From the technological point of view this book outlines the essential processes by which fissile materials can be produced for nuclear weapons. This is not only because of the paucity of open information on other aspects of nuclear weapons—publication of which would in any case serve no clear purpose—but also because it is generally recognized that acquisition of fissile materials in sufficient quantities is the most formidable barrier to nuclear weapon production.[8]

The critical technologies

Chapters 2 and 3 detail the major physical and technological processes of relevance to the production of fissile material for nuclear weapons. The most important uranium enrichment technologies from a proliferation standpoint, including electromagnetic isotope separation and centrifuge, aerodynamic and laser processes, are explained in chapter 2 in sufficient detail to enable an appreciation of their potential and to permit an informed evaluation by the reader of the subsequent discussion. Gaseous diffusion, the most widely used method, is also described at some length in order to introduce some of the fundamental concepts of enrichment.

In chapter 3, at about the same level of detail, plutonium production and extraction processes are discussed with specific reference to different types of reactor (commercial, research and military), their modes of operation and their efficiency in plutonium production.

Different ways of addressing the issue of the current surplus of plutonium, from civil power programmes as well as from military programmes, are examined as well as proposals to formalize the cessation of the production of plutonium and highly enriched uranium for weapon purposes. In the context of the NPT this would aid in providing assurance that obligations set out in Article VI of the Treaty, to strive for early disarmament, were being met.

The Iraqi case study

After the Persian Gulf War it was learned that Iraq had been pursuing a wide range of options for the production of fissile material, including electromagnetic isotope separation and centrifuge enrichment technology as well as plutonium separation. Against the background of the details of these and other processes described in the preceding chapters, the scope and the stage of development of these technologies by Iraq is analysed in chapter 4 with a view to assessing the implications for proliferation in other states.

Recommendations for specific measures to strengthen the nuclear non-proliferation regime, and thereby reduce the likelihood of further developments

[8] See, e.g., Miller, M. and Rathjens, G., 'Advanced technologies and nuclear proliferation', ed. R. H. Bruce, *Nuclear Proliferation: South Asia and the Middle East,* Monograph no. 2, Indian Ocean Centre for Peace Studies, Curtin University of Technology, University of Western Australia and University of Notre Dame (Australia), 1992, p. 107.

of the kind that occurred in Iraq, require a thorough understanding of the findings in that country. To facilitate such an understanding a detailed outline of the events and findings of the inspections carried out by the IAEA under UN Security Council Resolution 687 is presented. This illustrates the range of information that can be acquired through such an inspection effort as well as the methods that might be used by the inspected country to attempt to keep various pieces of information from the inspectors. While these inspections were carried out as part of a special mandate, the scope of which is unlikely to be repeated in the near future, it is none the less instructive to analyse the procedures and results as they may still provide valuable input for the implementation of special inspections of undeclared facilities that may be needed in the future.

Safeguards and export controls

The purpose, scope and objectives of existing safeguards are reviewed in chapter 5. While this book does not set out to provide a comprehensive description of nuclear safeguards, it highlights those elements that have shown themselves to be especially important or currently in a state of flux and discusses the changes that are currently under way. The unexpected discovery of a large nuclear weapon programme in Iraq led both to the submission of new proposals and the reaffirmation of long-standing proposals to strengthen nuclear safeguards and aid in the verification of nuclear non-proliferation in general.

While the positive implications for the nuclear non-proliferation regime of many of these proposals is beyond question, current political and fiscal realities may necessitate delay in the implementation of some and the abandonment of others, at least for the near future. It is thus essential to set and pursue goals that will be both attainable and most productive. The ways in which the short-notice 'special inspections', in some ways similar to those that have been carried out in Iraq, could be of use in other countries and situations are explored in particular.

It has often been expressed that export controls can have the potential to slow the progress of a country determined to develop a nuclear weapon capability, and this delay may provide sufficient time for security issues to be adequately addressed, for a change of leadership to occur, for a negotiated end to the programme to be reached or for the decision to be reversed for some other reason. There is, however, the ever-present danger that the rapid development of new technology and equipment that can be used in nuclear weapon construction can outpace the export controls in place. Until recently this was especially true of many currently available dual-use technologies. On the basis of the examination of the status of technologies of relevance to nuclear weapon construction and of the directions of current developments, recent improvements to the international export control regimes are discussed in chapter 6 with the aim of assessing areas in which further improvements may still be possible.

The potential for exports not only of nuclear equipment and materials but also of nuclear weapons themselves, as well as of scientists and engineers with knowledge relevant to the construction of nuclear weapons, has become an important issue since the demise of the Soviet Union. The various approaches being used to address this issue are also explored.

Information sharing, verification and intelligence

Valuable information of relevance to the proliferation of nuclear weapons and related technology is being collected and analysed by organizations ranging from national intelligence agencies, some with billion dollar budgets, to the media and other interested groups. In fact, its acquisition has become a major new priority for many of them. As developments in the Persian Gulf and North Korea have shown, such intelligence can be a valuable asset in monitoring activity related to nuclear proliferation. The resulting increased awareness has led to nations demonstrating their increased willingness to share such intelligence and expert assistance in order to stem the increasing danger of the spread of nuclear equipment and know-how.

Special inspections of undeclared facilities, which may prove necessary for sufficient confidence in the nuclear non-proliferation regime, depend to a large extent on the availability of such information. The various means and methods by which this type of information is being collected are discussed, along with a consideration of the impact they may have on the overall understanding of nuclear proliferation. The discussion in chapter 7 also covers the nuclear weapon programme in North Korea, including the means used to gather vital data on the programme as well as an assessment of their utility and potential for use in similar situations which may be encountered in the future.

2. Uranium enrichment technologies

I. Introduction

A 1971 US Atomic Energy Commission (AEC) advisory committee evaluated the potential of over 25 processes for enriching uranium.[1] The most important of these technologies, ranging from those in widespread use today—such as gaseous diffusion and the gas centrifuge—to those which may prove important for the near- or longer-term future—such as laser methods—are examined below with special emphasis on processes which may pose particular dangers for nuclear weapon proliferation. As the development of enrichment technology has shown, and as is described in this chapter, no one method of uranium enrichment can be said to be superior to all others. The method chosen has been and will continue to be based on the particular needs and circumstances of the state or corporation involved and on the enrichment level required.

This chapter does not set out to provide a complete coverage of all the various methods of enriching uranium. That has been done in considerable detail and with great thoroughness and competence elsewhere.[2] However, an assessment of technological capabilities requires an understanding of the various technologies available, so these are emphasized here to bring the current situation into focus and enable the reader better to assess the possible impact of future technological developments as they may occur.

Included below are somewhat detailed accounts of the two main forms of enrichment technology in existence today—gaseous diffusion and the gas centrifuge. Electromagnetic Isotope Separation (EMIS) is also presented in some detail as the emphasis on this method in the Iraqi nuclear programme raised concern. The newer methods of laser enrichment do not pose a substantial real threat at the present time but, because they may well have considerable implications for non-proliferation efforts in the near future, they are discussed in particular detail. For many methods of enrichment which, although useful in certain contexts, are not considered particularly dangerous in the proliferation context, only brief outlines are given or reference is made to more specialized works.

The two most prevalent methods for uranium enrichment employed worldwide are gaseous diffusion and the gas-centrifuge process, representing roughly

[1] Spindel, W., 'Isotope separation processes', ed. P. A. Rock, *Isotopes and Chemical Principles* (American Chemical Society: Washington, DC, 1975), p. 77.

[2] See in particular Krass, A. S. *et al.*, SIPRI, *Uranium Enrichment and Nuclear Weapon Proliferation* (Taylor & Francis: London, 1983), which also examines the link with nuclear non-proliferation issues. Other good overviews of the more technical aspects are contained in Villani, S. (ed.), *Topics in Applied Physics, Vol. 35, Uranium Enrichment* (Springer-Verlag: West Berlin, 1979); and Villani, S., *Isotope Separation* (American Nuclear Society: La Grange Park, Ill., 1976).

90 per cent and 10 per cent of the world enrichment market, respectively.[3] Recent assessment identifies low- to medium-level gas-centrifuge enrichment technology as a method that could become attractive to some countries for a number of reasons.[4] These include the open availability of information on the earlier centrifuge designs, relative ease of concealment, efficiency for producing highly enriched uranium (HEU) as well as the potential of equipment becoming available from the former Soviet Union. More sophisticated designs offer the advantage of even smaller, more efficient facilities.

The transfer of enrichment technology has not occurred on the same scale as the transfer of reprocessing technology. Official cooperation has been limited to the Urenco (the British, German, Netherlands Uranium Enrichment Company) gas-centrifuge project and to the German–Brazilian agreement of 1976 involving the sale of eight reactors. Assistance to South Africa was provided by FR Germany in the development of its stationary-walled centrifuge. In some cases centrifuge technology has been stolen, for example by Pakistan from the Netherlands.[5]

The status of research and development (R&D) of the newer techniques receives special attention here, as does the electromagnetic method employed by Iraq in its attempt to acquire nuclear weapon capability. For a number of reasons, including the large power requirements, and until Iraq demonstrated that a sizeable clandestine effort could probably be successful, the electromagnetic method was not previously considered to be a major concern as far as large-scale production of HEU was concerned.

Although there is no known facility producing substantial amounts of enriched uranium using laser techniques, proliferation concerns have been raised about the use of these techniques for HEU production since the processes themselves were understood in the early 1970s. One of the major concerns in the context of laser and other technologically advanced methods has been that the nature of these technologies could allow for smaller and more readily concealed enrichment facilities than other methods. Also, while the USA has not produced enriched uranium for weapon purposes since 1964,[6] and the former USSR announced in April 1989 that it had also halted its production,[7] the potentially small size of laser facilities, for example, for HEU production, is an important factor in assessing the verifiability of fissile material production cut-off proposals.

[3] Erkens, J. W., 'CRISLA aims to reduce costs', *Nuclear Engineering International*, vol. 34, no. 419 (June 1989), p. 48.

[4] Office of Technology Assessment (OTA), *Technologies Underlying Weapons of Mass Destruction*, OTA-BP-ISC-115 (US Government Printing Office: Washington, DC, Dec. 1993), p. 6.

[5] Fischer, D., *Stopping the Spread of Nuclear Weapons: The Past and the Prospects* (Routledge: London, 1992), p. 52. See also p. 98, where the author states that, in the case of Pakistan, 'At least Dr. Qadir Khan can claim that his motives in purloining industrial secrets were patriotic, not commercial or treasonable. . . . The main blame must fall on on those Western businessmen who, solely for profit, broke the law of their country.'

[6] *Energy and Water Development Appropriations for 1989*, Hearings before a Subcommittee of the Committee on Appropriations, House of Representatives, 100th Congress, 2nd Session (US Government Printing Office: Washington, DC, 1988), pp. 1034–35.

[7] *Arms Control Today*, vol. 19, no. 4 (May 1989), p. 25.

Table 1. Overview of the principal enrichment technologies, 1992

Technology	Status[a]	Countries involved[b]
Gaseous diffusion	Major industrial use	USA, Russia, UK, France, China, Argentina
Gas centrifuge	Major industrial use	Russia, UK, France, Germany, Holland, Japan, Pakistan, Brazil, Iraq, India, China
Separation nozzle	Large pilot plant built	Brazil
UCOR process	Commercial-size plant	South Africa
Chemical (CHEMEX process)	Pilot plant built	France
Chemical exchange (ASAHI process)	Pilot plant operating	Japan
Atomic Vapor Laser Isotope Separation (AVLIS)	Engineering development research only	USA, France, UK, Japan, Israel, Brazil
Molecular Laser Isotope Separation (MLIS)	Development	Japan, Germany, South Africa
Plasma separation (PSP)	Development	France

[a] This column on the status of the technology refers only to the largest programmes.

[b] Russia and China have R&D programmes in various enrichment technologies that are not listed in this table.

Source: Albright, D., Berkhout, F. and Walker, W., SIPRI, *World Inventory of Plutonium and Highly Enriched Uranium, 1992* (Oxford University Press: Oxford, 1993), excerpt from table A.1, p. 220.

Despite the current overcapacity for uranium enrichment,[8] the spread of laser enrichment technology in particular has proceeded rapidly in the past 15 years or so, with many countries—including many not party to the NPT—investing substantial amounts of time and effort in research and development. These developments may be hastened as nuclear power is re-examined in the light of growing evidence that other power sources have contributed to the greenhouse effect. New and supposedly safer reactors[9] may use uranium more highly enriched than that prevalent today, heightening proliferation concerns. Laser processes, now forecast to be capable of more economical uranium enrichment, could become the focus of much greater attention should such trends materialize.

[8] Clark, R. G. and Addington-Lee, F., 'Overcapacity leaves buyers in the driving seat', *Nuclear Engineering International,* vol. 34, no. 419 (June 1989), p. 42.

[9] Broad, W. H., 'Now, a meltdown-proof reactor', *International Herald Tribune*, 17 Nov. 1988.

While noting that the advanced technology necessary for the laser method makes it unlikely that it would enter significantly into the nuclear programme of a developing country for at least another decade, it is important that attempts to constrain such development be made as early as possible. It has also been recognized that the recent advances in ion-exchange and solvent-extraction enrichment techniques, particularly the published results of research in Japan and France, contribute to making these approaches 'a more serious proliferation concern than they had previously been thought', although important aspects remain proprietary at the present time.[10]

The choice of enrichment technology depends on the relative importance of several aspects of the processes concerned. These technical and economic factors are of course weighted differently when a decision is made on which method to use. Depending on whether a relatively small amount of HEU is desired for a few nuclear weapons or large amounts of inexpensively produced fuel are needed for a light water reactor (LWR), very dissimilar approaches may be chosen, for example. In order to understand clearly how such trade-offs are made and gain insight into the level of scientific expertise necessary for the various methods from a proliferation perspective, a basic knowledge of the technical characteristics of the various processes is required.[11] An overview of the enrichment programmes and technology known to be employed in 1992 is given in table 1.

II. The process of uranium enrichment

Natural uranium (containing only 0.7 per cent of the isotope uranium-235, ^{235}U, with ^{238}U making up the rest) can be used in heavy water and graphite reactors, but uranium must be enriched to 2–4 per cent ^{235}U to fuel the more prevalent light water reactors. Uranium must be enriched to more than 90 per cent ^{235}U for weapon purposes and to about 93–97 per cent for many nuclear-powered submarines and research reactors. (However, the former USSR revealed that its naval reactors used uranium enriched to only 10 per cent ^{235}U.[12]) In all the techniques described below for enriching uranium the process involves the separation of the input or 'feed' stream of material into two streams: a 'product' stream in which the ^{235}U is enriched and a 'tails' stream in which the ^{235}U is depleted.[13]

[10] OTA (note 4), pp. 126, 146, 149.

[11] As noted above a very thorough examination of uranium enrichment techniques can be found in Krass *et al.* (note 2).

[12] *Nuclear Fuel*, vol. 14, no. 15 (24 July 1989), p. 12.

[13] See, e.g., *Advanced Uranium Enrichment Technologies*, Hearing before the Subcommittee on Energy Research and Production of the Committee on Science and Technology, US House of Representatives, 96th Congress, 1st Session (US Government Printing Office: Washington, DC, 22 Sep. 1979), p. 86.

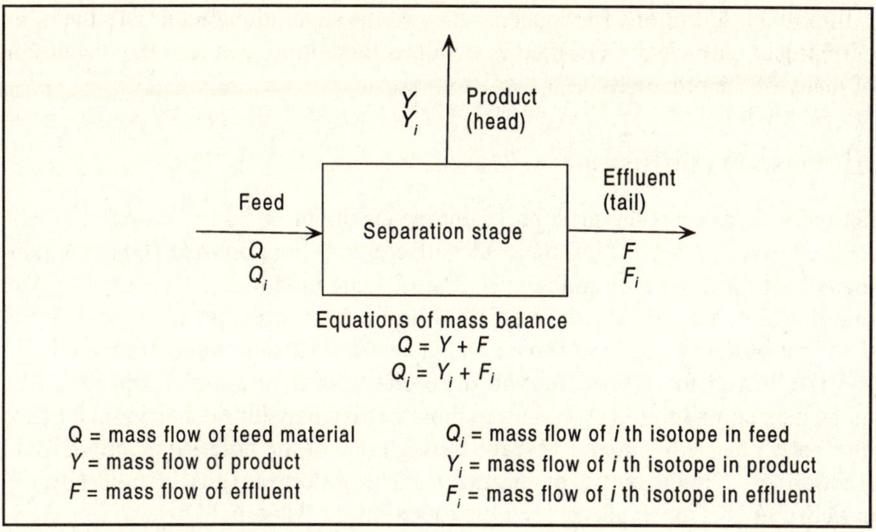

Figure 1. An isotope enrichment stage

Source: Based on Grossman, M. W. and Shepp, T. A., 'Plasma isotope separation methods', *IEEE Transactions on Plasma Science*, vol. 19, no. 6 (Dec. 1991), p. 1115.

This simple arrangement is illustrated in figure 1, where the box can be taken to represent an individual separation element or group of such elements arranged in parallel. Each enrichment method can be characterized by a single-stage elementary separation factor.[14] This separation factor can be defined for a simple two-component mixture of ^{235}U and ^{238}U (other isotopes are generally present in much smaller quantities and can be ignored for present purposes) as the percentage of ^{235}U in the product stream divided by the percentage of ^{235}U in the tails stream.

By definition, therefore, a separation factor of unity, corresponding to the same proportion of ^{235}U in the product and tails streams, indicates that no enrichment has occurred. A value slightly above unity indicates that a small amount of enrichment has occurred; as the separation factor increases further this implies that still higher enrichment is occurring. However, as discussed below, the processes that are used on a large scale at the present time all have enrichment factors of only slightly more than one, and so a given procedure must be repeated many times in order to reach the required enrichment values. Exceptions to this include the EMIS method and laser methods described in sections IV and VII, in which significant enrichments are possible with a single element.

[14] Massignon, D., 'Gaseous diffusion', ed. Villani, *Uranium Enrichment* (note 2), p. 58. See also, e.g., Rahn, F. J. *et al.*, *A Guide to Nuclear Power Technology: A Resource for Decision Making* (John Wiley: New York, 1984), p. 186; and Benedict, M., Pigford, T. H and Levi, H. W., *Nuclear Chemical Engineering*, 2nd edn (McGraw-Hill: New York, 1981), p. 648.

Important definitions for concepts such as the separation factor and that of an enrichment cascade are clarified in detail as they are relevant to the discussion of many of the processes.

III. Gaseous diffusion

Gaseous diffusion is the most prevalent means of enriching uranium today. The method involves separating molecules of uranium hexafluoride (UF_6) containing ^{235}U from those containing ^{238}U. The diffusion method is based on the fact that the lighter molecules in a gas will move with a greater average velocity than that of the heavier molecules. In a gaseous diffusion unit compressed UF_6 gas is allowed to diffuse through a porous barrier, the higher speed of the molecules containing ^{235}U leading to more collisions with the barrier and hence more of a chance for them to escape through one of the holes (typically a small fraction of a micrometre in diameter). The emerging gas is thus slightly enriched in UF_6 molecules containing the desired ^{235}U atom.

History and theory

Perhaps best known for being part of the Manhattan Project during World War II, the process involved—*molecular effusion*[15]—was first demonstrated in 1846 by Graham.[16] Molecular effusion refers to the passage of individual molecules essentially one-by-one through very small holes. In the resultant *molecular flow* the molecules transit the holes without colliding with other molecules. This situation should be contrasted with gas flowing as a continuous fluid in which such collisions occur very frequently.[17]

In 1920 Aston used a porous clay tube to enrich neon in the isotope ^{22}Ne. Complete separation of hydrogen and deuterium and almost complete separation of the ^{22}Ne and ^{20}Ne isotopes was accomplished in the early 1930s by Hertz, using 24–50 *stages* (defined below). The desire for the ^{235}U isotope during World War II led to a great deal of work on gaseous diffusion for uranium separation in England and the USA. The first enrichment plant was operated at Oak Ridge, Tennessee in 1945. The thousands of square metres of barrier to be used in the final plant were based on the type used in the early experiments, which was only a few square centimetres in area, however. Plants were later constructed at Paducah and Portsmouth in the USA and Capenhurst in the UK in 1950–56. The process was developed independently by France and its first plant was constructed at Pierrelatte in 1964–67.[18] Countries currently using this technology are listed in table 1.

[15] While strictly speaking the process involved is called molecular effusion, the processes based on it are referred to as gaseous diffusion. Glasstone, S. and Sesonske, A., *Nuclear Reactor Engineering*, 3rd edn (Van Nostrand Reinhold: New York, 1981), p. 483.

[16] London, H. (ed.), *Separation of Isotopes* (George Newnes: London, 1961), p. 332.

[17] Benedict *et al.* (note 14), pp. 818, 822.

[18] Tait, J. H., 'Uranium enrichment', ed. W. Marshall, *Nuclear Power Technology, Vol. 2: Fuel Cycle* (Clarendon Press: Oxford, 1983), p. 115; Benedict *et al.* (note 14), pp. 818–19; and Groves, L. R., *Now it can be Told: The Story of the Manhattan Project* (Harper & Row: New York, 1962), p. 113.

The manner in which separation of isotopes results from molecular flow can be seen as a straightforward result of the principle of equipartition of energy in statistical mechanics,[19] which states that in a gas consisting of several types of molecule each type will have the same average kinetic energy. Since the kinetic energy of a molecule of mass *m* with velocity *v* is equal to 1/2 mv^2 it is possible to equate the average kinetic energy of a UF_6 molecule containing ^{235}U with one containing ^{238}U:

$$\tfrac{1}{2}m_{(^{235}UF_6)}v^2_{(^{235}UF_6)} = \tfrac{1}{2}m_{(^{238}UF_6)}v^2_{(^{238}UF_6)}$$

Therefore, the ^{235}U molecules will on average move more quickly by the ratio:

$$\frac{v_{(^{235}UF_6)}}{v_{(^{238}UF_6)}} = \sqrt{\frac{m_{(^{238}UF_6)}}{m_{(^{235}UF_6)}}}$$

Their greater speed means that the lighter molecules (containing the ^{235}U atoms) will strike the sides of a container more often relative to their concentration and will, therefore, also more often enter the holes of a porous barrier if this is present. This increased relative frequency of entry into small holes defines the ideal separation factor alpha (α) for gaseous diffusion, which is equal to the velocity ratio given above:

$$\alpha = \frac{v_{(^{235}UF_6)}}{v_{(^{238}UF_6)}} = \sqrt{\frac{m_{(^{238}UF_6)}}{m_{(^{235}UF_6)}}}$$

$$= 1.00429$$

This ideal calculation gives a value for the separation factor which is larger than that which can be obtained in practical operation for several reasons.[20] First, since the pressure on the product side of the barrier is not zero there will always be some back-flow of already enriched product taking place, which will tend to offset the separation. Also, depending on the detailed barrier structure, there will be some flow which is of the continuous fluid type mentioned above, which does not provide any isotope separation at all. In addition, the concentration of $^{235}UF_6$ on the feed side of the barrier will decrease as more of these molecules diffuse through the barrier relative to the $^{238}UF_6$.[21] More realistic values of the separation factor for the gaseous diffusion process are probably around 1.003.[22]

[19] See, e.g., Kittel, C., *Thermal Physics* (John Wiley: New York, 1969), p. 165.

[20] Benedict *et al.* (note 14), p. 825.

[21] Krass *et al.* (note 2), p. 122.

[22] Cochran, R. G., and Tsoulfanidis, N., *The Nuclear Fuel Cycle: Analysis and Management* (American Nuclear Society: La Grange Park, Ill., 1990), p. 59; and Glasstone and Sesonske (note 15), p. 486.

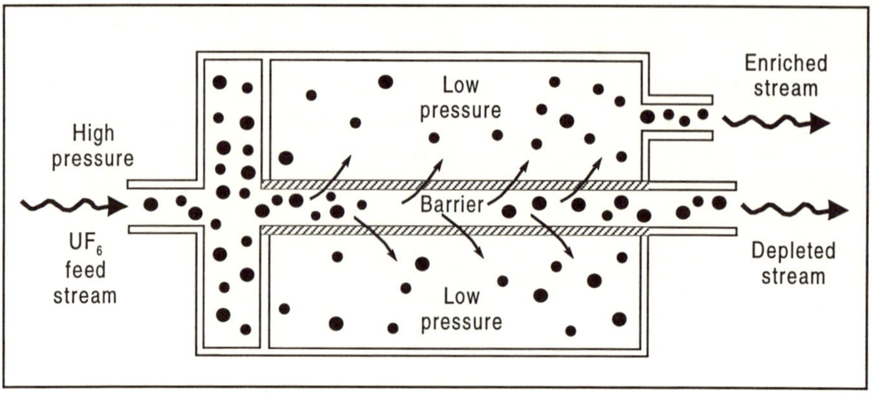

Figure 2. Simplified diagram of a diffusion stage

Source: Redrawn with permission from Glasstone, S. and Sesonske, A., *Nuclear Reactor Engineering*, 3rd edn (Van Nostrand Reinhold: New York, 1981), p. 485. © Van Nostrand Reinhold (1981).

Diffusion barriers

The qualities necessary for a suitable barrier are often in conflict with one another. Barriers should have small holes and yet high porosity, be as thin as possible and yet strong enough to hold up against large pressure gradients and have low chemical reactivity. Barriers may be of two basic types—the film type, in which holes are bored into a membrane, or the aggregate type, in which fine powders are either agglomerated or sintered.[23] Since performance of the barrier is the key to the diffusion process, much information on specific barrier types remains classified.

The barriers which are actually used are often far removed from those considered in theoretical models and contain crooked and non-circular holes of variable mean radius, from 0.005 to 0.03 micrometres (μm).[24] A French study has provided some information on five types developed by the Commissariat à l'Energie Atomique (CEA), and these are listed in table 2.

Barriers composed of two layers, one which provides the separation efficiency of very small pores and the other which is a strong macroporous layer, can permit higher operating pressures.[25] Molecular flow will occur if the mean free path of the gas in question is much larger than the dimensions of the holes. For UF_6 the mean free path at a pressure of 760 mm mercury (Hg) and at 20°C is 0.02 μm.[26] This illustrates that, in order for molecular flow and hence separation to occur, the holes must indeed be extremely small.

[23] Massignon, D., 'Gaseous diffusion', ed. Villani, *Uranium Enrichment* (note 2), p. 127.
[24] Benedict *et al.* (note 14), p. 823.
[25] Massignon, D., 'Gaseous diffusion', ed. Villani, *Uranium Enrichment* (note 2), p. 92.
[26] London (note 16), p. 339.

Table 2. Characteristics of some French diffusion barriers

Method of preparation	Mean pore radius (μm)
Dissolving silver from gold-silver alloy	0.03
Anodic oxidation of aluminium	0.01
Sintering alumina	0.025
Sintering nickel	0.020
Rolling Teflon powder into nickel gauze	0.015

Source: Frejacques, C. *et al.*, *PICG,* vol. 2, no. 4 (1958), p. 418, cited in Benedict, M., Pigford, T. H and Levi, H. W., *Nuclear Chemical Engineering*, 2nd edn (McGraw-Hill: New York, 1981), table 14.6, p. 830.

Cascade theory and operation

The separation factor of a given process is usually known beforehand and, given a desired enrichment, an appropriate arrangement of separating elements or machines can then be configured to meet the requirements. The small separation factor associated with processes like gaseous diffusion means that the feed must usually pass through several thousand separate elements before it is enriched in ^{235}U to the extent necessary for nuclear weapon production or even for use in a light water reactor. Very large plants are required to produce large quantities of enriched uranium by gaseous diffusion. Quantitative estimates of relevant parameters can be quite readily described as outlined below.

Individual separating elements or units can be operated in parallel in order to separate larger quantities of material and these *stages* are connected in series to produce higher enrichments. This arrangement is called a *cascade* and as is outlined below two very simple equations can be used to describe its basic operation. Figure 3 illustrates an enrichment cascade composed of seven stages—each stage being composed of a single element. This is referred to as a countercurrent cascade since (in contrast to a *simple* cascade in which no recycling takes place[27]) tails from each stage are recycled to a stage below as discussed further below.

The so-called equations of material balance basically state that what goes in must come out (albeit at different isotopic concentrations). The first of these states that the total amount of feed material must equal the amount of product plus the amount of waste or tails:[28]

$$F = P + W$$

where F, P and W are the amount of feed, product and tails in kilograms per unit time. The second equation states that the total amount of ^{235}U is con-

[27] Benedict *et al.* (note 14), p. 651.

[28] See, e.g., Graves, H. W., *Nuclear Fuel Management* (John Wiley: New York, 1979), pp. 30–33; Cochran and Tsoulfanidis (note 22), pp. 61–65; and Benedict *et al.* (note 14), pp. 647–701.

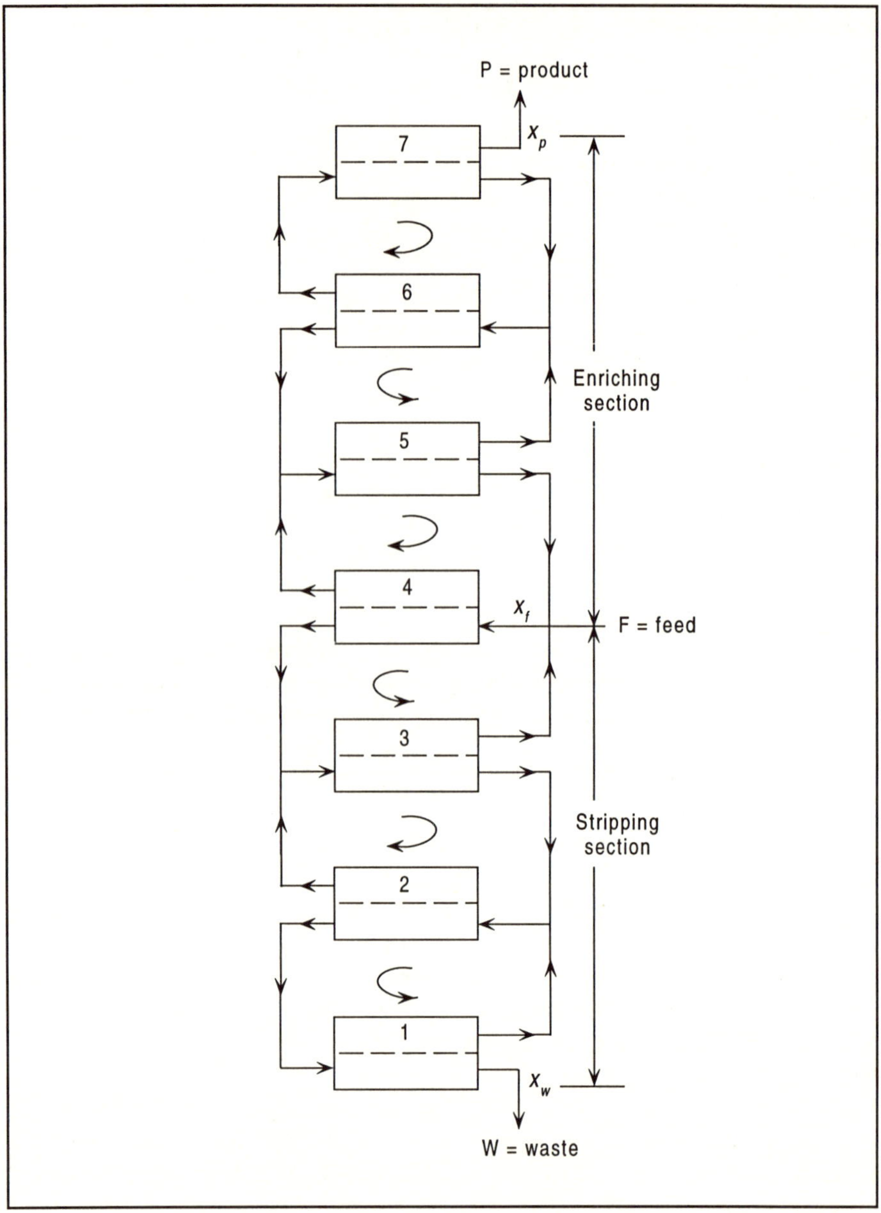

Figure 3. The symmetric countercurrent recycle cascade

Source: Redrawn from Graves, H. W., *Nuclear Fuel Management* (Wiley: New York, 1979), p. 31. © John Wiley & Sons, Inc. Reprinted by permission of John Wiley & Sons, Inc.

served—if x_f, x_p and x_w are the weight fractions (enrichment in ^{235}U) of the feed product and tails respectively—then this is expressed as:

$$x_f F = x_p P + x_w W$$

The variable x_f (the enrichment of the feed) will generally be that of natural uranium, that is, 0.71, and x_p is the desired enrichment level—about 3 per cent for light water reactor fuel or 97 per cent for weapon-grade uranium, for example. The tails enrichment x_w will generally affect the cost of enrichment. In the most common of the countercurrent recycle cascades—the *symmetric* cascade[29]—as figure 3 illustrates, the enriched product from a given stage is used as feed for the next higher stage (so that the enrichment can be increased) while the depleted waste is recycled as feed for the stage below. If, as is common, the enrichment is increased only slightly at each stage, the *cut,* defined as the fraction of the enriched product to the original feed, is very nearly equal to one-half in this case.

For instance, stage 6 in figure 3 further enriches the material which has already been enriched in stages 4 and 5, passing on its enriched product to stage 7 and recycling its waste back to stage 5. The waste from stage 6 is, therefore, seen to be mixed with the enriched product of stage 4. Ideally the ^{235}U concentrations would be the same in these two streams to be mixed—otherwise some of the separation already accomplished would be undone by the mixing. A cascade which has been so arranged that this is the case for all of its stages is the most efficient possible[30]—minimizing the total interstage flow[31] and specific power consumption[32]—and is termed an *ideal cascade*.

Stages above the stage at which the feed is introduced are part of what is referred to as the enriching section, while those below are part of the stripping section. The number of stages in each section is determined by the desired enrichment and tails levels of ^{235}U. In contrast to the simple cascade, the countercurrent cascade includes a stripping section, used to increase the recovery of ^{235}U from the feed.

From the two equations above the feed-to-product ratio can easily be found to be:[33]

$$F/P = \frac{(x_p - x_w)}{(x_f - x_w)}$$

Therefore to produce 1 kg of 3 per cent enriched light water reactor fuel with a nominal 0.3 per cent tails requires

$$F = \frac{(0.03 - 0.003)}{(0.0071 - 0.003)} = 6.6 \text{ kg}$$

[29] Tait (note 18), p. 111.
[30] Olander, D. R., 'The gas centrifuge', *Scientific American*, vol. 239, no. 2 (Aug. 1978), p. 43.
[31] Benedict *et al.* (note 14), pp. 631–32.
[32] Rahn *et al.* (note 14), p. 194.
[33] Benedict *et al.* (note 14), p. 655.

Figure 4. Aerial view of the gaseous diffusion plant at Portsmouth, Ohio
Source: Courtesy of US Department of Energy.

of natural uranium. To produce the same amount of 97 per cent enriched uranium on the other hand requires:

$$F = \frac{(0.97 - 0.003)}{(0.0071 - 0.003)} = 236 \text{ kg}.$$

The number (n) of stages in an ideal cascade can be shown to be:[34]

$$2\left\{ \ln\left[\frac{x_p(1-x_w)}{x_w(1-x_p)} \right] / \ln(\alpha) \right\} - 1$$

which, for the separation factor derived above for gaseous diffusion and for 3 per cent enriched uranium gives 1088 stages. For 90 per cent enriched uranium this becomes 3738 stages.

In fact the gaseous diffusion plant at Portsmouth, Ohio shown in figure 4 has been used to enrich uranium to 97 per cent in ^{235}U making use of a total of 4080

[34] Benedict *et al.* (note 14), p. 660.

stages.[35] It should also be noted that the minimum number of stages required to reach a given enrichment level is almost exactly one-half of the number in an ideal cascade.[36] However, use of this theoretical minimum number requires that the interstage flow rate to product ratio is infinite[37]—in other words that no enriched product is actually drawn off at all.

It is important from a proliferation point of view, however, to understand that, when power consumption is not an important constraint, cascades other than ideal (and with considerably fewer stages) may be operated to produce HEU. Another method by which to achieve higher enrichments with fewer stages is to recycle the product through a cascade more than once.

The amount of material produced at a given enrichment will be dependent on a number of factors. The most often-quoted measure of the effort which must be expended per unit quantity of enriched material is the separative work *S*. It may be applied to individual separation units, stages or an entire cascade to provide an idea of the energy which must be expended. The more enriched the product or the more depleted the tails desired the more the separative work which has to be performed. As has been aptly noted, 'the real product of an isotope-separation plant is separative work, not enriched uranium'.[38] The separative work required to produce an amount *P* of enriched product per unit time at enrichment x_p is given in terms of parameters defined above as:[39]

$$S = P(2x_p - 1)\ln\left[\frac{x_p}{(1-x_p)}\right] + W(2x_w - 1)\ln\left[\frac{x_w}{(1-x_w)}\right] - F(2x_f - 1)\ln\left[\frac{x_f}{(1-x_f)}\right]$$

The units are those of the material flow parameters *P*, *W* and *F*. For this measure of separating capability it is immaterial whether a given amount of separative work is performed by a large plant operating for a relatively short period of time or a small plant operating for a relatively long period of time. Proliferation concerns regarding clandestine plants, however, would probably be focused on the latter.

Using the equation above for *F/P* and an analogous one for *W/P*, the separative work per unit of product withdrawn is:

$$S/P = (2x_p - 1)\ln\left[\frac{x_p}{(1-x_p)}\right] + \left[\frac{(x_p - x_f)}{(x_f - x_w)}\right](2x_w - 1)\ln\left[\frac{x_w}{(1-x_w)}\right]$$
$$- \left[\frac{(x_p - x_w)}{(x_f - x_w)}\right](2x_f - 1)\ln\left[\frac{x_f}{(1-x_f)}\right]$$

[35] Benedict *et al.* (note 14), p. 632.

[36] To be precise the minimum number of stages possible for a given enrichment and tails assay can be obtained by adding one to the number of stages in an ideal cascade and *then* dividing by 2. See, e.g., Benedict *et al.* (note 14), p. 660.

[37] Benedict *et al.* (note 14), p. 657.

[38] Olander (note 30), p. 42.

[39] Benedict *et al.* (note 14), p. 669.

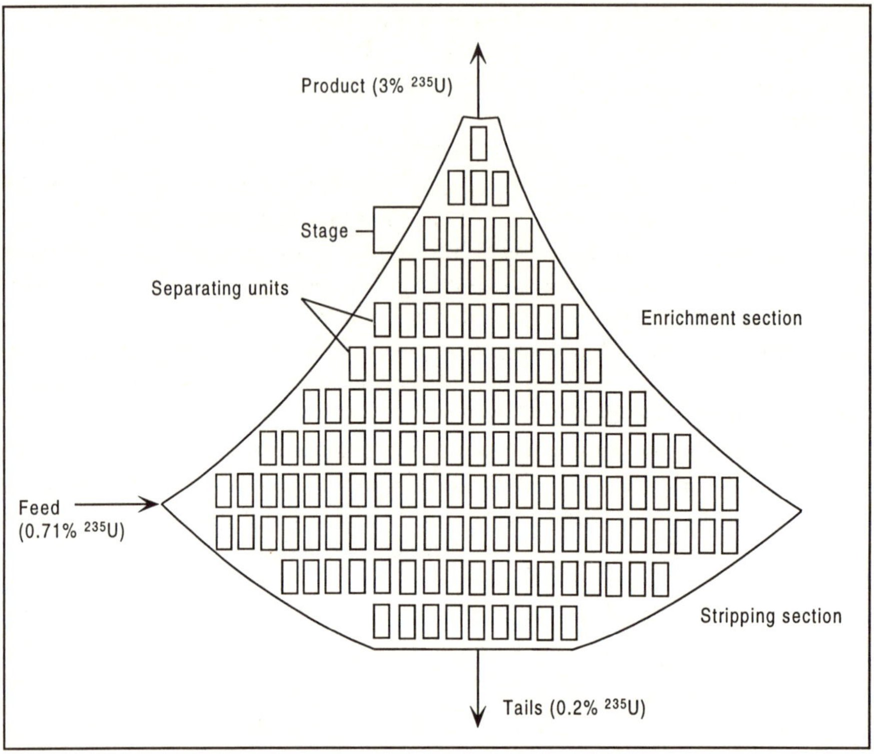

Figure 5. The ideal cascade

Source: Redrawn with permission from Olander, D. R., 'The gas centrifuge', *Scientific American*, vol. 239, no. 2 (Aug. 1978), p. 42. © 1978 by *Scientific American*, Inc. All rights reserved.

The numerical value is expressed in separative work units (SWU) (often quoted as kg SWU since the unit of product is usually expressed in kilograms). For example to produce 1 kg of 90 per cent enriched uranium from natural uranium with a tails assay (concentration of ^{235}U) of 0.3 per cent requires:[40]

$$\begin{aligned}S/P = &(2\times 0.9-1)\ln[0.9/(1-0.9)]\\&+[(0.9-0.0071)/(0.0071-0.003)](2\times 0.003-1)\ln[0.003/(1-0.003)]\\&-[(0.9-0.003)/(0.0071-0.003)](2\times 0.0071-1)\ln[0.0071/(1-0.0071)]\\&=193\ \text{SWU}\end{aligned}$$

[40] It should be noted here that for large enrichments the two isotope formulae become less strictly valid as a result of the increased proportion of ^{234}U in the product (which is enriched along with ^{235}U). For an enrichment of 98% ^{235}U, e.g., it will take about 8% more SWU than the simple two-component formula would indicate. See Cochran, T. B. *et al.*, NRDC, *Nuclear Weapons Databook, Vol. II, U.S. Nuclear Warhead Production* (Ballinger: Cambridge, Mass., 1987), p. 127 (table footnote).

To produce the 10–20 kg of HEU needed for a single atomic weapon[41] would therefore require about 2000–4000 SWU. This result should be borne in mind as different technologies for enriching uranium are discussed below. For example, a single gas centrifuge that Iraq had planned to use in its weapon programme had an estimated capacity of about 2 SWU per year[42]—it would take at least 1000–2000 such centrifuges one year to produce enough material for even a single weapon. Such calculations can provide quick and handy comparisons between different types of separating element once their capacity in SWU is known.

Examination of the material balance at each stage in an ideal cascade shows[43] that the size of the stages decreases away from the point at which the feed material is introduced, which usually means there are fewer elements. This is obvious when one considers that the final flow of product leaving the cascade must be much smaller than the amount being fed in. The *tapered* cascade can be illustrated as in figure 5 which displays the size of each stage in both the stripping and enriching sections as it varies with its place in the cascade.

Another useful quantity is the total interstage flow rate since this gives a good idea of the size and power needs of the plant concerned. In processes in which the separation factor is not much different from unity, the interstage flow is very simply given by:[44]

$$8/(\alpha-1)^2 \times \text{the separative work } S.$$

Taking the parameters from the above example, this means that the number of kilograms of UF_6 which must be pumped in total for every kilogram of 90 per cent enriched uranium produced in a gaseous diffusion plant is given by:

$$8/.00429^2 \times 193 = \text{almost 84 million kg !}$$

It should be emphasized that the total flow is inversely proportional to the difference of the separation factor from unity squared. Therefore, doubling $\alpha-1$ will mean that the total material flow necessary will be only one-quarter of what it would otherwise be—with all the attendant lessening in pumping and power requirements and thus overall plant size and cost.

It should be noted that the tapered ideal cascade is difficult if not impossible to implement in practice for the simple reason that the ideal number of elements in a given stage often turns out to be a non-integral value. In order to make use of the cost efficiency of mass production of large numbers of identical

41 A detailed discussion of the estimated amount of HEU or plutonium required for nuclear weapon construction appears in chapter 5 on safeguards.

42 See chapter 4, p. 116.

43 Avery, D. G. and Davies, E., *Uranium Enrichment by Gas Centrifuge* (Mills & Boon: London, 1973), p. 61.

44 Benedict *et al.* (note 14), p. 666. If the restriction to separation factors close to 1 is dropped the total flow rate is given by the expression on p. 664.

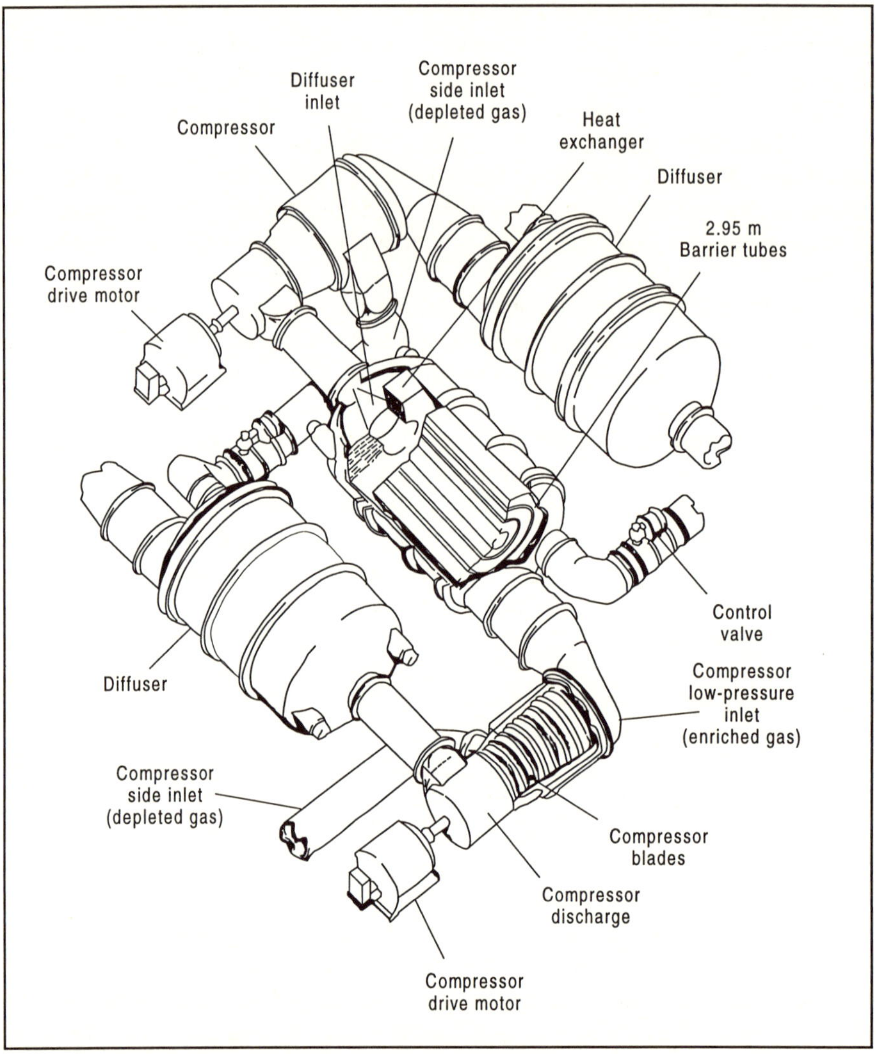

Figure 6. Stage arrangement and components in a US gaseous diffusion plant

Source: Redrawn by permission of the Oxford University Press from Tait, J. H., 'Uranium enrichment', ed. W. Marshall, *Nuclear Power Technology. Vol. 2, Fuel Cycle* (Clarendon Press: Oxford, 1983), p. 120.

elements, the ideal cascade is therefore approximated by what is referred to as a squared-off cascade in which the stages are composed of large numbers of identical elements in parallel.[45] This squaring off process is shown in figure 5 which overlays the squared-off cascade on the tapered cascade to which it approximates.

[45] Tait (note 18), p. 113; and Avery and Davies (note 43), pp. 62–63.

Another important concept connected with a particular enrichment technology and plant design is the start-up or *equilibrium time*. Before enriched material is withdrawn from a cascade the plant must be run long enough that its working inventory is built up and steady-state concentrations and flow rates are present throughout.[46]

Returning to the specifics of gaseous diffusion, after the UF_6 has flowed through a given separator it must then be recompressed and cooled (removing the heat of compression) before being fed into the next stage. Some pressure is also lost in the depleted stream which must also be recompressed. In US diffusion plants[47] each separating unit (called a converter) contains thousands of tubes made of diffusion barrier through which the higher pressure UF_6 flows. The portion flowing through the tube walls which is partially enriched is then pumped on to the next unit. The arrangement of compressors, heat exchangers and diffusing elements is shown in figure 6.

The vertical arrangement of converter, cooler, compressor and motor of the machines at the Eurodif facility in Tricastin France has the advantage of requiring less piping and floor space as illustrated in figure 7, in which the large size of these diffusion stages is illustrated by comparison with a human figure.[48]

Theoretical lower bounds to the energy consumption per SWU have been calculated to lie in the region of about 900 kilowatt-hours (kWh).[49] Factors such as compressor inefficiencies and pressure losses in the piping mean that practicably achievable values are usually several thousand kWh/SWU for an advanced diffusion technology.[50]

Why UF_6?

UF_6 is used in many uranium enrichment processes and it is therefore useful to understand why as well as to be aware of the very special problems which its use may pose. It is used since it is the only compound of uranium which has a large vapour pressure at room temperature.[51] Also fluorine has only a single stable isotope—keeping the isotope separation process as simple as possible—and a low atomic weight—helping to keep the mass of the gas as low as possible.

[46] Benedict *et al.* (note 14), p. 677; and Brigoli, B., 'Cascade theory', ed. Villani, *Uranium Enrichment* (note 2), p. 42.

[47] Benedict *et al.* (note 14), pp. 819–20.

[48] Benedict *et al.* (note 14), pp. 816, 821–22.

[49] Using various assumptions in his very thorough treatment Massignon obtained the values of 912, 948 and 876 kWh/SWU, while Tait obtained a value of 897 kWh/SWU. See Massignon, D., 'Gaseous diffusion', ed. Villani, *Uranium Enrichment* (note 2), pp. 112–13; and Tait (note 18), p. 121.

[50] Tait (note 18), p. 121. For the most efficient plants the AEC has estimated that 0.266 kW of electrical power would be necessary per year for each SWU—i.e., 2330 kWh/SWU. The figure of 0.266 kW is cited in Spindel, W., 'Isotope separation processes', ed. P. A. Rock, *Isotopes and Chemical Principles* (American Chemical Society: Washington, DC, 1975), p. 87. For the Tricastin plant a value of 2450 kWh/SWU is given in Villani, S., 'Review of separation processess', ed. Villani, *Uranium Enrichment* (note 2), p. 5.

[51] Massignon, D., 'Gaseous diffusion', ed. Villani, *Uranium Enrichment* (note 2), p. 56.

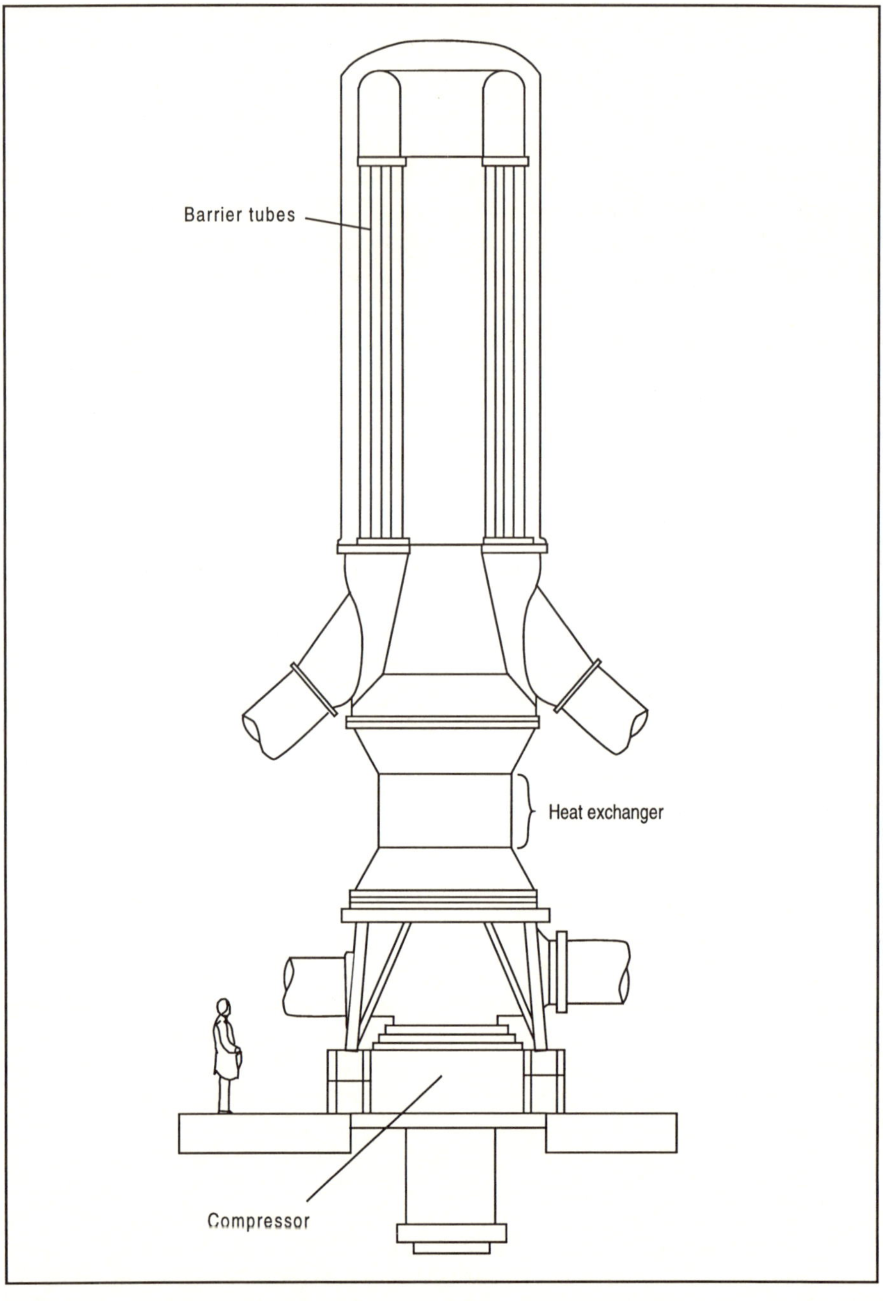

Figure 7. The integrated French gaseous diffusion unit

Source: Redrawn by permission of the Oxford University Press from Tait, J. H., 'Uranium enrichment', ed. W. Marshall, *Nuclear Power Technology. Vol. 2, Fuel Cycle* (Clarendon Press: Oxford, 1983), p. 123.

Disadvantages of its use include the ease with which it reacts with moisture, forming uranyl fluoride (UO_2F_2); and its corrosive attack on metals, forming metal fluorides, and on organic compounds, including lubricating oils, forming fluorinated organic compounds. This corrosiveness poses a problem for the barriers which should ideally keep their shape and pore size for long time periods. Some suitable barrier materials are described above. In general, any barrier or structural materials which may come into contact with the gas are therefore composed of materials such as nickel, nickel-coated steels, aluminium and teflon. Uranium hexafluoride also determines the operating pressures and temperatures. The temperature must remain above that at which it liquefies or crystallizes at a given pressure.[52]

IV. Electromagnetic isotope separation

History

As early as 1912, in experiments performed on helium by J. J. Thompson, it became apparent that electromagnetic fields could be used to separate isotopes. In early experiments the ^{20}N and ^{22}N isotopes were clearly discernible. Another pioneer of the method, F. W. Aston, stated in 1922, however, that 'the quantities produced under the most favourable estimates are hopelessly small'.[53] It was, of course, to be shown 25 years later that by employing the same basic idea with sufficient resources and ingenuity enough of a rare isotope of uranium could be created to produce a nuclear weapon. As detailed in chapter 4, using this proven technology, Iraq would decades later still attempt a similar endeavour, only to be thwarted before any substantial amount of fissile material was produced

The first separation of uranium using the electromagnetic method did not occur until 1940 when Alfred Nier and collaborators managed to separate 0.01 micrograms (μg) of ^{235}U using a separator with a radius of only 7 inches (17.8 cm).[54] With the realization of the possibility of using ^{235}U in an explosive chain reaction, the Manhattan Project invested substantial effort in a programme using EMIS to produce the material. In 1941 Lawrence at the University of California used the magnet of his 37-inch (94-cm) cyclotron[55] to separate uranium isotopes.[56] Subsequent experimentation with larger machines further increased confidence in the process, and the pressure of wartime then

[52] Rahn *et al.* (note 14), pp. 193–94; and Tait (note 18), p. 117.

[53] Quoted in Koch, J., Dawton, R. H. V. M., Smith, M. L. and Walcher, W., *Electromagnetic Isotope Separators and Applications of Electromagnetically Enriched Isotopes* (North-Holland: Amsterdam, 1958), p. 6.

[54] Nier, A. O., Booth, E. T., Dunning, J. R. and Grosse, A. V., 'Nuclear fission of separated uranium isotopes' and 'Further experiments on fission of separated uranium isotopes', Letters to the Editor, *Physical Review*, vol. 57 (1940), pp. 546, 748. Cited in Benedict *et al.* (note 14), p. 634.

[55] Hence the term calutron—a contraction of California University Cyclotron.

[56] Love, L. O., 'Electromagnetic separation of isotopes at Oak Ridge', *Science*, vol. 182, no. 4110 (26 Oct. 1973), p. 343; and Benedict *et al.* (note 14), p. 634.

led to simultaneous research, development, construction and operation of tailor-made separators called calutrons on a large scale.[57]

The plant for the ^{235}U production—code-named Y-12 and constructed near Oak Ridge, Tennessee—made use of two different-sized machines. The larger alpha calutrons performed the first stage of enrichment, which at best reached about 15 per cent ^{235}U—not sufficient for use in a bomb. The beta machines were used to further enrich the material which was output from the alpha separators to about 90 per cent, suitable for weapon production.

New problems presented themselves, especially in designing the vacuum systems and power supplies for the calutrons as compared to the earlier small- and medium-sized instruments.[58]

The ion beams in the alpha and beta calutrons traversed paths of radii of 48 inches (in.) and 24 in. (121.9 cm and 61.0 cm) respectively. The sizes of the tanks themselves were 12 feet (ft) × 8 ft by 28 in. (366 cm x 244 cm x 71 cm) and 6.5 ft × 5 ft by 23 in. (198 cm x 152 cm x 58 cm) weighing in at 10 tons and 9 tons, respectively. The calutrons were arranged in 'race tracks'—oval-shaped groupings of vacuum tanks and magnets—96 for the alpha and 36 for the beta machines. This arrangement was to be used as a virtual blueprint by the Iraqis in their nascent enrichment effort. Nine alpha and eight beta race tracks were eventually constructed—well over 1100 calutrons overall.[59]

In January 1945, the output from 864 alpha tanks was 258 grams of 10 per cent enriched product per day—just over one-quarter of a gram per machine. At the same time 204 grams of 80 per cent enriched product per day was being turned out by 36 beta tanks making use of accumulated alpha-machine product.[60]

Physical principles

The method depends on the basic physical principle that charged objects undergo acceleration as a result of motion perpendicular to a magnetic field. All else being equal, heavier ions will be deflected to a lesser extent. As shown in figure 8, therefore, the heavier ^{238}U ions (M_2; uranium tetrachloride is used as fuel) will not be deflected as much as the ^{235}U ions (M_1) and will thus move in a curved path of larger radius—arriving at a point offset from the arrival point of the ^{235}U ions. Appropriately placed ion collectors can then take advantage of this separation to collect the two isotopes in separate collector compartments.

An EMIS separator is thus essentially composed of an ion source which creates and expels ionized atoms of the element to be separated into a vacuum chamber, in which they travel through 180 degrees to be caught at the opposite end by collectors which are configured to take into account the different paths

[57] Groves (note 18), p. 96; and Koch *et al.* (note 53), p. 104.
[58] Koch *et al.* (note 53), p. vii.
[59] Groves (note 18), p. 98; Love (note 56), p. 344 (*re* size) and p. 352 (*re* enrichment factor).
[60] Rhodes, R., *The Making of the Atomic Bomb* (Penguin: London, 1988), p. 601.

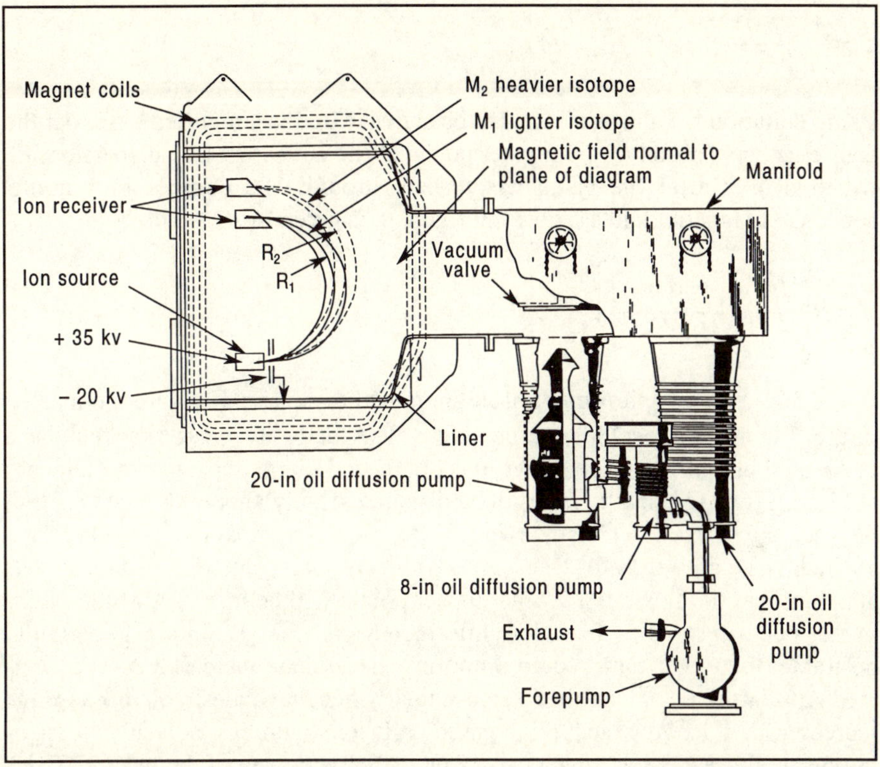

Figure 8. EMIS configuration

Source: Redrawn with permission from Love, L. O., 'Electromagnetic separation of isotopes at Oak Ridge', *Science*, vol. 182, no. 4110 (26 Oct. 1973), p. 344. © 1973 American Association for the Advancement of Science.

taken by different isotopes. As outlined in the combined report on the first and second inspections of Iraq following the Persian Gulf War, a successful EMIS enrichment programme requires mastery of a number of technologies, including those relevant to 'high current ion source development, high voltage DC power supply design and manufacture, high current power supply design and manufacture, large vacuum system design and operation, collector design and fabrication, and insulator design and fabrication.'[61] In addition equipment is needed to cool and purify the water used to cool the magnets and ion sources.[62]

Using elementary electromagnetic theory it is found that the radius of the trajectory of ions with charge Q and mass M, when accelerated by a voltage V in a magnetic field B is:

[61] Consolidated report on the first two IAEA inspections under Security Council Resolution 687 (1991) of Iraqi nuclear capabilities, UN document S/22788, 15 July 1991, pp. 9–10.

[62] Hibbs, M., 'Two Iraqi enrichment sites could host 200 calutrons', *Nucleonics Week*, vol. 32, no. 29 (18 July 1991), p. 4.

$$R = \frac{1}{B}\sqrt{\frac{2MV}{Q}} \qquad (1)$$

Using equation (1) above it can also be shown[63] in this simplified case that the theoretical separation of the impact points at the collectors (the dispersion, *d*), which occurs after the beam has turned through 180 degrees in a homogeneous[64] magnetic field as shown in figure 8, is given by

$$d = R\left[\frac{\left(M_{^{238}\mathrm{U}} - M_{^{235}\mathrm{U}}\right)}{M_{\mathrm{U}}}\right] \qquad (2)$$

where M_U is the atomic weight of uranium and $M_{^{238}U}$ and $M_{^{235}U}$ are the masses of the ^{238}U and ^{235}U isotopes respectively. The factor in square brackets has a value of about 0.013 and so for a typical radius of a large separator of 48 inches (122 cm), for example, there results a distance of only about 0.6 inch (1.5 cm) between the points at which the two isotopes would arrive at the collector. For a 24-inch (61-cm) separator, the value would be only half this distance. It is apparent that the separation of the impact points will be increased if the radius of the beam path is increased. While increasing this separation is certainly desirable, the larger radii required not only necessitate increased costs associated with larger equipment but also eventually become undesirable because the increased path length leads to increased collisions with gas molecules remaining inside the separator, which causes increased widening of the beam.[65] There are also a number of other factors which may cause spreading and fluctuation of the ion beams.

First, as is apparent from equation (1) above for the ion radius, this radius is dependent on both the stability of the magnetic field through which the ions move as well as the accelerating voltage.[66] Careful regulation of these parameters will help ensure that optimal performance is attained.

Since the beam is composed of like (positively) charged particles that repel one another, there is an inherent tendency for it to broaden and thus become less well defined, making collection more difficult. For beam currents appropriate to separation of uranium in reasonable quantities, these 'space charge effects' can be very important. Several methods can be used to alleviate the effect, including the formation of a compensating negative space charge resulting from electrons formed by the collision of the uranium ions with residual gas molecules in the chamber.[67]

It is also obviously desirable to minimize the divergence of the beam as it exits the ion source so that upon arrival at the collector it will not be so spread

[63] Taking differentials in equation (1); see e.g., Koch *et al.* (note 53), p. 102.
[64] Varying the magnetic field can lead to larger separations, but this is an added complication and also adds to the path length.
[65] London (note 16), p. 443.
[66] London (note 16), p. 439.
[67] London (note 16), p. 452.

out that overlap of beams of different isotopes results. A homogeneous magnetic field will, however, automatically compensate for some of this spreading and additional corrections can sharpen the focus even further. In addition, as the radius of curvature of the ions is proportional to their velocity it is important that the energy spread of the beam be kept as small as possible.[68]

It should also be stressed that experience from the Manhattan Project has shown that obtaining maximum performance involves a great deal of art as well as science. Technicians, their independent creativity and initiative being encouraged, developed intuitive skills with experience in tuning various machine parameters to optimize the machines' functioning.[69]

Ion sources and collectors

The output and efficiency of the separator depend in an essential way on the ion source,[70] which should be capable of providing a high density stream of ions, all as near to one another in energy as possible. Particularly if separation of uranium in quantity is desired it is also important that a stable source of ions can be provided for a long period of operation.[71] Rapid changes in the intensity of the beam can disturb the charge equilibrium which is desired to offset space charge effects and thus cause beam widening.[72]

The efficiency of the source is defined as the ratio of the amount of material in the form of ions which is emitted to the amount of source material which is introduced. Overall EMIS efficiency is essentially limited by the efficiency of the source which, for a variety of reasons, is basically restricted to the range of about 10–15 per cent for proper operation.[73] Much of this material is then further lost as it collects on surfaces within the tank itself before reaching the collector.

As shown in figure 9a, the uranium feed is vaporized in a furnace which leads to a (usually) graphite ionization chamber where electrons emitted by a filament (usually made of tantalum[74]) form a discharge and serve to dissociate the uranium tetrachloride (UCl_4) molecules and ionize the uranium atoms. These are then accelerated through a thin-walled extraction slit and into the main body of the vacuum chamber by an electric field produced by a pair of electrodes.[75] In the Y-12 machines each ion source had 30–40 1/16-inch slits.[76]

[68] Koch *et al.* (note 53), pp. 102–103.

[69] Allan Krass, personal communication.

[70] For a recent analysis of many of the difficulties involved with EMIS, especially the ion source, see Mozley, R. F., 'Uranium enrichment and other technical problems relating to nuclear weapons proliferation', Center for International Security and Arms Control, Stanford University, Stanford, Calif., July 1994, pp. 16–29.

[71] London (note 16), pp. 443–44.

[72] London (note 16), p. 454.

[73] London (note 16), pp. 448–49.

[74] Koch *et al.* (note 53), p. 130; and Love (note 56), p. 345.

[75] London (note 16), pp. 444–47; and Koch *et al.* (note 53), p. 129.

[76] Hibbs, M., 'Ion source problems held up Iraqi calutron program', *Nucleonics Week*, vol. 32, no. 32 (8 Aug. 1991), p. 9.

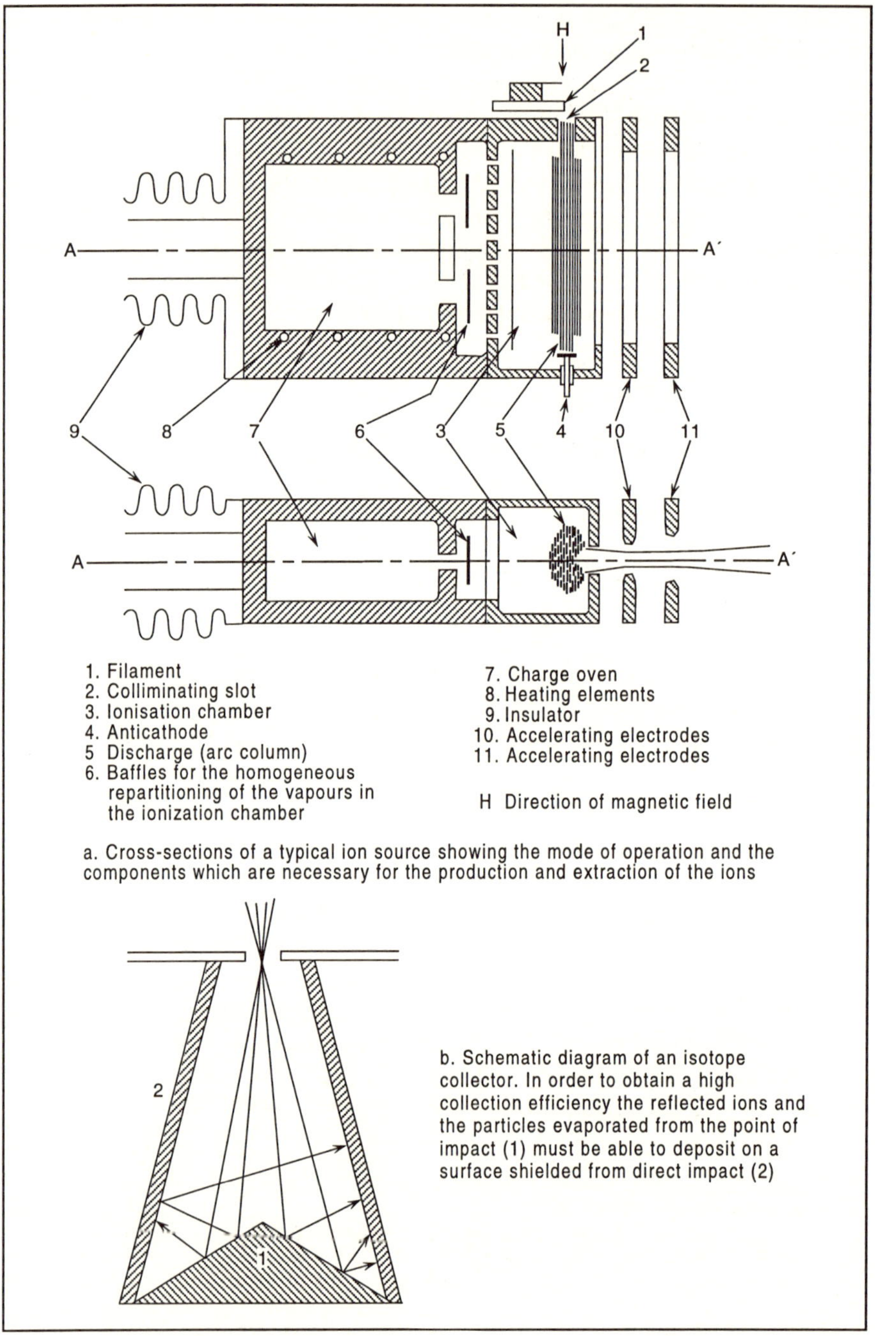

Figure 9. Ion source and isotope collector

Source: Based on Bernas, R. H., 'The electromagnetic separator', ed. H. London, *Separation of Isotopes* (George Newnes: London, 1961), figs 15.3 and 15.9, pp. 445 and 456.

Some unwanted ions are inevitably produced and this leads to lowered overall efficiency of the separator. For uranium isotope separation, UCl_4 is used as feed. Its vaporization temperature of approximately 400° C is much lower than that of uranium metal, making it easier to employ.[77] However, its use does lead to production of additional ions, mainly including UCl^+, UCl_2^+, UCl_3^+, UCl_4^+, Cl^+, Cl_2^+ (U^{++} is also produced) in addition to the desired U^+ ions. These latter ions do, none the less, comprise 60–70 per cent of total beam current.[78]

Problems with the (in principle straightforward) design and construction of collectors (see figure 9b) include dealing with rebound, re-evaporation and sputtering. These effects can reduce collector efficiency—the percentage of material entering the collector which remains there—to only about 50 per cent. Power dissipated in the collectors can be on the order of several thousand watts—for a typical 100 milliampere (mA) beam at 30 kilovolts (kV), 3 kilowatts (kW) are deposited.[79]

Calutrons operated during the Manhattan Project used up to four ion sources and collectors per vacuum tank. Experiments with up to 16 sources had been performed, but it was discovered that they were impracticable.[80]

Vacuum system and power supplies

The vacuum system is required to be able reliably to maintain a pressure of $2–5 \times 10^{-5}$ mm Hg with as short a pump-down time as possible. Although quite similar, four different types of large multiple-stage pump were manufactured for the Y-12 system. Regulated power-supply circuits to the source and accelerating electrodes and the magnet must all be controlled to within 0.1–0.2 per cent—more exacting than the usual requirements for large current circuits. For instance, since the mass difference of the isotopes of ^{235}U and ^{238}U differs by only 1.3 per cent, a decrease in the accelerating voltage of this magnitude would result in the ^{238}U ions falling into the ^{235}U collector pocket.[81]

Of course once the separation run has taken place the uranium must be recovered. Especially when enriched material is used as feed this involves substantial effort as the liner sources and collectors must be removed from the vacuum tank. The uranium is then reclaimed by a variety of processes.[82]

Although much less sophisticated, the EMIS method is somewhat analogous to laser separation in that large separation factors are achievable in a single machine taking up relatively little space, although EMIS requires many machines for significant output. The many problems with the method, including its small throughput, large space requirements and high power requirements, were not sufficient to prevent Iraq from pursuing the method in a large-scale

[77] Hibbs (note 76), p. 9.
[78] London (note 16), pp. 447–48: and Koch *et al.* (note 53), pp. 136–37.
[79] London (note 16), pp. 455–56.
[80] London (note 16), p. 455.
[81] Koch *et al.* (note 53), pp. 121, 123, 143–44. The last result follows from the fact that $2dR=RdV/V$, found by differentiating equation (1) in the same manner as equation (2) is obtained.
[82] Koch *et al.* (note 53), p. 119.

programme. Until the discovery of this programme the drawbacks of the EMIS method had led most observers to consider it unlikely to be used in a weapon programme.

V. The gas centrifuge

The gas-centrifuge method of enrichment is a more advanced technique in widespread commercial use that allows higher separation factors[83] than gaseous diffusion while still providing a reasonable throughput.[84] This method uses centrifugal acceleration created in a cylinder rotating at very high speed. Uranium hexafluoride gas is fed into the rotating cylinder and the acceleration of rotation increases the concentration of UF_6 molecules containing ^{238}U closer to the periphery of the cylinder and those containing ^{235}U closer to the centre for collection.[85] The rotor is contained in a highly evacuated enclosure, both to minimize drag and to contain the debris should a failure occur.[86]

Additional enrichment is usually attained by setting up a *countercurrent flow* which transports material along the outside wall in one direction and close to the axis of the spinning centrifuge in the other direction so that enriched and depleted UF_6 can be collected by scoops at the top and bottom. The high rate of rotation necessary to obtain useful enrichment factors is more effectively achieved using high-strength lightweight materials in cylinder construction and by operation in a highly evacuated container.[87]

Although gaseous diffusion is a tried and true technology, making use of an irreversible process—because of the expansion of the gas as it passes through the barrier—it requires much more energy per SWU than the gas-centrifuge method, which makes use of a reversible process. (In the gas centrifuge the isotopes are already separated before the product and waste are withdrawn; however, energy must be expended to accelerate the rotor, maintain its speed against friction, maintain the countercurrent flow and withdraw the gas. Therefore, the actual energy expended is still orders of magnitude more than the theoretical minimum.)[88]

There are several plants in operation in the world today as indicated in table 1. A portion of the plant at Almelo in the Netherlands in shown in figure 10.

[83] The separation factor is defined as the percentage of ^{235}U in the product stream divided by the percentage in the tails stream.

[84] Cochran *et al.* (note 40), p. 130

[85] Soubbaramayer, 'Centrifugation', ed. Villani, *Uranium Enrichment* (note 2), p. 186.

[86] Avery and Davies (note 43), p. 48.

[87] Krass *et al* (note 2), pp. 130–32. The report of the 7th IAEA inspection in Iraq contains information on the centrifuges that were under development by Iraq, and these are discussed in chapter 4. Report on the seventh IAEA on-site inspection in Iraq under Security Council Resolution 687 (1991), 11–22 October 1991, UN document S/23215, 14 Nov. 1991, p. 51.

[88] Tait (note 18), p. 113; and Whitley, S., 'Review of the gas centrifuge until 1962. Part I: Principles of separation physics', *Reviews of Modern Physics*, vol. 56, no. 1 (Jan. 1984), p. 61. Whitley (p. 62) estimates a power usage for the gas centrifuge of 100 times less than equivalent separation from the diffusion technology—but this is none the less still 10 000 times the theoretical minimum value for the centrifuge.

Figure 10. A Urenco cascade hall
Source: Courtesy of Urenco Ltd.

History

Experiments in the separation of mixtures of gases of different molecular weights using gravitational or centrifugal force fields were carried out as early as 1895 by Bredig.[89] High-speed liquid centrifuges had in fact been introduced much earlier with the development, beginning in 1877, of the cream separator by the Swedish engineer de Laval, which was capable of peripheral speeds of 400 metres per second (m/s).[90] Shortly after the discovery of the existence of isotopes it was suggested first by Lindemann and Aston in 1919 that a centrifugal field be applied to the purpose of enriching isotopes.[91]

The first successful experiments in isotope separation using the centrifuge were carried out by Beams and his collaborators, who achieved partial separation of the carbon isotopes ^{135}C and ^{137}C in 1938 using carbon tetrachloride (CCl_4). The use of countercurrent flow to increase the enrichment factor by heating the bottom and cooling the top of the centrifuge rotor was first proposed in 1939 by Urey.

At the commencement of the Manhattan Project the centrifuge was considered one of the most promising methods for uranium enrichment and a pilot plant was constructed. By 1941 uranium was reported to have been enriched in

[89] Avery and Davies (note 43), p. 21.
[90] Tait (note 18), p. 121.
[91] London (note 16), p. 249.

^{235}U by Beams and colleagues (1.2 g of 4 per cent enriched product) at the University of Virginia. Further research on larger machines continued in the USA, leading to a machine with a separative capacity of approximately 1 SWU/year. Although the results obtained were consistent with theoretical predictions, the technology associated with the high-speed rotating machines was not yet up to the task. This led by 1943 to the decision to abandon the process in favour of gaseous diffusion.[92]

During World War II in Germany, the use of internal scoops and baffles to establish the important countercurrent flow was suggested by Zippe. He continued his work after the war, first in the USSR and later in collaboration with Beams in Virginia. The light and durable machines developed were the forefathers of modern designs. During the 1950s, Groth and co-workers in Germany used thermal convection to establish countercurrent flow in a machine which was, however, more complex than the Zippe-type machines, and in 1956 a pilot facility was established in Japan.[93]

By the 1960s, as the technology matured, the main countries which had contributed substantially to its development—the FRG, the Netherlands, the UK and the USA—agreed to security restrictions on the technological description. Thus from this time forward, few specific details concerning operational centrifuge designs have become publicly available.[94]

Basic concepts

As outlined above the basic operating principle of the gas centrifuge depends on the centrifugal force set up in a rotating hollow body and the pressure gradient which results as gas molecules are forced towards the periphery. A simplified diagram of a centrifuge is given in figure 11.

If a gas of molecular weight M inside a centrifuge of radius a is rotating at an angular velocity of omega (ω) radians per second ($\omega = 2\,\pi f$, where f is the frequency of rotation in cycles per second), then equating the pressure gradient at a given point inside to the centrifugal force on a gas element at that point gives:[95]

$$p(a) = p(0)\exp\left[\frac{M(\omega a)^2}{2RT}\right]$$

where $p(a)$ is the pressure at the periphery, $p(0)$ is the pressure at the axis, the gas constant R= 8.314 joules/mole-°K and T is the temperature in degrees Kelvin. From Dalton's law of partial pressures this equation applies individu-

92 Avery and Davies (note 43), p. 15; Benedict *et al.* (note 14), pp. 848–89; and Olander (note 30), p. 37.

93 Benedict *et al.* (note 14), p. 849; Soubbaramayer, 'Centrifugation', ed. Villani, *Uranium Enrichment* (note 2), p. 183; and Cochran and Tsoulfanidis (note 22), p. 65.

94 Benedict *et al.* (note 14), p. 849.

95 See, e.g., Avery and Davies (note 43), p. 23; and Benedict *et al.* (note 14), pp. 856–57.

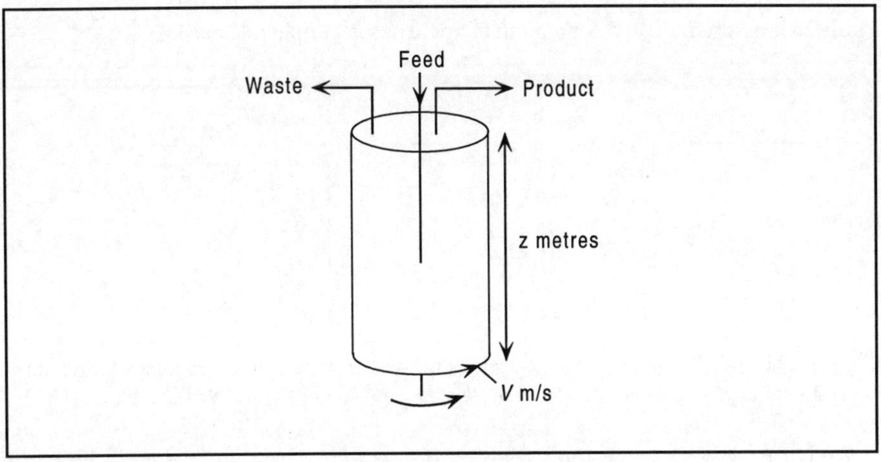

Figure 11. Simplified diagram of a centrifuge

ally to each component of a mixture of gases (in this case $^{235}UF_6$ and $^{238}UF_6$). So an equation analogous to the above could be written with M_1= 349 grams for $^{235}UF_6$ and with M_2 = 352 grams for $^{238}UF_6$. The ratio of these two partial pressures would also, from Avogadro's law, be the ratio of the molecular concentrations of the two different constituents[96] and thus the (equilibrium) separation factor for the centrifuge:

$$\alpha = \exp\left\{ \frac{[M_2 - M_1](\omega a)^2}{2RT} \right\}$$

Noting that the peripheral speed $v = \omega a$, this separation factor can also be expressed in terms of this more often-quoted value as :

$$\alpha = \exp\left\{ \frac{[M_2 - M_1]v^2}{2RT} \right\}$$

It is important to note the strong dependence of this factor on the peripheral speed v and the fact that it depends on the difference in the molecular weights of the two species in contrast to the case with gaseous diffusion where it depends on their ratio. It also decreases with increasing temperature. The above equation for the pressure at the periphery in terms of the pressure at the axis also displays this strong dependence on the rotational speed of the centrifuge rotor. Table 3 lists the pressure ratio (for $^{235}UF_6$) and the separation factor for various peripheral speeds. Particular note should be taken of the very rapid rise in pressure difference at high speeds.

[96] Whitley (note 88), p. 46.

Table 3. Pressure ratio and separation factor at some peripheral speeds

Peripheral speed (m/s)	Pressure ratio (for $^{235}UF_6$)	Separation factor (α)
300	573	1.056
400	80 x 10^3	1.101
500	46 x 10^6	1.162
600	11 x 10^{10}	1.242
700	10 x 10^{14}	1.343
800	41 x 10^{18}	1.469

Source: Adapted from Whitley, S., 'Review of the gas centrifuge until 1962. Part I: Principles of separation physics', *Reviews of Modern Physics*, vol. 56, no. 1 (Jan. 1984), p. 49.

It must be stressed that the values of α quoted above are for the equilibrium case—that is, no output from the centrifuge.[97] The non-equilibrium case is considered below.

Maximum separative power

The maximum separative power of a centrifuge can be shown to be related to the radius, gas density ρ, length Z, diffusion coefficient D and other variables already defined by:[98]

$$D\rho\left[\frac{(M_2 - M_1)(\omega a)^2}{(2RT)}\right]^2 \frac{\pi Z}{2}$$

This expression indicates that optimal performance can be obtained by (*a*) operating at low temperature; (*b*) using long rotors; and (*c*) attaining high peripheral velocity.

This equation implies, for example, that the maximum output of a 1-metre long centrifuge with a peripheral velocity of 300 m/s is just over 2 kg SWU/year.[99] As the speed increases, the output increases rapidly as the fourth power of the peripheral velocity. However, as table 3 shows, at very high peripheral speeds the pressure ratio becomes very large, which means that the pressure is so small near the centre of the rotor that no useful separation is contributed in this region. At high speeds it has been shown in fact that the output increases as the square of the peripheral speed rather than the fourth power.[100]

[97] Whitley (note 88), p. 48.

[98] Cohen, K., *The Theory of Isotope Separation as Applied to the Large-Scale Production of U^{235}* (McGraw-Hill: New York, 1951), p. 110; and Avery and Davies (note 43), p. 25.

[99] Whitley (note 88), p. 44 and the table on p. 49.

[100] Whitley (note 88), p. 48. A specific approximate theoretical calculation, e.g. (using the so-called Berman–Olander velocity distribution), gives the result that the exponent is 2.02 over the peripheral velocity range from 400–700 m/sec—see Benedict *et al.* (note 14), p. 867.

Types of centrifuge

There are three identifiable types of centrifuge. In the *evaporative centrifuge* the isotopic mixture is introduced in liquid form. The liquid is restricted to the periphery by the centrifugal force. When equilibrium is established between the liquid and vapour phase, vapour is withdrawn near the axis and the liquid phase is enriched in the heavier isotope. The simplest type of centrifuge which allows continuous flow of material is the *concurrent centrifuge*. In this type a steady stream of gas is introduced into one end of the centrifuge and two streams are withdrawn at the opposite end—one near the periphery and another closer to the axis.[101]

Both the evaporative and concurrent centrifuges are capable, even under the most ideal conditions, of achieving only the equilibrium separation factor derived above. Their use has mainly been confined to the laboratory[102] and the discussion here therefore focuses on the most productive—the *countercurrent centrifuge*—which, as outlined above, in setting up a circulating gas flow within the rotor is able to increase the separation factor substantially.

The countercurrent centrifuge

Countercurrent flow can be of either of two types. The first is called exogenous countercurrent, in which pumps maintain gas streams which enter the centrifuge at one end and exit at the opposite end at different radial positions. However, the countercurrent is usually of a second type—internal thermomechanical. This latter type of countercurrent flow may be set up by a combination of the following mechanisms.[103]

1. *Scoop type:* The flow is generated by rather complex effects of the stationary scoop which is used to withdraw gas depleted in ^{235}U.[104]
2. *End-cap thermal drive:* Here one end of the rotor is heated and the other end is cooled. The gas expands at the heated end and thus moves radially inwards away from the more dense gas at the periphery. The layer of gas is sufficiently thin that adequate transfer occurs between the rotor end cap and the enclosed gas. Similarly, gas flow at the cooled end is towards the outer edge of the rotor. The net result is that a countercurrent flow is induced, the gas flowing from the heated end to the cooled end along the centrifuge axis and from the cooled end to the heated end along the periphery.[105] (This is illustrated in figure 12 for the case of top heating and bottom cooling.)
3. *Wall thermal drive:* As with the end-cap thermal-drive type a temperature gradient along the wall induces a countercurrent flow.

[101] Avery and Davies (note 43), pp. 21–22; Tait (note 18), pp. 122–24; and Whitley (note 88), pp. 50–52.

[102] Villani, *Isotope Separation* (note 2), p. 207.

[103] Soubbaramayer, 'Centrifugation', ed. Villani, *Uranium Enrichment* (note 2), pp. 186–87.

[104] Olander (note 30), p. 38.

[105] Whitley (note 88), p. 56.

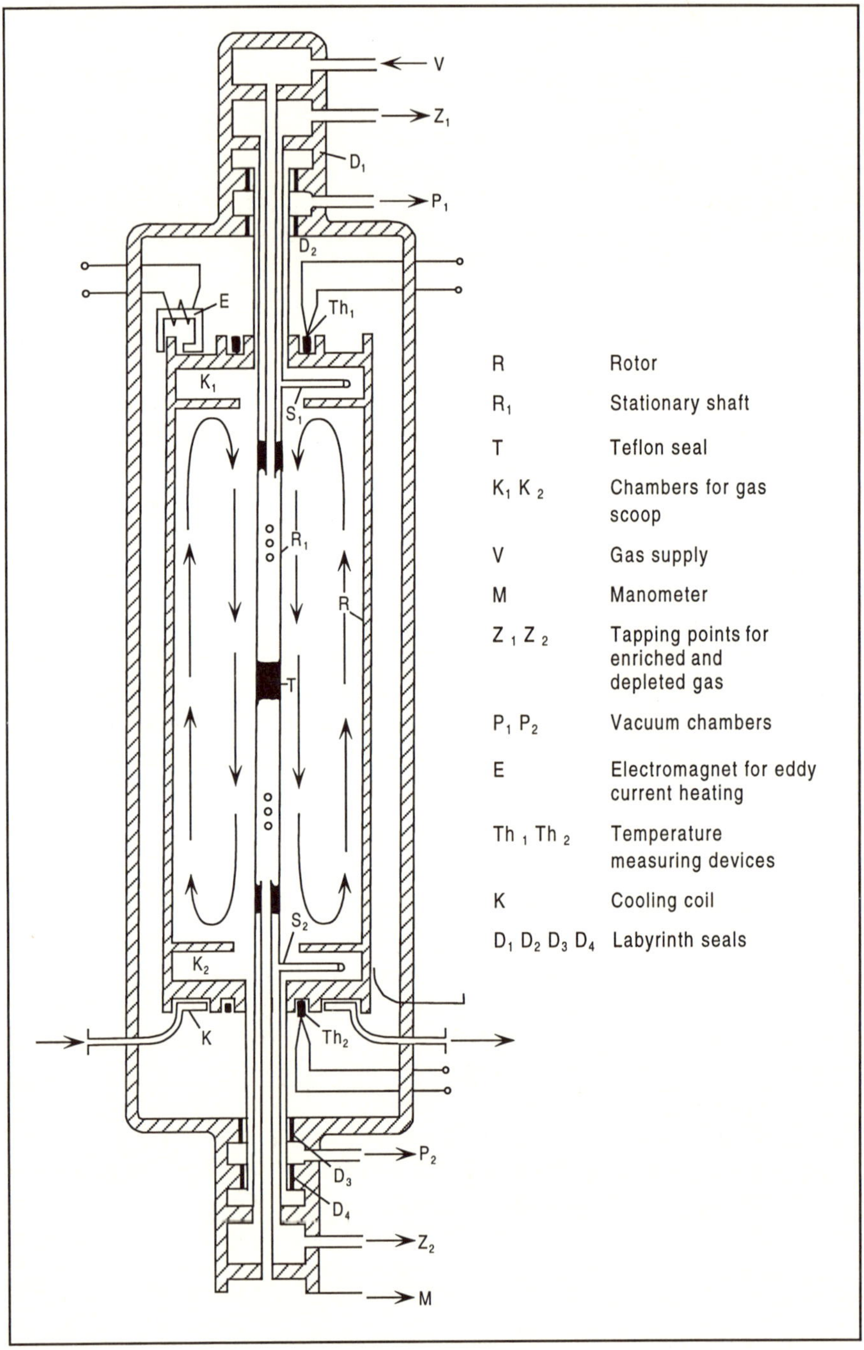

Figure 12. The Groth ZG5 centrifuge

Source: Based on Avery, D. G. and Davies, E., *Uranium Enrichment by Gas Centrifuge* (Mills & Boon: London, 1973), figure 18, p. 51.

4. *Feed drive:* Here flow is generated by a single feed point and two removal points within the rotor.

With countercurrent flow superposed on the radial flow, the centrifuge itself can be thought of as behaving like a miniature cascade, as the elementary separation factor α derived above for the case without countercurrent flow will be substantially increased.[106] Gas enriched in ^{235}U will flow along a path closer to the centrifuge axis and is withdrawn at one end of the centrifuge, while gas depleted in ^{235}U will flow in the opposite direction nearer to the periphery of the cylinder and is withdrawn at the opposite end.

Here again an estimate of the maximum value for the separation factor can be found—corresponding to zero withdrawal.[107]

$$\alpha_{max} = \exp\left\{\frac{(M_2 - M_1)\, v^2 Z}{\sqrt{2}\, RT\,(2a)}\right\}$$

The actual value of the separation factor for operational centrifuges depends on the specific parameters associated with the machine. Reputable sources quote values ranging from 1.2 to 1.5 and, while this is substantially larger than for gaseous diffusion, the separative work per centrifuge is generally smaller than that of a gaseous diffusion element since the throughput is very much lower.[108]

Some specific centrifuges

Rather detailed information is available for several types of centrifuge. Two types which indicate the basic design principles and which are most completely described in the open literature are the Groth and Zippe types.

The Groth centrifuge

Based on principles originating with Beams, the Groth ZG5 centrifuge achieves countercurrent flow by end-cap thermal drive, as illustrated in figure 12.

The top of the rotor is heated by an electromagnet *E* and the bottom is cooled by a cooling coil *K*. The rotor *R* is encased in a container which is either evacuated or contains hydrogen gas at low pressure. The UF_6 enters the rotor along the axis at R_1; enriched product is removed from the bottom scoop S_2 and withdrawn at Z_2 while depleted gas exits at Z_1, having been drawn off through the top scoop S_1. The two baffles K_1 and K_2 serve to prevent the scoops from disturbing the countercurrent flow. The double-walled centre shaft is highly elastic which, along with damping bearings, aids in stabilizing the rotor. The shaft is also connected to a motor (not illustrated). The top and bottom of the

106 Soubbaramayer, 'Centrifugation', ed. Villani, *Uranium Enrichment* (note 2), p. 186.

107 Whitley (note 88), p. 53; and Avery and Davies (note 43), p. 36.

108 International Nuclear Fuel Cycle Evaluation (INFCE), Report of the INFCE working group 2: *Enrichment Availability* (IAEA: Vienna, 1980), p. 40.

rotor shaft are connected to hollow shafts (not shown) which rotate within bearings lubricated with oil. Specially designed labyrinth bearings D_1, D_2, D_3 and D_4 are fed with hydrogen and prevent the mixing of oil and UF_6. The use of these seals and the oil-lubricated bearings make the machine expensive and complex to operate. However, the use of thermal convective drive permitted this machine to attain separative capacities as high as 75 per cent of the theoretical maximum in small machines.[109]

The Zippe Centrifuge

Easier to operate and not as costly as the Groth machine, the Zippe-type centrifuge has now generally been adopted by groups which remain committed to pursuing centrifuge technology.[110] As illustrated in figure 13, the Zippe centrifuge makes use of the scoop drive for generating the countercurrent and therefore a baffle is present only on the bottom, the top scoop being used to generate the countercurrent flow.

As with the Groth machine the rotor is housed in an evacuated container, but in this case it is supported at the bottom by a thin flexible steel needle (*P*) the point of which has been hardened by treatment with heat. The needle rotates in a hollowed-out portion of a highly tempered metal block (*S*). Lateral shifts are permitted by providing a footing (*T*) for the block which is supported by three steel balls. Surrounding oil provides cushioning for lateral motion as well as lubrication. Two magnets (*B* and *C*) hold the footing in place and one of them (*C*) is coupled by a spring to the metal block providing (along with the oil) cushioning of axial vibrations. The top of the rotor is held in place by magnetic coupling of a hollow permanent magnet (*E*) hung from the top of the rotor container with another magnet (*D*) attached to the rotor itself.

Concerning the delicate needle bearing it is interesting to note that tests conducted at the University of Virginia revealed that after an initial break-in time period, the needle was found to wear linearly but very slowly as required for long-term sustained operations.[111]

Feed enters the rotor through a tube (*G*) running along the axis which ends in the middle section. Enriched product and depleted product are withdrawn (*G′* and *G″*) from scoops at the bottom and top respectively. The outgoing gas flow is produced by the pressure of the rotating gas impacting on the scoops. Any gas which may leak from the top portion where gas enters and is withdrawn is removed from the area surrounding the rotor by a molecular pump (*Z*) which makes use of screw-type grooves in the wall of the centrifuge. The rotation of the cylinder itself then allows the near vacuum of 10^{-6} mm Hg to be maintained after an initial vacuum has been initiated by a pump acting through a valve (*U*).

[109] Avery and Davies (note 43), pp. 43, 49–53; and Benedict *et al.* (note 14), p. 850.
[110] Benedict *et al.* (note 14), pp. 632, 850.
[111] Villani, *Isotope Separation* (note 2), p. 220.

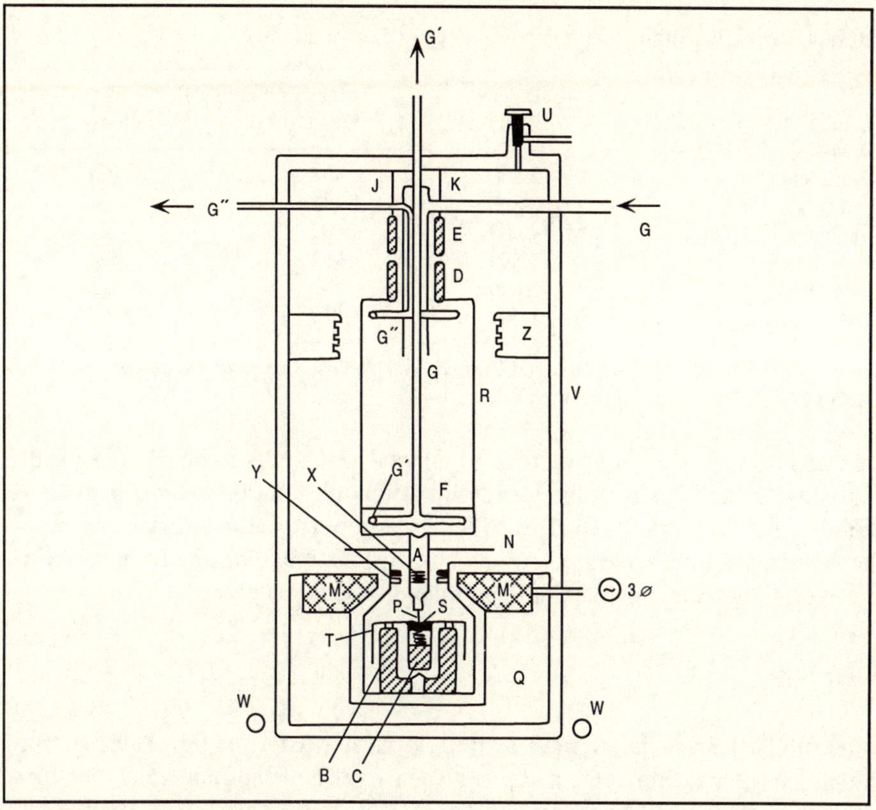

Figure 13. The Zippe Centrifuge

Source: Redrawn with permission from Villani, S. *Isotope Separation* (American Nuclear Society: La Grange Park. Ill., 1976), p. 219. © 1976 by the American Nuclear Society, La Grange Park, Illinois.

Rotation is induced in the armature (*N*) attached to the rotor and driven by the electric motor stator (*M*), the winding of which is immersed in an oil bath. Water flowing through the pipe system (*W*) is used to cool the entire lower portion of the centrifuge.[112]

Materials and construction

As with gaseous diffusion the use of UF_6 means that any components which will be exposed to the gas must be made of materials resistant to its corrosive properties.

[112] Avery and Davies (note 43), pp. 53–55; Benedict *et al.* (note 14), pp. 850–52; and Villani, *Isotope Separation* (note 2), pp. 218–21.

Table 4. Operating limits of some possible centrifuge materials

Material	Density kg/m^3 (ρ)	Tensile strength MPa (10^{-6} σ)	*V*max m/s
Aluminium alloys	2 800	448	400
High-tensile steel	7 800	1 381	421
Titanium	4 600	897	442
Maraging steel	7 800	1 932	498
Glass fibre	1 800	490	522
Carbon fibre/resin	1 600	829	720

Source: Benedict, M., Pigford, T. H and Levi, H. W., *Nuclear Chemical Engineering*, 2nd edn (McGraw-Hill: New York, 1981), table 14.11, p. 855.

In addition, as seen above a high peripheral velocity is to be desired for the centrifuge rotor. However, the speed of rotation must not be so high as to cause the rotor material to fail—that is, so high that the tangential stresses caused by the centrifugal forces are greater than the tensile strength of the rotor material. It can be shown that the maximum peripheral velocity is given by:[113]

$$v_{max} = \sqrt{\frac{\sigma}{\rho}}$$

where σ is the tensile strength in mega-Pascals (MPa) of the material from which the rotor is fabricated and ρ is its density. The maximum velocities for a number of materials considered for use in centrifuge construction are given in table 4.[114]

Materials must also be able to withstand the vibration caused by high-speed rotation as well as in many cases withstand passing through critical angular velocities (resonances) at which very large-scale vibrations may take place. Operating the centrifuge near any of these resonances will cause rotational energy to be transferred to energy of longitudinal vibrations, increasing their amplitude and resulting in the potential destruction of the rotor.

If the length and diameter are chosen such that resonances are avoided completely, the centrifuge is called subcritical. If on the other hand the rotor is sufficiently long that one or more resonant frequencies is attained it is termed supercritical. It is then important that the motors are sufficiently powerful to quickly accelerate the rotor through any such resonant frequencies.[115] Heavy-duty bearings and appropriate dampers may be used in such machines or short rotors may be connected with bellows, to ease the difficulty with critical frequencies.[116]

113 Avery and Davies (note 43), p. 43; and Benedict *et al.* (note 14), pp. 852–54.
114 For more details see Benedict *et al.* (note 14), p. 855.
115 Benedict *et al.* (note 2), pp. 855–56.
116 Tait (note 18), p. 127.

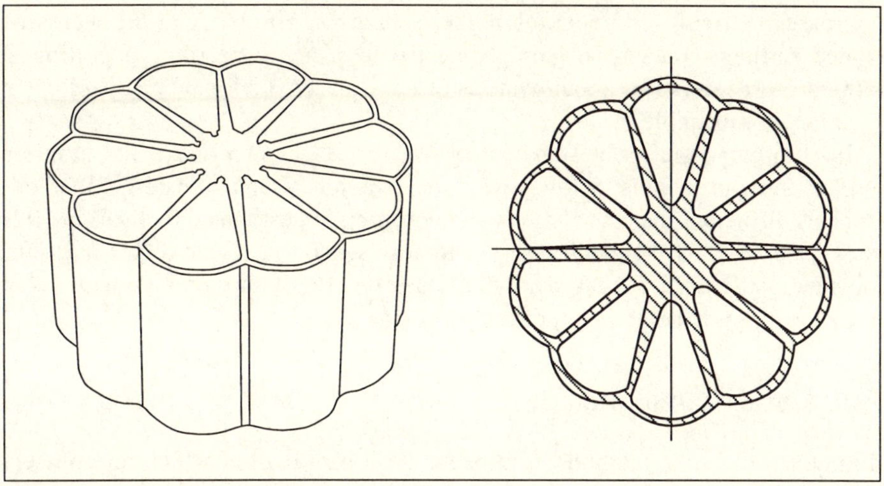

Figure 14. The rosette rotor

Source: Redrawn with permission from Whitley, S., 'Review of the gas centrifuge until 1962. Part II: Principles of high speed rotation', *Reviews of Modern Physics*, vol. 56, no. 1 (Jan. 1984), p. 85. © 1984 The American Physical Society.

Machines can in fact easily be classified according to the length-to-diameter ratio of the rotor (and thus are easily recognizable by inspection). The simplest is the short-bowl rotor with a length/diameter ratio of less than one, the sub-critical rotor which has a length/diameter ratio of 4 : 1 or 5: 1 and the super-critical rotor with length/diameter ratio of greater than 10: 1. Machines with length/diameter ratios intermediate to these are not normally employed, first because once a critical frequency has been passed it then makes sense to maximize the output of increased length before the next critical frequency is reached and second because intermediate machines would operate uncomfortably close to critical frequencies themselves.[117] When considering materials and optimal operating modes it should also be borne in mind that it is not certain that the simple cylindrical shape is the most optimal for the gas centrifuge. It was discovered during the centrifuge development in the UK from 1946 to 1954, for example, that a rosette rotor, shaped as shown in figure 14, is capable of being operated at peripheral speeds 50 per cent greater than would otherwise be the case for a given material.

The smaller radii of curvature of the loops making up the rotor surface (supported by spokes) reduce the stresses induced by rotation. Since the theoretical maximum output is proportional to the peripheral velocity to the fourth power, this 50 per cent increase in speed would theoretically allow for approximately a fivefold increase in output. However, the presence of the supporting spokes and the shape of the rotor itself decrease this theoretical estimate of the gain and reduce the increased output to just over a factor of about three. In addition,

[117] Whitley (note 88), pp. 73–74.

increased difficulty in obtaining higher separation efficiency at the increased speed further reduces the gain. None the less, a rosette rotor operating at 450 m/s turns out to be about twice as efficient as a cylindrical one operating at 300 m/s, for example.[118]

In summary, the greatest advantage[119] of the gas centrifuge for uranium enrichment purposes is its low power consumption when compared to methods such as diffusion (the centrifuge power consumption estimated by DOE in 1978 was 4 per cent of diffusion cost[120]). Its low separative capacity per machine, however, still requires that many thousands be used if substantial quantities of enriched product are to be produced.

VI. Aerodynamic methods

Many aerodynamic methods have been investigated, all of which rely on centrifugal forces in a flowing gas mixture to set up a pressure gradient which is then used to separate gas containing different isotopes into fractions enriched and depleted in a particular isotope. In principle it is therefore similar to the centrifuge method, although in this case the gas centrifugal force is generated by deflecting a gas jet. A recent OTA report has noted that in the longer term both laser (see section VII below) and aerodynamic uranium separation technologies have the potential to form a serious proliferation danger, especially if strict controls are not maintained on the technologies involved.[121]

The jet-nozzle method

This method was developed by E. W. Becker[122] and colleagues at the Nuclear Research Center at Karlsruhe in West Germany and was later exported for use in an enrichment programme in Brazil as well. In the jet-nozzle method a mixture of uranium hexafluoride and hydrogen is forced to flow along a curved wall as it expands through a nozzle. At the end of the deflecting surface the gas is split into a depleted and enriched fraction by a knife edge as illustrated in figure 15a. High velocity and resultant high acceleration is made possible by lowering the mean molecular weight by mixing hydrogen gas with UF_6 so that the percentage of UF_6 molecules is 4–15 per cent. The hydrogen also aids in prolonging the transient time during which the separation between the isotopic

[118] Whitley (note 88), pp. 69, 85.

[119] Benedict *et al.* (note 14), p. 856.

[120] Benedict *et al.* (note 14), p. 856.

[121] OTA (note 4), pp. 6, 126.

[122] See, e.g., Becker, E. W., *et al.*, 'Development and technical implementation of the separation nozzle process for enrichment of uranium-235', eds J. Merriman and M. Benedict, *Recent Developments in Uranium Enrichment,* AIChE Symposium Series, vol. 78, no. 221 (American Institute of Chemical Engineers: New York, 1982), p. 49; and Becker, E. W. *et al.*, 'Technological aspects of the separation nozzle process', ed. M. Benedict, *Developments in Uranium Enrichment,* AIChE Symposium Series, vol. 73, no. 169 (American Institute of Chemical Engineers: New York, 1977), p. 25.

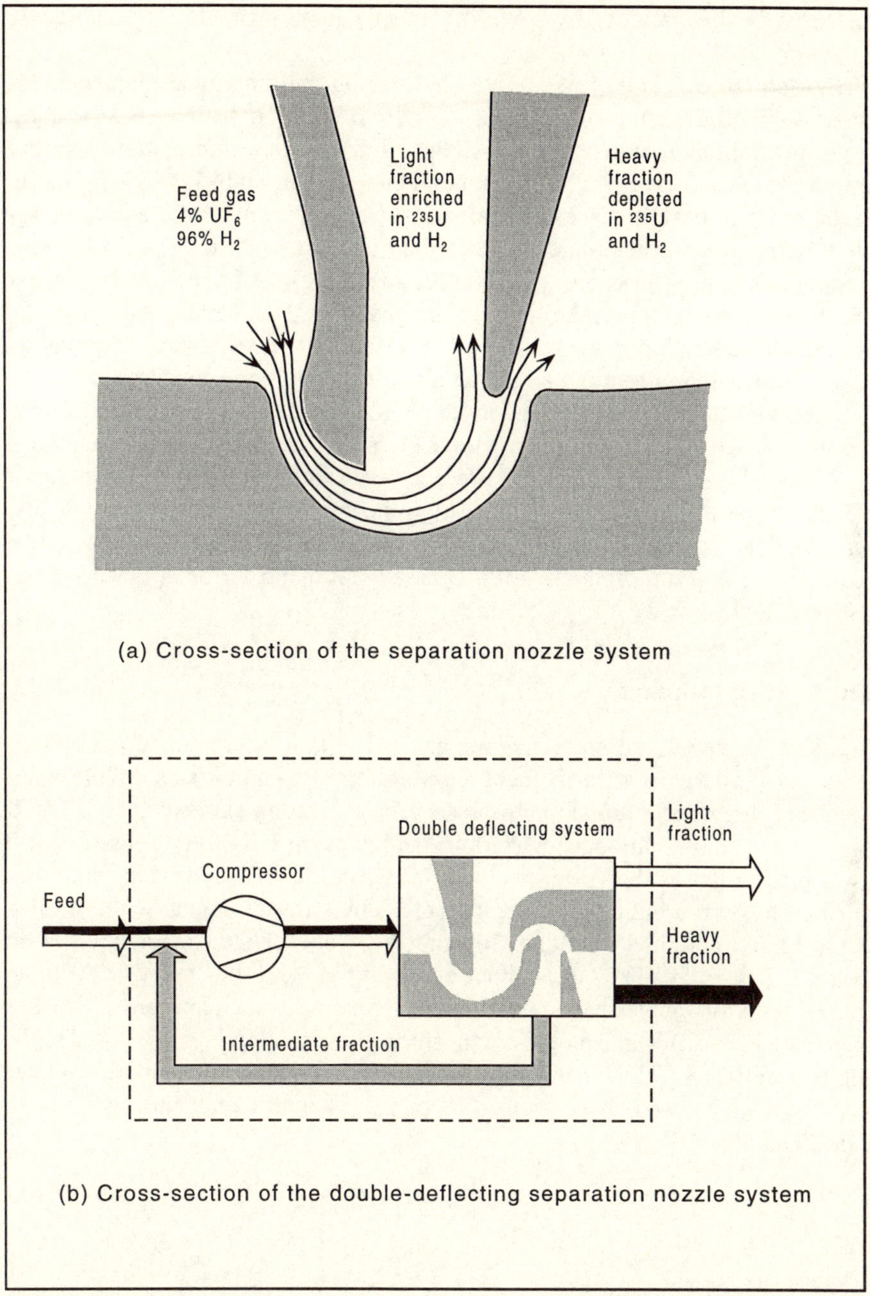

(a) Cross-section of the separation nozzle system

(b) Cross-section of the double-deflecting separation nozzle system

Figure 15. The jet-nozzle method

Source: Redrawn with permission from Becker, E. W., Nogueira Batista, P. and Völcker, H., 'Uranium enrichment by the separation nozzle method within the framework of German/ Brazilian cooperation', *Nuclear Technology*, vol. 52 (Jan. 1981), pp. 106 and 109. © 1976 by the American Nuclear Society, La Grange Park, Illinois.

mixtures is the greatest by lowering the frequency of UF_6 intermolecular collisions.[123]

High-pressure operation is allowed by making the individual elements very small (with the radius of curvature of the deflection wall typically about 0.1 mm or smaller), but this necessitates high-precision fabrication. Optimal enrichment is achieved with a cut of about one-quarter, requiring a modification in the cascade design described above so that the product from a given stage feeds three stages ahead and the tails feed the stage below. The power consumption is in general higher than that for gaseous diffusion, mainly because of the necessity to compress the light carrier gas as well as the UF_6. However, the achievable separation factor of about 1.0148 is significantly better than that for gaseous diffusion, meaning that the number of stages can be much less.[124]

In the newer double-deflecting system[125] illustrated in figure 15b the heavy fraction, which is depleted in ^{235}U from a classical system as described above, is fractionated again by a second knife edge. A significantly higher separation effect can be achieved than with a single nozzle and the optimal cut is also increased to one-third. A considerable reduction in the separation stages required for a given product and tails assay can therefore be achieved, along with a reduction in the energy requirements.

The Helikon technique

The UCOR process, often referred to as the Helikon technique, has been deployed by the Uranium Enrichment Corporation of South Africa. While many details of the process remain undisclosed, the separating element is based on 'a high performance stationary-walled centrifuge using UF_6 in hydrogen'.[126] It is probably similar to the vortex method, in which the UF_6–hydrogen mixture is allowed to swirl around in a separating element with subsequent withdrawal of depleted and enriched fractions. Separation factors for the elements are in the range 1.025–1.030. The cut is about one-twentieth and the cascade developed to deal with this makes use of axial-flow compressors that can transmit several streams which differ in isotopic composition without allowing appreciable mixing between them. Thus many stages can be incorporated into a single unit and the process is viewed as a combination of the separating elements and the cascaded technique.[127]

[123] Rahn *et al.* (note 14), pp. 216–17.

[124] Benedict *et al.* (note 14), pp. 878–80.

[125] Becker, E. W., Nogueira Batista, P. and Völcker, H., 'Uranium enrichment by the separation nozzle method within the framework of German/Brazilian cooperation', *Nuclear Technology*, vol. 52 (Jan. 1981), p. 106.

[126] Roux, A. J. A. and Grant, W. L., 'Uranium enrichment in South Africa', *Nuclear Energy Maturity, Proceedings of the European Center Nuclear Conference, Paris, 21–25 April, 1975, Invited Sessions* (Pergamon: New York, 1975), p. 167, quoted in Benedict *et al.* (note 14), p. 889.

[127] Tait (note 18), pp. 135–36; and Benedict *et al.* (note 14), pp. 888–89.

VII. Laser enrichment

For the past two decades research has been under way in many parts of the world to investigate the potential use of laser methods for enriching uranium (and purifying plutonium) which could then be used for the production of nuclear weapons. The impact of technological developments in the laser field on the nuclear non-proliferation regime has been a cause for concern since the processes themselves were first understood. Several important developments make it necessary to examine the potential impact of recent advances in these methods on the future of the nuclear non-proliferation regime.

In particular, many countries are currently investing substantial amounts of time and effort in laser isotope separation research and plans are being put in place to deploy several facilities at around the turn of the century. As laser technology in general becomes more widely available and its use for isotope separation rapidly reaches maturity, the possibility of its use for weapon-grade fissile material production in small, difficult-to-detect facilities becomes an ever more apparent danger. If the non-proliferation regime is to deal with this challenge adequately, a host of issues related to safeguards and export controls are sure to present themselves and will have to be addressed in the near future.

Although the United States announced in 1990 that it will no longer proceed with plans to construct a large facility for the laser purification of plutonium to weapon-grade, this method is examined here because of the concerns that future decisions to deploy this type of technology by the USA or other countries could pose for the non-proliferation regime.

Principles of laser enrichment

Perhaps surprisingly, photoselecting isotopes dates from experiments in the 1930s with mercury. The separation of uranium by selective photochemistry was also considered at the time of the Manhattan Project.[128] With the advent of the laser these methods were re-examined, and relatively efficient techniques have been found to separate both plutonium and uranium isotopes. The laser's ability to produce collimated light of a very precise frequency allows it to be used to deposit exact amounts of energy on given atoms or molecules—a fact that can be exploited in the isotopic separation process. Laser isotope separation has been discussed widely since the late 1960s,[129] and the fact that advanced lasers are useful for many other applications[130] ensures their continued development and increasing availability. Since some laser methods also use UF_6 as feed material, this has further implications for the ease with which they might be introduced into the enrichment processes now in widespread use.

[128] Robinson, C. P. and Jensen, R. J., 'Laser methods of uranium isotope separation', ed. Villani, *Uranium Enrichment* (note 2), p. 269.

[129] 'Uranium enrichment: rumors of Israeli progress with lasers', News and Comment, *Science*, vol. 183 (22 Mar. 1974), p. 1174.

[130] For example, atomic spectroscopy and chemical reaction research—see, e.g., Casper, B. M., 'Laser enrichment: a new path to proliferation?', *Bulletin of the Atomic Scientists*, vol. 33, no. 1 (Jan. 1977), pp. 31, 41.

Most of the details concerning the research and development of these advanced laser isotope separation processes remain classified and, therefore, some of the information presented below is, of necessity, lacking in detail in some specific areas.

Generic principles

A general laser enrichment process is most readily conceptualized as occurring in three stages:

1. Source preparation: the uranium or plutonium is put into a form amenable to the processing which will subsequently occur, such as UF_6 or uranium metal, depending on the particular process.
2. Excitation: the preferential modification of the source material associated with one of the isotopes (in most cases ^{235}U for uranium enrichment or ^{240}Pu for plutonium purification) through the use of one or more laser types.
3. Extraction: removal of the component which has been thus modified.[131]

Atomic Vapor Laser Isotope Separation

To illustrate the technology involved, the particular process in which the United States has invested most of its efforts is described. The Atomic Vapor Laser Isotope Separation (AVLIS) process has been developed at the Lawrence Livermore National Laboratory (LLNL) with support from the Oak Ridge National Laboratory[132] and is similar to processes being developed in several other countries. In the AVLIS process, the feed material is uranium metal, heated by bombarding it with a beam from an electron gun to produce a stream of uranium vapour.[133] This vapour contains both ^{235}U and ^{238}U atoms. The difference in size of the two respective nuclei (and to a lesser extent the difference in mass and other characteristics)[134] affects the specific wavelengths of light which produce allowable transitions between electron energy levels. These differences are very small, but with finely tuned lasers it is possible selectively to produce transitions leading to ionization in the ^{235}U atoms alone. Once thus positively charged, the ^{235}U atoms are selectively extracted from the vapour stream by attraction to negatively charged collector plates, leaving the uncharged ^{238}U atoms to continue on their path relatively unimpeded. The AVLIS separator is shown in figure 16.

[131] *Advanced Uranium Enrichment Technologies* (note 13), p. 70.
[132] 'DOE extends Martin Marietta contracts', *Nuclear Fuel*, vol. 13, no. 26 (26 Dec. 1988), p. 11.
[133] *Advanced Uranium Enrichment Technologies* (note 13), p. 72; and Cochran *et al.* (note 40), p. 132.
[134] Krass, A. S., 'Laser enrichment of uranium: the proliferation connection', *Science*, vol. 196, no. 4291 (13 May 1977), p. 723.

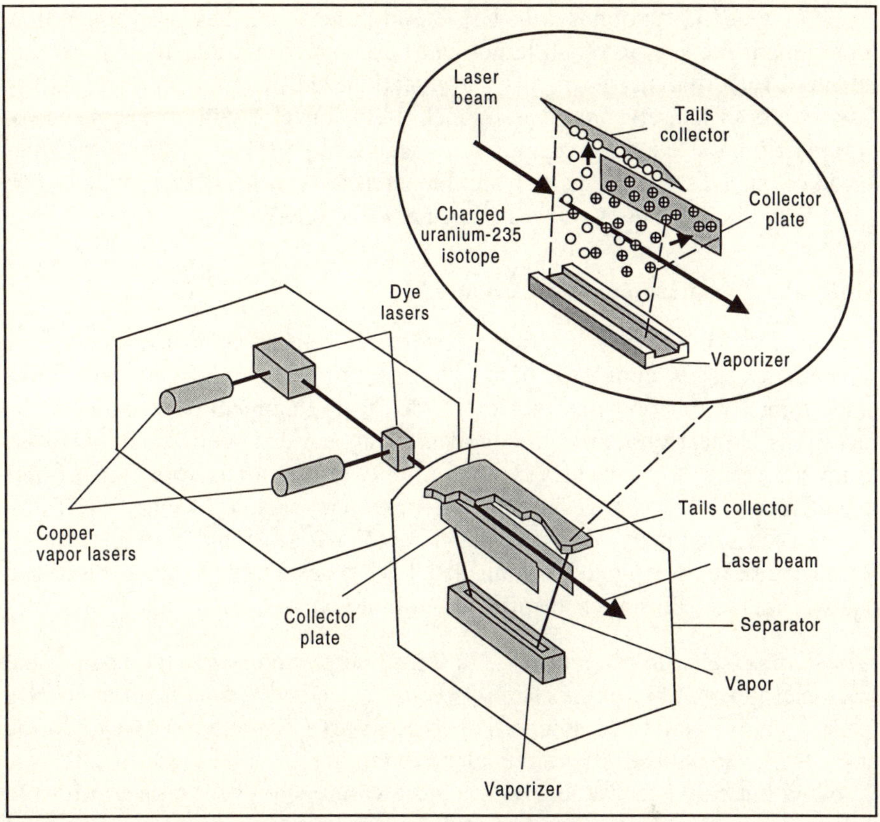

Figure 16. The AVLIS separator

Source: Redrawn from US General Accounting Office (GAO), *Uranium Enrichment: DOE Needs to Pursue Alternative AVLIS Deployment Options*, Report to Selected Congressional Committees, GAO/RCED-91-88 (US General Accounting Office: Washington, DC, Aug. 1991), p. 13.

In the laser system itself copper-vapour lasers[135] 'pump' (provide excitation energy for) dye lasers[136] that are tuned to the particular red-orange wavelengths that ^{235}U absorbs.[137] Four different laser frequencies are used: three to excite the ^{235}U atoms and a fourth to produce ionization. This complex procedure uses the part of the spectrum in which the dye lasers are more efficient[138] and enhances the selection of ^{235}U since each frequency takes advantage of a separate electron-energy level difference.[139]

135 See, e.g., Svelto, O., *Principles of Lasers,* 2nd edn (Plenum: New York, 1982), p. 210.
136 See, e.g., Svelto (note 135), p. 239.
137 Thurston, C., 'AVLIS program to gear up to full-scale 1-million SWU/yr module test by 1988', *Nuclear Fuel*, vol. 10, no. 15 (29 July 1985), pp. 3–5.
138 'Laser enrichment process called proliferation resistant', *Physics Today*, July 1979, p. 18.
139 Cochran *et al.* (note 40), p. 132.

For US AVLIS as opposed to UF_6-based processes it has been noted that: 'enrichment factors are much larger and raise significant questions regarding potential for criticality accidents and unauthorized material production. The laser systems themselves raise additional safety concerns with respect to use of organic fluids at elevated pressures, as well as dye toxicity'.[140] The USA is ahead of the substantial Japanese and French efforts in AVLIS by three to five years[141] and in 1992 costs were estimated at $25–50/SWU.[142]

Molecular Laser Isotope Separation

The chemical properties of molecules formed from different isotopes of the same element (UF_6 composed of six fluorine atoms and either one ^{235}U or one ^{238}U atom, for example) are basically identical. Chemical separation of the molecules is therefore correspondingly difficult. Lasers can be used, however, to impart energy to molecules containing only one of the isotopic forms, producing the chemical changes needed for subsequent chemical separation. These changes are principally of two types—photodissociation and photoreaction.[143] Both have been investigated in some detail and an example of each is discussed below. Figure 17 illustrates the principles of photodissociative separation.

1. *Photodissociative separation.* In a general photodissociative process the laser energy is used to *break chemical bonds* selectively—that is, in molecules made from one particular isotope. This process uses lasers to remove a fluorine atom from only those UF_6 molecules containing ^{235}U. The use of UF_6 was favoured not only because its high vapour pressure allows for high densities in the gaseous phase but also because of the substantial experience already gained in its production and handling for uranium separation using gas diffusion and centrifuge techniques.[144] The most advanced research in this method has been carried out in the FRG by a consortium led by Uranit (Uran-Isotopentrennungs-Gesellschaft mbH).[145] In the process, gas containing UF_6 is first cooled by expansion through a nozzle. Light from an infra-red laser is then used to excite molecular vibrations in the UF_6 molecules containing ^{235}U, leaving those containing ^{238}U unaffected. Subsequently, further irradiation by either an infrared

[140] Prepared testimony of Robert M. Bernero, Director, Office of Nuclear Material and Safeguards, NRC, 10 Apr. 1991, *Fiscal Year 1992 Department of Energy Authorization (Atomic Vapor Laser Isotope Separation R&D Program),* Hearing before the Subcommittee on Energy of the Committee on Science, Space, and Technology, US House of Representatives, 102nd Congress, 1st Session (US Government Printing Office: Washington, DC, 1991), p. 22.

[141] Statement of James I. Davis, Associate Director for Lasers, LLNL, 10 Apr. 1991, *Atomic Vapor Laser Isotope Separation R&D Program* (note 140), p. 47

[142] Dizard, W., '100-hour AVLIS test in December to be milestone for program', *Nuclear Fuel,* 23 Nov. 1992, p. 5.

[143] Robinson, C. P. and Jensen, R. J., 'Laser methods of uranium isotope separation', ed. Villani, *Uranium Enrichment* (note 2), p. 280.

[144] Robinson, C. P. and Jensen, R. J., 'Laser methods of uranium isotope separation', ed. Villani, *Uranium Enrichment* (note 2), p. 281.

[145] Hibbs, M., 'Laser team of West Germany's Uranit "fights for survival" of MLIS R&D', *Nuclear Fuel,* vol. 13, no. 19 (19 Sep. 1988), p. 4.

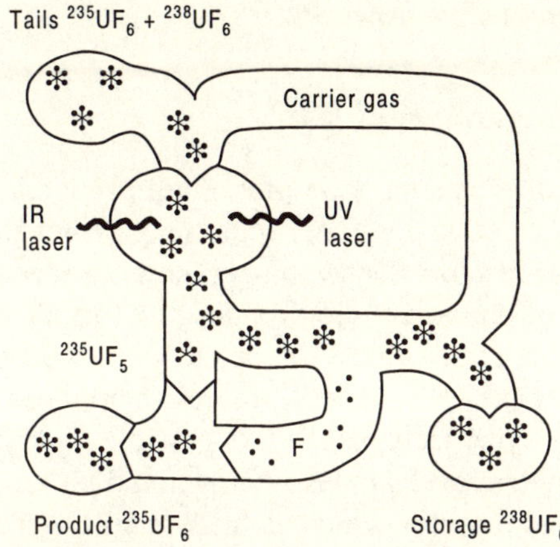

Figure 17. The photodissociative MLIS process

Source: Redrawn from Rahn, F. J. *et al.*, *A Guide to Nuclear Power Technology: A Resource for Decision Making* (John Wiley: New York, 1984), figure 6.20, p. 210. © 1984 by John Wiley & Sons, Inc. Reprinted by permission of John Wiley & Sons, Inc.

or ultraviolet laser then dissociates only the excited molecules into uranium pentafluoride (UF_5) and a fluorine atom. The desired UF_5 quickly condenses into a powdered form ('laser snow') which can be easily collected.[146]

2. *Photoreactive separation.* The US-based firm Isotopes Technologies (IT, once headed by a former Department of Energy Deputy Assistant Secretary for Uranium Enrichment) has claimed the feasibility of having a laser enrichment plant operating at a cost of under $50 million using a specific type of photo-reactive laser separation described here.[147] Employing 'off-the-shelf' modular technology,[148] the process has been called CRISLA (Chemical Reaction by Isotope Selective Laser Activation). As in photodissociative separation, UF_6 molecules containing ^{235}U are first preferentially excited by a laser (carbon monoxide in this case). The process then makes use of the fact that when a mixture of UF_6 and a proprietary reagent (called RX) is irradiated by the laser, the rate of reaction of the excited UF_6 molecules with RX is over 10 000 times[149] that of the unexcited molecules. The product of the reaction (called URX) is therefore enriched in ^{235}U and, being chemically and physically distinct from UF_6, is easily separated by standard techniques. The power of the lasers in this process is potentially lower than in the other methods described since the laser is used only for excitation and not for ionization or dissociation.

146 Krass *et al.* (note 2), p. 170.

147 'Longenecker to head Isotope Technologies', *Nuclear Fuel*, vol. 14, no. 13 (26 June 1989), pp. 1–2.

148 Lindeman, E., 'Isotope technologies marketing SWU on small scale to U.S. utilities', *Nuclear Fuel*, vol. 14, no. 4 (20 Feb. 1989), p. 4.

149 Erkens, J. W., 'CRISLA aims to reduce costs', *Nuclear Engineering International*, vol. 34, no. 419 (June 1989), p. 48.

Such techniques are sometimes referred to as 'laser-assisted' processes, and their number has continually grown.[150]

Plutonium isotope separation by laser

As further discussed in chapter 3 on plutonium production, the ^{239}Pu used in nuclear weapon construction does not occur in nature but can be produced from ^{238}U atoms in nuclear reactors. Depending on how the reactor is configured and run, other isotopes of plutonium are produced to varying degrees. US nuclear weapons, for example, are designed to operate with 'weapon-grade' plutonium composed of 6 per cent ^{240}Pu or less, the rest composed of ^{239}Pu (with very small amounts of the other isotopes).[151] It is possible to produce such plutonium in reactors, although this results in less than optimal power output. Commercial reactors discharge plutonium which is still mainly ^{239}Pu but also contains typically about 25 per cent ^{240}Pu and significant amounts of the other isotopes.[152] Chemical methods are then used to extract the plutonium and uranium separately as discussed in chapter 3.

In 1986 the USA selected the AVLIS process to convert fuel-grade ^{240}Pu (7–19 per cent)[153] owned by the Defense Department to weapon-grade plutonium.[154] Technologically there is considerable overlap in the uranium and plutonium AVLIS processes. In the LLNL facility most of this overlap has been in the laser systems. Copper vapour and dye lasers have been used for both, although tuned to slightly different frequencies.[155] In fact the laser hardware in the LLNL's Laser Demonstration Facility has been used to supply laser light for both the plutonium and uranium separation programmes.[156] There are differences in the operation and design of the production processes, however, primarily in the separator technology and with materials handling.

Although not as much is known (other than regarding the US programme) about the state of development of plutonium laser separation methods worldwide, the similarity in US AVLIS approaches to separating different isotopes of plutonium and uranium indicates the possibilities available for countries developing such techniques for uranium enrichment. In addition these tech-

[150] Krass *et al.* (note 2), pp. 171–72.

[151] *Energy and Water Development Appropriations for 1989* (note 6), pp. 1117, 1144.

[152] Lovins, A.B., 'Nuclear weapons and power-reactor plutonium', *Nature*, vol. 283, no. 5750 (28 Feb. 1980), p. 818.

[153] Hearings on National Defense Authorization Act for Fiscal Year 1989—H.R. 4264 and *Oversight of Previously Authorized Programs, DOE National Security Programs* before the Procurement and Military Nuclear Systems Subcommittee of the Committee on Armed Services, House of Representatives, 100th Congress, 2nd Session (US Government Printing Office: Washington, DC, 1988), p. 314.

[154] 'DOE selects AVLIS for Pu production also', *Nuclear Fuel*, vol. 11, no. 9 (5 May 1986), p. 13; *Energy and Water Development Appropriations for 1989* (note 6), p. 733; 'Laser technology', *Energy and Technology Review*, July/Aug. 1989, p. 20.

[155] *Fiscal Year 1987 Department of Energy Authorization*, Hearings before the Subcommittee on Energy Research and Production of the Committee on Science and Technology, House of Representatives, 99th Congress, 2nd Session (US Government Printing Office: Washington, DC, 1986), Vol. 1, p. 71.

[156] 'Special isotope separation program', *Energy and Technology Review*, July/Aug. 1989, p. 24.

niques have the potential for making reactor-grade plutonium more directly usable in a nuclear weapon by removing the unwanted even isotopes.[157]

The Special Isotope Separation controversy

As mentioned above, laser isotope separation has figured prominently in a long-standing debate, now resolved, involving the planned use of laser separation of plutonium isotopes by the United States for weapon purposes. Although the issue of plant construction in this case has now been put to rest, the technologies applicable for plutonium and uranium isotope separation have many elements in common and there are inherent proliferation dangers associated with any future development of this process by the USA or other countries. It is thus instructive to begin with a brief discussion of the issues surrounding this recent debate.

Implementation of the 1987 US–Soviet Treaty on the Elimination of Intermediate-Range and Shorter-Range Missiles (the INF Treaty) having proceeded as scheduled, and agreement on strategic arms reductions (the START I and II treaties) having been reached, there has been created a surplus of fissile material that can be used for nuclear weapons.[158] As seen in chapter 3, discussions of ways to eliminate current stocks of fissile material are proceeding.[159] With the exception of tritium (with a half-life of about 12 years) the important elements of nuclear weapons—^{239}Pu and ^{235}U—decay extremely slowly and therefore can be recycled from existing or retired weapons in order to construct more modern ones if need be. Such recycling has become common practice.

Although the USA expressed a desire to keep the warheads being withdrawn under the INF Treaty intact,[160] the Department of Energy (DOE) stated as far back as 1988 that reprocessed plutonium from warheads aboard newly retired Poseidon submarines would satisfy their near-term defence requirements.[161] At the same time, however, until late 1989 the DOE had continued to press for the creation of a new plutonium source 'technologically diverse from production reactors',[162] and the various issues associated with them, in order to provide 'flexibility in *rapid increases* in plutonium production capacity'.[163] For this purpose, a Special Isotope Separation (SIS) facility was planned for completion in 1995, to employ a sophisticated laser technique to remove the unwanted isotopes from Defense Department plutonium, upgrading it to weapon-grade material.

[157] See, e.g., Fischer (note 5), p. 48.

[158] See, e.g., Lockwood, D., 'Nuclear arms control', *SIPRI Yearbook 1993: World Armaments and Disarmament* (Oxford University Press: Oxford, 1993), pp. 549–73; and Lockwood, D., 'Nuclear arms control', *SIPRI Yearbook 1994* (Oxford University Press: Oxford, 1994), pp. 640–72.

[159] For a recent examination of the issues involved in the destruction of nuclear weapons and the disposal of fissile materials see Kokoski, R., 'Nuclear weapon destruction', *SIPRI Yearbook 1995: Armaments, Disarmament and International Security* (Oxford University Press: Oxford, 1995), appendix 16A, pp. 672–80.

[160] *DOE National Security Programs* (note 153), p. 257.

[161] *Energy and Water Development Appropriations for 1989* (note 6), Part 6, p. 773.

[162] *DOE National Security Programs* (note 153), p. 490.

[163] *Energy and Water Development Appropriations for 1989* (note 6), p. 1145; emphasis added.

Much concern arose over the inherent conflict in a policy which would authorize what could have amounted to several billion dollars to construct and operate a laser facility to produce material then unneeded, and which was likely to be in over-abundant supply in the not-too-distant future. In a December 1989 report, the National Academy of Sciences affirmed the adequacy of available plutonium to maintain a nuclear stockpile similar to the one in existence.[164]

Further implications involved the long-standing United States tenet on non-proliferation: to keep the military and civil uses of nuclear energy separate. Although the use of commercial spent fuel for weapon purposes is forbidden by the Hart–Simpson–Mitchell amendment[165] to the 1983 Nuclear Regulatory Commission Authorization Act, the DOE has admitted that, while the design life of the SIS plant was 30 years, given its planned capacity there was none the less only enough Defense Department feed to keep it occupied for about nine years. There had thus been concern that, once a plant was built and running, pressure would have been brought to bear on Congress to allow commercial spent fuel to be used.[166]

The purification of plutonium by the USA and perhaps other nuclear weapon states could complicate investigations of methods of nuclear warhead verification as well.[167] These rely on neutron emission from the plutonium-240 which makes up about 6 per cent of current weapon-grade plutonium. For example, the presence of ^{240}Pu in a warhead has been shown to be of potential use in verification of sea-launched cruise missiles (SLCMs).[168]

The DOE had planned to begin construction of the SIS facility in 1989,[169] and have it fully operational by 1995.[170] The Energy Secretary, strongly backing the project earlier in 1989, began questioning its necessity by the end of the year.[171] Finally, citing both the availability of plutonium from other sources and funding priorities, the DOE decided in early 1990 to cancel SIS construction.[172]

[164] *New York Times*, 21 Dec. 1989.

[165] Cochran *et al.* (note 40), p. 96; and Palmer, G. and Bolef, D. I., 'Laser isotope separation: the plutonium connection', *Bulletin of the Atomic Scientists*, vol. 40, no. 3 (Mar. 1984), p. 30.

[166] See also a 26 May 1989 letter from Paul Leventhal, President of the Nuclear Control Institute (NCI), to Sam Nunn, Chairman of the Senate Armed Services Committee. Co-signed by 28 leading arms control experts it recommended against SIS construction, stating that this could 'severely compromise U.S. non-proliferation objectives'. Concern was also expressed that the SIS operation 'would set a precedent for the use of such plutonium purification technology in the nuclear programs of other nations, including non-nuclear weapons states'. Regarding the technologies to be employed in the plant (see below) the authors pointed to 'unprecedented challenges to containing the nuclear programs of emerging and advanced industrial nations to exclusively peaceful purposes' and feared the precedent-setting nature of AVLIS demonstration in increasing the risks of diversion and terrorism. (Copy courtesy Deborah Holland, NCI)

[167] Letter from NCI to Sam Nunn (note 166).

[168] Cochran, T. B., 'Black Sea experiment only a start', *Bulletin of the Atomic Scientists*, vol. 45, no. 9 (Nov. 1989), pp. 13–16.

[169] *Energy and Water Development Appropriations for 1989* (note 6), p. 923.

[170] *DOE National Security Programs* (note 153), pp. 235, 263; and *Energy and Water Development Appropriations for 1989* (note 6), p. 1110.

[171] *Washington Post*, 28 Nov. 1989, p. A6; and 28 Jan. 1990, p. A4.

[172] Adams, P., 'DoE drops funds for Idaho plutonium plant', *Defense News*, vol. 5, no. 6 (5 Feb. 1990), p. 40.

The positive impact of the cancellation of the SIS programme in the USA notwithstanding, it has been recognized 'that the successful development of plutonium enrichment techniques would ease access to weapon-grade material and thus simplify the acquisition of high-performance weapons. Countries with nuclear power programmes could, in principle, obtain weapon-grade plutonium from their highly irradiated power reactor spent fuel if plutonium enrichment became a viable option'.[173]

Research and development

Further insight into the relative merits and potential dangers associated with high-technology enrichment techniques such as laser methods can be gained by looking at the vigour of current research, the planned facilities and the choices made by individual countries or companies and (where possible) the reasons for making them. These aspects are discussed in relative detail for laser technology, as this is believed by many of the technologically advanced countries to be the most promising new method. Potentially, therefore, it may pose the most dangers from a proliferation viewpoint. This is especially true if construction and operation of a clandestine facility were to be attempted.

Furthermore, since the laser process, even if developed only on a laboratory scale, could enable of the production of significant amounts of enriched uranium, it is especially critical that ongoing R&D efforts are followed in this area.[174]

Of the NPT states parties, the USA in 1982 selected the AVLIS process in preference to two other advanced uranium enrichment techniques for further development. In 1985 the AVLIS process was again selected for future US enrichment needs, this time in preference to the advanced gas centrifuge.[175] Former US Energy Secretary John Herrington has called AVLIS the 'technology of the future, the uranium enrichment process of the 21st Century'.[176] In its comparison study, the US Department of Energy evaluation board report stated that the advanced gas centrifuge would necessitate the 'development of machines that are at the upper limit of present technology in terms of materials components, design and manufacturing capabilities'.[177] At the time, LLNL's then Associate Director for Lasers contrasted this to the AVLIS programme,

[173] Albright, D., Berkhout, F. and Walker, W., SIPRI, *World Inventory of Plutonium and Highly Enriched Uranium*, 1992 (Oxford University Press: Oxford, 1993), p. 16.

[174] Liebert, W. and Neuneck, G., 'Civil-military ambivalence of science and the problem of qualitative arms control—an example of laser isotope separation', eds H. G. Brauch, H. J. van der Graaf, J. Grin and W. A. Smit, *Controlling the Development and Spread of Military Technology: Lessons from the Past and Challenges for the 1990s* (VU University Press: Amsterdam, 1992), p. 49.

[175] *DOE Uranium Enrichment Program*, Hearing before the Subcommittee on Energy Conservation and Power of the Committee on Energy and Commerce, US House of Representatives, 99th Congress, 2nd Session (US Government Printing Office: Washington, DC, 1986), p. 18; and Cochran *et al.* (note 40), p. 132.

[176] *Fiscal Year 1987 Department of Energy Authorization* (note 155), p. 48.

[177] Uranium Enrichment Technology Evaluation and Assessment, DOE Process Evaluation Board Report, 15 May 1985, p. 6, reprinted in *Nuclear Fuel*, vol. 10, no. 12 (17 June 1985), p. 19.

stating: 'we have taken relatively unsophisticated material and produced a sophisticated system.'[178]

The stated reasons for using AVLIS for uranium enrichment in the USA have been to remain competitive in the future and to 'assure the country has the military security that it requires for its Naval Propulsion Program and other programs'.[179] In its annual report for 1987, the DOE announced the successful demonstration of laser enrichment technology at one-half plant scale.[180] By the end of 1993 $1.3 billion had been spent on the AVLIS programme but there was still some debate as to whether the technology demonstrations had shown the process ready for commercialization.[181] In 1992 a full-scale prototype was run, demonstrating the ability to produce tens of kilograms of LEU product suitable for reactor use in a single step. In a single demonstration in December it was operated for more than 100 hours processing over 1 ton of uranium metal and producing hundreds of kilograms of enriched product.[182]

The 1992 Energy Policy Act established the US Enrichment Corporation (USEC) and the enrichment ernterprise was transferred from the DOE to the newly created government corporation in mid-1993. After much uncertainty over the fate of AVLIS in the USA the USEC decided in mid-1994 to commence taking the steps necessary to commercialize the technology. Funding is set at $3 million per month with a facility expected to be in operation by shortly after the year 2000 according to the USEC Chief Executive Officer.[183]

In *Japan* the Japan Atomic Energy Research Institute (JAERI) has been researching the AVLIS process since 1976. The Laser Atomic Separation Engineering Research Association of Japan (LASER-J) was formed in 1987[184] by nine commercial utilities, the Japan Atomic Power Company (JAPCO) and the Central Research Institute of the Electrical Power Industry (CRIEPI).[185] Mitsubishi, Hitachi and Toshiba have also joined LASER-J.[186] The MLIS process is being developed by the Institute of Physical & Chemical Research (IPCR), which in 1988 reported achieving a separation factor of 4.7. The process employed is a variant of the photodissociative process and quantities of 'laser snow' (solid UF_5 enriched in ^{235}U) measured in hundreds of milligrams

[178] Thurston (note 137), p. 4.

[179] *Fiscal Year 1987 Department of Energy Authorization* (note 155), pp. 8, 36.

[180] 'DOE reports '87 net loss of $385-million; SWU sales total nearly 1.13-billion', *Nuclear Fuel*, vol. 13, no. 12 (13 June 1988), p. 4.

[181] 'Outlook on USEC', *Nuclear Fuel*, 11 Oct. 1993, p. 11.

[182] Haynam, C., *et al.*, Status of gadolinium enrichment technology at LLNL', ed. J. A. Paisner, *Laser Isotope Separation*, Proceedings of the International Society for Optical Engineering, Los Angeles, Calif., 19–20 Jan 1993 (The International Society for Optical Engineering: Bellingham, Washington, DC, 1993), p. 2.

[183] Dizard, W. and Knapik, M., 'USEC approves AVLIS commercialization; SWU project to get $3 million monthly', *Nuclear Fuel*, 18 July 1994, p. 1.

[184] Usui, N., 'Japan's PNC commissions centrifuge enrichment demonstration plant', *Nuclear Fuel*, vol. 13, no. 9 (2 May 1988), p. 6.

[185] Usui, N., 'Japanese set up AVLIS research group', *Nuclear Fuel*, vol. 12, no. 3 (9 Feb. 1987), p. 12.

[186] Hiruo, E., 'U.S. share of enrichment market said to hinge on AVLIS operation date', *Nuclear Fuel*, vol. 13, no. 6 (21 Mar. 1988), p. 5.

were obtained.[187] Should laser enrichment prove reliable and economical it is possible that some of the new enrichment capacity which the Japan Nuclear Fuel Industries Company (JNFI) is planning may also use this technology.[188] Further, the Industrial Research Institute (IRI) has reportedly been evaluating the CRISLA process.[189] The Japanese Atomic Energy Commission decided in 1992 to develop a new generation of centrifuges that would use unspecified new materials and have 150–200 per cent increased capacity. Their commercial introduction is planned for 2004 at the latest at the Rokkasho enrichment plant.[190] None the less, the Japanese spending on laser enrichment is approaching $100 million per year in an effort to make up for lost time in this area.[191] After the completion of the first phase of the R&D process in 1992, the second phase involved full-scale AVLIS hardware development. In 1998 a decision will be made on whether to build a demonstration facility.[192]

The *Federal Republic of Germany*, now thought to have developed the most advanced MLIS technology, chose to concentrate on this method, believing it to be superior to the atomic laser process at least in part since it uses UF_6—not requiring high temperature or 'highly aggressive' uranium vapour.[193] The leader of MLIS research in the FRG has been Uranit, the German shareholder in Urenco, owned by Nukem GmbH, Preussenelektrika AG and Hoechst AG.[194] By the late 1980s a separation factor of 15 had been achieved on a laboratory scale, putting this effort well ahead of the Japanese MLIS (and of the US, British and French efforts, all of which abandoned MLIS after only achieving a separation factor of approximately 2.5).[195] In 1992, however, Urenco announced that its MLIS work would be abandoned and in 1994 its research on AVLIS was discontinued in favour of a next-generation advanced centrifuge design.[196]

In the *UK*, the United Kingdom Atomic Energy Authority (UKAEA), having originally concentrated on molecular laser separation, in 1984 decided in favour of the atomic separation process. British Nuclear Fuels plc (BNFL) initiated a laser isotope separation programme in 1982 and by 1986 felt it would be in a

[187] Usui, N., 'Japan's IPCR reports breakthrough using MLIS enrichment process', *Nuclear Fuel*, vol. 13, no. 8 (18 Apr. 1988), p. 7.

[188] 'NRC receives first license application to export U to Japan for enrichment', *Nuclear Fuel*, vol. 12, no. 12 (15 June 1987), p. 12.

[189] Ushio, S., 'Japanese move forward with AVLIS plans', *Nuclear Fuel*, vol. 11, no. 12 (16 June 1986), p. 8.

[190] Usui, N., 'Japan AEC formally approves new uranium enrichment policy', *Nuclear Fuel*, 17 Aug. 1992, p. 13.

[191] MacLachlan, A., 'French to continue laser enrichment until at least 1997 demonstration', *Nuclear Fuel*, 28 Mar. 1994, p. 16.

[192] Morioka, N., 'New Japanese AVLIS program', ed. J. A. Paisner, *Laser Isotope Separation*, Proceedings of the International Society for Optical Engineering, Los Angeles, Calif., 19–20 Jan 1993 (International Society for Optical Engineering: Bellingham, Washington, DC, 1993), p. 2.

[193] Hibbs, M., 'Laser team of West Germany's Uranit "fights for survival" of MLIS R&D', *Nuclear Fuel*, vol. 13, no. 19 (19 Sep. 1988), pp. 4–5.

[194] Hibbs, M., 'Late funding effort may save German laser enrichment project', *Nuclear Fuel*, vol. 13, no. 21 (17 Oct. 1988), p. 3.

[195] Hibbs (note 193), p. 5.

[196] 'Urenco to end AVLIS research', *Nuclear Fuel*, 28 Mar. 1994, p. 13.

position to consider plant installation in the late 1990s.[197] Development work in conjunction with the UKAEA is proceeding, and a small-scale demonstration was planned for the mid-1990s.[198]

Begun in 1985 in *France*, laser enrichment technology development is being pursued by the CEA although, as far as a commercial plant is concerned, its subsidiary Cogema, which is co-funding the research, will ultimately be the beneficiary.[199] Although believed to be behind the USA in laser enrichment development,[200] France is also pursuing AVLIS (the French acronym for which is 'SILVA'—Séparation Isotopique par Laser de la Vapeur Atomique d'uranium) and evaluated and abandoned centrifuge technology even before a similar decision was taken by the USA.[201] At the CEA's Saclay centre a pre-industrial SILVA process plant has been in operation for several years and by 1992 the process was used to produce 10 grams of pressurized water reactor (PWR)-grade uranium in 'just over two hours'.[202] This facility is now being expanded to allow full-scale tests to proceed and, with planned demonstration of the feasibility of the process by 1997, a pilot plant could be in operation between 2000 and 2005. With the eventual goal of developing the method to the point at which it can replace the 10.8 million SWU Georges Besse Eurodif gaseous diffusion plant, the current annual budget is over 400 million francs.[203]

Begun in 1973, research in *China* into laser isotope separation has involved both the molecular and atomic processes; but since 1985 emphasis has been on the atomic process.[204] The AVLIS process was used in October 1991 to re-enrich spent fuel and depleted uranium to give enrichment levels of over 3 per cent ^{235}U in one step.[205] Gas-centrifuge technology is also being investigated, and China hopes to decide on an enrichment priority by the turn of the century.[206] At Fudan University a replica of the CRISLA process developed by the US-based Isotope Technologies firm has been constructed using published data.[207]

[197] 'Enrichers discuss prospects for laser SWU', *Nuclear Fuel*, vol. 11, no. 18 (8 Sep. 1986), p. 5.

[198] Marshall, P., 'BNFL says operating profit is up while export earnings drop 12%', *Nuclear Fuel*, vol. 13, no. 23 (14 Nov. 1988), p. 5; and *Atom*, no. 389 (Mar. 1989), p. 46.

[199] MacLachlan, A., 'French "sages" could advise linking R&D, nuclear industry', *Nucleonics Week*, vol. 30, no. 16 (20 Apr. 1989), p. 15; and Norris, R. S., Burrows, A. S. and Fieldhouse, R. W., *Nuclear Weapons Databook Volume V: British, French, and Chinese Nuclear Weapons* (Westview Press: Boulder, Colo., 1994), p. 202.

[200] Thurston (note 137), p. 5.

[201] *Fiscal Year 1987 Department of Energy Authorization* (note 155), p. 44.

[202] *Programme for Promoting Nuclear Non-Proliferation (PPNN) Newsbrief*, no. 18 (summer 1992), p. 6; MacLachlan, A., 'French find chemical enrichment is a pleasant economic surprise', *Nuclear Fuel*, vol. 12, no. 2 (26 Jan. 1987), p. 2; Capron, J-P., 'Nuclear electricity, the answer to energy challenges', *Atom*, no. 388 (Feb. 1989), p. 34; and MacLachlan, A., 'Cogema will not deploy AVLIS for reprocessed U until after 2000', *Nuclear Fuel*, vol. 13, no. 10 (16 May 1988), p. 4.

[203] MacLachlan, A., 'French to continue laser enrichment until at least 1997 demonstration', *Nuclear Fuel*, 28 Mar. 1994, p. 15.

[204] 'China has been selling enriched uranium commercially since 1981, official says', *Nuclear Fuel*, vol. 13, no. 20 (3 Oct. 1988), p. 12; and Norris *et al.* (note 199), p. 345.

[205] Kong, Yan, 'China's nuclear bureaucracy', *Jane's Intelligence Review*, July 1993, p. 324.

[206] Lindeman, E., MacLachlan, A. and Hibbs, M., 'Nuclear fuel survey: views differ on market impact of Soviet, Chinese U/SWU', *Nuclear Fuel*, vol. 14, no. 1 (9 Jan. 1989), p. 7.

[207] Knapik, M., 'Looking ahead to the enrichment marketplace of the 1990s', *Nuclear Fuel*, vol. 14, no. 13 (26 June 1989), p. 2.

South Africa, having given up its nuclear weapon programme, has reportedly decided to develop laser uranium enrichment techniques in order to manufacture reactor fuel and hopes to become competitive on the international market.[208] Half of the South African Atomic Energy Corporation (AEC) R&D budget of R80-million (approximately US $24 million) is being spent on developing the molecular laser enrichment process and funding is projected until 1995 at this level. The AEC hope was to replace the indigenously developed stationary-wall centrifuge process by MLIS. Three of the major technical problems associated with the MLIS process have apparently been solved by the AEC: the micro-aerodynamics of flow cooling, repeating laser pulses at 2 kilohertz (kHz) as well as controlling UF_6 concentration in the flow-cooling network.[209] The technical feasibility of the method has now been proven and the technology developed to 'macro-scale' in the laboratories at Pelindaba.[210] A centrifuge development programme was recently abandoned on the verge of building a pilot cascade in favour of pursuing laser enrichment.[211] However, the start-up date for a pilot laser enrichment plant, which had been scheduled for 1995 with a theoretical capacity of 10 000 SWU, will now depend on ongoing discussions with potential partners, including both domestic and foreign companies. One of the main open questions now that South Africa has abandoned its nuclear weapon programme and become a state party to the NPT is whether it will maintain adequate control over the laser enrichment technology that the country will develop.[212]

Although information about the programme is rather sparse, research into uranium laser isotope separation was carried out in the former USSR at the Institute of Spectroscopy and the Kurchatov Institute.[213] The head of the development of laser uranium enrichment in the USSR reportedly stated in 1985 that the process had already been 'turned . . . over to industry' and they are thought to have made a great deal of progress.[214] However, a more recent report indicates that the USSR does not have plans to build additional enrichment capacity.[215]

Aspects of both MLIS and AVLIS have also been investigated in *the Netherlands*. In *Canada,* Atomic Energy Canada Ltd (AECL) expanded its activities

[208] Ottaway, D., 'Pretoria drops nuclear arms plan', *International Herald Tribune*, 18 Oct. 1991, p. 1.

[209] Cherry, M., 'A future for South Africa's nuclear agency?', *Nature*, vol. 364 (1 July 1993), p. 9.

[210] MacLachlan, A., 'South African AEC looking for partners to help fund laser enrichment facility', *Nuclear Fuel,* 29 Aug. 1994, p. 1.

[211] Hibbs, M., 'South African AEC restructuring from secrecy toward an open market', *Nucleonics Week,* 10 Mar. 1994, p. 7.

[212] Fischer, D., 'Reversing nuclear proliferation: South Africa', *Security Dialogue*, vol. 24, no. 3 (1993), p. 284.

[213] Central Intelligence Agency, *USSR Energy Atlas* (US Government Printing Office: Washington, DC, 1985), p. 43, cited in Cochran *et al.* (note 40), p. 94; and Robinson, C. P. and Jensen, R. J., 'Laser methods of uranium isotope separation', ed. Villani, *Uranium Enrichment* (note 2), p. 272.

[214] *Fiscal Year 1987 Department of Energy Authorization* (note 155), p. 44.

[215] 'European enrichers say they are hurt by Soviet/Chinese aggressiveness', *Nuclear Fuel,* vol. 14, no. 1 (9 Jan. 1989), p. 7.

in laser separation research in the late 1980s, and research has reportedly also been conducted in *Australia*.[216]

Of the non-signatories to the NPT, work on laser enrichment of uranium has also been pursued in *Brazil* at the Institute for Energy and Nuclear Research (IPEN) as well as at the Air Force's Aerospace Technology Center (CTA) in São José dos Campos, the principal site of Brazil's rocket research programme. While there have been reports that, as far as the CTA effort is concerned at least, the programme has now been de-emphasized,[217] both atomic and molecular laser enrichment methods continue to be developed at the Institute of Advanced Studies. Uranium has been enriched to 50 per cent ^{235}U by the atomic method and it has been judged recently that laser enrichment technology will be mastered by the next decade.[218]

As early as 1974 a physicist with the Ministry of Defence of *Israel* stated that Israel had demonstrated the feasibility of laser enrichment.[219] In 1986 Mordechai Vanunu told of the existence of an Israeli laser separation facility at the Dimona Centre, which could be used to enrich uranium and purify plutonium.[220] According to Vanunu, in 1981 Israeli scientists actually began to use lasers to separate uranium isotopes, expanding the unit to production-scale when he left Dimona in 1985.[221] A US report has stated that 'Israel has no known [uranium] enrichment capability, but it has been working to develop laser isotope separation that if successful could provide a new source of weapons materials'.[222] An LLNL source has also reported that Israel has been investigating the AVLIS process.[223]

In *Iran*, although officials have denied that their country is engaged in any work related to fissile material production, the CIA has claimed that there are indications that the current regime has reactivated a laser enrichment programme which it inherited from the regime of the former Shah.[224] *India* has also reportedly conducted research into laser enrichment techniques at the Bhabha Atomic Research Centre.[225]

Cooperative efforts involve Eurodif, a multinational uranium enrichment company, which is reported to be actively pursuing an AVLIS capability.[226] In

[216] Silver, R., 'Canadian officials looking at advances for fuel cycle, including enrichment', *Nuclear Fuel,* vol. 13, no. 13 (27 June 1988), p. 6; Casper (note 130), p. 40; and Krass *et al.* (note 2), p. 235.

[217] Hibbs, M., 'Bonn: there is "no military background" to Brazil's unsafeguarded program', *Nuclear Fuel*, vol. 14, no. 16 (7 Aug. 1989), p. 13.

[218] Institute for Defense and Disarmament Studies, *Arms Control Reporter* (IDDS: Brookline, Mass.), sheet 452.B.161, July 1994; and Spector, L. S., *The Undeclared Bomb* (Ballinger: Cambridge, Mass., 1988), pp. 259–60.

[219] Quoted in 'Uranium enrichment: rumors of Israeli progress with lasers' (note 129), p. 1172.

[220] Barnaby, F., *The Invisible Bomb: The Nuclear Arms Race in the Middle East* (I. B. Tauris: London, 1989), pp. 25–26.

[221] Barnaby (note 220), p. 40.

[222] Donnelly, W. H., 'Israel and nuclear weapons', Congressional Research Service (CRS) Issue Brief, IB87079, Library of Congress, Washington, DC, 17 Nov. 1989, p. 3.

[223] Thurston (note 137), p. 5.

[224] Hibbs, M., 'U.S. officials say Iran is pursuing fissile material production research', *Nuclear Fuel*, 7 Dec. 1992, p. 5.

[225] Spector, L. S., *The New Nuclear Nations* (Vintage: New York, 1985), p. 101.

[226] Hiruo, E., 'U.S. share of enrichment market said to hinge on AVLIS operation date', *Nuclear Fuel*, vol. 13, no. 6 (21 Mar. 1988), p. 5.

addition, in a joint statement,[227] the UK and the FRG have expressed receptivity to the proposal that laser enrichment technology be included in their Urenco cooperation. Until the mid-1990s, however, Urenco was planning to introduce in a modular fashion improved centrifuge designs with which laser technology will have to compete.[228] It has been agreed that any future collaboration on enrichment between France and Germany will involve laser methods.[229]

VIII. Comparison of uranium enrichment technologies

In addition to scientific feasibility the important features of any enrichment technology include: (*a*) the separation factor, (*b*) throughput, (*c*) inventory requirements, (*d*) energy requirements, (*e*) capital cost and (*f*) operating cost elements (including reliability).[230]

An advantage of gaseous diffusion and to some extent the gas centrifuge is that they involve to varying degrees tried and true technology. However, since the separation factor is so small for each stage, diffusion requires a 1200-stage 'cascade' (each stage enriching the uranium slightly more) in order to produce 3 per cent ^{235}U reactor-grade uranium from natural uranium.[231] Weapon-grade uranium requires about 4000 stages. In the case of the gas centrifuge only about 10 stages are required for reactor-grade and as few as 35 are needed to produce weapon-grade material. On the other hand the capacity of a given gas-centrifuge cascade is very small, and many thousands of individual centrifuges are required to produce substantial quantities of enriched product.[232] With lasers, however, the AVLIS process is expected to be able to enrich natural uranium to 3–5 per cent in a single stage[233] and 'possibly could be developed to produce HEU'.[234]

In addition, laser isotope separation of uranium can remove most of the ^{235}U from the uranium ore, whereas gaseous diffusion can leave more than a quarter of the ^{235}U. Lasers could also be used to remove the remaining ^{235}U from wastes of other types of separation.[235] Laser techniques can be more selective in their enrichment capability than either gaseous diffusion or centrifuges. Unwanted and potentially dangerous ^{232}U, ^{234}U and ^{236}U are not enriched by laser processes: decay products of ^{232}U emit gamma radiation and are a major health and materials handling problem; ^{234}U raises concerns about inhalation and internal

[227] Joint Declaration Between the UK and West Germany on the Peaceful Use of Nuclear Energy, signed in Bonn, 25 July 1989, reprinted in *Nuclear Fuel*, vol. 14, no. 16 (7 Aug. 1989), p. 5.

[228] 1988 Urenco Annual Report quoted in *Nuclear Fuel*, vol. 14, no. 7 (3 Apr. 1989), p. 5.

[229] MacLachlan, A., 'Potential French–German enrichment cooperation will be in lasers', *Nuclear Fuel*, vol. 14, no. 13 (26 June 1989), p. 4.

[230] *Advanced Uranium Enrichment Technologies* (note 13), pp. 69, 87.

[231] *Advanced Uranium Enrichment Technologies* (note 13), p. 10.

[232] Casper (note 130), p. 30.

[233] Lindeman, E., 'Less feed, fewer SWU, lower assay needed to enrich REPU with AVLIS, DOE says', *Nuclear Fuel*, vol. 12, no. 12 (15 June 1987), p. 9.

[234] *Fiscal Year 1989 Arms Control Impact Statements* (US Government Printing Office: Washington, DC, 1988), p. 145.

[235] Palmer and Bolef (note 165), p. 26.

Table 5. Efficiency of uranium enrichment technologies[a]

	Separation factor or enrichment factor[b]	No. of stages for 90% HEU[c]	kWh/SWU	kW for 4000 SWU/yr
Gaseous diffusion	1.004–1.0045	3500–4000	2500	1200
Gas centrifuge	1.2–1.5[d]	40–90	100–200	50–100
Aerodynamic				
Helikon/UCOR	1.030	540	4000	2000
Becker nozzle	1.015	1100	3600	1800
Chemical				
French Chemex	1.002–1.003	5000–8000[e]	600	300
Japanese Asahi	1.001–1.0013	12 000–16 000[e]	150	75
Electromagnetic[b]				
EMIS (calutron)	20–40	2–3	20 000–30 000[f]	10 000–15 000
Ion cyclotron resonance/ Plasma centrifuge	~(3–10)	(4–8)	(200–600)	(100–300)
Laser processes				
AVLIS	~(5–15)	(a few)	(100–200)	(50–100)
MLIS	~(3–10?)	(under 10?)	(200–250)	(100–125)
LAP (CRISLA)	~(1.5)	~(20)	(tens?)	(low)

[a] Estimates (in brackets) are uncertain and may not be achievable on an industrial scale.

[b] For electromagnetic and laser processes, estimates are for the *enrichment* factor, not the separation factor. 'Separation factor' is defined as the ratio of the relative (^{235}U-to-^{238}U) enrichment of the product to that of the tails in any one stage of a cascade, and is the figure given for diffusion, centrifuge, aerodynamic and chemical processes. 'Enrichment factor' is the ratio of relative enrichment of the product to that of the *feed*, which is more relevant to processes whose separation per stage is high enough that a many-stage cascade is not required, and in which the 'cut' (the ratio of the total amount of material in the product to that in the tails) is therefore not as relevant. The separation factor for a given process is always larger than its enrichment factor, but only slightly larger when the cut is much less than 50%, as it may be in some laser processes.

[c] Assumes tails with 0.3% ^{235}U content.

[d] The given range applies to modern centrifuges and is dependent on their length, rotational speed, and other factors. The earliest centrifuges operated at subcritical peripheral speeds of 250 m/sec and had separation factors of only 1.026.

[e] For chemical processes, a single physical item (e.g., an ion exchanger or pulse column) can contain tens or hundreds of effective 'stages', so that these large numbers can be misleading.

[f] This figure is sometimes given as 3000–4000, which would apply only to significantly improved calutrons that used multiple beams, permanent magnets, or other refinements. The figure given in the table is based on US 'alpha' machines used during the Manhattan Project, which produced only about 1/3 gram uranium-235 per machine per day in about a 20% enriched product, and used more than 50 kW per machine to power the electromagnets, pumps, and ion beams.

Source: Office of Technology Assessment (OTA), *Technologies Underlying Weapons of Mass Destruction*, OTA-BP-ISC-115 (US Government Printing Office: Washington, DC, Dec. 1993), table 4-5, p. 143.

dosage rates; and ^{236}U is a neutron absorber and unwanted in a nuclear reactor.[236] On the other hand, laser facilities are expected to require more frequent replacement of worn parts than gaseous diffusion equipment.[237] Comparing the advanced gas centrifuge to the AVLIS process for uranium enrichment, the DOE's then Deputy Assistant Secretary for Uranium Enrichment stated in 1986: 'The AVLIS technology is less capital intensive, requires significantly less investment prior to a decision to deploy, has a lower estimated (operating) cost, has greater potential for cost reductions through technology improvements, and is more adaptable to deployment in increments that can match the evolving needs of the enrichment marketplace'.[238] An overview of the efficiency of the various types of technology discussed is presented in table 5.

IX. Conclusions

Gaseous diffusion has been called 'one of the processes which has the lowest proliferation risk among the processes which have an equilibrium time short enough to reach weapon-grade enrichment assays from natural assay in less than a year of operation' for a number of reasons.[239] As shown here the low separation factors necessitate that a plant has thousands of stages, leading to very high capital as well as operation costs.[240] The skills involved in the R&D effort, as well as in the operation and maintenance of such a plant, can be acquired only over a long period of time.

The technological difficulties prove daunting even at a low production rate if high enrichment is desired. In this case the small size of the top stages would necessitate special construction, since the stages from a plant for production of low-enrichment assays would not be suitable. In addition, complex rearrangement of the interconnections would be necessary in order to modify an existing low-assay cascade to allow operation of an HEU side cascade. One of its main advantages is that the moving parts are basically confined to the compressors, making for reliability and long life—attributes which are not the most critical if reasonably small quantities of material are desired. The technology associated with the diffusion barriers and corrosion-resistant compressors has proven difficult to master for countries other than the nuclear weapon states. The process was abandoned by Iraq, for example, after six years of research.

Modifying a chemical enrichment plant used in low-enriched uranium (LEU) production would also require complex rearrangement, adding many additional stages or the reintroduction of already enriched uranium into the original feed.

[236] *Nuclear Fuel*, vol. 14, no. 6 (21 Mar. 1989), p. 4. The gas-diffusion and -centrifuge processes, which discriminate among isotopes based on their mass, enrich ^{232}U, ^{234}U and ^{236}U by factors of about 8, 5 and 10 times respectively as they enrich 0.8% ^{235}U to 3.2% ^{235}U. See *Nuclear Fuel*, vol. 12, no. 12 (15 June 1987), p. 9.

[237] MacLachlan, A., 'Sales increase for France's Pechiney', *Nuclear Fuel*, vol. 13, no. 11 (30 May 1988), p. 13.

[238] *Fiscal Year 1987 Department of Energy Authorization* (note 155), Vol. 1, pp. 26–27.

[239] Massignon, D., 'Gaseous diffusion', ed. Villani, *Uranium Enrichment* (note 2), p. 175.

[240] The three gaseous-diffusion plants in the USA used about 3 per cent of the total amount of electrical power produced in the USA in 1983, for example—quoted in Rahn *et al.* (note14), p. 188.

An added complication here might also be the necessity to reconfigure to smaller processing elements in order to avoid criticality problems.

The situation is less problematic, however, for the other major commercial enrichment process, namely, enrichment in gas-centrifuge plants. Here reconfiguration, reintroduction of feed or adjustment of feed rates could be used to increase the enrichment level, and time to reach equilibrium operation is only minutes for centrifuge enrichment plants compared to the weeks or months required for gaseous-diffusion plants. The possibility of detecting such reconfiguration has been enhanced, however, through the agreement among operators of such plants, at least in Japan and the European countries, to limited frequency unannounced access. This is a result of the Hexapartite Safeguards Project, which dealt with safeguards issues for centrifuge plants in the early 1980s.[241]

Centrifuge operation does, however, generate electromagnetic radiation at rotation frequencies which range from 600 to 2000 rotations per second. The long wavelength of this radiation means that it would be difficult to shield but also that no part of the facility would be likely to act as a very sufficient antenna. It has been noted that a corresponding signal might be found emanating from power lines leading to the facility, but such conjectures would have to be tested. It is also possible that an acoustic signal at these frequencies, or their harmonics, could be detected if appropriate instruments can be brought sufficently near to the facility under suspicion.[242]

Clandestine deployment

Unlike weapon-grade plutonium, which can be produced in a small nuclear reactor, the production of substantial quantities of HEU has, until now, required a large dedicated effort. As aptly remarked 'one of the hardest things on earth to hide is a gaseous diffusion plant; its mere presence on the landscape, easily detected by satellites, is a dead give-away of a nation's intentions'.[243] Even if only a relatively small quantity of HEU is being produced the large number of stages required when using this method necessitates a large facility. The fewer stages necessary and the subsequent smaller size of gas-centrifuge uranium enrichment plants means that their appearance is not as distinctive as that of diffusion plants, but the effort required for their construction might still permit identification. Laser enrichment plants need less uranium for processing and can be smaller still, which would contribute to the difficulty in detecting and monitoring them.[244] If these plants were large enough to produce substantial

[241] OTA (note 4), pp. 145–49.

[242] Fainberg, A., 'Strengthening IAEA safeguards: Lessons from Iraq', Center for International Security and Arms Control, Stanford University, Stanford: Calif., Apr. 1993, pp. 38–39.

[243] Uranium enrichment: rumors of Israeli progress with lasers' (note 129), pp. 1172–73.

[244] *Energy and Water Development Appropriations for 1989* (note 6), p. 1196; and *DOE Uranium Enrichment Program* (note 175), p. 192.

quantities (5 tonnes p.a.) it has been judged[245] that they would probably be detected by a 'larger intelligence effort', including analysis of human intelligence and communications intercepts, for example. Facilities capable of producing much smaller, but for many countries still militarily significant, quantities of uranium would, however, be substantially harder to find in a timely fashion.

Given the data in section VII on the number of states *known* to be involved in research and actively planning deployment of laser enrichment facilities, the possible construction of clandestine laser enrichment facilities is clearly a primary and increasing proliferation concern. An interesting suggestion has been made about how signatures specific to this type of enrichment activity might be detected, involving 'the distinctive electromagnetic signature of a [laser enrichment] plant resulting from the pulsed operation of the lasers, flash lamps and other items'.[246]

Any indication that a country was manufacturing or using uranium tetrachloride would point to a possible EMIS programme. The uranium compounds uranium hexafluoride or tetrafluoride, which are used in almost all other conversion and enrichment activity, have melting and boiling points which are too low for use in the ion sources which are employed in the EMIS process.[247]

In the context of clandestine deployment, a prominent cause for concern, should its developers' claims be borne out, is the CRISLA process. The size of the apparatus, about 7 metres in length, its modular design and the fact that it reportedly employs less complex technology than the AVLIS process[248] raise obvious proliferation concerns. The fact that China has used published drawings to construct a model of the same design demonstrates the inherent potential proliferation danger. It must be noted, however, that the CRISLA process has been developed as a commercial venture and uses a proprietary reactant. Independent assessment of its potential has therefore proven difficult, but scepticism has been voiced both about the claims made by the developer and the overall potential of the process itself.[249]

Although almost two decades of US research on AVLIS have not yet resulted in plant construction, it must be emphasized that the stated purpose of the LLNL uranium enrichment programme in the USA was 'to prove, by *large-scale* technology demonstrations, the *economic viability* of uranium enrichment for commercial reactor fuel'[250]—considerations which may not be very

[245] von Hippel, F., Albright, D. H. and Levi, B. G., 'Stopping the production of fissile materials for weapons', *Scientific American*, vol. 253, no. 3 (Sep. 1985), pp. 32–33.

[246] von Hippel, F. and Levi, B. G., 'Controlling nuclear weapons at the source: verification of a cut-off in the production of plutonium and highly enriched uranium', eds K. Tsipis, D. W. Hafemeister and P. Janeway, *Arms Control Verification: The Technologies that Make it Possible* (Pergammon Brassey's: Washington, DC, 1986), p. 376.

[247] Fainberg (note 242), p. 28.

[248] Lindeman, E., 'Isotope technologies marketing SWU on small scale to US utilities', *Nuclear Fuel*, vol. 14, no. 4 (20 Feb. 1989), p. 4.

[249] Marvin Miller, an expert in the field, has raised serious questions about the ability of CRISLA to live up to its development claims. See letter from Marvin Miller to FAS Study Group *re* 'CRISLA, AVLIS and all that', 18 Apr. 1990, 9 pp.

[250] 'Laser technology' (note 154), p. 20 [emphasis added].

important for other potential developers, in particular countries planning to produce a few nuclear weapons.

This point is further illustrated by the fact that workers at Avco-Everett, an earlier developer of the AVLIS-type laser process, 'had produced a small quantity of 50 percent enriched uranium in one pass through their apparatus'[251] within four months of filing a patent application in 1970. Also, in 1979, before R&D was moved to the Livermore government laboratories, Standard Oil of New Jersey (now the Exxon Corporation) had joined with Avco to form Jersey Nuclear-Avco Isotopes (JNAI), which felt that construction of a demonstration plant, if begun in 1981, could be completed by 1983. The US Government wanted to continue to carry out more research first and these plans never came to fruition, but they illustrate that there are likely to be more rapid routes to a deployed laser enrichment facility than that taken by large government projects—routes which would be more tempting for countries interested in a relatively small, but none the less significant, capability.

It is also important to point out that it may be advantageous, particularly for a less well developed country that may be having problems mastering a particular technology on a scale sufficient to produce significant quantities of weapon-grade uranium, to combine enrichment methods.[252] If 3 per cent enriched uranium was available from one enrichment technology (or was diverted from a LEU fuel cycle) a subsequent enrichment technology would only need to be about one-quarter the size that would be required if the starting point was natural uranium. If 25 per cent enriched uranium were produced by one method, a subsequent facility to enrich it to weapon-grade could be less than one-thirtieth the size of that required to enrich natural uranium. The smaller size of the facilities required to enrich diverted reactor-grade LEU in particular must be appreciated if efforts to prevent or uncover clandestine enrichment capabilities are to be fruitful.

When the Soviet Union embarked on its crash programme to produce atomic weapons after World War II, its gas-diffusion system at first failed to produce HEU because of stage losses in the pumping system. The system was efficient enough to produce 40 per cent enriched uranium, however, and a small—in comparison with the US calutron effort—EMIS separation capability allowed the 40 per cent ^{235}U from the diffusion plant to be enriched to weapon-grade.

[251] Palmer and Bolef (note 164), p. 26.
[252] Mozley (note 70), pp. 47–48.

3. Plutonium production

I. Introduction

From the standpoint of nuclear weapon proliferation the two most important parts of the nuclear fuel cycle are uranium enrichment, described in chapter 2, and reprocessing technology. Depending on the route taken these processes may be pursued independently or, if a reactor making use of enriched uranium is used to produce plutonium, in tandem to produce weapon-usable material. Especially for a clandestine nuclear weapon programme, where facility size would be an important consideration, the construction of a natural uranium reactor capable of producing plutonium, together with a reprocessing facility, would seem to have the advantage. Unlike enrichment technology, most of which remains highly classified, beginning with revelations concerning the basics of reprocessing technology at the Geneva Summit Conference in 1955 details of this path to obtaining fissile material are now well known. For example, by 1956 France had already agreed to sell the Dimona reactor along with reprocessing technology to Israel.[1]

Current reprocessing programmes (other than those associated with the declared nuclear weapon states) are listed in table 6. From the description of reprocessing technology below it is apparent that the chemicals involved are readily available commercially, although much of the equipment needed to deal with the high levels of radioactivity is under control. The construction time for large reprocessing facilities has generally been long, however, and even some smaller ones, for example, the Ezeiza plant in Argentina, remain uncompleted for a variety of economic and political as well as technical reasons.[2]

It remains unclear why Iraq, for example, chose to concentrate on the much more costly process of enriching uranium for its nuclear weapon programme. (The 1981 bombing of the Osiraq reactor by Israel before it became operational doubtless had some effect, but this would only have pressed Iraq to pursue a more clandestine programme. Details of investigations into the existence of such a reactor for the production of plutonium are discussed in chapter 4.) In general it was expected that a country wishing to acquire a clandestine nuclear weapon capability would do so through the operation of a relatively small nuclear reactor and the associated reprocessing facilities. This remains a problem of utmost concern as developments in the Democratic People's Republic of Korea (DPRK—North Korea) have shown. In order to appreciate the true scope

[1] Fischer, D., *Stopping the Spread of Nuclear Weapons: The Past and the Prospects* (Routledge: London, 1992), pp. 40, 50–51.

[2] Office of Technology Assessment (OTA), *Technologies Underlying Weapons of Mass Destruction*, OTA-BP-ISC-115 (US Government Printing Office: Washington, DC, Dec. 1993), pp. 138–39.

Table 6. Reprocessing programmes and capabilities outside the declared nuclear weapon states

Country	Reprocessing facility	Dates of operation	Capacity, actual or predicted (t HM/y)[a]	Safeguards?
Japan	Tokai-Mura	1981–present	90	Yes
	Rokkasho-mura	2005?	(800)	Yes
Germany	Karlsruhe	1971–90	35	Yes
Belgium	Eurochémic-Mol	1966–74	30	Yes
Israel	Dimona	1966?–	(50–100)?	No
India	Trombay	1966–74; (1983–present)?	30	No
	Tarapur	1982–present	100	Partly
	Kalpakkam	1993/94	(200)?	No
Pakistan	Chashma	Construction ended 1978?	(100)	. .
	Rawalpindi	Not operating?	(5)?	No
North Korea	Yongbyon	(1992)?	Pilot-scale?	(Yes)[b]
Iraq	Tuwaitha	1989–91 (destroyed)	Lab-scale	(Violation)
South Africa	Pelindaba	(1997–?)	Pilot-scale	Yes[c]
Argentina	Ezeiza	Suspended 1990	(5)	Partly
Brazil	Resende	Suspended 1980s	(3)	Yes
South Korea	. .	Abandoned 1970s	. .	. .
Taiwan	. .	Abandoned 1970s	. .	. .

[a] Tonnes of heavy metal per year. Items in (brackets) or with question marks represent estimates or substantial uncertainty, respectively.

[b] Although North Korea became a member of the NPT in 1985, its safeguards agreement with the IAEA was not signed until 1992.

[c] Prior to South Africa's accession to the NPT in 1991, this facility was only under safeguards when safeguarded fuel was present. Since then, it has come under full-scope safeguards.

Source: Office of Technology Assessment, *Technologies Underlying Weapons of Mass Destruction*, OTA-BP-ISC-115 (US Government Printing Office: Washington, DC, Dec. 1993), table 4-2, p. 139.

of the problem it is vital to understand the technological aspects of the processes involved and the ready availability of much of the technology of reprocessing.

It has been estimated that it would be possible secretly to obtain on the open market the materials to construct a reactor capable of producing enough plutonium for a few nuclear weapons per year for about $40 million.[3] Requiring only a relatively small facility for reprocessing the plutonium produced, such a clandestine programme could be remarkably easy to hide. Any country with a reasonable amount of experience in complex chemical processing, such as that

[3] Barnaby, F., 'Types of nuclear weapon', ed. F. Barnaby, *Plutonium and Security: The Military Aspects of the Plutonium Economy* (Macmillan: London, 1992), pp. 276–67.

involved in operating an oil refinery, would without much difficulty be able to construct a pilot plant for reprocessing fuel from a commercial reactor. If all that were required were the capability to extract plutonium produced by a reactor designed explicitly for this purpose (a production reactor) the task would be even easier, for reasons discussed below.[4]

South Africa chose another route which is also the cause of much concern—namely using a civilian nuclear programme as a guise for developing nuclear expertise and associated equipment which could then be used in a weapon programme. In fact the success of the South African programme, despite substantial obstacles including trade sanctions, indicates that the construction of nuclear weapons may not be as formidable a task as is often believed to be the case.[5]

II. The nuclear fuel cycle and the production of fissile material

Uranium production

Making up about four parts per million of the earth's crust, uranium is actually not a very rare element—being more abundant, for example, than either mercury or silver. High-grade ore deposits (pitchblende,[6] for example, contains 1–20 per cent uranium in the form of uranium oxide, U_3O_8) are relatively rare, however. The uranium content of the bulk of deposits is 0.001 per cent or less, which makes extraction uneconomical. The earth's oceans contain a great deal of uranium as well but, at a concentration of less than 3 parts per billion, its recovery from this source is not economic.

In the first step towards refining the uranium, depending on the type of ore, an appropriate compound is used to leach (dissolve) the uranium; most US ores are leached with sulphuric acid. The uranium is then separated from solution by solvent extraction or ion-exchange. The resulting uranium-bearing solution is treated with ammonia, and solid 'yellowcake' containing 75–85 per cent U_3O_8 is produced. Further purification is still necessary, however, in order to remove elements with an appreciable ability for neutron capture. Commercial processes for the conversion to high-purity uranium hexafluoride include a so-called 'dry' and a 'wet' (solvent extraction) process.

The dry or hydrofluor process involves grinding the U_3O_8 and heating it to 540°–650°C, at which point it is reduced by hydrogen gas producing mainly uranium dioxide or 'brown oxide' (UO_2). Two successive hydofluorination procedures can then be used to produce uranium tetrafluoride or 'green salt' (UF_4). Finally, uranium hexafluoride 'hex' (UF_6)—the form used in most enrichment processes—can be produced by treating the solid UF_4 with fluorine

[4] Greenwood, T., Rathjens, G. and Ruina, J., International Institute for Strategic Studies, *Nuclear Power and Weapons Proliferation*, Adelphi Paper no. 130 (IISS: London, 1977), p. 18.

[5] See, e.g., Smith, J. R., 'From dust to dust: history of S. Africa's bombs', *Washington Post*, 12 May 1993.

[6] Graves, H. W. Jr, *Nuclear Fuel Management* (Wiley: New York, 1979), p. 27.

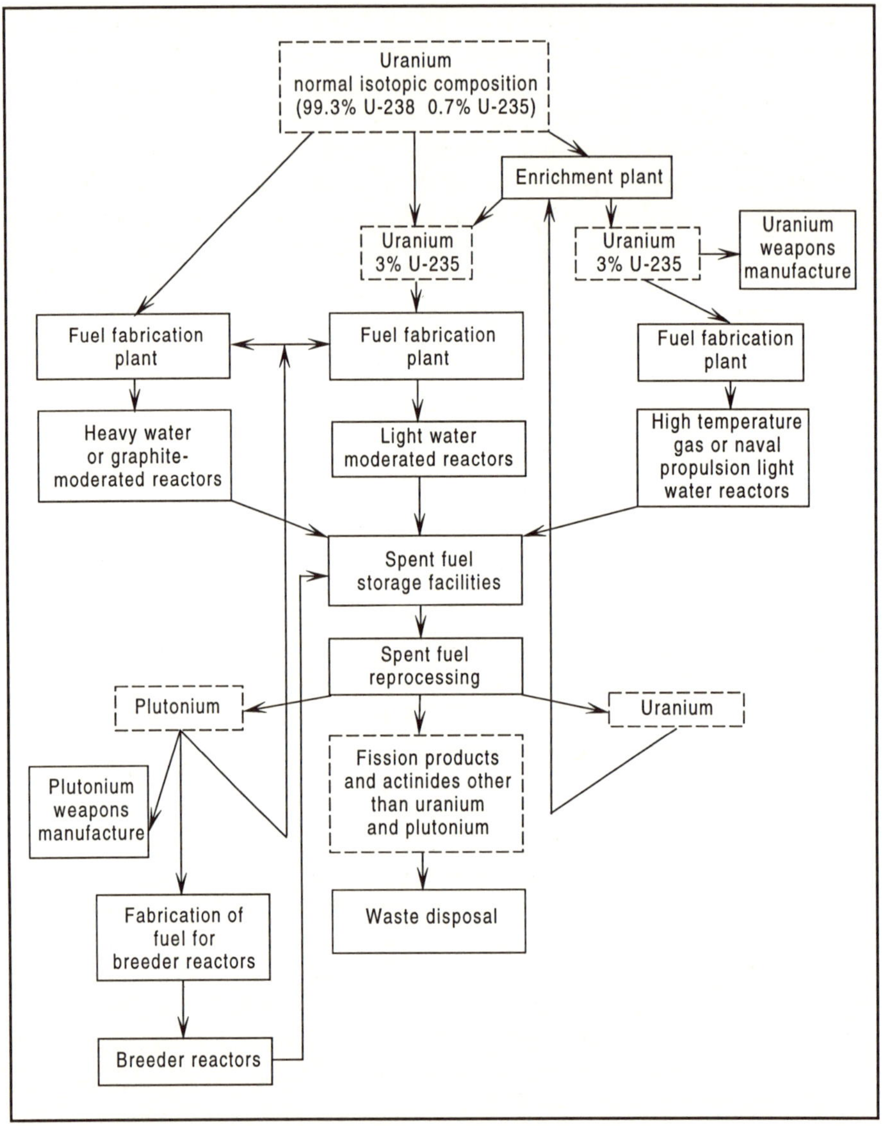

Figure 18. Nuclear reactors and nuclear weapon manufacture

Source: Redrawn by permission of the Oxford University Press from Greenwood, T., Rathjens, G. and Ruina, J., International Institute for Strategic Studies, *Nuclear Power and Weapons Proliferation*, Adelphi Paper no. 130 (IISS: London, 1977), p. 7.

gas and purifying by fractional distillation. In the wet process solvent extraction using *n*-tributyl phosphate is first used to produce uranium trioxide (UO_3), 'yellow oxide', which is reduced by hydrogen to UO_2 and then converted to UF_6 as in the dry process.

After enrichment and according to the type of reactor the UF_6 can be converted to uranium dioxide suitable for reactor fuel by first hydrolysing the UF_6, giving uranyl fluoride from which ammonium diuranate is precipitated using aqueous ammonia. The solid is finally separated and dried, and the residue is reduced by hydrogen to produce uranium dioxide.[7]

Plutonium production

There are a number of different types of nuclear reactor, each of which, for reasons detailed below, is more or less suitable for the production of plutonium that could be used in nuclear weapons. While reactors can be designed and used specifically for producing plutonium for use in nuclear weapons, plutonium can also be obtained from a peaceful nuclear power programme or research reactor.

An overview of the way in which plutonium is produced as an integral part of the nuclear fuel cycle can be obtained from figure 18, which also illustrates the processes involved in uranium enrichment as discussed in detail in chapter 2. The technical complexity of the production of weapon-grade uranium is demonstrated in chapter 2; in general the technology required to produce plutonium of sufficient quality for use in nuclear weapons using a nuclear reactor and appropriate plutonium separation methods is more accessible.

In general and in all reactor types, plutonium-239 is formed by the absorption of a neutron by ^{238}U to produce ^{239}U, followed by two subsequent beta decays (electron emission) according to the following process:

$$n + {}^{238}U \rightarrow {}^{239}U \rightarrow {}^{239}Np + e^- \rightarrow {}^{239}Pu + e^-$$

Not all of this plutonium survives, however. Further interactions with neutrons can result either in fission of the ^{239}Pu itself (about 65 per cent of the time) or, through neutron absorption, in the production of higher isotopes of plutonium—mainly ^{240}Pu, ^{241}Pu, ^{242}Pu and other elements.

The amount and isotopic composition of the plutonium produced are functions of several important variables,[8] including the specific type of reactor used and its detailed design characteristics and the composition and arrangement of the fuel. Most important for a given reactor design is the 'burnup', which is the extent to which the fuel has been exposed to neutrons. Burnup is usually defined in terms of the number of megawatt days of energy produced per tonne of fuel and is abbreviated MWd/t. Higher burnup can be achieved either by leaving the fuel in the reactor for a longer period of time or by exposing it to a higher flux of neutrons. In either case the greater exposure to neutrons in turn allows for a larger proportion of the higher isotopes of plutonium to build up in the fuel.

[7] See, e.g., Glasstone, S. and Sesonske, A., *Nuclear Reactor Engineering*, 3rd edn (Van Nostrand Reinhold: New York, 1981), pp. 478–82.

[8] Lovins, A. B., 'Nuclear weapons and power-reactor plutonium', *Nature*, vol. 283 (28 Feb. 1980), pp. 817–18.

Table 7. Typical isotopic concentrations of plutonium for various reactor types

Isotope	Weapon-grade isotopic concentrations (typical, %)	Reactor-grade isotopic concentrations (typical) PWR[a] (33 000 MWd/t[d])	Magnox[b] (5000 MWd/t)	CANDU[c] (7500 MWd/t)
^{238}Pu	. .	*1.3*	. .	. .
^{239}Pu	*93.0*	*56.6*	*68.5*	*66.6*
^{240}Pu	*6.5*	*23.2*	*25.0*	*26.6*
^{241}Pu	*0.5*	*13.9*	*5.3*	*5.3*
^{242}Pu	. .	*4.7*	*1.2*	*1.5*

[a] Pressurized water reactor.
[b] Magnesium oxide reactor.
[c] Canadian deuterium–uranium reactor.
[d] Megawatt-days per tonne of uranium fuel.

Source: Albright, D., Berkhout, F. and Walker, W., SIPRI, *World Inventory of Plutonium and Highly Enriched Uranium*, 1992 (Oxford University Press: Oxford, 1993), table 2.1, p. 17.

The burnup of the fuel is important in that it determines the relative proportion of the various plutonium isotopes which in turn influences the suitability of the plutonium for weapon production—as shown below the most desirable isotope for nuclear weapon production is ^{239}Pu.

First of all, only the isotopes of ^{239}Pu and ^{241}Pu are fissile—that is, fissionable by slow as well as fast neutrons. However, ^{241}Pu decays rather quickly to americium-241 (^{241}Am), which is an intense emitter of X-rays and gamma rays posing health and handling problems as well as producing heat which has to be dissipated. Plutonium-240 is also more radioactive than ^{239}Pu, and in addition it is particularly undesirable (along with ^{242}Pu) since it undergoes spontaneous fission at a much higher rate than ^{239}Pu. The neutrons emitted in this fission process increase the likelihood that the chain reaction in a bomb will begin before full compression of the plutonium has been achieved, thus causing pre-initiation. This can substantially reduce the yield of the device. Also, since ^{240}Pu and ^{242}Pu are not fissile, their presence in a bomb raises the critical mass of plutonium needed.[9]

For weapon purposes it is, therefore, more efficient to maximize the percentage of ^{239}Pu in the fuel discharged from a reactor. This can be achieved by keeping the burnup low, and in fact weapon-grade plutonium is usually produced by irradiating fuel for only a few weeks before it is discharged, usually keeping the burnup below 1000 MWd/t. On the other hand the burnup in power reactors ranges from 3000 to 8000 MWd/t for natural uranium reactors, such as the gas-cooled Magnox and the Canadian deuterium–uranium (CANDU), to a

[9] Greenwood, Rathjens and Ruina (note 4), p. 5; and Albright, D., Berkhout, F. and Walker, W., SIPRI, *World Inventory of Plutonium and Highly Enriched Uranium, 1992* (Oxford University Press: Oxford, 1993), p. 15.

typical burnup of 30 000–40 000 MWd/t for the pressurized water reactor using enriched uranium fuel. The isotopic concentrations for some typical reactor types are listed in table 7.[10]

The US Department of Energy defines weapon-grade plutonium as that containing less than 7 per cent ^{240}Pu; fuel-grade as that containing between 7 per cent and 19 per cent; and reactor-grade as that containing 19 per cent or more. Super-grade is defined as that containing 2–3 per cent ^{240}Pu and can be blended with the lower grades to produce weapon-grade material.[11] The plutonium in US nuclear warheads is composed of approximately 93 per cent ^{239}Pu and 6.5 per cent ^{240}Pu, along with very small amounts of other isotopes.[12]

It should be emphasized, however, that, while more difficult to construct and less predictable in yield, it is none the less possible to build a nuclear weapon even using reactor-grade plutonium (i.e., that discharged from commercial power reactors). In fact the USA successfully tested a bomb which used reactor-grade plutonium in 1962.[13] The IAEA and its Standing Advisory Group on Safeguards Implementation (SAGSI) considers any plutonium, with the exception of that containing more than 80 per cent ^{238}Pu, to be usable in a nuclear explosive device. Further, the former head of the theoretical division at Los Alamos National Laboratory in the USA, Carson Mark, has written that the assembly used in the first atomic bomb test in 1945 'would be capable of bringing reactor-grade plutonium of any degree of burnup to a state in which it could provide yields in the multi-kiloton range'.[14]

To indicate the quantities of plutonium which are regularly produced, a rule of thumb for reactors in which the fuel contains significant amounts of ^{238}U is that plutonium is produced at a rate of approximately 1 gram per day per megawatt-thermal (MWth) of reactor power.[15] Therefore a typical 1000 megawatt-electric (1000 MWe—equivalent to about 3000 MWth since only about one-third of the heat generated by a typical reactor is converted into electricity) commercial reactor would produce about 3 kg of plutonium per day if operated continuously, or about 1 tonne per year.

[10] Albright, Berkhout and Walker (note 9), pp. 16–17.

[11] *Fiscal Year 1992 Department of Energy Authorization (Atomic Vapor Laser Isotope Separation R&D Program)*, Hearing before the Procurement and Military Nuclear Systems Subcommittee of the Committee on Armed Services, US House of Representatives, 97th Congress, 1st Session (US Government Printing Office: Washington, DC, 1981), p. 170.

[12] Cochran, T. B., *et al.*, *Nuclear Weapons Databook, Vol. II, U.S. Nuclear Warhead Production* (Ballinger: Cambridge, Mass., 1987), p. 136.

[13] Lovins (note 8), p. 817; Oxford Research Group, *The Plutonium Legacy: Nuclear Proliferation out of Control*, Current Decisions Report, no. 12 (Apr. 1993), p. 6; and Carson Mark, J., 'Reactor-grade plutonium's explosive properties', Nuclear Control Institute, Washington, DC, Aug. 1990. It should be noted, however, that the definition of reactor-grade plutonium was different from that used today—at the time it was defined as plutonium containing more than 8% of the isotopes ^{240}Pu and ^{242}Pu. OTA (note 2), p. 133, footnote 5; and *PPNN Newsbrief*, no. 23 (third quarter 1994), p. 18.

[14] Carson Mark (note 13); 'Blix says IAEA does not dispute utility of reactor-grade Pu for weapons', *Nuclear Fuel*, vol. 15, no. 23 (12 Nov. 1990), p. 8; and 'US stirs plutonium dispute', *Financial Times*, 29 June 1994, p. 5.

[15] See, e.g., OTA (note 2), p. 131.

Reactor types

Nuclear reactors can be grouped into two basic categories: thermal reactors and fast reactors.[16] In thermal reactors the neutrons given off in fission are slowed down to thermal energies (i.e., so that they are in thermal equilibrium) before producing further fissions. A moderator, usually ordinary or heavy water or graphite, serves to slow the neutrons. This group includes most of the power reactors in current use. In fast reactors on the other hand the neutrons are not appreciably slowed down before fissioning other nuclei.

The dominant type of reactor is the *thermal reactor* using light water as a moderator, the light water reactor (LWR). There are two main types: the pressurized water reactor (PWR) and the boiling water reactor (BWR). The PWR heats water under high pressure to keep it below the boiling point within the reactor core. This water is then pumped from the core through a steam generator containing a secondary circuit within which the water is allowed to boil and then used to drive turbines. In the BWR coolant water within the reactor core is allowed to boil, and the resultant steam is used to drive the turbines directly. While clearly advantageous in that ordinary water is used as the moderator, LWRs must use enriched uranium (a few per cent ^{235}U, typically), which either means importing enriched uranium or developing an indigenous uranium enrichment capability. LWRs must also be shut down for refuelling every year or so and part of the fuel replaced while the rest is rearranged in the core.

If safeguards were in place it would be difficult to divert fuel from a light water reactor covertly since it is relatively straightforward to account for the fuel rods. Even if unsafeguarded, the shutting down of a large reactor would most likely create a signature (such as the reduction in heat output) observable from outside the reactor. Another advantage[17] from a proliferation standpoint is that light water reactors require the more difficult to obtain enriched uranium for operation. Further, as shown in table 7, the plutonium produced in normal operations of a PWR, for example, would contain almost one-quarter ^{240}Pu with substantial amounts of ^{241}Pu as well. While high levels of these isotopes do not preclude use for nuclear weapons the plutonium produced would be less suited to nuclear weapon use than the almost pure ^{239}Pu derived from reactors dedicated to producing weapon plutonium, for example. Higher proportions of ^{239}Pu would be possible with lower burnup in PWRs but this would require frequent shut-downs, which would be easily detectable with normal safeguards procedures.

Since it does not absorb neutrons as readily as light water, if heavy water is used as a moderator natural uranium can be used as fuel, obviating the need for enriched uranium. The CANDU pressurized heavy water (PHW) reactor makes use of heavy water in both coolant and moderator circuits in such a way that the

[16] For more details on reactor types see, e.g., Mounfield, P. R., *World Nuclear Power* (Routledge: London, 1991), pp. 1–16; Nero, A. V., Jr, *A Guidebook to Nuclear Reactors* (University of California Press: Berkeley, Calif., 1979); and Greenwood, Rathjens and Ruina (note 4), pp. 11–17.

[17] OTA (note 2), p. 139.

coolant cycle and generating system resemble those of the PWR. The fuel is contained in pressure tubes within the reactor core itself. While natural uranium is less expensive, a PHW reactor none the less has the disadvantage of relying on rather expensive heavy water.

The burnup in a typical PHW reactor is much lower than that of a typical PWR since the lower percentage of ^{235}U in the fuel means that criticality cannot be maintained after a certain point. Although such low burnups would produce plutonium with nearly 90 per cent ^{239}Pu in a light water reactor, the percentage of ^{239}Pu obtained from heavy water reactors is in fact close to that of LWRs. This is because the lower fraction of ^{235}U in the fuel leads to more neutron interactions with ^{239}Pu than occur in a LWR and subsequently more ^{239}Pu fissions as well as greater ^{240}Pu production.

However, heavy water reactors (HWRs) are fuelled while the reactor is in operation by passing the fuel bundles through fuelling channels. This feature could in principle be used to move some fuel quickly through a reactor with the resultant decrease in burnup causing an increase in the ^{239}Pu concentration. However, this would be at the expense of maintaining normal reactivity and would also produce local hot spots within the reactor core, resulting in less than optimal reactor performance. Use of the reactor in this way would also most likely be detected by the safeguards systems employed in CANDU reactors.[18]

It is of course unnecessary to use heavy water in the coolant circuit, and in fact the steam-generating heavy-water reactor (SGHWR) makes use of light water in the cooling circuit, which is allowed to boil and drive the turbines.

Graphite-moderated reactors have been designed in several different ways. The coolant in most designs is a gas—helium or carbon dioxide, for example—but many Russian designs use water in pressure tubes. Magnox reactors use natural uranium oxide fuel which is clad in a magnesium alloy canister and carbon dioxide coolant. This design has been superseded by the advanced gas-cooled reactor (AGR) which employs enriched (to a few per cent ^{235}U) ceramic uranium dioxide fuel and is much more efficient than the Magnox design. Still in the prototype stage, and using helium as coolant with graphite-coated spheres of enriched uranium dioxide, is the high-temperature gas-cooled reactor (HTGR). Although highly enriched uranium is used as fuel it is difficult to remove once it has been fabricated into the small spheres in which it is used.[19]

As mentioned above the *fast reactor* does not make use of a moderator at all. Typical of this type are the liquid metal fast breeder reactor (LMFBR), which uses sodium for a coolant, and the gas-cooled fast breeder reactor (GCFR), using helium as a coolant. In the basic fast breeder reactor a relatively small core (no moderator is contained), typically containing around 15–25 per cent fissile material, is surrounded by a blanket of fertile material. The main idea is to have neutrons emanating from the core 'breed' more fissile material by neutron capture in the ^{238}U blanket (producing ^{239}Pu) than were consumed in the first place—thus making use of the full uranium resource base. Several

[18] Greenwood, Rathjens and Ruina (note 4), pp. 11–13.

[19] Mounfield (note 16), p. 11; and Greenwood, Rathjens and Ruina (note 4), pp. 14–15.

difficulties, including high costs, operational difficulties and safety concerns, have now greatly dampened the expectations for these reactors. This is just as well from a proliferation point of view, since by processing the blanket material it is possible to obtain plutonium which contains over 90 per cent ^{239}Pu.[20]

Plans for the development of breeder reactors having been abandoned in Britain, France, Germany and the USA, at the present time it appears that the only country with serious plans for substantial use of breeder reactors is Japan. Russia is also keeping the breeder option open. Japan's policy is mainly the result of its strong ambitions to be more self-sufficient in energy. The Japanese breeder programme has been a cause of great international concern, especially since current plans involve the shipment of 30 tonnes of reprocessed plutonium from Britain and France during the next 10–15 years, raising a host of environmental and security concerns. An alternative plan has been proposed by Paul Leventhal and would have Japan establish a Strategic Uranium Reserve, taking advantage of the current low price of uranium resulting from its oversupply. Projected costs for relying on uranium are substantially less than those associated with the currently planned plutonium programme.[21]

In addition to the cost factors and the controversial nature of the plutonium shipments, Japan's utilities have also realized that the licensing of domestic reactors to use fuel which contains plutonium is a controversial issue domestically and that the world fabrication capacity for mixed-oxide fuel is not sufficient to absorb the amount of plutonium being separated. The utilities themselves have admitted that if they were given the choice to make again they would not take the reprocessing route. The important issue at present, therefore, is whether the long-term storage option will be permitted by the government. This would then allow the plutonium programme to be scaled back considerably, perhaps to an R&D effort only.[22] News of delays of perhaps decades in Japan's breeder reactor programme indicate that the country has realized the problems involved, both political and economic.[23]

[20] Albright, Berkhout and Walker (note 9), p. 20; Mounfield (note 16), pp. 13–15; Greenwood, Rathjens and Ruina (note 4), p. 15; and Nero (note 16), pp. 203–204.

[21] 'Pu—an element of concern in Japan', *Nuclear Engineering International*, July 1993, p. 17; Terazono, E. and Thomson, R., 'Nuclear outcry surprises Miti', *Financial Times*, 14–15 Nov. 1992, p. 2; McCarthy, T., 'Nuclear doubts sweep Japan', *The Independent*, 6 Jan. 1993, p. 10; and Oxford Research Group (note 13), p. 19. An analysis by British Nuclear Fuels plc (BNFL), Japan's supplier of reprocessing services, is not nearly as optimistic concerning the strategic reserve option. See 'Should Japan reprocess or build a strategic U reserve?', *Nuclear Engineering International*, Apr. 1994, p. 28. Cost factors may be almost a moot element in the official debate, however, as the low cost and ready availability of uranium which must be imported are of little importance in the decisions of politicians and bureaucrats in Japan, who concentrate mainly on reducing Japan's dependence on outside energy sources. Plutonium is 'quasi-domestic' in that it is produced from spent fuel even though the fuel itself must rely on imported uranium. Swinbanks, D., 'Japan committed to plutonium at all costs', *Nature*, vol. 359, no. 6396 (29 Oct. 1992), p. 766.

[22] von Hippel, F., Federation of American Scientists' Fund, *Cooperative Research Project on Arms Reductions*, Sixth Annual Report, 22 Aug. 1993, p. 4.

[23] Sanger, D. E., '20-year delay in nuclear plan', *International Herald Tribune*, 23 Apr. 1994, p. 1; and Swinbanks, D., 'Japan's fast reactor heads for the slow track', *Nature*, vol. 368, no. 6472 (14 Apr. 1994), p. 575.

Increasingly Japan's insistence on reprocessing spent nuclear fuel has been seen by some to reflect the desire in some quarters to keep open the nuclear weapon option. While concern for the nuclear programme in North Korea has generally been seen as the main reason for this, there are those in South Korea, both government officials and academics, who feel that Japan may eventually develop its own nuclear weapons regardless of the situation in North Korea.[24] The existence of any such plans has been categorically denied by the Japanese Foreign Ministry.[25]

Just as ^{239}Pu can be produced from ^{238}U by neutron capture, the fissile isotope ^{233}U can be created from thorium (^{232}Th) and be used to fuel a nuclear reactor. Uranium-233 is a good fissile material with a critical mass close to that of ^{239}Pu but it is doubtful that devices employing it for explosive use have ever even been tested. While this type of fuel cycle has potential for the future, only small quantities of ^{233}U have been produced and the thorium fuel cycle has moved little beyond the R&D stage to date.[26] It is therefore unlikely that the thorium fuel cycle represents a likely proliferation route.[27]

Historically the nuclear weapon states have made use of three reactor types to produce plutonium for nuclear weapons, all of which, at least in the early stages of the programmes, used natural uranium as fuel. Common in the USA, the former USSR and China was the light-water-cooled, graphite-moderated reactor, while the UK and France made use of the gas-cooled graphite-moderated type. The United States and the Soviet Union also made use of reactors which were cooled and moderated by heavy water to produce both plutonium and tritium.[28]

III. The technology of reprocessing

In general the main objective of reprocessing is to separate uranium and plutonium from fuel which has been irradiated in a reactor. If the goal is to produce plutonium for use in nuclear weapons the process is usually referred to as plutonium separation rather than reprocessing. As potentially useful products are separated from more radioactive materials, including fission fragments and other impurities which must be suitably dealt with, reprocessing has also been viewed as a form of waste management. However, it is now generally agreed that it is not intrinsically more difficult to store and dispose of spent fuel than to

[24] See, e.g., Harrison, S. S., 'The three-cornered nuclear suspense in Northeast Asia', *International Herald Tribune*, 2 Nov. 1993, p. 5; Jameson, S., 'Japan rattles nuclear saber at North Korea', *International Herald Tribune*, 30 July 1993, p. 4; and Opall, B., 'S. Korea fears Japanese nuclear capability', *Defense News*, 13–19 Dec. 1993, p. 6. There has been one report that Japan has in fact already acquired all of the components necessary for a nuclear weapon and has the capability to assemble a weapon in a short period of time. See 'Japan reported near nuclear status', *International Herald Tribune*, 31 Jan. 1994, p. 2.

[25] Nakamoto, M., 'Japanese scorn N-arms claims', *Financial Times*, 9–10 Apr. 1994, p. 2.

[26] Albright, Berkhout and Walker (note 9), p. 10; and Greenwood, Rathjens and Ruina (note 4), pp. 3, 6, 9.

[27] OTA (note 2), p. 129.

[28] This and more extensive information on the particular reactors and their locations can be found in Albright, Berkhout and Walker (note 9), pp. 25–27.

dispose of the high-level radioactive waste that results when fuel is reprocessed.[29]

The Purex method

Mainly because of the presence of highly radioactive fission products in the fuel discharged from a nuclear reactor, the spent fuel is stored for a period of at least five months before the uranium and plutonium can be safely separated. The fuel is stored in a water tank, the water providing both radiation shielding and a convenient way to remove the heat resulting from radioactive decay. This storage time allows the relatively short-lived isotopes present to decay almost completely, including the important and readily volatile iodine-131 isotope which has a half-life of 8.05 days.[30]

Although many processes have been developed for the separation of uranium and plutonium from irradiated fuel[31] the one in most common use today for both military and civil separation is the Purex (plutonium–uranium extraction) method. Now basically the universal choice for uranium and plutonium separation from spent fuel originating from low-enriched uranium, a version of the Purex process is also used for LMFBR spent fuel with appropriate modifications to take into account the higher plutonium and fission product concentrations.[32] Therefore, the Purex process is described here to give an overview of the types of chemical process required as well as to illustrate the level of sophistication required to obtain plutonium if a supply of spent fuel is available.

Decladding

Following an appropriate storage interval the first step in the reprocessing of spent fuel involves the separation of the fuel itself from the cladding material which surrounds it while in the reactor. This material can be of several different types, such as stainless steel, or magnox or zircalloy (alloys of magnesium and zirconium respectively), depending on the particular reactor from which the fuel originated. Separation of the cladding from the spent fuel itself is done in one of several ways, the two basic methods being mechanical and chemical decladding.

Chemical decladding involves the removal of the cladding material by dissolving it in an appropriate acid or other substance, leaving the fuel itself behind in easily separable solid form. The main disadvantages of this method are that the reaction products need more storage space than the original clad-

[29] Feiveson, H. A., von Hippel, F. and Albright, D., 'Breaking the fuel/weapons connection', *Bulletin of the Atomic Scientists*, vol. 42, no. 3 (Mar. 1986), p. 26.

[30] Glasstone and Sesonske (note 7), p. 513. For the major contributors to radioactivity which remain after 150 days see the table on p. 514.

[31] For a thorough review of the history of the development of the separation process and a description of many of the methods employed, see in particular Benedict, M., Pigford, T. H. and Levi, H. W., *Nuclear Chemical Engineering*, 2nd edn (McGraw-Hill: New York, 1981), pp. 458–514.

[32] Benedict, Pigford and Levi (note 31), p. 461.

ding and that there are problems associated with choosing appropriate storage container materials because the chemicals used will have been chosen to dissolve, for example, stainless steel cladding. Mechanical decladding, as the name implies, removes the cladding material by breaking or cutting it, or in some cases peeling it off in rather the same way as a banana skin is removed. The fuel is thus exposed so that it may react with a dissolvent that will leave the cladding material intact so that it can be removed as solid waste.[33]

Spent fuel dissolution

The feed for the actual solvent extraction process, which is used to separate the plutonium and uranium from the rest of the spent fuel material, is formed by dissolving the fuel in boiling nitric acid. This produces an aqueous solution containing uranium and plutonium as well as fission products as nitrates. The uranium is present in the form of uranyl nitrate ($UO_2(NO_3)_2$) but the plutonium is present in both the plutonium tetranitrate ($Pu(NO_3)_4$) and plutonyl nitrate ($PuO_2(NO_3)_2$) forms. Since the tetranitrate form is the more extractable, to increase the efficiency of the process the plutonyl nitrate is first converted to plutonium tetranitrate.[34]

Plutonium and uranium separation

Solvent extraction, which is used to separate the uranium and plutonium from the rest of the fission products and then to separate plutonium from uranium, can be defined simply as transferring a substance in solution in one liquid into solution in a second liquid, where this second liquid is either wholly or partly immiscible with the first.[35] The uranium and plutonium nitrates are much more readily dissolved in certain organic liquids than the bulk of the fission fragments. Therefore, if the aqueous acidic solution containing these nitrates is brought into intimate contact with such a liquid the uranium and plutonium nitrates will be transferred from the aqueous to the organic phase. Since the organic phase is immiscible with the aqueous phase, the organic solvent containing the uranium and plutonium can be readily separated from the aqueous solution.

In the case of the Purex process the organic substance is tributyl phosphate (TBP). The choice of TBP arises from its selectivity for the actinides, its reasonable stability against reaction with nitric acid, non-flammability, low cost and ready availability. To facilitate reprocessing it is diluted with a less dense, less viscous mixture of normal paraffins, mostly *n*-dodecane.[36]

[33] Allardice, R. H., Harris, D. W. and Miils, A. L., 'Nuclear fuel reprocessing in the UK', ed. W. Marshall, *Nuclear Power Technology, Vol. 2, Fuel Cycle* (Clarendon Press: Oxford, 1983), pp. 220–21, 235–38; and Benedict, Pigford and Levi (note 31), pp. 470–75.

[34] Allardice, Harris and Miils (note 33), p. 225.

[35] Allardice, Harris and Miils (note 33), p. 223.

[36] Benedict, Pigford and Levi (note 31), p. 508.

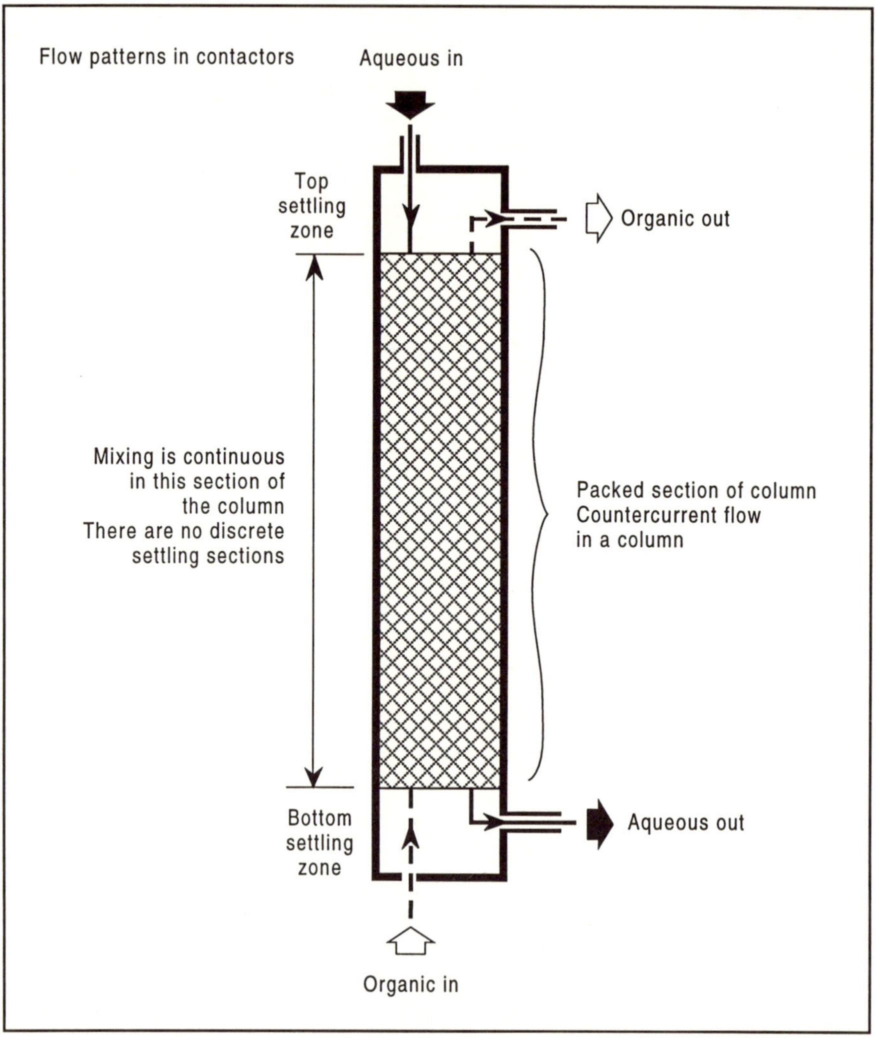

Figure 19. Counter-current solvent extraction

Source: Redrawn by permission of the Oxford University Press from Allardice, R. H., Harris, D. W. and Miils, A. L., 'Nuclear fuel reprocessing in the UK', ed. W. Marshall, *Nuclear Power Technology, Vol. 2, Fuel Cycle* (Clarendon Press: Oxford, 1983), p. 227.

In practice, the bringing into contact of the aqueous and organic phases can be accomplished either batchwise or continuously. In the latter method vertical columns are used and a counter-current flow established by having the organic solvent, being less dense, flowing upwards while the aqueous solution flows downwards (see figure 19). During this first solvent extraction process to separate uranium and plutonium from the fission products, 99.9 per cent of the uranium and 99.98 per cent of the plutonium are extracted into the organic phase with 99.5 per cent of the fission products in the aqueous phase.[37]

Plutonium separation

Solvent extraction can again be used in a further stage of the process to separate the plutonium from the uranium. This is because, unlike the tetranitrate form, the trinitrate form of plutonium is not soluble in the organic phase. A reagent, typically ferrous sulphamate, can therefore be used to convert the plutonium from the tetranitrate to the trinitrate form and, since it is no longer soluble in the organic medium, plutonium is back-extracted into the aqueous phase. Subsequent separation of the aqueous and the organic phases thus serves to separate the plutonium from the uranium and the uranium can be removed from the organic phase with very dilute nitric acid.

Further purification can then take place with further solvent extraction cycles on the separated uranium and plutonium streams. The uranium and plutonium would usually then be converted to oxide form with perhaps conversion of the uranium to uranium hexafluoride for subsequent enrichment.[38]

The Thorex process

For completeness it can also be mentioned that Thorex, a process comparable to the Purex process, is used to extract uranium and thorium from the fission products of a thorium reactor. The uranium and thorium are first separated from the fission fragments in the same manner as uranium and plutonium are in the Purex process, but the uranium is then separated from the thorium by making use of differences in the chemical equilibrium constants for the formation of uranium and thorium complexes with TBP.[39]

Tritium production

In addition to being a fission product, tritium is also produced in nuclear reactors, depending on the type, by the interactions of neutrons with boron control absorbers, lithium contaminants and/or with deuterium in water used as coolant and moderator. Since it can be used to boost the yield of nuclear weapons, tritium is also often produced in reactors, exposing lithium-6 targets to the thermal neutrons produced in a reactor according to the following reaction:

$$^{6}Li + n \rightarrow {}^{4}He + {}^{3}H$$

[37] Jones, P. M. S., 'The nuclear fuel cycle', ed. P. M. S. Jones, *Nuclear Power: Policy and Prospects* (Wiley: Chichester, 1987), p. 49; and Allardice, Harris and Miils (note 33), p. 226.

[38] Allardice, Harris and Miils (note 33), p. 226; Glasstone and Sesonske (note 7), p. 519; Wick, O. J. (ed.), *Plutonium Handbook: A Guide to the Technology, Volume II* (The American Nuclear Society: La Grange Park, Il., 1967), pp. 521–26; and Greenwood, Rathjens and Ruina (note 4), p. 36.

[39] Greenwood, Rathjens and Ruina (note 4), pp. 37–38.

High-energy neutrons will also interact with ^{7}Li (the predominant isotope) to produce tritium but with a lower cross-section.[40]

IV. Disposal of fissile material

Having discussed the manner in which plutonium is produced it is important to note that there is now a large stockpile of this material as a result of the nuclear power and nuclear weapon programmes of countries throughout the world, and various means are now under discussion to deal with the problem. The problem of how to deal with the large and growing stockpiles of plutonium is the subject of a great deal of current research. Detailed discussion of these issues abounds,[41] but it is important to draw attention to several crucial issues and facts.

In the first place the sheer size of the problem can be put into perspective when it is realized that the world inventory of plutonium produced by civil and military reactors is estimated for the end of 1993 at 1100 tonnes ±10 per cent, while only several kilograms are required to produce a nuclear device. Only about 250 tonnes of this is contained in the military inventory, the vast majority of which is weapon-grade. This is in contrast to the plutonium from civil nuclear programmes: of the estimated 845 tonnes, only about 17 per cent (about 144 tonnes) has been separated from spent fuel.[42] The amount of HEU in existence (not including some 100–200 tonnes dedicated to naval reactors) is currently estimated to be 1700 tonnes ±25 per cent, although, as discussed below, the problem of disposal is much less severe than for plutonium.[43]

Over 120 tonnes of plutonium had been separated from civil power reactor fuel by the end of 1991 and during the 1990s another approximately 190 tonnes of plutonium will have been separated as new reprocessing capacity is utilized in France and the UK. Part of this will be used in fast-neutron reactors and some as MOX (mixed plutonium oxide, PuO_2–uranium oxide, UO_2) fuel in light water power reactors—the latter being the only large-scale use of separated

[40] Benedict, Pigford and Levi (note 31), pp. 357, 391–92.

[41] For thorough discussions see especially Swahn, J., *The Long Term Nuclear Explosives Predicament: The Final Disposal of Militarily Usable Fissile Material in Nuclear Waste from Nuclear Power and from the Elimination of Nuclear Weapons* (Technical Peace Research Group, Institute of Physical Resource Theory: Gothenburg, 1992); von Hippel, F., Berkhout, F. and Feiveson, H. (eds), Report on the International Workshop 'Nuclear Disarmament and Non-Proliferation: Issues for International Action', Tokyo, 15–16 Mar. 1993; Berkhout, F. *et al.*, 'Disposition of separated plutonium', *Science & Global Security*, vol. 3, nos 3–4 (1993), pp. 161–213; and Allison, G. *et al.* (eds), *Cooperative Denuclearization: From Pledges to Deeds* (Center for Science and International Affairs, John F. Kennedy School of Government, Harvard University: Harvard, Mass., Jan. 1993).

[42] Figures presented in Albright, D., *et al.*, 'Inventories of fissile materials and nuclear weapons', *SIPRI Yearbook 1995: Armaments, Disarmament and International Security* (Oxford University Press: Oxford, 1995), pp. 318, 320, 325. Of these 144 tonnes about 34 tonnes have been recycled, leaving stocks of separated civil plutonium at about 110 tonnes at the end of 1993.

[43] Regarding the HEU estimate it should be noted that this figure is expressed in weapon-grade uranium (WGU) equivalent, defined as the amount of 93% ^{235}U that would have been produced (at a tails assay of 0.3%) by the same exertion of separative work units used in deriving HEU of the grade in question. Albright *et al.* (note 42), p. 318.

plutonium currently planned.[44] None the less, given current stockpiles and delays in licensing reactors which will accept the MOX fuel it is estimated that perhaps 200 tonnes[45] of separated plutonium will remain in existence by early in the next century. Given in addition the wide availability of the technology for separating plutonium from spent fuel it is apparent that the security of all plutonium stockpiles is of prime importance.

On 13 July 1992 President Bush formally made it government policy that the USA would no longer produce plutonium or HEU for nuclear weapons.[46] In fact, however, this announcement served only to codify a policy that was already effectively in place since the USA had not produced plutonium for weapons since 1988 and had halted the production of HEU for weapons in 1964.

Production of HEU ended in 1987 in the former Soviet Union and since then Russia has shut down 10 of its 13 military plutonium production reactors.[47] In early 1994 it agreed to shut down the remaining three nuclear reactors as soon as replacement energy sources have been constructed (the reactors also supply heat and electricity) with the aid of the United States. When the reactors are finally shut down in a few years time Russia will thus become the last of the five declared nuclear weapon states to stop producing fissile material for weapons.[48] The formal agreement signed in June 1994 also stipulated that verification arrangements be worked out, including on-site inspections of the currently operating Russian reactors as well as of Russian and US reactors which have produced weapon-grade plutonium in the past.[49]

Highly enriched uranium

Although stockpiles are estimated at 1700 tonnes, the problem of dealing with the growing stocks of HEU from weapon dismantlement is much less acute than that of dealing with plutonium. A small percentage of the HEU in existence could be used in naval-propulsion and research and isotope-production reactors, but the most natural method by which to dispose of it is to blend it

[44] Berkhout *et al.* (note 41), pp. 166, 191.

[45] Albright *et al.* (note 42), p. 11.

[46] *US Department of State Dispatch*, vol. 3, no. 29 (20 July 1992).

[47] Gordon, M. R., 'It's official; U.S. stops making material for nuclear warheads', *New York Times*, 14 July 1992, p. A16; and von Hippel, F., 'Nuclear disarmament: progress and problems. A US perspective', eds von Hippel, Berkhout and Feiveson (note 41), p. 4.

[48] While China has not announced that it has ceased production of plutonium for weapons, it is believed to have done so. The only countries which may still be producing plutonium for weapons are India and Israel. Albright *et al.* (note 42), p. 3.

[49] Lippman, T., 'Russia to stop producing weapons-grade plutonium', *International Herald Tribune*, 18 Mar. 1994, p. 1; 'Russia pledges to close reactors', *Jane's Defence Weekly*, 26 Mar. 1994, p. 6; and Lockwood, D., 'U.S., Russia agree to phase-out of nuclear weapons reactors', *Arms Control Today*, vol. 25, no. 6 (July/Aug. 1994), p. 24. Although as of the end of 1994 the agreement had not yet entered into force, Russia has stated that as of 1 Oct. 1994 it stopped using plutonium from the 3 reactors in nuclear warheads. Lockwood, D., 'U.S.–Russian talks on nuclear issues find progress slow at Moscow round', *Arms Control Today*, vol. 25, no. 1 (Jan./Feb. 1995), p. 22.

with either natural or depleted uranium to produce LEU, which can be used as fuel in nuclear reactors.[50]

There are several important considerations involved in the process of blending HEU down to LEU. First of all, at no time during the process should there be a possibility of a critical mass forming and thus creating a spontaneous chain reaction. In addition, it must be assured that the mixing is sufficiently complete that the isotopic content of the blended material does not vary to any significant degree throughout the final product. Furthermore, current industry safety standards limit the amount of the radioactive ^{234}U isotope which may be contained in commercial nuclear reactor fuel. HEU contains a higher proportion of ^{234}U and blending with depleted uranium would result in reactor fuel with a ^{234}U content which exceeds this standard. Therefore, blending of HEU will probably have to be restricted to blending with natural or slightly enriched uranium.[51]

An agreement was signed by the USA and Russia in February 1993 under which Russia is to sell 500 tonnes of HEU from its dismantled nuclear weapons to the USA over the next 20 years. It is to be blended down to LEU and used as reactor fuel.[52] Implementation of the agreement has been delayed as a result of disagreement over issues including the HEU price as well as profit sharing between Russia and Belarus, Kazakhstan and Ukraine.[53] The USA has, however, already paid $60 million of these funds in advance to help cover transportation and dismantlement costs for Ukrainian warheads transferred to Russia and fabrication of the reactor fuel assemblies which will be given to Ukraine in return.[54]

Plutonium

The disposal problems associated with plutonium are much more acute than those associated with HEU. It is not feasible isotopically to denature plutonium to preclude its use for weapons[55] and, as discussed in more detail below, it is not economical as a fuel at the present time. Proposals have been made to eliminate plutonium totally by such methods as launching it into the sun or

[50] See, e.g., von Hippel (note 47), pp. 1–2.

[51] Davis, Z., Humphries, M., Behrens, C. and Holt, M., 'Swords into energy: nuclear weapons materials after the cold war', CRS Report for Congress, 92-739 ENR, Library of Congress, Washington, DC, 29 Sep. 1992 (revised 9 Oct. 1992), pp. 7–8.

[52] For the technical aspects for making optimum use of HEU to produce low enrichment fuel see Neff, T. L., 'Integrating uranium from weapons into the civil fuel cycle', *Science & Global Security*, vol. 3, nos 3–4 (1993), pp. 215–22.

[53] Lockwood (note 49), p. 22; and 'Mikhailov considers uranium agreements', *Nuclear Engineering International*, Nov. 1993, p. 8.

[54] Statement released by the Office of the Spokesman, Washington, DC, Sep. 1994 in *U.S. Department of State Dispatch*, vol. 5, no. 41 (10 Oct. 1994), p. 677; and Annex to Trilateral Statement by the Presidents of the United States, Russia and Ukraine, 14 Jan 1994, reprinted in *Arms Control Today*, vol. 24, no. 1 (Jan./Feb. 1994), p. 21.

[55] It has been suggested that plutonium be denatured by increasing the relative amount of even isotopes because of the difficulties this causes in weapon design and material handling. For this purpose ^{238}Pu is the only isotope which can be produced in relatively large quantities (through irradiation of ^{237}Np), but the process would be difficult and costly. It would also not solve the long-term disposal problem since the half-life of ^{238}Pu is relatively short at 86.4 years. Swahn (note 41), pp. 163–64.

transmuting it by fissioning it totally, either by using fast neutron reactors or high-energy accelerators. Both of these options are not only somewhat daunting from a technological standpoint, but in addition they are probably only justifiable if most of the spent fuel in existence were to be reprocessed so that it could be eliminated in this manner, and current projections indicate that most of the spent fuel will remain unreprocessed in the near future.[56]

Other proposals to eliminate plutonium have included exploding a nuclear warhead in a cavity containing 100–1000 plutonium pits from nuclear weapons, thus diluting the plutonium in the resulting molten rock to about 1 part in 1000. This would, however, require adequate safeguarding of the sites after such explosions since 'plutonium mines' would have been created, and these are not likely to be acceptable to the public at large. Proposals to dilute plutonium in the ocean (especially given the difficulty in performing adequate dilution) or place plutonium in underwater subduction zones would undoubtedly also face the problem of public acceptance.[57]

Other more likely alternatives include first of all the recycling of plutonium in MOX fuel for light water reactors.[58] This route is being pursued or is proposed in Belgium, France, Germany, Japan and Switzerland. This type of recycling reduces by approximately 40 per cent the amount of fissile plutonium in the fuel in addition to mixing it with highly radioactive fission products—making the end-product more proliferation-resistant. However, given the current cost of uranium and even excluding reprocessing costs, MOX fuel—costing $1300–1600 per kilogram—is less economical than standard LEU reactor fuel costing approximately $1100 per kilogram.

There are other problems with this option, including the 'quantum leap' in the safeguards and physical security that would be necessary to ensure against diversion at large-scale reprocessing and MOX fuel fabrication facilities. In any case, projected capacity will only be able to handle about 50 per cent of the civil plutonium which will be produced during the next 10 years, not to mention the plutonium which will become available as a result of disarmament efforts.[59] This is largely because the properties of the plutonium contained in MOX fuel limit its use to about one-third of the reactor core in an unmodified LWR.[60] It has therefore been proposed that some reactors be modified to enable

[56] von Hippel (note 47), p. 2; Berkhout *et al.* (note 41), pp. 188–89; and Albright *et al.* (note 42), p. 324.

[57] Panofsky, W. K. H., 'Options for the long-term disposition of nuclear materials', Center for Security and Technology Studies, CSTS-35-93, Lawrence Livermore National Laboratory, Livermore, Calif., 16 Mar. 1993, pp. 2–3.

[58] Berkhout *et al.* (note 41), pp. 173–80, 192.

[59] Some proposals are geared especially towards dealing with the plutonium which is becoming available through deep cuts in nuclear arsenals. A Russian–US proposal, for example, would involve the use of a specially constructed modular HTGR estimated to cost $1.5 billion, which would be fuelled with the plutonium from dismantled nuclear warheads. A high percentage of the plutonium would be burned in the reactor and the plutonium remaining would have become part of radioactive spent fuel which would be less attractive for nuclear weapon production. Broad, W. J., 'U.S. team to work with Russians on joint reactor', *International Herald Tribune*, 7 Apr. 1993, p. 1.

[60] The CANDU reactor design makes it capable of handling a full MOX core and its use for plutonium disposal is being discussed. Silver, R., 'Canadian, U.S. officials discuss use of Candus for Pu disposition', *Nucleonics Week*, 14 July 1994, p. 5.

them to accept a full load of MOX fuel, and thus not only speed the recycling process but also ameliorate the difficulties associated with safeguarding the plutonium since this would presumably necessitate fewer facilities.

Using fast reactors to recycle plutonium has also been proposed. As discussed above, however, the fast reactor capacity in the mid-1990s is quite small. In addition fast reactors do not change the isotopic mix of the plutonium as much as LWRs at the same burnup, and the MOX fuel for fast reactors is more dangerous from a proliferation standpoint as it contains 15–20 per cent plutonium as compared with the 5–7 per cent contained in the MOX fuel for LWRs. The construction of new fast reactors has been considered, but considerable modifications to current designs would be necessary in converting plutonium breeders to plutonium burners, such as replacing the uranium in the reactor blanket with non-fertile material.[61]

As discussed further below, one of the most promising options is to dispose of plutonium by mixing it with high-level radioactive waste (HLW) which has been produced by past reprocessing before incorporating it into a suitable solid waste form (glass is preferred) and placing it in permanent storage in geological depositories. HLW is currently being glassified for final disposal in France, Russia and the UK, and this is also planned by Japan and the USA during the 1990s. This approach, sometimes referred to as 'anti-reprocessing', has several advantages,[62] including its simplicity, small incremental cost (less than MOX fuel fabrication), the relative inaccessibility of the plutonium compared with that in spent reactor fuel and, if carried out at a few sites, the relatively less burdensome safeguard measures required. A major disadvantage of this approach for weapon-grade plutonium is that it would remain weapon-grade after the glassification process, while if it were first used as MOX fuel it would have been converted to reactor-grade. As mentioned above, however, although less suitable, reactor-grade plutonium can also be used to construct nuclear weapons.

While less desirable from a proliferation perspective it is also possible, and would probably be less costly, to imbed plutonium in special materials such as silicate glass without the addition of high-level waste. The recovery process would be hazardous and costly but less so than in the case of plutonium which had first been blended with HLW.

Disposition of plutonium: the National Academy of Sciences study

The National Academy of Sciences (NAS) under the sponsorship of the Office of Nuclear Energy of the Department of Energy[63] released a detailed report on

[61] Berkhout *et al.* (note 41), pp. 178–80.

[62] Berkhout *et al.* (note 41), pp. 181–87, 190.

[63] The DOE completed the first phase of its study into long-term plutonium disposition in mid-1993 without making any policy recommendations but noting that the least expensive option would be to burn it in advanced light water reactors. Phase II of the study examines the various options in detail for both the USA and the former Soviet Union. Airozo, D., 'DOE study finds Pu burning in ALWRs is most economic option', *Nucleonics Week*, 29 July 1993, p. 1; and 'DOE says reprocessing cheapest for old warheads', *Nuclear Engineering International*, Sep. 1993, p. 14.

the Management and Disposition of Excess Weapons Plutonium in January 1994. An Office of Technology Assessment study released in 1993[64] had pointed to the need for national coherent policy direction in this area and the NAS study was able to narrow the options significantly. Stating the 'clear and present danger' which surplus material from nuclear weapons represents, the NAS study none the less notes that 'none of the options yet identified for managing this material can eliminate this danger; all they can do is reduce the risks'.[65]

Secure intermediate storage for the surplus weapon plutonium will be necessary for decades while the method of long-term disposal is decided upon and implemented. The NAS report notes that the optimal physical form in which plutonium should be stored remains a subject of debate but recommends for the immediate future that intact weapon components be stored. Sites which are or will be used to store fissile material should be monitored, and this should continue as the material leaves the sites for eventual long-term disposal. The IAEA could monitor the material within storage sites[66] and, should it be withdrawn, safeguard it to ensure that it is used for peaceful purposes. Russia could be offered financial or other incentives for depositing its fissile materials into storage, but from a proliferation and arms control perspective long-term plutonium storage in weapon-usable form is not recommended.[67]

When the risks of storage, handling and recovery are taken into account the study singles out two options as being particularly promising for the long-term disposition of plutonium. These are first, the use of the plutonium in existing or modified reactors as fuel, which would make the plutonium intensively radioactive and of the same basic form as spent reactor fuel now produced. This could be accomplished by using the plutonium in MOX fuel in LWRs, Russian VVER-1000 reactors or CANDU reactors, or by building special reactors for the purpose. The second option is to vitrify the plutonium once it has been mixed with radioactive high-level waste left over from plutonium separation or other defence activities. The glass logs which would be produced would then be placed in a geological depository. While technical issues remain to be worked out and are more substantial than those associated with the first option, the process appears to be feasible at the present time. The report also notes that another potentially attractive option which might be considered is burial in deep

[64] Airozo, D., 'OTA report says Pu disposition plans suffer from lack of policy direction', *Nuclear Fuel*, 27 Sep. 1993, p. 6.

[65] National Academy of Sciences (NAS), *Management and Disposition of Excess Weapons Plutonium*, Committee on International Security and Arms Control, Executive Summary (National Academy Press: Washington, DC, 1994) , p. 1.

[66] In the context of a storage facility for plutonium and/or HEU it should be borne in mind that the definitions of significant quantity (see chapter 5 on safeguards) as used in current safeguards procedures would require reassessment and probably new types of definition. For example, if the fissile material were to be stored in identical containers safeguards would most likely be designed to be capable of detecting tampering with or removal of a single container. Shea, T. E., 'On the application of IAEA safeguards to plutonium and highly enriched uranium from military inventories', *Science & Global Security*, vol. 3, nos 3–4 (1993), pp. 230–31.

[67] NAS (note 65), pp. 10–12.

boreholes. While significant uncertainties remain, this method has already been studied in several countries as a way of dealing with spent fuel and high-level waste.[68]

Consideration of the proliferation risks resulting from the civilian nuclear fuel cycle was beyond the mandate of the group, but it was noted in the report that 'the risks posed by plutonium in all forms must be addressed'.[69] The fact that for proliferation the danger from civil plutonium presents at least as great a danger as that from nuclear weapons was also an important conclusion of a 1993 RAND study.[70] It is expected that a final plan for the disposal of fissile material from weapons in the USA will be approved in 1995.[71]

International control

Several options are discussed above for dealing with the problem of ever-increasing stocks of surplus plutonium. Many of the methods would take some time to implement and the problem remains of what to do to ensure that stocks remain adequately safeguarded in the meantime. Especially as bilateral and unilateral reductions in the nuclear forces of the USA and the CIS states proceed, the possibility that the IAEA may be asked on a temporary or medium-term basis to aid in storage of newly surplused fissile materials is increasingly being investigated.[72] In addition, while a good case can clearly be made for the disposal of plutonium with radioactive waste, it seems clear at least for the present that the only option that the Russian Ministry of Atomic Energy (Minatom) is willing to consider is long-term storage. This may be at least in part the result of the offer of assistance by the USA to construct a long-term plutonium storage facility, but it must also be borne in mind that to many in Russia its plutonium, obtained as it was at great human and economic cost, is viewed as a 'national heritage'.[73]

As early as 1953, in proposing the creation of the International Atomic Energy Agency in his Atoms for Peace speech to the General Assembly of the United Nations, President Eisenhower proposed that the Agency serve to 'siphon off' fissile material from the nuclear weapon states to be used 'to serve the peaceful pursuits of mankind'.[74] Even the choice of a site for the IAEA headquarters, Vienna, was influenced by this desired role—its location between the (then) two hostile blocs would be mutually acceptable for storage of

[68] NAS (note 65), pp. 2, 12–17.

[69] NAS (note 65), p. 26.

[70] Chow, B. G. and Solomon, K. A., 'Limiting the spread of weapon-usable fissile materials', RAND Corporation, Santa Monica, Calif., 1993.

[71] Cooper, P. and Hitchens, T., 'DoE wrestles with fissile material disposal', *Defense News*, 21–27 Nov. 1994, p. 6; and Lippman, T., 'Plutonium surplus: bury or burn up?', *International Herald Tribune*, 21 Dec. 1995, p. 6.

[72] In fact the Clinton Administration has already said that it would place 7 of the 100 tonnes of plutonium produced for military purposes in storage subject to IAEA inspection. Also, 15 of the 750 tonnes of HEU which it has produced for nuclear weapons and to power navy vessels will be subject to safeguards. 'Beating swords into plowshares', *Atom*, no. 434 (June/July 1994), p. 39.

[73] von Hippel (note 22), pp. 2, 3.

[74] Fischer (note 1), pp. 34–35.

quantities of fissile materials.[75] With recent developments in nuclear arms control and concern over the fate of fissile material recovered from dismantled warheads, some type of role for the IAEA has been considered and should be considered further. Indeed, international confidence that plutonium is being securely and safely stored will probably only be forthcoming if the materials are under strict international safeguards.[76]

In several parts of Article IX, the Statute of the IAEA makes provision that: 'Members may make available to the Agency such quantities of special fissionable materials as they deem advisable and on such terms as shall be agreed with the Agency. The materials made available to the Agency may, at the discretion of the member making them available, be stored either by the member concerned or, with the agreement of the Agency, in the agency's depots.'[77]

For such material that is agreed to be stored the IAEA agrees to a number of responsibilities,

> The Agency shall ensure that these materials shall be safeguarded against (1) hazards of the weather, (2) unauthorized removal or diversion, (3) damage or destruction, including sabotage, and (4) forcible seizure. In storing special fissionable materials in its possession, the Agency shall ensure the geographical distribution of these materials in such a way as not to allow concentration of large amounts of such materials in any one country of the world.

and, with respect to reprocessing, Article XII of the IAEA statute affirms that the Agency has the right 'to require deposit with the agency of any excess of any special fissionable materials recovered or produced as a by-product over what is needed . . . in order to prevent stock-piling of these materials, provided that thereafter at the request of the member or members concerned special fissionable materials so deposited with the Agency shall be returned promptly.'[78]

Setting up International Plutonium Stores was considered in the 1980s, but the concept did not come to fruition. This was particularly because of issues related to withdrawal procedures and the geographical distribution of storage sites.[79] In 1990 the Fourth NPT Review Conference, in the light of projected developments in the peaceful nuclear fuel cycle and nuclear disarmament measures, reaffirmed the recommendation that the IAEA 'consider establishing arrangements as foreseen in its Statute for deposit with the Agency of any excess of plutonium and highly enriched uranium over what is needed, in order

[75] Fischer (note 1), p. 36.

[76] Oxford Research Group (note 13), p. 22. For arguments against the applications of international safeguards see, e.g., Bailey, K. C., 'International safeguards on special materials from weapons: why not?', ed. K. C. Bailey, *The Director's Series on Proliferation*, 1, Lawrence Livermore National Laboratory, Livermore, Calif., 7 June 1993, pp. 39–42 who states, e.g., that 'The high cost of international safeguards on US and Russian SNM is not worth the relatively low benefit'.

[77] International Atomic Energy Agency, IAEA Statute as amended up to 28 Dec. 1989 (IAEA: Vienna, June 1990), para. IX H.

[78] IAEA (note 77), para. IX H.

[79] Shea (note 66), pp. 227–28.

to prevent stockpiling of materials that could be diverted to direct use for nuclear weapons or other nuclear explosive devices'.[80]

There is a revival of interest in peaceful use or storage of the increasing stocks of plutonium, as indicated by remarks made by the Director General at IAEA General Conference meetings in the early 1990s. In January 1993 a meeting was held under the sponsorship of the IAEA at which the international plutonium storage concept was discussed. Japan, Russia and the USA were among the participants.[81]

In the new international climate efforts could prove more productive in making use of the above-mentioned IAEA provisions for storage of fissile materials as applied to plutonium and/or HEU from both NWS and NNWS. In particular, supervision of a ban on the production of fissile material for weapon use (see below) could be accomplished by the IAEA through application of safeguards to all nuclear materials outside those which would remain in military use.[82]

Part of President Clinton's new approach to the problem of proliferation enunciated in 1993 (see full discussion below) included a pledge to 'submit US fissile material no longer needed for our deterrent to inspection by the International Atomic Energy Agency'.[83] The first of these was carried out in September 1994 with the inspection of approximately 10 tonnes of surplus HEU at the Department of Energy's Y-12 plant near Oak Ridge, Tennessee and a second inspection was conducted in December at the DOE's Hanford facility.[84]

International control over plutonium stores does not necessarily have to involve the IAEA. A recommendation for an International Plutonium Depository for the storage of weapon-grade plutonium would involve existing storage facilities located in the country of origin meeting international safety and security standards. New facilities if and where needed would be constructed with the aid of the international community and all facilities would be under the custodianship of international guards. Appropriate safeguards would be applied by the nations cooperating in the denuclearization process. Depositing nations would be compensated for the plutonium according to the amount given up for storage by a Plutonium Depository Fund, which would be financed by the concerned members of the international community.[85]

Fissile material production ban

In 1992 the USA officially announced that it would no longer produce HEU or plutonium for nuclear weapons, thus codifying a policy which had already been

[80] IAEA document GC (XXXIV)/INF/291, 19 Sep. 1990, p. 3.

[81] Leopold, G. and Usui, N., 'Scientist fears nuclear proliferation, calls for watchdog agency in Japan', *Defense News*, 8–14 Feb. 1993, p. 34.

[82] Shea (note 66), p. 228.

[83] Fact Sheet: Non-Proliferation and Export Control Policy, as reprinted in *US Department of State Dispatch*, vol. 4, no. 40 (4 Oct. 1993), pp. 676–77.

[84] *PPNN Newsbriefs*, no. 28 (fourth quarter 1994), p. 11; and *Arms Control Today,* vol. 24, no. 8 (Oct. 1994), p. 24.

[85] Carter, A. B and Cote, O., 'Disposition of fissile materials', eds Allison *et al.* (note 41), pp. 125–27.

in effect since 1988 for HEU and since 1964 for plutonium.[86] HEU production ended in Russia in 1987 and most of its military production reactors have been shut down. Russia agreed in 1994 to shut down the rest as soon as replacement sources of the heat and electricity which the reactors also provide can be found. The time would therefore seem to be ripe for at least a formal bilateral agreement on a fissile material production ban.[87] The extension of safeguards over the civilian nuclear facilities of the United States and Russia[88] would cost at least as much as the current IAEA safeguards budget ($62 million for 1993) but this is a very small fraction of the current US nuclear weapon budget, for example.[89]

This bilateral ban would hopefully soon be followed by an extension to include the other declared nuclear weapon states. In addition there are indications that Israel, India and Pakistan would also consider adhering to such a ban if it were to be made universal.[90] Both North and South Korea have already pledged to refrain from constructing facilities for the production of fissile nuclear materials; Argentina and Brazil have informally agreed not to enrich uranium to weapon grade; and South Africa and Brazil have ceased their production of fissile materials.[91]

During his first speech to the UN General Assembly on 27 September 1993, US President Bill Clinton outlined a new non-proliferation plan. As detailed in a White House fact sheet[92] released on the same day, the plan included putting forward a 'comprehensive approach' to dealing with the increasing amount of fissile material from dismantled nuclear warheads and within civil nuclear programmes. Towards this end the USA proposed a multilateral convention with the goal of prohibiting the production of HEU and plutonium for nuclear

[86] von Hippel (note 47), p. 4; *US Department of State Dispatch*, vol. 3, no. 29 (20 July 1992); and Gordon, M. R., 'It's official; U.S. stops making material for nuclear warheads', *New York Times*, 14 July 1992, p. A16.

[87] For further discussions of issues associated with a cut-off of fissile material production and its verification in particular see, e.g., von Hippel, F., Albright, D. H. and Levi, B. G., 'Stopping the production of fissile materials for weapons', *Scientific American*, vol. 253, no. 3 (Sep. 1985), pp. 32–33; von Hippel, F. and Levi, B. G., 'Controlling nuclear weapons at the source: verification of a cutoff in the production of plutonium and highly enriched uranium for nuclear weapons', eds K. Tsipis, D. Hafemeister and P. Janeway, *Arms Control Verification: The Technologies that Make it Possible* (Pergamon: Elmsford, N.Y., 1985), pp. 339–88; Donnelly, W., 'Proposals for ending the US and Soviet production of fissile materials for nuclear weapons', Congressional Research Service (CRS) Issue Brief, IB89141, Library of Congress, Washington, DC, 8 Feb. 1991; and Sloss, D., 'Verifying a ban on production of special nuclear material for nuclear weapons', ed. J. Brown, *Challenges in Arms Control for the 1990s* (VU University Press: Amsterdam, 1992), pp. 129–38.

[88] The NPT mandates IAEA safeguards only for non-nuclear weapon states, nuclear weapon states voluntarily offering to accept safeguards on a small portion of their civil facilities.

[89] von Hippel, F., 'Controls on nuclear-warheads and materials', prepared statement for the Senate Armed Services Committee Hearings on the Disposition of US and CIS Strategic Nuclear Warheads under the START I Treaty and the June 17, 1992 U.S./Russian Joint Understanding on Further Reductions in Strategic Offensive Arms (START II), 4 Aug. 1992, pp. 10–11.

[90] von Hippel (note 47), p. 4.

[91] Spector, L. S. and Dean, J., 'Cooperative security: assessing the tools of the trade', ed. J. E. Nolan, *Global Engagement: Cooperation and Security in the 21st Century* (Brookings Institution: Washington, DC, 1994), p. 171.

[92] Note 83, pp. 676–77.

explosives or outside of safeguards and would seek to eliminate stockpiles of HEU and plutonium.[93]

While exploring ways to limit stockpiling of plutonium and minimizing the use of HEU in civil programmes, the approach would seek to constrain the production of fissile material in 'regions of instability and high proliferation risk', but at the same time it would not oppose civil nuclear programmes producing plutonium in Western Europe and Japan. This double standard, reportedly included in order not to alienate states such as France, Japan and the UK, which are currently engaged in reprocessing, has drawn some criticism, however.[94]

The USA further stated that it would allow all US fissile material not needed for weapons to be inspected by the IAEA, pursue the purchase of HEU from the former Soviet Union and other countries so that it can be used for peaceful purposes and begin study on the long-term options available for plutonium disposition. One serious weakness of the programme, however, is that it would legalize the stocks of fissile material already existing in the undeclared nuclear weapon states.[95]

A detailed plan for implementing the HEU and plutonium cut-off plan put forward by Jonathan Dean would, as a first-step agreement, have the declared nuclear weapon states stop production of fissile material and agree to IAEA inspections of their nuclear facilities. This would be followed by a phased-in approach to bring first the threshold nuclear states, and then the NPT states parties followed by all remaining states, into the regime. In the final phase production and storage of civil-use plutonium would be included as well, leading to a total ban on all plutonium production and reprocessing.[96] This goes somewhat further than the Clinton proposal in that it would in the final instance ban the production of plutonium even under safeguards and, importantly, including all civil plutonium as well—a much more useful goal.

In the bilateral sphere, in a potentially important first step towards a possible international control regime for plutonium, the USA and Russia agreed in March 1994 to permit inspection of each other's plutonium storage sites. Working group talks aimed at implementing the agreement were held in Moscow in 1994, and the Rocky Flats plant in Colorado in the USA and storage facilities at Tomsk-7 in Russia are sites being considered for the visits.[97]

[93] In a positive response to the Clinton initiative the British Foreign and Commonwealth Office recognized the 'potentially valuable contribution which a multilateral convention prohibiting the production of plutonium and highly-enriched uranium for explosives purposes could make to non-proliferation', *Trust and Verify*, Bulletin of the Verification Technology Information Centre, no. 41 (Oct. 1993), pp. 2–3.

[94] Goldemberg, J., 'A fair ban on production of plutonium would apply to all', *International Herald Tribune*, 23 Nov. 1993, p. 4; and *PPNN Newsbrief*, no. 23 (third quarter 1993), p. 5.

[95] Rauf, T., 'Strengthened safeguards and non-proliferation', ed. T. Rauf, *Strengthened IAEA Safeguards and Regional Non-Proliferation Strategies*, Canadian Centre for Global Security, Aurora Papers, 23 Mar. 1994, p. 10.

[96] Wilkenson, M., 'Forum on CTB, NPT, fissionable ban', *Disarmament Times*, 23 Nov. 1993, p. 4.

[97] 'U.S. and Russia reach accord on inspecting plutonium sites', *International Herald Tribune*, 17 Mar. 1994, p. 4; Lockwood, D., 'US, Russia begin detailed talks on fissile materials', *Arms Control Today*, vol. 24, no. 5 (June 1994), p. 25; and Lockwood, D., 'U.S.–Russian fissile material talks still face several hurdles', *Arms Control Today*, vol. 24, no. 10 (Dec. 1994), p. 21.

In addition, two technical working groups have been holding meetings in Moscow on fissile material issues. The group on Safeguards, Transparency and Irreversibility worked out details of the phasing out of Russian reactors producing plutonium for weapons. It is headed by Ambassador James Goodby and will also explore transparency measures relating to fissile material storage areas. The discussions of the group on the Disposition and Accumulation of Fissile Materials, headed by Frank von Hippel, include the management and disposal of plutonium extracted from nuclear warheads.[98]

At the end of 1993 the UN General Assembly adopted a consensus resolution which recognized that 'a non-discriminatory, multilateral and internationally and effectively verifiable treaty banning the production of fissile material for nuclear weapons or other nuclear explosive devices would be a significant contribution to nuclear non-proliferation in all its aspects'.[99] It is now accepted that the appropriate forum for negotiating a fissile material cut-off is the Conference on Disarmament (CD) and, while the CD appointed a special coordinator on the issue in early 1994, a year later there was still no consensus on a mandate. A key stumbling-block remained as to whether the mandate would include explicit reference to unsafeguarded, existing stocks.[100]

V. Conclusions

This chapter describes the technology required to produce plutonium from irradiated nuclear fuel. These techniques are widely available and, together with the relative availability of technology for producing a nuclear reactor, represent what has generally been considered to be the most dangerous path to nuclear proliferation. It is vital that the international community develop ways of detecting clandestine attempts to produce plutonium which could be used for nuclear weapons, and subsequent chapters examine appropriate ways and means of accomplishing this goal and discuss appropriate responses which could be taken should such activity be uncovered or suspected.

The difficulties involved in the long-term disposal of plutonium have become increasingly apparent and much more work needs to be done on this vital issue. The options explored to date are outlined above and the pros and cons of the various techniques are explored. IAEA-supervised storage seems a promising way of dealing with the problem in the near term, and priority should be given to studying the most rapid way to begin to implement a plan of action involving either this Agency or a consortium of concerned international parties.

There is a strong consensus that a ban on the further production of fissile material should be concluded, and several recent studies have recommended that commercial reprocessing of plutonium be discontinued as soon as is prac-

[98] Lockwood (note 49), p. 24; and Lockwood, June 1994 (note 97), p. 25.

[99] See Lockwood, D., 'Nuclear arms control', *SIPRI Yearbook 1994* (Oxford University Press: Oxford, 1994), pp. 659–60.

[100] *Nuclear Proliferation News*, no. 18 (17 Feb. 1995), p. 2; vol. 94, no. 17 (20 Dec. 1994), p. 5; vol. 94, no. 10 (2 Sep. 1994), p. 4; and *Disarmament Times*, Sep. 1994, pp. 3–4.

ticable as well.[101] If appropriate ways are to be found to deal with the problem of large stockpiles of plutonium and begin reducing amounts already accumulated, it is important that a verifiable halt to the production of fissile material for weapons be put into force and that further civil reprocessing be rapidly curtailed.

[101] Oxford Research Group (note 13), pp. 21, 41; and Berkhout *et al.* (note 41), p. 189.

4. The Iraqi nuclear programme

I. Introduction

The international community at large and the IAEA in particular were stunned to learn of the magnitude and scope of the clandestine programme that Iraq had undertaken to obtain nuclear weapons. Almost every conceivable method of obtaining fissile material, including both highly enriched uranium and weapon-grade plutonium, had been pursued alongside efforts to acquire the other necessary technological means to build a nuclear explosive device. The programme was an intricate and ingenious effort to obtain equipment, material and expertise from outside the country, in concert with developing and further improving an indigenous capability to the maximum extent feasible. Only after several years of inspections carried out by the IAEA, with the assistance and cooperation of the Special Commission of the United Nations (UNSCOM), were most of the details of the programme uncovered.

As a signatory of the 1968 Treaty on the Non-Proliferation of Nuclear Weapons, which it ratified in 1969, Iraq bound itself not only to forswear direct acquisition of nuclear weapons or nuclear explosive devices from other countries but also 'not to manufacture or otherwise acquire nuclear weapons or other nuclear explosive devices; and not to seek or receive any assistance in the manufacture of nuclear weapons or other nuclear explosive devices'.[1] Iraq failed to live up to this commitment and indeed attempted to acquire weapon-usable material in an elaborate and costly programme. As a further part of its NPT obligations Iraq was required to and did conclude a safeguards agreement with the IAEA 'for the exclusive purpose of verification of the fulfilment of its obligations assumed under [the NPT] with a view to preventing diversion of nuclear energy from peaceful uses to nuclear weapons or other nuclear explosive devices'.[2]

In two ground-breaking declarations the IAEA stated that Iraq had violated its safeguards agreement by its programmes to enrich uranium and produce plutonium and had in so doing violated its obligations under the NPT. The discovery and extent of these actions in violation of Iraq's international obligations sent shock waves through the international community. Calls for finding the means of avoiding such occurrences in the future were strong and immediate.

More specifically, under the auspices of Security Council Resolution 687, the United Nations authorized *inter alia* the carrying out of on-site inspections to

[1] Treaty on the Non-Proliferation of Nuclear Weapons, Article I (the text of the Treaty is reproduced in appendix A).

[2] NPT (note 1), Article III. The safeguards agreement was published as IAEA document INFCIRC/172, 22 Feb. 1973.

determine the full extent of the Iraqi nuclear programme. While it has been a matter of some dispute it was recently recognized that the comprehensive safeguards required of NPT signatories, for example, do in fact provide for on-site inspection at facilities other than those declared by the state party. Such inspections have, however, never been carried out and it is important to note that this remains the case even today—the many inspections carried out in Iraq since Resolution 687 was passed were performed *pursuant to* this resolution and not as part of any standard IAEA inspection responsibilities.[3]

The unique nature of the inspections in Iraq and the resulting findings, together with the consensus view that the IAEA does possess the legal means to carry out such inspections, has led to a re-examination of the IAEA's role in this and other areas.[4] The Director General of the IAEA, Hans Blix, summed up the problems and opportunities for improvement presented by the revelations in Iraq to the IAEA Board of Governors late in 1991:

> In the wake of these revelations the Agency has been both praised for its effective inspections under the Security Council mandate and been criticized for not having discovered through safeguards what was being done in Iraq. Warning voices are heard—primarily in the public debate—that there might be similar cases and that better guarantees must be offered against surprises.
>
> In my view, the Agency—the Board of Governors and the Secretariat—must take the concerns seriously and find remedies.[5]

To have better guarantees against such surprises implies, for example, that the traditional role of safeguards, assuring only that declared nuclear material be accounted for, be altered or supplemented to assure against undeclared material or clandestine facilities. The remedies of which Hans Blix spoke, to be effective, must involve a thorough re-examination of verification in the context of nuclear proliferation, including special inspections of undeclared facilities and also including much of the standard practice in the areas of nuclear safeguards and export controls in general. As was noted near the beginning of the inspections in Iraq, 'At long last, Saddam Hussein may be doing the world a favour. His country is now a giant laboratory for nuclear sleuthing experiments. Early results show that the old formula for stopping proliferation did not work. But a new one might'.[6]

While acknowledging the fact that the inspections which uncovered the specific nature of the Iraqi nuclear programme were carried out under procedures outside routine IAEA safeguards, Hans Blix points to the *information* supplied to the IAEA, which enabled the inspections to be carried out and to uncover the details of the programme, as the 'decisive factor'.[7]

[3] Such inspections have been called for in the case of North Korea (see chapter 7).

[4] For further discussion of these issues see chapter 5.

[5] Statement to the IAEA Board of Governors on safeguards matters, delivered by Hans Blix, Vienna, 5 Dec. 1991, p. 6.

[6] Milhollin, G. and White, G., 'Maybe Saddam did the world a favour', *International Herald Tribune,* 14 Aug. 1991, p. 4.

[7] Statement by Hans Blix (note 5), p. 7.

In fact, the situation in Iraq has expanded the agenda of the IAEA, particularly as far as information of relevance to verification is concerned. Although all of the specifics are not available from open sources, it is likely that information from highly protected sources, running the gamut from image and signals intelligence gathered from sophisticated satellites and aircraft to human intelligence, has been made available by member states to ascertain the situation in Iraq. It is unlikely that the Agency itself will be given responsibility for collecting this type of information directly in the foreseeable future. One of the main items on the agenda for immediate improvements in IAEA capabilities for monitoring a country's compliance with non-proliferation undertakings does involve the Agency accepting and analysing intelligence and other pertinent data, however. With the help of the national technical means of certain IAEA member states, such a development has the potential to bring about a watershed in its effectiveness in uncovering clandestine activity.

With the increased focus on the IAEA, nuclear safeguards and nuclear proliferation in general since the discoveries in Iraq, efforts towards improving safeguards are also being intensified in many specific areas. These renewed calls come at a time, however, when the IAEA budget—frozen in real terms for many years—is being asked to cope with a rapidly increasing list of responsibilities. The accessions of South Africa (1991), China (1992), France (1992) and Algeria (1995) to the NPT and the 1991 bilateral agreement between Argentina and Brazil[8] are among positive developments which will, however, necessitate further drain on the budget. Further responsibilities are also resulting from the breakup of the former USSR and the accession of many of the newly independent states to the NPT as non-nuclear weapon states (NNWS) and thus their agreement on full-scope safeguards.[9] As bilateral and unilateral reductions in the nuclear forces of the USA and the CIS proceed there is renewed interest in the IAEA having a major role in the accountancy and control of newly surplus fissile materials. In 1994 the USA allowed the IAEA to inspect some of its surplus highly enriched uranium to this end (see chapter 5). Also, the possibility of the IAEA being given a role in the context of a comprehensive test ban (CTB) treaty cannot be ignored.

Restrictions on exports of materials and equipment play a direct role in limiting access for their use in potential nuclear weapon programmes.[10] Monitoring of exports—keeping track of what is being acquired by which country at what time—can also perhaps somewhat indirectly aid other monitoring activities since procurement patterns may indicate that a particular route towards some illicit nuclear activity is being taken. Verification resources can then be concen-

[8] The safeguards agreement covering all Argentinian and Brazilian nuclear activities was signed between Argentina, Brazil, the joint Argentine–Brazilian Agency for Accounting and Control of Nuclear Materials (ABACC) and the IAEA on 13 Dec. 1991. This agreement puts the two largest South American threshold states on an equal footing with NPT states parties with respect to safeguards coverage.

[9] See appendix B for a list of states parties to the NPT and chapter 5 for further discussion of these matters.

[10] See chapter 6.

trated on a particular area looking for a particular type of facility—a centrifuge enrichment plant, for example.

With respect to the future involvement and role of the UN in nuclear non-proliferation, notice should be taken of the rather definitive statement made by the Security Council in January 1992. Noting 'the importance of the decision of many countries to adhere to the non-proliferation treaty and emphasize the integral role in the implementation of that treaty of fully effective I.A.E.A. safeguards, as well as the importance of effective export controls', it was stated that 'The members of the Council will take appropriate measures in the case of any violations notified to them by the I.A.E.A.'.[11]

Although agreement has been reached to put the North Korean nuclear programme on hold and to eliminate it after some years, the short time (by some estimates) within which it could acquire a nuclear weapon capability, coupled with apparent efforts to conceal elements of its programme, has left serious concerns about the country's intentions. As stated by François Heisbourg 'no single event [in Southeast Asia] would be more destabilizing than the North Korean bomb'.[12]

The importance of verification in the context of nuclear proliferation is amply demonstrated in the surprising amount which remained unknown even after intelligence resources had been amassed to concentrate on Iraq after its invasion of Kuwait—this in one of the most unstable areas of the world where the consequences of ignorance could well have been disaster. Uncertainties about other areas of the world are continuing to fuel fears of further such scenarios, and proposals to help avoid similar occurrences in the future, based to a large measure on the Iraqi experience, are addressed in chapters 5 and 6.

Before the 1991 Persian Gulf War there were certainly indications that Iraq was pursuing a nuclear weapon capability. At the time nothing was done since there was no consensus or precedent as to exactly what *should* be done or by whom. The lessons of the Iraqi experience, however, are beginning to push the international community as a whole in the direction which would minimize the risk of illicit nuclear activity and make some type of effective response more likely should serious attempts at weapon production be uncovered.

Many initial reports have turned out to be overly pessimistic and it now appears that it would probably have taken Iraq several more years to be able to produce its first atomic bomb. Even this estimate is based on the assumption that the knowledge they possessed could be smoothly transformed into production capability. None the less, the fact that the extent of the programme was virtually unknown and could have continued on its course for an undetermined and (for the world) possibly very dangerous stretch of time has forced the re-evaluation of many tenets of the nuclear non-proliferation regime.

The original NPT Model Safeguards Agreement between the IAEA and Iraq (see chapter 5) specifies two inspections per year in four facilities at

[11] UN Security Council Declaration quoted in *New York Times*, 1 Feb. 1992, p. A4.

[12] Smith, J. R., 'N. Koreans accused of arms ploy', *Washington Post*, 28 Feb. 1992, p. A29; and '2 Koreas caught in another snag', *New York Times*, 28 Feb, 1992, p. A9.

Al Tuwaitha. Up until the invasion of Kuwait in August 1990, 25 inspections had been performed by 13 inspectors.[13] After the invasion of Kuwait, IAEA inspections at Al Tuwaitha were carried out in November 1990 and (as was the case at the previous inspection in April) the conclusion was reached that all nuclear material under safeguards was accounted for.[14]

In fact before the 1991 Persian Gulf War, IAEA Safeguards Department Head Jon Jennekens praised the cooperation of Iraqi nuclear officials with the IAEA, saying they had 'made every effort to demonstrate that Iraq is a solid citizen' with respect to the NPT regime.[15] On a more technical note, a 1990 IAEA inspection report assured that three hot cells supplied by Italy and located in the Al Tuwaitha complex 'were sealed and "not capable" of reprocessing spent fuel'.[16] These were later found to have been used to separate a small quantity of plutonium, and Iraq's credentials as a 'solid citizen' were rather dramatically altered.

II. The inspections: an overview of the main findings

The first IAEA inspection under the UN mandate took place 15–21 May 1991. The discoveries made were surprising and dramatic with respect to the extent of Iraq's nuclear development and before detailing the inspections and their findings a basic overview of the programme is appropriate.[17]

The most surprising discovery was the extensive programme for enriching uranium using electromagnetic isotope separation (EMIS). This technology had been used by the USA during the Manhattan Project but was soon thereafter abandoned because of its relative inefficiency and high energy consumption.

[13] Hibbs, M. and Maclachlan, A., 'No bomb-quantity of HEU in Iraq, IAEA safeguards report indicates', *Nuclear Fuel*, vol. 15, no. 17 (20 Aug. 1990), p. 9.

[14] Hibbs, M., 'Iraqi nuclear threat warnings called unrealistic war rationale', *Nucleonics Week*, vol. 31, no. 48 (29 Nov. 1990), p. 7.

[15] Hibbs and Maclachlan (note 13), p. 8.

[16] Hibbs, M., '1982 report said 20 countries were pursuing EMIS research, *Nucleonics Week*, vol. 32, no. 30 (25 July 1991), p. 12. However, the existence of such assurance in any official document is challenged by the IAEA.

[17] See, e.g., Davis, Z. S. and Donnelly, W. H., 'Iraq and nuclear weapons', Congressional Research Service (CRS) Issue Brief, IB90113, Library of Congress, Washington, DC, 10 Dec. 1991; Müller, H., 'The non-proliferation regime beyond the cold war', *SIPRI Yearbook 1992: World Armaments and Disarmament* (Oxford University Press: Oxford, 1992); Chauvistré, E., *The Implications of IAEA Inspections under Security Council Resolution 687*, UNIDIR Research Paper no. 11 (United Nations: New York, 1992); Albright, D. and Hibbs, M., 'Iraq's bomb: blueprints and artifacts', *Bulletin of the Atomic Scientists,* vol. 48, no. 1 (Jan./Feb. 1992), p. 30; Albright, D. and Hibbs, M., 'Iraq's shop-til-you-drop nuclear program', *Bulletin of the Atomic Scientists,* vol. 48, no. 3 (Apr. 1992), p. 37; Albright, D. and Hibbs, M., 'Supplier-spotting', *Bulletin of the Atomic Scientists*, vol. 49, no. 1 (Jan./Feb. 1993), p. 8; Zimmerman, P., 'Iraq's nuclear achievements: components, sources, and stature', CRS Report for Congress, Library of Congress, Washington, DC, 18 Feb. 1993 (revised 4 June 1993); Trevan, T., 'The United Nations and Iraq: verification in the face of obstruction', eds J. B. Poole and R. Guthrie, VERTIC, *Verification 1993: Peacekeeping, Arms Control and the Environment* (Brassey's: London, 1993), p. 171; Trevan, T., 'The UN Special Commission's verification and monitoring activities in Iraq: 1993', eds J. B. Poole and R. Guthrie, VERTIC, *Verification 1994: Peacekeeping, Arms Control and the Environment* (Brassey's: London, 1994), p. 171; and Zifferero, M., 'IAEA activities and experience in Iraq under the relevant resolutions of the UN Security Council', *Proceeding of the 1994 Symposium on International Nuclear Safeguards, Vol. I* (IAEA: Vienna, 1994), pp. 211–21.

The technology was also largely declassified—a fact which, when coupled with the relative abundance of inexpensive electrical power that Iraq could make available—certainly had an impact on Iraq's decision to develop the technique. An 8-calutron facility had begun operational tests in September 1990[18] and had produced gram quantities of low-enriched uranium and milligram quantities of HEU. A full-scale plant designed for 90 separators was perhaps 36 months away from full operation with an identical 'back-up' facility being constructed at a separate location. Estimates are that one of these facilities could have produced close to 15 kg of HEU per year when operating as designed.[19]

It was also revealed that Iraq had conducted an R&D programme for centrifuge enrichment. This programme relied much less on indigenous production and involved a very well-organized international procurement effort set up to acquire the designs of model centrifuges as well as parts, manufacturing equipment and raw materials. A facility housing a cascade of about 100 centrifuges was to have been operational by 1993, with a larger 500-centrifuge plant running by 1996. In addition Iraq had also apparently been working on, although had subsequently abandoned, gaseous diffusion technology and had also explored chemical separation and laser techniques for uranium enrichment.

In addition, the production of gram quantities of plutonium had been accomplished in the safeguarded IRT-5000 research reactor supplied by the Soviet Union and which began operating in 1968. Subsequent reprocessing of this material took place in Italian-supplied hot cells.

Overall, as is detailed below, while the programme was advancing on several fronts it remained quite a long way from its goal.[20] Of the two most advanced elements, the mainly indigenous EMIS approach was facing difficulties and it would have taken several more years before sufficient uranium for military purposes could have been produced. The centrifuge programme, relying heavily on clandestinely acquired designs and the procurement of large quantities of materials and components, was at a very early stage in its development when the programme was stopped by the war. The nuclear weapon design effort was at an early stage as well, with a practicable design yet to be achieved.

III. UN Security Council Resolutions relating to Iraq

United Nations Security Council Resolution 687 adopted on 3 April 1991 called upon Iraq to:

unconditionally agree not to acquire or develop nuclear weapons or nuclear-weapons usable material or any subsystems or components or any research, development, support or manufacturing facilities related to the above; to submit to the Secretary-General and the Director-General of the International Atomic Energy Agency within fifteen

[18] Seneviratne, G., 'Blix asks new safeguards authority as IAEA says Iraq violated pledge', *Nucleonics Week*, vol. 32, no. 30 (25 July 1991), p. 11.

[19] The progress made in the various enrichment techologies is discussed in more detail below in the context of the individual inspections.

[20] For an overall assessment see IAEA Iraqi Action Team Fact Sheet, IAEA, Vienna, 18 Mar. 1993.

days of the adoption of the present resolution a declaration of the locations, amounts, and types of all items specified above; to place all of its nuclear-weapons-usable materials under the exclusive control, for custody and removal, of the International Atomic Energy Agency, with the assistance and cooperation of the Special Commission . . . to accept . . . urgent on-site inspection and the destruction, removal or rendering harmless as appropriate of all items specified above; and to accept the plan . . . for the future ongoing monitoring and verification of its compliance with these undertakings.[21]

With specific regard to the monitoring and verification arrangements the resolution further requested that the Director General of the IAEA, through the UN Secretary-General and with the assistance and cooperation of the Special Commission (formed to perform on-site inspection of the biological, chemical and missile capabilities of Iraq):

carry out immediate on-site inspection of Iraq's nuclear capabilities based on Iraq's declarations and the designation of any additional locations by the Special Commission; . . . develop a plan taking into account the rights and obligations of Iraq under the Treaty on the Non-Proliferation of Nuclear Weapons of 1 July 1968, for the future ongoing monitoring and verification of Iraq's compliance with [the obligations outlined above], including an inventory of all nuclear material in Iraq subject to the Agency's verification and inspections to confirm that Agency safeguards cover all relevant nuclear activities in Iraq.[22]

It is also worthy of note that these measures were to be taken as steps towards the establishment of a zone in the Middle East free from weapons of mass destruction.

Declarations of non-compliance

On 18 July 1991 the IAEA Board of Governors, considering a report by the Director General, declared that Iraq had not complied with its safeguards agreement.[23] This was based on information gained during the first two inspections and from declarations provided by Iraq on its uranium enrichment programme. In particular, nuclear material suitable for fuel fabrication and uranium enrichment (uranium dioxide, uranium tetrachloride and uranium hexafluoride) were not declared in accordance with Iraq's obligations under Article 34(c) of the NPT Model Safeguards Agreement. Under the same article Iraq should have reported the 0.5 kg of uranium which it was subsequently admitted had been enriched in the Iraqi programme.[24] This was the first time a state party to the NPT had been condemned for such a programme.

[21] UN Security Council Resolution 687, UN document S/RES/687, 8 Apr. 1991, para. 12. Resolution 687 is reproduced in appendix D.

[22] UN (note 21), para. 13.

[23] IAEA, Iraq's non-compliance with its safeguards obligations, Resolution adopted by the Board of Governors on 18 July 1991, IAEA document GOV/2532, 18 July 1991.

[24] IAEA, A report by the Director General on non-compliance by Iraq with its obligations under the safeguards agreement concluded with the Agency, IAEA document GOV/2530, 16 July 1991, pp. 4–5.

On 9 August 1991 the Director General reported an additional instance of non-compliance which 'included the undeclared production and separation of plutonium in safeguarded facilities'.[25] This involved the unreported production and irradiation of uranium dioxide fuel rods and pellets in the IRT-5000 reactor. While admitting that the IRT-5000 reactor had low potential for producing plutonium in substantial quantities, and that these activities were 'not comparable in terms of significance to Iraq's industrial-scale efforts to produce enriched uranium', he noted that 'the fact that the activities with respect to plutonium occurred in safeguarded facilities is of special concern'.[26]

On 15 August the UN Security Council adopted Resolution 707, which further condemned Iraq's non-compliance with its safeguards obligations and stated that this violated Iraq's commitments as a party to the NPT.[27] The Board of Governors declared on 13 September that there was evidence of further non-compliance by Iraq with its safeguards obligations. Then in taking up the two Board statements, the General Conference of the IAEA on 20 September strongly condemned Iraq's non-compliance with its nuclear non-proliferation obligations.[28]

Two months after Resolution 707, Security Council Resolution 715 was adopted.[29] This resolution approved plans submitted by the UN Secretary-General: 'Plan for the future and ongoing monitoring and verification of Iraq's compliance with relevant parts of section C of Security Council Resolution 687 (1991)'[30] and the Director General of the IAEA: 'Plan for future ongoing monitoring and verification of Iraq's compliance with paragraph 12 of part C of Security Council Resolution 687 (1991) and with the requirements of paragraphs 3 and 5 of Resolution 707 (1991)'.[31] As part of this latter detailed plan Iraq was to *inter alia* provide to the Agency a declaration of its facilities, materials and equipment at six-month intervals, beginning with a report covering the period from 1 January 1989. Appended to the document describing the plan were the specific types of information required (Annex 2) as well as a thorough list (Annex 3) of the items to be reported.[32] Not until late November 1993

[25] IAEA, A report by the Director General on non-compliance by Iraq with its obligations under the safeguards agreement concluded with the Agency, IAEA document GOV/2530/Add. 1, 9 Aug. 1991.

[26] IAEA (note 25), Annex, p. 2.

[27] UN Security Council Resolution 707, UN document S/RES/707, 15 Aug. 1991. The text of the resolution is reproduced in appendix D.

[28] IAEA document GC(XXXV)/RES/568, 20 Sep. 1991.

[29] UN Security Council Resolution 715, UN document S/RES/715, 11 Oct. 1991. The text of the resolution is reproduced in appendix D.

[30] UN, Plan for future ongoing monitoring and verification of Iraq's compliance with relevant parts of section C of Security Council Resolution 687 (1991), UN document S/22871/Rev.1, 2 Oct. 1991.

[31] UN, Plan for future ongoing monitoring and verification of Iraq's compliance with paragraph 12 of part C of Security Council Resolution 687 (1991), UN documents S/22872/Rev.1, 20 Sep. 1991 and S/22872/Rev.1/Corr. 1, 10 Oct. 1991.

[32] UN document S/22872/Rev.1 (note 31), pp. 11, 25. Annex 3 covers pp. 28–44 of the monitoring plan. Almost a year later Annex 3 was revised (and substantially expanded) in the light of experience gained in implementing Security Council Resolutions 687 and 707 and as a result of the agreement of the Nuclear Suppliers Group (NSG) on the Guidelines for Transfers of Nuclear-Related Dual-use Equipment, Materials and Technology. See the list of items to be reported to the Agency. Enclosure to the letter dated 14 July 1992 from the Director General of the International Atomic Energy Agency (IAEA) addressed to the Secretary-General, UN document S/24300, 16 July 1992. Annex 3 was expanded again in 1995 to a

would Iraq formally agree to accept the obligations contained in Resolution 715.

The IAEA has stated that 'for safeguards to be an effective deterrent it must be perceived that the international community will respond promptly and vigorously if the IAEA should ever have to "sound the alarm"'.[33] This perception has been enhanced in recent years even though the discoveries in Iraq in the main were not made as a result of routine safeguards procedures.

Addressing this before the Board during the meeting at which the first violations were being considered the Director General stated:

> It is now being asked, and we must ask ourselves, whether major changes are needed to strengthen the safeguards system. The case of Iraq demonstrates the challenges that may need to be met and the ability of the Agency to meet them. . . . I conclude that the lesson to be learnt from the present case is that a high degree of assurance can be obtained that the Agency can uncover clandestine nuclear activities if three major conditions are fulfilled: First, that access is provided to information obtained, inter alia through national technical means, regarding sites that may require inspection; second, that access to any such sites, even at short notice, is an unequivocal right of the Agency; and third, that access to the Security Council is available for backing and support that may be necessary to perform the inspection.[34]

The inspections to which he referred are a major element of new efforts in the verification of nuclear non-proliferation and are dealt with in particular detail in chapters 5 and 7.

IV. The inspections: a detailed account

The IAEA inspections in Iraq led to surprising revelations concerning the state of development of the Iraqi nuclear weapon programme. The inspections were able to build one upon the other with additional information continually being made available to develop a steadily clearer picture of the true state of affairs. In addition, areas found to be damaged from the bombing during the Persian Gulf War give at least some indication of which facilities were known about prior to the beginning of inspections. In order to appreciate fully the way in which information was built up over the inspection period, and the importance and limitations of such inspections for the future, their results are presented in chronological order. Thus this chapter also serves as a historical account of the important time during which the mission mandated by the Security Council was getting underway and of the trials and pitfalls which were encountered.

Although the implementation of the inspections is unique it none the less provides many valuable insights for future monitoring of nuclear activity. This is particularly true, for example, in the synergistic way in which various monitor-

63-page document, see UN documents S/1995/215, 23 Mar. 1995, S/1995/215/Corr.1, 7 Apr. 1995 and S/1995/215/Corr.2, Aug. 1995.

[33] *IAEA Safeguards: An Introduction* (IAEA: Vienna, 1981), p. 13.

[34] Quoted in IAEA Press Release, PR/91 24, 18 July 1991.

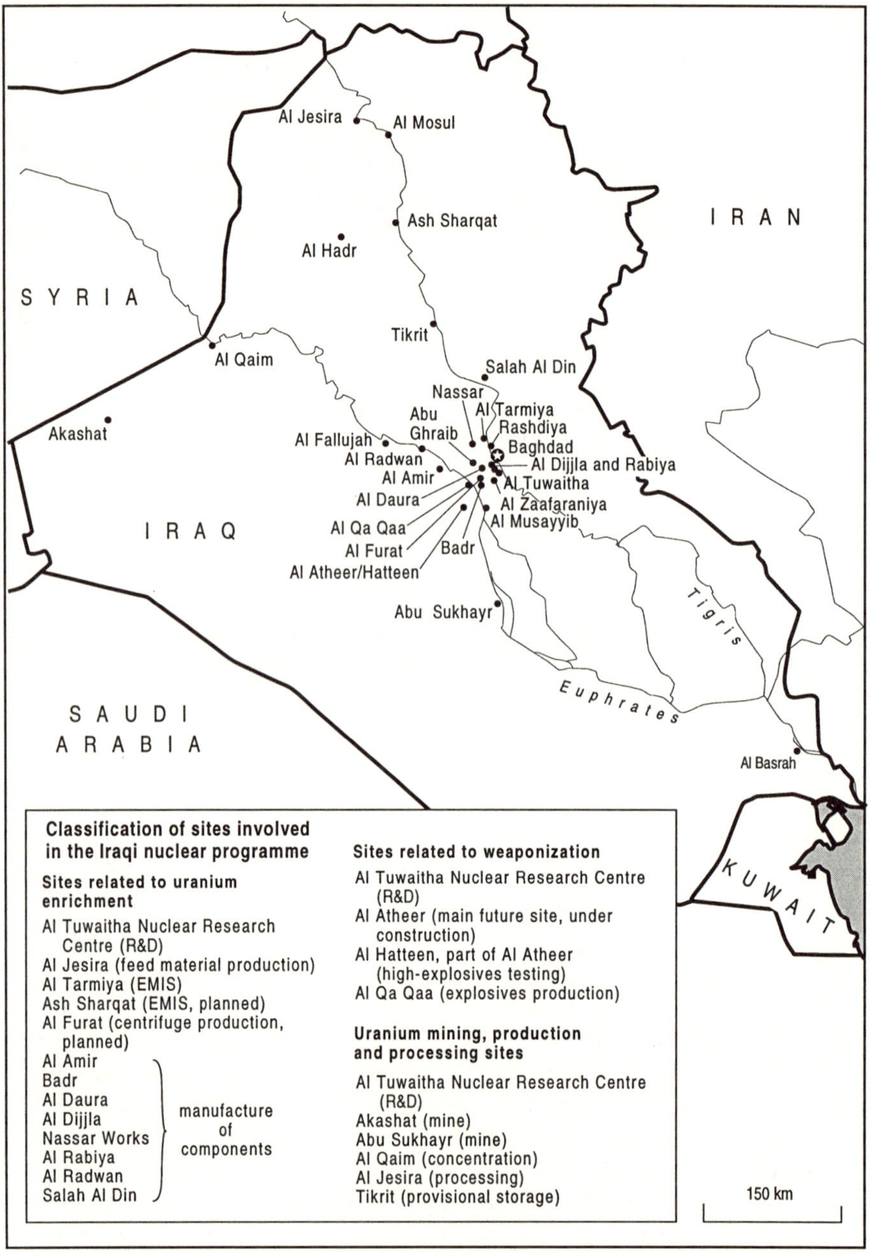

Figure 20. Map of Iraq showing the approximate locations of the main inspection sites

Sources: Based on maps contained in Report on the third IAEA on-site inspection in Iraq under Security Council Resolution 687 (1991), 7–18 July 1991, UN document S/22837, 25 July 1991, p. 13; Report on the seventh IAEA on-site inspection in Iraq under Security Council Resolution 687 (1991), 11–22 October 1991, UN document S/23215, 14 Nov. 1991, p. 63; IAEA, *IAEA Inspections and Iraq's Nuclear Capabilities* (IAEA: Vienna, Apr. 1992); and information supplied by Maurizio Zifferero, IAEA.

ing techniques were used. The employment of various forms of camouflage, concealment and deception (CC&D) at various times is revealed as well as the Iraqi practice of letting out only as much information as it thought necessary at a particular time.

Accounts of the earlier inspections are given individually and in detail, in part to illustrate the manner in which information was uncovered and thereby give a sense of the inspection process itself. Subheadings for EMIS, centrifuge enrichment and other key programme elements permit a quick review of the various elements to be readily made. The discussion necessarily concentrates on the aspects of the inspections relevant to the rest of the book—particularly uranium enrichment and plutonium separation—and the verification issues associated with nuclear weapon proliferation. The map in figure 20 shows the approximate locations of the major sites visited during the inspections, and illustrates their concentration in the area around and south of Baghdad.

The first and second inspections

The results of the first and second inspections conducted by the IAEA in Iraq were issued as a joint report.[35] The first was carried out 15–21 May 1991 by a team of 34 inspectors from 20 IAEA member states. The second occurred from 22 June to 3 July and was carried out by 18 personnel from 8 countries.

The three main objectives of these first inspections[36] were to verify the accuracy and completeness of the Iraqi declarations pursuant to Resolution 687, to inspect sites of possible undeclared nuclear activity or sites serving as storage for nuclear equipment as designated by UNSCOM, and lastly to develop an overall picture of the nature, direction and capabilities of the programme.

The first inspection team visited only two sites: Al Tuwaitha and Al Tarmiya.[37] The main purpose was to verify the 27 April declarations by Iraq concerning the nuclear materials at the Al Tuwaitha complex and full cooperation of the Iraqi Government was reported.[38] During the second inspection these sites were both revisited along with the designated sites of Abu Ghraib, Al Hamath, Al Musayyib, Al Fallujah and Al Zaafaraniya, the site later targeted in the January 1993 attack by the USA using 40–50 cruise missiles. (Maurizio Zifferero, who headed the first nuclear inspection to occur after the attack, said, however, that the site had been rearranged for peaceful purposes after the Persian Gulf War.[39])

[35] Consolidated report on the first two IAEA inspections under Security Council Resolution 687 (1991) of Iraqi nuclear capabilities, UN document S/22788, 15 July 1991.

[36] Report on the 1st and 2nd inspections (note 35), p. 4. *Note:* The inspection reports have usually been issued in both IAEA and UN Security Council versions. In noting the page references given in the footnotes here the reader should observe which version is cited at first mention of each inspection report.

[37] Report on the 1st and 2nd inspections (note 35), pp. 5, 9.

[38] MacLachlan, A., 'IAEA "takes custody" of Iraq material', *Nuclear Fuel,* vol. 16, no. 11 (27 May 1991), p. 15.

[39] 'Iraq says it tries, UN says no', *International Herald Tribune*, 1 Feb 1993, p. 5.

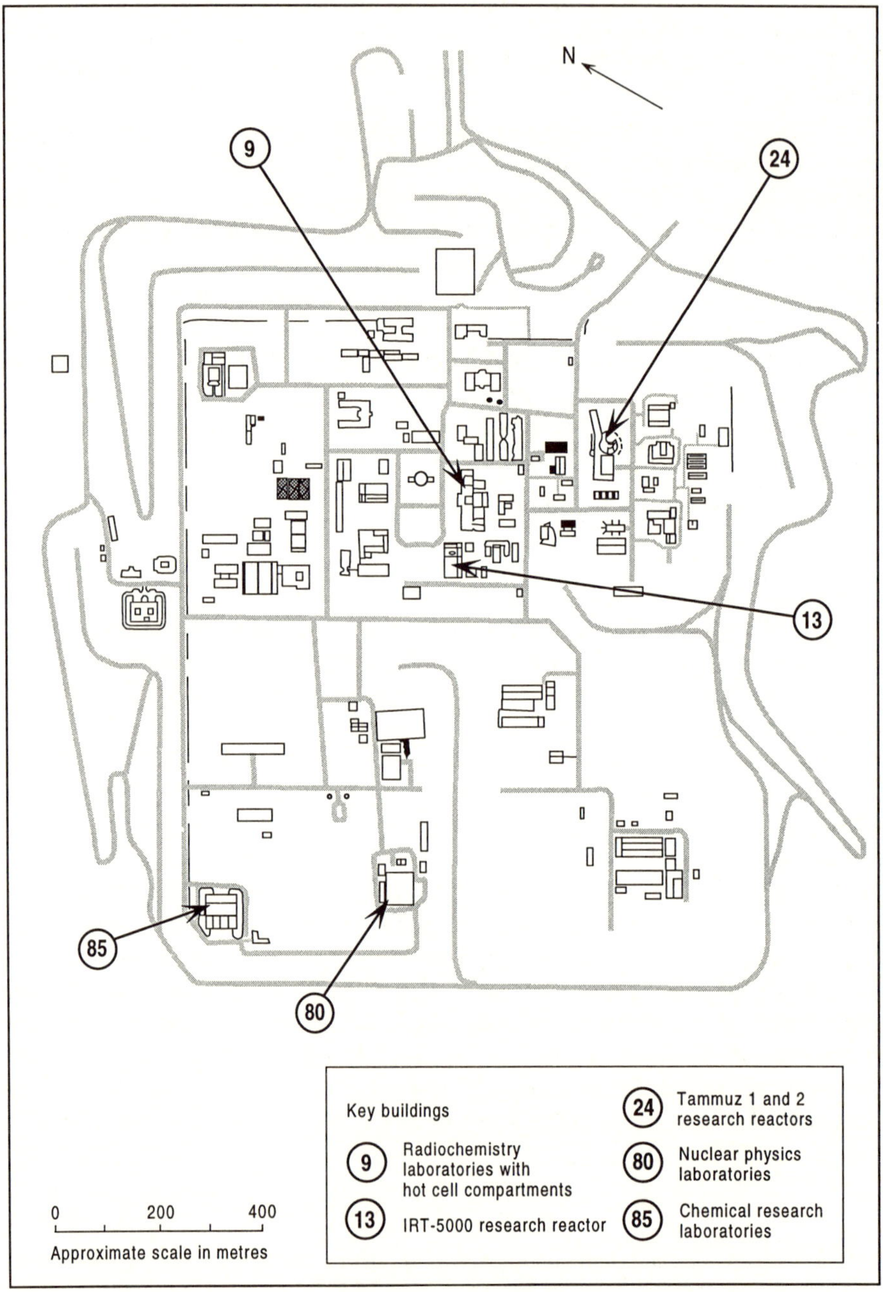

Figure 21. The Al Tuwaitha Nuclear Research Centre

Source: Report on the twenty-sixth IAEA on-site inspection in Iraq under Security Council Resolution 687 (1991), 22 August–7 September 1991, IAEA document GOV/INF/757, 28 Oct. 1994, p. 20. Redrawn by permission of the IAEA.

The Al Tuwaitha Nuclear Research Centre

Al Tuwaitha is the former site of the Tammuz 1 and 2 research reactors (building 24—see site map in figure 21) and the IRT-5000 reactor (building 13). All of the reactors were heavily damaged during the Persian Gulf War but no significant radiation problem was reported to have been encountered by the inspectors.[40] Despite the damage, HEU fuel for the IRT-5000 reactor was still inside the core, pool and external storage bay.[41]

Extensive verification of declared nuclear material—including fresh and irradiated HEU and irradiated LEU—involved the location, identification and characterization of the material as well as its placement under seals. A large amount of material had been relocated by Iraq to areas adjacent to and further removed from the Al Tuwaitha site.

In addition, 2.26 grams of plutonium recovered from spent fuel[42] and produced in the Radiochemistry Laboratories (building 9) was confirmed present. While this reprocessing activity was on a small scale, the report noted that it 'has a larger significance in establishing the capability for plutonium separation'.[43]

EMIS

Based at least in part on the information gathered from a defecting Iraqi engineer interviewed extensively in Germany,[44] the inspections were to shed important light on the extent of the EMIS programme which Iraq had been pursuing before the Persian Gulf War broke out. According to the defector, the programme was initiated at Al Tuwaitha in the early 1980s and was basically indigenous.

Evidence was uncovered indicating that several buildings at the Al Tuwaitha site were relevant to laboratory- or pilot-scale development of EMIS. These had been subject to heavy bomb damage during the Persian Gulf War as well as subsequent heavy clearing operations performed by the Iraqis. The inspection report noted that 'the sites where these buildings stood have been graded and cleared to an inexplicable extent. This action, in combination with the extraneous rubble . . . suggests an attempt to render difficult the identification of the activities and purposes of these buildings'.[45] The location of the equipment which had been removed from the site could not be ascertained at the time.

The building designated in the inspection reports as building 80 had been declared by Iraq to be for plasma and ion source physics, magnet development

[40] Seneviratne, G., 'North Korean safeguards pact and Iraq status reported to IAEA', *Nucleonics Week*, vol. 24, no. 24 (13 June 1991), p. 14.

[41] Report on the 1st and 2nd inspections (note 35), p. 5.

[42] Report on the 1st and 2nd inspections (note 35), p. 8.

[43] Report on the 1st and 2nd inspections (note 35), p. 6.

[44] Hibbs, M., 'Indigenous Iraqi calutron effort got under way in early 1980s', *Nuclear Fuel*, vol. 16, no. 13 (8 July 1991), p. 7.

[45] Report on the 1st and 2nd inspections (note 35), p. 10.

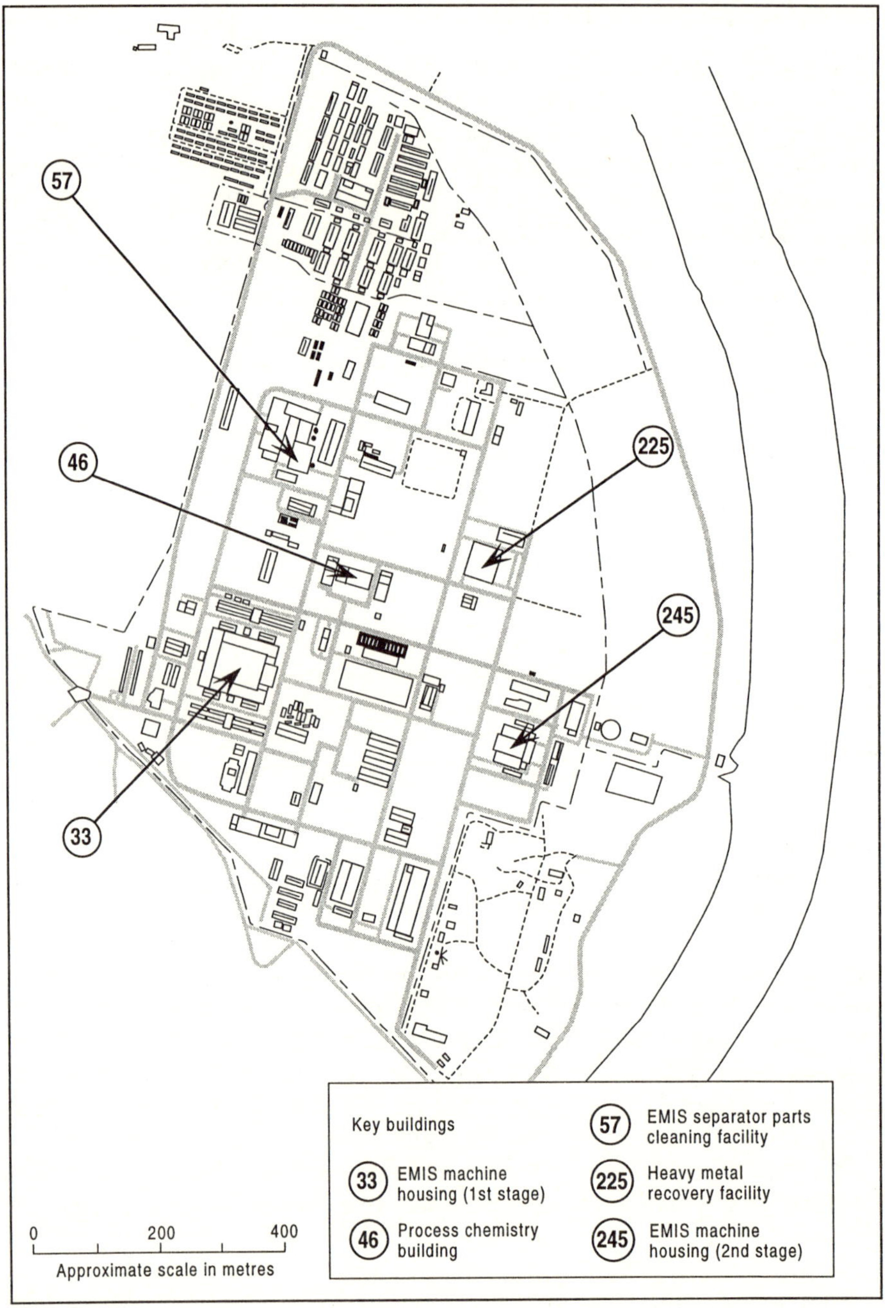

Figure 22. The Al Tarmiya facility

Source: Report on the twenty-sixth IAEA on-site inspection in Iraq under Security Council Resolution 687 (1991) 22 August–7 September 1991, IAEA document GOV/INF/757, 28 Oct. 1994, p. 21. Redrawn by permission of the IAEA.

and the operation of a cyclotron in the future. By the time of the first inspection the Iraqi clearing operations here included removal of all equipment except for two magnets and removal of a concrete reinforced floor. By the second inspection a level field was all that remained.[46] However, it was noted that 7.4 megawatts—'an inordinately large amount of power for a building of its size and declared function'—had previously been installed.[47]

The building designated as number 85 at Al Tuwaitha was declared by Iraq to be for chemical and chemical engineering-related R&D, including pilot-scale extraction of uranium from ore of high organic content.[48] It would, therefore, it was concluded, have allowed for the demonstration of pilot-scale EMIS process chemistry.[49] It was surmised that uranium isotope separation was carried out on a laboratory/pilot-scale in buildings 80 and 85, with perhaps five units in operation for an undetermined period of time.[50]

The characteristics of the Al Hamath workshop at Al Tuwaitha forced the inspectors to declare that its stated purposes—the Iraqis first stated it to be a truck maintenance site and later a machine shop—were not credible. It contained large cranes (one of which was found to be highly magnetized), and an electricity supply (1 MW) and water purification and chiller system beyond the needs of either declared purpose. Its characteristics led to the consensus that the site was used as a magnetic test facility and for engineering integration tests of the separators.[51]

Still more concrete discoveries were made at the Al Tarmiya site. As stated by the IAEA by the end of the second inspection, 'it was clear that the site was a multi-billion dollar EMIS facility'.[52] The Iraqi declaration that building 33 (see figure 22) at Al Tarmiya was for transformer fabrication was not judged to be credible by the inspectors—metal forming, coil winding and other necessary capabilities were clearly absent. However, the large power supply of over 100 megawatts, the presence of four large cranes, a chilled and purified water supply and the building configuration—including two parallel piers for electromechanical apparatus equipped with utility outlets—were judged to be consistent with a facility for approximately 100 EMIS units. It was surmised that building 33 was the first stage in the enrichment process and that building 245—serviced with 40 MW and basically a smaller version of building 33—was to have been for the second stage. Neither building was judged to have ever been functional, estimated as being 6–18 months from operation.[53]

Collocated buildings included building 46, suitable for high-quality batch chemistry, which could have been designated for processing uranium tetrachloride—which, as described in chapter 2, is the feed material used for EMIS.

[46] Report on the 1st and 2nd inspections (note 35), p. 7
[47] Report on the 1st and 2nd inspections (note 35), p. 10.
[48] Report on the 1st and 2nd inspections (note 35), p. 7
[49] Report on the 1st and 2nd inspections (note 35), p. 10
[50] Report on the 1st and 2nd inspections (note 35), p. 11.
[51] Report on the 1st and 2nd inspections (note 35), pp. 10–11.
[52] Report on the 1st and 2nd inspections (note 35), p. 11.
[53] Report on the 1st and 2nd inspections (note 35), pp 11–12.

It was the opinion of the inspectors that building 57, since it appeared designed to wash heavy objects of the appropriate size, was to be used for the vacuum chambers of the separators. Building 225, declared by Iraq as a heavy metal recovery facility, was judged suitable for recovering uranium for recycling. The building contained very large air handling and filtration equipment, the purpose of which would have been to conserve the enriched uranium as well as to prevent tell-tale isotopic signatures from escaping into the environment.

These facts left little room for doubt and the inspection report states that 'the configuration of buildings 33 and 245 with their unusual electrical and cooling utilities led the team to conclude that Al Tarmiya was an EMIS site. The collocated buildings containing all of the necessary ancillary functions completes the case'.[54]

Some EMIS-related equipment found at Al Tarmiya appeared to originate at the Al Dijjla Ministry of Industry site in Al Zaafaraniya. Capabilities in the manufacturing plants at this site included coil winding, chassis assembly, computer-aided design and assembly, and inspectors believed that EMIS electrical components could have been designed and fabricated here, but they concluded that the facility was not dedicated to EMIS work. Al Rabiya, another facility in Al Zaafaraniya, was also judged capable of fabricating major EMIS components.[55]

Based on all of the above, the inspection report concluded that there was declared evidence of EMIS R&D, documented evidence of Iraq's capability to manufacture all necessary EMIS components, evidence of successful laboratory or pilot-scale EMIS research and evidence that an EMIS plant had been under construction.

The third inspection

Inspections on the third mission to Iraq took place from 7 July to 19 July 1991. During the originally planned inspection period lasting until 12 July, 26 inspectors and 11 supporting staff of 22 nationalities took part. New declarations by Iraq on the first day of the inspection led to its extension until 19 July, and 20 inspectors remained for the extension period. A great deal of the work was related to verification of the new Iraqi information provided on 7 July and, at the request of the inspectors, supplemented on 14 July.

While the inspection report states that Iraq had been cooperative and that no access problems occurred,[56] the head of the team, Demetrius Perricos, stated in a subsequent briefing that the Iraqis were less than forthcoming—that inspectors had to 'pry a lot' in order to obtain information sought.[57]

[54] Report on the 1st and 2nd inspections (note 35), p. 12.

[55] Report on the 1st and 2nd inspections (note 35), p. 13.

[56] Report on the third IAEA on-site inspection in Iraq under Security Council Resolution 687 (1991), 7–18 July 1991, UN document S/22837, 25 July 1991, p. 5.

[57] Seneviratne, G., 'IAEA inspectors focus on Iraq centrifuge program', *Nucleonics Week*, vol. 32, no. 31 (1 Aug. 1991), p. 9.

It was learned that Iraq had examined not only EMIS but also gaseous-diffusion, gas-centrifuge and chemical-exchange methods for uranium enrichment. The emphasis on production-scale development and deployment of EMIS was based mainly on Iraq finding that the separators and magnets could be manufactured indigenously[58] and also on early success with the process itself. The first gleaning of a programme for using gas-centrifuge technology to enrich uranium came from the 7 July declaration which indicated that this was, however, second in priority.[59]

The Vice-Chairman of the Iraqi Atomic Energy Commission and Deputy Minister of Industry and Minerals, Dr J. D. Jaffar, was thought at the time to have been the head of the enrichment programme. He stated that the primary motive for the programme was the further development of the country's technological and industrial infrastructure, including production of fuel for research and possibly power reactors. While he noted that HEU production capability could create a political option for nuclear weapon development, he none the less denied that any decision on such an option had been taken.[60]

EMIS

Examinations of a videotape provided to the inspection team, as well as of components of calutrons and an ion source test stand, confirmed that research, development and testing of EMIS equipment had been carried out in building 80 at Al Tuwaitha (see figure 21) but that it was neither designed for nor capable of producing substantial quantities of HEU. Iraq declared that the only real obstacle remaining in its EMIS research was improving the ion sources. It was also concluded that building 85 at Al Tuwaitha contained a small uranium tetrachloride pilot production line.[61] Small amounts of uranium processed at the facility, including milligram quantities enriched to 40–45 per cent, were declared.[62]

In a return to Al Tarmiya, the inspectors were able to add to their knowledge of the location which Iraq had now confirmed to be an EMIS site. At the team's request, concrete, which had been used to conceal key components (the return irons and rails for the separators[63]), was removed by the Iraqis allowing for confirmation that Al Tarmiya had indeed been intended as a main EMIS production site. It was reported that eight separators had been installed in January–February 1990 and another 17-separator system was being installed when operations stopped.[64]

[58] As later discovered, large roughly finished iron cores for the 1200-mm machine magnets were procured outside the country. Report on the eighth IAEA on-site inspection in Iraq under Security Council Resolution 687 (1991), 11–18 November 1991, UN document S/23283, 12 Dec. 1991, p. 11.

[59] Seneviratne (note 57), p. 9; and Report on the 3rd inspection (note 56), p. 6.

[60] Report on the 3rd inspection (note 56), pp. 5–6.

[61] Report on the 3rd inspection (note 56), p. 6.

[62] Report on the 3rd inspection (note 56), p. 9

[63] Report on the 3rd inspection (note 56), p. 7.

[64] Report on the 3rd inspection (note 56), pp. 3, 8. It was later clarified that the first bank of 8 separators had actually been installed in the period Feb.–Oct. 1990 (at an average rate of 1 machine per month).

It was also learned that construction of what was apparently a duplicate of the Al Tarmiya facility located at Ash Sharqat was 85 per cent complete when it was destroyed. UNSCOM had designated this site since it was similar to Al Tarmiya, and it was later declared by the head of the inspection team to be 'a replica plant intended for use in a redundant situation in case something happened to the Al Tarmiya plant'.[65] It had not been declared by Iraq, and when first singled out for inspection the site was stated to be a machine-tool production and protective-coating plant. It was later admitted that it was to have been a twin of the Al Tarmiya facility and that, in fact, such replication of key facilities had become government policy.[66]

The Al Jesira facility for uranium tetrachloride (UCl_4) production, which included a conversion plant for the production of uranium dioxide (UO_2) to be combined with carbon tetrachloride (CCl_4) to produce UCl_4, was also inspected. It had suffered substantial bomb damage.[67]

In addition the team inventoried equipment from the Al Tuwaitha, Al Tarmiya and Al Jesira facilities (for UCl_4 production) which had been removed and transported to remote locations for destruction and concealment by the Iraqi Army. While much of this equipment had been destroyed beyond recognition, and no collectors and only a single ion source were discovered, what was uncovered was found to be consistent with Iraqi declarations.[68]

The third inspection report concluded that Iraq's stated broad goals for its enrichment programme 'neither require nor justify the construction of a facility the size of Al Tarmiya, much less two such facilities'. The 'combination of high-capacity/modest separation factor units and low-capacity/high separation factor units . . . is the type of arrangement that would be configured if the goal was to produce highly enriched uranium'.[69]

Enrichment by gas centrifuge

The third inspection team also discovered an indication of what was later to be a rather large and intricately structured programme to enrich uranium using gas-centrifuge technology. The declaration of 7 July included information on a projected 100-centrifuge facility, but it was claimed that only limited laboratory-scale activities had been performed with uranium hexafluoride (UF_6) and technical specifications of the machines were yet to be determined.[70]

It was concluded that all the Iraqi R&D with centrifuges (as well as all other uranium enrichment) had been performed at Al Tuwaitha.[71] In addition, on the last day of the inspection period the team was provided with information on single-centrifuge trial runs with uranium hexafluoride gas (465 grams of which

[65] Seneviratne (note 57), p. 9.
[66] Report on the 3rd inspection (note 56), p. 8
[67] Report on the 3rd inspection (note 56), p. 7
[68] Report on the 3rd inspection (note 56), p. 9
[69] Report on the 3rd inspection (note 56), p. 9
[70] Report on the 3rd inspection (note 56), p. 10
[71] Report on the 3rd inspection (note 56), p. 4.

were declared and verified[72]) but concluded that it was unlikely that the full extent of the programme had been disclosed at that time.[73] Centrifuge components were returned to Vienna for subsequent analysis.[74]

Further findings

A large inventory of natural uranium had been accumulated both through imports and domestic production. It was found that uranium extraction (for production of yellowcake) was carried out at a facility at Al Qaim which was fed by an open-cast phosphate mine in Akashat.[75]

Verification of nuclear material continued, including verification of irradiated HEU fuel elements in the IRT-5000 reactor. All hot cells and glove boxes at Al Tuwaitha were inspected and seals were applied to the undamaged manipulators.[76]

The fourth inspection

Much more knowledge was gained about the Iraqi centrifuge programme, which was given special priority during the fourth inspection. Visiting 22 sites in all, this inspection took place from 27 July to 10 August and involved 14 inspectors and 6 supporting staff of 11 nationalities. While no problems with access were encountered during the inspection, the report states that the inspection process was greatly hindered by the fact that questions on sensitive matters posed to officials other than those of high level, such as Dr Jaffar, were often met with untruthful responses.[77]

The centrifuge programme

While details of the full extent of the centrifuge enrichment programme, especially as concerning information on equipment suppliers, were not obtained during the fourth inspection, a good idea of the overall objectives of the programme was obtained. The plan as provided by the Iraqis included the following stages:

Mid 87 – Late 89	Trials on Model 1 Centrifuge
Mid 88 – Mid 91	Trials on Model 2 Centrifuge
Late 89 – Mid 91	Construct Centrifuge Production Facility
Mid 91 – End 91	Trial Operation of the Production Facility
Early 91 – End 92	Design and Construct 100-Machine Cascade
End 92 – Mid 93	Install Centrifuges and Pipework
Mid 93	Commence Operation of 100-Machine Cascade

72 Report on the 3rd inspection (note 56), p. 10.
73 Report on the 3rd inspection (note 56), p. 6.
74 Seneviratne (note 57), p. 9.
75 Report on the 3rd inspection (note 56), p. 7; Seneviratne (note 57), p. 9.
76 Report on the 3rd inspection (note 56), p. 11.
77 Report on the fourth IAEA on-site inspection in Iraq under Security Council Resolution 687 (1991), 27 July–10 August 1991, UN document S/22986, 28 Aug. 1991, p. 4.

Mid 92 – Mid 95	Design and Construct 500-Machine Cascade
Early 95 – End 95	Install Centrifuges and Pipework
Early 96	Commence Operation of 500-Machine Cascade[78]

As this plan makes clear, an ambitious programme was being undertaken. None the less, Iraq stated that only single-machine trials had been carried out up to late 1990—beginning with testing on an early aluminium oil-type (Beams type)[79] centrifuge, called Model 1, in 1987 and progressing to a magnetic/pivot bearing (Zippe type)[80] counter-current centrifuge, referred to as Model 2, by mid-1988. Both maraging-steel and carbon-composite cylinders were planned. Iraq also stated that a foreign source had been used to obtain 10 carbon-fibre cylinders. Tests on a carbon rotor design apparently yielded output of 1.9 separative work units (SWU)/year with 2.7 SWU/year expected after optimization.[81]

The Model 2 centrifuges that Iraq planned to use in the 100- and 500-machine cascades were very similar to the Urenco G-1 design.[82] It was very surprising that Iraq planned to proceed with such large cascades, given the limited experience which had apparently been accumulated in single machine trials and the rather rudimentary knowledge that Iraq was thought to possess concerning cascade design. It was speculated that the apparent confidence may have been at least partly the result of access to unknown outside expertise.[83]

Assuming that the G-1 type centrifuges planned for use have a throughput of about 2 SWU/year, the 500-machine cascade would have been capable of producing about 5 kg of uranium enriched to 93 per cent ^{235}U per year.[84]

The Al Furat Project for centrifuge production

The Badr General Establishment and the State Establishment for Heavy Engineering Equipment (SEHEE) joined together to construct a factory to manufacture all components for maraging-steel Model 2 centrifuges. This was code-named the Al Furat Project. Located at a site near An Walid, 20 km south of Baghdad, the production facility was also to be the site of the 100-machine cascade which was planned to have been operational by 1993.[85] Not previously

[78] Report on the 4th inspection (note 77), p. 12.

[79] See Report on the seventh IAEA on-site inspection in Iraq under Security Council Resolution 687 (1991), 11–22 October 1991, UN document S/23215, 14 Nov. 1991, p. 19.

[80] It was confirmed during the 7th inspection that the two lines of centrifuge development being pursued were both based on the Zippe-type sub-critical counter-current centrifuge. Report on the 7th inspection (note 79), p. 49

[81] Report on the 4th inspection (note 77), pp. 9–10.

[82] The G-1 centrifuge was designed in the late 1960s. An engineer who formerly worked for the Urenco centrifuge partner Machinenfabrik Augsburg-Nuernberg reported seeing blueprints for the G-1 in Iraq in 1988. See Hibbs, M., 'Experts believe Iraq program focused on Urenco's G-1 centrifuge', *Nuclear Fuel*, vol. 16, no. 16 (5 Aug. 1991), p. 6.

[83] Hibbs, M., 'Unresolved questions loom on Iraqi centrifuge effort', *Nucleonics Week*, vol. 69, no. 37 (12 Sep. 1991), p. 7.

[84] Hibbs, M., 'Iraqi-made centrifuge rotors "didn't work", inspectors told', *Nuclear Fuel*, vol. 16, no. 17 (19 Aug. 1991), p. 12; and Hibbs (note 82), p. 6.

[85] Report on the 4th inspection (note 77), p. 12.

known to be a nuclear-related site, it had not been subject to bomb damage during the Persian Gulf War.[86]

Some manufacturing equipment had been procured and vacuum casings and molecular pumps had been built along with other small components. Maraging-steel tubes had been flow-formed, but difficulties were encountered with the process and the components produced were not judged to be of adequate quality. The source of the maraging steel itself was not identified.[87] The equipment had been removed and dispersed prior to the inspection and inspectors observed many machines stored either outdoors or in warehouses. Here again, data on the source of the equipment were not provided, and in addition manufacturers' identification and serial numbers had been removed from all higher-quality equipment.

The site included two extremely large buildings (designated B00 and B02), approximately 80 m by 100 m. The declared target production capability was 200 centrifuges per year from a single shift, but inspectors estimated that eventually 600 could have easily been produced from equipment already available.[88] This estimate was, however, disputed by some experts, who noted that it is based on extrapolation of output based to a large extent on the size of the workshops and that evidence had yet to be found that many centrifuge components could be produced or that necessary supplies of maraging steel were accessible.[89]

Interestingly, the importation of a clean room facility from Interatom GmbH, which would have served in centrifuge rotor testing at Al Furat, was halted by German officials just days before Iraq's invasion of Kuwait. Overall, inspectors reportedly considered that the size and layout of the Al Furat installation 'compare favourably' with similar facilities operated by Urenco.[90]

Concerning the feed needed for the centrifuges, it was claimed by Iraq that the Al Jesira facility where the UCl_4 feed for calutrons was manufactured was also to have been the production site for UF_6.[91]

The inspection report noted the inconsistency in Iraq's construction of a large facility for producing centrifuges from maraging steel when the technology had yet to be mastered.[92] Analysis by mass spectrograph indicated that successful operation was achieved only with centrifuge rotors manufactured outside the country—no traces of uranium were found in the maraging-steel rotors which Iraq itself had produced but only on those made of carbon fibre and which were imported.[93]

[86] Report on the 4th inspection (note 77), p. 3.
[87] Report on the 4th inspection (note 77), p. 10.
[88] Report on the 4th inspection (note 77), p. 11.
[89] Hibbs (note 83), p. 7.
[90] Hibbs, M., 'Iraq tried to import Interatom lab for tests of centrifuge rotors', *Nuclear Fuel*, vol. 16, no. 19 (16 Sep. 1991), p. 9.
[91] Report on the 4th inspection (note 77), pp. 7, 16.
[92] Report on the 4th inspection (note 77), p. 12.
[93] Hibbs, M., 'Iraqi-made centrifuge rotors "didn't work", inspectors told', *Nuclear Fuel*, vol. 16, no. 17 (19 Aug. 1991), p. 12.

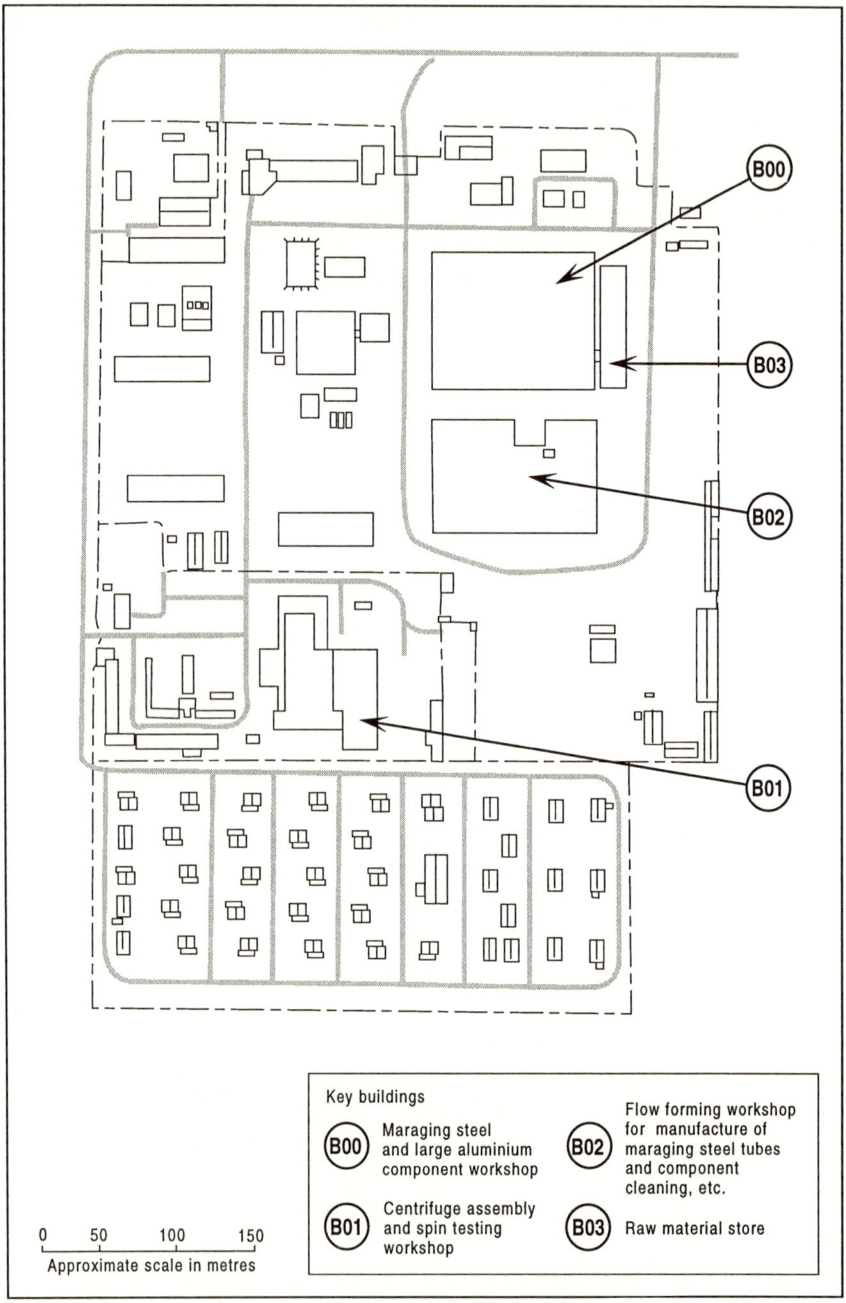

Figure 23. The Al Furat centrifuge production complex

Source: Report on the fifteenth on-site inspection in Iraq under Security Council Resolution 687 (1991), 8–18 November 1992, IAEA document GOV/INF/677, 17 Dec. 1992, p. 24. Redrawn by permission of the IAEA.

It is noteworthy, however, that Iraq was apparently very confident that export controls could be circumvented, allowing the country to obtain the large quantities of maraging steel it would require.[94] The inspectors were reasonably convinced that the programme was receiving assistance, probably including technical advice, from outside the country. They concluded that 'the nature of the economics of this effort makes it impossible to draw any other conclusion than that the effort was for non-peaceful purposes. The programme would have reached its objectives in time'.[95]

EMIS

Much more detailed information on the EMIS programme also came to light during the fourth inspection. The development of the separator at Al Tuwaitha (where work on EMIS was declared to have begun in 1982) moved through several stages, beginning with a 400-mm machine to test insulator and liner concepts and progressing to a 500-mm and three 1000-mm separators. Subsequently the effort progressed to the design of the actual 1200-mm and 600-mm separators for installation at Al Tarmiya.[96] Iraq declared that uranium enrichments of 17 per cent for gram quantities and 45 per cent for milligram quantities had been achieved.[97]

Eight of the 1200-mm first-stage separators, each requiring a loading of 6 kg of UCl_4, were declared to have begun some operations in 1990 from 23 February to 10 September at Al Tarmiya. The next set of 17 separators, which were being installed at the time of the Persian Gulf War, were to have an improved liner design. Six prototype magnets and vacuum chambers, along with six ion sources and collectors, had already been fabricated.[98]

Further indication that HEU production was intended came from criticality evaluations which had been included in the design of piping and vessels for buildings 57 and 225 at Al Tarmiya (see figure 22), which were for recovery of UCl_4 as UO_4 from the 1200-mm and 600-mm calutron liners. Uranium from the collector pockets was to be recovered as UO_3 in building 46, and it was noted that all three buildings had been sized for the ultimate site capacity.[99]

EMIS mechanical production facilities inspected included Al Daura (SEHEE, the State Establishment for Heavy Engineering Equipment), the Badr General Establishment and the three facilities of the Auqba Bin Nafi Establishment—Al Amin, Al Radwan and Al Ameer. Six-metre diameter vertical turning machines for production of the pole pieces for the separators at Al Tarmiya were found at

[94] Report on the 4th inspection (note 77), p. 12. Iraq was later to declare during the 9th inspection that 100 tonnes had in fact been acquired.

[95] Report on the 4th inspection (note 77), p. 13.

[96] This can be compared to the alpha and beta calutrons used in the Manhattan Project, which had radii of curvature of 48 and 24 inches (1220 mm and 610 mm) respectively (see chapter 2).

[97] Report on the 4th inspection (note 77), pp. 5–6.

[98] Report on the 4th inspection (note 77), pp. 6–8.

[99] Report on the 4th inspection (note 77), p. 8.

the latter two facilities. The electrical equipment facility at Al Zaafaraniya was judged to be capable of producing the necessary power supply units.[100]

The Al Jesira facility for uranium tetrachloride production was revisited. The design capacity for each of the two production lines was stated by Iraq to be 150 kg of UCl_4 per day; however, operational problems were encountered and only 1.2 tonnes of UCl_4 had been produced from one line during the two months of operations during 1990. Here again, much of the damage was discovered to be the result of Iraqi attempts at deception.[101]

It was estimated at the time that it may have been possible to achieve full production at Al Tarmiya within 18–36 months and that, at 55 per cent availability, the 90 planned separators at the facility could have produced about 15 kg of uranium per annum.[102] The site and the twin facility at Ash Sharqat were, however, effectively destroyed by bomb damage and subsequent clearing and dismantling operations performed by Iraq. The report notes that 'the thoroughness and scale of the industrialization of the Al Tarmiya site are evident from the use of bar coding and from the computerisation of source and collector part ordering and inventory maintenance'.[103]

It was also learned that the plant at Al Jesira which was to provide UCl_4 feedstock to Al Tarmiya, and possibly also to Ash Sharqat, had begun trial operations for UCl_4 production (as well as UO_2) before it was bombed.[104]

Weaponization

Although a number of sites had been designated as possible weaponization sites, and many questions were raised about the purpose of many Iraqi activities, no direct evidence was found of an on-going weaponization programme during the fourth inspection.

A firing bunker suitable for high-explosive testing belonging to the Al Hatteen Establishment at Al Musayyib was found near the Al Atheer materials research centre and had been used for testing conventional explosives. While no significant instrumentation was seen, the bunker was in the inspection report deemed capable of supporting experiments critical to nuclear weapon development.[105] In an internal memorandum, the chief inspector stated, however, that the inspecting team 'were of the opinion that the HE [high explosives] bunker examined was built as a nuclear weapons hydrodynamic test facility'.[106]

[100] Report on the 4th inspection (note 77), p. 6.

[101] Report on the 4th inspection (note 77), p. 15.

[102] Information which became available later suggested that this estimate may have been somewhat optimistic. An Iraqi report written in 1987 indicates that after two years the annual production rate might have been much lower if natural uranium were used as feed and notes that low-enriched feed would shorten this time. The plan outlined was to install 70 alpha and 20 beta calutrons from Aug. 1989 to Dec. 1992, but by Jan. 1991 progress was already about one year behind schedule. See Albright, D. and Hibbs, M., 'It's all over at Al Atheer', *Bulletin of the Atomic Scientists*, vol. 48, no. 5 (June 1992), p. 9.

[103] Report on the 4th inspection (note 77), p. 8

[104] Report on the 4th inspection (note 77), p. 7.

[105] Report on the 4th inspection (note 77), p. 13.

[106] Hibbs, M., 'IAEA thinks Iraq may have capability to make nuclear high-explosives', *Nuclear Fuel*, vol. 16, no. 18 (2 Sep. 1991), p. 11.

The inspectors were informed that Iraq had purchased hundreds of tonnes of HMX high explosives, which are conventional explosives suitable for nuclear weapon use.[107] Knowledge on the forming of shaped charges had been acquired by Iraq during the 1980–88 Iraq–Iran War, and the test range at Al Musayyib was deemed better than the facilities the USA had used in the Manhattan Project.[108]

At Al Qa Qaa, inspectors observed the fabrication of exploding bridge-wire detonators—ostensibly for use in rocket stage separation. However, for a nuclear weapon to ensure uniform compression, better simultaneity is needed than the 0.5 microseconds believed to have been achieved.[109] This facility had been flagged in 1990 by Western intelligence as 'concerned with the development of the non-nuclear components of a nuclear weapon'.[110]

The uranium metallurgy technology included a reduction, casting and machining capability, which was declared to be for a conventional armour penetrating weapon programme at Al Tuwaitha. The report concluded that the experience which had been gained provided the necessary capability for a nuclear weapon programme. Iraq also admitted that it had produced polonium-210 for steady-state neutron sources. This isotope can also be used in the initiator for a nuclear weapon, but its relatively short half-life of 138 days necessitates access to a steady supply.[111]

The inspection report declared that future monitoring of the Al Atheer site, and the companion facilities at Al Hatteen and Al Musayyib, was necessary as they: 'constitute a complete and sufficient potential nuclear weapons laboratory and production facility . . . so big and so well equipped that it can clearly do much more than the limited non-weapons activities that the Iraqis claim as its purpose'.[112]

Plutonium production and separation

The 2.26 grams of plutonium discovered on the first inspection was not deemed a safeguards violation since, as discussed in more detail in chapter 5, the material involved had been legally exempted from safeguards. However, after Iraqi declarations in July the fourth inspection report notes that: 'it was apparent that Iraq had embarked on a clandestine programme to produce natural uranium fuel elements from undeclared nuclear material (UO_2) in the Experimental Reactor Fuel Fabrication Laboratory (ERFFL) [at Al Tuwaitha], to irradiate this fuel in the IRT-5000 reactor and subsequently to chemically process the irradiated fuel in the Radiochemical Laboratory, to which safeguards inspectors had no

[107] Albright and Hibbs, 'Iraq's shop-til-you-drop nuclear program' (note 17), p. 37.

[108] Hibbs (note 106), p. 11.

[109] Albright, D. and Hibbs, M., 'Iraq's bomb: blueprints and artifacts', *Bulletin of the Atomic Scientists,* vol. 48, no. 1 (Jan./Feb. 1992), p. 35.

[110] Hibbs, M., 'Unresolved questions loom on Iraqi centrifuge effort', *Nucleonics Week*, vol. 69, no. 37 (12 Sep. 1991), p. 7.

[111] Hibbs, M., 'Iraq tried to import Interatom lab for tests of centrifuge rotors', *Nuclear Fuel*, vol. 16, no. 19 (16 Sep. 1991), p. 9.

[112] Report on the 4th inspection (note 77), p. 14.

access'.[113] As discussed in section III above, these activities were determined to be violations of Iraq's safeguards agreement with the IAEA. There is, however, little concern that quantities of plutonium significant for nuclear weapons could have been produced—estimates are that even had the hot cells operated continuously, a maximum of only 60–140 grams per year could have been produced.[114]

In particular, it was found that this second quantity of plutonium—about 3 grams (in addition to the previously accounted for 2.26 grams)—had been recovered from three fuel elements which had been manufactured at the ERFFL and irradiated in the IRT-5000 reactor. It was also noted that the irradiation was not continuous, which could have allowed the Iraqis to have avoided their detection by the twice-yearly IAEA inspections of the IRT-5000 reactor. The Radiochemical Laboratory at Al Tuwaitha, where the chemical processing and plutonium purification occurred, was not subject to access by inspectors.

Two additional fuel elements had been manufactured and irradiated but had not undergone the planned reprocessing. Iraq informed the fourth inspection team, which saw these elements, that before the first inspection the two elements were placed on a truck which, while remaining within the Al Tuwaitha complex, was continually moved around when the first three inspection teams were present to elude discovery. This tactic was labelled 'one of the most potentially dangerous deception activities encountered so far by the inspection teams'.[115]

In addition, 46 fuel elements were declared to have been produced which had, however, not been irradiated. In the complete absence of appropriate supporting documentation, the report states that a 'great deal of uncertainty' remained regarding the true extent of the fuel manufacturing capability and irradiation and plutonium separation activity.

The fifth inspection

The main objective of the fifth inspection, which took place on 14–20 September 1991, was to carry out follow-up activities to previous inspections and to ensure that inspectors were in Iraq in between major inspections. Fifteen people of 13 nationalities were involved, including nine inspectors of nine different nationalities.

The team included a chemical enrichment expert and experimental facilities were visited. No new information was acquired because of the clearing which had taken place subsequent to the site being bombed. The expert believed that other facilities must exist but was unable to provide supporting evidence. The overall results of the investigation were deemed inconclusive.[116]

[113] Report on the 4th inspection (note 77), p. 17.

[114] Hibbs, M., 'Loophole in safeguards rules allowed Iraq to reprocess', *Nucleonics Week*, vol. 33, no. 33 (15 Aug. 1991), p. 1.

[115] Report on the 4th inspection (note 77), p. 18.

[116] Report on the fifth IAEA on-site inspection in Iraq under Security Council Resolution 687 (1991), 14–20 September 1991, UN document S/23112, 4 Oct. 1991, pp. 5, 8.

Some progress was made towards creating an inventory of the nuclear material that had been collected at Al Tuwaitha by the two preceding inspections. Verification of previously emplaced seals was accomplished, routine sampling continued and sampling to complement earlier samples was carried out. Of the 24 seals applied to hot cells and associated manipulators during the third inspection, two had been cut but remained in place and one was missing. It was concluded, however, that no plausible sinister explanation existed. Other activity included the removal of 4.868 grams of the plutonium produced by Iraq, leaving 0.274 grams.[117]

Item-counts of the fresh fuel for the IRT-5000 and Tammuz reactors were accomplished, but difficulties were encountered in measuring the activity of all of the irradiated fuel because of high radiation levels.[118] The Iraqis stated that the heavy water which they possessed (at least 3 tonnes were known to have been acquired in 1980) had been stored at the Tammuz site but had been lost after the site was bombed by coalition forces. This could not, however, be verified after the amount of time that had elapsed.[119]

The sixth inspection

When a second Iraqi defector provided information on the location of documents an inspection was quickly organized to find them. This sixth inspection was held 22–30 September 1991. Tens of thousands of pages of documents, including computer printouts and blueprints,[120] dealing with the nuclear programme in Iraq, along with 19 hours of video tape and 70 rolls of film, were brought back by the inspectors. Inspectors could not, however, find documents at all locations which were flagged by the defector—material had apparently been removed from some areas. Although only a few[121] of the more important documents had been translated at the time the first report of the sixth inspection was released, the information was to represent a watershed in understanding the true purpose and scope of Iraq's nuclear programme—particularly concerning weaponization.

While a 'complete set' of procurement records related to the Iraqi effort to enrich uranium was believed to have been obtained, it was none the less felt that this information represented just a small portion of the total documentation on the overall nuclear effort.[122] All documents that were uncovered on the first inspection day at the Nuclear Design Center were confiscated by the Iraqis for several hours and not all were returned. In the opinion of the inspectors the

[117] Report on the 5th inspection (note 116), pp. 5, 6.

[118] Report on the 5th inspection (note 116), p. 7.

[119] Report on the 5th inspection (note 116), p. 8.

[120] Hibbs, M. and MacLachlan, A., 'IAEA condemns Baghdad again as Iraq protests "double standard"', *Nucleonics Week*, vol. 32, no. 39 (26 Sep. 1991), p. 11.

[121] First report on the sixth IAEA on-site inspection in Iraq under Security Council Resolution 687 (1991), 22–30 September 1991, UN document S/23122, 8 Oct. 1991, p. 3.

[122] Hibbs, M., 'Second Iraqi defector led IAEA to document trove', *Nucleonics Week*, vol. 32, no. 40 (3 Oct. 1991), p. 3.

more sensitive documents were withheld,[123] and IAEA officials believe these may have included information on the centrifuge enrichment effort.[124] At the second site, inspectors were interrupted in their work and detained for 96 hours when the Iraqis demanded the return of documents and film in their possession.[125]

Contrary to previous Iraqi pronouncements the group of inspectors uncovered 'conclusive evidence that the government of Iraq had a programme for developing an implosion-type nuclear weapon, and it found documents linking this programme—code named "Petrochemical Three" (PC-3)—to Iraq's Ministry of Industry and Military Industrialization, the Iraqi Atomic Energy Commission (IAEC) and Iraq's Ministry of Defense. Documents were found showing that the nuclear weapons program was supported by broad-based international procurement efforts'.[126] The substantial procurement effort attempted to avoid outside attention, in part by using cover explanations of a civilian nature for items to be used in the nuclear programme—while in actuality substituting indigenously produced items of similar description in their civilian sector.[127]

The documents indicated that centrifuge enrichment technology had been explored as early as 1982 (close to the time the EMIS programme was initiated) and gaseous diffusion as late as 1988.[128]

Suspicions about the potential role of the Al Atheer facility in nuclear weapon development, based on previous inspections, were shown to be well founded—a plant progress report covering the period 1 January 1990 to 31 May 1990 clearly reveals that the purpose of research was to design and produce a nuclear explosive device. It is very illuminating to examine the contents of this document—direct quotes are often useful not only to illustrate the clear intentions of the Iraqi research but also in explaining generic elements of a nuclear weapon itself of the type they were attempting to construct. The document begins:

> The goal of the Al-Athir [Al Atheer] plant program is the design and manufacture of the mechanism which is composed of the following principal parts:
> Nuclear initiator (Polonium-210 metal/Beryllium)
> Core (enriched uranium metal)
> Reflector (natural uranium metal)
> Tamper (hardened iron)
> Explosive lenses (prepared by the Al-Qa' Qa' [Al Qa Qaa] General Establishment)
> Electronic systems (triggering, control and guidance)[129]

[123] First report on the 6th inspection (note 121), pp. 6, 7.

[124] Hibbs, M., 'Speculation rampant while IAEA compiles Iraqi helpers list', *Nucleonics Week*, vol. 32, no. 41 (10 Oct. 1991), p. 9.

[125] First report on the 6th inspection (note 121), pp. 7, 8.

[126] First report on the 6th inspection (note 121), p. 3.

[127] First report on the 6th inspection (note 121), p. 5.

[128] First report on the 6th inspection (note 121), p. 4.

[129] 'Al-Athir [Al Atheer] plant progress report for the period 1 January 1990 to 31 May 1990', annex to the first report on the 6th inspection (note 121), p. 13.

The progress report goes on to state that preparations were underway for the fifth update of the basic implosion design. Theoretical calculations of various aspects of the weapon design were carried out using one- and two-dimensional hydrodynamic simulation and other computer codes.[130] Some of these were non-classified programmes which had been developed at the Los Alamos National Laboratory in the USA. It had been believed that Iraq would attempt to employ well known fission cross-sections developed in the Manhattan Project, but information discovered in some of the codes would reportedly have been highly classified in the USA or other nuclear weapon states. It was reported that the codes, some of which had been modified by the Iraqis,[131] were 'far more advanced than was thought to have been possible [in Iraq]'.[132] Twenty detonation tests were carried out on explosive lenses which had been prepared at Al Qa Qaa, and encouraging results were reported.[133]

While the purpose reported by Iraq to the fourth inspection team for the production of polonium-210 was for steady-state neutron sources, the Iraqi progress report states under the heading 'Production of Polonium-210' that 'Polonium-210 is considered one of the basic components for manufacturing the nuclear initiator'. It then describes the production of 6 milligrams of polonium by the irradiation of 14.85 kg of bismuth in a reactor.[134] It later continues:

> The nuclear initiator for the mechanism consists of two principal materials, polonium-210 and beryllium, separated by a thin gold coating. When the coating is ruptured as a result of the first explosion of the lenses and the shock wave, the neutrons are liberated through the interaction of the alpha particles emitted from the polonium-210 with the nucleus of the beryllium [atoms]. These neutrons are what cause the initiation of the fission chain reaction of the nuclei of the uranium-233 [235].[135]

Tests using the initiators produced are then described—final testing was said to be awaiting the completion of appropriate explosive lenses. Most design and construction information on this type of initiator is not classified; however, information concerning the actual placement of the initiator within the explosive device is highly classified in the USA.[136] Irradiation of fuel elements in the IRT-5000 reactor and reprocessing to obtain ^{239}Pu are also described, noting that the uranium dioxide used was derived from Iraqi phosphate ore.[137]

The report reveals that natural uranium was to be used in manufacturing the tamper rather than beryllium. This would imply that the nuclear device would

[130] Annex to the first report on the 6th inspection (note 121), pp. 13–15.

[131] First report on the 6th inspection (note 121), p. 4.

[132] Hibbs, M., 'Iraq made Be-Po initiators, got advanced fission codes', *Nucleonics Week*, vol. 32, no. 41 (10 Oct. 1991) p. 9.

[133] Annex to first report on the 6th inspection (note 121), p. 22.

[134] Annex to first report on the 6th inspection (note 121), p. 16.

[135] Annex to first report on the 6th inspection (note 121), p. 23.

[136] Hibbs (note 132), p. 9; and Hibbs, M., 'Iraqi execution of bomb design "two years away" data suggests', *Nuclear Fuel*, vol. 32, no. 42 (14 Oct. 1991), p. 8.

[137] Annex to first report on the 6th inspection (note 121), p. 17.

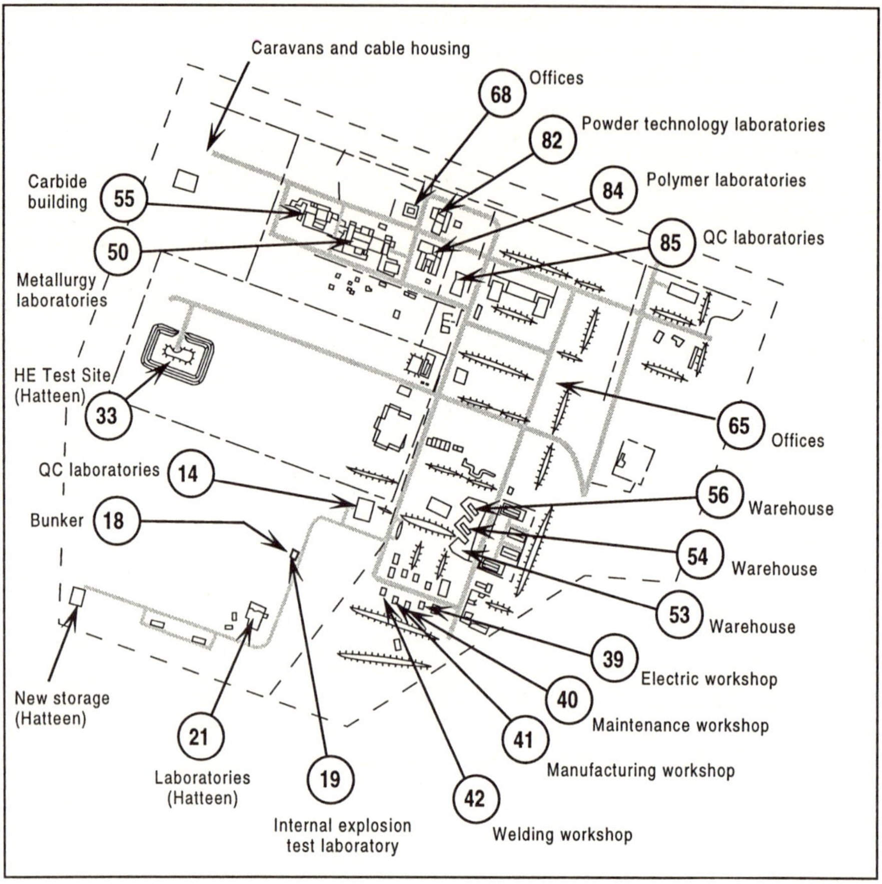

Figure 24. The Al Atheer materials research centre
Source: Report on the eighth IAEA on-site inspection in Iraq under Security Council Resolution 687 (1991), 11–18 November 1991, UN document S/23283, 12 Dec. 1991, p. 18. Redrawn by permission of the IAEA.

probably weigh at least several hundred kilograms.[138] Laboratory-scale production had apparently resulted in the equivalent of 254 kg of uranium metal produced from uranium tetrafluoride. As a result, design reports for semi-industrial systems for uranium tetrafluoride and uranium metal production were prepared. Melting and casting of uranium metal was also accomplished.[139]

The successful testing of a flash X-ray system[140] is also described as well as a detonation system with tolerances 'within time variations not exceeding 10 nanoseconds'[141]—far superior to tolerances discovered on the fourth inspection—and a miniature power system. In describing work on junction switches,

[138] Hibbs (note 136), p. 8.
[139] Annex to first report on the 6th inspection (note 121), pp. 18, 20.
[140] Annex to first report on the 6th inspection (note 121), p. 23.
[141] Annex to first report on the 6th inspection (note 121), p. 24.

the Iraqi report notes that 'the development and manufacture of this type of switch makes up for the use of other switches such as the krytron, which cannot be obtained commercially'.[142]

The IAEA inspection report specifically noted that Iraq had 'a complex, comprehensive nuclear weapons development program characterized by parallel approaches to fissile material production and by theoretical/experimental design work' and 'still has substantial facilities which were part of the clandestine program and which have not been declared'. It then concluded that from evidence gathered 'there was repeated and wilful non-compliance with Security Council Resolutions 687 and 707 and violation of the UN/IAEA-specified privileges and immunities agreed to by the Government of Iraq'.[143]

The seventh inspection

The seventh inspection, conducted 11–22 October, involved 26 inspectors and 13 supporting staff of 17 nationalities and visited 18 locations. The main objectives were the further assessment of weaponization and uranium enrichment activity as well as measurement and verification of nuclear material.

Weaponization

Confirming the validity of the documents uncovered during the sixth inspection Iraq acknowledged that weaponization research had been conducted, and that 'the objective in carrying out such research and studies was to establish the practical, technical and scientific requirements for a programme of this nature in the event that a political decision were to be taken to proceed in that direction'. They affirmed, however, that 'there was no political decision . . . to manufacture nuclear weapons'.[144]

The effort had involved several thousand people working over a period of years on an intermediary implosion-type design.[145] It was concluded that 'the explosive structure of an implosion-type device did not pose an insurmountable problem for Iraqi scientists'[146] but that the research accomplished had 'not yielded a workable production design'[147] and that experiments and other revelations, 'if taken at face value—indicate that Iraq still had a long way to go'.[148]

Computer simulations of several geometric configurations had been carried out. Uranium metallurgy had been carried out at Al Tuwaitha and a large building at Al Atheer had been destined for uranium metallurgy; it was concluded that the required knowledge and equipment in this field had been acquired.[149]

142 Annex to first report on the 6th inspection (note 121), p. 25.

143 First report of the 6th inspection (note 121), pp. 6, 7.

144 Letter from Iraqi Atomic Energy Commission to the chief inspector of the seventh team, 14 Oct. 1991, reprinted in Report on the 7th inspection (note 79), pp. 36–37.

145 Report on the 7th inspection (note 79), p. 6, 10.

146 Report on the 7th inspection (note 79), p. 15.

147 Report on the 7th inspection (note 79), p. 5.

148 Report on the 7th inspection (note 79), p. 18.

149 Report on the 7th inspection (note 79), pp. 10, 11.

Two types of explosive lens were believed to have been tested, and it was deemed 'prudent to assume that Iraqi scientists have a basic knowledge of the initiation of a spherical implosion'.[150] The presence of two high-speed streak X-ray cameras would have allowed precise detonation experiments but the state of development of a suitable firing system remained unknown. Iraqi documents mentioned studies on initiators other than polonium–beryllium but no indication was found that they had led to successful results.[151]

Uranium enrichment

EMIS. Inspectors visited the Ash Sharqat facility for the second time and confirmed that the site had never operated and that no EMIS equipment had ever been installed. While noting Iraqi claims that they had made a decision by mid-1989 to forgo use of the site for EMIS enrichment, inspectors could find no evidence to support it. Construction had apparently continued after this time, including installation of EMIS-related infrastructure, and the team believed that the site had remained designated to become a second EMIS enrichment site.

In compliance with a request by the third inspection team, the Iraqis moved all EMIS equipment to a location near Al Tuwaitha where it was compared with a new declaration. This declaration was judged generally consistent with the known extent of the EMIS programme, but there was some concern about absence of the ion sources and collectors from the Al Tuwaitha R&D units.[152] Of the EMIS equipment remaining after the damage caused by the bombing and Iraqi attempts at concealment, some was destroyed by the team and other remaining equipment was inventoried and marked for future destruction.[153]

Gas centrifuge. While some equipment was observed to still be in delivery packing cases it was stated that inspectors had seen 'everything necessary for mass-producing successful [maraging-steel] centrifuges'. Both maraging-steel and carbon-fibre lines of approach to centrifuge enrichment were in the early stages of development, but it was concluded that their ultimate success was highly likely. The estimate of the eventual potential manufacturing capability of the Al Furat complex was increased to 2000 or more centrifuges per year.[154] Manufacturers of some equipment were also identified, but they were not disclosed in the report.[155]

By the end of the seventh inspection all known centrifuge components had either been destroyed or removed from Iraq.[156] The report noted that Iraq would

[150] Report on the 7th inspection (note 79), p. 11.

[151] Report on the 7th inspection (note 79), p. 15.

[152] Report on the 7th inspection (note 79), pp. 46–48.

[153] Report on the 7th inspection (note 79), pp. 30–31.

[154] Report on the 7th inspection (note 79), p. 49.

[155] Report on the 7th inspection (note 79), p. 21. It was discovered some time later that Iraq had purchased just over 20 advanced carbon-fibre rotors from the German firm RO-SCH Verbundwerkstoff, Kaufbeuren and it is highly unlikely that significantly more than the 20 such rotors which were declared by Iraq were obtained. No evidence was found by the inspectors of equipment needed to produce this type of rotor. See Albright and Hibbs, 'Supplier-spotting' (note 17), p. 8.

[156] Report on the 7th inspection (note 79), pp. 30–31.

have difficulty in establishing the centrifuge project again after the destruction of equipment and tools if export controls were strictly enforced along with regular IAEA monitoring.[157] It was, however, added that 'since Iraq has not been forthcoming with procurement or project documentation and since there are marked anomalies as regards the numbers of individual components declared, it should be recognized that Iraq may still have an undisclosed programme'.[158]

Chemical enrichment. The seventh inspection report contained details of the Iraqi chemical enrichment effort at Al Tuwaitha, which was declared to have involved two methods—the ion-resin and the liquid–liquid processes.[159] Some equipment was inspected by the seventh team, but there was not a great deal of either physical or documented evidence of the programme to serve as confirmation of Iraqi accounts. The basic assessment was that the programme was not well advanced; Iraqi reports which were seen merely described results already available in the open literature. On a cautionary note, the report states that the physical space which had been allotted to this programme was 'appropriate to much larger-scale activities than those described to the inspection teams'.[160]

Other methods. Iraqi statements confirm that a serious theoretical/feasibility study, along with modest laboratory-scale work in gas diffusion, had taken place from 1982–87 at Al Tuwaitha. They had, however, concluded that they felt they did not have sufficient infrastructure to implement this technology.[161]

Inspections of lasers and related equipment, sampling, as well as interviews with Iraqi scientists led to the conclusion at the time that Iraq has not been involved in laser isotope separation.[162] Although there had been reports that a facility based on the jet-nozzle process had been obtained by Iraq from two German companies,[163] the seventh inspection report states that there was no evidence that this process had been pursued.[164]

The inspectors were also puzzled by the discovery of traces of uranium enriched to 93 per cent ^{235}U but with significant amounts of ^{236}U in areas in and near Al Tuwaitha. This material was unlikely to have resulted from Iraqi enrichment activity and was isotopically distinct from the French-supplied reactor fuel.[165] Speculation included reports of a secret store of HEU in Iraq obtained from China or Pakistan, indications that nuclear material used for instrument calibration may have been obtained from the US National Bureau of

[157] Report on the 7th inspection (note 79), p. 49.
[158] Report on the 7th inspection (note 79), p. 50.
[159] Report on the 7th inspection (note 79), pp. 19, 53.
[160] Report on the 7th inspection (note 79), p. 53.
[161] Report on the 7th inspection (note 79), pp. 19, 53.
[162] Report on the 7th inspection (note 79), pp. 19, 43, 54. This conclusion was later found to have been premature, as discussed under the subheading 'Laser enrichment activity' below.
[163] Hibbs, M., 'Speculation rampant while IAEA compiles Iraqi helpers list', *Nucleonics Week*, vol. 32, no. 41 (10 Oct. 1991), p. 9.
[164] Report on the 7th inspection (note 79), p. 19.
[165] Report on the 7th inspection (note 79), pp. 9, 21.

Standards or the possible occurrence of cross-contamination when the material was handled in the IAEA laboratory.[166]

Lithium production

Research on lithium was being conducted which was 'probably associated with efforts to develop higher-level explosive technology, most likely as part of a continuing long-term programme'.[167]

Enrichment had been performed using a solvent extraction technique, processing at a rate of 0.5–1.0 kg of lithium per year, but the laboratory was destroyed in the bombing. Iraq claimed the work on lithium-6 to be an extension of the IAEA contract on 'radiochemical separation for environmental purposes'.[168]

Further activities

Monitoring of the 36 per cent enriched fresh fuel, the 93 per cent irradiated French fuel and the fuel elements in the IRT-5000 reactor was also accomplished. In addition, the difficult task of producing an inventory and verification of other nuclear material including uranium ore, uranium oxide, uranium hexafluoride and uranium tetrafluoride continued.[169]

In addition, approximately 10 000 pages of documents at the PC-3 Headquarters were examined, and selected portions were returned to Vienna for further examination.[170]

The eighth inspection

With the completion of the eighth inspection the inspectors noted in the report that 'inspection efforts should gradually shift to monitoring, with occasional identification and characterisation activities performed when new information becomes available'.[171] Inspections continued and by the time their number reached 27 a permanent monitoring presence had been established.

The eighth inspection improved understanding of the procurement strategy of the Iraqi Atomic Energy Commission which involved using various other state establishments as buyers and contractors, procuring items both directly from manufacturers as well as indirectly through foreign intermediaries and completing the manufacture of some of the items obtained using indigenous capabilities.[172] A good example is the procurement of large iron pieces for use as cores for the double-pole magnets in the EMIS machines. At about the same time as orders were placed to a large West European foundry for six large pieces by the Iraqi State Electric Establishment, an order for six identical pieces was placed

[166] Hibbs, M. and Khan, Shahid-ur-Rehman, 'IAEA questions U.S. lab result implying hidden Iraqi HEU cache', *Nucleonics Week*, vol. 32, no. 49 (5 Dec. 1991), p. 7.

[167] Report on the 7th inspection (note 79), p. 18.

[168] Report on the 7th inspection (note 79), p. 30.

[169] Report on the 7th inspection (note 79), pp. 6, 24–25.

[170] Report on the 7th inspection (note 79), p. 35.

[171] Report on the 8th inspection (note 58), p. 7.

[172] Report on the 8th inspection (note 58), pp. 5, 10.

through a European company.[173] The components ordered by the State Electric Establishment were shipped directly to Iraq, while those ordered by the European company were first shipped to a German seaport before being re-routed to Iraq. The final machining of the components was done in Iraq so that the supplier would have been unaware of the final use.[174]

As part of a political decision to prevent the disclosure of information on their procurement network, the Iraqis engaged in activities such as removing name tags from equipment and filing away or painting over serial numbers and other procurement data. In spite of this the manufacturers of much of the equipment for use in the centrifuge production effort were firmly identified and listed in the inspection report. Manufacturers of substantial quantities of general-purpose and other equipment, including two streak video cameras, had also been identified but, as was pointed out, identifying a manufacturer does not necessarily mean that the supplier has been pin-pointed.[175]

As regards weaponization, the Iraqis stated that their research of the technical literature had indicated that gun-type explosive, while simpler in design, required more fissile material to construct. They had therefore concentrated their study on the implosion-type device.[176]

With regard to the lithium enrichment programme, although the reports on this work were classified as secret, the Iraqis maintained that the isotope separation activity was part of general scientific research and not directed towards a specific objective.[177]

The Iraqis had affirmed to the seventh inspection team that although the Al Atheer site was a national centre for research in material science and materials production, the design features of the buildings would meet the needs of a nuclear weapon programme should a decision to undertake such a programme be made. This site was revisited on the eighth inspection and of particular note was a multi-million dollar facility which contained an explosive chamber declared by the Iraqis to be for fragmentation studies for mortar shells. Such use was conclusively ruled out by the inspecting team.[178]

Destruction activities included the destruction of centrifuge-related equipment, EMIS components and chemical separation equipment. Verification activities related to nuclear material were completed during the eighth inspection based on random sampling with a 90 per cent confidence level. Iraq was requested to provide an explanation of some discrepancies in the nuclear material balance.[179]

[173] This order was along with another for an additional 22 halves—which were cut along the horizontal axis. Report on the 8th inspection (note 58), p. 11.

[174] Report on the 8th inspection (note 58), pp. 11, 14.

[175] Report on the 8th inspection (note 58), pp. 10, 11–14.

[176] Report on the 8th inspection (note 58), p. 15.

[177] Report on the 8th inspection (note 58), p. 16.

[178] Report on the 8th inspection (note 58), pp. 16–17.

[179] Report on the 8th inspection (note 58), pp. 19–21.

The condition of the Al Tarmiya site was reported to have changed little since the third inspection, building 245 being used for manufacture and repair of transformers.

The ninth inspection

The main purpose of the ninth inspection, conducted on 11–14 January 1992, was to verify information which had been made available to the IAEA from member states, in particular Germany, regarding Iraqi procurement of large quantities of materials and components suitable for gas-centrifuge manufacture. Iraq acknowledged procuring these materials, which included 300 tonnes of aluminium alloy tube extrusions used for producing vacuum housings (enough for about 2500 housings) and 84 tonnes for molecular pumps (enough for about 6000 pumps), as well as 240 000 ferrite magnet spacers and 10 000 soft iron ring band cores (enough for 10 000 centrifuge motor stators). They also declared procurement of 100 tonnes of 350-grade maraging steel (enough for 5000 centrifuges employing this material for rotors, end caps and baffles) and aluminium forgings (enough for several thousand top and bottom centrifuge vacuum housing flanges).[180] These components are indicated in the schematic centrifuge diagram included with the inspection report and reproduced here as figure 25. For reference this should be compared with the diagrams of more realistic designs in chapter 2.

The Iraqis stated that they had already destroyed or rendered harmless all of these materials and components before the start of the nuclear inspections and declared them available for inspection. The team inspected some of the material and took samples, but preliminary findings were not inconsistent with the Iraqi declarations.[181]

The acquisition by Iraq of such large stocks would seem to indicate that Iraq had plans for substantially more than the 500 centrifuge cascades which they admitted in the deployment schedule presented to the third and fourth inspection teams. Iraq, however, indicated that this was not inconsistent with its previous claims and that, as they were faced with increasingly tougher export controls, they pursued large-scale purchases as and whenever opportunities allowed, even though they may not have had immediate plans for the materials in the large quantities in which they were ordered.[182]

In describing the Iraqi centrifuge itself it is also interesting to note the inspection report assessment that the design 'conforms substantially to early west European designs. However, no component is identical in design; all showed evidence of intelligent adaptation and development based on sound principles.

[180] Report on the ninth IAEA on-site inspection in Iraq under Security Council Resolution 687 (1991), 11–14 January 1992, IAEA document GOV/INF/647, 31 Jan. 1992, p. 5.

[181] Report on the 9th inspection (note 180), pp. 7–9. As discussed below, however, in the 11th inspection it was to be revealed that the maraging steel which the Iraqis had declared to have 'rendered harmless' by melting could in fact be recovered from the melted ingots.

[182] Report on the 9th inspection (note 180), p. 7.

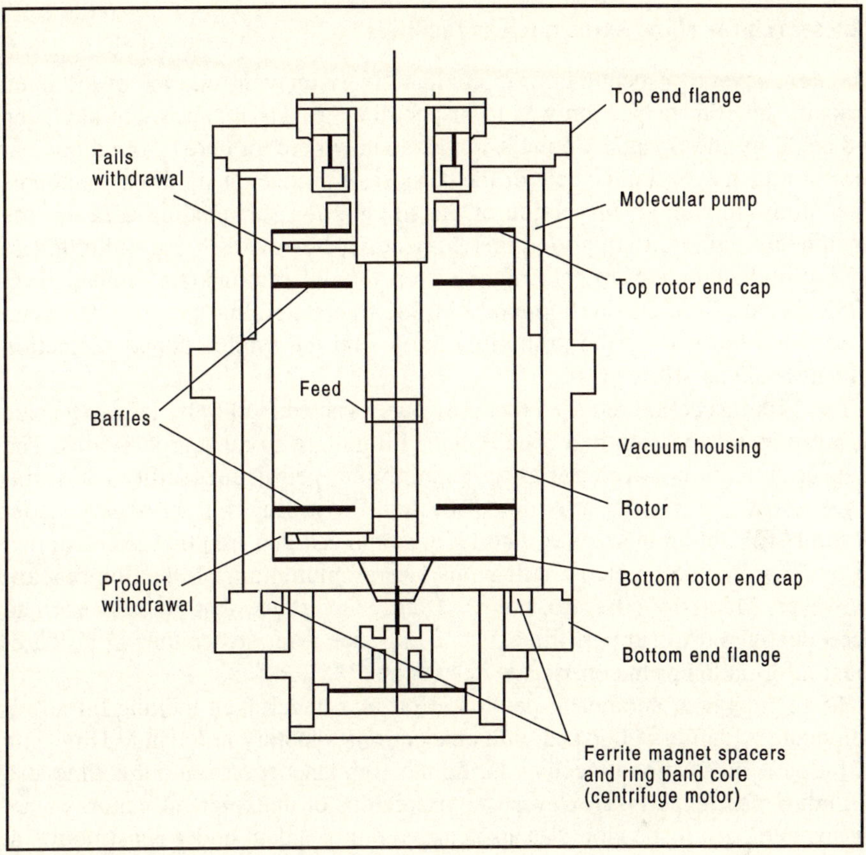

Figure 25. Schematic diagram of an Iraqi centrifuge

Source: Report on the ninth IAEA on-site inspection in Iraq under Security Council Resolution 687 (1991), 11–14 January 1992, IAEA document GOV/INF/647, 31 Jan. 1992, p. 6. Redrawn by permission of the IAEA.

A number of capable scientists and engineers were involved in the Iraqi centrifuge development effort, but it is unlikely that they were able to make the observed design modifications without outside help.'[183]

The existence of outside assistance has been confirmed by at least one expert involved, a former employee of the Urenco subcontractor MAN Technologie AG in Germany, who has admitted to helping Iraq with centrifuge design and assembly. He has stated that in the late 1980s Iraq had full-size centrifuge design drawings which were similar to those of the Urenco G1 machine and that he suggested improvements to them which were subsequently adopted. He also stated his belief that the drawings he was shown were acquired from outside Iraq and that Iraq could not have developed them unaided.[184]

183 Report on the 9th inspection (note 180), pp. 4–5.

184 Albright and Hibbs, 'Supplier-spotting' (note 17), pp. 8–9; and Albright, D., 'Engineer for hire', *Bulletin of the Atomic Scientists*, vol. 49, no. 10 (Dec. 1993), pp. 29–36.

The search for clandestine nuclear facilities

The next several inspections were comparatively uneventful. One of the main tasks of the 10th inspection was to inspect the SAAD-13 site which had been indicated by the Special Commission as a site where an underground nuclear reactor may have been located for the purpose of producing significant amounts of plutonium. Neither inspection of the site and the surrounding area nor the documents gathered supported this conjecture, however.[185] Iraq admitted to having studied the idea of constructing a reactor underground (for protection) in 1982–83, after the Osirak bombing of 1981, but stated that the idea had been abandoned because of the prohibitive costs and the limited added protection which would be afforded.[186]

The 14th inspection returned to a previously visited facility built into the side of a hill as information had been obtained linking it to nuclear activities. The inspection team confirmed it as an underground petroleum facility (oil refinery), however.[187] Shortly after this inspection David Kay, former deputy leader of the IAEA action team, was reportedly convinced that Iraq had either started to build or had completed a still undiscovered plutonium production reactor. However, Maurizio Zifferero, the chief inspector, stated that no evidence had been uncovered to support the existence of such a facility, either in procurement information or in confiscated documents.[188]

Six months later another inspection effort was undertaken looking for a hidden nuclear facility collocated with an electronics factory at Salah al Din—site of the same inspection objective during the 10th inspection—and this time also including new experts. However, 'no suspicious or unexplained features were discovered'. An inspection was also carried out of a dam under construction at Badoush, near Al Mosul, which displayed features that could be used to conceal an underground facility, but no hidden structures were found and no indication was discovered which would imply that the construction was being used to conceal any other facility. In addition four sites which were under consideration by Iraq as sites for power reactor construction in the 1980s were visited and no evidence of industrial development or construction activity was found.[189]

Throughout most of this time period destruction of installations and equipment continued, including most of the important elements of the EMIS programme by the 14th mission as well as of the Al Atheer–Al Hatteen weapon

[185] Report on the tenth IAEA on-site inspection in Iraq under Security Council Resolution 687 (1991), 5–13 February 1992, UN document S/23644, 26 Feb. 1992, p. 3.

[186] Report on the 10th inspection (note 185), p. 17.

[187] Report on the fourteenth IAEA on-site inspection in Iraq under Security Council Resolution 687 (1991), 31 August–7 September 1992, UN document S/24593, 28 Sep. 1992, p. 9.

[188] Hibbs, M., 'IAEA has no evidence pointing to secret Iraqi Pu production program', *Nuclear Fuel,* 14 Sep. 1992, p. 7.

[189] Report on the eighteenth IAEA on-site inspection in Iraq under Security Council Resolution 687 (1991), 3–11 March 1993, IAEA document GOV/INF/688, 28 Apr. 1993, pp. 17–19.

development site by the 11th mission.[190] Samples from the almost 100 tonnes of maraging steel which had been declared by Iraq during the ninth inspection, and which had been melted and poured into ingots, indicated that the material was as declared but that the material could also be recovered. It was determined, however, that this steel alloy could be destroyed by diluting it through remelting the ingots together with carbon steel, and this was done during the 15th inspection.[191]

Environmental sampling

Beginning in August–September 1992 with the 14th inspection, collection of environmental samples was initiated in the major watershed regions in Iraq at sites covering the entire country. This survey was to provide information on the impact of any present nuclear-related activities on the surface water systems, to detect possible as yet unknown nuclear facilities such as reactor operation or spent fuel reprocessing as well as to provide a baseline of hydrologic and radiometric conditions from which changes can be easily detectable to give indications of sizeable nuclear activity in the future. A total of 52 sites were visited during the 14th and 15th inspections.

Three different types of sample were taken: a 100 ml water sample, a sediment core and a filtering column used to concentrate dissolved and particulate matter from an approximately 300-litre water sample. The analysis of the samples was to include high-sensitivity gamma spectroscopy, radiochemical separations of the actinides (uranium and plutonium primarily), alpha spectrometry, high-sensitivity multi-stage surface ionization mass spectrometry, ultra-low background gas proportional counting for tritium and Inductively Coupled Plasma Mass Spectrometry for stable isotopes.[192]

Seven of the sampling locations were in the Kurdish-controlled regions and the Iraqi Government did not provide security at these locations. Some difficulties were encountered by the inspection team but they succeeded in collecting the samples required. As part of the long-term monitoring regime, plans were to revisit about 15 of the key sites twice a year, with spot checks to other more isolated locations.[193]

The first of the planned regular twice-yearly radiometric survey collecting samples of the surface waters of Iraq was conducted in spring 1993. Samples were collected from 15 sites for analysis and the results were consistent with

[190] Report on the eleventh IAEA on-site inspection in Iraq under Security Council Resolution 687 (1991), 7–15 April 1992, UN document S/23947, 22 May 1992, p. 3; and Report on the 14th inspection (note 187), p. 3.

[191] Report on the 11th inspection (note 190), p. 25; and Report on the fifteenth IAEA on-site inspection in Iraq under Security Council Resolution 687 (1991), 8–18 November 1992, IAEA document GOV/INF/677, 17 Dec. 1992, p. 16.

[192] Report on the 14th inspection (note 187), pp. 9–10.

[193] Report on the 15th inspection (note 191), pp. 4–5.

the baseline previously established from samples taken during the fourteenth and fifteenth inspections.[194]

Twice yearly (scheduled in the spring and autumn) samples of water, sediment and biota are taken in *ad hoc* campaigns which are part of the OMV regime. However, in the spring of 1994, for example, it was noted that while no problems were encountered, sampling points which had been established in the northern and north-eastern areas of Iraq were excluded from consideration for personnel security reasons.[195]

Annex 3 declarations

As noted above, Iraq was obliged to provide an inventory (the specific list of items covered was appended to the long-term monitoring plan as Annex 3) of all material, equipment and other items prohibited under Resolution 687 or others which may, depending on their use, also be prohibited or which are subject to the long-term monitoring plan. This information was finally provided by Iraq on 30 January 1993 at the end of the 17th inspection and covered the period from 1 January 1989.[196]

Subsequent inspection activity focused substantial activity on verification of the Annex 3 declarations. A particularly contentious issue concerned CNC (computer numerical controlled) machine tools, as only a few of the 54 Matrix Churchill CNC machines which had been seen by inspectors up until January 1993 had been declared. Iraq contended that many of these do not meet the Annex 3 specifications and so do not have to be declared.[197]

Attempts were made to resolve the issue concerning another 94 undeclared CNC Matrix Churchill turning machines, which were discovered during the first inspection after the Iraqi Annex 3 submission. After three technical meetings it was concluded by the inspection team that only 144 of the 148 machines do not meet the specifications of Annex 3 and so do not need to be declared, and that the other four required further evaluation.[198]

Subsequently a dual-use equipment committee was established by Iraq during this inspection to resolve differences in interpretation of reporting requirements related to Annex 3 as well as differences between procurement data obtained outside the country with the Iraqi declarations. This was overall a successful process. A common understanding was reached on the Annex 3 reporting

[194] Report on the nineteenth IAEA on-site inspection in Iraq under Security Council Resolution 687 (1991), 30 April–7 May 1993, IAEA document GOV/INF/704, 18 June 1993, p. 5; and Report on the twenty-second IAEA on-site inspection in Iraq under Security Council Resolution 687 (1991), 1–15 November 1993, UN document S/1994/31, 14 Jan. 1994, p. 6.

[195] Report on the 22nd inspection (note 194), p. 6; and Report on the twenty-fourth IAEA on-site inspection in Iraq under Security Council Resolution 687 (1991), 11–22 April 1994, IAEA document GOV/INF/746, 1 June 1994, p. 5.

[196] IAEA, The Implementation of United Nations Security Council Resolutions 687, 707 and 715 relating to Iraq, Report by the Director General, IAEA document GOV/2677-GC(XXXVII)/1069, 26 Aug. 1993, Attachment, p. 4.

[197] Report on the 18th inspection (note 189), p. 15; and Report on the 19th inspection (note 194), p. 8.

[198] Report on the 19th inspection (note 194), pp. 8–9.

requirements, and the revised Annex 3 submitted by Iraq at the conclusion of the inspection contained the required items. Although still more CNC machines were uncovered, the Iraqi declaration of the type, utilization and location of the Matrix Churchill machine tools was found to be consistent with the records of the company.[199] In addition a letter from the successor company to Matrix Churchill certified that none of the machines supplied to Iraq met the Annex 3 quality specification. It was therefore decided that none of the 280 Matrix-Churchill turning machines would be subject to declaration and monitoring under Annex 3 of the ongoing monitoring and verification (OMV) plan. In addition, a revised Annex 3 declaration has been provided by Iraq.[200]

Procurement network and supplier information

A source of constant frustration since the beginning of the inspections was the attempt to piece together the Iraqi procurement network given the reluctance of Iraq itself to provide substantial information on the subject. Some information had been provided during the 11th inspection, for example, on companies which had provided some centrifuge components and CNC machine tools and other equipment. During the next inspection, however, the team was informed of a decision by the Government 'not to provide specific information on suppliers' based on 'moral grounds'. The IAEA continued to seek this information, especially concerning the centrifuge programme, through other sources.[201]

Signals were given that the Iraqis were willing to deal positively with requests for such information, but they did not follow up by meeting the requests. On one occasion the Iraqi response was simply that all such requests should be submitted all at one time.[202] Responding to a specific request for information a few months later Iraq responded by saying that the IAEA already had a great deal of information on the subjects addressed in the request and that dealing with 'general questions, as the ones [*sic*] included in your letter is impractical.'[203]

Difficulties related to obtaining information continued until long-awaited revelations concerning the Iraqi procurement activities and sources of technical advice were made during the second series of high-level technical talks in Baghdad in early October 1993 (prior to the 22nd inspection held 1–15 November). Iraq could be declared to have complied with requirements concerning disclosure of its past nuclear activities under Resolutions 687 and

[199] Report on the 22nd inspection (note 194), pp. 7–8.

[200] Report on the twenty-third IAEA on-site inspection in Iraq under Security Council Resolution 687 (1991), 4–11 February 1994, IAEA document GOV/INF/733, 28 Mar. 1994, p. 5; and Report on the 22nd inspection (note 194), p. 3.

[201] Report on the 11th inspection (note 190), pp. 17–18; and Report on the twelfth IAEA on-site inspection in Iraq under Security Council Resolution 687 (1991), 26 May–4 June 1992, UN document S/24223, 2 July 1992, p. 22.

[202] Report on the sixteenth IAEA on-site inspection in Iraq under Security Council Resolution 687 (1991), 5–8 December 1992, IAEA document GOV/INF/678, 29 Dec. 1992, pp. 4–5 and Annexes 1 and 2.

[203] Report on the 18th inspection (note 189), pp. 12–13, Attachment 2.

707 once the information had been verified for accuracy and completeness.[204] It was noted shortly thereafter by the Director General that the information appeared to be 'complete and verifiable'. [205]

The agent who procured the 100 tonnes of maraging steel was identified, as was its transportation route from a northern European port, but Iraq stated that they did not know and could only speculate on the country of origin. The source of the maraging steel (the country of origin) and the manufacturer were later identified with the assistance of the government concerned.[206] Iraq also provided some information on the 'sources and circumstances' of outside technical advice received for their centrifuge programme at the high level talks. Details on these matters were then supplied to the 22nd inspecting team, including the names of individuals, and details of how they became involved as well as the type of assistance provided were disclosed. The information was not released pending decisions on legal action.[207]

Areas in which technical assistance was provided include:

- vacuum and clean room technologies, heat treatment of maraging steel and advice regarding machine tools;
- simulation software for design and evaluation applications;
- advice regarding the procurement of specific components and equipment;
- two general assembly drawings and 10–12 drawings of specific components;
- technical specification for some specific components.[208]

Iraq pointed to the usefulness of earlier work on the Beams-type centrifuge before moving on to the Zippe-type machine and the advantage this afforded in focusing and managing the search for outside assistance. The Iraqis stated that their plan, which had already been underway at the time of the Persian Gulf War, was to obtain from outside the country the components for about 50 machines while at the same time developing their own manufacturing capability. They acknowledged that the general assembly and component drawings obtained from outside the country served to greatly accelerate the centrifuge programme.[209]

Inspection procedures

With some exceptions—especially early on, the inspections themselves proceeded in a fairly routine manner. During the 16th inspection, however, which included inspection of PC-3 Project headquarters (the location of the parking lot stand-off during the 6th inspection) documents were observed being removed by the Iraqis. Attempts were also made to remove or hide other docu-

[204] IAEA, The Implementation of United Nations Security Council Resolutions 687, 707 and 715 (1991) Relating to Iraq, IAEA document GOV/2747-GC(XXXVIII)/10, 11 Aug. 1994, Attachment, p. 1.

[205] Hibbs, M., 'IAEA verifying procurement data after Baghdad disclosure session', *Nucleonics Week*, 21 Oct. 1993, p. 6.

[206] Maurizio Zifferero, personal communication.

[207] Report on the 22nd inspection (note 194), p. 14.

[208] Report on the 22nd inspection (note 194), p. 15.

[209] Report on the 22nd inspection (note 194), p. 15.

ments which were subsequently recovered but found not to be relevant to Resolution 687.[210] The attempts constituted a violation of the rights of the IAEA and the Special Commission.

Iraq temporarily attempted to restrict access of the inspectors after they made a request for a no-notice inspection to the University of Baghdad, but access was gained 45 minutes after notification. In reference to the university facilities themselves, which were inspected at the College of Science, the report notes that they were 'not adequate for graduate research or for a serious industrial development program.'[211]

Many short-notice and no-notice inspections were conducted, which were able to convince the teams that quick access was achievable. A short-notice inspection was carried out of the Taji-Nassr State Establishment with notice given just 10 minutes prior to passing the site on the way to another site. Access was obtained within 30–35 minutes from the time of notification, and it was noted in the inspection report that 'A time interval from the notification to the beginning of the inspection of 15 minutes is easily achievable'.[212] Short-notice inspections were performed to six other sites during the subsequent inspection visit to test procedures for long-term monitoring of various equipment. No difficulties were reported and the period of time between the notification of the desire to inspect and entry ranged from 6–11 minutes.[213]

Several facilities previously involved in the nuclear programme and which are being developed for alternate use were visited.

The Al Nidaa (formerly Al Rabiya) Establishment (bombed in a January 1993 US cruise missile attack) was revisited (end-April–early May 1993) and was found to be entirely rebuilt and 'turned into a showcase', including landscaping and monuments and an exhibition centre which documents the reconstruction effort.[214]

Several additional inspections were undertaken of the eight 'core' sites of the former nuclear programme: Al Tarmiya, Al Sharqat, Al Jesira, Al Furat, Rashdiya, Al Tuwaitha, Al Firnas (Al Atheer) and Al Qaim, and modifications, construction and future plans in converting the first four of the sites to non-nuclear applications were reviewed. Work was being carried out to convert Al Tarmiya into a national centre for industrial chemistry R&D, a new facility is being created at Ash Sharqat for producing ammonium nitrate and sulphuric acid and some construction was observed at Al Jesira to establish a centre for the development of processes to recover minerals from ores. Nothing was noticed to be indicative of prohibited activities.[215]

[210] Report on the 16th inspection (note 202), pp. 2–3.

[211] Report on the 18th inspection (note 189), pp. 19–20.

[212] Report on the seventeenth IAEA on-site inspection in Iraq under Security Council Resolution 687 (1991), 25–31 January 1993, UN document S/25411, 13 Mar. 1993, pp. 9–10.

[213] Report on the 18th inspection (note 189), p. 14.

[214] Report on the 19th inspection (note 194), p. 11.

[215] Report on the 18th inspection (note 189), p. 22; Consolidated report on the twentieth (25–30 June 1993) and twenty-first (24–27 July 1993) IAEA on-site inspections under Security Council Resolution 687 (1991), IAEA document GOV/INF/707, 25 Aug. 1993. p. 1; Report on the 22nd inspection (note 194), pp. 4, 15–21; and Report on the 23rd inspection (note 200), p. 4.

Preparations for OMV

By June 1994, with the 25th inspection much of the focus shifted to preparing for the implementation of the OMV.[216] This included inspections to check the adequacy of information in the OMV reports which had been provided by Iraq and checking sites for their current status and use. Future inspection frequencies were also assigned. In addition several days of discussions took place regarding the quality and completeness of the information contained in the Iraqi reports.[217]

A 10-camera multiplexed closed-circuit video-surveillance system (MUX) was installed and tested to monitor production of the flow-forming machines at the Nassr engineering establishment which have the capability to produce centrifuge rotors. In addition another video-surveillance system was installed to improve the coverage of the surveillance system previously installed in the milling and boring machine tool workshop at Um Al Ma'arik where EMIS components had previously been manufactured.[218]

Laser enrichment activity

Although it had been concluded in 1991 that Iraq had not been involved in laser isotope separation, one of the main tasks of the 26th inspection was to investigate information which had been received from IAEA member states indicating that Iraq had invested in a substantial effort towards laser isotope separation, including both the molecular and atomic vapour processes. Iraq had denied any laser enrichment to the seventh inspection team but the new information prompted further investigation; searches of the Action Team data base pointed to several activities which related to laser component manufacture and included an abstract of an unclassified Iraqi report on 'Dissociation of UF_6 molecules by UV laser'.[219]

The five-day investigation was carried out by a team including five experts in laser technology and included a thorough search of several facilities. Although nothing suggesting laser isotope separation-related activities resulted from the inspections themselves,[220] information received from the Iraqis indicated that there had been some modest investigations into this method of enrichment. In particular during a seminar delivered to the team by Iraqi experts, the head of the Department of Physics at Al Tuwaitha stated: 'I received an objective [in 1981] from the Atomic Energy Commission to work in Laser Isotope Separation . . . We [Laser Section 6240] started in two lines; one which is looking after the molecular and the other the atomic direction'. Information was also provided, however, that in 1987, when the achievements of this group were

[216] The second, and last, shipment of irradiated enriched uranium fuel had been removed from Iraq and shipped to Russia in Mar. 1994. Report on the 23rd inspection (note 200), p. 10.

[217] Report on the twenty-fifth IAEA on-site inspection in Iraq under Security Council Resolution 687 (1991), 22 June–1 July 1994, IAEA document GOV/INF/752, 25 Aug. 1994, pp. 3, 5, 7.

[218] Report on the 25th inspection (note 217), pp. 6–7.

[219] Report on the twenty-sixth IAEA on-site inspection in Iraq under Security Council Resolution 687 (1991), 22 August–7 September 1994, IAEA document GOV/INF/757, 28 Oct. 1994, pp. 3–4.

[220] Report on the 26th inspection (note 219), pp. 11, 15–16.

evaluated, its work was downgraded to a 'watching brief' and a number of key personnel were transferred to other programmes, EMIS in particular.[221]

There were no indications that work had progressed to the point of an integrated experiment achieving isotopic separation or that even rudimentary capabilities in AVLIS or MLIS had been achieved. Overall the team was satisfied with information it acquired regarding the activities of Section 6240, the inspection report stating that it 'was consistent with a loosely co-ordinated and largely empirical approach to LIS, but not consistent with the achievement of substantial progress in what is a complex technology'.[222] It was also apparent to the team that export controls as well as voluntary refusals by several suppliers 'had severely hampered the Iraqi LIS activities' by preventing them from acquiring key pieces of equipment, in particular copper vapour laser systems.

Concurrent with the 26th inspection a continuous IAEA presence was established in Iraq prepared to implement the OMV plan.[223] The head of the Iraqi National Monitoring Directorate (NMD) informed the team that personnel had been designated to facilitate the ongoing monitoring activities. The establishment of a continuous IAEA presence in Iraq resulted in a decrease in the frequency of visits by large inspection teams to the country, but such inspections will continue as special circumstances warrant.

The report of the 27th inspection team which visited Iraq in October 1994 was the last in a series of mission-specific inspection reports, and detailed descriptions of IAEA activity in Iraq are now to appear only in semi-annual reports to the UN Security Council. Teams composed of a chief inspector and one or more experts are now assigned to tours of duty at the Baghdad Monitoring and Verification Center (BMVC) established in consultation with the IAEA by the Special Commission.[224]

V. Ongoing and long-term monitoring

With the acceptance by Iraq on 26 November 1993 during the third round of high-level talks with the IAEA and the UN Special Commission of its obligations under Security Council Resolution 715, setting forth the plans for future ongoing monitoring and verification, the way was paved for the IAEA and UNSCOM to satisfy themselves that they were in a position to implement the plan for monitoring and verification. One especially outstanding issue had been the refusal of Iraq to disclose information regarding its foreign suppliers, but the most significant information was finally released in autumn 1993.

Installation proceeded in 1994 of 20 tonnes of sensors and equipment, including live video cameras at key industrial plants to ensure that Iraq does not restart its nuclear, chemical or biological weapon or missile programmes. An

221 Report on the 26th inspection (note 219), p. 18.
222 Report on the 26th inspection (note 219), p. 19.
223 Report on the 26th inspection (note 219), p. 7.
224 Report on the twenty-seventh IAEA on-site inspection in Iraq under Security Council Resolution 687 (1991), 14–21 October 1994, IAEA document GOV/INF/760, 29 Dec. 1994, p. 2.

80-person team will monitor Iraq's industry from the UN office. In Baghdad a 90-metre tower has been constructed to receive the signals from all of the cameras and sensors as well as to relay messages to inspectors in the field who will monitor several hundred sites throughout the country.[225]

The destruction, removal or rendering harmless of all of the weapon-usable nuclear material known to exist in Iraq has been completed, and since August 1994 the IAEA has maintained a continuous presence in Iraq. IAEA staff will undertake both routine and non-routine inspection visits to sites selected for ongoing monitoring. The IAEA monitoring programme involves more than 200 sites, including places where nuclear activity was occurring before the Persian Gulf War, sites of previous supporting activity for the nuclear programme directed by sub-contractor organizations and places where other activities were occurring with possible connections to the nuclear programme. Inspectors will monitor the usage of equipment including dual-use machine tools to ensure they are not used for disallowed nuclear activity.

Environmental monitoring is an ongoing activity but major campaigns are carried out on a twice-yearly basis in Iraq,[226] and there is now a strong possibility that routine safeguards procedures in other countries will also include some form of environmental monitoring in the future. Stringent measures are necessary to ensure that the sampling materials are free from contamination and that the integrity of the sample is maintained once the sampling procedure has been performed, and subsequent analysis must be performed under exacting conditions. The Iraqi samples were analysed in several IAEA member states and the IAEA is now moving to establish a specialized laboratory dedicated to the handling of environmental samples.[227]

As of 23 August 1994 the IAEA had established a permanent presence in Iraq and by September all elements of the ongoing monitoring and verification activities had been put in place, including the Baghdad Monitoring and Verification Center. According to Rolf Ekeus, the monitoring system would have to run for about six months before enough confidence is gained in Iraqi intentions that a recommendation to lift sanctions could be made.[228]

Once the UN has lifted its sanctions on Iraq an Import–Export Monitoring Mechanism will be put in place that will require Iraq to report any imports of items appearing on a list of dual-use commodities as well as oblige all countries to report exports of such listed items to Iraq.[229]

[225] Lewis, P., 'UN monitoring stops Iraqi A-weapons, but Saddam survives', *International Herald Tribune*, 27 July 1994, p. 2.

[226] IAEA Press Release 94 PR/33 (19 Sep. 1994); Hibbs, M., 'Permanent IAEA monitors now on the job in Iraq', *Nucleonics Week*, 1 Sep. 1994, p. 17; and Maurizio Zifferero, personal communication.

[227] Donohue, D., Deron, S. and Kuhn, E., 'Environmental monitoring & safeguards: reinforcing analytical capabilities', *IAEA Bulletin*, no. 3 (1994), p. 20.

[228] 'Inspectors resume watch on Iraq', *Jane's Defence Weekly*, 20 Aug. 1994, p. 10; and *PPNN Newsbrief*, no. 27 (third quarter 1994), p. 14.

[229] Wolfsthal, J. B., 'UNSCOM outlines long-term monitoring plan for Iraq', *Arms Control Today*, Nov. 1994, p. 29.

VI. Conclusions: summary of the inspection findings and lessons learned

Iraq had invested enormous resources in its nuclear programme in a long-term and far-reaching attempt to acquire by whatever means possible[230] the required knowledge, materials and technology for nuclear weapon development. By 2 September 1992 it was stated by the Deputy Director General of the IAEA that, as a result of the UN inspections as well as the bomb damage suffered during the war, the Iraqi nuclear weapon programme had been 'neutralised'. While some equipment remained to be destroyed and verification would continue to ensure that covert activity was not resumed he asserted that no evidence had been uncovered that the programme was continuing.[231]

By the end of August 1994 the IAEA had a continuous monitoring presence in Iraq, a well established system of periodic environmental monitoring was in place, all special fissionable material had been removed and all items associated with the clandestine nuclear weapon programme had been destroyed, rendered harmless or removed.[232]

A report filed after the 18th inspection by the IAEA Iraqi Action Team[233] responsible for enforcing Resolution 687 presented a number of conclusions and assessments. Regarding EMIS, while the programme was a clever indigenous approach it was facing serious difficulties in implementation as a result of 'lack of technical depth'. The report noted that it would have been 'some years' before it could have produced militarily significant quantities of uranium. Facilities and equipment related to the programme were damaged during the war, as a result of the post-war Iraqi concealment effort as well as by the cruise missile attack in January 1993. Other facilities were destroyed by the Iraqis under IAEA supervision and equipment was either destroyed or inventoried.

All centrifuge components and special tooling were destroyed in 1991 with dual-use equipment related to the programme remaining under IAEA seal. The Action Team assessment is that the Iraqi centrifuge programme was in a 'very early stage'. Using designs obtained clandestinely and materials obtained illicitly only a few research machines were built in Iraq itself, and a small number of more advanced carbon-fibre rotors were obtained from abroad. Hundreds of tonnes of special metals and components were procured—enough for thousands of centrifuges—but all of these materials have been either seized by the inspection teams or destroyed. One clue as to why so much was invested in this method was gained from senior Iraqi technical specialists, who stated that

[230] As an indication of the many avenues available to obtain information, it has been reported that Iraq used the Internet electronic bulletin board to obtain some useful information related to their nuclear weapon programme by simply disguising problems in an innocuous manner and waiting for replies. Burrows, W. E. and Windrem, R., *Critical Mass: The Dangerous Race for Superweapons in a Fragmenting World* (Simon&Schuster: New York, 1994), p. 46.

[231] Nicholson, M., 'UN says Iraqi N-threat is over', *Financial Times*, 3 Sep. 1992, p. 7.

[232] See the seventh semi-annual report on the implementation by the International Atomic Energy Agency of the plan for the destruction, removal or rendering harmless of items listed in paragraph 12 of Security Council Resolution 687 (1991), UN document S/1994/1438, 22 Dec. 1994.

[233] IAEA Iraqi Action Team Fact Sheet (note 20).

meetings were held in mid-1987 at which it was acknowledged that gas diffusion had failed and that EMIS was not making the expected progress because of ion source difficulties; gas diffusion[234] was therefore cancelled and support for the centrifuge effort was dramatically increased.[235]

The assessment of the Action Team regarding weaponization was that although 'sophisticated concepts and development were under consideration', the weaponization effort was 'at an early stage and consisted of a very broadly based study of all aspects of producing a uranium core implosion weapon'. The Iraqis had failed to achieve development of a practical design for a nuclear weapon.[236] It was noted in their report that while the facilities and hardware supporting the programme have been destroyed 'the concepts remain'.

The reactors at Al Tuwaitha have been totally destroyed as a result of the Persian Gulf War. Searches for other clandestine reactors were made by the inspection teams but no verifiable evidence was uncovered to indicate the existence of such a reactor. The long-term environmental monitoring programme is in place, with baseline measurements taken and several semi-annual sampling missions accomplished. There has been no evidence of the operation of any clandestine nuclear facility in the recent past.

There have been a number of important consequences of the Iraqi experience in the areas of safeguards and export controls in particular. Overall lessons learned include: (*a*) as it functioned at the time, the nuclear non-proliferation regime did not in this case prevent a determined proliferation effort from achieving substantial progress towards the development of nuclear weapons; (*b*) measures then in place were not adequate to warn of the full extent of the type of clandestine activity which was taking place. Even verification of compliance with the NPT (admittedly with the letter of the requirements since only a small amount of plutonium had been separated) could not be verified; and (*c*) although a nuclear programme may be destroyed down to and including the infrastructure level, the capability remains none the less to restart with the accumulated knowledge, personnel and perhaps also equipment which may have been hidden from destruction.[237]

In the Iraqi case it has been possible to implement a programme of long-term monitoring which will serve to detect with a fairly high degree of confidence any substantial efforts to restart a nuclear weapon programme in Iraq. This

[234] The Iraqi gas diffusion uranium enrichment programme apparently did not evolve beyond the unsuccessful work on diffusion barrier development. Documents found during the 6th inspection suggest that the facility at Al Rabiya would have had a role in manufacturing had this programme continued. Report on the 17th inspection (note 211), p. 6.

[235] Report on the 15th inspection (note 191), p. 9.

[236] The simplest route, even if identified by the Iraqis as such, was not always that which Iraq decided to pursue. E.g., one of the inspection reports notes that regarding weaponization, 'the Iraqi authorities had decided to go for the most complicated solution, i.e. an implosion system, because, in their view, defining its requirements would generate the expertise needed for a simpler system, such as a gun-type system. The weapons studies had been based on HEU rather than plutonium as the fissile material because it had been considered by the Iraqi side to be the more difficult route'. The Iraqis acknowledged that explosives technology was a weak point in their design work. Report on the 11th inspection (note 190), pp. 20–21.

[237] Bailey, K. C., *Strengthening Nuclear Nonproliferation* (Westview Press: Boulder, Colo., 1993), pp. 34–35.

degree of confidence in the absence of clandestine nuclear activity in other areas of the globe of high proliferation concern is highly unlikely in the near future. Further efforts directed towards uncovering attempted clandestine nuclear activity including enhanced safeguards and effective and adequately enforced export controls as well as development and refinement of national or multinational intelligence-gathering measures are therefore necessary to ensure the maximum transparency possible. These subjects are dealt with in the following chapters.

5. Safeguards: present and future

I. The role, scope and limitations of safeguards

As early as 1945 the term 'safeguards' was used by Britain, Canada and the USA in a declaration which stipulated that only 'when effective enforceable safeguards' against the use of atomic energy for destructive purposes could be worked out would information on its use for industrial purposes be made publicly available.[1] In 1946 the MacMahon Act was passed by the US Congress, stipulating that there be 'no exchange of information with other nations with respect to the use of atomic energy for peaceful purposes' until effective nuclear safeguards were in place.[2] These restrictions were not revoked until the Atomic Energy Act was adopted in 1954.[3]

As currently formalized, the nuclear safeguards agreements of the International Atomic Energy Agency involve a complex array of rights and obligations. While they serve the broad purpose of halting the further spread of nuclear weapons, they may involve quite different specific objectives and obligations depending on whether they are undertaken as a requirement of a particular treaty (the NPT, the 1967 Treaty of Tlatelolco and the 1985 Treaty of Rarotonga all make provision for the application of IAEA safeguards on relevant nuclear activities) or for the supply of nuclear materials, equipment or facilities. As discussed below, the new challenges of recent years are requiring re-evaluation and reassessment of the role and scope of safeguards activities. As noted by the IAEA Deputy Director General for Safeguards in early 1994, 'to an important degree the application of international safeguards has moved from a phase of consolidation in the 1980s to a phase of transition in the 1990s as we respond to dynamic political and technological developments'.[4]

There are two important 'model' safeguards agreements. The safeguards agreement between Iraq and the IAEA (IAEA document INFCIRC/172, 22 February 1973), for example, was based on the 1971 NPT Model Safeguards Agreement (set forth in IAEA document INFCIRC/153) drawn up to cover nuclear material in the fuel cycle of non-nuclear weapon states parties to the NPT. Specific elements of this agreement are discussed in this chapter with regard to particular obligations, limitations and the potential for improvement. The NPT Model Safeguards Agreement is in two parts—the first involving the political and general obligations of an NPT state party and the IAEA, and the second stating the specific technical aspects of the safeguards which are to be

[1] Noted, e.g., in Fischer, D., *Stopping the Spread of Nuclear Weapons: The Past and the Prospects* (Routledge: London, 1992), p. 5.

[2] Fischer (note 1), p. 264.

[3] Fischer (note 1), p. 36.

[4] Statement of Bruno Pellaud at the IAEA International Symposium on Safeguards, Mar. 1994 as quoted in *IAEA Press Release*, PR 94/8 (18 Mar. 1994).

applied.[5] Its specific form is used as a basis for all safeguards agreements with non-nuclear weapon states parties to the NPT as well as for parties to the Treaty of Tlatelolco, the Treaty of Rarotonga and the 1991 Agreement on the Exclusively Peaceful Uses of Nuclear Energy between Argentina, Brazil, the IAEA and ABACC (Argentine–Brazilian Agency for Accounting and Control of Nuclear Materials).

A state entering into such an agreement must agree to accept safeguards on all source or special fissionable material 'for the exclusive purpose of verifying that such material is not diverted to nuclear weapons or other nuclear explosive devices'.[6] It agrees to establish and maintain a system of accounting for the nuclear material subject to safeguards and to provide the IAEA with appropriate information on this nuclear material as well as the features of facilities which may be relevant to the safeguarding of the material.[7] So-called 'subsidiary arrangements' are also negotiated for the detailed implementation of the safeguards. Included in these arrangements are specifically tailored 'facility attachments' for the detailed safeguarding of particular nuclear facilities.[8]

The basic framework for safeguards applied in countries which have not made binding the multilateral or bilateral non-proliferation commitments mentioned above, the second model safeguards agreement, is embodied in the IAEA Safeguards System of 1965–68.[9] As it must deal with a very broad range of particular supply and other arrangements this framework is cast in much more general terms than the NPT Model Safeguards Agreement. The IAEA Safeguards System does not require all the nuclear activities of a country to be placed under safeguards, whereas under paragraph 62 of the NPT Model Safeguards Agreement a state must report all nuclear material in its peaceful nuclear activities. IAEA safeguards are not restricted to following the flow of nuclear material alone as is the case with the NPT Model Safeguards Agreement (although paragraph 42 of the latter does stipulate that the state provide design information on existing facilities as well as on new facilities as early as possible before nuclear material is introduced into the facility). The fundamental difficulty with the IAEA Safeguards System is that it does not go far enough, leaving 'the door open to construct unsafeguarded facilities, a door through which Israel, India, South Africa and Pakistan have long since passed'.[10]

There also remains a grey area in safeguards application in that while only nuclear weapons or other nuclear explosive devices are prohibited by the NPT,

[5] See, e.g., IAEA, *IAEA Safeguards: Aims, Limitations, Achievements* (IAEA: Vienna, 1983), p. 16.

[6] IAEA, The Structure and Content of Agreements between the International Atomic Energy Agency and States Required in Connection with the Treaty on the Non-Proliferation of Nuclear Weapons (the NPT Model Safeguards Agreement), IAEA document INFCIRC/153, 10 Mar. 1971, para. 1. The text of the NPT Model Safeguards Agreement is reproduced in appendix C in this volume.

[7] NPT Model Safeguards Agreement (note 6), paras 7, 8.

[8] NPT Model Safeguards Agreement (note 6), paras 39, 40; and Fischer, D. and Szasz, P., ed. J. Goldblat, SIPRI, *Safeguarding the Atom: A Critical Appraisal* (Taylor & Francis: London, 1985), p. 27.

[9] The IAEA Safeguards System of 1965–68, IAEA document INFCIRC/66/Rev.2, 16 Sep. 1968. The text of the IAEA Safeguards System is reproduced in appendix C in this volume.

[10] Fischer and Szasz (note 8), pp. 24, 92. South Africa has now given up its nuclear weapon programme and become the first country to pass back through that door, signing the NPT in 1991 and placing its nuclear materials and facilities under safeguards.

safeguards are required in the NNWS only on source or special nuclear material in all *peaceful* nuclear activities.[11] Therefore the non-explosive *military* use of such materials would be permitted without safeguards. This includes such applications as nuclear-powered submarines and military research reactors, and were a country to take advantage of this grey area its nuclear activities would be bifurcated into those that are covered by safeguards and those that are not. This issue was first brought to prominence when Canada made a decision to acquire nuclear-powered submarines in 1987. Although the decision was later rescinded the grey area remains.

As of 31 December 1994, 199 safeguards agreements were in force with 118 states, an increase from 194 safeguards agreements in force with 116 states at the end of 1993, 188 agreements with 110 states at the conclusion of 1992 and 180 agreements with 105 states at the end of 1991. At the end of 1994, 102 safeguards agreements pursuant to the NPT were in force, and while 61 non-nuclear weapon states parties to the Treaty had no safeguards agreement in force only six of these have significant nuclear activities. Of the 29 states parties to the Treaty of Tlatelolco, 20 had concluded safeguards agreements pursuant to that Treaty, 18 of them were in force and two states with territories in the Treaty's zone of application also had agreements in force. In addition all 11 signatories of the Rarotonga Treaty had NPT safeguards in force. During 1994, 2349 inspections were performed making use of a total of 9152 person-days of inspection.[12]

II. The objectives of safeguards

The technical objective of safeguards as stated in the NPT Model Safeguards Agreement is 'the timely detection of diversion of significant quantities of nuclear material from peaceful nuclear activities to the manufacture of nuclear weapons or other nuclear explosive devices or for purposes unknown, and deterrence of such diversion by the risk of early detection'.[13]

The deterrent function of safeguards in general is, however, secondary to their main function, which is the building of confidence among nations.[14] Thus the IAEA describes the two main political objectives of nuclear safeguards as:

To assure the international community that States are complying with their non-proliferation and other 'peaceful use' undertakings.

[11] This issue, with particular reference to the Canadian case, is thoroughly addressed in Desjardins, M-F. and Rauf, T., 'Opening Pandora's box: nuclear powered submarines and the spread of nuclear weapons', Aurora Papers 8, Canadian Centre for Arms Control and Disarmament, Ottawa, June 1988.

[12] The Agency also applies safeguards to nuclear installations in Taiwan. IAEA, *The Annual Report for 1994*, GC(39)/3 (IAEA: Vienna, July 1995), pp. 174–75, 194; IAEA, *The Annual Report for 1993*, GC(XXXVIII)/2 (IAEA: Vienna, July 1994), pp. 141–42, 157; and IAEA, *The Annual Report for 1992*, GC(XXXVII)/1060 (IAEA: Vienna, July 1993), p. 136.

[13] NPT Model Safeguards Agreement (note 6), para. 28.

[14] Fischer and Szasz (note 8), pp. 5–6.

To deter (a) the diversion of safeguarded nuclear materials to the production of nuclear explosives or for other military purposes and (b) the misuse of safeguarded facilities with the aim of producing unsafeguarded nuclear material.[15]

The IAEA employs three safeguards methods or measures—material accountancy, containment and surveillance—by making use of four procedures—design review, maintenance of plant-operating records, reports on plant operation and on-site inspection.

Material accountancy, as the main safeguards measure, is founded on so-called material balance areas (MBAs), which may be parts of or entire plants such that all material brought into, removed from and present in the area is measurable—thus allowing for a material balance to be established. By keeping track of the material flow into and out of the MBA, a book value for the amount of material present in each MBA can be maintained. Through a system of records and reports the IAEA is kept informed of the inventory, and it can be checked periodically by the operator of the facility as well as by the IAEA through inspections. The difference between the expected amount (the book value) and the amount actually found is referred to as the material unaccounted for (MUF), which thus represents a possible diversion of nuclear material.[16]

Inspections

The NPT Model Safeguards Agreement allows for three types of inspection: (*a*) *ad hoc inspections* for verifying initial inventories of nuclear materials subject to safeguards, and changes thereto, as well as transfers into or out of the state; (*b*) *routine inspections* to verify the consistency of reports filed by the state with records, the location, identity, quantity and composition of nuclear material subject to safeguards, and information on possible causes of any uncertainties which may exist; and (*c*) *special inspections,* which the Agency may make to verify information in special reports[17] or 'if the Agency considers that information made available by the State, including explanations from the State and information obtained from routine inspections, is not adequate for the Agency to fulfil its responsibilities'. An inspection is considered special 'when it is either additional to the routine inspection effort . . . or involves access to information or locations in addition to the access . . . for ad hoc and routine inspections, or both'. It is further stated that the Agency 'may obtain access in agreement with the State to information or locations in addition to the access specified . . . for ad hoc and routine inspections'.[18]

[15] IAEA, *IAEA Safeguards: An Introduction* (IAEA: Vienna, 1981), p. 12.

[16] Sanders, B., 'IAEA safeguards: a short historical background', eds D. Fischer, B. Sanders, L. Sheinman and G. Bunn, *A New Nuclear Triad: The Non-Proliferation of Nuclear Weapons, International Verification and The International Atomic Energy Agency*, Programme for Promoting Nuclear Non-Proliferation (PPNN) Study Three, Mountbatten Centre for International Studies, Southampton, Sep. 1992, pp. 6–7; and Fischer and Szasz (note 8), pp. 26–29, 41.

[17] Special Reports deal with unusual incidents involving possible loss of nuclear material or important changes in containment. NPT Model Safeguards Agreement (note 6), para. 68.

[18] NPT Model Safeguards Agreement (note 6), paras 73 and 77.

In addition, the IAEA Statute states the Agency's right 'to send into the territory of the recipient State or States inspectors . . . who shall have access at all times to all places and data and to any person who by reason of his occupation deals with materials, equipment or facilities which are required by this Statute to be safeguarded.'[19]

Instances where states are found not to be in compliance with their safeguards agreements are reported to the Board of Governors. Failure to comply can result in a report to the Security Council and the General Assembly. The Board can instruct the Director General to withdraw technical assistance to the state concerned and the Security Council can impose wider sanctions.[20] As reaffirmed by the IAEA Board of Governors in 1992, however, and as discussed below, these provisions are now seen to form a legal basis for special inspections to undeclared facilities as well in all countries with comprehensive safeguards agreements.[21]

Problems and limitations

It is already admittedly the case that 'Acceptance of the NPT and the safeguards that go with it obviously entails a significant concession of national sovereignty'.[22] None the less, the International Nuclear Fuel Cycle Evaluation (INFCE) made it clear in 1980 that there is no easy technical means to prevent the acquisition of nuclear material for explosives purposes, emphasizing political solutions to the problem of proliferation by strengthening safeguards in particular.[23]

The limitations on IAEA inspectors and inspections, such as prescribed limitations on the total time which may be spent inspecting various types and sizes of facility and on what inspectors are and are not allowed to do, are difficult to reconcile with parts of the IAEA Statute. Article XII, paragraph A.6, for example, states that inspectors 'shall have access at all times to all places and data and to any person who by reason of his occupation deals with materials, equipment or facilities which . . . are required to be safeguarded'. In addition, while automatic monitoring devices cannot replace the inspectors,[24] advanced technology for remote monitoring and unattended measurement are increasingly important in strengthened and more efficient safeguards.

Pointing to another issue concerning inspections, a report prepared for the US Congress states: 'The Iraqi bomb project has clearly revealed the limitations of enforcement of the no-weapons pledge of the Non-proliferation Treaty (NPT) via inspection of solely those nuclear facilities and materials facilities that a country chooses to declare. The IAEA would require access to intelligence

[19] IAEA Statute as amended up to 28 Dec. 1989, Vienna, 28 Dec. 1989, Article XII, para. A6.

[20] NPT Model Safeguards Agreement (note 6), paras 18, 19; and IAEA Statute (note 19), Article XII, para. C.

[21] IAEA Press Release, PR 92/12 (26 Feb. 1992).

[22] IAEA (note 15), p. 4.

[23] IAEA (note 15), pp. 4–5.

[24] Fischer (note 1), pp. 122, 289.

about suspicious nuclear activities or authority to conduct surprise inspections of suspicious facilities whether or not they have been declared'.[25] As discussed below, it is clear that a suitable framework for facilitating access to the appropriate information and the ability to act on this information has become a priority of IAEA Director General Hans Blix.

There remain many other important issues involving the present scope of safeguards, which are also under active review. In September 1990, before the extent of the Iraqi nuclear programme had been discovered, many recommendations for improvements to safeguards were included in the report of Main Committee II of the Fourth NPT Review Conference. These included the streamlining of safeguards, broadening export controls to include non-nuclear materials which may be of use in nuclear weapons, such as tritium, the use of randomized inspections, stricter separation of civilian and military fuel cycles and increased safeguards coverage of NWS, making full use of special inspections and increasing the transparency of safeguards.[26]

Of course since no official final document was issued the recommendations have no formal status, but an IAEA document containing the suggestions of the draft final document concerning the work of the IAEA (and importantly for safeguards improvements) was circulated.[27] This empowered but did not oblige the IAEA to pursue further studies on how best to implement paragraphs 73 and 77 of the NPT Model Safeguards Agreement on special inspections, for example.[28] As shown below, progress is now being made towards strengthening safeguards in several areas.

Regarding exemptions, the NPT Model Safeguards Agreement states that

nuclear material that would otherwise be subject to safeguards shall be exempted from safeguards at the request of the State, provided that *nuclear material* so exempted in the State may not at any time exceed:

(*a*) One kilogram in total of special fissionable material which may consist of one or more of the following: (i) Plutonium; (ii) Uranium with an *enrichment* of 0.2 (20%) and above, taken account of by multiplying its weight by its *enrichment;* and (iii) Uranium with an *enrichment* below 0.2 (20%) and above that of natural uranium, taken account of by multiplying its weight by five times the square of its *enrichment.*

(*b*) Ten metric tons in total of natural uranium and depleted uranium with an enrichment above 0.005 (0.5%);

(*c*) Twenty metric tons of depleted uranium with an enrichment of 0.005 (0.5%) or below; and

[25] Davis, Z. S. and Donnelly, W. H., 'Iraq and nuclear weapons', CRS Issue Brief, IB90113, Library of Congress, Washington, DC, 10 Dec. 1991, p. 1.

[26] A full explication of this and other activity of the Fourth NPT Review Conference can be found in Müller, H., Fischer, D. and Kötter, W., SIPRI, *Nuclear Disarmament and Global Ord*er (Oxford University Press: Oxford, 1992), pp. 86–87.

[27] IAEA, Fourth Review Conference of the Parties to the Treaty on the Non-Proliferation of Nuclear Weapons, Geneva, 20 August to 14 September 1990, Extracts from NPT/CONF.IV/DC/ADD.3(A) and text of NPT/CONF.IV/DC/ADD.3(B), circulated as IAEA document GC(XXXIV)/INF/291, 19 Sep. 1990.

[28] Müller, Fischer and Kötter (note 26), p. 106.

(*d*) Twenty metric tons of thorium; or such greater amounts as may be specified by the Board of Governors for uniform application.[29]

This paragraph was included so that special nuclear material could be used in nuclear research programmes and has been commonly used to exempt small quantities of materials. Iraq, for example, was granted an exemption for several fuel elements, on which subsequent experimentation allowed the separation of small quantities of plutonium. Importantly, the Agreement does not address the issue of the use to which the exempted material may be put. In the wake of the Iraqi nuclear activity there has been concern that the amounts allowed—particularly 1 kg of plutonium—may have to be reconsidered.[30]

More difficult to safeguard than individual nuclear reactors are the commercial bulk-handling facilities, such as fuel-fabrication plants, reprocessing facilities and uranium enrichment facilities. It is hard to keep track of the large amounts of nuclear materials they handle in non-discrete form.[31] Enrichment plants are of particular concern since, while almost all civil power production utilizes uranium which is no more than low-enriched, they may be reconfigured for the production of highly enriched uranium. The ease with which this can be accomplished is an important factor (discussed further in chapter 2). Safeguards on reprocessing facilities are also important, as even the reactor-grade plutonium which is produced in commercial reactors can be used for weapon purposes (see chapter 3).

New technological developments will pose additional challenges for safeguards in the years to come. In particular, employing AVLIS for uranium enrichment will require the development of new safeguards methods and devices, a fact acknowledged by the USA, which is in the forefront of research in this area.[32] A former divisional director in the IAEA Department of Safeguards saw no difficulty in developing safeguards appropriate for uranium enrichment plants using laser methods and expected them to progress as the technology itself matured.[33] The inventory at any one time would be relatively small and the sensitive enrichment technology is confined to one step. The major safeguards problem may turn out to be the construction of small clandestine HEU production facilities.[34]

Should it be brought into practice, however, a senior Western safeguards official believes that the laser upgrading of plutonium, by blurring the civilian–

[29] NPT Model Safeguards Agreement (note 6), para. 37.

[30] Hibbs, M., 'Loophole in safeguards rules allowed Iraq to reprocess', *Nucleonics Week*, vol. 32, no. 33 (15 Aug. 1991), p. 1.

[31] Office of Technology Assessment (OTA), *Technologies Underlying Weapons of Mass Destruction*, OTA-BP-ISC-115 (US Government Printing Office: Washington, DC, Dec. 1993), p. 123.

[32] *Energy and Water Development Appropriations for 1989*, Hearings before a Subcommittee of the Committee on Appropriations, House of Representatives, 100th Congress, 2nd Session (US Government Printing Office: Washington, DC, 1988), p. 1229.

[33] Seneviratne, G., 'Former IAEA official warns of problems ahead for IAEA safeguards regime', *Nuclear Fuel*, vol. 12, no. 2 (26 Jan. 1987), p. 10.

[34] von Baeckmann, A., 'Modern fuel cycle technologies: challenges to IAEA safeguards?', eds D. Fakley and A. von Baeckmann, *New Technologies, Nuclear Non-Proliferation and IAEA Safeguards*, PPNN Occasional Paper 4 (Centre for International Policy Studies: Southampton, Oct. 1989), p. 9.

military distinction in relation to nuclear energy, would 'pose a major challenge to the international safeguards regime'.[35] Facilities like the formerly proposed SIS plant discussed in chapter 2 would require substantial new efforts on the part of the IAEA, as safeguards would be needed for the large amounts of ^{240}Pu and ^{241}Pu which would be produced in addition to the ^{239}Pu.[36]

III. Options for improvement and assessment

In the wake of the revelations about the Iraqi nuclear weapon programme described in chapter 4, many proposals to strengthen the nuclear non-proliferation regime and the system of verification, safeguards and export controls have been put forward. Many of them had been proposed in the past but, because of political, fiscal or other constraints, had not yet been implemented. New impetus has been added to these efforts because of the findings in Iraq and the situation in North Korea, which could lead to profound changes in the scope of international efforts to curb nuclear proliferation.

Special inspections of undeclared facilities

Perhaps the most important of these new efforts to forestall proliferation efforts involves special inspections of undeclared facilities. Although the inspections in Iraq have been carried out under unique circumstances, the experience has made clear that even when this type of inspection is undertaken—even in large numbers—it may be difficult to obtain complete assurance as to whether or not clandestine nuclear activity is being pursued. In addition, verification of nuclear proliferation in general will increasingly involve an analysis of the means available and necessary to acquire the type of information which would be used to cue such inspections.

It has been suggested that the political aim of safeguards, in so far as their intention is to serve as a deterrent, should be 'to confront a would-be NWS with such risk of detection that it would prefer to withdraw from the NPT'.[37] This aim could be considerably enhanced in the future by allowing for the credible possibility of the use of special inspections. Special inspections would also contribute to the confidence-building role of safeguards.

An outline of the cases in which special inspections of undeclared facilities would take place, and the conditions under which they would be authorized, is given below. The use of special inspections in countries which have concluded comprehensive safeguards agreements has long been contemplated and recommendations have been under discussion for many years. The draft final document of the Fourth NPT Review Conference made particular reference to the potential of special inspections to restore confidence 'in the event of questions

[35] Hibbs, M. and MacLachlan, A., 'Soviet Union postpones completion of Siberian reprocessing plant', *Nuclear Fuel*, vol. 14, no. 21 (16 Oct. 1989), p. 2.

[36] Letter of 26 May 1989 from Paul Leventhal, President of the Nuclear Control Institute (NCI), to Sam Nunn, Chairman of the Senate Armed Services Committee, p. 2.

[37] Fischer and Szasz (note 8), p. 45.

arising about the commitment to the non-proliferation objectives of the Treaty of any State Party, and in particular about the safeguards coverage of its source or special fissionable materials'. The Conference in fact urged the Agency: 'not to hesitate to take full advantage of its rights, including the use of special inspections as outlined in paragraphs 73 and 77 of INFCIRC/153'.[38] The language was sponsored by Canada, Great Britain, Hungary and the Netherlands, whose delegates were motivated by the surfacing of serious doubts concerning Iraq's non-proliferation credentials.

The discussion was not confined to Iraq, however, and possible *ad hoc* inspections of North Korea were also discussed.[39] The draft final document also stated that the Conference would welcome an Agency study of 'the possible scope, application and procedures of such inspections, including their implications for the information requirements and policy of the Agency'.[40]

In an interview in late 1991, the Director General of the IAEA stated that it had not been possible for the Agency to inspect sites other than an NPT state party's declared facilities because such places had never been indicated to the IAEA as suspicious. Stressing the seriousness with which clandestine facilities should be viewed he urged that safeguards be strengthened to reduce the risks of their going undetected, stating that 'the crucial and evident lesson of Iraq is the importance of information'. He followed this up with a call to member states 'to give us information based upon whatever intelligence they have'.[41]

He stressed on several occasions in explicit reference to the Iraqi experience three key lessons to be drawn in order to ensure a high degree of confidence that undeclared nuclear material and facilities are detected in the future.[42]

The first is the importance of information of relevance to nuclear proliferation. Without such information it would obviously be impossible for special inspections to proceed. Categories of information outlined include that collected in the course of regular safeguards activities, safety and technical cooperation, information which is publicly available, as well as information collected by member states through their own national intelligence means.[43]

[38] IAEA (note 27), p. 5.

[39] Hibbs, M., 'Iraq, North Korea activities prompt call at NPT Conference for new inspections', *Nuclear Fuel*, vol. 15, no. 19 (17 Sep. 1990), p. 6; and 'Officials say IAEA could inspect centrifuge equipment in Iraq', *Nucleonics Week*, vol. 31, no. 38 (20 Sep. 1990), p. 1.

[40] IAEA (note 27), p. 5.

[41] 'IAEA Director Hans Blix: keeping an eye on a nuclear world', interview by Spurgeon M. Keeny, Jr and Jon W. Wolfsthal on 23 Oct. 1991, *Arms Control Today*, vol. 21, no. 9 (Nov. 1991), p. 4.

[42] Hans Blix, Statement to the Forty-Sixth Session of the United Nations General Assembly, 21 Oct. 1991 (as delivered mimeo), pp. 5–7; Statement to the Board of Governors of the IAEA, 11 Sep. 1991 (as delivered mimeo), pp. 7–9; and Blix, H., 'IAEA safeguards: new challenges', *Disarmament*, vol. 15, no. 2 (1992), p. 43.

[43] It has been suggested that acquisition, collation and evaluation of information could be enhanced by reinstating the system of country desk officers at the IAEA. These officers would be the point of convergence for information relevant to or provided by each state and would also perform valuable functions in briefing and debriefing of inspectors. This system could also be extended to ensure the existence of a permanent and comprehensive institutional data base on each country. Scheinman, L., 'Assuring the nuclear non-proliferation safeguards system', Occasional Paper Series, Atlantic Council of the United States, Washington, DC, Oct. 1992, p. 24.

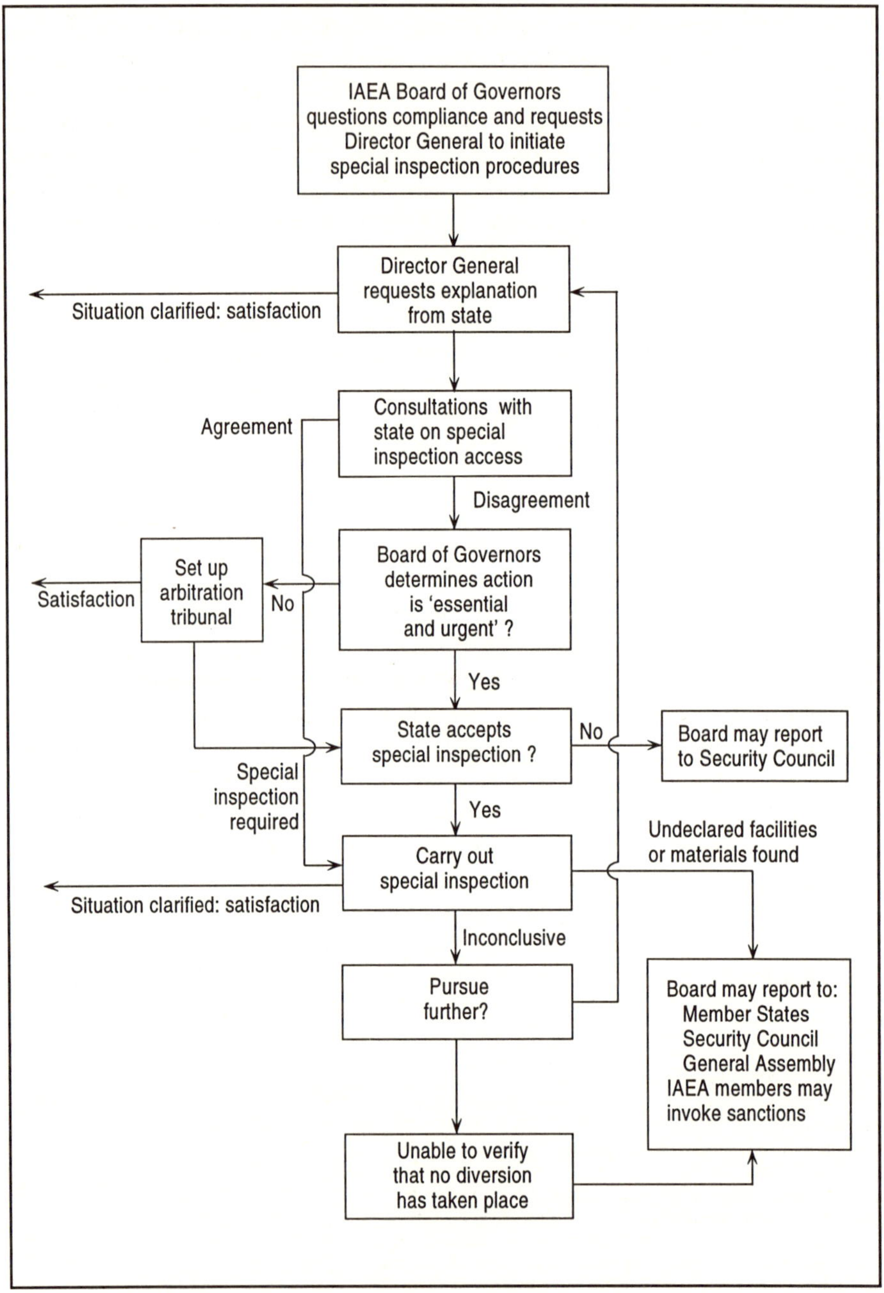

Figure 26. Procedures for initiating and carrying out special inspections

Source: Based on the sequence of events described in IAEA, Strengthening of Agency Safeguards, IAEA document GOV/2554, Attachment 1, 12 Nov. 1991, pp. 4–7.

Information of the latter type, being highly sensitive in nature, would need to be dealt with in a very confidential manner to protect sources and methods among other things. The Director General thus proposed setting up an advisory group to receive such information, composed of only two members who would report directly to him.[44] At the outset of 1991 a single IAEA official was placed in such an advisory position with another such position remaining to be filled. While this is certainly insufficient for the task at hand it does represent an important qualitative change in the manner in which information is being handled by the Agency.[45]

The second is the need to assure the unequivocal right of inspectors to visit suspect sites unimpeded. The Board of Governors reaffirmed[46] at its February 1992 meeting the 'right to undertake special inspections in Member States with comprehensive safeguards agreements, when necessary and appropriate, and to ensure that all nuclear materials in peaceful nuclear activities are under safeguards . . . and to have access to additional information and locations in accordance with the Agency's Statute'.[47]

The third lesson is the value of strong support (specifically in the Security Council) to back up these rights of inspection in the event that such appropriate access is denied. Under the IAEA Statute the Agency may report non-compliance directly to the Security Council. Further action would then be determined by this body but the events in Iraq make it more likely today that firm backing would be forthcoming.

In the event that the Board of Governors or the Director General deems it appropriate that a special inspection be conducted, this would first involve consultations on the subject with the state concerned. In the event of continued refusal by the state to accept a special inspection, or the discovery of undeclared facilities or materials by means of inspection, the matter would be turned over to the Security Council for further consideration.[48] The specific procedures involved are illustrated in the flowchart in figure 26.

The seriousness with which the Security Council views developments of concern for proliferation was explicitly stated in the Declaration of the Security Council summit meeting of 31 January 1992, wherein it is stated that 'the proliferation of all weapons of mass destruction constitutes a threat to international peace and security' and that Council members will be committed to 'prevent the spread of technology related to the research for or production of such weapons and to take appropriate action to that end'. With specific reference to

[44] Hans Blix, Statement to the IAEA Board of Governors on Safeguards Matters, 5 Dec. 1991 (mimeo), p. 10.

[45] Fainberg, A., 'Strengthening IAEA safeguards: lessons from Iraq', Center for International Security and Arms Control, Stanford University, Stanford, Calif., Apr. 1993, pp. 47, 51–52.

[46] As the negotiating record demonstrates, by accepting the NPT, NNWS are obliged to 'permit inspection in places where reasonable evidence can be shown by the IAEA that nuclear material, or facilities that customarily use such material, are present'. Bunn, G., 'Does the NPT require its non-nuclear-weapon parties to permit inspection by the IAEA of nuclear activities that have not been reported to the IAEA?', eds Fischer *et al.* (note 16), Annex, p. 54.

[47] IAEA Press Release, PR 92/12 (26 Feb. 1992).

[48] IAEA, Strengthening of Agency Safeguards, IAEA document GOV/2554, Attachment 1, 12 Nov. 1991, pp. 4–7.

nuclear proliferation the declaration acknowledged the role of fully effective IAEA safeguards and effective export controls and stated that 'appropriate measures' will be taken in case of violations reported by the IAEA.[49]

These pronouncements will clearly help forge a stronger link between the IAEA and the Security Council in addition to helping ensure that appropriate internationally sanctioned action is taken should developments of proliferation concern occur. At the very least it can be said that the beginnings of a new consensus on the seriousness of proliferation have been demonstrated.[50] The statement of the resolve of the Security Council makes it more clear that the weight of the Council may be brought to bear even on a suspect proliferant state lying outside the scope of special IAEA inspections.[51]

As discussed above, however, a state which is under suspicion and which has been requested to be the subject of special inspection in compliance with its obligation to do so does have the right to refuse, albeit at the risk of ultimate Security Council intervention. It has, therefore, been suggested that depriving the IAEA of the opportunity to carry out a special inspection be automatically considered a breach of the safeguards agreement unless convincing arguments are provided that the triggering suspicions are groundless.[52]

Soon after the uncovering of the Iraqi nuclear programme the Netherlands proposed on behalf of the EC that safeguards be strengthened by allowing unannounced special inspections (without spelling out exactly how the inspections should be carried out).[53] Premature announcement of inspections may give the country an opportunity to hide its activity. Once suspect activity has been detected, steps should be taken to ensure the implementation of the inspections before such concealment is possible or practicable.

The confidence-building aspect of special inspections should be noted—they should not always be seen as adversarial. They are expected to occur only rarely, but it is possible that such inspections would be invited by a state under suspicion, for example, to assure the Agency and the world at large that suspicions are unfounded. There was a period during which IAEA safeguards were suspected by many nations to be a form of industrial espionage. Were the IAEA to begin to develop its own intelligence agency, such fears might recur. This also points to the extreme care which should surround the handling of sensitive information which may be acquired through nuclear inspections.[54]

One key element of the inspections in Iraq is that they included people from outside the IAEA with expertise in nuclear weapons. This is to be recommended in the future for special inspections the IAEA may intend to make—it should attempt to add to its cadre of inspectors (perhaps on a call-up basis)

[49] 'Security Council Summit Declaration: New Risks for Stability and Security', text of SC resolution, 31 Jan. 1992, reprinted in *New York Times*, 1 Feb. 1992, p. A4.

[50] See, e.g., Scheinman (note 43), p. 6.

[51] Fainberg (note 45), p. 59.

[52] Goldblat, J., 'The Non-Proliferation Treaty: How to remove the residual threats', UNIDIR Research Paper no. 13 (United Nations: New York, 1992), p. 9.

[53] Hibbs, M., 'Europeans outline new effort to strengthen IAEA safeguards', *Nucleonics Week*, vol. 32, no. 38 (19 Sep. 1991), p. 11.

[54] Imai, R., 'NPT safeguards today and tomorrow', *Disarmament*, vol. 15, no. 2 (1992), pp. 48–49.

several people who possess adequate knowledge in this area. Were an inspection limited to such individuals,[55] who would almost by definition be citizens of nuclear weapon states, this would have the added advantage of reducing the threat of spread of nuclear knowledge in general and eliminating the possibility that such inspections would provide an opportunity for states of proliferation concern directly to acquire information of relevance to nuclear weapon design or construction.

Given the time and effort needed to be reasonably sure of the status of the Iraqi programme, the possible limitations of the information gained by conducting a small number of special inspections in other states—under conditions sure to be much less favourable—must be realized and taken into account.

Challenge inspections

In terms of verification of nuclear-related activity in general, special inspections could become a part of further inspection efforts. For example, a report by the Federation of American Scientists on ending the production of fissile materials in the USA and the FSU, stated that: 'As in the case of the Non-proliferation treaty, the primary task of detection of any clandestine (undeclared) production facilities would be left to the national intelligence agencies of each country. However, as with the verification arrangements for the proposed ban on chemical-weapon production, on-site inspections at declared facilities could be supplemented by challenge inspections at suspect sites'.[56]

The 1993 Chemical Weapons Convention (CWC) states that: 'Each State Party has the right to request an on-site challenge inspection of any facility or location in the territory or in any other place under the jurisdiction or control of any other State Party for the sole purpose of clarifying and resolving any questions concerning possible non-compliance with the provisions of the Convention . . . '.[57] This request is submitted to the Executive Council, which has the power to decide against carrying out the inspection if it is deemed to be 'frivolous, abusive or clearly beyond the scope of this Convention' but must do so by a vote of three-quarters of its members and within 12 hours of receipt of the request.[58]

A similar procedure of nuclear challenge inspections being initiated by concerned states would have the advantage of eliminating charges of partiality levelled at the IAEA or accusations that it is acting as a proxy for a certain state or states, as can be perceived to be the case with special inspections. Challenge

[55] Fainberg (note 45), p. 51.

[56] Ending the production of fissile material for weapons, Verifying the dismantlement of nuclear warheads, A preliminary report of the Federation of American Scientists in collaboration with the Committee of Soviet Scientists for Global Security and the Center for Program Studies of the USSR Academy of Sciences, June 1991, p. 2.

[57] Convention on the Prohibition of the Development, Production, Stockpiling and Use of Chemical Weapons and on their Destruction, 13 Jan. 1993, Article IX, para. 8. The text is reproduced in *SIPRI Yearbook 1993: World Armaments and Disarmament* (Oxford University Press: Oxford, 1993), pp. 735–56.

[58] CWC (note 57), paras 13, 17.

inspections could be particularly effective in detecting clandestine facilities since the consent of the inspected party would not be required.

By their nature, however, such inspections might not afford sufficient time for diplomatic initiatives which could settle issues without the intergovernmental confrontation that could also be inherent in challenge inspections. They would also be viewed by many as discriminatory as a nuclear weapon state could request an inspection of any area in a NNWS, but sensitive facilities in a NWS would be exempt from reciprocal inspections. Perhaps once the CWC has come into force and experience has been gained in initiating challenge inspections they could be successfully applied in the nuclear sphere to complement existing IAEA procedures.[59]

Tightening requirements for prior declaration of nuclear facilities

Besides reaffirming the right of the Agency to perform special inspections in countries subject to comprehensive safeguards, the February 1992 meeting of the IAEA Board of Governors further strengthened safeguards and increased transparency by addressing the need for more timely design information. The NPT Model Safeguards Agreement stipulates the provision of design information 'as early as possible before nuclear material is introduced into a new facility'.[60] Model subsidiary arrangements which supplement a state's safeguards agreement more precisely stipulate 180 days as the specific time period, but in practice this is often as short as 30 days.[61]

The fact that no information need be provided until shortly before the introduction of nuclear material has been a cause of concern. For example, officially the IAEA had no information on the supply of the hot-cell facility by Italy to Iraq—reportedly one of the reasons that Israel destroyed the Tammuz 1 reactor in 1981. Later Iraq was also able to claim that its centrifuge enrichment facilities did not have to be declared since no nuclear material had been introduced.[62]

At the February 1992 meeting the Board called on parties subject to comprehensive safeguards 'to provide preliminary information as early as possible on programmes for new nuclear facilities and activities, as well as modifications to existing facilities as soon as the decision to construct, to authorize construction or to modify a facility has been taken'.[63] It also called for continual updating of the information as the project passes through the project definition, preliminary design, construction and commissioning phases. In most countries in fact this type of information is quite openly available in trade journals and government

[59] For further discussion see Fischer, D., 'Innovations in IAEA safeguards to meet the challenges of the 1990s', eds Fischer *et al.* (note 46), pp. 6–7; and Fischer, D., 'The future of the IAEA', *PPNN Issue Review*, no. 2 (Dec. 1993), p. 4.

[60] NPT Model Safeguards Agreement (note 6), para. 42.

[61] IAEA (note 48), p. 1.

[62] Fischer and Szasz (note 8), p. 80; and Scheinman (note 43), p. 15.

[63] IAEA Press Release, PR 92/12 (26 Feb. 1992).

reports. Failure to disclose such information should alert the IAEA to direct extra attention to the countries concerned.[64]

The earlier provision of this information would be useful on a number of fronts. It would be an important confidence-building measure, providing reassurance of the peaceful nature of the undertaking. As affirmed at the Fourth NPT Review Conference, it is important that states 'take safeguards requirements into account while planning, designing and constructing new nuclear facilities and while modifying existing ones'.[65] More timely information would thus facilitate steps leading to a final facility which would be more 'safeguards friendly'. Early information would allow the Agency to pursue the R&D it felt was necessary to better implement effective safeguards. This will be especially important should new types of reactor, or enrichment plants employing laser technology, for example, be constructed. It would allow for more efficient planning of budgetary details and the installation of appropriate safeguards equipment at optimal stages of construction, and it would also facilitate verification of the actual facility design.[66]

It should be remembered that the NPT Model Safeguards Agreement states that 'In examining design information, the Agency shall, at the request of the State, be prepared to examine on premises of the State design information which the State regards as being of particular sensitivity. Such information would not have to be physically transmitted to the Agency provided that it remained available for ready further examination by the Agency on the premises of the State'.[67] This way of handling sensitive information could also be applied in procedures allowing earlier access to design information while at the same time allaying legitimate fears about the spread of sensitive information.

It has been proposed that, should access to appropriate information eventually enable adequate verification that all nuclear plants in a non-nuclear weapon state party to the NPT had been declared, the NPT Model Safeguards Agreement could be strengthened by requiring initial declaration of all nuclear plants and nuclear materials and further notification of subsequent construction.[68] Recent developments in both better intelligence data acquisition by the IAEA for verification and increasing requirements on provision of design information make such proposals more likely to be adopted.

Prioritizing and streamlining of safeguards.

Several proposals have been made with the intention of promoting more effective and efficient safeguards procedures. For example, more than half of the inspection programme is devoted to safeguards in a handful of Western coun-

[64] Imai (note 54), pp. 53–54.
[65] IAEA (note 27), p. 3.
[66] Statement by Hans Blix (note 44), p. 12; see also IAEA (note 48), Attachment 2, pp. 1, 2.
[67] NPT Model Safeguards Agreement (note 6), para. 8.
[68] Fischer and Szasz (note 8), p. 90.

tries with good non-proliferation credentials. This issue has raised a great deal of concern and led to exploration of ways in which to remedy the situation.

The draft final document of the Fourth NPT Review Conference reiterated 'calls for the continued pursuit of the principle of universal application of safeguards to all peaceful nuclear activities in all States'.[69] At the same time, Main Committee II of the Conference recommended studying the application of randomized inspections. Such a recommendation would certainly not have been possible 10 years ago as it would imply, for example, that the frequency of inspections in Germany would have been reduced—a situation which would have been quite unacceptable to the USSR.[70] Especially now, as the Agency finds itself forced by budgetary constraints to cut back on inspections, it is more important than ever that priorities be well analysed.

In order better to prioritize safeguards activities, some countries with proven non-proliferation records could be subject to less scrutiny while those under some suspicion could be subject to more. For example, Harold Denton, the Director of the Office of International Programs of the US Nuclear Regulatory Commission (NRC), has stated that the IAEA 'can respond to new safety and safeguards demands without seriously undermining other essential activities if less valuable efforts were discontinued' and suggested in particular that the safeguards effort in Canada, Japan and Western Europe could be appropriately curtailed, enabling a more focused effort on the countries where it is most needed.[71] Of course a difficulty with such processes is that it requires specifically naming and increasing the scrutiny on countries which are deemed to have less than ideal non-proliferation credentials—and this specific type of discrimination is not allowed within the IAEA.

It has been suggested that one way in which such political barriers could be overcome would be to involve special inspections in the process. All countries could be given the chance to open their facilities to 'any-time–anywhere' special inspections with an attendant end to, or great reduction in, routine inspections.[72] If this opportunity were not taken by a given state—a state which might have something to hide, for example—its alternative might be to accept the maximum allowed routine inspections if the IAEA so wished. This would avoid directly calling into question any state's commitment to non-proliferation but would provide a *de facto* mechanism to focus safeguards activity in a more efficient manner.

[69] IAEA (note 27), p. 2.

[70] Müller, Fischer and Kötter (note 26), p. 86.

[71] 'U.S. says prioritizing projects is answer to IAEA budget woes', *Nucleonics Week*, vol. 32, no. 48 (28 Nov. 1991), p. 9.

[72] Elaborations on proposals to this effect, along with discussion of enhancing the cost-effectiveness of safeguards by their more selective application at key fuel cycle points, can be found in Scheinman (note 43), p. 21. In addition see Fischer, D., 'Innovations in IAEA safeguards to meet the challenges of the 1990s', eds Fischer *et al.* (note 16), pp. 32–37, on the possibility of the creation of partnerships between the IAEA and Euratom or other regional agency for sharing rather than duplicating nuclear inspections.

More specifically, it has recently been argued[73] that if states such as Canada, for example, could convincingly demonstrate that there were no enrichment or reprocessing facilities within the country, this would make the question of diversion of nuclear material irrelevant. Given that 600 of the 700 person-days of inspection in Canada in 1992 and almost 80 per cent of the 170 site visits were focused on spent reactor fuel—of no value for nuclear weapon use in the absence of reprocessing capability—curtailing this inspection activity could provide a potential for substantial savings. It has been recommended that a minimum series of steps needed to ensure the absence of reprocessing or enrichment facilities would include allowing inspectors to travel without notice or restriction with the same freedom as a state citizen would have, monitor radiation levels and take environmental samples. In addition access should be permitted as well to sites which would not be accessiblc to the public under normal circumstances with careful arrangements made in order to ensure that the state's security interests were maintained.

The adoption of these latter measures would contribute to a more healthy and robust state–Agency relationship but, mainly as a result of the level of intrusiveness required, would unfortunately certainly not be applicable in many states at the present time. However, given the dramatic savings which may be incurred, along with the substantial increase in transparency which would result, the proposal is certainly worthy of further exploration. The Standing Advisory Group on Safeguards Implementation (SAGSI), which serves as an international advisory group to the Director General on the effectiveness and efficiency of safeguards, has expressed the opinion that the principle of a trade-off between an improved ability to detect undeclared nuclear facilities and a decrease in some routine inspections—including the elimination of interim inspections of spent fuel—is a valid one. It identified the areas of environmental monitoring and freer access to sites in particular as measures which would increase the capability to detect such clandestine facilities and activities.[74]

Although the three countries Canada, Germany and Japan are the target of more than 70 per cent of the IAEA inspections, and this is the result of the democratic nature of the safeguards system, it should be noted that there is a provision in the NPT Model Safeguards Agreement which has already been used to decrease the number of inspections in the European Atomic Energy Community (EURATOM) countries and Japan[75] and could be applied to decrease inspections to less 'suspect' countries even more in the future. This provision[76] stipulates that a set of criteria to be used to determine 'the actual number, intensity, duration, timing and mode of routine inspections of any

[73] Sinden, D. B. and McManus, J. G., 'A new safeguards approach', ed. T. Rauf, *Strengthened IAEA Safeguards and Regional Non-proliferation Strategies*, Aurora Papers 23, Canadian Centre for Global Security, Ottawa, Mar. 1994, pp. 35–42.

[74] IAEA, Strengthening the Effectiveness and Improving the Efficiency of the Safeguards System, IAEA document GC(XXXVII)/1073, 6 Sep. 1993, pp. 5, 7.

[75] Fischer (note 1), p. 132.

[76] NPT Model Safeguards Agreement (note 6), para. 81.

facility'—factors which would influence the cost—depend on, among other things, 'the effectiveness of the State's accounting and control system, including the extent to which the operators of the facilities are functionally independent of the State's accounting and control system'.

Another possibility to relieve some of the burden on the IAEA is to make more use of well-developed national and regional accounting systems. Delegation to or sharing of duties with EURATOM, Canada, Japan and perhaps Finland, Sweden, Switzerland and several other countries with such accounting and control systems could be combined with unlimited challenge inspections.[77] In the same vein, a 'New Partnership Approach' (NPA) has been established between the IAEA and EURATOM based on 'optimization of the necessary practical arrangements and the use of commonly agreed safeguards approaches and inspection planning, procedures, activities, instruments, methods and techniques'. The programme was expected to save 1000 person-days of inspection in the first year, with twice this annual saving when the programme is fully implemented.[78]

The role of inspectors

The Fourth NPT Review Conference took note of the request of the Director General that states 'facilitate the designation of inspectors and their entry into the States, in particular with regard to visa requirements', appealing to states to 'respond as fully as possible so as to maximize the efficient use of Agency inspection resources'.[79] Iraq, for example, had before the 1991 Persian Gulf War restricted inspectors to those from countries with which it had friendly relations'.[80]

At present a state can attempt to impede inspections through employing a number of tactics—it can delay reply to proposals to designate inspectors, reject the proposals, attempt to limit the number of inspectors, hold up visa requests or refuse outright the admission of inspectors on grounds of security, for example.[81] While granting that inspectors' rights may not be the most serious problem on the agenda, the Director General has recognized the need to improve upon present rules and practices in this area.[82]

In the past inspectors have not been encouraged to question activities in areas beyond the defined strategic points while conducting routine inspections. In fact IAEA policy had reportedly been to refrain from any official acknowledgement of suspect activities which may have related to clandestine facilities or material—thus severely limiting any role routine inspections may have

[77] Fischer (note 1), pp. 133–34.

[78] IAEA (note 74), pp. 7–8.

[79] IAEA (note 27), p. 3.

[80] Hibbs, M., 'Iraq protests IAEA action, may reconsider commitment', *Nucleonics Week,* vol. 31, no. 39 (27 Sep. 1991), p. 3; and 'U.S. may send NEST to Iraq; IAEA sets up task force', *Nucleonics Week*, vol. 32, no. 16 (18 Apr. 1991), p. 9.

[81] Fischer and Szasz (note 8), p. 42.

[82] Statement by Hans Blix (note 44), p. 7.

played in triggering further investigations of this type of activity. In general the overall confidence in safeguards could be improved by granting greater latitude to inspectors through, for example, employing special inspections as part of routine verification visits by having inspectors seek access to additional locations at a given site. To take full advantage of possibilities for greater access in its various aspects, including special inspections, it will be necessary to improve the process of inspector designation and granting of visas, perhaps including the initiation of a universally recognized IAEA passport. Routine inspections could also be used to collect environmental samples.[83]

Extension of safeguards

The Fourth Review Conference recognized that 'there are items of equipment and materials, including tritium, not identified in NPT Article III.2 which are relevant to the proliferation of nuclear weapons and therefore to the NPT as a whole' and called for 'early consultations among States to ensure that their supply and export controls are appropriately coordinated'.[84]

On behalf of the European Community (EC) the Netherlands proposed at the General Conference in September 1991 that in the light of Iraqi behaviour, safeguards should be strengthened by applying them to yellowcake (U_3O_8), which had been exempt since 1971.[85] While states with NPT safeguards agreements must report amounts of yellowcake which are imported or exported there are no verification provisions attached to this obligation and yellowcake is effectively subject to safeguards only when introduced into a declared conversion plant.[86] Iraq had amassed tonnes of yellowcake which, after appropriate conversion, would have provided substantial feed material to its calutron and centrifuge programmes.

Although it may not be among the first priorities of the IAEA, especially at a time when financial constraints are being strongly felt, it is recommended that studies on the feasibility of extending safeguards to cover such materials fully be continued and that means of obtaining the (not insubstantial) funds adequate for the necessary additional safeguards procedures be addressed. The discoveries in Iraq have amply demonstrated that the resources expended would provide returns in terms of added assurance and security.

Increasing transparency: increased availability of safeguards results

It has been noted within the IAEA that a somewhat ironic state of affairs exists whereby the annual safeguards implementation report (SIR) is classified and its information thus not accessible to the legislatures and informed public whose confidence it was designed to enhance.[87] The draft final document of the Fourth

[83] Fainberg (note 45), pp. 47–48; and Scheinman (note 43), pp. 22–23, 27.
[84] IAEA (note 27), p. 3.
[85] Hibbs (note 53), p. 11.
[86] OTA (note 31), p. 138.
[87] Müller, Fischer and Kötter (note 26), p. 87.

NPT Review Conference recommended that the IAEA 'improve upon the transparency of presentation of the results of its safeguards activities so that information on these results can be made available to the public in order to prevent possible misinformation and misunderstanding'.[88]

While a list of facilities under safeguards or containing safeguarded material is published in the IAEA Annual Report, increased transparency on the verification of and compliance with non-proliferation obligations, including the release of information contained in documents such as the SIR, which outlines both successes and problems with safeguards implementation, would help to increase confidence in the Agency's work.

Care must be taken, however, that the information released neither is of use to potential proliferators nor compromises legitimate commercial concerns, so a careful balance must be struck and the pros and cons of releasing particular information must be carefully weighed.[89] Here it must be acknowledged that there is some conflict between the interests of more effective safeguards and widespread confidence in their operation on the one hand and the potential for spreading information concerning technology which would increase the danger of proliferation on the other.

Originally, the concerns of the technically advanced NNWS that details of new processes and designs or performance, for example, would be of commercial value, and that their disclosure would place them at a commercial disadvantage *vis-à-vis* the NWS, led to the strict rules concerning publication of the details of safeguards results. The fact that it is very difficult to keep secrets within an organization the size of the IAEA makes it unlikely, however, that important industrial or commercial secrets would be made available to the IAEA in the first place.[90] If strong resistance to publishing documents such as the SIR persists it might be worthwhile considering beginning the process of increasing transparency by publishing appropriately sanitized versions.

Redefinition of safeguards terminology

Among the terms which require quantification for planning the implementation and evaluating the performance of safeguards, 'significant quantity' (SQ) receives continued attention. A significant quantity is defined as 'the approximate quantity of nuclear material in respect of which, taking into account any conversion process involved, the manufacturing of a nuclear explosive cannot be excluded'.[91] For direct-use material (i.e., that which would not require further enrichment or transmutation) an SQ is currently 8 kg of plutonium containing less than 80 per cent ^{238}Pu, 25 kg of ^{235}U contained in uranium enriched to 20 per cent or more, or 8 kg of ^{233}U.

[88] IAEA (note 27), p. 5.

[89] Scheinman, L., 'Safeguards: new threats and new expectations', *Disarmament*, vol. 15, no. 2 (1992), p. 70.

[90] Fischer and Szasz (note 8), pp. 31, 55, 83.

[91] IAEA (note 5), p. 26.

As the SQ definition directly affects the detection and inspection goals of the IAEA it is important that quantitative values correctly represent the potential dangers of diversion. The Director General stated at the February 1991 Board of Governors' meeting that the definition of an SQ 'has important implications for safeguards approaches. If this tenet were no longer to give adequate confidence, it should be re-examined'. He also stated that 'only the nuclear weapons states can completely address' this question. The USA has reportedly recommended a considerable reduction in the SQ for uranium—the 25 kg figure is based on a compromise contained in a 1968 UN study.[92]

The Director General has noted that if what is currently considered a 'significant quantity' is reduced, then 'the cost of the safeguards and the manpower needed for safeguards would increase very quickly as that figure declined'.[93] However, estimates of a Western official are that if the SQ for HEU were halved, the resulting increased inspections (of appropriate research reactors) would add only about 1–2 man-days per reactor per year of inspections.[94]

In general the amount of uranium or plutonium needed for a weapon is a function of many parameters, including fissile isotope ratio levels and the sophistication of the device itself. As computers and software capable of performing the hydrodynamic calculations needed to model the implosion shockwave created by conventional explosives to detonate a nuclear device are increasingly available, the possibility of sophisticated bomb designs requiring less and less fissile material must be taken into account.

The case for reformulating the definition of a significant quantity has been strengthened somewhat by a study by the Natural Resources Defense Council (NRDC),[95] which points out that, even for relatively unsophisticated devices, the amount of fissile material needed to create a significant nuclear yield is much less than has been commonly assumed. For example, the 1945 Fat Man bomb used 6.1 kg of weapon-grade plutonium to produce a 20-kt yield, but if only half this amount had been used and subjected to the same compression by the implosion mechanism the resulting bomb would still have produced the quite substantial yield of 1 kt. While about 3 kg of weapon-grade plutonium would therefore be needed for a 1-kt blast using this relatively 'low-tech' design, a 'high-tech' device could achieve the same explosive result with as little as 1 kg of weapon-grade plutonium—one-eighth of the current SQ definition. In addition, data presented in the NRDC report indicate that a 1-kt explosion could also be obtained using about 8 kg of HEU, even in the case of a

[92] Hibbs, M., 'Iraqi report to UN raises issue of adequacy of IAEA safeguards on HEU', *Nuclear Fuel*, vol. 16, no. 10 (13 May 1991), pp. 4–8. Also, for example, the representative of Japan's Permanent Mission to the IAEA has recommended that the definition of significant quantity be lowered 'to accommodate technical progress since 1970'. The EC has also had discussions about the strengthening of safeguards by redefining terms such as significant quantity. Usui, N., 'Japanese ambassador urges beefed-up IAEA NPT inspection', *Nucleonics Week*, vol. 32, no. 16 (18 Apr. 1991), p. 10; and Hibbs (note 53), p. 11.

[93] Hans Blix, IAEA Director interview (note 41), p. 5.

[94] He notes as well, however, that inspection sensitivity would have to double, as would the amount of certain sampling tests. Hibbs (note 92), pp. 4–8.

[95] Cochran, T. B. and Paine, C. E., 'The amount of plutonium and highly-enriched uranium needed for pure fission nuclear weapons', Nuclear Weapons Databook Working Paper, Natural Resources Defense Council, Washington, DC, 22 Aug. 1994.

'low-tech' device; if a 'high-tech' design could be employed then just over 2 kg would be needed.

While it remains open to reviewing the issue, the US Department of Energy has not confirmed the NRDC figures. The DOE has stated that a bomb can be made with 4–6 kg of plutonium, and in recent remarks an expert from the Lawrence Livermore National Laboratory said that a weapon can be made with 4 kg but 'whether you can or can't do it below 4 kg is classified'.[96]

In any case it appears that the time is ripe for a thorough re-examination of the definition of significant quantity and the possibility of quite dramatic changes in the definition should be considered. The NRDC study by Cochran and Paine discussed above recommends an eightfold reduction in the amounts of uranium and plutonium, which would be considered a significant quantity—3 kg of ^{235}U enriched to 20 per cent or more, 1 kg ^{233}U and 1 kg plutonium (containing less than 80% ^{238}Pu). Other seasoned observers, such as Richard Garwin, propose a somewhat less dramatic revision of the current IAEA definition[97] (at least down to 4 kg or perhaps less for plutonium, for example), but it is becoming generally agreed that the definition should be revised.

It could also be argued that the definition should depend on the enrichment of the uranium since the potential to turn 25 kg of 90 per cent enriched uranium into a weapon without further processing already exists, while 25 kg of 20 per cent enriched uranium is not nearly so threatening in terms of proliferation.

Assuming that funds would be available to handle the increased inspection burden it might also be advisable to reduce the time frame considered in the safeguards objective of 'timely detection of diversion of significant quantities of nuclear material'. The current definition of 'timely', 7–10 days for plutonium or HEU in metallic form, 1–3 months for plutonium in irradiated nuclear fuel and approximately one year for natural uranium or LEU, could be shortened, especially for the direct-use nuclear material including plutonium contained in spent nuclear fuel.[98]

Exemptions

As discussed in chapter 4, during the first inspection in Iraq 2.26 g of plutonium were found in a hot cell. This reprocessing did not constitute a safeguards violation because Iraq had made requests to exempt some material from safeguards from 1982 to 1988, including one fuel pin which had been irradiated in the IRT-5000 reactor. The fuel pin was then reprocessed in the three hot cells which had been provided by Italy. The NPT Model Safeguards Agreement allows such exemptions to allow for nuclear research.[99] Exemption for up to 1 kg of plutonium is allowed. This is a substantial quantity and may have to be

[96] Hart, K., 'NRDC seeks drastic reduction in IAEA nuclear threshold figure', *Nucleonics Week*, 25 Aug. 1994, p. 12.

[97] Quoted in Broad, W. J., 'Bombs need less plutonium now', *International Herald Tribune*, 22 Aug. 1994, p. 4.

[98] See, e.g., Goldblat (note 52), p. 7.

[99] NPT Model Safeguards Agreement (note 6), para. 37.

reduced, especially given that the material can be reprocessed without the further consent of the IAEA.[100]

Among other countries France reportedly wanted to require that before amounts of plutonium are exempted from safeguards the proposal first be submitted to the Board of Governors for approval, a step which could allow for increased control on this type of activity.[101]

New initiatives

Building on decisions in 1991 and 1992 on early provision and use of design information and the reporting of exports and imports of nuclear material, the IAEA has been evaluating measures in six specific areas to strengthen and improve the cost-effectiveness of the safeguards system through a two-year development programme to be completed in 1995 and named 'Programme 93+2'. The areas include a cost analysis of current safeguards implementation, an assessment of possible measures to cut costs, environmental techniques for application in safeguards, increased cooperation with State Systems of Accounting and Control (SSACs), improved analysis of data on nuclear activities of states and enhanced safeguards training. The areas recommended for scrutiny were put forward by SAGSI, and results are to be integrated into proposals to the Board of Governors by 1995.[102]

Further transparency will result from a trial programme of environmental monitoring including air, water and soil samples designed to ascertain the presence or level of certain nuclear activities. Suggestions have also been made for a separate environmental monitoring regime, the existence of which could allow for a reduction of the burden on routine safeguards measures currently in place. These types of measure would aid in providing warning of inconsistencies between declared and indicated nuclear programmes as well as a basis on which further, more thorough, verification means could be requested and carried out. Another measure under consideration would involve the systematic exchange of information on nuclear-related research and development activity (while at the same time allowing for adequate protection of proprietary information) striving towards a system of 'total programmatic transparency' for countries involved.[103]

Unilateral initiatives which are aiding in the increased transparency of nuclear activities include agreement by such countries as Australia, Japan and Sweden to cooperate in pilot projects on environmental monitoring and renewed openness of countries such as Iran to IAEA visits. Further, Canada

[100] Hibbs (note 30), p. 1.

[101] Hibbs, M. and MacLachlan, A., 'IAEA condemns Baghdad again as Iraq protests "double standard"', *Nucleonics Week*, vol. 32, no. 39 (26 Sep. 1991), p. 13.

[102] *IAEA Newsbriefs*, vol. 9, no. 1 (Feb./Mar. 1994), p. 3; and *IAEA Bulletin*, no. 1 (1994), p. 46. [The process of formalizing the implementation of new strengthening and efficiency measures was begun after the June 1995 session of the IAEA Governing Board. Details are published in a series of annexes to IAEA document GC(39)/17, 22 Aug. 1995, which became available as this book went to press.]

[103] Sheinman, L., 'Strengthened IAEA safeguards and special inspections', ed. Rauf (note 73), pp. 24–25.

offered in December 1993 to permit the IAEA 'effectively unlimited and unannounced access to declared nuclear facilities in order to perform activities over and above nuclear material accounting', and included an offer to assure access to other locations which the IAEA might identify.[104]

In addition, while still in the preliminary definitional stages, adoption of a new safeguards mechanism referred to as 'enhanced safeguards analysis' may serve to complement traditional verification measures in a significant way. Routine systematic reviews will be undertaken of information related to states' nuclear activities including design information, information from all the state's nuclear facilities and data obtained through normal inspection activity as well as data on the state's nuclear transactions. The plan is to couple this with information from analysis of water, air and soil samples to provide as complete a picture as possible of nuclear activities.[105]

Budgetary considerations

Doubtless many of the options discussed in this section would, if implemented, add to the Agency's operating costs. The Fourth NPT Review Conference requested that the IAEA 'continue to identify all resources needed for effective and efficient safeguards' and urged that these resources be provided 'through the important mechanism of continued assured regular budget financing' and welcomed efforts to 'find a lasting and equitable solution to the question of a safeguards financing formula'.[106] However, the IAEA has been forced to operate under a zero real growth budget since 1985. The 1995 budget appropriation was $211.6 million compared with the 1994 figure of $201.1 million. Safeguards were allotted a 4.6 per cent increase in 1993 to $62 million in order to cover new activities in Argentina, Brazil, North Korea and South Africa but taking account as well of a lessening of safeguard activities in EURATOM countries. The 1995 safeguards appropriations totalled $72.7 million[107] compared with $68.6 million in 1994.[108]

Bringing new materials such as yellowcake and tritium under safeguards, reducing the amount of fissile material which denotes a significant quantity and expanding full-scope safeguards would all place extra burdens on the safeguards budget. The financial problems have already led to missed opportunities to make safeguards and their procedures more effective overall and more cost-

[104] Coll, S., 'Nuclear inspectors check sites in Iran', *Washington Post,* 20 Nov. 1993, p. A13; and Sheinman, L., 'Strengthened IAEA safeguards and special inspections', ed. Rauf (note 73), p. 31.

[105] Rauf, T., 'Strengthened safeguards and non-proliferation', ed. Rauf (note 73), p. 17.

[106] IAEA (note 27), p. 3.

[107] It should be noted, however, that some safeguards activities are supported by member countries outside the regular budget including research and development and instrument costs as well as the service of experts on a cost-free basis. Extrabudgetary contributions in 1993 amounted to over $8.6 million. *The Annual Report for 1993* (note 12), p. 182; and Scheinman (note 43), p. 42.

[108] *The Annual Report for 1993* (note 12), p. 1; *PPNN Newsbrief,* no. 27 (3rd quarter 1994), p. 12 and no. 18 (summer 1992), p. 4.

effective in particular—leading one observer to note that 'the future will pay for the thrift of the present'.[109]

However, many of the options discussed in this chapter have the potential to bring about substantial cost reductions. Many of the improvements discussed are either cost-free to the IAEA or have the potential to produce a large increase in overall assurance with respect to nuclear activities at a very small price. In particular, prioritizing and streamlining inspections as discussed above could aid in the current budgetary crunch. One of the most important changes to the non-proliferation regime as a whole could come about as a result of information provided to the Agency which would form the basis upon which special inspections to undeclared sites would be made. While the national intelligence agencies which would in theory supply some of this information would cull it from that which is acquired at a cost of billions of dollars annually,[110] the only costs incurred for the Agency would be for the office in charge of receiving and assessing the information unless specific actions were required as a result.[111]

In addition, any changes which do occur to the safeguards system are likely to come about gradually and so a sharp rise in the budget in a short time should certainly not be seen as a likely possibility. It must also be taken into consideration, however, that any additional expenditure on safeguards will likely have to be matched by an equal increase in technical assistance in keeping with the wishes of the Group of 77.[112]

While acknowledging that there is a problem with the budget, especially with Argentina and Brazil[113] and with South Africa coming under comprehensive safeguards, the Director General has noted, however, that the financial problem is exacerbated by the simple fact that many countries simply do not pay their share of the budget until very late in the year.[114] This is something that should be amenable to quick and relatively painless agreement with the parties concerned provided the necessary political will can be mustered.

The Russian Federation has taken over the rights and obligations of the former USSR in the IAEA. In the former USSR safeguards were being applied voluntarily to only a few facilities. However, as the former republics accede to the NPT appropriate safeguarding of all of their facilities will have to be negotiated, further increasing the already straining safeguards burden. One sug-

[109] Fischer (note 1), p. 132.

[110] The US intelligence-gathering apparatus alone has been estimated to consume approximately $28 billion annually. While all of the information collected and analysed is certainly not related to proliferation, one of the three major tasks which have been defined for the CIA in the years to come involves the proliferation of weapons of mass destruction.

[111] Seneviratne, G., 'IAEA Governors defer decision on expanding safeguards powers', *Nucleonics Week*, vol. 32, no. 50 (12 Dec. 1991), p. 9.

[112] See, e.g., Fainberg (note 45), p. 54.

[113] The 1991 Argentine–Brazilian agreement alone (which establishes an inspection agency—the Argentine–Brazilian Agency for Accounting and Control of Nuclear Material, ABACC) is expected to involve substantial additional cost to the safeguards budget. The IAEA in cooperation with ABACC will apply safeguards to all nuclear material and facilities in Argentina and Brazil under the Quadripartite Agreement between the two countries, ABACC and the IAEA, which entered into force in Mar. 1994. Redick, J. R., 'Argentina-Brazil nuclear non-proliferation initiatives', *PPNN Issue Review*, no. 3 (Jan. 1993); and IAEA Press Release, PR 94/11 (8 Apr. 1994).

[114] Interview with Hans Blix (note 41), p. 6.

gestion to help deal with this problem would be the setting up of a system of transnational ownership and a safeguards system for the peaceful nuclear programmes in these countries similar to that of EURATOM.[115]

IV. Developments in the former USSR

While the basic physics and engineering knowledge associated with many aspects of the development of nuclear weapons is well known, and is taught throughout the world, outside expertise particular to weapon design could be particularly useful to a nascent nuclear weapon programme by enabling various dead ends to be avoided. By shortening the time and effort required access to such expertise would make a clandestine programme more likely to succeed before discovery and hence perhaps more likely to be instigated in the first place.[116]

There has arisen increasing concern that some of the experts on nuclear weapon design and materials production in the former USSR may sell their expertise. There are estimates that some 3000–5000 individuals involved in fissile material production reportedly have access to sensitive information, while about 100 000 reportedly have official nuclear security clearance.[117] Viktor N. Mikhailov, director of the nuclear military programme of the former Soviet Union, has said that about 100 000 people were employed in the Soviet nuclear military–industrial complex, that 10 000–15 000 nuclear scientists possess 'really secret' information and that about 200–3000 of these have 'information of paramount importance in sophisticated technologies'.[118]

Strict control of the nuclear defence sector has meant that such concerns were not a major worry until the breakup of the USSR. Now with nuclear experts reportedly in most of the newly independent states there is an ever-present risk that some may find their way to areas of the globe where their knowledge could create new problems for the non-proliferation regime. New initiatives to help this situation include the establishment by the USA, the EC and Japan of an International Science and Technology Centre in Russia with possible branches in other former republics. As noted by then Secretary of State James Baker the Centre would 'receive, review, generate and fund proposals for projects . . . help match projects with qualified scientists and individuals. Actual projects themselves could be carried out by top scientists throughout the new independent states'.[119] While it was anticipated that the first grants would be issued from the Centre by May 1992, by early 1994 the Centre had yet to be fully operational, but fortunately there was still no indication that scientists

[115] Simpson, J., 'Regional approaches offer non-proliferation benefits', *Atom*, Sep./Oct. 1993, p. 32.

[116] OTA (note 31), pp. 154–55.

[117] Hibbs, M., '"Vulnerable" Soviet nuclear experts could aid clandestine weapons aims', *Nuclear Fuel*, vol. 16, no. 22 (28 Oct. 1991), p. 4.

[118] Friedman, T., 'U.S. to offer plan to keep scientists at work in Russia', *New York Times*, 8 Feb. 1992, p. A1.

[119] Secretary of State James Baker quoted in Friedman, T. L., 'Ex-Soviet atom scientists ask Baker for West's help', *New York Times*, 15 Feb. 1992, p. A1.

from the former Soviet military research establishment had gone abroad. Initial delays were the result of disagreements on details of the plan by the sponsoring nations followed by additional domestic difficulties with the plan resulting from infighting between hard-line conservatives and Yeltsin loyalists.[120]

The Centre was opened in Moscow[121] on 3 March 1994.[122] Funding included $25 million in financial assistance made available under the Soviet Nuclear Threat Reduction Act (or 'Nunn–Lugar Act'). This legislation has allocated a total of $1.2 billion in US financial assistance from 1992–94 for the safe destruction, transportation and secure storage of nuclear weapons and to set up verifiable safeguards against their spread. The USA is assisting the dismantlement of nuclear weapons in the former USSR and safeguarding nuclear material through the Safe and Secure Dismantlement Program.[123]

The problem of the export of nuclear expertise should not be considered to be limited to the former Soviet Union. As has been pointed out, US nuclear weapon scientists are potentially much more aggressive than their ex-Soviet counterparts in marketing their skills. In addition a given US scientist will probably have been exposed to a broader range of information concerning nuclear weapons than those in the more compartmentalized ex-Soviet programme.[124] With the end of the South African nuclear programme there may be further dangers of experts looking to sell nuclear weapon expertise. It has been reported, for example, that a group of 16 disgruntled scientists who had been laid off from the South African nuclear programme would be willing to sell their expertise to any nation willing to pay. A gag order has been issued by the Supreme Court of the Transvaal in order to block any such action.[125]

Reports of the acquisition of actual nuclear weapons by states of proliferation concern are repeatedly found in the press reflecting uncertainty especially in the physical security of the nuclear weapons of the FSU. In May 1993, for example, it was reported in the German press, based on information from a former Iranian scientist who had defected to the USA, that Iran had acquired at least two nuclear warheads, one of which came from the former Soviet military. However, no hard evidence has yet been uncovered that such weapons have found themselves in the wrong hands.[126] It is essential that programmes initiated to assist in alleviating these problems be rapidly implemented. There have been delays in the US Government's implementation of the programme based on

[120] 'Russian science aid falls short', *Science*, vol. 261 (10 Sep. 1993), p. 380; and Tigner, B., 'Center aims to keep Russian scientists in friendly camp', *Defense News*, 28 Mar.–3 Apr. 1994, p. 12.

[121] In Oct. 1993 the USA pledged $10 million to establish an international science centre in Kiev, with Canada agreeing to a $2 million contribution and Sweden $1.5 million. Mann, P., 'U.S. wins accord on Kiev warheads', *Aviation Week & Space Technology*, 17 Jan. 1994, p. 23.

[122] Fact Sheet: Russia, *US Department of State Dispatch*, vol. 5, no. 23 (6 June 1994), p. 370.

[123] Lockwood, D., 'Nuclear arms control', *SIPRI Yearbook 1993: World Armaments and Disarmament* (Oxford University Press: Oxford, 1993), pp. 566–70; and *Proliferation and the Former Soviet Union*, Office of Technology Assessment, Congress of the United States (US Government Printing Office: Washington, DC, Sep. 1994), pp. 24–26.

[124] Bailey, K. C., *Strengthening Nuclear Nonproliferation* (Westview Press: Boulder, Colo., 1993), pp. 43–44.

[125] *PPNN Newsbrief*, no. 26 (2nd quarter 1994), p. 19.

[126] *PPNN Newsbrief*, no. 22 (2nd quarter 1993), p. 14.

Nunn–Lugar funds (referred to as the Cooperative Threat Reduction, CTR, programme), but earlier delays which resulted from problems in coming to agreement with recipient states have now generally been resolved.[127]

Recent positive developments include Ukraine agreeing to remove all nuclear warheads from its territory in compliance with the START treaties and to accede to the NPT as a NNWS, and the signing of the Treaty by Belarus and Kazakhstan. The new President of Ukraine has agreed to remove all nuclear weapons from the country but has advised that aid will be required to keep this promise.[128] Consolidation of the nuclear weapons of the FSU within Russia can now proceed to completion.

V. Conclusions: the future of safeguards

While the system of safeguards has been evolving and improving steadily—in the overall assessment of the IAEA with regard to its verification goals in 1982 these goals were fully achieved at only 47 per cent of safeguarded plants, while already by 1989 this figure had risen dramatically to 80 per cent[129]—recent events have indicated that renewed reassessment is necessary. As discussed above much needed change is now occurring in attempts to improve the overall safeguards regime, but more remains to be accomplished.

There had been reluctance within the IAEA to Secretariat proposals to reopen various elements of the safeguards provisions to changes because of fears on the part of those that support strict safeguards that changes which might occur could actually create a weaker system 'than that approved by a more compact and less politicized Board of Governors nearly twenty years ago'. In addition, the changes would have to be incorporated into the safeguards agreements already in existence, be they within the NPT or outside it. It may be possible to alleviate the somewhat daunting prospect of renegotiating the agreements, however, by introducing an additional protocol into agreements in their present form rather than renegotiating the existing agreements.[130]

Provided adequate political and financial commitments are forthcoming it should be possible for the IAEA to operate a more extensive and effective safeguards regime. Many of those tasked with carrying out the various aspects of present safeguards within the Agency are looking forward to the prospect of increased challenges and the attendant responsibility possible in the new international climate. None the less, as with all international institutions exercising wide-ranging powers, there exists the danger that some nations serve as a hindering force against useful reform. Even countries with strong non-proliferation credentials have resisted and continue in many instances to resist safeguards reforms that they may see as placing unwanted burdens on themselves.[131]

[127] *Proliferation and the Former Soviet Union* (note 123), p. 24.
[128] 'Ukraine upholds nuclear pledge', *International Herald Tribune,* 18 July 1994, p. 2.
[129] Fischer (note 1), p. 129.
[130] Fischer (note 1), p. 130.
[131] See discussions in Scheinman (note 43), pp. 28–29.

Iraqi nuclear activities did raise serious concerns about the system of safeguards in general and in particular the ability of the nuclear non-proliferation regime as a whole to detect even serious efforts in the direction of the acquisition of nuclear weapons. This has pointed to the need to examine current safeguards procedures to determine the extent to which they can be amended or reinterpreted so as to provide increased assurance.

Contrary to the view expressed in some quarters, however, the IAEA safeguards system as it existed at the time cannot be said to have seriously failed with respect to the nuclear programme in Iraq. The small quantities of plutonium which were produced, while constituting a theoretical violation, were, in terms of potential for near-term acquisition of significant quantities of fissile material, not serious. It could not have been expected that the uranium enrichment effort, while extensive and surprising, would have been uncovered through normal safeguards procedures. Those expecting that the existence of a substantial clandestine weapons effort would be uncovered, if not by the IAEA then by other verification or intelligence means, were of course very surprised and discomforted by the discoveries in Iraq, and renewed efforts are under way to ensure that similar surprises do not occur.

The issue of special inspections will be one of the most important in the coming years. Questions related to technologies and methods associated with the information-gathering prerequisite to such inspections are dealt with in chapter 7 on verification. A potential organizational structure within the IAEA to deal with acquired intelligence has been outlined by the Director General in a very broad sense and an office has been set up, but it is yet to be seen how such a structure will function effectively and efficiently in such a large organization with many differing interests and priorities.

The right to undertake special inspections themselves has been reaffirmed and this should be viewed as a very positive development. It remains to be seen how effectively the procedures will operate—how willing countries will be to provide information, how capable the IAEA will be in its analysis, and ultimately how well states under suspicion will react. North Korea has already provided an interesting test case and it is still unclear whether the country will live up to its promise to open itself up to this type of inspection, which is critical to understanding the history of their nuclear programme.

The analysis and use of the information available regarding suspect nuclear activity are very important. To avoid embarrassment, the IAEA would probably not wish to attempt a special inspection unless first, the evidence was overwhelming that illicit activity was actually taking place and, second, the activity could be confirmed by the inspection before, for example, it could be hidden. This would breed caution into the analysis of intelligence and other material collected. Conflicting with this, however, would be the fear of reacting too slowly to available information and having an advanced programme revealed by other circumstances—a situation which would also cause embarrassment.

Resolving and formalizing ways in which short-notice challenge inspections could be conducted might help in this regard and could also hinder efforts at concealment. In general, such inspection teams should include experts in all facets of nuclear weaponry and fissile material production where at all possible so that the most is gained from each inspection.

To allay suspicion concerning motives of the information sources on whose evidence an inspection is requested, all ways to corroborate the evidence which can be made public should be explored. This would include encouraging commercial satellite programmes, allowing as much open access to data as possible, further exploring the establishment of international or regional satellite monitoring agencies with verification of non-proliferation as a high priority, as well as keeping files of acquired images of suspect facilities in high-risk countries.

Recent proposals for creating a data base based on reporting of nuclear and nuclear-related exports should be further pursued. In conjunction with ensuring that new requirements on provision of design information on facilities are complied with, possible extension of safeguards and the new trend towards requiring full-scope safeguards as a condition of exports will contribute to an ever more complete picture of nuclear activity. Greater openness on the part of the IAEA concerning information on the implementation and effectiveness of safeguards would ensure that this clearer picture would be not only more widely scrutinized but also better understood and appreciated.

Prioritizing and streamlining safeguards could, if properly put into action, increase confidence as well as save money. Political obstacles may make some proposals, especially those targeting specific countries for increased scrutiny, difficult to bring to fruition, but concepts involving special inspections in lieu of many routine inspections could lead to a workable solution.

In order to prevent the flow of nuclear materials and equipment from the former Soviet republics, cooperation with the West in effective safeguards measures should be ensured. With respect to the danger of the export of nuclear knowledge, the establishment of International Science and Technology Centres should be further encouraged in the former Soviet republics and ways should be found as quickly as possible to have them operating in an efficient manner.

While further financial resources will clearly need to be sought to ensure the Agency's ability to carry out its increasing responsibilities, member states should be strongly encouraged to provide the Agency with their due financial contribution promptly.

Viktor N. Mikhailov, director of the nuclear weapon programme of the FSU, has forewarned that 'the number of countries that possess nuclear weapons will increase markedly over the next 10 years and the situation could become unpredictable'.[132] Increased effort must be expended now to ensure that this is not allowed to happen, in part through strengthened and more far-reaching safeguards which can help ensure that an adequate verification mechanism is in place to provide the required assurance. Another area which can help keep a lid on the speed at which nuclear technology is spreading, and the subject of chapter 6, is that of controlling nuclear exports.

[132] Friedman (note 118), p. A1.

6. Export controls: progress and problems

I. Introduction

While the threat of nuclear weapon proliferation may have receded from a political perspective since the NPT was opened for signature, from a technological perspective it may well be said to have increased as nuclear technology has become more widespread.[1] Particularly in the wake of events in Iraq this has put increased emphasis on controls on technology which may be important in nuclear weapon development. It should be noted, however, that export controls are only really useful to the extent that they can be successfully implemented, and they may often serve at best (although importantly) as a delaying tactic to prevent countries attempting to develop nuclear weapons from acquiring nuclear weapon-related technology until—hopefully—other methods can be found to dissuade the pursuit.[2] The new concern caused by the nuclear programme in Iraq has led to a substantial tightening of export controls on technology of use for nuclear weapon development and in their likely effectiveness as well.

Effective restrictions on exports of materials and equipment can play a direct role in limiting access to their use in potential nuclear weapon programmes. Monitoring of exports can also perhaps somewhat indirectly aid other monitoring activities since procurement patterns may indicate that a particular route towards some clandestine nuclear activity is being taken. Verification resources can then be concentrated on a particular area, looking for a particular type of activity—a centrifuge enrichment facility, for example.

Monitoring for signs of nuclear-related activity can help ensure that export controls are functioning as designed and indicate where improvements or increased vigilance may be necessary. As noted in the report of the seventh IAEA inspection in Iraq, after the destruction of equipment and tools related to its centrifuge enrichment effort Iraq 'will have difficulty in re-establishing the centrifuge project—provided that there is strict maintenance of export controls by the industrial nations backed up by regular monitoring by the IAEA of Iraq's nuclear industry'.[3] At the same time, it was recognized that without access to

[1] See, e.g., Goldblat, J., *The Non-Proliferation Treaty: How to Remove the Residual Threats*, UNIDIR Research Paper No. 13 (United Nations: New York, 1992), pp. 13–14.

[2] For a recent overview of multilateral export controls in general, and the various schools of thought on their goals and utility, see Anthony, I., De Geer, A., Kokoski, R. and Stock, T., 'Multilateral export control measures', *SIPRI Yearbook 1995: Armaments, Disarmament and International Security* (Oxford University Press: Oxford, 1995), pp. 605–41.

[3] Report on the seventh IAEA on-site inspection in Iraq under Security Council resolution 687 (1991) 11–22 October 1991, UN document S/23215, 14 Nov. 1991, p. 49.

the appropriate procurement and other documentation it could not be ruled out that an undisclosed centrifuge programme still existed.[4]

In many circumstances, however, export controls may not be able to have a substantial impact on a nuclear weapon programme. In the case of South Africa, for example, the programme used a sufficiently 'low-tech' approach that substantial reliance on outside help could be avoided—aid which trade sanctions in force at the time would have made particularly difficult in any case. The prototype bomb completed in 1977 was of the fairly primitive gun-barrel type design—the Director of Armscor has reportedly commented that a self-propelled howitzer that the company produced in 1992, for example, was much more difficult to engineer. Additionally, great efforts were taken to keep fabrication and storage sites from the prying eyes of intelligence collection agencies.[5]

With the realization of the poor state of the accounting and control system in the newly independent states of the former Soviet Union there is increased concern about the possibility of smuggling of fissile material. Export control regimes *per se* can do little to stop such activity. There is clearly a need for national vigilance, including increased security at the source as well as increased sharing of information about persons involved in smuggling activity in order to preclude the potential diversion of this material to persons or states which could use it to make nuclear weapons.

There are two main bodies which coordinate multilateral export controls on nuclear materials today—the Nuclear Exporters Committee, known as the Zangger Committee, and the Nuclear Supplier's Group (NSG), or London Club, as it is sometimes known. In the past few years there have been substantial revisions to the list of items under control as well as the addition of a regime to cover dual-use items. In addition a new universal reporting scheme on imports and exports of nuclear-related equipment has been implemented, albeit on a voluntary basis at the present time, which should make it possible to gain further insight into the trade patterns of the nations involved.

II. International restrictions on exports of nuclear materials and equipment

The Zangger Committee

The first important multilateral instrument of control for nuclear technology was put in place in 1974 by the Zangger Committee.[6] Article III of the NPT

[4] Report on the 7th inspection (note 3), p. 50.

[5] See, e.g., Smith, J. R., 'From dust to dust: history of S. Africa's bombs', *Washington Post*, 12 May 1993.

[6] At the end of 1994 the Zangger Committee consisted of 29 states: Australia, Austria, Belgium, Bulgaria, Canada, the Czech Republic, Denmark, Finland, France, Germany, Greece, Hungary, Ireland, Italy, Japan, Luxembourg, the Netherlands, Norway, Poland, Portugal, Romania, Russia, Slovakia, South Africa, Spain, Sweden, Switzerland, the United Kingdom and the United States. Anthony *et al.* (note 2), p. 598.

obliges that a party 'undertakes not to provide: (*a*) source or special fissionable material, or (*b*) equipment or material especially designed or prepared for the processing, use or production of special fissionable material, to any non-nuclear-weapon State for peaceful purposes, unless the source or special fissionable material shall be subject to [IAEA] safeguards'.[7] However, as the IAEA is only involved here in administering the safeguards in the importing state it is up to the exporters themselves to interpret and implement this article.[8]

In particular the ambiguity in the phrase 'equipment or material especially designed or prepared for the processing, use or production of special fissionable material' needed clarification. Over a period of several years in the early 1970s, under the chairmanship of Claude Zangger, a group of suppliers met to discuss these issues with the aim of reaching consensus on interpretation. In August 1974 they informed the Director General that they had agreed upon a 'trigger list' of categories of equipment or material which would, if exported to a NNWS not party to the NPT, trigger the application of IAEA safeguards on 'the source or special fissionable material produced, processed or used in the facility for which the item is supplied' and that this material 'shall not be diverted to nuclear weapons or other nuclear explosive devices'.[9] In addition it is required that the importing country provide satisfactory assurances, in the event of re-export to another NNWS not a party to the NPT, that safeguards would also be applied in the country receiving the re-export.[10]

Items on the original trigger list included nuclear reactors and specified equipment therefor, including pressure vessels, fuel-charging and -discharging machines, control rods, pressure tubes, zirconium tubes and primary coolant pumps. Also included were exports of deuterium and heavy water exceeding specific amounts, nuclear-grade graphite, reprocessing plants and equipment designed or prepared for them, fuel fabrication plants and also equipment (not including analytical instruments) designed or prepared for uranium isotope separation.[11] Periodic updates to the list have been made since it was first drawn up.[12]

[7] Treaty on the Non-Proliferation of Nuclear Weapons, Article III, para. 2. The text of the Treaty is reproduced in appendix A.

[8] For more details on this and the following see SIPRI, *Safeguards against Nuclear Proliferation* (Almqvist & Wiksell: Stockholm, 1975), pp. 17–23; Fischer, D. and Szasz, P., ed. J. Goldblat, SIPRI, *Safeguarding the Atom: A Critical Appraisal* (Taylor & Francis: London, 1985), pp. 101–102; and OECD, *The Regulation of Nuclear Trade: Non-Proliferation–Supply–Safety, Vol. 1, International Aspects*, Nuclear Regulation Series (OECD Nuclear Energy Agency: Paris, 1988).

[9] IAEA document INFCIRC/209, 3 Sep. 1974, Memorandum B, paras 3(a), and 3(b). The text is also reproduced in OECD (note 8), pp. 97–98.

[10] INFCIRC/209, Memorandum B (note 9), para. 5.

[11] INFCIRC/209, Memorandum B (note 9), para. 2.

[12] Clarifications have been made in IAEA documents INFCIRC/209/Mods. 1, 2, 3 and 4 which were then consolidated in INFCIRC/209/Rev.1. The latest clarification—concerning plants for the production of heavy water, deuterium and deuterium compounds and equipment especially designed and prepared therefor—was made in early 1992 and appears in IAEA document INFCIRC/209/Rev.1/Mod.1, May 1992.

The Nuclear Suppliers Group

After initial consultations in 1974 between the UK, the USA and the USSR on the desirability of further coordinating export policy, and with increased concern over the transfer of nuclear technology resulting from the explosion of a nuclear device by India, the Nuclear Suppliers Group met in 1975–78. The countries initially involved were Canada, France, the FRG, Japan, the UK, the USA and the USSR. A major reason for the group's creation was the inclusion of France, a major supplier and at the time not a party to the NPT and thus not a participant in the Zangger Committee.[13]

An outline agreement had already been reached by 1976, at which time eight other states—Belgium, Czechoslovakia, the German Democratic Republic, Italy, the Netherlands, Poland, Sweden and Switzerland—were also invited to participate in further consultations. In early 1978, using a procedure similar to that adopted by the Zangger Committee, all the countries involved sent letters to the Director General of the IAEA to inform that they would abide by the principles which had been agreed in 1977. The Guidelines for the Export of Nuclear Material, Equipment or Technology (the so-called London Guidelines for Nuclear Transfers) are contained in IAEA document INFCIRC/254.[14] These London Guidelines, which only apply to exports to non-nuclear weapon states, placed more stringent requirements[15] on nuclear exports than the Zangger Committee understandings and included requirements for assurances of non-explosive use on the part of recipients, safeguards, as well as the control of re-transfer.

The Zangger trigger list in the form it had taken by the end of 1978 was incorporated to Annex A, the trigger list of the London Guidelines, which also includes common criteria for technology transfers under the Guidelines.

The three basic principles of the Guidelines are: (*a*) that transfer of items on the trigger list should be authorized only after formal assurances from the government of the recipients, which explicitly excludes uses which would result in a nuclear explosive device; (*b*) materials and facilities appearing on the trigger list should be 'placed under effective physical protection to prevent unauthorized use and handling'; and (*c*) trigger list items should only be transferred when covered by appropriate IAEA safeguards.[16] The first and third of these principles are also part of the Zangger Committee agreements.

The Guidelines stipulate that these three requirements should also apply to facilities for reprocessing, enrichment or heavy-water production which utilize technology 'directly transferred from the supplier or derived from transferred

[13] Carnahan, B. M., 'Export law and policy of the emerging nuclear suppliers: a basis for cautious optimism', *Eye on Supply*, no. 5 (fall 1991), p. 67.

[14] Guidelines for the Export of Nuclear Material, Equipment and Technology, IAEA document INFCIRC/254, Feb. 1978. The text is also reproduced in OECD (note 8), p. 79. Timerbaev, R., 'A major milestone in controlling nuclear exports', *Eye on Supply*, no. 6 (spring 1992), p. 58.

[15] Strulak, T., 'The Nuclear Suppliers Group', *The Nonproliferation Review*, fall 1993, p. 2.

[16] These principles appeared originally in 1977. The most recent (amended) version of the London Guidelines for Nuclear Transfers was published in IAEA document INFCIRC/254/Rev. 1/Part 1/Mod. 3, Nov. 1994. See paras 2, 3 and 4. The text of this document is reproduced in appendix C.

facilities, or major critical components thereof'. In addition, the transfer of any such facilities, major critical components thereof, or related technology requires that IAEA safeguards also apply to any facilities of the same type which may also be constructed and that a safeguards agreement allow the IAEA to apply safeguards to facilities identified as using transferred technology.[17]

The Guidelines include other important stipulations. Suppliers are urged to exercise restraint in transferring sensitive facilities, technology and weapon-usable materials.[18] This has generally been interpreted to mean *no* transfer of such sensitive items, the single exception to this rule being the sale of a heavy water plant by a Swiss firm to Argentina.[19]

A supplier nation must also be informed if an enrichment facility or technology therefor is to be operated in such a manner as to produce uranium enriched to greater than 20 per cent ^{235}U; this also applies to facilities based on such supplied technology.[20]

There is also a prior consent clause calling on supplier and recipient to agree on arrangements for reprocessing, storage, alteration, use, transfer or re-transfer of weapon-usable material which has either been transferred or derived from transferred facilities. It should be noted here, however, that this is not a firm commitment—it is only stated that suppliers 'should endeavour to include such provisions whenever appropriate and practicable'.[21] In addition, if transferred trigger list items or items derived from transferred facilities or with the help of such equipment or technology are re-transferred, the same assurances must be given by the recipient as were required for the original transfer.[22]

Also included were measures to improve the effectiveness and adequacy of safeguards and agreement on consultations in the case of violations in order to give an appropriate response. Unanimous consent is required if any of the Guidelines are to be changed. An important omission in the Guidelines was the absence of the stipulation of full-scope safeguards. While full-scope safeguards had been recommended by the UK and the USSR in a joint proposal, objections by France, the FRG and Japan foreclosed the adoption of such an agreement.[23]

It is also important to take note of the fact that the Guidelines are implemented through national mechanisms of legislation and enforcement leaving open the possibility of differences in interpretation and application. Provision for consultations to minimize such effects was included in the Guidelines but in fact, other than isolated bilateral consultations, the NSG did not meet again until 1991 by which time the Zangger list had been systematically updated so that it had become more detailed that the NSG list.[24]

[17] The London Guidelines (note 16), para. 6.
[18] The London Guidelines (note 16), para. 7.
[19] Goldblat (note 1), p. 14; and Timerbaev (note 14), pp. 58–59.
[20] The London Guidelines (note 16), para. 8.
[21] The London Guidelines (note 16), para. 9.
[22] The London Guidelines (note 16), para. 10.
[23] Timerbaev (note 14), p. 59.
[24] Strulak (note 15), p. 3.

Newer initiatives

While the NSG had always demonstrated an ability to transcend most of the difficulties associated with the East–West divide, the conclusion of the cold war and the resulting decreased tensions, together with the new focus on proliferation, especially as a regional concern, produced an environment which was much more conducive to further agreement within the group. At the same time concern had grown that many countries were evading export controls by obtaining dual-use technology using methods that included concealing the actual end-use of equipment, transhipment of materials through third countries and exploiting the existing and often diverse national dual-use export regulations. These factors, together with the uncovering of the clandestine Iraqi nuclear programme and the realization that many of the NSG countries had exported much of the technology and equipment, nuclear and otherwise, which had been used,[25] led the (then) 26 members of the Nuclear Suppliers Group to meet for the first time since 1978 in the Netherlands 5–7 March 1991.

Support was expressed by several countries, including Germany and the USA, to require full-scope safeguards as a prerequisite for supply of nuclear equipment (see also chapter 5) but this opinion was still not expressed by all states. This informal meeting came to the consensus that, while not expressly controlled by the group, dual-use technology controls should be addressed because of 'steady revelations over the last two or three years of misuse of dual-use technology in nuclear weapons programmes'.[26] A working group was set up to study this issue. New nuclear suppliers, including Argentina, Brazil and China, were also given an open invitation to adhere to the Guidelines.

At the follow-up meeting in Warsaw in April 1992 the group[27] (enlarged to 27 members with the joining of Austria in 1991, and with Ukraine and the European Community also present with observer status[28]) agreed on three important initiatives. The first would make acceptance of comprehensive safeguards mandatory for countries receiving any new significant nuclear exports. The second established specific guidelines on the export of a wide variety of dual-use technology items; these were laid out in the 1992 Guidelines for Transfers of Nuclear-related Dual-Use Equipment, Material and Related Technology (INFCIRC/254/Rev.1/Part 2). Third, amendments to the 1977 trigger list were made.

Such rapid agreement was possible to a great extent as a result of the increasing irrelevance of Co-ordinating Committee on Multilateral Export Controls

[25] Simpson, J. and Howlet, D., 'The NPT renewal conference: stumbling toward 1995', *International Security*, vol. 19, no. 1 (summer 1994), p. 48; and Strulak (note 15), pp. 4–5.

[26] Hibbs, M., 'London Suppliers Club forms working group on dual-use', *Nucleonics Week*, vol 32, no. 11 (14 Mar. 1991), p. 4.

[27] Membership at the end of 1994 is almost the same as that of the Zangger Committee except that Argentina and New Zealand, while *not* Zangger Committee members, are members of the NSG. Anthony *et al.* (note 2), p. 598.

[28] Timerbaev (note 14), pp. 60, 65.

(COCOM) controls as well as to the realization of the impact this could have on proliferation efforts.[29]

The updated trigger list

Dealing first with the third of these initiatives, the all-important trigger list to which the NSG Guidelines refer has been revised and is much more specific in several areas.[30] Regarding fuel reprocessing plants and equipment especially designed or prepared for them, where the earlier list mentions only fuel chopping machines and critically safe tanks the new list not only expands upon these items but also includes solvent extractors and solvent extraction equipment, chemical holding or storage vessels, plutonium nitrate to oxide conversion systems and plutonium oxide to metal production systems.[31]

The new trigger list is much more detailed in particular with respect to specific components useful for isotope separation for uranium enrichment. Whereas the earlier list had simply mentioned equipment of relevance in the centrifuge method of enrichment, the new list contains highly specific enumeration of rotating and static components in addition to specially designed auxiliary equipment such as feed and tails withdrawal systems and frequency changers.[32]

Similarly, where the older list simply mentions gaseous diffusion barriers and gaseous diffuser housings, the new list is more specific on these two types of equipment and also includes compressors, gas blowers, rotary shaft seals, heat exchangers for cooling UF_6 as well as details on auxiliary equipment for use in gaseous diffusion enrichment.[33] Systems, equipment and components for use in laser-based enrichment and aerodynamic enrichment are also covered in detail as well as those for chemical exchange and ion exchange and plasma enrichment.[34] The new list is also much more specific regarding plants or equipment designed for the production of heavy water.

The type of equipment necessary to construct the type of electromagnetic isotope separation units,[35] which Iraq was on the verge of employing to separate large quantities of uranium, is also included.

[29] Burrus, C. and Cohen, E., 'Enhancing the effectiveness of nonproliferation export controls', report prepared for Office of Export Controls and International Safeguards, Department of Energy (USA), Science Applications International Corporation, 4 Mar. 1993, p. 2.

[30] Some of the changes discussed below, including detailed mention of laser and aerodynamic enrichment technology, were not part of the 1992 amendments but do appear as part of the most recently amended trigger list in IAEA document INFCIRC/254/Rev. 1/Part 1/Mod 2, Apr. 1994, Annex B. The text is reproduced in appendix C.

[31] Amended trigger list (note 30), para. 3.

[32] Amended trigger list (note 30), paras 5.1 and 5.2.

[33] Amended trigger list (note 30), paras 5.3 and 5.4.

[34] Amended trigger list (note 30), paras 5.5–5.9.

[35] It is interesting to note that a 1982 report prepared by the DOE and Los Alamos National Laboratory, while identifying 20 countries conducting R&D in EMIS (not necessarily for uranium isotope separation, however), some of which had relevance from a proliferation standpoint, did not include Iraq in the list. Hibbs, M., 'IAEA names some manufacturers of equipment found in Iraq', *Nucleonics Week*, vol. 32, no. 50 (12 Dec. 1991), p. 7.

Control of dual-use items

Until the Warsaw meeting, one of the important gaps in the non-proliferation regime involved dual-use items. Problems in gaining cooperation among suppliers are exacerbated since the number of countries able to supply such equipment is large and suppliers of dual-use items are not normally thought of as nuclear suppliers. According to the US State Department the most difficult part of the national export system to administer is the control of dual-use items. Approximately 12 000 Commerce licence applications are reviewed each year with about 300 of these referred to the Subgroup on Nuclear Export Control for review. Of this latter number about two-thirds are approved, the rest of the requests being either withdrawn or denied. With the easing of COCOM controls, new problems were added to the non-proliferation regime in the area of dual-use items; in particular this list supplied the legal basis for many countries to control many dual-use items such as computers.[36]

The USA through the Nuclear Non-Proliferation Act of 1978 and several other countries as well have placed controls on the export of dual-use items which could be of potential use in a nuclear explosives programme.[37] It was, however, a major turning point in international control when the Nuclear Suppliers Group agreed in Warsaw in March–April 1992 on the Guidelines for Transfers of Nuclear-Related Dual-Use Equipment, Material and Related Technology—the so-called Warsaw Guidelines.[38]

With the stated objective of averting the proliferation of nuclear weapons the Group committed itself to the basic principle of refraining from transferring equipment, material or related technology as identified in an attached annex either

– for use in a non-nuclear weapon state in a nuclear explosive or an unsafeguarded nuclear fuel cycle activity, or
– in general, when there is an unacceptable risk of diversion to such an activity, or when the transfers are contrary to the objective of averting the proliferation of nuclear weapons.[39]

While the Guidelines are to be implemented in accordance with national legislation and international commitments, for any prospective transfers of

[36] 'Outlook on Nuclear Nonproliferation', special report in *Nuclear Fuel*, vol. 16, no. 2 (21 Jan. 1991), p. 3.

[37] With some exceptions, national export legislation is not covered here since a thorough exposition and analysis would require a volume in itself. To cite just one example, in the USA no less than 5 different government agencies administer nuclear export controls involving 5 distinct control regimes which act under the authority of 4 separate statutes. This is obviously the cause of some confusion for suppliers as more than one agency may have jurisdiction and licencing authority over a single export. This does, however, carry the advantage of providing checks and balances and, while certainly not perfect, the control system has usually proven effective. See Crocker, T. E., 'Basic lessons of the nuclear nonproliferation export control system for the former Soviet Union', *Eye on Supply*, no. 8 (winter 1993), pp. 82–83.

[38] Guidelines for Transfers of Nuclear-Related Dual-Use Equipment, Material and Related Technology (the Warsaw Guidelines), IAEA document INFCIRC/254/Rev.1/Part 2, July 1992. See appendix C for the complete text of the Guidelines and the accompanying annex.

[39] The Warsaw Guidelines (note 38), para 2.

items listed in the Guidelines' annex, procedures—including enforcement measures should violations occur—are to be established. In practice, however, differences in the legal systems of the countries involved may make it difficult to adopt standardized enforcement measures.[40]

Several factors are listed which are to be taken into account when considering whether to carry out such transfers. These include (*a*) whether the state is a party to the NPT, Treaty of Tlatelolco or similar nuclear non-proliferation agreement with an agreement on IAEA safeguards on all peaceful nuclear activities; (*b*) if the state is not a party to any such international agreement, whether facilities associated with nuclear fuel cycle activity are not or will not be subject to safeguards; (*c*) whether items are appropriate to the stated end-use and also whether this stated end-use is considered appropriate for the end-user; (*d*) whether the item is to be used in a reprocessing or enrichment facility; and (*e*) demonstrated support for nuclear non-proliferation by the recipient and compliance with existing obligations in this area. Also to be considered are the previous activities of the recipient, in particular: (*f*) whether illegal or clandestine procurement activities have been engaged in; and (*g*) whether a transfer has not been authorized or whether any authorized transfer has been diverted for purposes inconsistent with the Guidelines. It should be noted, however, that these conditions are not strictly required. While they approach making full-scope safeguards a condition of supply, the final decision is left to the supplier.

Transfers are also to be conditional on specifications from the recipient regarding the end-uses and end-use locations as well as assurance that neither transferred items nor their replicas will be used in any nuclear explosive activity or unsafeguarded nuclear fuel-cycle activity. For transfers to states not adhering to the Guidelines, assurances must also be given that supplier consent will be secured before any transferred items or replicas are re-transferred.

Computers and several other items which are currently controlled by the USA, for example, are not on the new list, but on the other hand 12 items on the Nuclear Suppliers List are not currently subject to controls in the USA and will have to be added to the Nuclear Referral List. (It should, however, be noted that high-performance computers are not required in order to design first-generation fission weapons and so strict export controls on them would be of minimal importance especially compared to technology useful for nuclear materials production.[41]) Overall, for example, the US State Department called the agreement 'the most important export control initiative of recent years' and stated that it would 'fill a crucial gap in existing controls and will greatly assist in our efforts to halt the spread of nuclear weapons'.[42]

[40] Müller, H., 'Reform of the system of nuclear export controls', eds H. Müller and L. A. Dunn, *Nuclear Export Controls and Supply Side Restraints: Options for Reform*, PPNN Study four, Mountbatten Centre for International Studies, Southampton, Oct. 1993, p. 12.

[41] See, e.g., Office of Technology Assessment, *Technologies Underlying Weapons of Mass Destruction*, OTA-BP-ISC-115 (US Government Printing Office: Washington, DC, Dec. 1993), p. 5.

[42] Suppliers agree on dual-use controls, full-scope safeguards export policy', *Nuclear Fuel*, vol. 17, no. 8 (13 Apr. 1992), p. 4; and Knapik, M., 'Nuclear suppliers reach agreement on control of dual use items', *Nucleonics Week*, vol. 33, no. 15 (9 Apr. 1992), p. 1.

The list of dual-use equipment is made up of eight main categories:[43]

1. Industrial equipment (e.g., spin-forming or flow-forming equipment, and vacuum induction furnaces).
2. Materials (e.g. Beryllium, high strength aluminium and maraging steel).
3. Uranium isotope separation equipment and components (e.g., rotor and bellows equipment, filament winding machines, superconducting solenoidal electromagnets, high-voltage direct current power supplies, electromagnetic isotope separators and specified lasers, laser amplifiers and oscillators).
4. Heavy water production plant-related equipment (e.g., hydrogen-cryogenic distillation columns).
5. Implosion systems development equipment (e.g., flash X-ray equipment, specialized instruments for hydrodynamic experiments).
6. Explosives and related equipment (e.g., detonators and multipoint initiation systems).
7. Nuclear testing equipment and components (e.g., high-speed pulse generators).
8. Other (e.g., neutron generator systems, tritium, tritium compounds and mixtures).

While cooperation between the Zangger Committee and the NSG has remained informal, given the almost identical membership of the two organizations the necessity of keeping two separate groups has been raised. While this issue has in fact been discussed, agreement has been reached that for some time to come the organizations will remain separate largely because of the desirability of giving the option to those outside the control regimes to join either organization.

While there is no formal cooperation between the NSG and the Missile Technology Control Regime (MTCR) or the Australia Group there are similarities in the organizational and procedural set-ups. For example, as with the MTCR a Point-of-Contact responsible for information exchanges between members, meeting organization, consultation coordination and record keeping has been established for the administration of the dual-use nuclear export control regime.[44]

Full-scope safeguards

One of the most serious limitations of international safeguards has been in the failure of all NNWS to accept comprehensive control of their nuclear activities.[45] NNWS which are NPT states parties are required to subject all nuclear activities to safeguards, whereas those that are not states parties have in general enjoyed the luxury of being required to accept safeguards only on specific

[43] Annex to the Warsaw Guidelines, List of Nuclear-Related Dual-Use Equipment, Materials and Related Technology, IAEA document INFCIRC/254/Rev.1/Part 2, July 1992, reproduced in appendix C.
[44] Strulak (note 15), p. 8.
[45] Fischer and Szasz (note 8), p. xi.

individual imports. Recently, in large measure because of discoveries in Iraq, changes have occurred which are helping to ameliorate this problem. In particular, more countries are now requiring full-scope safeguards as a condition for exports to NNWS.

At the Fourth Review Conference of the NPT the NNWS which had not already done so were urged 'to accept IAEA safeguards on all their peaceful nuclear activities, both current and future and to verify that commitment'. In addition nuclear supplier states were urged 'to require as a necessary condition for the transfer of relevant nuclear supplies to non-nuclear-weapon States under new supply arrangements, such a commitment and the acceptance of such safeguards'.[46] In the Nuclear Non-Proliferation Act of 1978 the USA had already pledged to restrict nuclear exports to countries accepting full-scope safeguards,[47] a policy which was also adopted as well by Canada in 1976, Australia and Sweden in 1977, Poland and Czechoslovakia in 1978, and Japan in 1989.[48]

An important step was taken more recently when Germany announced a policy of application of full-scope safeguards as a condition of nuclear exports at the Fourth NPT Review Conference. France announced its adherence to this policy in October 1991—the French change in policy was apparently at least partly because of the failure of the export controls in place to prevent the large-scale Iraqi nuclear programme. The same full-scope policy was then also accepted by Belgium, Switzerland and the UK and, interestingly, at about the same time the Ministry of Atomic Power and Industry in the (then) USSR was first able to agree on the full-scope provision only in principle since it lacked an executive organ to implement the policy. By March 1992, however, President Yeltsin had announced that the newly created Russian Federation had accepted the provision.[49]

Capping the flurry of unilateral initiatives of the previous year and a half was agreement at the March 1992 Warsaw meeting on full-scope safeguards as a condition of export of nuclear supplies. The Nuclear Suppliers Group agreed that 'the transfer of nuclear facilities, equipment, components, material and technology as referred to in the export trigger list of the Guidelines for Nuclear Transfers (see INFCIRC/254), should not be authorised to a non-nuclear weapon State unless that State has brought into force an agreement with the IAEA requiring the application of safeguards on all source and special fissionable material in its current and future peaceful nuclear activities'.[50]

[46] IAEA document GC (XXXIV)/INF/291, 19 Sep. 1990, p. 13.

[47] The Symington Amendment had already been passed in 1976. It restricted economic and military assistance to any country which either exported or imported reprocessing or enrichment equipment, materials or technology unless full-scope safeguards were brought into force. See, e.g., Beckman, R. L., *Nuclear Non-Proliferation: Congress and the Control of Peaceful Nuclear Activities* (Westview Press: Boulder, Colo., 1985), pp. 242–44.

[48] Timerbaev (note 14), p. 61; and Strulak (note 15), p. 4.

[49] Hibbs, M., 'USSR Foreign Ministry denies full-scope safeguards decision', *Nucleonics Week*, vol. 32, no. 46 (14 Nov. 1991), p. 11; Hibbs, M. and MacLachlan, A., 'More countries agree to full-scope safeguards as condition for export', *Nuclear Fuel*, vol. 16, no. 22 (28 Oct. 1991), p. 12; and Pilarski, L., 'Swiss Government says it will require full-scope safeguards', *Nucleonics Week*, vol. 32, no. 45 (7 Nov. 1991), p. 11; and Timerbaev (note 14), p. 61.

[50] IAEA document INFCIRC/405, May 1992, Attachment, p. 1.

However, the policy was not considered applicable to existing agreements and contracts existing at the time. It was also agreed that transfers to states without full-scope safeguards can be authorized in exceptional cases when they are felt to be necessary for the safe operation of existing facilities to which safeguards are applied.

Attention is focused ever more on the emerging nuclear suppliers and those not yet members of the Nuclear Suppliers' Group. They could hamper the effectiveness of the nuclear export control regimes now in place as well as the non-proliferation regime as a whole. Although China has engaged in serious dialogue with the NSG it is unlikely to join either the NSG or the Zangger Committee in the near term. China remains the major source of nuclear supplies still not requiring stringent safeguards, but it holds to the belief that the NSG is discriminatory and that the controls act as impediments to the transfer of technology necessary for the energy programmes of developing countries.[51] Other suppliers, including Brazil, India and South Africa as well as most of the former Soviet republics, should all be encouraged to join the NSG. Particular efforts have been made to attract the former Soviet republics into the NSG, but problems such as differences in views on the NSG between the nuclear sector and politicians and absence of adequate legislation or an effective system for controlling nuclear trade have stood in the way.[52] It is important that further efforts are undertaken to remedy this situation.

Another important issue facing the international nuclear export control regime is how to deal with countries which through various and sundry ingenious methods manage to acquire technology which may be used for non-peaceful nuclear purposes. Here the newly established Universal Reporting scheme (see chapter 5) if utilized to its full potential, as well as increased inter-governmental exchange of sensitive information concerning such activity,[53] could help to increase transparency in the area of nuclear-related trade and uncover such activity.

III. Current prospects and concerns

Developments in the wake of the Iraqi programme

As discussed above, in the wake of the Persian Gulf War and revelations concerning the nuclear programme in Iraq steps have been taken to broaden and strengthen export controls. Within a short while of its being uncovered the unexpected nature of the Iraqi nuclear programme and the technological approaches used had a large direct impact on improvements to export regulations. The improvements to the NSG trigger list and the items listed in the Guidelines for Transfers of Nuclear-Related Dual-Use Equipment included

[51] Hu, Weixing, 'China's nuclear export controls: policy and regulations', *Nonproliferation Review*, winter 1994, pp. 5–6; and Hibbs, M., 'Moscow says it will now apply full-scope safeguards on exports', *Nuclear Fuel*, 12 Oct. 1992, p. 4.

[52] Strulak (note 15), p. 7.

[53] Strulak (note 15), pp. 9, 10.

detailed descriptions of many of the technological methods that had been explored by Iraq, particularly in the area of centrifuge technology and EMIS. While developed mostly indigenously, Iraq's EMIS programme—given its unexpected use—indicated the desirability of controlling this technology in order to make it more difficult to deploy it for uranium enrichment purposes. Its inclusion on the NSG list of dual-use items represented the first time that this technology has appeared on any such list of guidelines.[54] The fact that the centrifuge and several other methods were being developed as well indicated the need for the overall re-evaluation of export controls. These have included detailed amendments to the NSG trigger list as well as inclusions on the dual-use list.

Concerning the EMIS method in particular, the technology needed to construct calutrons of the type used by the USA at the Oak Ridge National Laboratory was declassified in the 1950s. The equipment needed includes large amounts of copper or silver cable, industrial power supplies, large magnets, vacuum chambers, collectors, high capability insulators and ion sources.[55] Existing controls would have been incapable of affecting the programme in Iraq even if its existence were known and this prompted calls to improve this situation with respect to specific components.

As described in chapter 2, the calutron method relies on the acceleration by electromagnetic fields of ionized beams of particles which, by virtue of the slightly different masses of different isotopes, follow slightly different curved paths. In order that the different isotopes reach their appropriate collectors it is necessary to maintain a precisely defined beam current. Only about 30 companies in the USA, for example, are capable of manufacturing the appropriate power supplies and so it may be feasible to control their export for clandestine weapon activity.[56] Electrical generators worth $1.2 million rated at 40 000–45 000 kv and 5 amperes, which were ostensibly for use in induction welding but now believed to have been power supplies for calutrons, were purchased from the USA by Iraq in the late 1980s.[57]

At the time of the discoveries recommendations were made to control this type of technology and it was also realized that controls on ion sources which create charged uranium atoms that are then accelerated to separate the different isotopes could be beneficial.[58] Consistent with the experience of the IAEA in countries other than Iraq, inspectors were told by the Iraqis that 'the only real obstacle remaining in the development of an efficient [calutron] system was an

[54] Müller (note 40), p. 8.

[55] Hibbs, M. and Seneviratne, G., 'US believes Iraq has built magnetic isotope enrichment plant', *Nucleonics Week*, vol. 32, no. 25 (20 June 1991), p. 2; Hibbs, M., '1982 Report said 20 countries were pursuing EMIS research', *Nucleonics Week*, vol. 32, no. 30 (25 July, 1991), p. 12; and Hibbs, M., 'Controls on EMIS equipment on agenda of NSG meeting', *Nucleonics Week*, vol. 32, no. 41 (10 Oct. 1991), p. 11.

[56] Hibbs, M., 'Iraqi purchase of power supplies may have aided enrichment effort', *Nucleonics Week*, vol. 32, no. 26 (27 June 1991), p. 11.

[57] Hibbs and Seneviratne (note 55), p. 2.

[58] Hibbs (note 56), p. 11.

improved ion source'.[59] The new NSG trigger list includes EMIS separation and equipment and components related to them, including ion sources, collectors, vacuum housings, large magnet pole pieces and power supplies.[60]

In addition, the list of items covered under the Guidelines for Transfers of Nuclear-Related Dual-Use Equipment included the electromagnetic isotope separation process. In particular, high-voltage power supplies of the type which could be useful for operating such equipment, as well as EMIS separators themselves which are capable of providing a total ion beam current of 50 milliamperes (mA) or greater, are controlled. Regarding the latter restriction it should be noted that less than 3 grams of HEU can be obtained per year from a single 50-mA ion source from natural uranium feed. Ion sources (at least as part of molecular beam mass spectrometers) have also been included along with vacuum pumps with particular characteristics.[61]

The extension of export controls for critical elements of new enrichment technologies is very important. A US Government report stated in 1988 that while 'equipment for economic production of LEU or HEU is readily distinguishable from that needed for most other applications . . . it could be difficult to detect and hence control the export of equipment suitable for AVLIS smaller scale experimentation'.[62] Laser enrichment technology was addressed for the first time[63] in the NSG guidelines on dual-use items, which included a detailed list[64] of specific lasers, laser amplifiers and oscillators. They are also covered in detail in the most recent NSG trigger list of April 1994.[65] It is important that new developments in this and other advanced technologies are followed closely so that with the advent of newer approaches employing novel but perhaps somewhat less sophisticated technology, such as the CRISLA process, the guidelines can be further refined and suitably updated.

Former WTO states and former Soviet republics

There are fears regarding the new democracies of Eastern Europe, most of whom were dependent heavily on the former Soviet Union for nuclear technology and hence may not have sufficient experience in preventing the export of sensitive nuclear-related exports.[66] With respect to former Soviet republics concerns range from the export of nuclear knowledge to the export of relevant materials and actual weapons.

[59] Hibbs, M., 'Ion source problems held up Iraqi calutron program', *Nucleonics Week*, vol. 32, no. 32 (8 Aug. 1991), p. 9.

[60] Amended trigger list (note 30), para. 5.9.

[61] Annex to the Warsaw Guidelines (note 43), paras 3.11 and 3.14.

[62] *Fiscal Year 1989 Arms Control Impact Statements* (US Government Printing Office: Washington, DC, 1988), p. 165.

[63] Müller (note 40), p. 8.

[64] Annex to the Warsaw Guidelines (note 43), para. 3.6.

[65] Amended trigger list (note 30), para. 5.7.

[66] Outlook on Nuclear Nonproliferation, Special report in *Nuclear Fuel*, vol. 16, no. 2 (21 Jan. 1991), p. 2.

The Russian Federation Export Control Commission came into existence as a result of President Yeltsin's April 1992 decree number 388, which outlined 'Measures to Establish an Export Control System in Russia' and was given responsibility for the implementation of five control lists. The Russian dual-use items list for nuclear equipment corresponds closely to that of the NSG Warsaw Guidelines.[67] According to testimony in early 1993 from R. James Woolsey, Jr, then Director of Central Intelligence for the USA, however, Russia still did not have a system which is effective for controlling exports of sensitive military equipment and technology, including that in the nuclear area. At the same time he noted that there were no credible reports that nuclear weapons, nuclear weapon design information or significant quantities of weapon-grade fissile material had escaped from Russia.[68]

While Russia can be said to have taken some positive steps in its efforts to further the effectiveness of its nuclear export controls, the situation in many of the other former Soviet republics has in fact deteriorated in the time since they became independent. A formerly rigid export control regime is no longer in existence and nuclear export control systems anywhere similar to those in existence in the West are still 'embryonic or non-existent'.[69] The agreement on export control coordination signed by Armenia, Belarus, Kazakhstan, Kyrgyzstan, Russia, Tajikistan, Turkmenistan and Uzbekistan on 26 June 1992 was designed to ensure the creation of national export control systems and coordination of export control policies. Unfortunately, however, little progress has been made in the implementation of the agreement.[70]

Smuggling

Overall, the problem of smuggling of fissile material has in fact been much smaller than might have been expected. As of the end of 1994 there was still no hard evidence that nuclear weapons, weapon components or any militarily significant quantities of fissile material had been exported illicitly from the former Soviet Union. While there have been scores of reported cases[71] along with many arrests, the material involved has in many cases been radioactive but not weapon-related—i.e., material such as caesium, cobalt and strontium.

[67] Bertsch, G. K. and Cupitt, R. T., 'Nonproliferation in the 1990s: enhancing international cooperation on export controls', *Washington Quarterly*, vol. 16, no. 4 (autumn 1993), pp. 64–65; and Kripunov, I., 'Nonproliferation export controls in the former Soviet Union', ed. K. C. Bailey, Director's Series on Proliferation 1, Lawrence Livermore National Laboratory, Livermore, Calif., 7 June 1993, pp. 13–14.

[68] Testimony of R. James Woolsey in *Proliferation Threats of the 1990's*, Hearing before the Committee on Governmental Affairs, United States Senate, 103rd Congress, 1st Session, 24 Feb. 1993 (US Government Printing Office: Washington, DC, 1993), p. 11; and Smith, R. J., 'Nuclear-export control in Russia called weak', *International Herald Tribune*, 26 Feb. 1993, p. 2.

[69] Coll, S., 'On Russia's rim, problems of nuclear control', *International Herald Tribune*, 17 May 1993, p. 3; and Potter, W. C., 'Nuclear exports from the former Soviet Union: what's new, what's true', *Arms Control Today*, vol. 23, no. 1 (Jan./Feb. 1993), pp. 6–7.

[70] Potter (note 69), p. 7.

[71] For a chronology of reported or attempted exports of controlled nuclear-related materials from the former Soviet Union see Potter, W. C., *Nuclear Profiles of the Soviet Successor States,* Monograph no. 1, Program for Nonproliferation Studies, Monterey Institute of International Studies, Monterey, Calif., May 1993, Appendix One.

Nevertheless there is cause for concern. On the evidence gained through criminal justice and intelligence investigations of smuggling activity from Eastern Europe and the CIS, Klaus Toepfer, Federal Minister of Environment and Nuclear Safety in Germany, assessed the level of safeguards and physical protection for nuclear items within the CIS to be seriously inadequate.[72]

While confirming that there was no evidence that such activity has yet occurred, the Director of the CIA in the USA warned in mid-1994 of the possibility that organized crime groups in Russia could gain access to and sell nuclear weapons or weapon-grade fissile material. One of the particular targets is to gain control of tactical nuclear warheads.[73]

Cause for concern heightened in mid-1994 at the first discovery of weapon-grade plutonium on the black market. Approximately 6 grams of plutonium-239 were uncovered in the residence of a German businessman, which during preliminary analysis was traced back to the Russian nuclear weapon industry. The German Government has warned of the increased danger of nuclear material being smuggled. According to the person found to be in possession of this material it represents only a small portion of that on the European black market. Concern that this might represent only a small part of the weapon-grade material on the illicit market was also voiced by Canadian, German, Italian, Russian and US law enforcement officials. International crime organizations as well as officials of the Russian Government were reportedly possibly involved.[74] In a subsequent find 560 grams of mixed uranium/plutonium oxide were discovered at Munich airport, containing over 400 grams of plutonium, 87 per cent of which was plutonium-239.[75]

Senior officials of German and Russian intelligence services have held discussions on the issue and agreed to work together to try and stop the smuggling activity by exchanging information and tightening border controls.[76] The Director of the Federal Bureau of Investigation in the USA in June 1994 stated in congressional testimony that 'the greatest long-term threat to the security of the United States' was the possibility that 'organized crime, rogue nations or bands of terrorists' would obtain nuclear weapons or materials from Russia.[77] He met with law enforcement officials in Russia and signed a memorandum of understanding with Russia's Interior Ministry providing for joint efforts to

[72] 'Germans hunt a smuggling ring dealing Soviet nuclear materials', *Nucleonics Week*, 15 Oct. 1992, p. 12.

[73] 'CIA fears theft of nuclear arms', *International Herald Tribune*, 28 June 1994, p. 1; and *Programme for Promoting Nuclear Non-Proliferation (PPNN) Newsbrief*, no. 26 (2nd quarter 1994), p. 20.

[74] 'German alert on nuclear smuggling', *International Herald Tribune*, 18 July 1994, p. 2; and Vogel, S., 'Illicit nuclear cache called a "harbinger"', *International Herald Tribune*, 21 July 1994, p. 7. Several officials are sceptical regarding this particular businessman's claims of the existence of large amounts of additional material based on the plutonium's composition which is 99.7% plutonium-23— much more pure than that usually employed in nuclear weapons and more likely to have been produced for laboratory use than to have come from a nuclear stockpile. Smith, S., 'European authorities seek a rumored plutonium cache', *International Herald Tribune*, 26 July 1994, p. 5.

[75] *PPNN Newsbrief*, no. 27 (3rd quarter 1994), p. 20.

[76] *PPNN Newsbrief* (note 75), p. 22.

[77] Hockstader, L., 'Moscow insists criminals can't get at nuclear weapons', *International Herald Tribune*, 1 July 1994, p. 2.

combat organized crime and, reportedly, pave the way for offices to be established in the Russian and US capitals.[78]

While the IAEA itself is not involved in import or export authorizations, IAEA stationary has apparently been used in attempts to legitimize export of certain materials by some individuals. These exports are usually misrepresented—for example, as 'red mercury' and more recently Osmium-187, which is non-radioactive and can be obtained legitimately quite readily. The dealers attempt to give these substances an aura of mystery and make them seem more rare than they actually are.[79] While such fraudulent schemes have yet to be of any major import they indicate some of the lengths to which those trying desperately to get their hands on hard currency are willing to go.

In addition, the many reports of smuggling do introduce an unwanted amount of noise into the system which could make it more difficult to distinguish cases which may pose a real threat and should be investigated further. In addition these reported cases do indicate that there exists a substantial number of individuals who are willing to take on the role of middlemen in such transactions and who may have access to covert channels which could prove to be a problem in the future.[80]

The only victims which nuclear smuggling has claimed so far have been the smugglers themselves, many of whom are unaware of the dangers involved in the safe care and transport of the items with which they are dealing. In addition the smuggling rings have so far been shown to be very susceptible to police penetration—so much so that it has been hypothesized that undercover police activity may in fact be helping to create a perceived market for smuggled nuclear material.[81] A serious problem with the current situation, however, as pointed out by former IAEA chief inspector David Kay, is the fact that as the whereabouts of nuclear materials becomes more uncertain it is increasingly difficult to dismiss as a hoax a terrorist claim to be in possession of a nuclear device.[82]

It has been proposed that an international agency should be set up to deal with the governments and sub-national groups who are willing to expend substantial resources to obtain fissile materials in particular. Such a 'nuclear Interpol' would of course have to be equipped with adequate power and resources to perform such a task adequately.[83] Further efforts towards improving the situation include a decree issued by President Boris Yeltsin on 15 September 1994 establishing a new agency for material accountancy, physical security and

[78] *PPNN Newsbrief* (note 75), p. 22.

[79] Seneviratne, G., 'IAEA finds name used by "rare" metal fraudsters', *Nucleonics Week*, 8 Oct. 1992, p. 13.

[80] OTA (note 41), p. 135.

[81] Sullivan, S., 'Nukes for sale', *Time*, 29 Aug. 1994, pp. 11, 13.

[82] Hughes, D., 'Plutonium incident alarms Lufthansa', *Aviation Week & Space Technology*, 5 Sep. 1994, p. 133.

[83] Oxford Research Group, *The Plutonium Legacy: Nuclear Proliferation Out of Control*, Current Decisions Report, no. 12 (Apr. 1993), p. 33.

collaborative efforts with Germany and the USA to help prevent illegal diversion of nuclear material.[84]

Universal reporting of exports, imports and production

The agreement by the Nuclear Suppliers Group on the application of full-scope safeguards as a condition of nuclear supply is sure to have a positive impact on the non-proliferation regime. With China the only major supplier still not adhering to the full-scope safeguards policy the emphasis must shift to the newly emerging nuclear suppliers.

Even full-scope safeguards do not require comprehensive reporting of export, import and production of nuclear material. Transfers of nuclear material not yet suitable for either fuel fabrication or enrichment, or material which is exported for peaceful non-nuclear purposes, or to a nuclear weapon state, for example, do not have to be reported. Nor is it necessary to report domestic production and stockpiling of nuclear material. The realization of the increase in transparency which would result from a universal reporting scheme on the export, import and production of such materials has led to important recent progress in this area.[85]

During the February 1992 Board meeting proposals on 'reporting on and verification of the export, import and production of nuclear material, of sensitive equipment and certain non-nuclear materials' were taken up. While no concrete action was taken at the time, the proposals included the provision of information by states to the IAEA for the purpose of verification of the consistency of reported inventories and the state's nuclear activities.[86]

During the February 1993 Board of Governors meeting a universal reporting scheme including both nuclear and non-nuclear material was endorsed. Member states were encouraged to provide 'relevant information relating to their exports and imports of nuclear material and exports of specified equipment and non-nuclear material' and also invited to 'provide information on their production of nuclear material and on their imports of specified equipment and non-nuclear material'.[87] Special forms were circulated for the purpose. While participation in the scheme remains voluntary it is hoped that all states would eventually subscribe.[88]

This type of information could be coupled with other data, including open source data such as that from press and scientific reports and other data bases such as that compiled by the Monterey Institute of International Studies, possibly revealing important correlations. Newly developed expert system tech-

[84] Goodby, J. E. *et al.*, 'Nuclear arms control', *SIPRI Yearbook 1995* (note 2), p. 666.

[85] Scheinman, L., 'Assuring the nuclear non-proliferation safeguards system', Atlantic Council of the United States, Occasional Paper Series, Oct. 1992, p. 16.

[86] IAEA Press Release, PR 92/12 (26 Feb. 1992).

[87] Strengthening the Effectiveness and Improving the Efficiency of the Safeguards System, IAEA document GC(XXXVII)/1073, 6 Sep. 1993, pp. 3–4.

[88] IAEA (note 87), p. 3; and *IAEA Bulletin*, no. 1 (1993), p. 40.

niques could be employed to help filter and analyse the data, possibly aiding in providing new insights into possible clandestine nuclear activity.[89]

The current situation

Although the Zangger trigger list has been updated from time to time over the years and the NSG trigger list has undergone a fairly major revision, especially as further revelations from special inspections in Iraq have thrown more light on their nuclear programme and procurement methods, still further reassessment and revisions to export control lists and policy may be necessary. The opinion had been expressed in 1992[90] that any further refining of the list of dual-use items could lead to 'a technological and political swamp' and it is perhaps more important to concentrate effort where it is most needed—in the areas of national and international controls of items whose significance for nuclear weapons is beyond dispute and which may remain outside present controls or are not yet adequately controlled. It is, however, important that the lists be continually re-examined, especially so that the definitions and scope may be altered in response to technological evolution.

In this context it is important to note that in an important new development, annual plenary meetings of the NSG are now held to air concerns and form decisions. At the 1994 Madrid meeting lists of export licence denials were exchanged and guidelines for the transfer of nuclear materials and equipment to NPT member states which are, none the less, causes of proliferation concern—Iran, North Korea, Libya and Syria, as well as to China, the only declared nuclear weapon state not an NSG member, were discussed.[91]

It is, of course likely that countries and individual companies and countries will be more cautious in the future because of outcries over sales to Iraq. For example, days after Iraq admitted to UN inspectors that it had procured specialized centrifuge equipment that could be of use in the construction of nuclear weapons from suppliers in Germany, long-stalled legislation that would tighten export controls on arms was approved by an embarrassed German Parliament in January 1992. Investigators of a new government agency created by the bill to monitor exports will reportedly be given the power to open mail and tap telephones in order to acquire evidence against suppliers.[92]

The universal reporting of information on exports, imports and production would be further enhanced by increasing sharing of information acquired by intelligence sources related to these matters between countries involved. Such exchanges, whether routinized as the twice-yearly United States–Russian 'non-proliferation bilaterals' or held on a more *ad hoc* basis would shed further light

[89] Fainberg, A., 'Strengthening IAEA safeguards: lessons from Iraq', Center for International Security and Arms Control, Stanford University, Stanford, Calif., Apr. 1993, pp. 44–45

[90] Leventhal, P. L., 'Nuclear export controls: can we plug the leaks?', ed. J-F. Rioux, *Limiting the Proliferation of Weapons: The Role of Supply-Side Strategies* (Carleton University Press: Ottawa, 1992), p. 47.

[91] *Arms Control Today*, vol. 24, no. 4 (May 1994), p. 24; and Strulak (note 15), p. 8.

[92] Kinzer, S., 'Germany acts to curb arms exports', *New York Times*, 24 Jan. 1992, p. A3.

on procurement patterns and procedures and could also enhance the credibility of information exchanged through political channels.[93]

IV. Conclusions

Since the experience with Iraq there has been substantial progress in attempts to tighten export controls, particularly in the area of dual-use items. While improved export controls may help to slow the spread of nuclear weapon-related technology, it is apparent from the revelations of the Iraqi nuclear programme that the strong temptation arising from the lucrative profits to be had in sales of controlled items can prove too great for many companies. It is apparent that the risks involved in such transactions have not provided sufficient barriers to their being carried out. In attempting to alleviate this, positive inducements[94] for good behaviour should perhaps also be used in conjunction with supply-side controls, including such measures as increased access to technology and technological development aid and positive security assurances.

The new nuclear suppliers—countries which may become involved in the export of nuclear technology and material without the application of safeguards—could provide new challenges for the NPT regime. These include Argentina, Brazil, China, India, Israel, South Korea and South Africa—although Argentina and South Africa have recently become members of the NSG and Argentina has ratified the Tlatelolco Treaty.[95] It is important that nuclear exports which do take place be adequately safeguarded. The view that prevails among the countries of the Nuclear Suppliers Group is that merely political commitments to peaceful use of nuclear technology on the part of importers are insufficient and may hide a hidden nuclear programme agenda. The requirement of full-scope safeguards (FSS) as a condition of supply, now adopted by the NSG, will have a positive impact and should be encouraged for all suppliers. Care must be taken to recognize states of proliferation concern that seek to join the regime in order to help bolster an image as responsible countries simply to take advantage of the benefits resulting from increased technology transfer. [96]

Control of dual-use items is inherently difficult for a number of reasons. First of all there is often a lack of consensus on the necessity or propriety of controlling such items since it can be argued to have a negative impact on the economic development of many countries. By their nature, dual-use items are also usually widely available and hence difficult to control. Indeed it could be the

[93] Dunn, L. A., 'Buttressing nuclear export controls and supply-side restraints: initiatives and actions', eds Müller and Dunn (note 40), p. 26.

[94] Zimmerman, P. D., 'Proliferation: bronze medal technology is good enough', *Orbis*, winter 1994, pp. 78, 80–81.

[95] Rauf, T., 'Strengthened safeguards and non-proliferation', ed. T. Rauf, *Strengthened IAEA Safeguards and Regional Non-Proliferation Strategies*, Canadian Centre for Global Security, Ottawa, Aurora Papers 23, Mar. 1994, p. 11.

[96] Bailey, K. C., *Strengthening Nuclear Nonproliferation* (Westview Press: Boulder, Colo., 1993), pp. 20–21.

case that placing such items on control lists may actually lead to some countries manufacturing them in order to fill a perceived need in the face of diminished supply (and correspondingly higher price—this increased profit motivation may, of course, not only be present in the case of dual-use items but for direct-use items as well). Finally the nature of dual-use items also means that it is often easy to manufacture or obtain substitutes for them—their acquisition is often attempted merely as a cost or time saving expedient.[97]

The future success of export controls could be greatly enhanced if companies supplying items of possible concern were to exercise voluntary restraint in selling dual-use as well as direct-use equipment to countries suspected of attempting to develop nuclear weapons. For example, in 1993 the Leybold AG firm, having received negative publicity after its sales of electron-beam welding equipment to Iraq, adopted a voluntary restraint programme on the sale of dual-use items, even those which are legal.[98]

Where export controls are being effective, more effort may be expended by a country interested in developing nuclear weapons in improving its indigenous capability. Ways of improving these capabilities may involve approaching foreign companies—which should be on the alert for such inquiries—in attempts to obtain technical information. Iraq, for example, would have foreign firms bid for a particular transfer of technology in an attempt to gain access to technical data from the supplier vying for a contract. Contact would be broken off without a deal actually having been made when Iraq acquired all the information it thought it could from the process. Examples of this procedure are the discussions held by Iraq with the Soviet Union, a French–Belgian consortium and China between 1982 and 1986 for the construction of an underground nuclear reactor. Iraq announced that the project was too expensive only after receiving a large amount of technical information. This particular episode was responsible at least in part for the suspicion that Iraq may indeed have constructed an underground reactor for producing plutonium.[99]

Some countries may attempt to obtain materials and equipment by working through another country with an established supplier network. It has been reported, for example, that Saudi Arabia had provided Iraq with financial assistance totalling up to $5 billion as well as specialized equipment for its nuclear programme that could not be obtained elsewhere. In return Iraq was to share the nuclear technology that it had acquired, which would then help enable Saudi Arabia to obtain a nuclear capability.[100] Saudi Arabia was previously reported as interested in buying a nuclear weapon.[101] Although it has signed the NPT

[97] Bailey (note 96), pp. 23–24.

[98] Hart, K., 'Trade group urges more sharing of proliferation information', *Nuclear Fuel,* 5 July 1993, p. 15.

[99] Bailey (note 96), p. 29. See chapter 4 for an account of the attempts to locate such a reactor.

[100] 'Saudi says Riyadh aided Iraqi atom plan', *International Herald Tribune,* 25 July 1994, p. 2; and Lewis, P., 'Defector says Saudis sought reactors to build weapons', *International Herald Tribune*, 8 Aug. 1994, p. 5.

[101] Nitze, P. H. and Stafford, M. F., 'Better to persevere with sanctions than launch all-out war', *International Herald Tribune*, 8 Jan. 1990, p. 6.

Saudi Arabia has yet to conclude a comprehensive safeguards agreement with the IAEA.

Also, the possibility of bringing those states which frequently act as intermediaries in the shipment of nuclear or related equipment into the export control system should not be overlooked. Related to this, while verification of end-use may not be feasible for all exports, an examination could be made of the possibilities of implementing some form of end-use controls perhaps on a select list of goods.[102]

The one single measure which has the potential to help alleviate many of the problems with export controls discussed above is the universal reporting of imports, exports and production of nuclear-related material and equipment. As more countries hopefully become involved in this reporting system it will provide increased transparency which should enable it to become less difficult to uncover procurement patterns and strategies which may be pursued as part of an effort to develop nuclear weapons.

While no serious export of nuclear weapon-related material has yet occurred from the countries of the former USSR conditions are certainly 'ripe for export control abuse'. Action is needed quickly to correct the current situation of inadequately safeguarded nuclear facilities, large stockpiles of weapon-usable fissile material, nuclear experts who are either unemployed or under-employed, huge segments of the populations desperate for hard currency and governments which displayed far less than the necessary concern for the proper control of nuclear exports. It would be useful in combating nuclear smuggling if international arrangements were to be set up to supply all governments involved with information which becomes available on smuggling activity.[103] Of the former Soviet republics only Russia is a member of the NSG. The other former republics should be encouraged to join as quickly as possible and effective individual export control systems should be ensured.

[102] Müller, H., 'Reform of the system of nuclear export controls', eds Müller and Dunn (note 40), pp. 11, 12.

[103] Potter (note 69), p. 9; and Fischer, D., 'Plutonium smuggling: assessing the risk', *Bulletin of Arms Control*, no. 16 (Nov. 1994) p. 6.

7. Verification and intelligence

I. Introduction

The ways in which safeguards contribute to assurances that nuclear non-proliferation objectives and obligations are met are discussed in chapter 5 While safeguards are an extremely important measure their effect is somewhat limited in the critical area of uncovering clandestine nuclear weapon activity. It may be argued that the detection of this type of activity, rather than the acquisition of fissile material through diversion from peaceful nuclear activity, is the major focus of concern today. Since the discovery of the Iraqi nuclear weapon programme there is also an increased effort to uncover such clandestine activity before facilities are actually completed and operating.[1] Extension or expansion of the traditionally accepted concept of safeguards into the arena of uncovering non-declared nuclear material and activities of relevance to nuclear weapon proliferation has gained and continues to gain support. Special inspections as explained in chapter 5 may well come to play a significant role in this regard, but it is of course also important to examine the methods that can be used to trigger such inspections or otherwise to indicate clandestine activity, whether it be illegal activity by an NPT state party or an activity by a state not party to the NPT which, although not illegal, would be of concern to the international community.

While this renewed focus originated largely with developments in Iraq, a more recent and important test case involves the nuclear programme in the DPRK. North Korea announced its decision to withdraw from the NPT in order to avoid special inspections, only to suspend this decision at the last moment while still claiming that its resultant 'unique status' also meant that it was not obliged to accept such inspections. It is suspected that North Korea has already produced enough plutonium for one or two bombs using material from a 5-MWe reactor. Before the 21 October 1994 framework agreement stopped the nuclear programme, two new larger reactors were being completed and the capacity of the North Korean reprocessing plant was being increased and could have given North Korea the capability to produce plutonium for many bombs per year.

Because of the closed nature of North Korean society, much of the information about the scope of the country's nuclear programme has been derived from intelligence collection activity. Although North Korea chose the path to proliferation that experts in non-proliferation issues would most expect—namely, plutonium production and reprocessing—only with the recent agreement on

[1] See, e.g., Scheinman, L., 'Safeguards: new threats and new expectations', *Disarmament*, vol. 15, no. 2 (1992), p. 59; and Hibbs, M., 'U.S. officials say Iran is pursuing fissile material production research', *Nuclear Fuel*, 7 Dec. 1992, p. 5.

freezing the nuclear programme will it hopefully be possible to obtain detailed information on its history. Much of this information will require special inspections and these are probably still years away.

In general, the verification of nuclear non-proliferation commitments and the uncovering of nuclear weapon research, development and production will continue to be a primary focus of the international community. According to a UN study verification is, by definition, 'a process which establishes whether the States Parties are complying with their obligations under an agreement. The process includes: collection of information relevant to obligations under arms limitation and disarmament agreements; analysis of the information; and reaching a judgement as to whether the specific terms of an agreement are being met'.[2] While the collection of information tends to be more of an objective technical activity, more care must be taken in the stages involving interpretation and analysis of the information collected, and the judgements reached at these stages may be influenced by a host of political factors.[3]

The verification regimes of bilateral or multilateral arms control agreements incorporate many agreed-upon cooperative monitoring methods, including a variety of on-site inspection (OSI) methods. To date, such methods have mainly been employed in detecting and deterring violations at known sites which are declared in advance. Such cooperative monitoring characterizes much of the IAEA activity in the area of safeguards, as discussed in chapter 5. For the detection of clandestine activity related to arms control agreements, however, various intelligence collection methods remain a primary source of valuable information.

The effectiveness of some aspects of intelligence collection has been recognized in many arms control agreements—it is stipulated in the 1991 and 1993 START treaties and the 1990 Treaty on Conventional Armed Forces in Europe (CFE), for example, that states parties shall 'not interfere' with national technical means (NTM) or use 'concealment methods that impede verification'; cooperative procedures were negotiated in the START agreements to 'enhance the effectiveness' of NTM. While challenge inspections such as those introduced in the 1993 Chemical Weapons Convention may provide valuable information, indications of where to inspect must be obtained in general from other sources. The use of such information in detecting clandestine nuclear weapon-related activity is now recognized more than ever in the wake of events in both Iraq and North Korea.

Inspections may be cued by a variety of information originating from other inspection activity, as well as various intelligence methods, including the use of

[2] UN Department for Disarmament Affairs, *Study on the Role of the United Nations in the Field of Verification* (United Nations: New York, 1991), p. 4.

[3] The substantial US intelligence resources which are involved in monitoring nuclear programmes in other countries include the Joint Atomic Energy Intelligence Committee, the Central Intelligence Agency, the Defense Intelligence Agency, the Department of Energy Office of Intelligence, the Air Force Technical Applications Center and the Z (Special Projects) Division of the Lawrence Livermore National Laboratory. Richelson, J. T., 'Can the intelligence community keep pace with the threat?', eds M. Reiss and R. S. Litwak, *Nuclear Proliferation after the Cold War* (Woodrow Wilson Center Press: Washington, DC, 1994), p. 305, footnote 2.

satellites and aircraft for imagery and signals collection in addition to human intelligence.

The important question of what needs to be verified from the perspective of nuclear weapon proliferation of course depends on who is asking the question. This book is mainly concerned with international obligations concerning the IAEA and the NPT. Individual countries may also have particular proliferation concerns and their own intelligence and analysis operations which attempt to answer them. With recent initiatives within the IAEA to make use of intelligence and other information available to national organizations these two concerns are, however, likely to overlap even further in the future.

The agenda for verification and intelligence collection can be expanded to include pressing concerns of the moment and those of the near and distant future. Fortunately some of the means overlap, but the above discussion accentuates the need to be constantly asking the question: How much is enough? For near-term concerns this question can be more effectively answered since the political situation is an important factor to be considered in the determination. In the longer term, however, this question is more difficult to address, and perhaps the best that can be done is to design current and near-term verification elements with longer-term objectives in mind as well.

II. Verification of nuclear non-proliferation: monitoring means, methods and organization

As demonstrated above the prerequisite for carrying out special inspections is a source of pertinent information on clandestine activity related to nuclear weapon development. This information is, of course, also of prime importance for the verification of nuclear non-proliferation in general. It is therefore important to examine the manner in which such information may be collected, analysed and shared, as well as the ways in which states may attempt to practice deception in order to hide behaviour that conflicts with international non-proliferation goals.

Information sharing

The sharing of intelligence information is becoming increasingly important. While new efforts are being made to increase this type of activity, such cooperation is certainly not new. For example, with converging interests in nuclear non-proliferation during the détente of the 1960s, the USA and the USSR began a long history of cooperation in these matters impervious to the ups and downs of their relationship in other realms. It is known, for example, that meetings between US and Russian experts in non-proliferation—the 'non-proliferation bilaterals'—have taken place twice yearly.[4]

[4] Dunn, L. A., 'Buttressing nuclear export controls and supply-side restraints: initiatives and actions', eds H. Müller and L. A. Dunn, *Nuclear Export Controls and Supply Side Restraints: Options for Reform*,

In a statement before the IAEA Board of Governors in 1991 the Director General reaffirmed that 'a key modification of our practices must be to use more extensively such information as we already possess and be open to accept and critically examine information that may be offered to us from the outside'. There are certainly potential problems in making use of such information. Acknowledging the risks that some information would be supplied with 'ulterior motives', for example, he none the less stressed that all information, whether from official or non-official sources, should be examined and of course also carefully and critically assessed.[5]

He also stated that the IAEA would not concern itself with the manner in which the intelligence was collected and that the IAEA would 'want to receive only sufficient evidence to lead us to conclude that requesting a special inspection was justified. We would have to evaluate the evidence. I imagine that photographs, satellite photographs or surveillance aircraft photographs, would be of value.'[6]

However, some IAEA officials have reportedly been concerned about relying too heavily on the intelligence of a particular member state, since they felt that the USA did not share pertinent information in a timely enough manner. Preference has been expressed for intelligence operations to be conducted by the IAEA itself by some Agency officials.[7] Such a procedure would, however, be unlikely to meet with general approval and would also require additional funds, possibly cast suspicion on the motives of the IAEA in taking up such a role and raise concerns about the information collected. It would probably not provide the detailed intelligence which member states could make available in any case.

The idea of setting up a separate unit within the IAEA to collect intelligence information provided from outside, which had surfaced shortly after the revelations in Iraq, has only been implemented on a small scale. This was probably in part because of the fears of Third World states that the IAEA would be manipulated, thus posing a danger to their security concerns, as well as the US concern that information might subsequently be leaked from the IAEA once in its possession. None the less the USA and other member states continue to supply the IAEA with intelligence information, the most sensitive of which is supplied directly to the Director General.[8] One proposal that would lessen the dangers of

Programme for Promoting Nuclear Non-Proliferation (PPNN) Study Four, Mountbatten Centre for International Studies, Southampton, Oct. 1993, p. 26; and Fischer, D., *Stopping the Spread of Nuclear Weapons: The Past and the Prospects* (Routledge: London, 1992), pp. 36–37, 57 and footnote 35, p. 265.

[5] Statement to the IAEA Board of Governors on Safeguards Matters, delivered by Hans Blix, Vienna, 5 Dec. 1991, pp. 7–8. In this regard, e.g., it has been reported that the US Department of Defense and the National Security Council gave 'inflated estimates' of Iraqi uranium enrichment capability to various press organizations, among other things to enhance support for removing Saddam Hussein by military means. Hibbs, M., 'Inspectors find four calutron enrichment plants in Iraq', *Nuclear Fuel*, vol. 16, no. 15 (22 July 1991), p. 6.

[6] 'IAEA Director Hans Blix: keeping an eye on a nuclear world', interview by Spurgeon M. Keeny, Jr and Jon W. Wolfsthal on 23 Oct. 1991, *Arms Control Today*, vol. 21, no. 9 (Nov. 1991), p. 4.

[7] Hibbs, M., 'Europeans outline new effort to strengthen IAEA safeguards', *Nucleonics Week*, vol. 32, no. 38 (19 Sep. 1991), p. 11.

[8] Hibbs, M., 'US warned not to try using IAEA to isolate or destabilize Iran', *Nucleonics Week*, 8 Oct. 1992, p. 9.

politicization that might otherwise be associated with provision of sensitive intelligence information would be for the USA, for example, to pool its information not only with that from other Western countries but also with that from Russia before providing it to the IAEA.[9]

The Director General has also stated that information gleaned from open sources would be used as well as voluntary reporting by states regarding relevant imports and exports. Concerning press reports, it has been demonstrated by an IAEA working group that these alone may be of somewhat limited value, however. Their study assessed whether reports in the media would have provided an indication of relevant nuclear activity in past cases, including reprocessing and unsafeguarded nuclear reactors in North Korea, the clandestine nuclear activity in Iraq, gaseous diffusion enrichment in Argentina and the unsafeguarded enrichment activities in South Africa. They came to the conclusion that relying on these sources alone would not have been helpful in bringing the clandestine activity to light.[10]

None the less it is worthwhile and important for intelligence agencies in general to collect as much unclassified material concerning activities related to nuclear weapon proliferation as possible, not only to supplement classified information but also to serve as a source of information which can be used in unclassified discussions with allies or in public revelations concerning proliferation activity.[11] A focal point of expanding the information extracted from open source intelligence (sometimes referred to as OSCINT) may result from the appointment of an open source coordinator within the Central Intelligence Agency (CIA) in 1992.[12] As discussed in chapter 5 on safeguards, combining various sources of open source data, including existing data bases, and employing newly developed expert systems techniques may also prove effective in enhancing the clues to proliferation derived from this type of information.

Identifying clandestine activities

For many processes, particularly involving uranium enrichment, it should be noted that in so far as indigenous equipment is used not only can the facility intended for enrichment be searched for, and hopefully detected, but so can the manufacturing plants which produce the equipment used in the enrichment process. The more effective the export controls, the more indigenous methods must be employed and the greater the chance of detection—because more people are involved, more facilities are needed, and so on. This should be particularly true in the case of the massive equipment involved in EMIS enrichment, for example, but in fact it was only after the Persian Gulf War that the installation for centrifuge manufacture at Al Furat was discovered in Iraq.[13]

[9] Bailey, K. C., *Strengthening Nuclear Nonproliferation* (Westview Press: Boulder, Colo., 1993), p. 73.
[10] Bailey (note 9), p. 72.
[11] Sokolski, H., 'Fighting proliferation with intelligence', *Orbis*, spring 1994, p. 257.
[12] Steele, R. D., 'Open source intelligence clarifies global threats', *Signal*, Sep. 1992, p. 65.
[13] Richelson (note 3), p. 292.

Information contained in the special inspection reports indicates that the Iraqi calutron enrichment buildings were over 100 m long and would be easily detectable even with commercial satellites. The problem, however, in such situations is in trying to piece together enough collateral information to identify nuclear facilities as such. This may also require communications and other signals intercepts, human intelligence sources, and so on.

In the case of centrifuges, the problem is exacerbated as the facilities involved could be quite small and difficult to locate with satellite imagery, for example. In general a certain trade-off must be made between building a very complex and difficult-to-manufacture centrifuge, which would necessitate fewer machines and a facility of correspondingly reduced size, and relying on relatively simple technology requiring more machines and a larger facility.[14]

Reprocessing activity in general requires very thick shielding for protection from the intense radioactivity involved and also involves distinctive emissions which can be detected over distances of several kilometres. Attempts to hide such facilities underground and prevent tell-tale emissions would be difficult and expensive. Such activity could potentially be concealed by building a reprocessing facility near an existing safeguarded reprocessing facility, the emissions from which would help mask those from a clandestine activity.[15] It could, therefore, perhaps be advisable to focus image intelligence collection assets from time to time in the area around such legal activity, especially if there is a suspicion that a country may be carrying out clandestine reprocessing.

With specific regard to hiding clandestine activity, Robert Gates, then Director of the CIA, reported that classified information indicated that North Korea had a deception plan in order to hide some of its nuclear activities. Information used in this assessment was derived from sources including intensive aerial and satellite reconnaissance.[16] This further points to the need for special inspections as countries which are known to have been working towards weapon development become a part of the NPT regime—especially since in the same testimony Gates said that the CIA believed that North Korea was 'a few months to as much as a couple of years' away from producing its first nuclear weapon.

The use of satellites and aerial means to collect information on nuclear proliferation-related activity has been well demonstrated in the Iraqi situation (albeit with a somewhat less than perfect record). The USA was also reportedly able to ascertain that the North Korean reactor at Yongbyon was still in operation at the end of 1993 by keeping track of its temperature[17]—the reactor would have to be shut down and thus cool substantially in order to remove the

[14] Hibbs, M., 'Iraqi evidence points to unknown enrichment mentor', *Nucleonics Week*, vol. 32, no. 34 (22 Aug. 1991), p. 7.

[15] Bailey (note 9), p. 76.

[16] Sciolino, E., 'CIA Chief says North Koreans are hiding nuclear arms projects', *New York Times*, 26 Feb. 1992, p. A1.

[17] Smith, J., 'When cool-off is the tip-off: U.S. satellites watch for chilling of North Korean reactor', *International Herald Tribune*, 14 Dec. 1993, p. 10.

spent fuel and this cooling could be detected by infrared sensors on board satellites.[18] As this fuel could then be reprocessed to produce plutonium, this monitoring capability was very useful in easing fears of the acquisition of further plutonium by that country, forestalling a potential crisis situation and allowing negotiations to proceed.

As the above indicates it is important to understand the capabilities of the various intelligence-gathering platforms now or soon to be in existence along with some of their strengths and weaknesses with respect to the task at hand. As regards the most technologically advanced sources operated by the United States and Russia it should be noted that decades of experience and large sums of money have been invested in intelligence collection, some of which has focused directly on nuclear proliferation-related activities, but because of their highly classified nature the actual capabilities can to a large extent only be surmised.

Satellite observations[19]

The most detailed information available from satellites is gathered by the United States and Russia. It is important that the US and Russian capabilities be understood now that the IAEA is willing to accept and analyse information from member states and, perhaps more important, willingness has been shown on the part of the collectors to share some of the data acquired. In addition to these capabilities, an increasing number of commercial satellites are expected to be launched in the next several years. To varying degrees these assets are capable of providing visible-light, infrared and radar imagery of the earth in addition to collecting signals intelligence.

In recent years the USA has had the largest constellation of image-collecting satellites in its history, probably including as many as three each of the Lacrosse radar satellite, the KH-11 Keyhole digital imaging satellite and the advanced KH-11.[20] In 1994 the overall US intelligence budget was estimated at approximately $28 billion per year.[21] US military space programmes were allocated over $14 billion in 1993 and about $15 billion in 1994, approximately $5 billion of which is to be spent on classified spy satellites alone. Although a decline in the overall military space budget of 15 per cent is expected by the year 2000, much of this will come about as a result of such factors as use of

[18] While it is possible that the reactor could be shut down for very short periods of time without being detected by the satellite sensors, the amount of plutonium which could be removed in such short periods would not be significant; see *PPNN Newsbrief*, no. 24 (4th quarter 1993), p. 4.

[19] More detailed information on the use of satellites for verification can be found, e.g., in Koulik, S. and Kokoski, R., *Verification of the CFE Treaty*, SIPRI Research Report, Stockholm International Peace Research Institute, Stockholm, Oct. 1991, pp. 32–51.

[20] Pike, J., Lang, S. and Stambler, E., 'Military use of outer space', *SIPRI Yearbook 1992: World Armaments and Disarmament* (Oxford University Press: Oxford, 1992), pp. 121–41.

[21] 'Congress putting the clamps on CIA', *International Herald Tribune*, 4 July 1994, p. 3; and Sciolino, E., 'CIA chief rejects a spying shake-up', *International Herald Tribune*, 3 Apr. 1992, p. 3.

newer technology, increased reliance on commercially available technology and increased lifetimes of satellites.[22]

The Director of the CIA has recently asked that the satellite intelligence collection systems operated by the National Reconnaissance Office (NRO) be consolidated into five satellite programmes. Three of these are low-altitude satellites: the KH-11C/13 photographic-intelligence satellite with high-resolution, narrow-field-of-view and wide-area, moderate-resolution (about 1 m) sensors; a new, lighter and smaller version of the Lacrosse satellite, the Lacrosse 2 radar satellite; and a wide-area surveillance satellite using a combination of radar and infrared sensors. The other systems include the signals-intercept satellites in geosynchronous-orbit and the satellites in elliptical-orbit, which detect missile launches.[23]

The Lacrosse satellite's radar is capable of day–night, all-weather imagery but its resolution (on the order of 1 m) is substantially less than that of the Keyhole satellites, which can in principle achieve resolutions approaching 10 cm. The infrared imaging capability of the latter is, however, substantially lower.

Russian capabilities for visible-light imagery are comparable in resolution but they remain reliant to some extent on photographic film which must be returned to the earth for processing (whereas all US satellites relay imagery in near-real time to the earth for analysis). Unlike many other verification tasks, however, when attempting to locate clandestine facilities engaging in illicit nuclear activity the ability to receive information within very short time intervals is not critical. Such facilities would be fixed and thus could be repeatedly photographed over long periods of time. As mentioned above the main task would be to ascertain the actual use to which a facility is being put.

Answering this latter question can often be aided by intercepting communications to, from or pertaining to a particular facility. Here again, satellites can provide a wealth of information. The USA most likely has the lead with a variety of platforms, including several Magnum satellites in geostationary orbit with antennas reportedly 100 m in diameter and able to pick up broadcasts from even tiny transmitters. Russia also has a large number of three different kinds of signals intelligence (SIGINT) platform in orbit. Communications can, of course, be encrypted to hinder efforts to uncover sensitive programmes such as those to develop nuclear weapons. In addition to advanced high-speed computers, which can sometimes foil such attempts, it should also be noted that the 'externals' of communications—including point of origin, priority and volume of traffic—can often be very useful in themselves even though the content of the message may remain a mystery.

[22] Munro, N. and Polsky Werner, D., 'Officials predict spy satellite industry shakeout', *Space News*, 13–19 Dec. 1993, p. 3; Kiernan, V., 'Spy satellite budget request cut by 18 percent', *Space News*, 20–26 July 1992, p. 3; and Iannotta, B., 'US spy satellite spending static in 1995', *Space News*, 14–20 Feb. 1994, p. 4.

[23] Fulghum, D. A., 'USAF pursues stealthy UAV to improve reconnaissance', *Aviation Week & Space Technology*, 17 Jan. 1994, p. 46.

Despite the political and economic turmoil following the breakup of the Soviet Union the Russian space programme has shown itself to be surprisingly resilient. While the number of photoreconnaissance satellites launched in 1993 was substantially lower in comparison with 1989, for example—10 as opposed to 31—the longevity of several types of this satellite continues to increase. All basic space-based activities, including those providing valuable imagery and signals intelligence, have continued since the collapse of the USSR, and Russia is believed to have recently orbited a new and more advanced reconnaissance satellite employing digital-image transmission.[24]

Comparatively little is known about the Chinese photoreconnaissance capability. Employing a film-camera imaging system, the FS-1 Recoverable Satellite Programme photographic intelligence satellite, which began development in 1966, was later superseded by the larger FS-2 satellite first launched in 1992.[25]

Concern was raised among European commanders during the Persian Gulf War as the extent to which they were dependent on the USA for their intelligence became apparent. This led to increased momentum in developing a variety of intelligence-gathering capabilities.[26] The Helios satellite programme, which was initiated by France and joined by Italy and Spain, set a precedent in cooperative space-based verification when it launched its first satellite in mid-1995.[27] In an important policy reversal the French Government agreed to share information gathered from this military programme with its allies. Sensors carried by Helios will allow visible-light images at a resolution of approximately 1 m as well as infrared and signals intercept. A Helios 2 satellite with improved capabilities, including a resolution of perhaps 50 cm, has also been approved and should be operational by the year 2001. France is hoping to involve other European nations in this more advanced satellite programme.

A small experimental signals-intelligence satellite called Cerise was also carried on board the rocket launching Helios. By the beginning of the 21st century a large French signals-intelligence satellite, Zenon, is expected to be operational. Supplementing the Helios imagery with space-based military radar, the French Osiris satellite is also planned to be on station by around the year 2000. It is hoped that Osiris will become a European satellite programme perhaps organized under the Western European Union (WEU).[28] Germany has already

[24] 'Russia launches military satellite on SL-16', *Aviation Week & Space Technology*, 5 Sep. 1994, p. 33; Iannotta, B., 'Despite turmoil, Russia launched 47 rockets in 1993', *Space News,* 24–30 Jan. 1994, p. 8; and 'Russian reconnaissance upgrades', *Aviation Week & Space Technology*, 10 Jan. 1994, p. 15.

[25] Pike, J., 'Military use of outer space', *SIPRI Yearbook 1991: World Armaments and Disarmament* (Oxford University Press: Oxford, 1991), p. 74; Pike, J., 'Military satellites launched in 1992', *SIPRI Yearbook 1993: World Armaments and Disarmament* (Oxford University Press: Oxford, 1993), appendix 8A, p. 330; and Covault, C., 'Chinese space program sets aggressive pace', *Aviation Week & Space Technology*, 5 Oct. 1992, p. 49.

[26] Lenorovitz, J., Covault, C. and Shifrin, C. A., 'European forces seeking better standoff capability', *Aviation Week & Space Technology,* 17 Jan. 1994, p. 60.

[27] Covault, C., 'Helios 1A bolsters European recon', *Aviation Week & Space Technology,* 17 July 1995, p. 26.

[28] de Selding, P. B., 'France confirms work on new spy satellite systems', *Space News*, 6–19 July 1992, p. 1; Covault, C., 'Tight budgets, new priorities pressure global space programs', *Aviation Week & Space*

indicated its interest in playing a role in the Osiris programme and has signalled likely German participation in the Helios 2 effort.[29]

While their sophistication may be substantially less than that of classified satellites, the number of commercial satellites and their capabilities will expand substantially in the next several years as discussed below, making available information not only to agencies such as the IAEA but also to the general public. Important commercial platforms currently in orbit include Landsat, with a multispectral capability and 30-m resolution (120 m in the thermal infrared); the SPOT satellites[30] with 10-m and 20-m resolutions for panchromatic and multispectral images, respectively; and Russian satellites supplying the Sojuzkarta company with photographs with varying resolutions as high as 3 m and better. A British company has now gained access to literally millions of Russian archived satellite photographs with resolutions as high as 2 m which it is digitizing (for ease of subsequent computer processing) and offering for sale.[31] Canada's Radarsat, set for launch in September 1995, will provide radar images with a resolution of approximately 10 m with a follow-on planned for launch by 2000.[32]

France hopes to have a new SPOT satellite capable of 5-m resolution (beginning with SPOT 5) as early as 1999. It is also hoped that other European countries will invest in the newer satellites.[33] The European Space Agency (ESA) operates a 25-m resolution radar satellite—Earth Remote Sensing Satellite (ERS-1)—with a follow-on to be launched in 1995.

A successor to the first Russian Almaz commercial radar satellite, which operated from April 1991 to October 1992, the Almaz 1B will include a three-band radar and optical imager with a resolution of 2.5 m and is scheduled for launch in 1995. It will be capable of monitoring proliferation-related activity through keeping track of 'activities at facilities designed to produce nuclear and chemical weapons'.[34] Russia is also planning a civilian remote-sensing satellite by the late 1990s, with a resolution of 5 m and thus comparable to the SPOT 5 satellite, but images are expected to be less expensive than the data from the French satellite.[35]

Technology, 7 Sep. 1992, p. 121; de Selding, P. B., 'Advanced Helios to give France a keener eye from space', *Defense News*, 21–27 Mar. 1994, p. 12; 'Helios satellite project gets funding go-ahead', *Jane's Defence Weekly*, 7 May 1994, p. 5; and de Selding, P., 'Spain abandons Helios 2 project', *Defense News*, 19–25 Sep. 1994, p. 4.

[29] 'Germany ready to take role in Helios program', *Space News*, 23–29 May 1994, p. 2.

[30] As of the end of 1993 SPOT 2 and SPOT 3 (which became operational in Nov. 1993) were in operation with the older SPOT 1 satellite being held in reserve in orbit. de Selding, P. B., 'SPOT wins financing to operate a pair of satellites in 1994', *Space News*, 31 Jan.–6 Feb. 1994, p. 17.

[31] de Selding, P., 'UK firm begins to market Russian satellite images', *Space News*, 15–28 Nov. 1993, p. 21.

[32] Knapp, B., 'Canada commits $175 million to build follow-on Radarsat', *Space News*, 11–17 July 1994, p. 4; and *Space News*, 28 Mar.–3 Apr. 1994, p. 12.

[33] Riccitiello, R., 'France, SPOT plan new satellite design before 2000', *Space News*, 25–31 Jan. 1993, p. 18.

[34] Hitchens, T. and Munro, N., 'U.S., Russian efforts to target chemical, nuclear weapons', *Defense News*, 14–20 Mar. 1994, p. 34; and 'Russians prepare Almaz 1B for 1995 Proton launch', *Space News*, 9–15 Aug. 1993, p. 12.

[35] Covault, C., 'New Russian spacecraft to compete against Spot', *Aviation Week & Space Technology*, 23 May 1994, p. 57.

In addition, the WEU has established a joint satellite interpretation centre. The facility, which will employ about 100 people, was inaugurated in March 1993. An initial three-year experimental phase with a budget of 38.25 million ECUs will be used to train experts from the WEU countries in satellite data interpretation, using at first only commercially available imagery from the SPOT, Landsat and ERS satellites. An agreement was reached that at a later stage the much higher resolution data which will be derived from the Helios satellite will also be made available to the centre on a case-by-case basis. The dual main objectives of the programme are verification of arms control agreements and crisis monitoring, and the information will be distributed to the WEU and member states.[36]

While its JERS-1 (Japan Earth Resources Satellite) radar and optical sensor satellite orbited in 1992 has been shut down owing to sensor malfunctions, Japan, traditionally reliant to a large extent on US imagery for its intelligence needs, is also planning a new platform—the Advanced Land Observation Satellite (ALOS)—with a 2.5-m panchromatic and 10-m multispectral capability. The first South African Green Sat, which includes a 1.5-m resolution visible-light imagery capability, is to be launched in 1995.[37] In 1995 India will launch an improved version of its existing IRS-1A and IRS-1B remote-sensing satellites, including a camera with a resolution of 10 m.[38]

As the majority of the information given to the UN Special Commission on Iraq was collected by the USA,[39] the acquisition and sharing of high-quality imagery and other intelligence by other states, as well as by commercial satellites, would help alleviate fears that intelligence provided by the USA, for example, was being used for political purposes.

Commercial satellites

A study which assessed the potential of satellites such as SPOT and Landsat for monitoring nuclear activities concluded that 'such imaging from space can make a limited but valuable contribution to nuclear non-proliferation'.[40] One major problem outlined in this study is that, even though a facility may be observable from a satellite photograph with 10-m resolution, it is virtually impossible in the absence of collateral information to ascertain its purpose. A

[36] *Atlantic News*, no. 2521 (20 Apr. 1993), p. 4; de Selding, P., 'France to provide imagery to WEU', *Space News*, 3–9 May 1993, p. 9; and Interview with Barry Blaydes, Director, Western European Satellite Center, Newsmaker Forum, *Space News*, 15–28 Aug. 1994, p. 22.

[37] Asker, J. R., 'High-resolution imagery seen as threat, opportunity', *Aviation Week & Space Technology*, 23 May 1994, p. 51; Ebata, K., 'Japan plans satellite launch program', *Jane's Defence Weekly*, 11 June 1994, p. 22; and Sekigawa, E. and Mecham, M., 'Japan confirms delays in M-5 booster launch', *Aviation Week & Space Technology*, 27 June 1994, p. 82. The ALOS spacecraft, previously called HIROS, was renamed to avoid possible confusion with an existing high-resolution US satellite programme.

[38] Raghuvanshi, V., 'India prepares second generation IRS spacecraft for 1995 launch', *Space News*, 1–7 Aug. 1994, p. 18.

[39] Hibbs, M., 'US experts divided on whether Iraqi calutrons produced U-235', *Nuclear Fuel*, vol. 16, no. 13 (24 June 1991), p. 3.

[40] Spector, L. S., 'Monitoring nuclear proliferation', eds M. Krepon *et al.*, *Commercial Observation Satellites and International Security* (St. Martin's Press: New York, 1990), pp. 125–41.

photograph from the SPOT satellite was in fact able to identify Pakistan's Kahuta enrichment facility only as a 'massive structure' within a security perimeter. At this resolution Israel's Dimona reactor dome could not be discerned. The capacities of such plants could obviously not be estimated from these data, but the study concluded that such photographs could have value in that they may provide 'some tangible evidence' of a plant's existence and thus 'focus public attention on . . . growing nuclear capabilities'.

However, the capabilities of commercial satellites for monitoring proliferation-related and other activities are likely to grow by a quantum leap in the very near future after a decision by President Clinton in March 1994 allowing US firms to produce and sell satellite imagery of high resolution. While no firm restriction was placed on the resolution, it was made clear to industry officials that 1-m resolution would be acceptable. Decisions to license the satellites will be made to the Commerce Department, which will also have the power to stop data transmission from the satellites in times of national security or foreign policy crisis.[41] In the wake of this announcement the CIA has apparently learned that Russia may soon be offering images with resolution as fine as 0.75 m.[42] In the case of France on the other hand extended negotiations between the government and SPOT Image were required for the government to agree to even the 5-m resolution sensor to be orbited on the SPOT 5 commercial satellite at the turn of the century.[43]

Soon after the new US policy was announced, both Lockheed Corporation, through its Space Imaging Corporation, and Eyeglass International—a joint venture of Orbital Sciences Corporation, Litton's Itek Optical Systems Division and GDE Systems Inc.—received licences from the Commerce Department to orbit satellites with resolutions of 1 m. A third project, that of Worldview Imaging Corporation and CTA Inc., licensed in 1993 for a system with 3-m resolution which it hoped to have ready by 1996, also hoped to orbit a satellite with 1-m resolution capability once its 3-m resolution system is in place as a foundation. Both Lockheed and Eyeglass plan to be offering data by 1997. US firms are required to keep a list of the images which they acquire and to share their records with the government. It has been projected in some quarters at least that the commercial market for satellite imagery will lie in the $2–15 billion range by the end of the decade. The CIA, which has already recently opened up its satellite archives to allow a small group of environmental scientists to assess their potential use in understanding such areas as land use and climatic change, has reportedly also been discussing plans to market commercially some of its

[41] Mintz, J., 'Clinton approves sales of space photos, jarring the CIA', *International Herald Tribune,* 12–13 Mar. 1994, p. 1; and Lawler, A., 'Image policy opens new market for US', *Space News*, 14–20 Mar. 1994, p. 1.

[42] Iannotta, B., 'Russia expected to raise ante in satellite image market, *Space News*, 18–24 Apr. 1994, p. 18; and *Aviation Week & Space Technology*, 11 Apr. 1994, p. 19.

[43] de Selding, P., 'French doubt market for sharper images', *Space News*, 21–27 Mar. 1994, p. 1.

archived satellite data with 1-m resolution. These would, however, be restricted to images taken before 1972.[44]

The commercial availability of higher-resolution images should make the identification of nuclear facilities, or at least the raising of suspicions, much more likely. Use of the newer high-resolution platforms could in fact be cued by the lower-resolution satellites now in orbit, which have a much broader field of view, and the newer instruments can be used to get a closer look at interesting developments.

Commercial satellites are most promising if used to detect changes—for example, to identify whether major construction is under way at a known nuclear facility—and thus trigger appropriate political action or other means of investigation. If such information were available to the IAEA it could lead to a request for explanations if the state is party to the NPT. If the facility were not already subject to safeguards, the information could still be of use by alerting the Agency to monitor nearby facilities which might be safeguarded more closely, to try to ensure that no transfer of nuclear material is occurring.

Potentially, the *status* of known nuclear facilities could be monitored if they give off sufficient heat to be detectable by specific means such as satellites or aircraft. Such knowledge would be valuable in general and specifically with respect to monitoring possible agreements to halt production of fissionable material. The SPOT satellite, for example, by providing infrared images of the cooling pond, was able to demonstrate that the Chernobyl plant had been shut down after the accident in 1986. Heat from some reactors is discharged into the atmosphere. This could also be detected in principle, although an experiment performed in this area using 120-m resolution Landsat infrared images was not successful. Improvements in capabilities may make such undertakings feasible, however. It should also be noted that classified satellites are surely better equipped to deal with this type of problem as is demonstrated in the North Korean case discussed below.

Especially as more detailed images become available, it would be recommended that the IAEA keep a continuously updated file of commercial satellite images. In addition to the information provided by these images, more detailed and conclusive information is received from intelligence sources. Commercial photographs could also be used, for example, to help assuage public or national concerns regarding the purpose of a proposed special inspection. In a related area, perhaps now is the time to seek renewed support for an International Satellite Monitoring Agency for verification such as that first proposed by France in 1978.[45]

[44] Iannotta, B., 'Satellites challenge aerial photos', *Space News*, 21–27 Mar. 1994, p. 4; Anselmo, J. C., 'High-resolution satellite competition heats up', *Aviation Week & Space Technology*, 11 July 1994, p. 56; Asker, J. R., 'High-resolution imagery seen as threat, opportunity', *Aviation Week & Space Technology*, 23 May 1994, p. 51; Seitz, P., 'Worldview hones marketing strategy for imaging system', *Space News*, 5–11 Sep. 1994, p. 18; Interview with John Neer, President, Space Imaging Corp., *Space News*, 8–14 Aug. 1994, p. 22; de Selding (note 43), pp. 1 and 20; Gries, D. D., 'Opening up secret intelligence', *Orbis*, summer 1993, p. 372; and 'Green espionage', *New Scientist*, 16 Apr. 1994, p. 10.

[45] United Nations, *The Implications of Establishing an International Satellite Monitoring Agency*, (United Nations: New York, 1983).

Aerial reconnaissance

Aerial reconnaissance has a number of advantages over the use of satellites for verification and for verification of nuclear proliferation-related activity in particular. First and foremost is the simple fact that most states are in a technological and financial position to make use, at least in some modest form, of this monitoring method. There are probably more than 50 countries in possession of some reconnaissance capability, although in many cases this is still quite rudimentary. Other than the USA and the former Soviet Union (FSU), countries which routinely carry out reconnaissance flights include Australia, Canada, Denmark, France, Germany, Greece, Italy, Japan, the Netherlands, Norway, Spain, Sweden, Turkey and the UK.[46]

It has also been noted that, unlike satellites, which usually follow predictable orbits (changes require expense of limited and precious fuel), aircraft can 'change speed abruptly, fly in any direction, drop under clouds with their cameras, return to a target as often as necessary, and even loiter until an intelligence-gathering opportunity ripens . . . [and] are also more mission-adaptable than satellites because they can be loaded with specialised equipment as often as necessary'.[47] In addition aircraft offer virtually limitless resolution if allowed to fly low enough. Of course satellites can overfly large stretches of territory very quickly, but any detailed imagery requires limiting each photograph to a relatively small area. Satellites do not cause the legal difficulties that would pose problems for aircraft in the absence of appropriate agreements. These may often be eliminated, however, by flying outside the borders of unfriendly states and peering inside. The U-2 aircraft, for example, can obtain oblique-angle photographs from a range of 100 km.

As is well known, coalition aircraft, the mission of many of which was solely or partially reconnaissance, were able to roam the skies unhindered for the most part during the Persian Gulf War. Much of this reconnaissance was devoted to targeting, battle damage assessment (BDA) and other intelligence tasks, but one important mission was the uncovering of Iraq's nuclear potential. Because of the classified nature of the data collected, however, it is difficult to know the relative value of such flights compared with satellite intelligence in gathering information concerning proliferation activity.

Of course it should be remembered that these two types of monitoring are by no means mutually exclusive. Satellites would have been used to cue aerial overflights to get a clearer picture of the situation and, particularly in a situation in which hostile ground fire is a distinct possibility or when questions of sovereignty make aircraft imagery politically inexpedient, a brief sighting by an aircraft could be used to focus satellite attention on a specific area from the

[46] Krepon, M. and Tracey, J. P.,'"Open Skies" and UN peacekeeping', *Survival*, vol. 32, no. 3 (May/June 1990), p. 263.

[47] Burrows, W. E., *Deep Black: Space Espionage and National Security* (Berkeley Books: New York, 1988), p. 148.

safety of space to collect imagery or for long-duration communications monitoring.

In a related area, new efforts in the USA to reduce the costs of intelligence gathering led to an exploration of the ways in which unmanned spy drones could be used as a substitute for both satellite intelligence collection and manned aerial platforms in some instances.[48] In fact the Defense Airborne Reconnaissance Office (DARO), created in late 1993, will reportedly push for development of unmanned aerial vehicles (UAVs) which can be used for surveillance of countries such as North Korea and Bosnia and Herzegovina at the expense of more traditional programmes such as the U-2 spy plane.[49] A long-endurance UAV is currently under development in three phases in a joint effort involving the CIA and the Defense Department at a cost of $93 million. A classified follow-on to this effort with a very large budget is reportedly also under way.[50] Long-endurance UAVs would be particularly useful in covering areas of interest continuously or nearly so, unlike satellites which are usually limited to brief glimpses.

A US U-2 aircraft was put at the disposal of UNSCOM and together with three CH-53 helicopters from the German Government flew regular missions in Iraq. It was noted that:

> The commission has few doubts about the importance of aircraft to their mission. Its long-term monitoring plans, approved by the Security Council, include the right to overfly at any time, without hindrance, any area, site, or facility in Iraq, in fixed- or rotary-wing aircraft equipped with appropriate sensors. The commission's insistence on aerial inspection is the result of first-hand U.N. experience [in the Sinai, Angola, the Western Sahara, Cambodia and other areas].[51]

The mode of operation was to announce to Iraq a 48-hour period during which the flights, which originated in Saudi Arabia, would be conducted, specifying entry and exit points but giving no further details regarding the flight itself. The situation in Iraq, however, allowed for access which is unlikely to be repeated in future areas of interest. For example, Iranian incursions into Iraq in April 1992 prompted the Government of Iraq to request that the UN flights be halted lest they be mistaken for Iranian warplanes and shot down. The reaction of the Security Council was to threaten 'serious consequences' if the safety of the flights was not ensured.[52]

Concern over developments in North Korea prompted decisions to reactivate three of the SR-71 Blackbird reconnaissance aircraft, originally retired in 1990,

[48] Hitchens, T. and Munro, T., 'Pentagon review might terminate nuclear, spy plans', *Defense News*, 18–24 Oct. 1993, p. 3.

[49] Munro, N., 'Pentagon to buy UAV spy craft', *Defense News*, 20–26 Dec. 1993, p. 1.

[50] Fulghum, D. A., 'USAF stresses UAVs for recon', *Aviation Week & Space Technology*, 27 Sep. 1993, p. 44; and Morrocco, J. D., 'Pentagon-CIA UAV gains new significance', *Aviation Week & Space Technology*, 8 Nov. 1993, p. 28.

[51] Smithson, A. E., 'Open skies ready for takeoff', *Bulletin of the Atomic Scientists*, vol. 48, no. 1 (Jan/Feb. 1992), p. 17.

[52] Lewis, P., 'Iraq tells UN that surveillance flights might be shot down', *New York Times*, 11 Apr. 1992, p. 4.

for 'wide-area reconnaissance and intelligence support'. To be equipped with a new synthetic-aperture radar (SAR), a broad-area optical bar and other cameras, the Mach 3 plus aircraft is also capable of defeating deceptive practices known to be employed by some nations that know the exact times at which satellites will be passing overhead. These aircraft are quite expensive to maintain, however, and have prompted some of those concerned with the nuclear proliferation threat to suggest using large numbers of small and inexpensive satellites instead, especially when the target may not be able to be specified in advance, as noted by David Kay, former chief inspector for the IAEA in Iraq.[53]

The Joint Surveillance Target Attack Radar System (JSTARS), which was employed with success in the Persian Gulf War, has had its SAR capability increased since its employment in that conflict from about 1-m to about 0.3-m resolution over a distance of 300 miles (480 km).[54] While still considered a wartime capability,[55] this long-range asset could prove particularly effective in long-range information collection from outside a nation's borders.

Obtaining information on the operational status of nuclear facilities from thermal discharges, which has been seen to be a difficult task using, for example, commercial satellites alone, has been shown to be feasible from aircraft.[56] In 1977, during the time in which the USA was pressuring South Africa with regard to its preparations for a nuclear weapon test in the Kalahari Desert, intelligence efforts included surreptitious aerial reconnaissance. The CIA reportedly equipped the aircraft of the US Ambassador, which was flown for sport on occasion by the US military attaché in Pretoria, with cameras and an infrared sensor. Instructions were given to the attaché to fly in a circular pattern around the Valindaba enrichment plant in order to measure its thermal emissions to estimate its activity.[57]

While more intrusive than satellites, aircraft are less intrusive than on-site inspections and in some regions or with respect to certain agreements could therefore be more politically acceptable than on-the-ground inspections. Such overflights could be part of future regional accords. A study of the feasibility of such Open Skies regimes for verification of nuclear proliferation-related activity notes that aerial inspections would be of particular use in certain countries, including Iran, Iraq, Libya and North Korea, which, while having signed the NPT, are known to have sought nuclear weapons.[58] That these countries do not have significantly developed civilian nuclear fuel cycles facilitates the identification of weapon-related activity since the chance of confusing covert and

[53] Boatman, J., 'Blackbird revived for contingency role', *Jane's Defence Weekly,* 27 Aug. 1994, p. 12; Weber, S., 'Proposal to revive SR-71 ruffles feathers' *Defense News*, 29 Aug.–4 Sep. 1994, p. 6; and 'Conferees approve $263.8 billion in defense spending for FY 1995', *Arms Control Today*, vol. 24, no. 7 (Sep. 1994), p. 26.

[54] Fulghum (note 23), p. 46; Janssen Lok, J., 'J-STARS Gulf role detailed', *Jane's Defence Weekly*, 29 June 1991; and Kolcum, E. H., 'Joint-STARS E-8s return to US; 20-aircraft fleet believed assured', *Aviation Week & Space Technology*, 11 Mar. 1991, p. 20.

[55] Fulghum, D. A., 'Moving target indicators pushed for Korea watch', *Aviation Week & Space Technology*, 8 Aug. 1994, p. 23.

[56] Spector (note 39), pp. 137–38.

[57] Smith, J., 'S. Africa's nuclear file to be age-tested', *Washington Post,* 13 May 1993.

[58] Ramberg, B., 'Open Skies and nuclear nonproliferation', unpublished manuscript, 1992.

legitimate activity is minimized. As regards countries not party to the NPT and of particular concern, aerial monitoring would be much more useful in Pakistan and Israel, which have a relatively small number of dedicated facilities, than in India, where the weapon capability is embedded in a large civilian power programme. In countries which have recently declared their abandonment of nuclear weapon activity, including Argentina, Brazil and South Africa, an important confidence-building role could be played by aerial reconnaissance in ensuring that the new pledges are being honoured.

It is also noted in the same study that even the success of the Open Skies negotiations among the participating states of the then Conference on Security and Co-operation in Europe (renamed the Organization for Security and Co-operation in Europe, OSCE, from January 1995), while demonstrating the feasibility of such regimes, might be unable to provide sufficient impetus to overcome political barriers in regions where 'secrecy, not transparency is a *sina qua non* for security'. Forums considered for negotiating such agreements range from the UN Committee on Disarmament, to the IAEA, which would consider amendments by the Board of Governors to the 1971 NPT Model Safeguards Agreement to include aerial inspection. However, given the difficulties likely to be encountered in attempting to implement the latter it would perhaps be preferable to attempt regional aerial monitoring agreements as a first step.

Other types of information and synergistic effects

The usefulness of satellite and aerial imagery is well known and acknowledged. However, while SIGINT or the more specialized collection of communications intelligence (COMINT) are often overlooked in discussions of verification and intelligence collection, their role is by no means an unimportant one. Furthermore, communications intercepts can be acquired from much less expensive ground-based stations in addition to aerial or space-based systems. Overhead photography cannot peer inside buildings and, even with the highest-resolution photographs, what goes on inside a particular facility may remain a mystery. A few key phrases intercepted from communications, however, may provide initial indications or corroborate suspicions.

For example, evidence that employees of a German firm were directly involved in the nuclear programme of North Korea is based on telecommunications intercepts between the two countries made by the US National Security Agency (NSA).[59] Telecommunications intercepts have also led to the conclusion that Iran is 'seeking indiscriminately a wide range of nuclear technology and nuclear-related equipment, from a wide range of potential sources'.[60] Evidence of this sort can then cue further investigations involving stepped-up efforts using other intelligence resources and perhaps other countries to focus

[59] Hibbs, M., 'Agencies trace some Iraqi Urenco know-how to Pakistan re-export', *Nucleonics Week*, vol. 32, no. 48 (28 Nov. 1991), pp. 7–8.

[60] Hibbs, M., Patri, N. and Sandler, N., 'US, Europe doubt Israeli claim of Iranian nuclear weapons effort', *Nuclear Fuel*, vol. 16, no. 24 (25 Nov. 1991), p. 8.

attention on potential problem states before their progress reaches an advanced stage.

There are, therefore, synergistic effects involving aerial and satellite reconnaissance, imagery and signals collection. It is also important to realize that human inspectors undertaking legal activity for the IAEA may provide additional information to help target other monitoring resources. In addition there is always the possibility that human intelligence will provide important information, as was the case with Iraqi defectors. Human sources could be particularly valuable in helping to piece together information acquired from other sources by providing information on the state of development of a programme, including details of what is actually taking place inside certain facilities, or by supplying lists of foreign suppliers and other documents related to a nuclear programme. They may also provide soil samples from the vicinity of a facility under suspicion which could be analysed for nuclear clues—uranium hexafluoride, for example, in the case of a suspected enrichment plant.[61]

Information supplied by an Iraqi defector was reportedly corroborated by intelligence information on file in the USA, including satellite photographs taken months before the defector's revelations. These photographs were originally thought to show a facility unrelated to the nuclear programme in Iraq but, when reviewed in light of the defector's statements, were determined to reveal nuclear-related activity.[62] This highlights the possible synergistic effects of using multiple resource types—while one source of information may be of limited or no use in a given situation, information from another source may greatly enhance its value in identifying a particular facility or activity. Weapon proliferation is a prime concern of the CIA and its former Director, R. James Woolsey, has noted the necessity of coordinating the information gained from human intelligence with that from NTM, particularly in order to understand the various procurement systems that are being used.[63]

The offering of rewards for providing information related to a country's nuclear programme could be considered, but this might lead to an inordinate number of false alarms being generated which could easily overload a system set up to deal with information. However, willing governments could conceivably pursue this concept for acquiring information which could then be filtered before perhaps being passed on to the IAEA.

It should be very advantageous for nations to pool the information acquired from their various intelligence resources before submitting it to the IAEA. Correlating and analysing information from different sources and from different countries could be a valuable function of an IAEA information receiving and analysis unit—in receiving information from diverse sources and methods it would be in a better position perhaps than individual countries to assess various activities of potential proliferation concern.

[61] Richelson (note 3), p. 296.

[62] Hibbs, M. and Seneviratne, G., 'US believes Iraq has built magnetic isotope enrichment plant', *Nucleonics Week*, vol. 32, no. 25 (20 June 1991), p. 2.

[63] Prados, J., 'Woolsey and the CIA', *Bulletin of the Atomic Scientists*, vol. 49, no. 6 (July/Aug. 1993), p. 33.

It is very important to note that valuable experience has been gained in Iraq in acquiring and analysing intelligence of relevance for nuclear proliferation and then assessing the results through inspections with, if not a totally uncooperative, certainly a less-than-forthcoming state. The many-tiered approach of space-based, aerial- and ground-based sensors, coupled with OSI, was employed. It would be hard to imagine a better proving ground to assess the various methods. These specific lessons, while outside the scope of detailed analysis without access to classified information, will undoubtedly be of great benefit to any future verification of nuclear potential. Of course in future cases it may not be possible to use one or more of these methods immediately (or at all), but it is much more likely that the methods which are available will be able to provide much more useful information than they have done in the past as a result of lessons learned in Iraq.

While intelligence capabilities have also proved effective in the case of North Korea in providing information on the status of its nuclear reactors, operational bureaucracy must still be put in place before this type of information can be used to its full effect. While the IAEA acknowledged the US information, for example, the Agency none the less stressed that independent confirmation was required for political reasons and to preserve the credibility of the regime as a whole.[64]

Detection of clandestine facilities which are part of an effort to develop nuclear weapons could be accomplished by a variety of techniques which are often specific to a given type of facility.[65] Verification of clandestine enrichment activity is discussed in chapter 2. Newer and more technologically sophisticated technologies, such as laser enrichment and centrifuge methods, will be much more difficult to uncover directly through detection of an associated facility. The high power requirements of many enrichment techniques may provide some further clues. Some quantitative estimates of the power requirements for the various types of enrichment activity have been made,[66] but these are in general very dependent on the efficiency of operation for a given enrichment process and thus on the technical prowess of the developer. In addition, if a facility is designed to produce only enough material for one or two bombs per year—which as reported in chapter 5 may be a very few kilograms—it is much less likely that it could be detected using remote-sensing techniques such as satellite monitoring.

For example, the power necessary for an enrichment plant using gas diffusion to produce HEU has been estimated at approximately 0.900–3.0 MWh/SWU,

[64] Smith, J., 'When cool-off is the tip-off: U.S. satellites watch for chilling of North Korean reactor', *International Herald Tribune,* 14 Dec. 1993, p. 10.

[65] See, in particular, Greenwood, T., Rathjens, G. W. and Ruina, J., *Nuclear Power and Weapons Proliferation*, Adelphi Paper no. 130 (IISS: London, 1977), p. 36; von Hippel, F. and Levi, B. G., 'Controlling nuclear weapons at the source: verification of a cutoff in the production of plutonium and highly enriched uranium', eds K. Tsipis, D. W. Hafemeister and P. Janeway, *Arms Control Verification: The Technologies that Make it Possible* (Pergammon Brassey's: Washington, DC, 1986), pp. 377–80; and Fainberg, A., 'Strengthening IAEA safeguards: Lessons from Iraq', Center for International Security and Arms Control, Stanford University, Stanford: Calif., Apr. 1993, pp. 28–35.

[66] A recent compilation is given in Fainberg (note 65), p. 25.

which translates to about 3600–12 000 MWh for 20 kg of 90 per cent enriched uranium (given the requirement of about 200 SWU for each kilogram of 90 per cent enriched uranium as discussed in chapter 2). If centrifuges are used, this figure is reduced to the estimated range of 0.050–0.600 MWh/SWU or 200–2400 MWh for 20 kg. For EMIS the estimated range is 3–4 MWh/SWU or 12 000–16 000 MWh for 20 kg. This latter factor would be increased if the sophistication of the machines were only at the level of the alpha machines that were used in the Manhattan Project, that is, 20–30 MWh/SWU[67] or about 80 000–120 000 MWh for 20 kg. For laser techniques, however, the power consumption would be much lower than any of the above figures.

Assuming a 50 per cent capacity factor these figures translate at most into about 2.7 MW of power for each 20 kg of HEU produced per year by gas diffusion, 27 MW for Manhattan Project-level EMIS machines or 3.7 MW for more advanced EMIS separators. For centrifuge enrichment the figure is only about 0.5 MW. The somewhat limited usefulness of such estimates should be noted, however. The Iraqi enrichment effort was to require 200–400 MW of power for EMIS production of about 30 kg of HEU per year, while the above figures would indicate that only about 40 MW would be required even for Manhattan Project machines. While detection of an enrichment effort requiring only a few megawatts would be likely to go undetected, an effort requiring hundreds of megawatts is well above the detection threshold (which is probably in the tens of megawatts range) and could be expected to be discovered.[68] In this context it should also be mentioned, as discussed below, that the small North Korean reactor which has been producing plutonium has a heat output of about 25 MW and is capable of producing approximately 6–7 kg of plutonium per year.

It should also be noted that if the production capacity of either HEU or plutonium is spread out among several smaller enrichment plants or reactors then it could be substantially more difficult to uncover a given facility from its thermal emissions. On the other hand, however, discovery of just one of the more numerous facilities would be sufficient to sound an alarm revealing the presence of a clandestine effort.[69]

While the most conspicuous signature of a reactor being used for the clandestine production of plutonium would be its heat output it is possible that some tell-tale radioactive gases may be released, such as krypton-85 (half-life 10.8 years) or argon-41 and argon-42.[70] In principle these could be detected, but air

[67] Office of Technology Assessment (OTA), *Technologies Underlying Weapons of Mass Destruction*, OTA-BP-ISC-115 (US Government Printing Office: Washington, DC, Dec. 1993), p. 143. Table 5 in chapter 2 gives the power requirements for various technologies.

[68] Fainberg (note 65), p. 26.

[69] von Hippel and Levi (note 65), p. 377.

[70] Although the amount of argon-42 produced in a reactor is in general much smaller than the amount of argon-41, its half-life of about 33 years makes it much more amenable to sampling than the relatively short lived argon-41 isotope whose half-life is only 110 min. This short time period creates potential logistical difficulties since a sample would have to be analysed fairly rapidly after having been taken. If a direct detection method were to be used the detector would have to be close to the site and the reactor would have to have been operating very recently for any appreciable amount of argon-42 to be remaining to be detected. Fainberg (note 65), p. 28.

samples would probably be necessary in the vicinity of the plant and these may not be possible to obtain.

Perhaps more likely would be the detection of radioactive noble gas fission products which are released when spent fuel is reprocessed to obtain plutonium. Levels of krypton-85 in the atmosphere are in fact monitored by US intelligence and this has long been considered to be the most reliable method by which to estimate the amount of plutonium produced in the FSU for military purposes.[71] While the detection of clandestine facilities would depend on the background levels it is to be expected that even for a small plant, processing perhaps a few tens of kilograms of plutonium per year, the krypton-85 plume could be detected at distances of around 15–20 km. The gas is almost always released into the atmosphere in current reprocessing activity, but it is possible to use cryogenic and other techniques to trap it. Although well over 99 per cent of the gas could be collected by such methods, there remains the problem of storage as well as the possibility of uncontrolled accidental releases.

If any uranium or plutonium, or their fission products, were to escape from a reprocessing plant this could indicate that a clandestine effort is under way. As outlined in chapter 3, reprocessing requires many substances which, although perhaps not as specific to nuclear activity as plutonium or uranium, if discovered could at least serve to raise suspicions and perhaps prompt further investigation. These include acids, mainly nitric acid, used to dissolve the fuel as well as organic solvents such as dodecane. The nitrous acid effluents resulting from the dissolution of the spent fuel in nitric acid might also be observed, possibly using laser techniques. High-level radioactive waste may also be detected by its heat signature or, as was the case in North Korea, by its effect on plant life.

Much of the above discussion points to the utility of air and water sampling at specific sites for the possible detection of clandestine nuclear activity in the short term, but also on a routine long-term basis to establish a baseline level of the many possible indicators for future reference. Promising current investigations in this area are discussed below.

Other possible indicators of clandestine nuclear activity might include the discovery of unexplained high-security areas through either overhead reconnaissance or other means. Discovery of a high-explosive test site might also indicate the existence of a nuclear weapon programme, but it could be very difficult to distinguish such a site from a high-explosive testing area for conventional weapons. However, if subcritical tests for nuclear weapon development are being conducted, bright streamers caused by burning uranium might be detectable. These streamers would radiate symmetrically in all directions from a spherical implosion test or preferentially in a single direction from a test of a gun barrel-type device.[72]

[71] Albright, D., Berkhout, F. and Walker, W., SIPRI, *Plutonium and Highly Enriched Uranium 1995: World Inventories, Capabilities and Policies* (Oxford University Press: Oxford, forthcoming), chapter 3 : 'Inventories of military plutonium in the nuclear weapon states', section III, subsection on 'measuring krypton-85 emissions'.

[72] Fainberg (note 65), p. 38.

Citizen verification

As discussed above, crucial information on the Iraqi nuclear programme was obtained through defectors who were willing to share the appropriate information with those in a position to act on it. Another important case of information about a country's nuclear programme coming to light through a citizen who had access to much information was the widely publicized case of Mordechai Vanunu and his revelations concerning the Israeli nuclear weapon programme.[73]

These examples indicate that, especially with treaty-related activities which are very difficult to verify by more standard measures—such as clandestine deployment of nuclear facilities—it could be useful to set up some type of international mechanism which would allow those in a position to offer information of potential use in the verification process to come forward. Such an authority could be headed by a small group whose eminence is such that their opinion would be highly valued by the international community. Those possessing valuable information could come forward in confidence to such a body perhaps through and protected by the UN. Where violation of an international treaty is involved, the international obligation to come forward with information would transcend any obligation to the nation state. Encouraging an appropriate forum could aid significantly in strengthening the NPT.[74]

Such an authority could also be potentially useful in dealing with information which may come to light as a result of the acquisition and analysis of information obtained through the use of commercial satellites.

Camouflage, concealment and deception

Compounding the difficulties in locating and identifying facilities and equipment related to the production of materials for nuclear weapons, potential proliferators could and almost certainly would employ camouflage, concealment and deception (CC&D) techniques. It is well known that Iraq employed such techniques throughout the Persian Gulf War and in particular in attempting to conceal its nuclear programme.

The full extent and effectiveness of this effort may never be known, but the resources employed were apparently extensive. For example, the IAEA was informed by Iraq that it had been building the redundant facilities which had been uncovered so that, if one location were discovered, another would serve to allow the programme to continue. Thus, the calutron facility at Al Tarmiya had an identical twin (although less complete) at Ash Sharqat.[75] In a building apparently designed for recovering uranium from calutrons, inspectors found

[73] For a highly interesting and detailed account see Barnaby, F., *The Invisible Bomb: The Nuclear Arms Race in the Middle East* (I. B. Tauris: London, 1989).

[74] Oxford Research Group, *The Plutonium Legacy: Nuclear Proliferation out of Control*, Current Decisions Report, no. 12 (Apr. 1993), pp. 34–35.

[75] Hibbs, M., 'Unresolved questions loom on Iraqi centrifuge effort', *Nucleonics Week*, vol. 32, no. 37 (12 Sep. 1991), p. 7.

equipment for extensive air handling and filtration which would not only conserve the material itself but also prevent tell-tale isotopic signatures from escaping.[76] In addition, for example, evidence which could have pointed to the large power requirements of the EMIS enrichment programme was hidden by burying power lines, and great pains were taken to secure communications to prevent tell-tale information from being intercepted by foreign signals intelligence operations.[77] The entire facility at Al Tarmiya—including almost 400 buildings in an area of more than 2 square miles—was surrounded by a light fence so as to fool satellite photo interpreters by giving them the impression that nothing of great importance was taking place inside.[78]

In addition Iraq used several methods to hinder IAEA inspectors. This included providing information on the last day of a particular inspection so that it would be too late to act on it, overwhelming the team with information on the first day of an inspection and causing unnecessary translation delays by providing answers to questions in Arabic. In addition they physically prevented the free movement of inspectors as they tried to acquire data, destroyed entire facilities to attempt to conceal activities which had taken place, painted over areas to hamper sampling activity, removed electrical grids to hide evidence of power consumption levels and covered items with concrete.

The Iraqis also videotaped inspections, presumably to examine inspectors' behaviour for weaknesses to be exploited in the future and better monitor the flow of information from their own people, and as an intimidation tactic for both sides. More physical intimidation of inspectors included firing warning shots, death-threat notes slipped under hotel-room doors and splattering them with paint. These tactics certainly had an effect on the ability of some inspectors to perform their tasks in an optimal manner.[79]

There are indications that in the mid-1980s China was considering constructing a nuclear power plant in Iraq. It is interesting to note that, although there is no public evidence that discussions ever went beyond the feasibility stage, Iraqi requirements included 'the defensibility of area from possible attacks' as well as the 'ability to camouflage from satellites'.[80]

It is also important to note here that concern over the possibility of Iraq losing the war with Iran led to the transfer of highly classified intelligence to Iraq by the USA from 1982 to 1988. Reportedly, imagery from satellites as well as communications intercepts and CIA assessments were provided to Iraqi commanders. From this information they were able to learn about appropriate methods of camouflaging their systems and activities.[81] Thus, while Iraq is a

[76] Hibbs, M., 'Inspectors find four calutron enrichment plants in Iraq', *Nuclear Fuel*, vol. 16, no. 15 (22 July, 1991), p. 7.

[77] Bailey (note 9), p. 29.

[78] Burrows, W. E. and Windrem, R., *Critical Mass: The Dangerous Race for Superweapons in a Fragmenting World* (Simon&Schuster: New York, 1994), p. 44.

[79] Bailey (note 9), pp. 32–33.

[80] Knapik, M., 'US document says China studied building Iraq a power reactor', *Nucleonics Week*, vol. 32, no. 27 (4 July 1991), p. 2.

[81] Hersh, S. M., 'US secretly gave aid to Iraq early in its war against Iran', *New York Times*, 26 Jan. 1992, p. A1; 'U.S. data dump to Iraq hurt Gulf recon efforts', *Space News*, 7–13 Mar. 1994, p. 2; Tim-

special case in that so much intelligence was indeed focused on it during the war without evidence of a large fraction of its weapon programme being found, it must be borne in mind that a great deal can be learned with respect to enhancing CC&D if one has access to information on the types of collection which are occurring. Access to some raw intelligence would certainly have allowed Iraq to assess the US national technical means and thus aid in thwarting them.

In fact, shortly after the Israeli bombing of the Osiraq reactor in 1981, Saddam Hussein stated in an interview that the bombing taught Iraq and all Arabs that 'they must shelter their vital projects from all attack, so that even an atomic bomb will not be able to knock them out'.[82]

In an example from another part of the world, in South Africa the Advens Laboratory, where most of the work on the South African nuclear bomb was carried out, was reportedly not identified as a nuclear facility by the IAEA or the CIA until its function was finally disclosed by the South African Government in March 1993. Great pains had been taken to hide the facility from satellites including, for example, installing the green roof of the building before either its internal walls were constructed or any recognizable equipment was delivered to the site. US suspicion was as a result focused on another site closer to Valindaba, the main nuclear research centre, instead—a site where South Africa now asserts that no nuclear weapon work ever took place.[83] Thus detecting facilities even in the construction stage—before a permanent form of camouflage is employed—may be thwarted by camouflaging the construction itself. This further accentuates the necessity to avoid relying on any one means to uncover nuclear-related activity, as discussed above.

III. The case of North Korea

Following closely on the heels of the Iraqi experience the IAEA and the international nuclear non-proliferation regime have faced a new challenge in North Korea. Intelligence collection has had a large impact on this case owing to the closed nature of North Korea. This aspect of the case is given particular attention below along with the implications for monitoring nuclear proliferation-related activity in the future.

North Korea acceded to the NPT in 1985.[84] Although the Treaty obligates states parties to conclude a safeguards agreement with the IAEA within

merman, K. R., *The Death Lobby: How the West Armed Iraq* (Houghton Mifflin Co.: New York, 1991), pp. 130–31; and Woodward, B., *Veil: The Secret Wars of the CIA 1981–1987* (Pocket Books: New York, 1988), pp. 507, 556.

[82] Saddam Hussein, interview with Barbara Walters, 23 June 1981, quoted in Timmerman (note 81), p. 104.

[83] Smith, J. R., 'From dust to dust: history of S. Africa's bombs', *Washington Post*, 12 May 1993.

[84] The historical sequence of events reported here is drawn from a number of sources, including 'Report by the Director General on the implementation of the agreement between the Government of the Democratic People's Republic of Korea and the International Atomic Energy Agency for the application of safeguards in connection with the Treaty on the Non-Proliferation of Nuclear Weapons (INFCIRC/403)', IAEA document GC(XXXVII)/1084 Attachment, 26 Sep. 1993; Lehman, R. F. II, 'A North Korean nuclear-weapons program', *Security Dialogue*, vol. 24, no. 3 (1993), pp. 257–72; Albright, D., 'North Korean plutonium production', Institute for Science and International Security (ISIS),

18 months of signature, it was not until April 1992 that the safeguards agreement between North Korea and the IAEA finally entered into force. In May of that year North Korea submitted its initial report on nuclear materials and in the same month the IAEA began *ad hoc* inspections to verify the correctness and completeness of the report. Based on inconsistencies between the results of these inspections and the initial report made by North Korea and in order to resolve the discrepancies, the IAEA requested further information as well as access to two locations at which it was believed nuclear waste was being stored.

The disagreement concerned the amount of plutonium that North Korea had reprocessed—plutonium produced in its 5-MWe (approximately 25-MWth) gas-cooled, graphite-moderated experimental nuclear reactor situated at the Yongbyon Nuclear Research Center.[85] From the isotopic content of collected samples the IAEA inspections determined that a reprocessing plant[86] being constructed by North Korea at Yongbyon (referred to as a 'Radiochemical Laboratory' by the North Koreans) had been used on a small scale during 1989–91. The DPRK declared that it had separated only 100 grams of plutonium in 1990 taken from a few damaged fuel rods in 1990.

As discussed in chapter 3, one of the decay products of plutonium-241 is americium-241. Hence the amount of ^{241}Am present in samples taken in 'smear' or 'swipe' samples from the glove boxes used to handle the purified plutonium can be used as an indicator of how much time has passed since the plutonium was separated. This was used by the IAEA to arrive at the conclusion that separation efforts occurred at three distinct times. The isotopic ratios of the plutonium isotopes ^{239}Pu, ^{240}Pu and ^{241}Pu were also determined for plutonium contained in the waste and the separated plutonium, and significantly less plutonium-240 was found in the waste. These ratios should have been the same if the waste and the separated plutonium resulted from processing the same batch of spent fuel. The fact that they were different indicates that North Korea probably has more waste than has been declared—although the uncertainty in this latter conclusion is reportedly larger than that concerning the americium. A further problem was found in the isotope ratios of ^{239}Pu, ^{240}Pu and ^{241}Pu, which

Washington, DC, 3 June 1994; Davis, Z. S., 'International Atomic Energy Agency: strengthen verification authority?', CRS Issue Brief, IB91109, Library of Congress, Washington, DC, 14 Feb. 1994; Albright, D., 'North Korea and the "worst-case" scare-nario', *Bulletin of the Atomic Scientists*, vol. 50, no. 2 (Jan./Feb. 1994), p. 3; Albright, D., 'How much plutonium does North Korea have?', *Bulletin of the Atomic Scientists*, vol. 50, no. 5 (Sep./Oct. 1994), p. 46; and *PPNN Newsbrief*, no. 22 (2nd quarter 1993), no. 23 (3rd quarter 1993), no. 24 (4th quarter 1993), no. 25 (1st quarter 1994) and no. 26 (2nd quarter 1994).

[85] The reactor is rated at about 5 MWe, which is approximately 20–30 MWth. Using the rule of thumb given in chapter 3, that plutonium is produced at a rate of approximately 1 g per day per MWth of reactor power (this is a very rough estimate as the amount varies with reactor type), if operated continuously at full power this reactor would be capable of producing about 7–11 kg of plutonium annually—roughly enough for one bomb. The operation would normally be at less than full efficiency, however.

[86] It is believed that construction of the 180-m long, 6-storey high facility began in 1987. By the 1992 IAEA inspections it was estimated to be 80% complete and recent estimates are that it could be complete and operational by 1996. It is estimated that its capacity will be sufficient to reprocess all the spent fuel from the 5-, 50- and 200-MWe reactors North Korea is operating or constructing. Bermudez, J. S., 'North Korea's nuclear infrastructure', *Jane's Intelligence Review*, Feb. 1994, pp. 77–78; and Albright, ISIS (note 84).

were not only different in the separated material and the waste samples that were taken but also inconsistent with the declared reactor history as well.[87]

North Korean declarations were therefore at odds with the IAEA findings and, together with intelligence information received from member states[88] concerning the existence of two undeclared nuclear-related sites (thought to store nuclear waste), prompted the request for access to the sites where waste from the plutonium reprocessing was believed to be stored.

Citing the perceived threat posed by the upcoming 'Team Spirit' military exercise involving the USA and South Korea, North Korea refused to allow the requested special inspections unless the exercise was cancelled. The refusal having been reported by the Director General to the Board of Governors of the IAEA, they in February and again in March 1993 called upon North Korea to comply with the Agency's request, having decided that access to the sites was essential and urgent. On 12 March, citing the 'Team Spirit' exercise, the impartiality of the IAEA and the defence of its supreme interests, North Korea began the three-month process of withdrawal from the NPT—the first time that such a decision had been taken.

On 1 April 1993 the Board found North Korea in non-compliance with its safeguards agreement, deciding to report this as well as the inability of the Agency to verify non-diversion of nuclear material required to be safeguarded to Agency members as well as to the UN Security Council and General Assembly. This was followed by Security Council Resolution 825 (adopted on 11 May 1993) calling on North Korea to comply with its IAEA safeguards agreement. Sanctions were not called for at that time, apparently to avoid a veto from China which favoured the continuation of dialogue. The resolution was immediately rejected; but then, on 11 June, just before the three-month period of notice required by Article X of the NPT was about to come to an end, North Korea announced that it was suspending its withdrawal from the Treaty. While it was announced that the IAEA would be allowed to continue to apply safeguards the issue of allowing the special inspections to take place remained unsettled.

Senior-level bilateral talks on nuclear issues had begun with the USA on 2 June 1993 and by July discussion involving the USA had reportedly offered aid in shifting North Korea from its graphite-moderated reactors to light-water reactors. These pose less proliferation concern especially since they will require enriched uranium fuel which will have to be imported and the plutonium produced under typical operating conditions will contain a large fraction of isotopes other than ^{239}Pu. The aid would be contingent, however, on North Korea

[87] See Albright, D., 'North Korea drops out', *Bulletin of the Atomic Scientists,* May 1993, p. 10; and Hileman, B., 'North Korea suspected of hiding plutonium', *Chemical & Engineering News*, 11 Apr. 1994, p. 5.

[88] It was apparently necessary for former CIA Director Robert Gates to overcome powerful objections within the CIA in order to share information collected by satellites with the IAEA. McCurdy, D., 'Glasnost for the CIA', *Foreign Affairs*, vol. 73, no. 1 (Jan./Feb. 1994), p. 135.

living up to its international commitments.[89] Meanwhile, inspections of the maintenance and replacement of safeguards equipment were allowed to continue in May and August at the 25-MWth reactor[90] and the Radiochemical Laboratory, but inspectors were unable to complete all of the required inspection activities.

There followed a period of haggling during which North Korea offered to accept certain limited inspections and the IAEA expressed the view that it did not wish to carry out inspections unless the Agency was allowed full access. North Korea for its part claimed 'unique status' with respect to the NPT—having suspended its withdrawal from the Treaty—which the North Koreans claimed meant that they were not obliged to accept full IAEA safeguards.[91] Inspections continued in February and March 1994 to all seven of the declared nuclear facilities but they followed an agreed list of permitted activities which were mainly limited to gaining sufficient information for the IAEA to verify that no diversion of nuclear material had occurred since previous inspections.[92] None the less even some of the limited procedures which had been agreed to beforehand were reportedly not allowed, including the collection of samples which would have allowed determination to be made of whether recent plutonium separation had occurred.

[89] Although ideal for the production of weapon-grade plutonium, North Korea has said that its reactors—the 5-MWe operating reactor and the 50-MWe and 200-MWe reactors under construction and scheduled for start-up in 1995 and 1996 respectively—are solely for the production of electricity, stating that the graphite-moderated design was chosen because it could be developed without foreign assistance. The spent fuel of this type of gas-cooled, graphite-moderated reactor requires reprocessing for safety reasons as the magnesium compound used for the fuel cladding is very difficult to store safely—storage in water or exposure to moisture breaks down the cladding. Subsequent exposure of the spent fuel to the air can lead to escape of radionuclides as well as corrosion and subsequent spontaneous ignition of the uranium metal and significant release of radioactive material. These concerns enable the North Koreans to nominally justify their reprocessing on the basis of safety concerns—such justification would not be possible in the case of light water reactors. Panofsky, W. K. H., 'Options for the long-term disposition of nuclear materials', Center for Security and Technology Studies, CSTS-35-93, Lawrence Livermore National Laboratory, Livermore, Calif., 1993, pp. 4–5; and Albright, ISIS (note 84). The type of fuel used in the North Korean reactor can be stored under optimal conditions in water for up to 2 years and for up to 5 years by placing the fuel in special canisters in the spent fuel ponds. Conditions in the Korean facilities were far from ideal, however, when the fuel was placed in them—lacking adequate filtration and purification systems. If special dry storage facilities are constructed (North Korea's small dry storage area is not sufficiently maintained) the spent fuel can be stored safely for periods perhaps as long as decades. Albright, D., 'North Korea's corroding fuel', An Occasional ISIS Report, ISIS, Washington, DC, 2 Aug. 1994.

[90] North Korea also possesses a 0.1 MWth critical assembly and a 8 MWth modified IRT-2000 reactor, both acquired from the former Soviet Union, the latter having been upgraded to 8 MWth by North Korea using indigenous technology. They are used for producing radioactive isotopes for medicine and industry as well as for scientific research. See Spector, L. S., *Nuclear Ambitions: The Spread of Nuclear Weapons 1989–1990* (Westview Press: Boulder, Colo., 1990), p. 139; and Bermudez, J. S., 'North Korea's nuclear infrastructure', *Jane's Intelligence Review*, Feb. 1994, p. 78.

[91] As a North Korean official who was involved in the bilateral talks with the USA put it, after withdrawing from the NPT in March: 'In June, we then agreed in a bilateral note to the U.S. that we would suspend the withdrawal. But that is not legally sufficient to balance out our instrument of withdrawal under NPT Article 10 . . . So we are legally and technically out (of the NPT) and politically in'. Quoted in Hibbs, M., 'Pyongyang may end IAEA access to monitored sites, envoy says', *Nucleonics Week*, 7 Oct. 1993, p. 11.

[92] *IAEA Newsbriefs*, vol. 9, no. 1 (Feb./ Mar. 1994); *IAEA Press Release*, PR94/4, 15 Feb. 1994; and *IAEA Press Release*, PR94/7, 16 Mar. 1994.

As a result, at a Board of Governors meeting in March, a resolution was adopted finding North Korea in further non-compliance with its safeguards agreement and that the Agency remained 'unable to verify that there has been no diversion of nuclear material required to be safeguarded under the terms of the safeguards agreement to nuclear weapons or other explosive devices'.[93]

In April North Korea advised the IAEA that it would soon shut down the reactor for safety reasons and begin the process of fuel replacement. The IAEA then requested full access to the fuel-removal operation, including random selection of several hundred of the fuel rods for subsequent examination. Knowledge of the position of the rods[94] and isotopic analysis of their contents would allow a history of the reactor core to be constructed. In particular this would enable determination of how much fuel may have been replaced during the 1989 shut-down and thus how much may have already been reprocessed to produce plutonium.

The capacity of the 25 MWth reactor has been estimated at approximately 6–7 kg of weapon-grade plutonium per year.[95] At the time the fuel was removed US officials estimated that the fuel rods from the reactor contained 20–30 kg of plutonium, or enough for 4 or 5 nuclear weapons, and that reprocessing could be completed by the end of 1994 even without the second production line which was being constructed at the reprocessing plant.[96] The capacity of the 50 MWe reactor has been estimated at about 50 kg of weapon-grade plutonium per year, and that of the 200 MWe reactor at about 180 kg.[97]

North Korea rejected the IAEA proposal to sample the fuel but announced that it would permit inspectors to be present at the refuelling. The shut-down occurred in May and the refuelling commenced, at first without IAEA inspectors present—a technical violation of the safeguards agreement. When the inspectors did arrive, about 5 per cent of the fuel had been removed and placed in a monitored cooling pond and they were allowed to perform maintenance on

[93] Resolution by the Board of Governors of the International Atomic Energy Agency of 24 Mar. 1994: Implementation of the Agreement between the Agency and the Democratic People's Republic of Korea for the application of safeguards in connection with the Treaty on the Non-Proliferation of Nuclear Weapons (INFCIRC/403), reprinted in *IAEA Press Release*, PR94/9, 21 Mar. 1994, Attachment, p. 2.

[94] The IAEA wished to sample about 300 fuel pins from a radial cross-section of the reactor core. The amount of plutonium produced would normally be expected to follow a well-defined pattern increasing in fuel rods towards the centre of the core. If any irradiated fuel has been removed and replaced with fresh fuel in the past this would skew the normal pattern and this would be detected in the radial sampling technique. Hibbs, M. and Hart, K., 'IAEA, US agencies underestimated North Korea's refuelling capacity', *Nuclear Fuel*, 6 June 1994, p. 6.

[95] This particular published estimate assumes that the reactor is operated at 25 MWth for an average of 80% of the time, although it is not considered likely that the reactor operated this efficiently from its start-up in 1986. Albright, ISIS (note 84).

[96] Gordon, M. R., 'US says North Korea could have plutonium for 4 bombs this year', *International Herald Tribune*, 8 June 1994, p. 6.

[97] These estimates assume thermal power outputs of 200 MW and 800 MW and operation at full power for 80% and 70% of the time, respectively. In addition the 200 MWe reactor is probably not optimized for producing weapon-grade plutonium but rather for electricity production, in which case its annual output would be about 120 kg. Albright, ISIS (note 84).

monitoring equipment, including cameras, so that they were able to ascertain that there had not been any diversion of the spent fuel.[98]

The fuel had not been marked in any way, however, nor was the IAEA permitted its request, which it called 'indispensable', to select, segregate and secure fuel rods. This would have allowed the IAEA, through subsequent analysis of a representative sample of the fuel rods, to determine that no fuel had been diverted in the past by obtaining a proper history of the reactor core and, in particular, establishing whether it had been the first core as was declared by North Korea. In its refusal of the IAEA requests North Korea again claimed its 'unique status' under the NPT.

As North Korea made clear to the IAEA this unique status is 'based on its [North Korea's] temporary suspension of the effectuation of the announced withdrawal from the non-proliferation treaty' and on the fact that the decision for this suspension was undertaken 'on the premise that the DPRK–USA negotiations for a peaceful resolution of the nuclear issue will continue on an equal and unprejudiced basis'.[99] They also stated that their unique status meant that they were 'only obliged to provide the continuity of safeguards through the verification of the non-diversion of nuclear material' and that 'such inspection activities falling under the categories of routine and ad hoc inspections as selection and preservation of some of the fuel rods can never be allowed'.[100] It was based on this interpretation of their obligations that the North Koreans restricted other inspection activities requested by the Agency, such as smear sampling at the reprocessing plant in March.[101]

On 19 May a report was made to the Board of Governors and the Security Council that in discharging the fuel without compliance with IAEA-requested safeguards measures North Korea had committed a serious violation of its safeguards agreement.[102] Inspectors were, however, permitted to complete their inspection of the reprocessing plant which had been interrupted in March, although they were not allowed to sample the dissolver liquids.

US officials continued warnings that they would seek to have the Security Council impose sanctions on North Korea if proper inspection of the fuel unloading was not permitted, and in early June they called for UN economic sanctions. Failing Security Council backing, the USA was also considering organizing sanctions outside the UN.[103] None the less both the CIA and its

[98] 'Senate chiefs speak out for sanctions on North Korea', *International Herald Tribune*, 16 May 1994, p. 1; 'N Korea cleared in new arms row', *Financial Times*, 22 May 1994, p. 4; 'Nuclear inspectors complete work at Korean plant', *International Herald Tribune*, 26 May 1994, p. 4; and 'IAEA says Pyongyang's fissile material is under safeguards', *Arms Control Today*, vol. 24, no. 5 (June 1994), p. 24.

[99] Communication dated 20 April 1994 received from the permanent mission of the Democratic People's Republic of Korea to the International Atomic Energy Agency, IAEA document INFCIRC/442, 9 May 1994, Attachment, p. 1.

[100] Communication dated 14 May 1994 received from the permanent mission of the Democratic People's Republic of Korea to the International Atomic Energy Agency, IAEA document INFCIRC/444, 30 May 1994, Attachment, p. 2.

[101] IAEA document INFCIRC/442, 9 May 1994, Attachment, pp. 5–6.

[102] IAEA document INFCIRC/443, 18 May 1994; and *IAEA Press Release*, PR 94/24, 28 May 1994.

[103] Smith, J. R., 'Experts find North Koreans defied UN', *International Herald Tribune*, 20 May 1994, p. 1; Dunne, N. and Walker, T., 'US may seek N Korea sanctions ouside of UN', *Financial Times*, 6 June

counterpart in South Korea had determined that sanctions would not prove effective in convincing North Korea to give up its nuclear programme, one high South Korean official remarking, 'How do you isolate the world's most isolated country? . . . The truth is it can't be done'.[104] North Korea has repeatedly threatened that the imposition of sanctions would constitute an act of war.[105]

On 10 June the IAEA Board of Governors adopted another resolution, stating that the limited opportunity to select, segregate and secure the fuel rods had been lost and that 'the Agency's ability to ascertain, with sufficient confidence, whether nuclear material from the reactor had been diverted in the past'[106] had been lost as well. The North Koreans had stated that the refuelling was being conducted 'in such a manner as to fully preserve the technical possibility of measuring the fuel rods as requested by the IAEA when our unique status comes to an end'.[107] (In a more independent challenge to the IAEA claim it has been noted that there may still be enough information to ascertain the needed historical information regarding the length of time that the fuel has been in the reactor, and whether any diversion took place, by randomly sampling the fuel rods and hence determining their average age and burnup rates.[108]) In addition, the IAEA found that North Korea continued to 'widen its non-compliance with its safeguards agreement', and as a result of the non-compliance decided to suspend hundreds of thousands of dollars in non-medical assistance.[109]

As a result, it was noted by the Agency's Director General that the inspections of the two suspected waste sites were now even more important. None the less, North Korea stated that it would never allow outside access to the sites, in part at least because of the fact that they had been discovered by satellite photographs.[110] On 13 June 1994 North Korea announced that it was withdrawing from the IAEA and would no longer allow Agency inspectors inside the country.[111] The safeguards agreement between North Korea and the IAEA pursuant to the NPT remained valid and unaffected by this withdrawal, however.

1994, p. 1; Smith, J., 'U.S. maps plan for UN sanctions against North Korea', *International Herald Tribune*, 2 June 1994, p. 7; and Gordon, M. R., 'U.S. will ask the UN to impose sanctions against North Korea', *International Herald Tribune*, 3 June 1994, p. 1.

[104] Sanger, D., 'Analyzing North Korea: "somebody miscalculated"', *International Herald Tribune*, 7 June 1994, p. 1.

[105] Reid, T. R., 'North Korea links sanctions and war', *International Herald Tribune*, 7 June 1994, p. 5; and 'China vow to North Korea sets back sanctions effort', *International Herald Tribune*, 8 June 1994, p. 1.

[106] 'Implementation of the Agreement between the Agency and the Democratic People's Republic of Korea for the application of safeguards in connection with the Treaty on the Non-Proliferation of Nuclear Weapons (INFCIRC/403)', Resolution adopted by the Board on 10 June 1994, *IAEA Press Release*, PR 94/25, 13 June 1994, Attachment, p. 1.

[107] 'Statement dated 1 June 1994 by a spokesman for the foreign ministry of the Democratic People's Republic of Korea', IAEA document INFCIRC/450, 13 July 1994, Attachment, p. 3.

[108] Opall, B., 'US arms control group backs N. Korea claim', *Defense News*, 6–12 June 1994, p. 6.

[109] 'Implementation of the agreement between the Agency and the Democratic People's Republic of Korea' (note 106), Attachment, p. 2; and *PPNN Newsbrief*, no. 26 (2nd quarter 1994), p. 5.

[110] Ottaway, D. B., '"Never!" the Kim regime declares on nuclear access', *International Herald Tribune*, 8 June 1994, p. 6.

[111] The withdrawal of the Democratic People's Republic of Korea from the International Atomic Energy Agency, IAEA document INFCIRC/447, 21 June 1994; and Sanger, D. E., 'North Korea declares an immediate pullout from atomic agency; Seoul alerts reserves', *International Herald Tribune*, 14 June 1994, p. 1.

Soon afterwards, however, in the wake of discussions between visiting former US President Jimmy Carter in North Korea with leader Kim Il Sung it was announced on 22 June that North Korea had agreed to freeze its nuclear programme. This included a pledge to refrain from refuelling the 25-MWth nuclear reactor or reprocessing the spent fuel removed and to allow continued access to the fuel removed from the reactor as long as bilateral talks with the USA continued and in exchange for US agreement to suspend its efforts to impose sanctions. New talks between the USA and North Korea began on 8 July. They were temporarily suspended after only one day by the death of Kim Il Sung, but they were resumed on 5 August when discussions included the North Korean request for a light water reactor to replace its graphite reactors.[112]

Agreement was reached later in the month on the elements which 'should be part of a final resolution of the nuclear issue'. North Korea agreed to freeze its nuclear activities and maintain the continuity of safeguards, stating that it was prepared to replace its graphite-moderated reactors with light water reactors. The USA stated that it would be prepared to arrange for supplying them as well as for supplying the required energy alternatives to the graphite reactors in the interim. Upon receiving these assurances from the USA, North Korea would freeze its reactor construction, forgo reprocessing and seal its reprocessing plant. This would then be monitored by the IAEA. South Korea offered to supply technology and financing for light water reactors provided that North Korea demonstrated that it is not developing nuclear weapons.

Both the USA and North Korea also affirmed their preparedness to establish diplomatic and economic relations with one another, the USA to provide assurances that it would not threaten or use nuclear weapons against North Korea and North Korea that it would be prepared to implement the 1994 North–South Joint Declaration on the Denuclearization of the Korean Peninsula. Furthermore North Korea pledged to remain party to the NPT and to 'allow implementation of its safeguards agreement under the Treaty'.[113]

North Korea continued to refuse access to the two waste sites, however, but meetings continued in September and October. The USA agreed to allow North Korea to store its spent fuel rods in welded steel containers as an interim measure and that the special inspections could be conducted months or even years after a settlement has been reached.[114]

[112] Hibbs, M., ''Threat by China led North Korea to call on Carter to mediate', *Nucleonics Week*, 30 June 1994, p. 8; Riding, A., 'US–North Korea talks resume but go nowhere', *International Herald Tribune*, 6–7 Aug. 1994, p. 5; and 'Clinton says North Korea yields in nuclear dispute', *International Herald Tribune*, 23 June 1994, p. 1.

[113] Agreed statement between the United States and North Korea, Geneva, 12 Aug. 1994 as reprinted in *Arms Control Today*, vol. 24, no. 7 (Sep. 1994), p. 23; Pollack, A., 'Seoul offers to provide reactors for North Korea', *International Herald Tribune*, 15 Aug. 1994, p. 1; Pollack, A., 'On unity for Korea, decades of enmity die hard', *International Herald Tribune*, 16 Aug. 1994, p. 4; 'Nuclear fears dispelled by N Korean accord', *Jane's Defence Weekly*, 27 Aug. 1994, p. 6; and Hibbs, M., 'U.S.: cap North Korean program, then seek unreported activities', *Nucleonics Week*, 18 Aug. 1994, p. 12.

[114] New U.S. concession to North Korea', *International Herald Tribune*, 12 Sep. 1994, p. 2; and 'U.S. eases stance on North Korea', *International Herald Tribune*, 10–11 Sep. 1994, p. 2.

Finally, building on the preliminary accord reached in August the USA and North Korea agreed on 21 October 1994 on a timetable for implementing an end to the North Korean nuclear weapon programme.[115] The agreement first provides for the replacement of North Korea's graphite-moderated reactors with the more proliferation-resistant light water reactors to produce electric power.[116] The USA is to arrange for the provision of these reactors with a total capacity of 2000 MW installed by the year 2003.

In the interim, the USA will also arrange for the power forgone through the abandonment of North Korea's graphite-moderated reactors to be replaced by 500 000 tons of oil annually until the first LWR is completed. In return North Korea agreed to freeze—within a month of signing the agreement—and eventually dismantle its graphite-moderated reactors and related facilities. The dismantlement is to be completed when the LWR project is completed. The DPRK agreed to allow the IAEA to monitor the freeze and to cooperate with the USA in storing the spent fuel rods from the 5-MWe (25-MWth) reactor while the LWRs are being constructed pending their eventual disposal in a way which does not involve reprocessing in North Korea.

North Korea agrees to remain a party to the NPT and, once a 'significant portion' of the new LWR project has been completed, but before 'key nuclear components' have been delivered, agrees to 'come into full compliance with its safeguards agreement'. Therefore it is not until this time—perhaps five years from the signing of the agreement—that inspections of the suspect nuclear waste sites may provide clues to North Korea's plutonium reprocessing history and this element has led to the expression of some scepticism regarding the agreement from within the IAEA.[117] North Korea agrees to resume *ad hoc* and routine IAEA inspections once the supply contract for the reactors has been concluded.

The two sides also agreed to move towards normalization of economic and political relations and work towards peace and security for the Korean Peninsula. Their efforts include a US pledge to provide assurances that it will not use or threaten to use nuclear weapons against North Korea and a North Korean pledge to work towards implementation of the North–South Joint Declaration on the Denuclearization of the Korean Peninsula.

Although the agreement halts construction of the operation of the 5 MWe reactor and construction of the other two North Korean reactors, the fuel from the 5 MWe reactor will remain in the country for several years—albeit monitored by the IAEA. While North Korea announced soon after the agreement was signed that its nuclear reactor programme had been frozen as promised, there has been some concern that North Korea could abrogate the agreement

[115] Smith, J., 'Pact fleshes out earlier deal with North Korea', *International Herald Tribune*, 19 Oct. 1994.

[116] Agreed Framework of 21 October 1994 between the United States of America and the Democratic People's Republic of Korea, IAEA document INFCIRC/457, 2 Nov. 1994.

[117] James, B., 'UN agency doubtful of North Korea deal', *International Herald Tribune*, 21 Oct. 1994, p. 1.

and proceed to reprocess the fuel at a later time.[118] Only with the eventual dismantlement of the reprocessing capability and removal of the fuel will these fears be totally removed.

The reactors will be financed by a US-led consortium with South Korea most likely providing more than half of the $4 billion or more costs as well as playing a dominant role in construction. Other possible contributors include Japan and European nations. Considerable dissatisfaction has been expressed in the USA by Republican congressional leaders, who believe the deal was too generous and have sought to block it through denying funds for its execution—in particular funds that would provide alternate energy sources for North Korea while the new LWRs are being built.[119]

Assessment

The situation in North Korea has resulted in the focusing of a great deal of resources by the intelligence community on trying to ascertain the full extent of the nuclear programme. As is usually the case in such situations it is not possible to be sure exactly how much is known within the various intelligence communities at the present time. In early 1993 the Director of Central Intelligence for the USA stated that 'of greatest concern is the real possibility that North Korea has already manufactured enough fissile material for at least one nuclear weapon, and is hiding this from the IAEA. We assess that two North Korean-produced reactors at Yongbyon were built for plutonium production, despite North Korean claims that the reactors are part of an electric power programme'.[120]

At the same time Woolsey noted that the new emphasis on non-proliferation would first stress an increased reliance on human intelligence in order to provide information which can 'pull together seemingly unrelated technical titbits to build a convincing, accurate picture'. Second, intelligence collection should be usable and accessible to those in a position to make decisions on non-proliferation policy—'actionable intelligence'—rather than facts alone.[121] At about the same time the Principal Deputy Under Secretary of Defense for Policy, Walter Slocombe, stated that the amount of plutonium in the possession of North Korea was 'highly uncertain' but that if all of the fuel rods had been removed during the 1989 three-month shut-down they could have enough plutonium to construct one or two nuclear devices.[122]

[118] Sanger, D. E., 'Clinton approves a plan to give aid to North Koreans', *New York Times,* 19 Oct. 1994, p. 1.

[119] Sterngold, J., 'North Korea moves on pact, freezing nuclear reactors', *International Herald Tribune,* 19–20 Nov. 1994, p. 1; and Greenhouse, S., 'Republicans seek to scuttle accord with North Korea', *International Herald Tribune*, 26–27 Nov. 1994, p. 1.

[120] Testimony of James Woolsey in *Proliferation Threats of the 1990's*, Hearing before the Committee on Governmental Affairs, United States Senate, 103rd Congress, 1st Session, 24 Feb. 1993 (US Government Printing Office: Washington, DC, 1993), p. 14.

[121] Testimony of James Woolsey (note 120), pp. 16–17.

[122] Statement by Walter Slocombe before the House Armed Services Committee, 24 Mar. 1994, mimeo, p. 8.

By the end of 1993 the assessment of all segments of the intelligence community in the United States, including the CIA, the Defense Intelligence Agency, the National Security Agency as well as the Department of Energy as embodied in a National Intelligence Estimate, was that there was a 'better than even' chance that North Korea had already developed and was in possession of a nuclear bomb. While hard evidence is still apparently lacking, the report estimated that as much as 12 kg of plutonium could have been extracted—enough for perhaps two bombs. Craters which would be consistent with experiments on the conventional explosives used in detonating a nuclear device had been detected near Yongbyon. The State Department was alone in disputing the claim of weapon possession and some of its officials, as well as some within the Pentagon, have concluded that a worst-case scenario has been put forward by others in order to avoid the type of intelligence failure which occurred in the Iraqi case. The causes of this dispute resided in a difference in assessment of the level of scientific development in the country as well as disagreement of North Korea's basic intentions—the intelligence analysts holding a much more pessimistic view.[123]

This is a good demonstration of the ambiguity often involved in the verification process, especially when hard evidence is difficult to come by. Differing presuppositions and preconceptions can lead to quite different overall assessments which can seriously affect the choice of appropriate policy decisions. Here the choices included how long to continue to try to negotiate with moderates which are perceived to exist within the North Korean establishment or to abandon all hope of success of this type of action and begin considering other more drastic options such as sanctions or even military force. The importance of and types of inspection necessary would also be affected if North Korea was found to be already in possession of a nuclear device.

In March 1994 Woolsey reiterated 'the Agency's view that North Korea has stockpiled enough plutonium for at least one nuclear device'. In addition, as reported in the Japanese magazine *Weekly Bunshun*, a classified Russian Defence Ministry document dated 22 October 1993 states that North Korea is in possession of over 30 kg of enriched nuclear materials and that 22 Russian specialists are employed in its nuclear programme making use of 1980s Soviet technology.[124] Russian Foreign Minister Andrey Kozyrev has said that he is very sceptical about whether North Korea has developed nuclear weapons as yet, but uncertain about whether they possess plutonium.[125]

Until inspections of the two waste sites are allowed the amount of plutonium already separated by North Korea will probably remain uncertain. CIA estimates quoted in July 1994 are that the 25-MWth reactor was only shut down

[123] Engelberg, S. and Gordon, M. R., 'North Korea likely to have developed own atomic bomb, CIA tells president', *International Herald Tribune*, 27 Dec. 1993, p. 1.

[124] Lee, C. S. *et al.*, 'Pyongyang's endless game', *Newsweek*, 28 Mar. 1994, p. 29.

[125] 'Q&A: Moscow official sees "positive signs" in nuclear dispute', *International Herald Tribune*, 25 July 1994, p. 5; and 'Envoy says Russia doubts North Korea has atomic weapons', *International Herald Tribune*, 27 May 1994, p. 4;

for 75 days, not the 100 days previously thought.[126] It is believed by many to be unlikely that all of the fuel rods could have been changed in that time and, therefore, at worst North Korea could have obtained enough plutonium for a single bomb. Fuel removed in 1994 contains 30–40 kg of plutonium, according to US intelligence.[127]

In his own independent analysis Frank Barnaby has noted that North Korea would probably wish to be conservative in weapon construction and so would use plutonium in the delta phase (density 15.9 g/cm^3), in which it is most stable and for which the critical mass is about 15.5 kg (this is larger than for plutonium in the alpha phase with a density of 19.8 g/cm^3 and a critical mass of about 10 kg). North Korea would also choose a core mass only slightly less than the critical mass to ensure that a supercritical mass is created by its implosion device. Barnaby estimates that North Korea would use 13 kg plutonium for each device. Using estimates for the burnup of about 660 MWd/t, he calculates that North Korea could obtain about 26 kg of 95 per cent ^{239}Pu from the core of its 25-MWth reactor in its seven years of operation, or enough for about two bombs.[128]

Other recent independent analysis by David Albright,[129] assuming that the reactor shut-down in 1989 allowed an amount of fuel ranging from one-half the core to the full core being replaced at that time, estimates that 7–14 kg of plutonium could have been obtained by the North Koreans. In this same analysis estimates of the plutonium in the core removed in 1994 range from 14 kg to 33 kg. He notes that even though about 5 kg is required per bomb a first bomb would require about 10 kg, since about half this amount would be lost in the manufacturing process. Most of that lost could, however, be recovered for use in subsequent devices. He also notes that many experts hold the opinion that development of an implosion bomb is within the technical capabilities of the North Koreans.

It should be further pointed out here that, as outlined in chapter 5, recently released estimates confirm that it may be possible to construct a workable nuclear bomb with significantly lower amounts of plutonium than heretofore assumed in many quarters.[130] Depending on the sophistication of the device, 1–3 kg of plutonium would be sufficient to produce a 1-kt bomb. If a rough estimation drawn from the above discussion of the plutonium made available to North Korea is that about 25 kg of fuel is removed from its 25-MWth reactor, this may represent enough fissile material for at least eight such nuclear weapons, even assuming a relatively 'low-tech' approach is used in the design.

[126] A more recent article appearing in the South Korean newspaper *Chosin Ilbo*, however, states that the reactor was shut down for 71 days in 1989, one month in 1990 and 50 days in 1991, allowing for the extraction of 22–27 kg of plutonium or enough for 3–4 bombs.'New clue on North Korea plutonium', *International Herald Tribune*, 8 Aug. 1994, p. 2.

[127] Lewis, P., 'US sets terms for Pyongyang', *International Herald Tribune*, 1 July 1994, p. 12.

[128] Barnaby, F., 'How many bombs? North Korea's nuclear-weapon program', *International Defense Review*, no. 8 (1994), p. 12.

[129] Albright, D., 'How much plutonium does North Korea have?', *Bulletin of the Atomic Scientists*, vol. 50, no. 5 (Sep./Oct. 1994), p. 51.

[130] See the definition of significant quantity in chapter 5, pp. 166–68.

The spent fuel must first be reprocessed to remove the plutonium, but North Korea has extensive knowledge of this technology and its reprocessing plant (the 'Radiochemical Laboratory') may have the capacity to reprocess a full core from the 25 MWth reactor in as little as three months,[131] although US intelligence estimates are that it could be done in 6–9 months.[132] A second reprocessing line in the reprocessing facility had not yet been completed at the time of the March 1994 inspection to the safeguarded line, but it would have allowed a doubling of the reprocessing capacity if it had ever become operational.[133]

It has been noted that part of the difficulties raised by the North Koreans about the call for special inspections in their country could have resulted from the negative connotations resulting from the fact that such inspections had previously only been used in connection with the Iraqi nuclear programme, along with an international outcry against that country.[134] As a result the move to inspect could have seemed particularly condemnatory to the North Korean leadership. The use of *ad hoc* inspections, designed to verify initial inventories of nuclear materials and changes thereto as discussed in chapter 5—which is appropriate to the North Korean situation in any case—would have allowed the side-stepping of any perceived stigma associated in the North Korean leadership with special inspections. While it is certainly far from clear that such a change in tactics would have made any difference in the North Korean case, the option for future use of *ad hoc* inspections, given that they can also be conducted in 'any location where the initial report or any inspections carried out in connection with it indicate that nuclear material is present',[135] should be considered as a further recourse before special inspections are initiated.

Although much is still unknown about the programme, it must be judged that overall North Korea was less capable than Iraq or South Africa in hiding its activities. Samples of plutonium collected by the IAEA inspections at Yongbyon revealed that several batches had been separated in contrast to the single batch admitted by North Korea. In addition, buried nuclear waste had effects on nearby plant life which were visible to satellite observation.[136]

In an important development related to delivery capability, the naval intelligence community in the USA has stated that the North Korean No Dong 1

[131] Albright (note 129), p. 53.

[132] Hibbs, M., 'North Korea needs 6–9 months to reprocess discharged core', *Nucleonics Week*, 26 May 1994, p. 17.

[133] Hibbs, M., 'Second, hidden reprocessing line feared opened at Yongbyon plant', *Nucleonics Week*, 24 Mar. 1994, p. 1.

[134] Sheinman, L., 'Strengthened IAEA safeguards and special inspections', ed. T. Rauf, *Strengthened IAEA Safeguards and Regional Non-proliferation Strategies*, Aurora Papers 23, Canadian Centre for Global Security, Ottawa, Mar. 1994, pp. 22–23.

[135] This access clause holds 'until such time as the *strategic points* have been specified in the Subsidiary Arrangements'. IAEA, The Structure and Content of Agreements between the International Atomic Energy Agency and States Required in Connection with the Treaty on the Non-Proliferation of Nuclear Weapons (the NPT Model Safeguards Agreement), IAEA document INFCIRC/153, 10 Mar. 1971, para. 76(a). The text of the NPT Model Safeguards Agreement is reproduced in appendix C.

[136] Bracken, P., 'Nuclear weapons and state survival in North Korea', *Survival*, vol. 35, no. 3 (autumn 1993), pp. 140–41.

missile will 'probably be able to be equipped with a nuclear warhead by 2000', and it is believed by some in the intelligence community that a No Dong nuclear warhead could be complete by 1995.[137]

Repercussions

It was imperative, both for the credibility of the international non-proliferation regime as a whole and in particular for the success of the 1995 NPT Extension and Review Conference, that a satisfactory conclusion to the North Korean situation be obtained. Given North Korea's record as an arms dealer, particularly in the Middle East, the possibility that the nuclear technology developed by North Korea would be sold to other countries in the same way is, to say the least, worrying.[138]

Henry Kissinger had expressed his belief that a freeze of the North Korean programme, leaving open the possibility that it is in possession of a few nuclear weapons, should be viewed as unsatisfactory and that a roll-back of the North Korean nuclear programme was necessary. Otherwise a 'no-lose' prospect is placed before other aspiring nuclear weapon states and the message is sent that 'they can extract blackmail for abandoning their programmes or they will be left with nuclear weapons. They have been given no incentive whatsoever to avoid the road toward nuclear weapon technology'. He advocated serious diplomatic action with a deadline, to be followed by possible military action unless North Korea agrees to open all sites to IAEA inspection, account for past plutonium production and return to the NPT.[139] As pointed out elsewhere, however, probably the only feasible case of a nation of proliferation concern copying the North Korean example is that of Iran—currently already the subject of intense US efforts to deny supplies which could contribute to a nuclear programme.[140]

Others have taken an even more pessimistic line than Kissinger. The former deputy for non-proliferation of the US Defense Department (1989–93) was of the opinion that North Korea's withdrawal from the NPT should be accepted and that 'we should use this occasion to dispel our long time fantasy that we can take assurances from secretive, militant nations like North Korea and safeguard dangerous activities merely by inspecting them'.[141]

It was abundantly clear, however, that as long as diplomacy held out the promise of a peaceful and mutually satisfactory solution then it should continue to be pursued. In addition to the political difficulty of pursuing the military option against North Korean nuclear facilities before less risky alternatives of persuasion and sanctions have been tried, Andrew Mack pointed to the practical

[137] Starr, B., 'No Dongs may soon be nuclear, warns USN', *Jane's Defence Weekly*, 18 June 1994, p. 1.

[138] Lehman, R. F. II, 'A North Korean nuclear-weapons program', *Security Dialogue*, vol. 24, no. 3 (1993), p. 269.

[139] Kissinger, H. A., 'Tell it straight to North Korea—but talking may not be enough', *International Herald Tribune*, 4 July 1994, p. 5.

[140] Perkovich, G., 'Carrots for Koreans: alas, the safest way', *International Herald Tribune*, 30 Sep. 1994, p. 8.

[141] Sokolski, H., 'Non-proliferation fantasy: NPT will not quell N. Korean nuclear ambitions', *Defense News*, 12–18 Apr. 1993, p. 20.

difficulty of locating all the potential North Korean targets as well as the military counter-strikes that would doubtless follow on the South. He also appropriately asked that the US and South Korean officials and commentators who suggest that Yongbyon be attacked militarily 'try and imagine how South Koreans would feel if the boot were on the other foot—if the North Korean Defence Minister had threatened military strikes against US bases in South Korea if nuclear weapons allegedly stored at them were not removed'.[142]

With respect to monitoring means and methods, the destabilizing developments in general on the peninsula are leading to new independent initiatives. South Korea, which has been dependent on the USA for most of its intelligence information, while admitting no direct link between the North Korean nuclear programme and its desire to acquire its own intelligence-gathering means, is planning to develop its own tactical intelligence capability. The programme is to be implemented in two stages. The first, lasting from 1993 to 1998, would involve the purchase of SIGINT aircraft, remotely controlled unmanned vehicles and a synthetic-aperture radar system plus an intelligence-gathering ship. During the second phase, from 1999 to 2004, attempts will be made to produce a sound-surveillance system (SOSUS) as well as to develop military satellites.[143]

A competition for an airborne intelligence capability worth up to $1 billion has already been initiated as a result of what is viewed as an increasing threat from the North. The Korean Air Reconnaissance System and the Airborne Remote Control Signals Intelligence System will include eight aircraft, four each, equipped with signals intelligence collection and SAR capabilities. It is reported that the USA has used the promise of classified technology as well as greater access to specialized intelligence to try to gain the contract for a US company. Other Association of South-East Asian Nations (ASEAN) countries, including Taiwan, Japan and Malaysia, are also considering the acquisition of this type of intelligence gathering capability.[144]

Japan, also concerned about developments in North Korea and now dependent largely on US intelligence, is giving consideration to acquiring its own reconnaissance satellite. Such an undertaking would not be difficult for a country which has already launched many satellites including the JERS-1 which, with visible, infrared and radar imaging capability, can, according to Japan's National Space Development Agency, also be used for military reconnaissance purposes.[145]

[142] Mack, A., 'North Korea's nuclear program: the options are shrinking', working paper 1994/5, Department of International Relations, Research School of Pacific Studies, Australian National University, Canberra, July 1994, pp. 6, 13–14.

[143] Kiernan, T., 'S. Korea seeks to bolster intelligence abilities', *Defense News*, 29 Mar.–4 Apr. 1993, p. 6.

[144] Opall, B., 'Seoul seeks spy plane fleet: South Korea launches high-stakes competition for aircraft', *Defense News*, 6–12 Dec. 1993, p. 1.

[145] Usui, N., 'Japan awaits launch of 1st spy satellite', *Defense News*, 24–30 Jan. 1994, p. 1; Riccitiello, R., 'Japanese elated as JERS-1 rescue works', *Space News*, 13–19 Apr. 1992, p. 1; and Usui, N. and Opall, B., 'Japan eyes space for defense', *Space News*, 1–7 Aug. 1994, p. 4.

IV. New priorities

With the end of the cold war, priorities of intelligence collection are shifting more and more to issues connected with weapon proliferation in general and nuclear weapon proliferation in particular. US intelligence agencies are adjusting to the new world situation by organizing around three main concepts, one of which is the proliferation of weapons of mass destruction. The first steps, resulting at least in part from experience with Iraq, have included the creation of a Non-Proliferation Center (NPC) by then CIA Director Robert Gates in September 1991 with a staff of 100 to coordinate the intensification of collection and analysis.[146] The broadly defined agenda of the Center covers the 'world-wide development or acquisition of production technology, designs, components, and complete military systems in the areas of mass destruction and advanced conventional weapons'.[147]

The responsibilities and scope of the Center were expanded in 1993 by James Woolsey and especially noteworthy is the increased reliance being placed on human intelligence. Transfer Network Groups within the NPC will seek to identify suppliers and understand networks of trade in various technologies of relevance to proliferation.[148] The Center has already proved to be a valuable link between policy and intelligence officials in their work to counter proliferation.[149]

New technical capabilities, including enhanced space-based imagery and communications collection capability, along with a new focus in the past few years on proliferation activity itself, are substantially increasing the available information on potential proliferators. It is important that this information be used in the most effective manner and it is therefore recommended that the information collected by the several distinct intelligence organizations within the USA, for example, be further integrated.[150] Pooling of information between countries collecting data on nuclear proliferation is also to be further encouraged.

With the ending of the cold war the weapon laboratories in the USA have turned their energies to verification activity in general and to ways of detecting and controlling the proliferation of nuclear weapons in particular. Investigations will hopefully include research into 'alternate nuclear technology', which would involve exploring all of the possible routes and designs which a country might pursue in the development of nuclear weapons. As the Iraqi experience has shown, methods long ignored or abandoned may appear with little warning. This is particularly true with today's rapid advances in nuclear weapon-related

[146] Sciolino, E., 'CIA casting about for new missions', *New York Times*, 4 Feb. 1992, p. A1; and Church, G. J., 'Who else will have the bomb?', *Time*, 16 Dec. 1991, p. 14.

[147] Testimony of James Woolsey (note 120), p. 16.

[148] Starr, B., 'Woolsey tackles proliferation as the problem gets worse', *Jane's Defence Weekly*, 13 Nov. 1993, p. 23.

[149] Sokolski (note 11), p. 255.

[150] Richelson (note 3), p. 304.

technology, including computers, advanced measuring techniques and electronics.[151]

To meet the obvious need for increased information on nuclear weapon proliferation in the wake of the experience with Iraq and North Korea, new techniques are being explored to increase the capabilities of space-based detection techniques. The Los Alamos National Laboratory, for example, is developing new satellites to enhance the detection of nuclear explosions in the atmosphere and new multispectral imaging techniques which could be applied to future Landsat spacecraft, for instance, to aid in monitoring proliferation. More advanced techniques are also being investigated which would employ lasers to reveal the composition of materials on the ground.[152]

According to the Senate Armed Services Committee in its 1992 recommendation to further develop Lidar (laser imaging detection and ranging) systems, 'Lidar technology would provide a capability to classify trace elements of a variety of materials suspended in the air or lying on the surface of objects, the ground or water. This capability can be used . . . to detect, locate, classify and assess the clandestine production of chemical, biological, or nuclear weapons.'[153] The Brookhaven, Lawrence Livermore, Los Alamos, Pacific Northwest and Sandia national laboratories have been assigned a new project by the Department of Energy called CALIOPE (Chemical Analysis by Laser Interrogation of Proliferation Effluents). Using laser illumination from ultraviolet to infrared the system under study is focused on uncovering nuclear proliferation-related activity by detecting relevant chemical indicators. This system will also be of use in detecting proscribed chemical and biological warfare-related activities.[154]

As discussed, there is a strong need to improve the capabilities for detecting clandestine nuclear activity. This is included in a proposal by the Department of Defense that $400 million in new funding be spent annually from Fiscal Year (FY) 1996 on technology to counter weapons of mass destruction, including a $25 million increase in funds for technology which would detect, locate and disarm not only nuclear but also chemical and biological weapons in a global context and another $25 million for enhanced collection and analysis of intelligence.[155] Specific proposals involved in the counter-proliferation effort include substantial funding to detect underground structures and to develop capabilities for attacking such structures even if hardened; ground sensors to monitor sites of interest; and expanding the 'Threat Anticipation Skunkworks' at the Sandia National Laboratory to include the analysis of weapons development in the

[151] Henderson, B. W., 'US labs target better nuclear arms reliability and safety after drawdowns', *Aviation Week & Space Technology*, 17 Feb. 1992, p. 43.

[152] Foley, T., 'New satellites may aid nuclear inspectors', *Space News*, 31 Jan.–6 Feb. 1994, p. 6.

[153] Tuttle, R., 'Airborne sensors draw new interest', *Aviation Week & Space Technology*, 10 Jan. 1994, p. 61.

[154] *Energy & Technology Review*, Jan./Feb. 1994, p. 14.

[155] Report on Nonproliferation and Counterproliferation Activities and Programs, Office of the Deputy Secretary of Defense, Washington, DC, May 1994, pp. 32–33.

developing countries. It is additionally proposed that the CALIOPE programme be expanded.[156]

The Lawrence National Livermore Laboratory is currently developing new technology to obtain thermal imagery with enhanced temperature and spatial resolution. The TAISIR (Temperature and Imaging System Infrared) programme is developing space-based or airborne sensors which will be used to detect thermal emissions such as those from smoke stacks or cooling ponds emanating from facilities which may be involved in nuclear activity. Techniques used include methods to enhance defraction-limited imagery and high-resolution spectroscopy to increase robustness to atmospheric effects which degrade thermal imagery.[157]

Ground sensors may also prove useful in keeping track of activity around nuclear sites. The Defense Intelligence Agency in the USA, for example, is developing measurements and signatures intelligence (MASINT) sensors known as unattended ground sensors (UGS) which detect and process acoustic and seismic signals. Activated by either their acoustic signals detection or day–night imagery capability, UGS sensors could be employed around North Korean nuclear sites or other critical areas of proliferation concern where their continuous operation and covert two-way communications capability could provide an important adjunct to satellite imagery, for example, in confirming site activities.[158]

British Prime Minister John Major has announced that countering the proliferation of weapons of mass destruction will be a 'priority task' for the Secret Intelligence Service (MI6), Government Communications Headquarters (GCHQ) and the Security Service (MI5). The resources available to these agencies for this particular purpose have now been increased.[159]

After a meeting between US Secretary of State Warren Christopher and the European Community (EC) foreign ministers, at which he called 'the long-term threat of proliferation the most urgent arms-control problem of the 1990s', the USA and the EC agreed to pool some of their intelligence related to the acquisition by Iraq of weapons of mass destruction.[160]

In a report on the strengthening of the UN role in crisis management and prevention, which proposed that a permanent pool of troops be made available to the UN by member states to enforce peace, a request was also made that members provide timely intelligence to the Secretary-General. Such intelligence would help to enable the seeking of diplomatic solutions to security threats

[156] Starr, B., 'Proliferation the new high ground for USA', *Jane's Defence Weekly*, 14 May 1994, p. 1; and Foley, T., 'Defense, energy departments push counterproliferation', *Space News*, 16–22 May 1994, p. 10.

[157] Note 154, pp. 14, 27.

[158] Starr, B., 'Super sensors will eye the new proliferation frontier', *Jane's Defence Weekly,* 4 June 1994, p. 19.

[159] *Trust and Verify*, Bulletin of the Verification Technology Information Centre, London, no. 43 (Dec. 1993), p. 4.

[160] Goshko, J. M., 'US urges halt to Iran sales; Christopher warns on arms technology', *Washington Post*, 10 June 1993.

before a conflict actually erupts.[161] More specifically, discussions are reportedly under way concerning the establishment of a UN organization which, aided by the intelligence organizations of some member states including agents from the British MI6, the CIA and Russia's Foreign Intelligence Service, would help combat the proliferation of nuclear weapons.[162]

A consultants group was convened by the IAEA in 1993 in order to evaluate the potential of environmental monitoring techniques and concluded that a range of signatures exist which would in principle identify undeclared nuclear facilities. The primary signature for uranium enrichment would be the detection of disturbed isotopic ratios, for example, and while environmental monitoring techniques would not always provide unambiguous identification of clandestine activity they would be able to point to specific areas or states for further investigation. The study concluded that sensitive analytical techniques applied to water and sediment samples would allow detection of the appropriate signatures and recommended a series of field trials. These began in August 1993 and sampling has already been carried out in Argentina, Australia, Hungary, Indonesia, Japan, the Republic of Korea, South Africa, Sweden and the USA. As discussed in chapter 4 on the Iraqi nuclear programme, these sampling techniques are playing an important part in the ongoing monitoring and verification procedures in that country.[163]

V. Conclusions

Verification of nuclear non-proliferation is today being accomplished by a variety of means ranging from the routine (but not unimportant) and well-entrenched IAEA nuclear safeguards to the highly esoteric (and highly classified) intelligence collection methods of technologically advanced countries such as the United States. One important problem which arises even given all of these methods is that—as has often been said—'we don't know what we don't know'. No one can ever be 100 per cent sure that a clandestine nuclear activity is not taking place except perhaps in the cases of extraordinarily intrusive on-site inspections and even then only in a given limited area and for a very limited time.

To be sure monitoring and verification techniques and expertise are continually advancing. Especially with respect to efforts that are ongoing but highly secretive within the intelligence community it is difficult to assess the capabilities of current methods and systems. Clues are often released which give cryptic hints of capabilities which can only be guessed at. This is exemplified, in a recent award given by the CIA and the NSA, for a secret project carried out by

[161] Lewis, P., 'UN Chief asks for armed force to serve as permanent deterrent', *New York Times,* 19 June 1992, p. 1.

[162] *Nucleonics Week*, 9 June 1994, p. 16; and *PPNN Newsbrief*, no. 26 (2nd quarter 1994), p. 8.

[163] Puchkarev, V., Kuhn, E. and Rundquist, D. E., 'Strengthening safeguards: progress in R&D', *IAEA Yearbook 1994* (IAEA: Vienna, 1994), pp. E15–16; and Coll, S., 'Nuclear inspectors check sites in Iran', *Washington Post,* 20 Nov. 1993, p. A13.

LLNL which resulted in success 'on a series of technical problems of enormous complexity, resulting in an extremely powerful operational capability that can be used to gather intelligence from unique sources not exploitable by other means'.[164]

Extensive intelligence-gathering capabilities in states such as the USA and Russia remain out of reach for most countries of the world, most of which share the desire to limit nuclear proliferation. As this chapter demonstrates, increased sharing and openness seem to be the watchwords for the near future with regard to intelligence information and, in addition, commercial information-gathering capabilities are being steadily improved and expanded.

In the regional context[165] it will be important to develop new verification approaches and techniques specially adapted to creating the required transparency and aiding in confidence building on a regional level. These could include information sharing from national intelligence measures (NIM), using experience gained in aerial monitoring regimes such as that of the 1992 Open Skies Treaty, to develop protocols for aerial-monitoring of nuclear non-proliferation and development of new specific technologies for environmental monitoring as well as other more intrusive means of verification.

Perhaps one of the most worthwhile additions to the verification of nuclear non-proliferation would be implementation of regional agreements allowing aerial overflights, especially in proliferation-prone regions. The successful negotiation of such accords is probably not very likely, at least in the short term, but this should in no way discourage pursuing discussions on such matters. Allowing aircraft to be used for special inspections by the IAEA could be an important step in this direction. This could perhaps most easily be implemented at first in cases where a willing state wishes to dispel rumoured clandestine activity and allows aerial inspection as part of the overall inspection effort. Aside from the implications of greater assurance which improved verification methods would provide, it should also be stressed that, as stated by the IAEA Director General, 'the very existence of a verification system with more teeth would have a certain deterrent effect on potential violators'.[166]

The Iraqi situation has provided new impetus for the sharing of intelligence information of relevance to nuclear proliferation. In congressional testimony a former CIA Director has stated that, among other nations, the USA 'is committed to providing the United Nations the information and support it needs to complete its mission . . . an unprecedented amount of information has been shared with the United Nations, changing the previous rules of the game'.[167] The new 'rules of the game' have received their first real test case in North Korea and for the moment have provided at least some cause for confidence.

Intelligence can of course never provide all the answers. As stated by the CIA Deputy Director for Intelligence John Helgerson, 'Proliferation—it's a growth

[164] 'Award given for . . . er . . . better not say', *New Scientist,* 22 Jan. 1994, p. 5.

[165] See Pilat, J. F., 'Regional non-proliferation strategies', ed. Rauf (note 134), pp. 66–67.

[166] Hans Blix, Statement to the Forty-Sixth Session of the United Nations General Assembly, 21 Oct. 1991, p. 7

[167] Testimony of James Woolsey (note 120), p. 17.

industry at the moment like no other. We could put everyone in the agency in proliferation and narcotics and we still wouldn't solve the problems'.[168] As the North Korean situation has shown, the acquisition of fairly unambiguous information on that country's nuclear programme was able to spur on determined efforts to control it—efforts that have now apparently succeeded in containing what may otherwise have been a threat discovered all too late. Determined efforts must remain focused on countries of proliferation concern to ensure that this type of information continues to be acquired and analysed in a still more thorough and timely fashion in order to allow for an appropriate and rapid response in the future.

[168] Sciolino (note 146), p. A1.

8. Conclusions

The pace of international events, the successful conclusion of key arms control agreements and the political realities of the 1990s, including the breakup of the former Soviet Union, require that measures aimed at helping to ensure international security be assessed from new perspectives. This is especially true of efforts aimed at curbing the spread of nuclear weapons and the associated technology. While such an assessment underlines the latent or manifest defects of the measures employed, it also provides new opportunities for their more efficient and effective implementation. The concern generated by the Iraqi and North Korean nuclear weapon programmes in particular has resulted in further efforts to control the spread of nuclear technology and in increased transparency measures in a broad-based endeavour to ensure that such situations are not allowed to recur.

Attempting to control exports of nuclear materials and the development of nuclear weapon technology, while certainly important, can only be near- and medium-term solutions to the horizontal spread of nuclear weapons as the technology becomes more accessible to an ever-increasing number of countries. The ultimate solution must of course involve appropriately addressing the security concerns of individual nations and regions and the introduction of adequate transparency measures to provide confidence that security and stability are ensured well into the future—in short, political measures. At present, controls on the spread of nuclear-related technology and assurance that nuclear materials are not being diverted for clandestine weapon use remain vital. A further key to curbing nuclear weapon proliferation in areas where appropriate and necessary means have not been put in place to ensure adequate security is political warning. It will remain critical to ascertain which countries are developing or acquiring which technologies so that appropriate efforts may then be made to deal effectively with such developments.

It could be argued that the successfully negotiated settlement bringing the North Korean nuclear weapon programme to a halt has demonstrated the power of persistent political pressure in situations where a nuclear weapon programme is known to be already under way. None the less, increased vigilance will be necessary in order to ensure that the relevant technology, which is increasingly widely available, is not used for purposes of nuclear weapon development as it was in North Korea.

In the case of the dismantlement of the South African nuclear weapon programme and the accession of South Africa to the NPT in 1991, several important conclusions relevant to the proliferation of nuclear technology can be drawn. From a technological standpoint this case clearly demonstrates that, with the political will and a less than enormous investment,[1] a sufficiently industrially advanced nation can develop a fair-sized nuclear arsenal without necessarily testing the devices. This demonstrates the somewhat limited effectiveness of technology-denial policies, at least and especially for the technologically more advanced nations. Once a political decision is made and the resources are committed, such policies may only serve to delay the inevitable unless other more political questions and security concerns are addressed. This latter was certainly true in the case of South Africa.

Second, and perhaps more important, the fact that South Africa was willing to declare its previous activity and give up its nuclear weapons to accede to the NPT as a non-nuclear weapon state party, and place its nuclear industry under international safeguards, serves to vindicate the value of the Treaty itself. Also, and related to this, the IAEA has shown that, once it has a mandate to become involved, it is capable of demonstrating through appropriate measures, including inspections, that a nuclear weapon programme is no longer in existence and posing a threat.[2]

In addition, the events in both South Africa and North Korea may at last have demonstrated that nuclear proliferation is in fact reversible. In the case of Argentina and Brazil their change in direction towards policies more in line with non-proliferation goals was achieved before they actually acquired a nuclear weapon capability—so, while certainly laudable, the change was not so dramatic. The same was true of Iraq, although in this case the reversal had to be forced on that country. In the case of North Korea there remains some uncertainty with regard to the future status of its nuclear weapon programme, but here again if current trends continue the now halted nuclear programme will eventually be totally reversed.

Recent examples and positive trends thus demonstrate that the policy of 'managing' proliferation long advocated by many is perhaps better replaced by one of reversing proliferation, at least as an ultimate goal.[3] In any case a knowledge of the essential technology associated with nuclear weapon development—the primary focus of this book—will be a necessary and invaluable tool.

I. Uranium enrichment technologies

Advances in uranium enrichment technologies and the associated know-how are spreading. Use by Iraq of the electromagnetic isotope separation method,

[1] At 1994 exchange rates the total cost of the South African nuclear weapon programme amounted to about $200 million and was accomplished with a peak workforce of about 400 and involved about 1000 people in total during a 10-year period. Although these figures do not include the construction force or those involved in the mining of uranium they are none the less in stark contrast to the Iraqi figure of 15 000 people in total employed during 1981–91. Zimmerman, P. D., 'Proliferation: Bronze medal technology is good enough', *Orbis*, winter 1994, pp. 78–79.

[2] Simpson, J., 'South Africa; considering the implications', *Nuclear Engineering International*, May 1993, p. 12.

[3] Fischer, D., 'Reversing nuclear proliferation: South Africa', *Security Dialogue*, vol. 24, no. 3 (1993), p. 283.

previously thought by most observers to be of little concern from a proliferation standpoint, has made clear that it may be difficult to ascertain which types of enrichment technology should be the focus of concern. None the less, for a variety of reasons several methods stand out as worthy of particular attention. In addition to the EMIS method, the gas centrifuge—increasingly the choice of commercial enrichment enterprises—must be viewed as a high proliferation risk. The updated London Guidelines of the Nuclear Suppliers Group are now much more detailed with regard to specific components associated with this enrichment technology.

Developments in laser enrichment in the past two decades have shown this technology to be advanced to the point at which some countries are on the verge of making decisions on full-scale laser enrichment plant construction and many others are considering deployment of demonstration or prototype facilities. This technology, already developed to the point of commercial production capability, will doubtless be mastered by many more countries in the next decade. The precedent-setting nature of developments in more technologically advanced nations coupled with new, potentially more accessible, methods of laser isotope separation is a combination which gives cause for concern with regard to nuclear weapon proliferation.

It has been predicted that the projected lower cost of laser enrichment will possibly force world enrichment prices down in the future. In addition, developers of the process have predicted that, because the feed and product material are quite different from the uranium hexafluoride gas used in most of today's separation processes, the AVLIS process has the potential to change the nuclear fuel cycle.[4] Although it would doubtless take some time, should the AVLIS approach gain a foothold there will be potential economic and logistical incentives likely to further the spread of this laser enrichment technology to other nations interested in a share of the world uranium market. From the proliferation standpoint the danger would then arise that this laser technology could be used in the production of HEU and its subsequent mixing with natural uranium for LWR fuel, creating the danger of diversion to weapon production. (Of course, if this HEU were being produced for reactors utilizing HEU, there is a diversion potential independent of the materials source.[5]) The US Department of Energy has, in fact, acknowledged a primary concern that laser enrichment presents certain risks of proliferation and in the mid-1980s stated a desire to focus much attention on this, as it tried to do with diffusion and the gas centrifuge.[6]

[4] Hiruo, E., '10-year enrichment services pacts may be outdated, ex-DOE official says', *Nuclear Fuel*, vol. 13, no. 10 (16 May 1988), p. 11.

[5] Greenwood, T., Rathjens, G. W. and Ruina, J., *Nuclear Power and Weapons Proliferation*, Adelphi Paper no. 130 (IISS: London, 1977), p. 28.

[6] *Fiscal Year 1987 Department of Energy Authorization*, Hearings before the Subcommittee on Energy Research and Production of the Committee on Science and Technology, House of Representatives, 99th Congress, 2nd Session (US Government Printing Office: Washington, DC, 1986), vol. 1, p. 36.

Decisions to discontinue work on or to de-emphasize laser enrichment in some countries reflect more the market situation[7] in which these methods will not be needed until perhaps the second decade of the 21st century rather than problems with developing the basic technology. Countries which continue to develop advanced laser enrichment techniques, and which are not as yet members of the Nuclear Suppliers Group, need to be brought into the regime and encouraged to develop appropriate domestic legislation so that proper controls can be applied to the technology.[8]

II. The production and disposal of plutonium

The updated London Guidelines are now more detailed on specific equipment that could be used in producing plutonium as part of an effort to produce nuclear weapons. However, owing to the wide availability of most of the technology involved, the focus of efforts to halt clandestine production of plutonium for nuclear weapon use must be on detecting facilities associated with such a programme. As detailed in chapter 7, such efforts include visual identification of facilities and the detection of heat signatures from reactors and other emissions, including fission products, which are known to be associated with reprocessing facilities. New efforts are being made to systematize collection of such information and are likely to open up new possibilities in this important endeavour.

Recent progress in nuclear disarmament is releasing a great deal of plutonium and HEU, which it will be necessary to deal with in some way. While the most appropriate means of disposal remains a topic of active research, these developments also provide what can be looked upon as an ideal opportunity to deal as well with weapon-usable material from all sources, including the substantial plutonium from civil sources.

Were the United States and Russia to agree to internationally monitored storage of the nuclear materials from retired nuclear weapons as a first step, a number of benefits would be immediately forthcoming. These would include the demonstration of the feasibility of such storage arrangements, providing an important precedent for extending such arrangements to other sources of fissile material. The material would also be much safer from any sort of diversion including that from terrorist groups, for example. In bringing more nuclear material from the nuclear weapon states under safeguards, this and other such potential new agreements would also help to deal with arguments concerning the alleged discriminatory nature of the nuclear non-proliferation regime. Further measures bringing excess civil nuclear material under IAEA authority

[7] Usui, N., 'Japan's AEC may approve plan to stress centrifuge and not laser enrichment', *Nuclear Fuel,* 3 Aug. 1992, p. 4.

[8] Fischer (note 3), p. 283.

as well would be a logical next step and would aid in the long-term objectives of the nuclear non-proliferation regime.[9]

III. Safeguards

The need to improve the effectiveness of the IAEA system of safeguards has long been recognized and, especially following the results of the investigations into the Iraqi nuclear weapon programme, the process of amending and reinterpretation has begun. The right to undertake special inspections has been reaffirmed, various approaches to gathering and interpreting information important to cueing such inspections are being put in place and the UN Security Council has indicated the seriousness with which it regards nuclear proliferation threats. Development of open source data to corroborate classified information obtained from intelligence agencies should be further explored in order to allay fears of politicization which could be associated with the conduct of special inspections based on classified data.

New requirements on the early reporting of design information on new nuclear facilities and modifications to existing facilities should not only provide an important confidence-building measure, providing additional assurance of peaceful intent, but also a vital step in ensuring 'safeguards friendly' construction of such facilities.

The weight of expert opinion indicates that serious consideration should be given to the adoption of a lower 'significant quantity' threshold, perhaps initially about 50 per cent below the present level, in order to reflect more accurately the amount of fissile material required for nuclear weapon construction.

Methods which could be used to re-prioritize standard safeguards activities in order to concentrate valuable resources where they are in fact most needed should be further explored. Giving countries a chance to open themselves up to special inspection on an any-time–anywhere basis, in return for substantial relief from routine inspection activity, is one approach worthy of further study. Improvements in inspector designation and the efficiency of visa processing, including perhaps the initiation of a universally recognized IAEA passport, should be considered.

Even without the adoption of these improvements, new responsibilities for the International Atomic Energy Agency will necessitate budgetary increases if they are to be carried out effectively. States should demonstrate their willingness to contribute further resources to the IAEA since the resultant increase in transparency and security would be well worth additional expenditures.

[9] Scheinman, L. and Fischer, D. A. V., 'Managing the coming glut of nuclear weapon materials', *Arms Control Today*, vol. 22, no. 2 (Mar. 1992), pp. 9–10.

IV. Export controls

Although much of what was discovered in Iraq, including the large-scale construction of electromagnetic enrichment capability, apparently resulted from indigenous technology, it also became apparent that a large part of the programme was aided by sources outside the country. The success of the calutron programme was at least partly the result of the fact that export controls on related equipment were almost non-existent, while in the centrifuge enrichment programme export controls were blatantly circumvented.[10] As noted in chapter 6, multilateral export controls have been substantially revised since these discoveries were made and controls on dual-use technology have been introduced. It is vital that these controls and the national infrastructures which are to bring the changes into effect be implemented in an effective manner and constantly reassessed to keep pace with technological change.

It is also important to recognize that even should the non-proliferation regime fail in a particular case, export controls can still play a role in constraining the sophistication, scope and size of activities following the acquisition of a first nuclear weapon.[11]

The poor state of export controls in most of the countries of the former Soviet Union is a source of particular concern. While there has not yet been a case of substantial amounts of fissile material being smuggled from this area, appropriate measures must be taken to strengthen the relevant national bodies in these states to ensure against such an eventuality. Efforts should also be made to bring these states into the Nuclear Suppliers Group. Of course inadequate controls have not only been seen in the former USSR. Although much has been done to improve the situation since the revelations about the nuclear programme in Iraq, in some of the supplier nations, such as Germany, for example, increased efforts must be upheld and further vigilance encouraged.[12]

Expanded use of full-scope safeguards, including the decision by the NSG to require full-scope safeguards as a condition of supply, is a positive development which should be encouraged for all suppliers. New challenges to the export control regime from the new nuclear suppliers must be guarded against. The new universal reporting scheme involving imports, exports and production will increase confidence in the non-proliferation regime and could prove a valuable source of information regarding not only those countries that participate but

[10] Albright, D. and Hibbs, M., 'Iraq's shop-till-you-drop nuclear program', *Bulletin of the Atomic Scientists*, vol. 48, no. 3 (Apr. 1992), pp. 28–29.

[11] Dunn, L A., 'Buttressing nuclear export controls and supply-side restraints: initiatives and actions', eds H. Müller and L. A. Dunn, *Nuclear Export Controls and Supply Side Restraints: Options for Reform*, PPNN Study four, Mountbatten Centre for International Studies, Southampton, Oct. 1993, p. 20.

[12] In the context of the Iraqi programme, it has been noted that 'German export controls were perfectly meaningless. To receive shipments of sensitive equipment from West Germany, all they [Iraq] had to do was pay off an inspector at Eschborn or falsify documents, since nobody checked what was actually being shipped. Timmerman, K. R., *The Death Lobby: How the West Armed Iraq* (Houghton Mifflin: New York, 1991), p. 132.

also non-participants, by increasing overall transparency in worldwide nuclear trade. In particular, in the case of a known transaction, by allowing certain participating states to be ruled out, the source could be pinned down at least to some degree through a process of elimination. Obviously, the more countries that become party to this reporting scheme the more effectively it will be able to provide an overall picture of nuclear activity.

V. Verification, intelligence and proliferation

As discussed throughout the book, the key to further progress in curbing the proliferation of nuclear weapons is *information*. This information may be acquired through a number of channels as discussed in chapter 7. Some nuclear activities, such as the use of gaseous diffusion to produce significant quantities of enriched uranium, require very large structures which under most circumstances should be relatively easy to detect by observation from satellites, for example. Even commercial satellites, with their somewhat limited resolution, could prove capable of adding to evidence pointing to illicit activity.

Smaller facilities, such as those using more advanced methods of enrichment, including gas centrifuges or laser technology, for example, would be much more difficult to uncover. The United States set an important precedent in providing intelligence for inspectors in Iraq in their quest to discover the full extent of Iraq's nuclear programme. The Director General of the IAEA has stated that such intelligence information is of crucial importance. Capabilities which could be of use in the non-proliferation context range from sophisticated image and signals intelligence satellites to human intelligence. The latter may be an important source of information which in many instances may not be available through other means, including those providing early-warning of nuclear weapon-related activity or in some cases even the intent to pursue such a programme.

As discussed, information may also be obtained through special inspections, but much valuable information has been and is being collected routinely by the International Atomic Energy Agency in its safeguards activities as well. The universal reporting procedure involving information exchange between countries and the IAEA, although in its formative stages, has the potential to increase transparency and thus aid in the overall effort to monitor proliferation-related activity.

To build additional confidence and enhance deterrence, other methods of collecting appropriate information on a regional or international scale should be further explored, with specific reference to their capabilities for monitoring nuclear activities which carry the risk of nuclear weapon proliferation. While political obstacles may still abound, here, as in other areas, the current international state of affairs could provide an opportune climate for progress.

VI. Regional developments

There have been several regional developments in the past several years which give rise to optimism. These include the abandonment of the South African nuclear weapon programme and its accession to the NPT as well as the 1991 Agreement on the Exclusively Peaceful Utilization of Nuclear Energy between Argentina, Brazil, the IAEA and ABACC. However, especially with the recent demise of the effects of superpower rivalry, many regional powers find themselves not only with decreased restraints, or with no restraints at all, but also without many of the important assurances which the old alliances may have provided. Therefore, regional security concerns are creating incentives for many countries to invest more heavily in military programmes to enhance their perceived security, including possible incentives to acquire or develop the appropriate technology for nuclear weapons.

The desirability of implementing regional verification measures in such regions as the Middle East and the Korean Peninsula[13] is well appreciated. Problems in these areas, and perhaps in the former Soviet Union too, could create difficulties for the non-proliferation regime, while it is still perhaps too early to ascertain the full impact of diminished security ties between India and the former Soviet Union, and between Pakistan and the USA.

Therefore, while international efforts including supply-side controls need to be continued, additional focus is needed in parallel at the regional level to develop new and effective approaches to alleviate such concerns and thus aid in curbing nuclear proliferation from the demand side. Confidence- and security-building measures, as well as assurance that verification systems are in place that will provide adequate detection capabilities at the regional level, are important ways to pursue this goal. With the end of the cold war there are positive prospects for substantial US–Russian cooperation in new approaches to regional non-proliferation structures.[14]

Such approaches will of necessity be different for different regions. In the Middle East the long-term monitoring being implemented as a result of the Persian Gulf War could provide the beginning of a basis for a regional arms control agreement.[15] However, a safeguards regime tailored for the Middle East, which might need to include a ban on reprocessing and enrichment and posses-

[13] The Non-Nuclear Korean Peninsula Agreement, which entered into force in 1992, has yet to be implemented. It specifies the strictly peaceful use of nuclear energy, provides for mutual inspections and prohibits the testing, manufacturing, producing, receiving, possession, storing, deployment or use of nuclear weapons on the Korean Peninsula as well as banning enrichment and reprocessing facilities. See, e.g., Pilat, J. F., 'Regional non-proliferation strategies', ed. T. Rauf, *Strengthened IAEA Safeguards and Regional Non-Proliferation Strategies*, Aurora Papers 23, Canadian Centre for Global Security, Ottawa, Mar. 1994, p. 60.

[14] See, e.g., Pilat, J. F., 'Regional non-proliferation strategies', pp. 57–66; Rauf, T., 'Strengthened safeguards and non-proliferation', pp. 17–18; and Sheinman, L., 'Strengthened IAEA safeguards and special inspections', pp. 19, 25–26—all in Rauf (note 13). See also Simpson, J. and Howlet, D., 'The NPT renewal conference: stumbling toward 1995', *International Security*, vol. 19, no. 1 (summer 1994), pp. 50–52, and references therein.

[15] Simpson and Howlet (note 14), pp. 52–53.

sion of reprocessed plutonium or HEU, together with a system of bilateral inspections with the threat of punishment in order to offer credible assurance, may be unsuitable for Western Europe, the CIS or North America, for example.[16]

VII. Iraq, North Korea and dealing with nuclear proliferation

The vast array of weaponry, not only nuclear, that was acquired by Iraq with the aid of other countries illustrates 'what can happen when monumental greed meets boundless ambition'.[17] As early as 1975, when France first agreed to sell two reactors to Iraq, Saddam Hussein had reportedly said that the agreement was 'the first concrete step toward the production of the Arab atomic weapon'.[18] The desire on the part of the Iraqi leader to develop nuclear weapons[19] was not a surprise, but the extent of the programme which had been conducted under cover for many years certainly was. This discovery of how little could be known about such a substantial programme has, however, had a substantial effect on the nuclear non-proliferation regime, helping to effect improvements in safeguards, export controls and other measures as delineated in this volume.

In addition, although conducted under unique circumstances, the inspections by the IAEA under UN auspices in Iraq have provided a wealth of valuable experience which should be useful in the conduct of nuclear-related inspections in the future. This includes the use of a vast array of national technical means in conjunction with the inspection activity and, while many of the lessons learned may not be publicly available, it is certain that they will be useful not only in improving NTM capability but also, especially, in the way in which the information acquired is fused with other data, such as those acquired from human sources, and analysed. While admittedly a very special case, developments in Iraq have been important in demonstrating the willingness of the UN Security Council to take decisive action with respect to the proliferation of weapons of mass destruction.

While the special inspections which are needed to uncover the full extent of the North Korean nuclear programme are unlikely to be conducted in the near future, it is important that the country's nuclear programme has been frozen. Continued patient diplomacy may well be needed to assure that all elements of

[16] Fischer, D., 'The future of the IAEA', *PPNN Issue Review*, no. 2 (Dec. 1993), p. 6.

[17] Timmerman (note 12), p. x.

[18] Interview in *Al Usbu al-Aarai,* quoted in Timmerman (note 12), p. 30.

[19] Some parallels can be drawn between the Iraqi nuclear weapon programme and the Manhattan Project that are interesting from the point of view of a nascent nuclear weapon programme in general. As with the Manhattan Project many methods were pursued simultaneously, as it was not clear which would be most effective, including uranium separation by several methods as well as plutonium production. As with the Manhattan Project the Iraqi effort also apparently would 'proceed vigorously on major phases of the work despite large gaps in basic knowledge', and the general philosophy consistently adhered to was that 'nothing would be more fatal to success than to try to arrive at a perfect plan before taking any important step'. Groves, L. R., *Now it can be Told: The Story of the Manhattan Project* (Harper&Row: New York, 1962), pp. 11, 42.

the agreement are brought to completion, but it must be regarded as an important success.

Although an agreed halt to the North Korean programme has been reached, should that country fail to follow through on its obligations the threat of sanctions which loomed throughout a large part of the negotiated settlement will doubtless be reconsidered. They may also be considered in the future to cope with other situations in other countries, whether political, economic, military or some combination of these. The effectiveness of sanctions will generally depend on a number of factors:[20] the extent of the overall reliance on the commodities under sanction, the relative amount which those applying sanctions actually contribute to the withheld commodities, availability of alternate suppliers, possibility of the sanctioned nation to retaliate to an unacceptable degree, and the determination of the sanctioning countries to see that the sanctions are actually applied as agreed. The threatened sanctions would also have to pose a threat to the countries concerned strong enough to outweigh the advantages sought by the acquisition of nuclear weapons, whether they be national security objectives or merely prestige.

As the experience in Iraq has shown, even under circumstances when most of these conditions have been well met, the effectiveness of sanctions has not been substantial. This is not to say that they may not prove to be an effective weapon against nuclear proliferation in the future, and certainly they express the resolve of those involved in imposing them, but careful consideration should be given to the above factors before any decision is taken. Such an analysis should also not fail to take account of the moral considerations that may be involved in depriving a civilian population of a reasonable standard of living, which might be the result if sanctions are implemented.

In extreme situations, when all other options have failed, the option of military force may come under consideration. It is important to remember several drawbacks of this option, including possible retaliation, nuclear contamination resulting from an attack on nuclear facilities, and the fact that the results may only be a temporary setback unless other means are employed to change a proliferator's reasons for trying to acquire a nuclear capability in the first place.

Security assurances have been and may continue to prove an effective tool in countering proliferation. Positive security assurances by the USA, for example, have contributed to the abandonment of nuclear programmes by South Korea in the face of the threat from the North as well as in the case of Taiwan. The 1994 Agreed Framework between the USA and North Korea provides for assurances that the USA will refrain from using or threatening to use nuclear weapons against North Korea. None the less the provision of positive security assurances is perhaps less likely in the future as they are viewed in increasingly negative terms. The spread of technology provides more nations with increasingly

[20] Bailey, K. C., *Strengthening Nuclear Nonproliferation* (Westview Press: Boulder, Colo., 1993), pp. 79–85.

sophisticated weapons, perhaps including nuclear weapons, which could threaten a state that might consider providing such assurances.[21]

Perhaps one of the most effective means of countering proliferation is through education.[22] If a well-informed cost-benefit analysis can convince countries that acquiring a nuclear capability is not in their best interests, then they may forgo the option. Important concrete factors should be considered, including: (*a*) the enormous cost of a nuclear weapon effort, both in financial terms and in terms of diverted industrial and intellectual resources from civilian (as well as conventional military) enterprise; (*b*) that the acquisition of nuclear weapons may decrease crisis stability by creating 'use them or lose them' scenarios; (*c*) that they may encourage regional nuclear arms races; and (*d*) that their production creates difficult and expensive environmental problems.

The spread of nuclear technology will continue to present serious challenges to the nuclear non-proliferation regime. Concrete steps now being taken and recommendations for further action to address these challenges are explored in this volume. Ultimately, however, their implementation will be most effective only when underlying security concerns, and other political factors that lead states or groups of individuals to seek nuclear weapon technology, are appropriately analysed and addressed.

[21] Simpson, J., 'Nuclear arms control and an extended nonproliferation regime', *SIPRI Yearbook 1994* (Oxford University Press: Oxford, 1994), pp. 612–13; and Bailey (note 20), pp. 88–91, 107.

[22] Bailey (note 20), pp. 97–104.

Appendix A. The Treaty on the Non-Proliferation of Nuclear Weapons

Signed at London, Moscow and Washington, DC, on 1 July 1968
Entered into force on 5 March 1970
Depositaries: UK, US and Soviet governments

The States concluding this Treaty, hereinafter referred to as the 'Parties to the Treaty',

Considering the devastation that would be visited upon all mankind by a nuclear war and the consequent need to make every effort to avert the danger of such a war and to take measures to safeguard the security of peoples,

Believing that the proliferation of nuclear weapons would seriously enhance the danger of nuclear war,

In conformity with resolutions of the United Nations General Assembly calling for the conclusion of an agreement on the prevention of wider dissemination of nuclear weapons,

Undertaking to co-operate in facilitating the application of International Atomic Energy Agency safeguards on peaceful nuclear activities,

Expressing their support for research, development and other efforts to further the application, within the framework of the International Atomic Energy Agency safeguards system, of the principle of safeguarding effectively the flow of source and special fissionable materials by use of instruments and other techniques at certain strategic points,

Affirming the principle that the benefits of peaceful applications of nuclear technology, including any technological by-products which may be derived by nuclear-weapon States from the development of nuclear explosive devices, should be available for peaceful purposes to all Parties to the Treaty, whether nuclear-weapon or non-nuclear-weapon States,

Convinced that, in furtherance of this principle, all Parties to the Treaty are entitled to participate in the fullest possible exchange of scientific information for, and to contribute alone or in co-operation with other States to, the further development of the applications of atomic energy for peaceful purposes,

Declaring their intention to achieve at the earliest possible date the cessation of the nuclear arms race and to undertake effective measures in the direction of nuclear disarmament,

Urging the co-operation of all States in the attainment of this objective,

Recalling the determination expressed by the Parties to the 1963 Treaty banning nuclear weapon tests in the atmosphere, in outer space and under water in its Preamble to seek to achieve the discontinuance of all test explosions of nuclear weapons for all time and to continue negotiations to this end,

Desiring to further the easing of international tension and the strengthening of trust between States in order to facilitate the cessation of the manufacture of nuclear weapons, the liquidation of all their existing stockpiles, and the elimination from national arsenals of nuclear weapons and the means of their delivery pursuant to a Treaty on general and complete disarmament under strict and effective international control,

Recalling that, in accordance with the Charter of the United Nations, States must refrain in their international relations from the threat or use of force against the territorial integrity or political independence of any State, or in any other manner inconsistent with the Purposes of the United Nations, and that the establishment and maintenance of international peace and security are to be promoted with the least diversion for armaments of the world's human and economic resources,

Have agreed as follows:

Article I

Each nuclear-weapon State Party to the Treaty undertakes not to transfer to any recipient whatsoever nuclear weapons or other nuclear explosive devices or control over such weapons or explosive devices directly, or indirectly; and not in any way to assist, encourage, or induce any non-nuclear-weapon State to manufacture or otherwise acquire nuclear weapons or other nuclear explosive devices, or control over such weapons or explosive devices.

Article II

Each non-nuclear-weapon State Party to the Treaty undertakes not to receive the transfer from any transferor whatsoever of nuclear weapons or other nuclear explosive devices or of control over such weapons or explosive devices directly, or indirectly; not to manufacture or otherwise acquire nuclear weapons or other nuclear explosive devices and not to seek or receive any assistance in the manufacture of nuclear weapons or other nuclear explosive devices.

Article III

1. Each non-nuclear-weapon State Party to the Treaty undertakes to accept safeguards, as set forth in an agreement to be negotiated and concluded with the International Atomic Energy Agency in accordance with the Statute of the International Atomic Energy Agency and the Agency's safeguards system, for the exclusive purpose of verification of the fulfilment of its obligations assumed under this Treaty with a view to preventing diversion of nuclear energy from peaceful uses to nuclear weapons or other nuclear explosive devices. Procedures for the safeguards required by this Article shall be followed with respect to source or special fissionable material whether it is being produced, processed or used in any principal nuclear facility or is outside any such facility. The safeguards required by this Article shall be applied on all source or special fissionable material in all peaceful nuclear activities within the territory of such State, under its jurisdiction, or carried out under its control anywhere.

2. Each State Party to the Treaty undertakes not to provide: (*a*) source or special fissionable material, or (*b*) equipment or material especially designed or prepared for the processing, use or production of special fissionable material, to any non-nuclear-weapon State for peaceful purposes, unless the source or special fissionable material shall be subject to the safeguards required by this Article.

3. The safeguards required by this Article shall be implemented in a manner designed to comply with Article IV of this Treaty, and to avoid hampering the economic or technological development of the Parties or international co-operation in the field of peaceful nuclear activities, including the international exchange of nuclear material and equipment for the processing, use or production of nuclear material for peaceful purposes in accordance with the provisions of this Article and the principle of safeguarding set forth in the Preamble of the Treaty.

4. Non-nuclear-weapon States Party to the Treaty shall conclude agreements with the International Atomic Energy Agency to meet the requirements of this Article either individually or together with other States in accordance with the Statute of the International Atomic Energy Agency. Negotiation of such agreements shall commence within 180 days from the original entry into force of this Treaty. For States depositing their instruments of ratification or accession after the 180-day period, negotiation of such agreements shall commence not later than the date of such deposit. Such agreements shall enter into force not later than eighteen months after the date of initiation of negotiations.

Article IV

1. Nothing in this Treaty shall be interpreted as affecting the inalienable right of all the Parties to the Treaty to develop research, production and use of nuclear energy for peaceful purposes without discrimination and in conformity with Articles I and II of this Treaty.

2. All the Parties to the Treaty undertake to facilitate, and have the right to participate in, the fullest possible exchange of equipment, materials and scientific and technological information for the peaceful uses of nuclear energy. Parties to the Treaty in a position to do so shall also co-operate in contributing alone or together with other States or international organizations to the further development of the applications of nuclear energy for peaceful purposes, especially in the territories of non-nuclear-weapon States Party to the Treaty, with due consideration for the needs of the developing areas of the world.

Article V

Each Party to the Treaty undertakes to take appropriate measures to ensure that, in accordance with this Treaty, under appropriate international observation and through appropriate international procedures, potential benefits from any peaceful applications of nuclear explosions will be made available to non-nuclear-weapon States Party to the Treaty on a non-discriminatory basis and that the charge to such Parties for the explosive devices used will be as low as possible and exclude any charge for research and development. Non-nuclear-weapon States Party to the Treaty shall be able to obtain such benefits, pursuant to a special international agreement or agreements, through an appropriate international body with adequate representation of non-nuclear-weapon States. Negotiations on this subject shall commence as soon as possible after the Treaty enters into force. Non-nuclear-weapon States Party to the Treaty so desiring may also obtain such benefits pursuant to bilateral agreements.

Article VI

Each of the Parties to the Treaty undertakes to pursue negotiations in good faith on effective measures relating to cessation of the nuclear arms race at an early date and to nuclear disarmament, and on a treaty on general and complete disarmament under strict and effective international control.

Article VII

Nothing in this Treaty affects the right of any group of States to conclude regional treaties in order to assure the total absence of nuclear weapons in their respective territories.

Article VIII

1. Any Party to the Treaty may propose amendments to this Treaty. The text of any proposed amendment shall be submitted to the Depositary Governments which shall circulate it to all Parties to the Treaty. Thereupon, if requested to do so by one-third or more of the Parties to the Treaty, the Depositary Governments shall convene a conference, to which they shall invite all the Parties to the Treaty, to consider such an amendment.

2. Any amendment to this Treaty must be approved by a majority of the votes of all the Parties to the Treaty, including the votes of all nuclear-weapon States Party to the Treaty and all other Parties which, on the date the amendment is circulated, are members of the Board of Governors of the International Atomic Energy Agency. The amendment shall enter into force for each Party that deposits its instrument of ratification of the amendment upon the deposit of such instruments of ratification by a majority of all the Parties, including the instruments of ratification of all nuclear-weapon States Party to the Treaty and all other Parties which, on the date the amendment is circulated, are members of the Board of Governors of the International Atomic Energy Agency. Thereafter, it shall enter into force for any other Party upon the deposit of its instrument of ratification of the amendment.

3. Five years after the entry into force of this Treaty a conference of Parties to the Treaty shall be held in Geneva, Switzerland, in order to review the operation of this Treaty with a view to assuring that the purposes of the Preamble and the provisions of the Treaty are being realised. At intervals of five years thereafter, a majority of the Parties to the Treaty may obtain, by submitting a proposal to this effect to the Depositary Governments, the convening of further conferences with the same objective of reviewing the operation of the Treaty.

Article IX

1. This Treaty shall be open to all States for signature. Any State which does not sign the Treaty before its entry into force in accordance with paragraph 3 of this Article may accede to it at any time.

2. This Treaty shall be subject to ratification by signatory States. Instruments of ratification and instruments of accession shall be deposited with the Governments of the United Kingdom of Great Britain and Northern Ireland, the Union of Soviet Socialist Republics and the United States of America, which are hereby designated the Depositary Governments.

3. This Treaty shall enter into force after its ratification by the States, the Governments of which are designated Depositaries of the Treaty, and forty other States signatory to this Treaty and the deposit of their instruments of ratification. For the purposes of this Treaty, a nuclear-weapon State is one which has manufactured and exploded a nuclear weapon or other nuclear explosive device prior to 1 January, 1967.

4. For States whose instruments of ratification or accession are deposited subsequent to the entry into force of this Treaty, it shall enter into force on the date of the deposit of their instruments of ratification or accession.

5. The Depositary Governments shall promptly inform all signatory and acceding States of the date of each signature, the date of deposit of each instrument of ratification or of accession, the date of the entry into force of this Treaty, and the date of receipt of any requests for convening a conference or other notices.

6. This Treaty shall be registered by the Depositary Governments pursuant to Article 102 of the Charter of the United Nations.

Article X

1. Each Party shall in exercising its national sovereignty have the right to withdraw from the Treaty if it decides that extraordinary events, related to the subject matter of this Treaty, have jeopardized the supreme interests of its country. It shall give notice of such withdrawal to all other Parties to the Treaty and to the United Nations Security Council three months in advance. Such notice shall include a statement of the extraordinary events it regards as having jeopardized its supreme interests.

2. Twenty-five years after the entry into force of the Treaty, a conference shall be convened to decide whether the Treaty shall continue in force indefinitely, or shall be extended for an additional fixed period or periods. This decision shall be taken by a majority of the Parties to the Treaty.

Article XI

This Treaty, the English, Russian, French, Spanish and Chinese texts of which are equally authentic, shall be deposited in the archives of the Depositary Governments. Duly certified copies of this Treaty shall be transmitted by the Depositary Governments to the Governments of the signatory and acceding States.

Source: *Treaty Series,* Vol. 729 (United Nations, New York).

Appendix B. Implementation of the NPT

RAGNHILD FERM*

I. Summary of provisions

The Treaty on the Non-Proliferation of Nuclear Weapons (NPT) was signed at London, Moscow and Washington, DC, on 1 July 1968 and entered into force on 5 March 1970. The Treaty prohibits the transfer by nuclear weapon states, to any recipient whatsoever, of nuclear weapons or other nuclear explosive devices or of control over them, as well as the assistance, encouragement or inducement of any non-nuclear weapon state to manufacture or otherwise acquire such weapons or devices. It prohibits the receipt by non-nuclear weapon states from any transferor whatsoever, as well as the manufacture or other acquisition by those states of nuclear weapons or other nuclear explosive devices.

Non-nuclear weapon states undertake to conclude safeguards agreements with the International Atomic Energy Agency (IAEA) with a view to preventing diversion of nuclear energy from peaceful uses to nuclear weapons or other nuclear explosive devices.

The states parties undertake to facilitate the exchange of equipment, materials and scientific and technological information for the peaceful uses of nuclear energy and to ensure that potential benefits from peaceful applications of nuclear explosions will be made available to non-nuclear weapon parties to the Treaty. They also undertake to pursue negotiations in good faith on effective measures relating to cessation of the nuclear arms race at an early date and to nuclear disarmament, and on a treaty on general and complete disarmament.

In 1995, 25 years after the entry into force of the Treaty, in accordance with Article X, a conference was convened to decide whether the Treaty would continue in force indefinitely or would be extended for an additional fixed period or periods. It was decided that the Treaty should remain in force indefinitely.

II. Status of implementation as of 15 April 1995

The Non-Proliferation Treaty provides for three depositaries—the Governments of the UK, the USA and the USSR. The dates indicated in table B are the earliest dates on which countries deposited their instruments of ratification, accession or succession—whether in London, Washington, DC, or Moscow.

The designation 'SA' in table B indicates that an IAEA nuclear safeguards agreement is in force as required by the Treaty or concluded by a nuclear weapon state on a voluntary basis.

* This appendix is updated from Ferm, R., 'Major multilateral arms control agreements', *SIPRI Yearbook 1995: Armaments, Disarmament and International Security* (Oxford University Press: Oxford, 1995), Annexe A.

Table B. States parties to the NPT, as of 15 April 1995

Country	Year		Country	Year	
Afghanistan	1970	SA	Croatia	1992	
Albania	1990		Cyprus	1970	SA
Algeria	1995		Czech Republic	1993	SA
Antigua and Barbuda	1985		Denmark	1969	SA
Argentina	1995		Dominica	1984	
Armenia	1993	SA	Dominican Republic	1971	SA
Australia	1973	SA	Ecuador	1969	SA
Austria	1969	SA	Egypt	1981[2]	SA
Azerbaijan	1992		El Salvador	1972	SA
Bahamas	1976		Equatorial Guinea	1984	
Bahrain	1988		Eritrea	1995	
Bangladesh	1979	SA	Estonia	1992	
Barbados	1980		Ethiopia	1970	SA
Belarus	1993		Fiji	1972	SA
Belgium	1975	SA	Finland	1969	SA
Belize	1985		France	1992	SA[3]
Benin	1972		Gabon	1974	
Bhutan	1985	SA	Gambia	1975	SA
Bolivia	1970		Georgia	1994	
Bosnia and Herzegovina	1994		Germany	1975[4]	SA
Botswana	1969		Ghana	1970	SA
Brunei	1985	SA	Greece	1970	SA
Bulgaria	1969	SA	Grenada	1975	
Burkina Faso	1970		Guatemala	1970	SA
Burundi	1971		Guinea	1985	
Cambodia	1972		Guinea-Bissau	1976	
Cameroon	1969		Guyana	1993	
Canada	1969	SA	Haiti	1970	
Cape Verde	1979		Holy See	1971[5]	SA
Central African Republic	1970		Honduras	1973	SA
Chad	1971		Hungary	1969	SA
China	1992[1]		Iceland	1969	SA
Colombia	1986		Indonesia	1979[6]	SA
Congo	1978		Iran	1970	SA
Costa Rica	1970	SA	Iraq	1969	SA
Côte d'Ivoire	1973	SA	Ireland	1968	SA

Country	Year	Country	Year
Italy	1975[7] SA	Morocco	1970 SA
Jamaica	1970 SA	Mozambique	1990
Japan	1976[8] SA	Myanmar (Burma)	1992
Jordan	1970 SA	Namibia	1992
Kazakhstan	1994	Nauru	1982 SA
Kenya	1970	Nepal	1970 SA
Kiribati	1985 SA	Netherlands	1975 SA
Korea, North	1985 SA	New Zealand	1969 SA
Korea, South	1975[9] SA	Nicaragua	1973 SA
Kuwait	1989	Niger	1992
Kyrgyzstan	1994	Nigeria	1968 SA
Laos	1970	Norway	1969 SA
Latvia	1992 SA	Palau	1995
Lebanon	1970 SA	Panama	1977
Lesotho	1970 SA	Papua New Guinea	1982 SA
Liberia	1970	Paraguay	1970 SA
Libya	1975 SA	Peru	1970 SA
Liechtenstein	1978[10] SA	Philippines	1972 SA
Lithuania	1991 SA	Poland	1969 SA
Luxembourg	1975 SA	Portugal	1977 SA
Macedonia (Former Yugoslav Republic of)	1995	Qatar	1989
		Romania	1970 SA
Madagascar	1970 SA	Russia	1970 SA[12]
Malawi	1986 SA	Rwanda	1975
Malaysia	1970 SA	Sant Kitts and Nevis	1993
Maldives	1970 SA	Saint Lucia	1979 SA
Mali	1970	Saint Vincent and the Grenadines	1984 SA
Malta	1970 SA		
Marshall Islands	1995	Samoa, Western	1975 SA
Mauritania	1993	San Marino	1970
Mauritius	1969 SA	Sao Tome & Principe	1983
Mexico	1969[11] SA	Saudi Arabia	1988
Micronesia	1995	Senegal	1970 SA
Moldova	1994	Seychelles	1985
Monaco	1995	Sierra Leone	1975
Mongolia	1969 SA	Singapore	1976 SA

Table B, *contd*

Country	Year	Country	Year
Slovakia	1993 SA	Trinidad and Tobago	1986 SA
Slovenia	1992	Tunisia	1970 SA
Solomon Islands	1981 SA	Turkey	1980[13] SA
Somalia	1970	Turkmenistan	1994
South Africa	1991 SA	Tuvalu	1979 SA
Spain	1987 SA	Uganda	1982
Sri Lanka	1979 SA	UK	1968 SA[14]
Sudan	1973 SA	Ukraine	1994
Suriname	1976 SA	Uruguay	1970 SA
Swaziland	1969 SA	USA	1970 SA[15]
Sweden	1970 SA	Uzbekistan	1992
Switzerland	1977[10] SA	Venezuela	1975 SA
Syria	1969 SA	Viet Nam	1982 SA
Taiwan	1970	Yemen	1979
Tajikistan	1995	Yugoslavia	1970[16] SA
Tanzania	1991	(Serbia & Montenegro)	
Thailand	1972 SA	Zaire	1970 SA
Togo	1970	Zambia	1991 SA
Tonga	1971 SA	Zimbabwe	1991

Notes

[1] China stated that the nuclear weapon states should undertake: (*a*) not to be the first to use nuclear weapons at any time and under any circumstances; (*b*) not to use or threaten to use nuclear weapons against non-nuclear weapon countries or nuclear-free zones; and (*c*) support the establishment of nuclear weapon-free zones, respect the status of such zones and assume corresponding obligations. All states that have nuclear weapons deployed outside of their boundaries should withdraw all those weapons back to their own territories. China also declared that it regards the signing and ratification of the NPT by Taiwan in the name of China as illegal and null and void.

[2] Egypt stated that since it was embarking on the construction of nuclear power reactors, it expected assistance and support from industrialized nations with a developed nuclear industry. It called upon nuclear weapon states to promote research and development of peaceful applications of nuclear explosions in order to overcome all the difficulties at present involved therein. Egypt also appealed to these states to exert their efforts to conclude an agreement prohibiting the use or threat of use of nuclear weapons against any state, and expressed the view that the Middle East should remain completely free of nuclear weapons.

[3] An agreement between France, the European Atomic Energy Community (EURATOM) and the IAEA for the application of safeguards in France had entered into force in 1981. The agreement covers nuclear material and facilities notified to the IAEA by France.

[4] FR Germany declared that it reaffirmed its expectation that the nuclear weapon states would intensify their efforts in accordance with the undertakings under Article VI of the Treaty, as well as its understanding that the security of FR Germany continued to be ensured by NATO; it stated that no provision of the Treaty may be interpreted in such a way as to hamper further development of European unification; that research, development and use of nuclear energy for peaceful purposes, as well as international and multinational cooperation in this field, must not be prejudiced by the Treaty; that the application of the Treaty, including the implementation of safeguards, must not lead to dis-

crimination of the nuclear industry of FR Germany in international competition; and that it attached vital importance to the undertaking given by the USA and the UK concerning the application of safeguards to their peaceful nuclear facilities, hoping that other nuclear weapon states would assume similar obligations.

[5] The Holy See stated, *inter alia*, that the Treaty will attain in full the objectives of security and peace and justify the limitations to which the states party to the Treaty submit, only if it is fully executed in every clause and with all its implications.

[6] On signing the Treaty, Indonesia stated, *inter alia*, that it attaches great importance to the declarations of the USA, the UK and the USSR affirming their intention to provide immediate assistance to any non-nuclear weapon state party to the Treaty that is a victim of an act of aggression in which nuclear weapons are used. Of utmost importance, however, is not the action *after* a nuclear attack has been committed but the guarantees to prevent such an attack. Indonesia trusts that the nuclear weapon states will study further this question of effective measures to ensure the security of the non-nuclear weapon states. On depositing the instrument of ratification, Indonesia expressed the hope that the nuclear countries would be prepared to cooperate with non-nuclear countries in the use of nuclear energy for peaceful purposes and implement the provisions of Article IV of the Treaty without discrimination. It also stated the view that the nuclear weapon states would observe the provisions of Article VI of the Treaty relating to the cessation of the nuclear arms race.

[7] Italy stated that nothing in the Treaty was an obstacle to the unification of the countries of Western Europe; it noted full compatibility of the Treaty with the existing security agreements; it noted further that when technological progress would allow the development of peaceful explosive devices different from nuclear weapons, the prohibition relating to their manufacture and use shall no longer apply; it interpreted the provisions of Article IX, para. 3 of the Treaty, concerning the definition of a nuclear weapon state, in the sense that it referred exclusively to the five countries which had manufactured and exploded a nuclear weapon or other nuclear explosive device prior to 1 Jan. 1967, and stressed that under no circumstance would a claim of pertaining to such category be recognized by Italy for any other state.

[8] Japan declared that it urged a reduction of nuclear armaments and a comprehensive ban on nuclear testing; appealed to all states to refrain from the threat or use of force involving either nuclear or non-nuclear weapons; expressed the view that peaceful nuclear activities in non-nuclear weapon states party to the Treaty should not be hampered and that Japan should not be discriminated against in favour of other parties in any aspect of such activities. It also urged all nuclear weapon states to accept IAEA safeguards on their peaceful nuclear activities.

[9] The Republic of Korea (South Korea) took note of the fact that the depositary governments of the three nuclear weapon states had made declarations in June 1968 to take immediate and effective measures to safeguard any non-nuclear weapon state which is a victim of an act or an object of a threat of aggression in which nuclear weapons are used.

[10] Liechtenstein and Switzerland stated that activities not prohibited under Articles I and II of the Treaty include, in particular, the whole field of energy production and related operations, research and technology concerning future generations of nuclear reactors based on fission or fusion, as well as production of isotopes. Liechtenstein and Switzerland define the term 'source or special fissionable material' in Article III of the Treaty as being in accordance with Article XX of the IAEA Statute, and a modification of this interpretation requires their formal consent; they will accept only such interpretations and definitions of the terms 'equipment or material especially designed or prepared for the processing, use or production of special fissionable material', as mentioned in Article III of the Treaty, that they will expressly approve; and they understand that the application of the Treaty, especially of the control measures, will not lead to discrimination of their industry in international competition.

[11] On signing the Treaty, Mexico stated, *inter alia*, that none of the provisions of the Treaty shall be interpreted as affecting in any way whatsoever the rights and obligations of Mexico as a state party to the Treaty of Tlatelolco. It is the understanding of Mexico that 'at the present time' any nuclear explosive device is capable of being used as a nuclear weapon and that there is no indication that 'in the near future' it will be possible to manufacture nuclear explosive devices that are not potentially nuclear weapons. However, if technological advances modify this situation, it will be necessary to amend the relevant provisions of the Treaty in accordance with the procedure established therein.

[12] The agreement provides for the application of IAEA safeguards in Soviet [Russian] peaceful nuclear facilities designated by the USSR [Russia].

[13] Turkey underlined the non-proliferation obligations of the nuclear weapon states, adding that measures must be taken to meet adequately the security requirements of non-nuclear weapon states.

[14] This agreement, signed by the UK, EURATOM and the IAEA, provides for the submission of British non-military nuclear installations to safeguards under IAEA supervision.

[15] This agreement provides for safeguards on fissionable material in all facilities within the USA, excluding those associated with activities of direct national security significance.

[16] Yugoslavia stated, *inter alia*, that it considered a ban on the development, manufacture and use of nuclear weapons and the destruction of all stockpiles of these weapons to be indispensable for the maintenance of a stable peace and international security; it held the view that the chief responsibility for progress in this direction rested with the nuclear weapon states, and expected these states to undertake not to use nuclear weapons against the countries which have renounced them as well as against non-nuclear weapon states in general, and to refrain from the threat to use them.

Appendix C. International Atomic Energy Agency documents

THE IAEA SAFEGUARDS SYSTEM OF 1965–68

The Agency's safeguards system (1965, as provisionally extended in 1966 and 1968)

I. GENERAL CONSIDERATIONS

A. The purpose of this document

1. Pursuant to Article II of its Statute the Agency has the task of seeking 'to accelerate and enlarge the contribution of atomic energy to peace, health and prosperity throughout the world'. Inasmuch as the technology of nuclear energy for peaceful purposes is closely coupled with that for the production of materials for nuclear weapons, the same Article of the Statute provides that the Agency 'shall ensure, so far as it is able, that assist-ance provided by it or at its request or under its supervision or control is not used in such a way as to further any military purpose'.

2. The principal purpose of the present document is to establish a system of controls to enable the Agency to comply with this statutory obligation with respect to the activities of Member States in the field of the peaceful uses of nuclear energy, as provided in the Statute. The authority to establish such a system is provided by Article III.A.5. of the Statute, which authorizes the Agency to 'establish and administer safeguards designed to ensure that special fissionable and other materials, services, equipment, facilities, and information made available by the Agency or at its request or under its supervision or control are not used in such a way as to further any military purpose'. This Article further authorizes the Agency to 'apply safeguards, at the request of the parties, to any bilateral or multilateral arrangement, or at the request of a State, to any of that State's activities in the field of atomic energy'. Article XII.A sets forth the rights and responsibilities that the Agency is to have, to the extent relevant, with respect to any project or arrangement which it is to safeguard.

3. The principles set forth in this document and the procedures for which it provides are established for the information of Member states, to enable them to determine in advance the circumstances and manner in which the Agency would administer safeguards, and for the guidance of the organs of the Agency itself, to enable the Board and the Director General to determine readily what provisions should be included in agreements relating to safeguards and how to interpret such provisions.

4. Provisions of this document that are relevant to a particular project, arrangement or activity in the field of nuclear energy will only become legally binding upon the entry into force of a *safeguards agreement*[1] and to the extent that they are incorporated therein. Such incorporation may be made by reference.

5. Appropriate provisions of this document may also be incorporated in bilateral or multilateral arrangements between Member States, including all those that provide for the transfer to the Agency of responsibility for administering safeguards. The Agency will not assume such responsibility unless the principles of the safeguards and the procedures to be used are essentially consistent with those set forth in this document.

6. Agreements incorporating provisions from the earlier version of the Agency's safeguards system[2] will continue to be administered in accordance with such provisions, unless all States parties thereto request the Agency to substitute the provisions of the present document.

7. Provisions relating to types of *principal nuclear facilities,* other than *reactors,* which may produce, process or use safeguarded *nuclear material* will be developed as necessary.

8. The principles and procedures set forth in this document shall be subject to periodic review in the light of the further experience gained by the Agency as well as of technological developments.

---

[1] The use of italics indicates that a term has a specialized meaning in this document and is defined in Part IV.

[2] Set forth in documents INFCIRC/26 and Add. 1.

B. General principles of the Agency's safeguards

The Agency's obligations

9. Bearing in mind Article II of the Statute, the Agency shall implement safeguards in a manner designed to avoid hampering a State's economic or technological development.

10. The safeguards procedures set forth in this document shall be implemented in a manner designed to be consistent with prudent management practices required for the economic and safe conduct of nuclear activities.

11. In no case shall the Agency request a State to stop the construction or operation of any *principal nuclear facility* to which the Agency's safeguards procedures extend, except by explicit decision of the Board.

12. The State or States concerned and the Director General shall hold consultations regarding the application of the provisions of the present document.

13. In implementing safeguards, the Agency shall take every precaution to protect commercial and industrial secrets. No member of the Agency's staff shall disclose, except to the Director General and to such other members of the staff as the Director General may authorize to have such information by reason of their official duties in connection with safeguards, any commercial or industrial secret or any other confidential information coming to his knowledge by reason of the implementation of safeguards by the Agency.

14. The Agency shall not publish or communicate to any State, organization or person any information obtained by it in connection with the implementation of safeguards, except that:

(*a*) Specific information relating to such implementation in a State may be given to the Board and to such Agency staff members as require such knowledge by reason of their official duties in connection with safeguards, but only to the extent necessary for the Agency to fulfil its safeguards responsibilities;

(*b*) Summarized lists of items being safeguarded by the Agency may be published upon decision of the Board; and

(*c*) Additional information may be published upon decision of the Board and if all States directly concerned agree.

Principles of implementation

15. The Agency shall implement safeguards in a State if:

(*a*) The Agency has concluded with the State a *project agreement* under which materials, services, equipment, facilities or information are supplied, and such agreement provides for the application of safeguards; or

(*b*) The State is a party to a bilateral or multilateral arrangement under which materials, services, equipment, facilities or information are supplied or otherwise transferred, and:

(i) All the parties to the arrangement have requested the Agency to administer safeguards; and

(ii) The Agency has concluded the necessary *safeguards agreement* with the State; or

(*c*) The Agency has been requested by the State to safeguard certain nuclear activities under the latter's jurisdiction, and the Agency has concluded the necessary *safeguards agreement* with the State.

16. In the light of Article XII.A.5 of the Statute, it is desirable that *safeguards agreements* should provide for the continuation of safeguards, subject to the provisions of this document, with respect to produced special fissionable material and to any materials substituted therefor.

17. The principal factors to be considered by the Board in determining the relevance of particular provisions of this document to various types of materials and facilities shall be the form, scope and amount of the assistance supplied, the character of each individual project and the degree to which such assistance could further any military purpose. The related *safeguards agreement* shall take account of all pertinent circumstances at the time of its conclusion.

18. In the event of any non-compliance by a State with a *safeguards agreement,* the Agency may take the measures set forth in Articles XII.A.7 and XII.C of the Statute.

II. CIRCUMSTANCES REQUIRING SAFEGUARDS

A. Nuclear materials subject to safeguards

19. Except as provided in paragraphs 21–28, *nuclear material* shall be subject to the Agency's safeguards if it is being or has been:

(*a*) Supplied under a *project agreement;* or

(*b*) Submitted to safeguards under a *safeguards agreement* by the parties to a bilateral or multilateral arrangement; or

(*c*) *Unilaterally submitted* to safeguards under a *safeguards agreement;* or (*d*) Produced, processed or used in a *principal nuclear facility* which has been:

(i) Supplied wholly or substantially under a *project agreement;* or

(ii) Submitted to safeguards under a *safeguards agreement* by the parties to a bilateral or multilateral arrangement; or

(iii) *Unilaterally submitted* to safeguards under a *safeguards agreement;* or

(*e*) Produced in or by the use of safeguarded *nuclear material;* or

(*f*) Substituted, pursuant to paragraph 26(*d*), for safeguarded *nuclear material.*

20. A *principal nuclear facility* shall be considered as substantially supplied under a *project agreement* if the Board has so determined.

B. Exemptions from safeguards

General exemptions

21. *Nuclear material* that would otherwise be subject to safeguards shall be exempted from safeguards at the request of the State concerned, provided that the material so exempted in that State may not at any time exceed:

(*a*) 1 kilogram in total of special fissionable material, which may consist of one or more of the following:

(i) Plutonium;

(ii) Uranium with an *enrichment* of 0.2 (20%) and above, taken account of by multiplying its weight by its *enrichment;*

(iii) Uranium with an *enrichment* below 0.2 (20%) and above that of natural uranium, taken account of by multiplying its weight by five times the square of its *enrichment;*

(*b*) 10 metric tons in total of natural uranium and depleted uranium with an *enrichment* above 0.005 (0.5%);

(*c*) 20 metric tons of depleted uranium with an *enrichment* of 0.005 (0.5%) or below; and

(*d*) 20 metric tons of thorium.

Exemptions related to reactors

22. Produced or used *nuclear material* that would otherwise be subject to safeguards pursuant to paragraph 19(*d*) or (*e*) shall be exempted from safeguards if:

(*a*) It is plutonium produced in the fuel of a *reactor* whose rate of production does not exceed 100 grams of plutonium per year; or

(*b*) It is produced in a *reactor* determined by the Agency to have a maximum calculated power for continuous operation of less than 3 thermal megawatts, or is used in such a *reactor* and would not be subject to safeguards except for such use, provided that the total power of the *reactors* with respect to which these exemptions apply in any State may not exceed 6 thermal megawatts.

23. Produced special fissionable material that would otherwise be subject to safeguards puruant only to paragraph 19(*e*) shall in part be exempted from safeguards if it is produced in a *reactor* in which the ratio of fissionable isotopes within safeguarded *nuclear material* to all fissionable isotopes is less than 0.3 (calculated each time any change is made in the loading of *the reactor* and assumed to be maintained until the next such change). Such fraction of the produced material as corresponds to the calculated ratio shall be subject to safeguards.

C. Suspension of safeguards

24. Safeguards with respect to *nuclear material* may be suspended while the material is transferred, under an arrangement or agreement approved by the Agency, for the purpose of processing, reprocessing, testing, research or development within the State concerned or to any other Member State or to an international organization, provided that the quantities of *nuclear material* with respect to which safeguards are thus suspended in a State may not at any time exceed:

(*a*) 1 *effective kilogram* of special fissionable material;

(*b*) 10 metric tons in total of natural uranium and depleted uranium with an *enrichment* above 0.005 (0.5%);

(*c*) 20 metric tons of depleted uranium with *an enrichment* of 0.005 (0.5%) or below; and

(*d*) 20 metric tons of thorium.

25. Safeguards with respect to *nuclear material* in irradiated fuel which is transferred for the purpose of reprocessing may also be suspended if the State or States concerned have, with the agreement of the Agency, placed under safeguards substitute *nuclear material* in accordance with paragraph 26(*d*) for the period of suspension. In addition, safeguards with respect to plutonium contained in irradiated fuel which is transferred for the purpose of reprocessing may be suspended for a period not to exceed six months if the State or States concerned have, with the agreement of the Agency, placed under safeguards a quantity of uranium whose *enrich-*

ment in the isotope uranium-235 is not less than 0.9 (90%) and the uranium-235 content of which is equal in weight to such plutonium. Upon expiration of the said six months or the completion of reprocessing, whichever is earlier, safeguards shall, with the agreement of the Agency, be applied to such plutonium and shall cease to apply to the uranium substituted therefor.

D. Termination of safeguards

26. *Nuclear material* shall no longer be subject to safeguards after:

(*a*) It has been returned to the State that originally supplied it (whether directly or through the Agency), if it was subject to safeguards only by reason of such supply and if:

(i) It was not *improved* while under safeguards; or

(ii) Any special fissionable material that was produced in it under safeguards has been separated out, or safeguards with respect to such produced material have been terminated; or

(*b*) The Agency has determined that:

(i) It was subject to safeguards only by reason of its use in a *principal nuclear facility* specified in paragraph 19(*d*);

(ii) It has been removed from such facility; and

(iii) Any special fissionable material that was produced in it under safeguards has been separated out, or safeguards with respect to such produced material have been terminated; or

(*c*) The Agency has determined that it has been consumed, or has been diluted in such a way that it is no longer usable for any nuclear activity relevant from the point of view of safeguards, or has become practicably irrecoverable; or

(*d*) The State or States concerned have, with the agreement of the Agency, placed under safeguards, as a substitute, such amount of the same element, not otherwise subject to safeguards, as the Agency has determined contains fissionable isotopes:

(i) Whose weight (with due allowance for processing losses) is equal to or greater than the weight of the fissionable isotopes of the material with respect to which safeguards are to terminate; and

(ii) Whose ratio by weight to the total substituted element is similar to or greater than the ratio by weight of the fissionable isotopes of the material with respect to which safeguards are to terminate to the total weight of such material;

provided that the Agency may agree to the substitution of plutonium for uranium-235 contained in uranium whose *enrichment* is not greater than 0.05 (5.0%); or

(*e*) It has been transferred out of the State under paragraph 28(*d*), provided that such material shall again be subject to safeguards if it is returned to the State in which the Agency had safeguarded it; or

(*f*) The conditions specified in the *safeguards agreement* pursuant to which it was subject to Agency safeguards, no longer apply, by expiration of the agreement or otherwise.

27. If a State wishes to use safeguarded source material for non-nuclear purposes, such as the production of alloys or ceramics, it shall agree with the Agency on the circumstances under which the safeguards on such material may be terminated.

E. Transfer of safeguarded nuclear material out of the State

28. No safeguarded *nuclear material* shall be transferred outside the jurisdiction of the State in which it is being safeguarded until the Agency has satisfied itself that one or more of the following conditions apply:

(*a*) The material is being returned, under the conditions specified in paragraph 26(*a*), to the State that originally supplied it; or

(*b*) The material is being transferred subject to the provisions of paragraph 24 or 25; or

(*c*) Arrangements have been made by the Agency to safeguard the material in accordance with this document in the State to which it is being transferred; or

(*d*) The material was not subject to safeguards pursuant to a *project agreement* and will be subject, in the State to which it is being transferred, to safeguards other than those of the Agency but generally consistent with such safeguards and accepted by the Agency.

III. SAFEGUARDS PROCEDURES

A. General procedures

Introduction

29. The safeguards procedures set forth below shall be followed, as far as relevant, with respect to safeguarded *nuclear materials,* whether they are being produced, processed or used in any *principal nuclear facility* or are outside any such facility. These procedures also extend to facilities containing or to con-

tain such materials, including *principal nuclear facilities* to which the criteria in paragraph 19(*d*) apply.

Design review

30. The Agency shall review the design of *principal nuclear facilities,* for the sole purpose of satisfying itself that a facility will permit the effective application of safeguards.

31. The design review of a *principal nuclear facility* shall take place at as early a stage as possible. In particular, such review shall be carried out in the case of:

(*a*) An Agency project, before the project is approved;

(*b*) A bilateral or multilateral arrangement under which the responsibility for administering safeguards is to be transferred to the Agency, or an activity *unilaterally submitted* by a State, before the Agency assumes safeguards responsibilities with respect to the facility;

(*c*) A transfer of safeguarded *nuclear material* to a *principal nuclear facility* whose design has not previously been reviewed, before such transfer takes place; and

(*d*) A significant modification of a *principal nuclear facility* whose design has previously been reviewed, before such modification is undertaken.

32. To enable the Agency to perform the required design review, the State shall submit to it relevant design information sufficient for the purpose, including information on such basic characteristics of the *principal nuclear facility* as may bear on the Agency's safeguards procedures. The Agency shall require only the minimum amount of information and data consistent with carrying out its responsibility under this section. It shall complete the review promptly after the submission of this information by the State and shall notify the latter of its conclusions without delay.

Records

33. The State shall arrange for the keeping of records with respect to *principal nuclear facilities* and also with respect to all safeguarded *nuclear material* outside such facilities. For this purpose the State and the Agency shall agree on a system of records with respect to each facility and also with respect to such material, on the basis of proposals to be submitted by the State in sufficient time to allow the Agency to review them before the records need to be kept.

34. If the records are not kept in one of the working languages of the Board, the State shall make arrangements to facilitate their examination by inspectors.

35. The records shall consist, as appropriate, of:

(*a*) Accounting records of all safeguarded *nuclear material*; and

(*b*) Operating records for *principal nuclear facilities.*

36. All records shall be retained for at least two years.

Reports

General requirements

37. The State shall submit to the Agency reports with respect to the production, processing and use of safeguarded *nuclear material* in or outside *principal nuclear facilities.* For this purpose the State and the Agency shall agree on a system of reports with respect to each facility and also with respect to safeguarded *nuclear material* outside such facilities, on the basis of proposals to be submitted by the State in sufficient time to allow the Agency to review them before the reports need to be submitted. The reports need include only such information as is relevant for the purpose of safeguards.

38. Unless otherwise provided in the applicable *safeguards agreement*, reports shall be submitted in one of the working languages of the Board.

Routine reports

39. Routine reports shall be based on the records compiled in accordance with paragraphs 33–36 and shall consist, as appropriate, of:

(*a*) Accounting reports showing the receipt, transfer out, inventory and use of all safeguarded *nuclear material.* The inventory shall indicate the nuclear and chemical composition and physical form of all material and its location on the date of the report; and

(*b*) Operating reports showing the use that has been made of each *principal nuclear facility* since the last report and, as far as possible, the programme of future work in the period until the next routine report is expected to reach the Agency.

40. The first routine report shall be submitted as soon as:

(*a*) There is any safeguarded *nuclear material* to be accounted for; or

(*b*) The *principal nuclear facility* to which it relates is in a condition to operate.

Progress in construction

41. The Agency may, if so provided in a *safeguards agreement*, request information as to when particular stages in the construction of a *principal nuclear facility* have been or are to be reached.

Special reports

42. The State shall report to the Agency without delay:

(*a*) If any unusual incident occurs involving actual or potential loss or destruction of, or damage to, any safeguarded *nuclear material* or *principal nuclear facility*; or

(*b*) If there is good reason to believe that safeguarded *nuclear material* is lost or unaccounted for in quantities that exceed the normal operating and handling losses that have been accepted by the Agency as characteristic of the facility.

43. The State shall report to the Agency, as soon as possible, and in any case within two weeks, any transfer not requiring advance notification that will result in a significant change (to be defined by the Agency in agreement with the State) in the quantity of safeguarded *nuclear material* in a facility, or in a complex of facilities considered as a unit for this purpose by agreement with the Agency. Such report shall indicate the amount and nature of the material and its intended use.

Amplification of reports

44. At the Agency's request the State shall submit amplifications or clarifications of any report, in so far as relevant for the purpose of safeguards.

Inspections

General procedures

45. The Agency may inspect safeguarded *nuclear materials* and *principal nuclear facilities.*

46. The purpose of safeguards inspections shall be to verify compliance with *safeguards agreements* and to assist States in complying with such agreements and in resolving any questions arising out of the implementation of safeguards.

47. The number, duration and intensity of inspections actually carried out shall be kept to the minimum consistent with the effective implementation of safeguards, and if the Agency considers that the authorized inspections are not all required, fewer shall be carried out.

48. Inspectors shall neither operate any facility themselves nor direct the staff of a facility to carry out any particular operation.

Routine inspections

49. Routine inspections may include, as appropriate:

(*a*) Audit of records and reports;

(*b*) Verification of the amount of safeguarded *nuclear material* by physical inspection, measurement and sampling;

(*c*) Examination of *principal nuclear facilities*, including a check of their measuring instruments and operating characteristics; and

(*d*) Check of the operations carried out at *principal nuclear facilities* and at *research and development facilities* containing safeguarded *nuclear material.*

50. Whenever the Agency has the right of access to a *principal nuclear facility* at all times[3], it may perform inspections of which notice as required by paragraph 4 of the *Inspectors Document* need not be given, in so far as this is necessary for the effective application of safeguards. The actual procedures to implement these provisions shall be agreed upon between the parties concerned in the *safeguards agreement*.

Initial inspections of principal nuclear facilities

51. To verify that the construction of a *principal nuclear facility* is in accordance with the design reviewed by the Agency, an initial inspection or inspections of the facility may be carried out, if so provided in a *safeguards agreement*:

(*a*) As soon as possible after the facility has come under Agency safeguards, in the case of a facility already in operation; or

(*b*) Before the facility starts to operate, in other cases.

52. The measuring instruments and operating characteristics of the facility shall be reviewed to the extent necessary for the purpose of implementing safeguards. Instruments that will be used to obtain data on the *nuclear materials* in the facility may be tested to determine their satisfactory functioning. Such testing may include the observation by inspectors of commissioning or routine tests by the staff of the facility, but shall not hamper or delay the construction, commissioning or normal operation of the facility.

---

[3] See para. 57.

Special inspections

53. The Agency may carry out special inspections if:

(*a*) The study of a report indicates that such inspection is desirable; or

(*b*) Any unforeseen circumstance requires immediate action.

The Board shall subsequently be informed of the reasons for and the results of each such inspection.

54. The Agency may also carry out special inspections of substantial amounts of safeguarded *nuclear material* that are to be transferred outside the jurisdiction of the State in which it is being safeguarded, for which purpose the State shall give the Agency sufficient advance notice of any such proposed transfer.

B. Special procedures for reactors

Reports

55. The frequency of submission of routine reports shall be agreed between the Agency and the State, taking into account the frequency established for routine inspections. However, at least two such reports shall be submitted each year and in no case shall more than 12 such reports be required in any year.

Inspections

56. One of the initial inspections of a *reactor* shall if possible be made just before the reactor first reaches criticality.

57. The maximum frequency of routine inspections of a *reactor* and of the safeguarded *nuclear material* in it shall be determined from the following table:

Whichever is the largest of: (a) Facility inventory (including loading); (b) Annual throughput; (c) Maximum potential annual production of special fissionable material (*Effective kilograms of nuclear material*)	Maximum number of routine inspections annually
Up to 1	0
More than 1 and up to 5	1
More than 5 and up to 10	2
More than 10 and up to 15	3
More than 15 and up to 20	4
More than 20 and up to 25	5
More than 25 and up to 30	6
More than 30 and up to 35	7
More than 35 and up to 40	8
More than 40 and up to 45	9
More than 45 and up to 50	10
More than 50 and up to 55	11
More than 55 and up to 60	12
More than 60	Right of access at all times

58. The actual frequency of inspection of a *reactor* shall take account of:

(*a*) Whether the State possesses irradiated-fuel reprocessing facilities;

(*b*) The nature of the *reactor*; and

(*c*) The nature and amount of the *nuclear material* produced or used in the *reactor*.

C. Special procedures relating to safeguarded nuclear material outside principal nuclear facilities

Nuclear material in research and development facilities

Routine reports

59. Only accounting reports need be submitted in respect of *nuclear material* in *research and development facilities*. The frequency of submission of such routine reports shall be agreed between the Agency and the State, taking into account the frequency established for routine inspections; however, at least one such report shall be submitted each year and in no case shall more than 12 such reports be required in any year.

Routine inspections

60. The maximum frequency of routine inspections of safeguarded *nuclear material* in a *research and development facility* shall be that specified in the table in paragraph 57 for the total amount of material in the facility.

Source material in sealed storage

61. The following simplified procedures for safeguarding stockpiled source material shall be applied if a State undertakes to store such material in a sealed storage facility and not to remove it therefrom without previously informing the Agency.

Design of storage facilities

62. The State shall submit to the Agency information on the design of each sealed storage facility and agree with the Agency on the method and procedure for sealing it.

Routine reports

63. Two routine accounting reports in respect of source material in sealed storage shall be submitted each year.

Routine inspections

64. The Agency may perform one routine inspection of each sealed storage facility annually.

Removal of material

65. The State may remove safeguarded source material from a sealed storage facility after informing the Agency of the amount, type and intended use of the material to be removed, and providing sufficient other data in time to enable the Agency to continue safeguarding the material after it has been removed.

Nuclear material in other locations

66. Except to the extent that safeguarded *nuclear material* outside of *principal nuclear facilities* is covered by any of the provisions set forth in paragraphs 59–65, the following procedures shall be applied with respect to such material (for example, source material stored elsewhere than in a sealed storage facility, or special fissionable material used in a sealed neutron source in the field).

Routine reports

67. Routine accounting reports in respect of all safeguarded *nuclear material* in this category shall be submitted periodically. The frequency of submission of such reports shall be agreed between the Agency and the State, taking into account the frequency established for routine inspections; however, at least one such report shall be submitted each year and in no case shall more than 12 such reports be required in any year.

Routine inspections

68. The maximum frequency of routine inspections of safeguarded *nuclear material* in this category shall be one inspection annually if the total amount of such material does not exceed five *effective kilograms*, and shall be determined from the table in paragraph 57 if the amount is greater.

IV. DEFINITIONS

69. 'Agency' means the International Atomic Energy Agency.

70. 'Board' means the Board of Governors of the Agency.

71. 'Director General' means the Director General of the Agency.

72. 'Effective kilograms' means:

(*a*) In the case of plutonium, its weight in kilograms,

(*b*) In the case of uranium with an *enrichment* of 0.01 (1%) and above, its weight in kilograms multiplied by the square of its *enrichment*;

(*c*) In the case of uranium with an *enrichment* below 0.01 (1%) and above 0.005 (0.5%), its weight in kilograms multiplied by 0.0001; and

(*d*) In the case of depleted uranium with an *enrichment* of 0.005 (0.5%) or below, and in the case of thorium, its weight in kilograms multiplied by 0.00005.

73. 'Enrichment' means the ratio of the combined weight of the isotopes uranium-233 and uranium-235 to that of the total uranium in question.

74. 'Improved' means, with respect to *nuclear material*, that either:

(*a*) The concentration of fissionable isotopes in it has been increased; or

(*b*) The amount of chemically separable fissionable isotopes in it has been increased; or

(*c*) Its chemical or physical form has been changed so as to facilitate further use or processing.

75. 'Inspector' means an Agency official designated in accordance with the *Inspectors Document*.

76. 'Inspectors Document' means the Annex to the Agency's document GC(V)/INF/39.

77. 'Nuclear material' means any source or special fissionable material as defined in Article XX of the Statute.

78. 'Principal nuclear facility' means a *reactor*, a plant for processing *nuclear material* irradiated in a *reactor*, a plant for separating the isotopes of a *nuclear material*, a plant for processing or fabricating *nuclear material* (excepting a mine or ore-processing plant) or a facility or plant of such other type as may be designated by the Board from time to time, including associated storage facilities.

79. 'Project agreement' means a *safeguards agreement* relating to an Agency project and containing provisions as foreseen in Article XI.F.4(b) of the Statute.

80. 'Reactor' means any device in which a controlled, self-sustaining fission chain-reaction can be maintained.

81. 'Research and development facility' means a facility, other than a *principal nuclear facility*, used for research or development in the field of nuclear energy.

82. 'Safeguards agreement' means an

agreement between the Agency and one or more Member States which contains an undertaking by one or more of those States not to use certain items in such a way as to further any military purpose and which gives the Agency the right to observe compliance with such undertaking. Such an agreement may concern:

(*a*) An Agency project;

(*b*) A bilateral or multilateral arrangement in the field of nuclear energy under which the Agency may be asked to administer safeguards; or

(*c*) Any of a State's nuclear activities *unilaterally submitted* to Agency safeguards.

83. 'Statute' means the Statute of the Agency.

84. 'Throughput' means the rate at which *nuclear material* is introduced into a facility operating at full capacity.

85. 'Unilaterally submitted' means submitted by a State to Agency safeguards, pursuant to a *safeguards agreement*.

ANNEX I. PROVISIONS FOR REPROCESSING PLANTS

Introduction

1. The Agency's Safeguards System (1965) is so formulated as to permit application to *principal nuclear facilities* other than *reactors* as foreseen in paragraph 7. This Annex lays down the additional procedures which are applicable to the safeguarding of *reprocessing plants*. However, because of the possible need to revise these procedures in the light of experience, they shall be subject to review at any time and shall in any case be reviewed after two years' experience of their application has been gained.

Special procedures

Reports

2. The frequency of submission of routine reports shall be once each calendar month.

Inspections

3. A *reprocessing plant* having an annual *throughput* not exceeding 5 *effective kilograms of nuclear material*, and the safeguarded *nuclear material* in it, may be routinely inspected twice a year. A *reprocessing plant* having an annual *throughput* exceeding 5 *effective kilograms of nuclear material*, and the safeguarded *nuclear material* in it, may be inspected at all times. The arrangements for inspections set forth in paragraph 50 shall apply to all inspections to be made under this paragraph.[1]

4. When a *reprocessing plant* is under Agency safeguards only because it contains safeguarded *nuclear material*, the inspection frequency shall be based on the rate of delivery of safeguarded *nuclear material*.

5. The State and the Agency shall co-operate in making all the necessary arrangements to facilitate the taking, shipping or analysis of samples, due account being taken of the limitations imposed by the characteristics of a plant already in operation when placed under Agency safeguards.

Mixtures of safeguarded and unsafeguarded nuclear material

6. By agreement between the State and the Agency, the following special arrangements may be made in the case of a *reprocessing plant* to which the criteria in paragraph 19(*d*) do not apply, and in which safeguarded and unsafeguarded *nuclear materials* are present:

(*a*) Subject to the provisions of subparagraph (*b*) below, the Agency shall restrict its safeguards procedures to the area in which irradiated fuel is stored, until such time as all or any part of such fuel is transferred out of the storage area into other parts of the plant. Safeguards procedures shall cease to apply to the storage area or plant when either contains no safeguarded *nuclear material*; and

(*b*) Where possible, safeguarded *nuclear material* shall be measured and sampled separately from unsafeguarded material, and at as early a stage as possible. Where separate measurement, sampling or processing are not possible, the whole of the material being processed in that *campaign* shall be subject to the safeguards procedures set out in this Annex. At the conclusion of the processing the *nuclear material* that is thereafter to be safeguarded shall be selected by agreement between the State and the Agency from the whole output of the plant resulting from that *campaign*, due account being taken of any processing losses accepted by the Agency.

---

[1] It is understood that for plants having an annual *throughput* of more than 60 *effective kilograms*, the right of access at all times would normally be implemented by means of continuous inspection.

Definitions

7. 'Reprocessing plant'[2] means a facility to separate irradiated *nuclear materials* and fission products, and includes the facility's head-end treatment section and its associated storage and analytical sections.

8. 'Campaign' means the period during which the chemical processing equipment in a *reprocessing plant* is operated between two successive wash-outs of the *nuclear material* present in the equipment.

---

[2] This term is synonymous with the term 'a plant for processing nuclear material irradiated in a reactor' which is used in paragraph 78.

ANNEX II. PROVISIONS FOR SAFEGUARDED NUCLEAR MATERIAL IN CONVERSION PLANTS AND FABRICATION PLANTS

Introduction

1. The Agency's Safeguards System (1965, as Provisionally Extended in 1966) is so formulated as to permit application to *principal nuclear facilities* other than *reactors* as foreseen in paragraph 7. This Annex lays down the additional procedures which are applicable to safeguarded *nuclear material* in *conversion plants* and *fabrication plants*.[1] However, because of the possible need to revise these procedures in the light of experience, they shall be subject to review at any time and shall in any case be reviewed after two years' experience of their application has been gained.

Special procedures

Reports

2. The frequency of submission of routine reports shall be once each calendar month.

Inspections

3. A *conversion plant* or *fabrication plant* to which the criteria in paragraph 19(*d*) apply and the *nuclear material* in it, may be inspected at all times if the plant inventory at any time, or the annual input, of *nuclear material* exceeds five *effective kilograms*. Where neither the inventory at any time, nor the annual input, exceeds five *effective kilograms* of *nuclear material*, the routine inspections shall not exceed two a year. The arrangements for inspection set forth in paragraph 50 shall apply to all inspections to be made under this paragraph.[2]

4. When a *conversion plant* or *fabrication plant* to which the criteria in paragraph 19(*d*) do not apply contains safeguarded *nuclear material* the frequency of routine inspections shall be based on the inventory at any time and the annual input of safeguarded *nuclear material*. Where the inventory at any time, or the annual input, of safeguarded *nuclear material* exceeds five *effective kilograms* the plant may be inspected at all times. Where neither the inventory at any time, nor the annual input, exceeds five *effective kilograms* of safeguarded *nuclear material* the routine inspections shall not exceed two a year. The arrangements for inspection set forth in paragraph 50 shall apply to all inspections to be made under this paragraph.[2]

5. The intensity of inspection of safeguarded *nuclear material* at various steps in a *conversion plant* or *fabrication plant* shall take account of the nature, isotopic composition and amount of safeguarded *nuclear material* in the plant. Safeguards shall be applied in accordance with the general principles set forth in paragraphs 9–14. Emphasis shall be placed on inspection to control uranium of high enrichments and plutonium.

6. Where a plant may handle safeguarded and unsafeguarded *nuclear material*, the State shall notify the Agency in advance of the programme for handling safeguarded batches to enable the Agency to make inspections during these periods, due account being also taken of the arrangements under paragraph 10 below.

7. The State and the Agency shall cooperate in making all the necessary arrangements to facilitate the preparation of inventories of safeguarded *nuclear material* and the taking, shipping and/or analysis of samples, due account being taken of the limitations imposed by the characteristics of a plant

---

[1] This terminology is intended to be synonymous with the term 'a plant for processing or fabricating *nuclear material* (excepting a mine or ore-processing plant') which is used in paragraph 78.

[2] It is understood that for plants having an inventory at any time, or an annual input, of more than 60 *effective kilograms* the right of access at all times would normally be implemented by means of continuous inspection.

Where neither the inventory at any time nor the annual input exceeds one *effective kilogram* of *nuclear material* the plant would not normally be subject to routine inspection.

already in operation when placed under Agency safeguards.

Residues, scrap and waste

8. The State shall ensure that safeguarded *nuclear material* contained in residues, scrap or waste created during conversion or fabrication is recovered, as far as is practicable, in its facilities and within a reasonable period of time. If such recovery is not considered practicable by the State, the State and the Agency shall co-operate in making arrangements to account for and dispose of the material.

Safeguarded and unsafeguarded nuclear material

9. By agreement between the State and the Agency, the following special arrangements may be made in the case of a *conversion plant* or a *fabrication plant* to which the criteria in paragraph 19(*d*) do not apply, and in which safeguarded and unsafeguarded *nuclear material* are both present:

(*a*) Subject to the provisions of sub-paragraph (*b*) below, the Agency shall restrict its safeguards procedures to the area in which safeguarded *nuclear material* is stored, until such time as all or any part of such *nuclear material* is transferred out of the storage area into other parts of the plant. Safeguards procedures shall cease to be applied to the storage area or plant when it contains no safeguarded *nuclear material;* and

(*b*) Where possible, safeguarded *nuclear material* shall be measured and sampled separately from unsafeguarded *nuclear material,* and at as early a stage as possible. Where separate measurement, sampling or processing is not possible, any *nuclear material* containing safeguarded *nuclear material shall* be subject to the safeguards procedures set out in this Annex. At the conclusion of processing, *the nuclear material* that is thereafter to be safeguarded shall be selected, in accordance with paragraph 11 below when applicable, by agreement between the State and the Agency, due account being taken of any processing losses accepted by the Agency.

Blending of nuclear material

10. When safeguarded *nuclear material* is to be blended with either safeguarded or unsafeguarded *nuclear material,* the State shall notify the Agency sufficiently in advance of the programme of blending to enable the Agency to exercise its right to obtain evidence, through inspection of the blending operation or otherwise, that the blending is performed according to the programme.

11. When safeguarded and unsafeguarded *nuclear material* are blended, if the ratio of fissionable isotopes in the safeguarded component going into the blend to all the fissionable isotopes in the blend is 0.3 or greater, and if the concentration of fissionable isotopes in the unsafeguarded *nuclear material* is increased by such blending, then the whole blend shall remain subject to safeguards. In other cases the following procedures shall apply:

(*a*) Plutonium/plutonium blending. The quantity of the blend that shall continue to be safeguarded shall be such that its weight, when multiplied by the square of the weight fraction of contained fissionable isotopes, is not less then [*sic*] the weight of originally safeguarded plutonium multiplied by the square of the weight fraction of fissionable isotopes therein, provided however that:

(i) In cases where the weight of the whole blend, when multiplied by the square of the weight fraction of contained fissionable isotopes, is less than the weight of originally safeguarded plutonium multiplied by the square of the weight fraction of fissionable isotopes therein, the whole of the blend shall be safeguarded; and

(ii) The number of fissionable atoms in the portion of the blend that shall continue to be under safeguards shall in no case be less than the number of fissionable atoms in the originally safeguarded plutonium;

(*b*) Uranium/uranium blending. The quantity of the blend that shall continue to be safeguarded shall be such that the number of *effective kilograms* is not less than the number of *effective kilograms* in the originally safeguarded uranium, provided however that:

(i) In cases where the number of *effective kilograms* in the whole blend is less than in the safeguarded uranium, the whole of the blend shall be safeguarded; and

(ii) The number of fissionable atoms in the portion of the blend that shall continue to be under safeguards shall in no case be less than the number of fissionable atoms in the originally safeguarded uranium;

(*c*) Uranium/plutonium blending. The whole of the resultant blend shall be safeguarded until the uranium and the plutonium constituents are separated. After separation of the uranium and plutonium, safeguards shall apply to the originally safeguarded component; and

(*d*) Due account shall be taken of any processing losses agreed upon between the State and the Agency.

Definitions

12. 'Conversion plant' means a facility (excepting a mine or ore-processing plant) to *improve* unirradiated *nuclear material,* or irradiated *nuclear material* that has been separated from fission products, by changing its chemical or physical form so as to facilitate further use or processing. The term *conversion plant* includes the facility's storage and analytical sections. The term does not include a plant intended for separating the isotopes of a *nuclear material.*

13. 'Fabrication plant' means a plant to manufacture fuel elements or other components containing *nuclear material* and includes the plant's storage and analytical sections.

Source: IAEA document INFCIRC/66/Rev. 2, IAEA, Vienna, 1968.

THE STRUCTURE AND CONTENT OF AGREEMENTS BETWEEN THE INTERNATIONAL ATOMIC ENERGY AGENCY AND STATES REQUIRED IN CONNECTION WITH THE TREATY ON THE NON-PROLIFERATION OF NUCLEAR WEAPONS (NPT MODEL SAFEGUARDS AGREEMENT)

Agreed at Vienna on 10 March 1971
On 20 April 1971 the IAEA Board of Governors authorized the Director General to use the material reproduced below as the basis for negotiating safeguards agreements between the IAEA and non-nuclear weapon states parties to the NPT.

PART I

Basic undertaking

1. The Agreement should contain, in accordance with Article III.1 of the Treaty on the Non-Proliferation of Nuclear Weapons, an undertaking by the State to accept safeguards, in accordance with the terms of the Agreement, on all source or special fissionable material in all peaceful nuclear activities within its territory, under its jurisdiction or carried out under its control anywhere, for the exclusive purpose of verifying that such material is not diverted to nuclear weapons or other nuclear explosive devices.

Application of safeguards

2. The Agreement should provide for the Agency's right and obligation to ensure that safeguards will be applied, in accordance with the terms of the Agreement, on all source or special fissionable material in all peaceful nuclear activities within the territory of the State, under its jurisdiction or carried out under its control anywhere, for the exclusive purpose of verifying that such material is not diverted to nuclear weapons or other nuclear explosive devices.

Co-operation between the Agency and the State

3. The Agreement should provide that the Agency and the State shall co-operate to facilitate the implementation of the safeguards provided for therein.

Implementation of safeguards

4. The Agreement should provide that safeguards shall be implemented in a manner designed:

(*a*) To avoid hampering the economic and technological development of the State or international co-operation in the field of peaceful nuclear activities, including international exchange of *nuclear material;*

(*b*) To avoid undue interference in the State's peaceful nuclear activities, and in particular in the operation of *facilities*; and

(*c*) To be consistent with prudent management practices required for the economic and safe conduct of nuclear activities.

5. The Agreement should provide that the Agency shall take every precaution to protect commercial and industrial secrets and other confidential information coming to its knowledge in the implementation of the Agreement. The Agency shall not publish or communicate to any State, organization or person any information obtained by it in connection with the implementation of the Agreement, except that specific information relating to such implementation in the State may be given to the Board of Governors and to such Agency staff members as require such knowledge by reason of their official duties in connection with safeguards, but only to the extent neces-

sary for the Agency to fulfil its responsibilities in implementing the Agreement. Summarized information on *nuclear material* being safeguarded by the Agency under the Agreement may be published upon decision of the Board if the States directly concerned agree.

6. The Agreement should provide that in implementing safeguards pursuant thereto the Agency shall take full account of technological developments in the field of safeguards, and shall make every effort to ensure optimum cost-effectiveness and the application of the principle of safeguarding effectively the flow of *nuclear material* subject to safeguards under the Agreement by use of instruments and other techniques at certain *strategic points* to the extent that present or future technology permits. In order to ensure optimum cost-effectiveness, use should be made, for example, of such means as:

(*a*) Containment as a means of defining *material balance areas* for accounting purposes;

(*b*) Statistical techniques and random sampling in evaluating the flow of *nuclear material*; and

(*c*) Concentration of verification procedures on those stages in the nuclear fuel cycle involving the production, processing, use or storage of *nuclear material* from which nuclear weapons or other nuclear explosive devices could readily be made, and minimization of verification procedures in respect of other *nuclear material,* on condition that this does not hamper the Agency in applying safeguards under the Agreement.

National system of accounting for and control of nuclear material

7. The Agreement should provide that the State shall establish and maintain a system of accounting for and control of all *nuclear material* subject to safeguards under the Agreement, and that such safeguards shall be applied in such a manner as to enable the Agency to verify, in ascertaining that there has been no diversion of *nuclear material* from peaceful uses to nuclear weapons or other nuclear explosive devices, findings of the State's system. The Agency's verification shall include, inter alia, independent measurements and observations conducted by the Agency in accordance with the procedures specified in Part II below. The Agency, in its verification, shall take due account of the technical effectiveness of the State's system.

Provision of information to the Agency

8. The Agreement should provide that to ensure the effective implementation of safeguards thereunder the Agency shall be provided, in accordance with the provisions set out in Part II below, with information concerning *nuclear material* subject to safeguards under the Agreement and the features of *facilities* relevant to safeguarding such material. The Agency shall require only the minimum amount of information and data consistent with carrying out its responsibilities under the Agreement. Information pertaining to *facilities* shall be the minimum necessary for safeguarding *nuclear material* subject to safeguards under the Agreement. In examining design information, the Agency shall, at the request of the State, be prepared to examine on premises of the State design information which the State regards as being of particular sensitivity. Such information would not have to be physically transmitted to the Agency provided that it remained available for ready further examination by the Agency on premises of the State.

Agency inspectors

9. The Agreement should provide that the State shall take the necessary steps to ensure that Agency inspectors can effectively discharge their functions under the Agreement. The Agency shall secure the consent of the State to the designation of Agency inspectors to that State. If the State, either upon proposal of a designation or at any other time after a designation has been made, objects to the designation, the Agency shall propose to the State an alternative designation or designations. The repeated refusal of a State to accept the designation of Agency inspectors which would impede the inspections conducted under the Agreement would be considered by the Board upon referral by the Director General with a view to appropriate action. The visits and activities of Agency inspectors shall be so arranged as to reduce to a minimum the possible inconvenience and disturbance to the State and to the peaceful nuclear activities inspected, as well as to ensure protection of industrial secrets or any other confidential information coming to the inspectors' knowledge.

Privileges and immunities

10. The Agreement should specify the privileges and immunities which shall be granted

to the Agency and its staff in respect of their functions under the Agreement. In the case of a State party to the Agreement on the Privileges and Immunities of the Agency, the provisions thereof, as in force for such State, shall apply. In the case of other States, the privileges and immunities granted should be such as to ensure that:

(*a*) The Agency and its staff will be in a position to discharge their functions under the Agreement effectively; and

(*b*) No such State will be placed thereby in a more favourable position than States party to the Agreement on the Privileges and Immunities of the Agency.

Termination of safeguards

Consumption or dilution of nuclear material

11. The Agreement should provide that safeguards shall terminate on *nuclear material* subject to safeguards thereunder upon determination by the Agency that it has been consumed, or has been diluted in such a way that it is no longer usable for any nuclear activity relevant from the point of view of safeguards, or has become practicably irrecoverable.

Transfer of nuclear material out of the State

12. The Agreement should provide, with respect to *nuclear material* subject to safeguards thereunder, for notification of transfers of such material out of the State, in accordance with the provisions set out in paragraphs 92–94 below. The Agency shall terminate safeguards under the Agreement on *nuclear material* when the recipient State has assumed responsibility therefor, as provided for in paragraph 91. The Agency shall maintain records indicating each transfer and, where applicable, the re-application of safeguards to the transferred *nuclear material.*

Provisions relating to nuclear material to be used in non-nuclear activities

13. The Agreement should provide that if the State wishes to use *nuclear material* subject to safeguards thereunder in non-nuclear activities, such as the production of alloys or ceramics, it shall agree with the Agency on the circumstances under which the safeguards on such *nuclear material* may be terminated.

Non-application of safeguards to nuclear material to be used in non-peaceful activities

14. The Agreement should provide that if the State intends to exercise its discretion to use *nuclear material* which is required to be safeguarded thereunder in a nuclear activity which does not require the application of safeguards under the Agreement, the following procedures will apply:

(*a*) The State shall inform the Agency of the activity, making it clear:

(i) That the use of the *nuclear material* in a non-proscribed military activity will not be in conflict with an undertaking the State may have given and in respect of which Agency safeguards apply, that the *nuclear material* will be used only in a peaceful nuclear activity; and

(ii) That during the period of non-application of safeguards the *nuclear material* will not be used for the production of nuclear weapons or other nuclear explosive devices;

(*b*) The State and the Agency shall make an arrangement so that, only while the *nuclear material* is in such an activity, the safeguards provided for in the Agreement will not be applied. The arrangement shall identify, to the extent possible, the period or circumstances during which safeguards will not be applied. In any event, the safeguards provided for in the Agreement shall again apply as soon as the *nuclear material* is re-introduced into a peaceful nuclear activity. The Agency shall be kept informed of the total quantity and composition of such unsafeguarded *nuclear material* in the State and of any exports of such material; and

(*c*) Each arrangement shall be made in agreement with the Agency. The Agency's agreement shall be given as promptly as possible; it shall only relate to the temporal and procedural provisions, reporting arrangements, etc., but shall not involve any approval or classified knowledge of the military activity or relate to the use of the *nuclear material* therein.

Finance

15. The Agreement should contain one of the following sets of provisions:

(*a*) An agreement with a Member of the Agency should provide that each party thereto shall bear the expenses it incurs in implementing its responsibilities thereunder. However, if the State or persons under its jurisdiction incur extraordinary expenses as a result of a specific request by the Agency, the Agency shall reimburse such expenses provided that it has agreed in advance to do so. In any case the Agency shall bear the cost of any additional measuring or sampling which inspectors may request; or

(*b*) An agreement with a party not a Member of the Agency should in application of the provisions of Article XIV.C of the Statute, provide that the party shall reimburse fully to the Agency the safeguards expenses the Agency incurs thereunder. However, if the party or persons under its jurisdiction incur extraordinary expenses as a result of a specific request by the Agency, the Agency shall reimburse such expenses provided that it has agreed in advance to do so.

Third party liability for nuclear damage

16. The Agreement should provide that the State shall ensure that any protection against third party liability in respect of nuclear damage, including any insurance or other financial security, which may be available under its laws or regulations shall apply to the Agency and its officials for the purpose of the implementation of the Agreement, in the same way as that protection applies to nationals of the State.

International responsibility

17. The Agreement should provide that any claim by one party thereto against the other in respect of any damage, other than damage arising out of a nuclear incident, resulting from the implementation of safeguards under the Agreement, shall be settled in accordance with international law.

Measures in relation to verification of non-diversion

18. The Agreement should provide that if the Board, upon report of the Director General, decides that an action by the State is essential and urgent in order to ensure verification that *nuclear material* subject to safeguards under the Agreement is not diverted to nuclear weapons or other nuclear explosive devices the Board shall be able to call upon the State to take the required action without delay, irrespective of whether procedures for the settlement of a dispute have been invoked.

19. The Agreement should provide that if the Board upon examination of relevant information reported to it by the Director General finds that the Agency is not able to verify that there has been no diversion of *nuclear material* required to be safeguarded under the Agreement to nuclear weapons or other nuclear explosive devices, it may make the reports provided for in paragraph C of Article XII of the Statute and may also take, where applicable, the other measures provided for in that paragraph. In taking such action the Board shall take account of the degree of assurance provided by the safeguards measures that have been applied and shall afford the State every reasonable opportunity to furnish the Board with any necessary reassurance.

Interpretation and application of the Agreement and settlement of disputes

20. The Agreement should provide that the parties thereto shall, at the request of either, consult about any question arising out of the interpretation or application thereof.

21. The Agreement should provide that the State shall have the right to request that any question arising out of the interpretation or application thereof be considered by the Board; and that the State shall be invited by the Board to participate in the discussion of any such question by the Board.

22. The Agreement should provide that any dispute arising out of the interpretation or application thereof except a dispute with regard to a finding by the Board under paragraph 19 above or an action taken by the Board pursuant to such a finding which is not settled by negotiation or another procedure agreed to by the parties should, on the request of either party, be submitted to an arbitral tribunal composed as follows: each party would designate one arbitrator, and the two arbitrators so designated would elect a third, who would be the Chairman. If, within 30 days of the request for arbitration, either party has not designated an arbitrator, either party to the dispute may request the President of the International Court of Justice to appoint an arbitrator. The same procedure would apply if, within 30 days of the designation or appointment of the second arbitrator, the third arbitrator had not been elected. A majority of the members of the arbitral tribunal would constitute a quorum, and all decisions would require the concurrence of two arbitrators. The arbitral procedure would be fixed by the tribunal. The decisions of the tribunal would be binding on both parties.

Final clauses

Amendment of the Agreement

23. The Agreement should provide that the parties thereto shall, at the request of either of

them, consult each other on amendment of the Agreement. All amendments shall require the agreement of both parties. It might additionally be provided, if convenient to the State, that the agreement of the parties on amendments to Part II of the Agreement could be achieved by recourse to a simplified procedure. The Director General shall promptly inform all Member States of any amendment to the Agreement.

Suspension of application of Agency safeguards under other agreements

24. Where applicable and where the State desires such a provision to appear, the Agreement should provide that the application of Agency safeguards in the State under other safeguards agreements with the Agency shall be suspended while the Agreement is in force. If the State has received assistance from the Agency for a project, the State's undertaking in the Project Agreement not to use items subject thereto in such a way as to further any military purpose shall continue to apply.

Entry into force and duration

25. The Agreement should provide that it shall enter into force on the date on which the Agency receives from the State written notification that the statutory and constitutional requirements for entry into force have been met. The Director General shall promptly inform all Member States of the entry into force.

26. The Agreement should provide for it to remain in force as long as the State is party to the Treaty on the Non-Proliferation of Nuclear Weapons.

PART II

Introduction

27. The Agreement should provide that the purpose of Part II thereof is to specify the procedures to be applied for the implementation of the safeguards provisions of Part I.

Objective of safeguards

28. The Agreement should provide that the objective of safeguards is the timely detection of diversion of significant quantities of *nuclear material* from peaceful nuclear activities to the manufacture of nuclear weapons or of other nuclear explosive devices or for purposes unknown, and deterrence of such diversion by the risk of early detection.

29. To this end the Agreement should provide for the use of material accountancy as a safeguards measure of fundamental importance, with containment and surveillance as important complementary measures.

30. The Agreement should provide that the technical conclusion of the Agency's verification activities shall be a statement, in respect of each *material balance area,* of the amount of *material unaccounted for* over a specific period, giving the limits of accuracy of the amounts stated.

National system of accounting for and control of nuclear material

31. The Agreement should provide that pursuant to paragraph 7 above the Agency, in carrying out its verification activities, shall make full use of the State's system of accounting for and control of all *nuclear material* subject to safeguards under the Agreement, and shall avoid unnecessary duplication of the State's accounting and control activities.

32. The Agreement should provide that the State's system of accounting for and control of all *nuclear material* subject to safeguards under the Agreement shall be based on a structure of material balance areas, and shall make provision as appropriate and specified in the Subsidiary Arrangements for the establishment of such measures as:

(*a*) A measurement system for the determination of the quantities of *nuclear material* received, produced, shipped, lost or otherwise removed from inventory, and the quantities on inventory;

(*b*) The evaluation of precision and accuracy of measurements and the estimation of measurement uncertainty;

(*c*) Procedures for identifying, reviewing and evaluating differences in shipper/receiver measurements;

(*d*) Procedures for taking a *physical inventory;*

(*e*) Procedures for the evaluation of accumulations of unmeasured inventory and unmeasured losses;

(*f*) A system of records and reports showing, for each *material balance area,* the inventory of *nuclear material* and the changes in that inventory including receipts into and transfers out of the *material balance area*;

(*g*) Provisions to ensure that the accounting procedures and arrangements are being operated correctly; and

(*h*) Procedures for the provisions of reports to the Agency in accordance with paragraphs 59–69 below.

Starting point of safeguards

33. The Agreement should provide that safeguards shall not apply thereunder to material in mining or ore processing activities.

34. The Agreement should provide that:

(*a*) When any material containing uranium or thorium which has not reached the stage of the nuclear fuel cycle described in subparagraph (*c*) below is directly or indirectly exported to a non-nuclear-weapon State, the State shall inform the Agency of its quantity, composition and destination, unless the material is exported for specifically non-nuclear purposes;

(*b*) When any material containing uranium or thorium which has not reached the stage of the nuclear fuel cycle described in sub-paragraph (*c*) below is imported, the State shall inform the Agency of its quantity and composition, unless the material is imported for specifically non-nuclear purposes; and

(*c*) When any *nuclear material* of a composition and purity suitable for fuel fabrication or for being isotopically enriched leaves the plant or the process stage in which it has been produced, or when such *nuclear material,* or any other *nuclear material* produced at a later stage in the nuclear fuel cycle, is imported into the State, the *nuclear material* shall become subject to the other safeguards procedures specified in the Agreement.

Termination of safeguards

35. The Agreement should provide that safeguards shall terminate on *nuclear material* subject to safeguards thereunder under the conditions set forth in paragraph 11 above. Where the conditions of that paragraph are not met, but the State considers that the recovery of safeguarded *nuclear material* from residues is not for the time being practicable or desirable, the Agency and the State shall consult on the appropriate safeguards measures to be applied. It should further be provided that safeguards shall terminate on *nuclear material* subject to safeguards under the Agreement under the conditions set forth in paragraph 13 above, provided that the State and the Agency agree that such *nuclear material* is practicably irrecoverable.

Exemptions from safeguards

36. The Agreement should provide that the Agency shall, at the request of the State, exempt *nuclear material* from safeguards, as follows:

(*a*) Special fissionable material, when it is used in gram quantities or less as a sensing component in instruments;

(*b*) *Nuclear material,* when it is used in non-nuclear activities in accordance with paragraph 13 above, if such *nuclear material* is recoverable; and

(*c*) Plutonium with an isotopic concentration of plutonium-238 exceeding 80%.

37. The Agreement should provide that *nuclear material* that would otherwise be subject to safeguards shall be exempted from safeguards at the request of the State, provided that *nuclear material* so exempted in the State may not at any time exceed:

(*a*) One kilogram in total of special fissionable material, which may consist of one or more of the following:

(i) Plutonium;

(ii) Uranium with an *enrichment* of 0.2 (20%) and above, taken account of by multiplying its weight by its *enrichment;* and

(iii) Uranium with an *enrichment* below 0.2 (20%) and above that of natural uranium, taken account of by multiplying its weight by five times the square of its *enrichment;*

(*b*) Ten metric tons in total of natural uranium and depleted uranium with an *enrichment* above 0.005 (0.5%);

(*c*) Twenty metric tons of depleted uranium with an *enrichment* of 0.005 (0.5%) or below; and

(*d*) Twenty metric tons of thorium; or such greater amounts as may be specified by the Board of Governors for uniform application.

38. The Agreement should provide that if exempted *nuclear material* is to be processed or stored together with safeguarded *nuclear material,* provision should be made for the re-application of safeguards thereto.

Subsidiary arrangements

39. The Agreement should provide that the Agency and the State shall make subsidiary Arrangements which shall specify in detail, to the extent necessary to permit the Agency to fulfil its responsibilities under the Agreement in an effective and efficient manner, how the procedures laid down in the Agreement are to be applied. Provision should be made for the possibility of an extension or change of the Subsidiary Arrangements by agreement between the Agency and the State without amendment of the Agreement.

40. It should be provided that the Subsidiary Arrangements shall enter into force at the same time as, or as soon as possible after,

the entry into force of the Agreement. The State and the Agency shall make every effort to achieve their entry into force within 90 days of the entry into force of the Agreement, a later date being acceptable only with the agreement of both parties. The State shall provide the Agency promptly with the information required for completing the Subsidiary Arrangements. The Agreement should also provide that, upon its entry into force, the Agency shall be entitled to apply the procedures laid down therein in respect of the *nuclear material* listed in the inventory provided for in paragraph 41 below.

Inventory

41. The Agreement should provide that, on the basis of the initial report referred to in paragraph 62 below, the Agency shall establish a unified inventory of all *nuclear material* in the State subject to safeguards under the Agreement, irrespective of its origin, and maintain this inventory on the basis of subsequent reports and of the results of its verification activities. Copies of the inventory shall be made available to the State at agreed intervals.

Design information

General

42. Pursuant to paragraph 8 above, the Agreement should stipulate that design information in respect of existing *facilities* shall be provided to the Agency during the discussion of the Subsidiary Arrangements, and that the time limits for the provision of such information in respect of new *facilities* shall be specified in the Subsidiary Arrangements. It should further be stipulated that such information shall be provided as early as possible before *nuclear material* is introduced into a new *facility*.

43. The Agreement should specify that the design information in respect of each *facility* to be made available to the Agency shall include, when applicable:

(*a*) The identification of the *facility*, stating its general character, purpose, nominal capacity and geographic location, and the name and address to be used for routine business purposes;

(*b*) A description of the general arrangement of the *facility* with reference, to the extent feasible, to the form, location and flow of *nuclear material* and to the general layout of important items of equipment which use, produce or process *nuclear material*,

(*c*) A description of features of the *facility* relating to material accountancy, containment and surveillance; and

(*d*) A description of the existing and proposed procedures at the *facility* for *nuclear material* accountancy and control, with special reference to *material balance areas* established by the operator, measurements of flow and procedures for *physical inventory* taking.

44. The Agreement should further provide that other information relevant to the application of safeguards shall be made available to the Agency in respect of each *facility*, in particular on organizational responsibility for material accountancy and control. It should also be provided that the State shall make available to the Agency supplementary information on the health and safety procedures which the Agency shall observe and with which the inspectors shall comply at the *facility*.

45. The Agreement should stipulate that design information in respect of a modification relevant for safeguards purposes shall be provided for examination sufficiently in advance for the safeguards procedures to be adjusted when necessary.

Purposes of examination of design information

46. The Agreement should provide that the design information made available to the Agency shall be used for the following purposes:

(*a*) To identify the features of *facilities* and *nuclear material* relevant to the application of safeguards to *nuclear material* in sufficient detail to facilitate verification;

(*b*) To determine *material balance areas to* be used for Agency accounting purposes and to select those *strategic points* which are *key measurement points* and which will be used to determine the *nuclear material* flows and inventories; in determining such *material balance areas* the Agency shall, inter alia, use the following criteria:

(i) The size of the *material balance area* should be related to the accuracy with which the material balance can be established;

(ii) In determining the *material balance area* advantage should be taken of any opportunity to use containment and surveillance to help ensure the completeness of flow measurements and thereby simplify the application of safeguards and concentrate measurement efforts at *key measurement points;*

(iii) A number of *material balance areas* in

use at a *facility* or at distinct sites may be combined in one *material balance area* to be used for Agency accounting purposes when the Agency determines that this is consistent with its verification requirements; and

(iv) If the State so requests, a special *material balance area* around a process step involving commercially sensitive information may be established;

(*c*) To establish the nominal timing and procedures for taking of *physical inventory* for Agency accounting purposes;

(*d*) To establish the record and reports requirements and records evaluation procedures;

(*e*) To establish requirements and procedures for verification of the quantity and location of *nuclear material;* and

(*f*) To select appropriate combinations of containment and surveillance methods and techniques and the *strategic points* at which they are to be applied.

It should further be provided that the results of the examination of the design information shall be included in the Subsidiary Arrangements.

Re-examination of design information

47. The Agreement should provide that design information shall be re-examined in the light of changes in operating conditions, of developments in safeguards technology or of experience in the application of verification procedures, with a view to modifying the action the Agency has taken pursuant to paragraph 46 above.

Verification of design information

48. The Agreement should provide that the Agency, in co-operation with the State, may send inspectors to *facilities* to verify the design information provided to the Agency pursuant to paragraphs 42–45 above for the purposes stated in paragraph 46.

Information in respect of nuclear material outside facilities

49. The Agreement should provide that the following information concerning *nuclear material* customarily used outside *facilities* shall be provided as applicable to the Agency:

(*a*) A general description of the use of the *nuclear material,* its geographic location, and the user's name and address for routine business purposes; and

(*b*) A general description of the existing and proposed procedures for *nuclear material* accountancy and control, including organizational responsibility for material accountancy and control.

The Agreement should further provide that the Agency shall be informed on a timely basis of any change in the information provided to it under this paragraph.

50. The Agreement should provide that the information made available to the Agency in respect of *nuclear material* customarily used outside *facilities* may be used, to the extent relevant, for the purposes set out in sub-paragraphs 46(*b*)–(*f*) above.

Records system

General

51. The Agreement should provide that in establishing a national system of accounting for and control of *nuclear material as* referred to in paragraph 7 above, the State shall arrange that records are kept in respect of each *material balance area.* Provision should also be made that the Subsidiary Arrangements shall describe the records to be kept in respect of each *material balance area.*

52. The Agreement should provide that the State shall make arrangements to facilitate the examination of records by inspectors, particularly if the records are not kept in English, French, Russian or Spanish.

53. The Agreement should provide that the records shall be retained for at least five years.

54. The Agreement should provide that the records shall consist, as appropriate, of:

(*a*) Accounting records of all *nuclear material* subject to safeguards under the Agreement; and

(*b*) Operating records for *facilities* containing such *nuclear material.*

55. The Agreement should provide that the system of measurements on which the records used for the preparation of reports are based shall either conform to the latest international standards or be equivalent in quality to such standards.

Accounting records

56. The Agreement should provide that the accounting records shall set forth the following in respect of each *material balance area:*

(*a*) All *inventory changes,* so as to permit a determination of the *book inventory* at any time;

(*b*) All measurement results that are used for determination of the *physical inventory*;

and

(*c*) All *adjustments* and *corrections* that have been made in respect of *inventory changes, book inventories* and *physical inventories.*

57. The Agreement should provide that for all *inventory changes* and *physical inventories* the records shall show, in respect of each *batch* of *nuclear material:* material identification, *batch data* and *source data.* Provision should further be included that records shall account for uranium, thorium and plutonium separately in each *batch* of *nuclear material.* Furthermore, the date of the *inventory change* and, when appropriate, the originating *material balance area* and the receiving *material balance area* or the recipient, shall be indicated for each *inventory change.*

Operating records

58. The Agreement should provide that the operating records shall set forth as appropriate in respect of each *material balance area:*

(*a*) Those operating data which are used to establish changes in the quantities and composition of *nuclear material;*

(*b*) The data obtained from the calibration of tanks and instruments and from sampling and analyses, the procedures to control the quality of measurements and the derived estimates of random and systematic error;

(*c*) A description of the sequence of the actions taken in preparing for, and in taking, a *physical inventory,* in order to ensure that it is correct and complete; and

(*d*) A description of the action taken in order to ascertain the cause and magnitude of any accidental or unmeasured loss that might occur.

Reports system

General

59. The Agreement should specify that the State shall provide the Agency with reports as detailed in paragraphs 60–69 below in respect *of nuclear material* subject to safeguards thereunder.

60. The Agreement should provide that reports shall be made in English, French, Russian or Spanish, except as otherwise specified in the Subsidiary Arrangements.

61. The Agreement should provide that reports shall be based on the records kept in accordance with paragraphs 51–58 above and shall consist, as appropriate, of accounting reports and special reports.

Accounting reports

62. The Agreement should stipulate that the Agency shall be provided with an initial report on all *nuclear material* which is to be subject to safeguards thereunder. It should also be provided that the initial report shall be dispatched by the State to the Agency within 30 days of the last day of the calendar month in which the Agreement enters into force, and shall reflect the situation as of the last day of that month.

63. The Agreement should stipulate that for each *material balance area* the State shall provide the Agency with the following accounting reports:

(*a*) *Inventory change* reports showing changes in the inventory of *nuclear material.* The reports shall be dispatched as soon as possible and in any event within 30 days after the end of the month in which the *inventory changes* occurred or were established; and

(*b*) Material balance reports showing the material balance based on a physical *inventory* of *nuclear material* actually present in the *material balance area.* The reports shall be dispatched as soon as possible and in any event within 30 days after the *physical inventory* has been taken.

The reports shall be based on data available as of the date of reporting and may be corrected at a later date as required.

64. The Agreement should provide that *inventory change* reports shall specify identification and *batch data* for each *batch* of *nuclear material,* the date of the *inventory change* and, as appropriate, the originating *material balance area* and the receiving *material balance area* or the recipient. These reports shall be accompanied by concise notes:

(*a*) Explaining the *inventory changes,* on the basis of the operating data contained in the operating records provided for under subparagraph 58(*a*) above; and

(*b*) Describing, as specified in the Subsidiary Arrangements, the anticipated operational programme, particularly the taking of a *physical inventory.*

65. The Agreement should provide that the State shall report each *inventory change, adjustment and correction* either periodically in a consolidated list or individually. The *inventory changes* shall be reported in terms of *batches,* small amounts, such as analytical samples, as specified in the Subsidiary Arrangements, may be combined and reported as one *inventory change.*

66. The Agreement should stipulate that the Agency shall provide the State with semi-annual statements of *book inventory* of *nuclear material* subject to safeguards, for each *material balance area,* as based on the *inventory change* reports for the period covered by each such statement.

67. The Agreement should specify that the material balance reports shall include the following entries, unless otherwise agreed by the Agency and the State:

(*a*) Beginning *physical inventory;*

(*b*) *Inventory changes* (first increases, then decreases);

(*c*) Ending *book inventory;*

(*d*) *Shipper/receiver differences;*

(*e*) Adjusted ending *book inventory;*

(*f*) Ending *physical inventory;* and

(*g*) *Material unaccounted for.*

A statement of the *physical inventory*, listing all *batches* separately and specifying material identification and *batch data* for each *batch*, shall be attached to each material balance report.

Special reports

68. The Agreement should provide that the State shall make special reports without delay:

(*a*) If any unusual incident or circumstances lead the State to believe that there is or may have been loss of *nuclear material* that exceeds the limits to be specified for this purpose in the Subsidiary Arrangements; or

(*b*) if the containment has unexpectedly changed from that specified in the Subsidiary Arrangements to the extent that unauthorized removal of *nuclear material* has become possible.

Amplification and clarification of reports

69. The Agreement should provide that at the Agency's request the State shall supply amplifications or clarifications of any report, in so far as relevant for the purpose of safeguards.

Inspections

General

70. The Agreement should stipulate that the Agency shall have the right to make inspections as provided for in paragraphs 71–82 below.

Purposes of inspections

71. The Agreement should provide that the Agency may make ad hoc inspections in order to:

(*a*) Verify the information contained in the initial report on the *nuclear material* subject to safeguards under the Agreement;

(*b*) Identify and verify changes in the situation which have occurred since the date of the initial report; and

(*c*) Identify, and if possible verify the quantity and composition of, *nuclear material* in accordance with paragraphs 93 and 96 below, before its transfer out of or upon its transfer into the State.

72. The Agreement should provide that the Agency may make routine inspections in order to:

(*a*) Verify that reports are consistent with records;

(*b*) Verify the location, identity, quantity and composition of all *nuclear material* subject to safeguards under the Agreement; and

(*c*) Verify information on the possible causes of *material unaccounted for, shipper/receiver differences* and uncertainties in the *book inventory.*

73. The Agreement should provide that the Agency may make special inspections subject to the procedures laid down in paragraph 77 below:

(*a*) In order to verify the information contained in special reports; or

(*b*) If the Agency considers that information made available by the State, including explanations from the State and information obtained from routine inspections, is not adequate for the Agency to fulfil its responsibilities under the Agreement.

An inspection shall be deemed to be special when it is either additional to the routine inspection effort provided for in paragraphs 78–82 below, or involves access to information or locations in addition to the access specified in paragraph 76 for ad hoc and routine inspections, or both.

Scope of inspections

74. The Agreement should provide that for the purposes stated in paragraphs 71–73 above the Agency may:

(*a*) Examine the records kept pursuant to paragraphs 51–58;

(*b*) Make independent measurements of all *nuclear material* subject to safeguards under the Agreement;

(*c*) Verify the functioning and calibration of instruments and other measuring and control equipment;

(*d*) Apply and make use of surveillance and containment measures; and (*e*) Use other objective methods which have been demonstrated to be technically feasible.

75. It should further be provided that within the scope of paragraph 74 above the Agency shall be enabled:

(*a*) To observe that samples at *key measurement points* for material balance accounting are taken in accordance with procedures which produce representative samples, to observe the treatment and analysis of the samples and to obtain duplicates of such samples;

(*b*) To observe that the measurements of *nuclear material* at *key measurement points* for material balance accounting are representative, and to observe the calibration of the instruments and equipment involved;

(*c*) To make arrangements with the State that, if necessary:

(i) Additional measurements are made and additional samples taken for the Agency's use;

(ii) The Agency's standard analytical samples are analysed;

(iii) Appropriate absolute standards are used in calibrating instruments and other equipment; and

(iv) Other calibrations are carried out;

(*d*) To arrange to use its own equipment for independent measurement and surveillance, and if so agreed and specified in the Subsidiary Arrangements, to arrange to install such equipment;

(*e*) To apply its seals and other identifying and tamper-indicating devices to containments, if so agreed and specified in the Subsidiary Arrangements; and

(*f*) To make arrangements with the State for the shipping of samples taken for the Agency's use.

Access for inspections

76. The Agreement should provide that:

(*a*) For the purposes specified in sub-paragraphs 71(*a*) and (*b*) above and until such time as the *strategic points* have been specified in the Subsidiary Arrangements, the Agency's inspectors shall have access to any location where the initial report or any inspections carried out in connection with it indicate that *nuclear material* is present;

(*b*) For the purposes specified in sub-paragraph 71(*c*) above the inspectors shall have access to any location of which the Agency has been notified in accordance with sub-paragraphs 92(*c*) or 95(*c*) below;

(*c*) For the purposes specified in paragraph 72 above the Agency's inspectors shall have access only to the *strategic points* specified in the Subsidiary Arrangements and to the records maintained pursuant to paragraphs 51–58; and

(*d*) In the event of the State concluding that any unusual circumstances require extended limitations on access by the Agency, the State and the Agency shall promptly make arrangements with a view to enabling the Agency to discharge its safeguards responsibilities in the light of these limitations. The Director General shall report each such arrangement to the Board.

77. The Agreement should provide that in circumstances which may lead to special inspections for the purposes specified in paragraph 73 above the State and the Agency shall consult forthwith. As a result of such consultations the Agency may make inspections in addition to the routine inspection effort provided for in paragraphs 78–82 below, and may obtain access in agreement with the State to information or locations in addition to the access specified in paragraph 76 above for ad hoc and routine inspections. Any disagreement concerning the need for additional access shall be resolved in accordance with paragraphs 21 and 22; in case action by the State is essential and urgent, paragraph 18 above shall apply.

Frequency and intensity of routine inspections

78. The Agreement should provide that the number, intensity, duration and timing of routine inspections shall be kept to the minimum consistent with the effective implementation of the safeguards procedures set forth therein, and that the Agency shall make the optimum and most economical use of available inspection resources.

79. The Agreement should provide that in the case of *facilities* and *material balance areas* outside *facilities* with a content or *annual throughput*, whichever is greater, of *nuclear material* not exceeding five *effective kilograms*, routine inspections shall not exceed one per year. For other *facilities* the number, intensity, duration, timing and mode of inspections shall be determined on the basis that in the maximum or limiting case the inspecion régime shall be no more intensive than is necessary and sufficient to maintain continuity of knowledge of the flow and inventory of *nuclear material*.

80. The Agreement should provide that the maximum routine inspection effort in respect

of *facilities* with a content or *annual throughput* of *nuclear material* exceeding five *effective kilograms* shall be determined as follows:

(*a*) For reactors and sealed stores, the maximum total of routine inspection per year shall be determined by allowing one sixth of a *man-year of inspection* for each such *facility* in the State;

(*b*) For other *facilities* involving plutonium or uranium enriched to more than 5%, the maximum total of routine inspection per year shall be determined by allowing for each *such facility* 30 x $\sqrt{E}$ man-days of inspection per year, where E is the inventory or *annual throughput of nuclear material,* whichever is greater, expressed in *effective kilograms. The* maximum established for any such *facility* shall not, however, be less than 1.5 *man-years of inspection;* and

(*c*) For all other *facilities,* the maximum total of routine inspection per year shall be determined by allowing for each *such facility* one third of a *man-year of inspection* plus 0.4 x E man-days of inspection per year, where E is the inventory or *annual throughput* of *nuclear material,* whichever is greater, expressed in *effective kilograms.*

The Agreement should further provide that the Agency and the State may agree to amend the maximum figures specified in this paragraph upon determination by the Board that such amendment is reasonable.

81. Subject to paragraphs 78–80 above the criteria to be used for determining the actual number, intensity, duration, timing and mode of routine inspections of any *facility* shall include:

(*a*) The form of *nuclear material,* in particular, whether the material is in bulk form or contained in a number of separate items; its chemical composition and, in the case of uranium, whether it is of low or high *enrichment;* and its accessibility;

(*b*) The effectiveness of the State's accounting and control system, including the extent to which the operators of *facilities* are functionally independent of the State's accounting and control system; the extent to which the measures specified in paragraph 32 above have been implemented by the State; the promptness of reports submitted to the Agency; their consistency with the Agency's independent verification; and the amount and accuracy of the *material unaccounted for,* as verified by the Agency;

(*c*) Characteristics of the State's nuclear fuel cycle, in particular, the number and types of *facilities* containing *nuclear material* subject to safeguards, the characteristics of such *facilities* relevant to safeguards, notably the degree of containment; the extent to which the design of such *facilities* facilitates verification of the flow and inventory of *nuclear material*; and the extent to which information from different *material balance areas* can be correlated;

(*d*) International interdependence, in particular, the extent to which *nuclear material* is received from or sent to other States for use or processing; any verification activity by the Agency in connection therewith; and the extent to which the State's nuclear activities are interrelated with those of other States; and

(*e*) Technical developments in the field of safeguards, including the use of statistical techniques and random sampling in evaluating the flow of *nuclear material.*

82. The Agreement should provide for consultation between the Agency and the State if the latter considers that the inspection effort is being deployed with undue concentration on particular *facilities.*

Notice of inspections

83. The Agreement should provide that the Agency shall give advance notice to the State before arrival of inspectors at *facilities* or *material balance areas* outside facilities, as follows:

(*a*) For ad hoc inspections pursuant to sub-paragraph 71(*c*) above, at least 24 hours, for those pursuant to sub-paragraphs 71(*a*) and (*b*), as well as the activities provided for in paragraph 48, at least one week;

(*b*) For special inspections pursuant to paragraph 73 above, as promptly as possible after the Agency and the State have consulted as provided for in paragraph 77, it being understood that notification of arrival normally will constitute part of the consultations; and

(*c*) For routine inspections pursuant to paraph 72 above, at least 24 hours in respect of the *facilities* referred to in sub-paragraph 80(*b*) and sealed stores containing plutonium or uranium enriched to more than 5%, and one week in all other cases.

Such notice of inspections shall include the names of the inspectors and shall indicate the *facilities* and the *material balance areas* outside *facilities* to be visited and the periods during which they will be visited. If the inspectors are to arrive from outside the State the Agency shall also give advance notice of the place and time of their arrival in the State.

84. However, the Agreement should also provide that, as a supplementary measure, the Agency may carry out without advance notification a portion of the routine inspections pursuant to paragraph 80 above in accordance with the principle of random sampling. In performing any unannounced inspections, the Agency shall fully take into account any operational programme provided by the State pursuant to paragraph 64(*b*). Moreover, whenever practicable, and on the basis of the operational programme, it shall advise the State periodically of its general programme of announced and unannounced inspections, specifying the general periods when inspections are foreseen. In carrying out any unannounced inspections, the Agency shall make every effort to minimize any practical difficulties for *facility* operators and the State, bearing in mind the relevant provisions of paragraphs 44 above and 89 below. Similarly the State shall make every effort to facilitate the task of the inspectors.

Designation of inspectors

85. The Agreement should provide that:

(*a*) The Director General shall inform the State in writing of the name, qualifications, nationality, grade and such other particulars as may be relevant, of each Agency official he proposes for designation as an inspector for the State;

(*b*) The State shall inform the Director General within 30 days of the receipt of such a proposal whether it accepts the proposal;

(*c*) The Director General may designate each official who has been accepted by the State as one of the inspectors for the State, and shall inform the State of such designations; and

(*d*) The Director General, acting in response to a request by the State or on his own initiative, shall immediately inform the State of the withdrawal of the designation of any official as an inspector for the State.

The Agreement should also provide, however, that in respect of inspectors needed for the purposes stated in paragraph 48 above and to carry out ad hoc inspections pursuant to sub-paragraphs 71(*a*) and (*b*) the designation procedures shall be completed if possible within 30 days after the entry into force of the Agreement. If such designation appears impossible within this time limit, inspectors for such purposes shall be designated on a temporary basis.

86. The Agreement should provide that the State shall grant or renew as quickly as possible appropriate visas, where required, for each inspector designated for the State.

Conduct and visits of inspectors

87. The Agreement should provide that inspectors, in exercising their functions under paragraphs 48 and 71–75 above, shall carry out their activities in a manner designed to avoid hampering or delaying the construction, commissioning or operation of *facilities,* or affecting their safety. In particular inspectors shall not operate any *facility* themselves or direct the staff of a *facility* to carry out any operation. If inspectors consider that in pursuance of paragraphs 74 and 75, particular operations in a *facility* should be carried out by the operator, they shall make a request therefor.

88. When inspectors require services available in the State, including the use of equipment, in connection with the performance of inspections, the State shall facilitate the procurement of such services and the use of such equipment by inspectors.

89. The Agreement should provide that the State shall have the right to have inspectors accompanied during their inspections by representatives of the State, provided that inspectors shall not thereby be delayed or otherwise impeded in the exercise of their functions.

Statements on the Agency's verification activities

90. The Agreement should provide that the Agency shall inform the State of:

(*a*) The results of inspections, at intervals to be specified in the Subsidiary Arrangements; and

(*b*) The conclusions it has drawn from its verification activities in the State, in particular by means of statements in respect of each *material balance area,* which shall be made as soon as possible after a *physical inventory* has been taken and verified by the Agency and a material balance has been struck.

International transfers

General

91. The Agreement should provide that *nuclear material* subject or required to be subject to safeguards thereunder which is transferred internationally shall, for purposes of the Agreement, be regarded as being the responsibility of the State:

(*a*) In the case of import, from the time that

such responsibility ceases to lie with the exporting State, and no later than the time at which the *nuclear material* reaches its destination; and

(*b*) In the case of export, up to the time at which the recipient State assumes such responsibility, and no later than the time at which the *nuclear material* reaches its destination.

The Agreement should provide that the States concerned shall make suitable arrangements to determine the point at which the transfer of responsibility will take place. No State shall be deemed to have such responsibility for *nuclear material* merely by reason of the fact that the *nuclear material* is in transit on or over its territory or territorial waters, or that it is being transported under its flag or in its aircraft.

Transfers out of the State

92. The Agreement should provide that any intended transfer out of the State of safeguarded *nuclear material* in an amount exceeding one *effective kilogram,* or by successive shipments to the same State within a period of three months each of less than one *effective kilogram* but exceeding in total one *effective kilogram,* shall be notified to the Agency after the conclusion of the contractual arrangements leading to the transfer and normally at least two weeks before the *nuclear material* is to be prepared for shipping. The Agency and the State may agree on different procedures for advance notification.

The notification shall specify:

(*a*) The identification and, if possible, the expected quantity and composition of the *nuclear material* to be transferred, and the *material balance area* from which it will come;

(*b*) The State for which the *nuclear material* is destined;

(*c*) The dates on and locations at which the *nuclear material* is to be prepared for shipping;

(*d*) The approximate dates of dispatch and arrival of the *nuclear material;* and

(*e*) At what point of the transfer the recipient State will assume responsibility for the *nuclear material,* and the probable date on which this point will be reached.

93. The Agreement should further provide that the purpose of this notification shall be to enable the Agency if necessary to identify, and if possible verify the quantity and composition of, *nuclear material* subject to safeguards under the Agreement before it is transferred out of the State and, if the Agency so wishes or the State so requests, to affix seals to the *nuclear material* when it has been prepared for shipping. However, the transfer of the *nuclear material* shall not be delayed in any way by any action taken or contemplated by the Agency pursuant to this notification.

94. The Agreement should provide that, if the *nuclear material* will not be subject to Agency safeguards in the recipient State, the exporting State shall make arrangements for the Agency to receive, within three months of the time when the recipient State accepts responsibility for the *nuclear material* from the exporting State, confirmation by the recipient State of the transfer.

Transfers into the State

95. The Agreement should provide that the expected transfer into the State of *nuclear material* required to be subject to safeguards in an amount greater than one *effective kilogram,* or by successive shipments from the same State within a period of three months each of less than one *effective kilogram* but exceeding in total one *effective kilogram,* shall be notified to the Agency as much in advance as possible of the expected arrival of the *nuclear material,* and in any case not later than the date on which the recipient State assumes responsibility therefor. The Agency and the State may agree on different procedures for advance notification.

The notification shall specify:

(*a*) The identification and, if possible, the expected quantity and composition of the *nuclear material*;

(*b*) At what point of the transfer responsibility for the *nuclear material* will be assumed by the State for the purposes of the Agreement, and the probable date on which this point will be reached; and

(*c*) The expected date of arrival, the location to which the *nuclear material* is to be delivered and the date on which it is intended that *the nuclear material* should be unpacked.

96. The Agreement should provide that the purpose of this notification shall be to enable the Agency if necessary to identify, and if possible verify the quantity and composition of, *nuclear material* subject to safeguards which has been transferred into the State, by means of inspection of the consignment at the time it is unpacked. However, unpacking shall not be delayed by any action taken or contemplated by the Agency pursuant to this notification.

Special reports

97. The Agreement should provide that in the case of international transfers a special report as envisaged in paragraph 68 above shall be made if any unusual incident or circumstances lead the State to believe that there is or may have been loss of *nuclear material,* including the occurrence of significant delay during the transfer.

Definitions

98. 'Adjustment' means an entry into an accounting record or a report showing a *shipper/receiver difference* or *material unaccounted for.*

99. 'Annual throughput' means, for the purposes of paragraphs 79 and 80 above, the amount of *nuclear material* transferred annually out of a *facility* working at nominal capacity.

100. 'Batch' means a portion of *nuclear material* handled as a unit for accounting purposes at a *key measurement point* and for which the composition and quantity are defined by a single set of specifications or measurements. The *nuclear material* may be in bulk form or contained in a number of separate items.

101. 'Batch data' means the total weight of each element of *nuclear material* and, in the case of plutonium and uranium, the isotopic composition when appropriate. The units of account shall be as follows:

(*a*) Grams of contained plutonium;

(*b*) Grams of total uranium and grams of contained uranium-235 plus uranium-233 for uranium enriched in these isotopes; and

(*c*) Kilograms of contained thorium, natural uranium or depleted uranium.

For reporting purposes the weights of individual items in the *batch* shall be added together before rounding to the nearest unit.

102. 'Book inventory' of a *material balance area* means the algebraic sum of the most recent *physical inventory* of that *material balance area* and of all *inventory changes* that have occurred since *that physical inventory* was taken.

103. 'Correction' means an entry into an accounting record or a report to rectify an identified mistake or to reflect an improved measurement of a quantity previously entered into the record or report. Each correction must identify the entry to which it pertains.

104. 'Effective kilogram' means a special unit used in safeguarding *nuclear material.* The quantity in 'effective kilograms' is obtained by taking:

(*a*) For plutonium, its weight in kilograms;

(*b*) For uranium with an *enrichment* of 0.01 (1%) and above, its weight in kilograms multiplied by the square of its *enrichment;*

(*c*) For uranium with an *enrichment* below 0.01 (1%) and above 0.005 (0.5%), its weight in kilograms multiplied by 0.0001; and

(*d*) For depleted uranium with an *enrichment* of 0.005 (0.5%) or below, and for thorium, its weight in kilograms multiplied by 0.00005.

105. 'Enrichment' means the ratio of the combined weight of the isotopes uranium-233 and uranium-235 to that of the total uranium in question.

106. 'Facility' means:

(*a*) A reactor, a critical facility, a conversion plant, a fabrication plant, a reprocessing plant, an isotope separation plant or a separate storage installation; or

(*b*) Any location where *nuclear material* in amounts greater than one *effective kilogram* is customarily used.

107. 'Inventory change' means an increase or decrease, in terms of *batches,* of *nuclear material* in a *material balance area;* such a change shall involve one of the following:

(*a*) Increases:

(i) Import;

(ii) Domestic receipt: receipts from other *material balance areas,* receipts from a non-safeguarded (non-peaceful) activity or receipts at the starting point of safeguards;

(iii) Nuclear production: production of special fissionable material in a reactor; and

(iv) De-exemption: reapplication of safeguards on *nuclear material* previously exempted therefrom on account of its use or quantity.

(*b*) Decreases:

(i) Export;

(ii) Domestic shipment: shipments to other *material balance areas* or shipments for a non-safeguarded (non-peaceful) activity;

(iii) Nuclear loss: loss of *nuclear material* due to its transformation into other element(s) or isotope(s) as a result of nuclear reactions;

(iv) Measured discard: *nuclear material* which has been measured, or estimated on the basis of measurements, and disposed of in such a way that it is not suitable for further nuclear use;

(v) Retained waste: *nuclear material* generated from processing or from an operational accident, which is deemed to be unrecoverable for the time being but which is stored;

(vi) Exemption: exemption of *nuclear material* from safeguards on account of its use or quantity; and

(vii) Other loss: for example, accidental loss (that is, irretrievable and inadvertent loss of *nuclear material* as the result of an operational accident) or theft.

108. 'Key measurement point' means a location where *nuclear material* appears in such a form that it may be measured to determine material flow or inventory. 'Key measurement points' thus include, but are not limited to, the inputs and outputs (including measured discards) and storages in *material balance areas.*

109. 'Man-year of inspection' means, for the purposes of paragraph 80 above, 300 man-days of inspection, a man-day being a day during which a single inspector has access to a *facility* at any time for a total of not more than eight hours.

110. 'Material balance area' means an area in or outside of a *facility* such that:

(*a*) The quantity of *nuclear material* in each transfer into or out of each 'material balance area' can be determined; and

(*b*) The *physical inventory* of *nuclear material* in each 'material balance area' can be determined when necessary, in accordance with specified procedures, in order that the material balance for Agency safeguards purposes can be established.

111. 'Material unaccounted for' means the difference between *book inventory* and *physical inventory.*

112. 'Nuclear material' means any source or any special fissionable material as defined in Article XX of the Statute. The term source material shall not be interpreted as applying to ore or ore residue. Any determination by the Board under Article XX of the Statute after the entry into force of this Agreement which adds to the materials considered to be source material or special fissionable material shall have effect under this Agreement only upon acceptance by the State.

113. 'Physical inventory' means the sum of all the measured or derived estimates of *batch* quantities of *nuclear material* on hand at a given time within a *material balance area,* obtained in accordance with specified procedures.

114. 'Shipper/receiver difference' means the difference between the quantity *of nuclear material* in a *batch* as stated by the shipping *material balance area and* as measured at the receiving *material balance area.*

115. 'Source data' means those data, recorded during measurement or calibration or used to derive empirical relationships, which identify *nuclear material* and provide *batch data.* 'Source data' may include, for example, weight of compounds, conversion factors to determine weight of element, specific gravity, element concentration, isotopic ratios, relationship between volume and manometer readings and relationship between plutonium produced and power generated.

116. 'Strategic point' means a location selected during examination of design information where, under normal conditions and when combined with the information from all 'strategic points' taken together, the information necessary and sufficient for the implementation of safeguards measures is obtained and verified; a 'strategic point' may include any location where key measurements related to material balance accountancy are made and where containment and surveillance measures are executed.

Source: IAEA document INFCIRC/153 (corrected), IAEA, Vienna, 1983.

GUIDELINES FOR NUCLEAR TRANSFERS (REVISED 1977 LONDON GUIDELINES)

1. The following fundamental principles for safeguards and export controls should apply to nuclear transfers for peaceful purposes to any non-nuclear-weapon State and, in the case of controls on retransfer, to transfers to any State. In this connection, suppliers have defined an export trigger list and agreed on common criteria for technology transfers.

Prohibition on nuclear explosives

2. Suppliers should authorize transfer of items identified in the trigger list only upon formal governmental assurances from recipients explicitly excluding uses which would result in any nuclear explosive device.

Physical protection

3. (*a*) All nuclear materials and facilities identified by the agreed trigger list should be placed under effective physical protection to

prevent unauthorized use and handling. The levels of physical protection to be ensured in relation to the type of materials, equipment and facilities, have been agreed by suppliers, taking account of international recommendations.

(*b*) The implementation of measures of physical protection in the recipient country is the responsibility of the Government of that country. However, in order to implement the terms agreed upon amongst suppliers, the levels of physical protection on which these measures have to be based should be the subject of an agreement between supplier and recipient.

(*c*) In each case special arrangements should be made for a clear definition of responsibilities for the transport of trigger list items.

Safeguards

4. (*a*) Suppliers should transfer trigger list items to a non-nuclear-weapon State only when the receiving State has brought into force an agreement with the IAEA requiring the application of safeguards on all source and special fissionable material in its current and future peaceful activities.

(*b*) Transfers covered by paragraph 4 (*a*) to a non-nuclear-weapon State without such a safeguards agreement should be authorized only in exceptional cases when they are deemed essential for the safe operation of existing facilities and if safeguards are applied to those facilities. Suppliers should inform and, if appropriate, consult in the event that they intend to authorize or to deny such transfers.

(*c*) The policy referred to in paragraph 4 (*a*) and 4 (*b*) does not apply to agreements or contracts drawn up on or prior to April 3, 1992. In case of countries that have adhered or will adhere to INFCIRC/254/Rev. 1/Part 1 later than April 3, 1992, the policy only applies to agreements (to be) drawn up after their date of adherence.

(d) Under agreements to which the policy referred to in paragraph 4 (*a*) does not apply (see paragraphs 4 (*b*) and (*c*)) suppliers should transfer trigger list items only when covered by IAEA safeguards with duration and coverage provisions in conformity with IAEA doc. GOV/1621. However, suppliers undertake to strive for the earliest possible implementation of the policy referred to in paragraph 4 (*a*) under such agreements.

(*e*) Suppliers reserve the right to apply additional conditions of supply as a matter of national policy.

5. Suppliers will jointly reconsider their common safeguards requirements, whenever appropriate.

Safeguards triggered by the transfer of certain technology

6. (*a*) The requirements of paragraphs 2, 3 and 4 above should also apply to facilities for reprocessing, enrichment, or heavy-water production, utilizing technology directly transferred by the supplier or derived from transferred facilities, or major critical components thereof.

(*b*) The transfer of such facilities, or major critical components thereof, or related technology, should require an undertaking (1) that IAEA safeguards apply to any facilities of the same type (i.e. if the design, construction or operating processes are based on the same or similar physical or chemical processes, as defined in the trigger list) constructed during an agreed period in the recipient country and (2) that there should at all times be in effect a safeguards agreement permitting the IAEA to apply Agency safeguards with respect to such facilities identified by the recipient, or by the supplier in consultation with the recipient, as using transferred technology.

Special controls on sensitive exports

7. Suppliers should exercise restraint in the transfer of sensitive facilities, technology and weapons-usable materials. If enrichment or reprocessing facilities, equipment or technology are to be transferred, suppliers should encourage recipients to accept, as an alternative to national plants, supplier involvement and/or other appropriate multinational participation in resulting facilities. Suppliers should also promote international (including IAEA) activities concerned with multinational regional fuel cycle centres.

Special controls on export of enrichment facilities, equipment and technology

8. For a transfer of an enrichment facility, or technology therefor, the recipient nation should agree that neither the transferred facility, nor any facility based on such technology, will be designed or operated for the production of greater than 20% enriched uranium without the consent of the supplier nation, of which the IAEA should be advised.

Controls on supplied or derived weapons-usable material

9. Suppliers recognize the importance, in order to advance the objectives of these guidelines and to provide opportunities further to reduce the risks of proliferation, of including in agreements on supply of nuclear materials or of facilities which produce weapons-usable material, provisions calling for mutual agreement between the supplier and the recipient on arrangements for reprocessing, storage, alteration, use, transfer or retransfer of any weapons-usable material involved. Suppliers should endeavour to include such provisions whenever appropriate and practicable.

Controls on retransfer

10. (*a*) Suppliers should transfer trigger list items, including technology defined under paragraph 6, only upon the recipient's assurance that in the case of:

(1) retransfer of such items, or

(2) transfer of trigger list items derived from facilities originally transferred by the supplier, or with the help of equipment or technology originally transferred by the supplier;

the recipient of the retransfer or transfer will have provided the same assurances as those required by the supplier for the original transfer.

(*b*) In addition the supplier's consent should be required for: (1) any retransfer of trigger list items and any transfer referred to under paragraph 10 (*a*) (2) from any State which does not require full scope safeguards, in accordance with paragraph 4 (*a*) of these Guidelines, as a condition of supply; (2) any retransfer of the facilities, major critical components, or technology described in paragraph 6; (3) any transfer of facilities or major critical components derived from those items; (4) any retransfer of heavy water or weapons-usable material.

Non-proliferation Principle

11. Notwithstanding other provisions of these Guidelines, suppliers should authorize transfer of items identified in the trigger list only when they are satisfied that the transfers would not contribute to the proliferation of nuclear weapons or other nuclear explosive devices.

SUPPORTING ACTIVITIES

Physical security

12. Suppliers should promote international co-operation on the exchange of physical security information, protection of nuclear materials in transit, and recovery of stolen nuclear materials and equipment.

Support for effective IAEA safeguards

13. Suppliers should make special efforts in support of effective implementation of IAEA safeguards. Suppliers should also support the Agency's efforts to assist Member States in the improvement of their national systems of accounting and control of nuclear material and to increase the technical effectiveness of safeguards.

Similarly, they should make every effort to support the IAEA in increasing further the adequacy of safeguards in the light of technical developments and the rapidly growing number of nuclear facilities, and to support appropriate initiatives aimed at improving the effectiveness of IAEA safeguards.

Sensitive plant design features

14. Suppliers should encourage the designers and makers of sensitive equipment to construct it in such a way as to facilitate the application of safeguards.

Consultations

15. (*a*) Suppliers should maintain contact and consult through regular channels on matters connected with the implementation of these Guidelines.

(*b*) Suppliers should consult, as each deems appropriate, with other Governments concerned on specific sensitive cases, to ensure that any transfer does not contribute to risks of conflict or instability.

(*c*) In the event that one or more suppliers believe that there has been a violation of supplier/recipient understandings resulting from these Guidelines, particularly in the case of an explosion of a nuclear device, or illegal termination or violation of IAEA safeguards by a recipient, suppliers should consult promptly through diplomatic channels in order to determine and assess the reality and extent of the alleged violation.

Pending the early outcome of such consultations, suppliers will not act in a manner that could prejudice any measure that may be adopted by other suppliers concerning their current contacts with that recipient.

Upon the findings of such consultations, the suppliers, bearing in mind Article XII of the IAEA Statute, should agree on an appropriate response and possible action which could include the termination of nuclear transfers to that recipient.

16. In considering transfers, each supplier should exercise prudence having regard to all the circumstances of each case, including any risk that technology transfers not covered by paragraph 6, or subsequent retransfers, might result in unsafeguarded nuclear materials.

17. Unanimous consent is required for any changes in these Guidelines, including any which might result from the reconsideration mentioned in paragraph 5.

Source: IAEA document INFCIRC/254/Rev. 1/ Part 1/Mod. 3 (amended), IAEA, Vienna, Nov. 1994.

ANNEX A. TRIGGER LIST REFERRED TO IN GUIDELINES

PART A. Material and equipment

1. Source and special fissionable material

As defined in Article XX of the Statute of the International Atomic Energy Agency:

1.1. 'Source material'

The term 'source material means uranium containing the mixture of isotopes occurring in nature; uranium depleted in the isotope 235; thorium; any of the foregoing in the form of metal, alloy, chemical compound, or concentrate; any other material containing one or more of the foregoing in such concentration as the Board of Governors shall from time to time determine; and such other material as the Board of Governors shall from time to time determine.

1.2. 'Special fissionable material'

(i) The term 'special fissionable material' means plutonium-239; uranium-233; uranium enriched in the isotopes 235 or 233; any material containing one or more of the foregoing; and such other fissionable material as the Board of Governors shall from time to time determine; but the term 'special fissionable material does not include source material.

(ii) The term 'uranium enriched in the isotopes 235 or 233' means uranium containing the isotopes 235 or 233 or both in an amount such that the abundance ratio of the sum of these isotopes to the isotope 238 is greater than the ratio of the isotope 235 to the isotope 238 occurring in nature.

However, for the purposes of the Guidelines, items specified in subparagraph (a) below, and exports of source or special fissionable material to a given recipient country, within a period of 12 months, below the limits specified in subparagraph (b) below, shall not be included:

(a) Plutonium with an isotopic concentration of plutonium-238 exceeding 80%.

Special fissionable material when used in gram quantities or less as a sensing component in instruments; and

Source material which the Government is satisfied is to be used only in non-nuclear activities, such as the production of alloys or ceramics;

(b) Special fissionable material	50 effective grams;
Natural uranium	500 kilograms;
Depleted uranium	1000 kilograms;
and	
Thorium	1000 kilograms.

2. Equipment and Non-nuclear Materials

The designation of items of equipment and non-nuclear materials (hereafter referred to as the 'Trigger List') adopted by the Government is as follows (quantities below the levels indicated in the Annex B being regarded as insignificant for practical purposes):

2.1. Reactors and equipment therefor (see Annex B, section 1.);

2.2. Non-nuclear materials for reactors (see Annex B, section 2.);

2.3. Plants for the reprocessing of irradiated fuel elements, and equipment especially designed or prepared therefor (see Annex B, section 3.);

2.4. Plants for the fabrication of fuel elements (see Annex B, section 4.);

2.5. Plants for the separation of isotopes of uranium and equipment, other than analytical instruments, especially designed or prepared therefor (see Annex B, section 5.);

2.6. Plants for the production of heavy water, deuterium and deuterium compounds and equipment especially designed or prepared therefor (see Annex B, section 6.);

2.7. Plants for the conversion of uranium and equipment especially designed or prepared therefor (See Annex 8, Section 7.).

PART B. Common criteria for technology transfers under paragraph 6 of the Guidelines

(1) 'Technology' means technical data in physical form designated by the supplying country as important to the design, construction, operation, or maintenance of enrichment, reprocessing, or heavy water production facilities or major critical components thereof, but excluding data available to the public, for example, in published books and periodicals, or that which has been made available internationally without restrictions upon its further dissemination.

(2) 'Major critical components' are:

(*a*) in the case of an isotope separation plant of the gas centrifuge type: *gas centrifuge assemblies, corrosion-resistant to UF_6;*

(*b*) in the case of an isotope separation plant of the gaseous diffusion type: *diffusion barrier*;

(*c*) in the case of an isotope separation plant of the jet nozzle type: the *nozzle units;*

(*d*) in the case of an isotope separation plant of the vortex type: the *vortex units;*

(3) For facilities covered by paragraph 6 of the Guidelines for which no major critical component is described in paragraph 2 above, if a supplier nation should transfer in the aggregate a significant fraction of the items essential to the operation of such a facility, together with the knowhow for construction and operation of that facility, that transfer should be deemed to be a transfer of 'facilities or major critical components thereof'.

(4) The definitions in the preceding paragraphs are solely for the purposes of paragraph 6 of the Guidelines and this Part B, which differ from those applicable to Part A of this Trigger List, which should not be interpreted as limited by such definition.

(5) For the purposes of implementing paragraph 6 of the Guidelines, the following facilities should be deemed to be 'of the same type (i.e. if their design, construction or operating processes are based on the same or similar physical or chemical processes)':

Where the technology transferred is such as to make possible the construction in the recipient State of a facility of the following type, or major critical components thereof:	The following will be deemed to be facilities of the same type:
(a) an isotope separation plant of the gaseous diffusion type	any other isotope separation plant using the gaseous diffusion process.
(b) an isotope separation plant of the gas centrifuge type	any other isotope separation plant using the gaseous diffusion process.
(c) an isotope separation plant of the jet nozzle type	any other isotope separation plant using the jet nozzle process.
(d) an isotope separation plant of the vortex type	any other isotope separation plant using the vortex process.
(e) a fuel reprocessing plant using the solvent extraction process	any other fuel reprocessing plant using the solvent extraction process.
(f) a heavy water plant using the exchange process	any other heavy water plant using the exchange process.
(g) a heavy water plant using the electrolytic process	any other heavy water plant using the electrolytic process.
(h) a heavy water plant using the hydrogen distillation process	any other heavy water plant using the hydrogen distillation process.

Note: In the case of reprocessing, enrichment, and heavy water facilities whose design, construction, or operation processes are based on physical or chemical processes other than those enumerated above, a similar approach would be applied to define facilities 'of the same type', and a need to define major critical components of such facilities might arise.

The reference in paragraph 6(b) of the Guidelines to 'any facilities of the same type constructed during an agreed period in the recipient's country' is understood to refer to such facilities (or major critical components thereof), the first operation of which commences within a period of at least 20 years from the date of the first operation of (1) a facility which has been transferred or incorporates transferred major critical components or of (2) a facility of the same type built after the transfer of technology. It is understood that during that period there would be a conclusive presumption that any facility of the same type utilized transferred technology. But the agreed period is not intended to limit the duration of the sateguards imposed or the duration of the right to identify facilities as being constructed or operated on the basis of or by the use of transferred technotogy in accordance with paragraph 6 (b)(2) of the Guidelines.

Source: IAEA document INFCIRC/254/Rev. 1/Part 1/Mod. 2 (amended), IAEA, Vienna, Apr. 1994.

ANNEX B. CLARIFICATION OF ITEMS ON THE TRIGGER LIST

(as designated in Section 2 of Part A of Annex A)

1. Reactors and equipment therefor

1.1. Complete nuclear reactors

Nuclear reactors capable of operation so as to maintain a controlled self-sustaining fission chain reaction, excluding zero energy reactors, the latter being defined as reactors with a designed maximum rate of production of plutonium not exceeding 100 grams per year.

EXPLANATORY NOTE

A 'nuclear reactor' basically includes the items within or attached directly to the reactor vessel, the equipment which controls the level of power in the core, and the components which normally contain or come in direct contact with or control the primary coolant of the reactor core.

It is not intended to exclude reactors which could reasonably be capable of modification to produce significantly more than 100 grams of plutonium per year. Reactors designed for sustained operation at significant power levels, regardless of their capacity for plutonium production, are not considered as 'zero energy reactors'.

EXPORTS

The export of the whole set of major items within this boundary will take place only in accordance with the procedures of the Guidelines. Those individual items within this functionally defined boundary which will be exported only in accordance with the procedures of the Guidelines are listed in paragraphs 1.2. to 1.7. The Government reserves the right to apply the procedures of the Guidelines to other items within the functionally defined boundary.

1.2. Reactor pressure vessels

Metal vessels, as complete units or as major shop-fabricated parts therefor, which are especially designed or prepared to contain the core of a nuclear reactor as defined in paragraph 1.1. above and are capable of withstanding the operating pressure of the primary coolant.

EXPLANATORY NOTE

A top plate for a reactor pressure vessel is covered by item 1.2. as a major shop-fabricated part of a pressure vessel.

Reactor internals (eg support columns and plates for the core and other vessel internals, control rod guide tubes, thermal shields, baffles, core grid plates, diffuser plates, etc.) are normally supplied by the reactor supplier. In some cases, certain internal support components are included in the fabrication of the pressure vessel. These items are sufficiently critical to the stability and reliability of the operation of the reactor (and, therefore, to the guarantees and liability of the reactor supplier), so that their supply, outside the basic supply arrangement for the reactor itself, would not be common practice. Therefore, although the separate supply of these unique, especially designed and prepared, critical, large and expensive items would not necessarily be considered as falling outside the area of concern, such a mode of supply is considered unlikely.

1.3. Reactor fuel charging and discharging machines

Manipulative equipment especially designed or prepared for inserting or removing fuel in a nuclear reactor as defined in paragraph 1.1. above capable of on-load operation or employing technically sophisticated positioning or alignment features to allow complex off-load fuelling operations such as those in which direct viewing of or access to the fuel is not normally available.

1.4. Reactor control rods

Rods especially designed or prepared for the control of the reaction rate in a nuclear reactor as defined in paragraph 1.1. above.

EXPLANATORY NOTE

This item includes, in addition to the neutron absorbing part, the support or suspension structures therefor if supplied separately.

1.5. Reactor pressure tubes

Tubes which are especially designed or prepared to contain fuel elements and the primary coolant in a reactor as defined in paragraph 1.1. above at an operating pressure in excess of 5.1 MPa (740 psi).

1.6. Zirconium tubes

Zirconium metal and alloys in the form of tubes or assemblies of tubes, and in quantities exceeding 500 kg in any period of 12 months, especially designed or prepared for use in a reactor as defined in paragraph 1.1. above, and in which the relation of hafnium to zirconium is less than 1:500 parts by weight.

1.7. Primary coolant pumps

Pumps especially designed or prepared for circulating the primary coolant for nuclear reactors as defined in paragraph 1.1. above.

EXPLANATORY NOTE

Especially designed or prepared pumps may include elaborate sealed or multi-sealed systems to prevent leakage of primary coolant, canned-driven pumps, and pumps with inertial mass systems. This definition encompasses pumps certified to NC-1 or equivalent standards.

2. Non-nuclear materials for reactors

2.1. Deuterium and heavy water

Deuterium, heavy water (deuterium oxide) and any other deuterium compound in which the ratio of deuterium to hydrogen atoms exceeds 1:5000 for use in a nuclear reactor as defined in paragraph 1.1. above in quantities exceeding 200 kg of deuterium atoms for any one recipient country in any period of 12 months.

2.2. Nuclear grade graphite

Graphite having a purity level better than 5 parts per million boron equivalent and with a density greater than 1.50 g/cm^3 in quantities exceeding 3.10^4 kg (30 metric tons) for any one recipient country in any period of 12 months.

3. Plants for the reprocessing of irradiated fuel elements, and equipment especially designed or prepared therefor

INTRODUCTORY NOTE

Reprocessing irradiated nuclear fuel separates plutonium and uranium from intensely radioactive fission products and other transuranic elements. Different technical processes can accomplish this separation. However, over the years Purex has become the most commonly used and accepted process. Purex involves the dissolution of irradiated nuclear fuel in nitric acid, followed by separation of the uranium, plutonium, and fission products by solvent extraction using a mixture of tributyl phosphate in an organic diluent.

Purex facilities have process functions similar to each other, including: irradiated fuel element chopping, fuel dissolution, solvent extraction, and process liquor storage. There may also be equipment for thermal denitration of uranium nitrate, conversion of plutonium nitrate to oxide or metal, and treatment of fission product waste liquor to a form suitable for long term storage or disposal. However, the specific type and configuration of the equipment performing these functions may differ between Purex facilities for several reasons, including the type and quantity of irradiated nuclear fuel to be reprocessed and the intended disposition of the recovered materials, and the safety and maintenance philosophy incorporated into the design of the facility.

A 'plant for the reprocessing of irradiated fuel elements', includes the equipment and components which normally come in direct contact with and directly control the irradiated fuel and the major nuclear material and fission product processing streams.

These processes, including the complete systems for plutonium conversion and plutonium metal production, may be identified by the measures taken to avoid criticality (eg by geometry), radiation exposure (eg by shielding), and toxicity hazards (eg by containment).

EXPORTS

The export of the whole set of major items within this boundary will take place only in accordance with the procedures of the Guidelines.

The Government reserves to itself the right to apply the procedures of the Guidelines to other items within the functionally defined boundary as listed below.

Items of equipment that are considered to fall within the meaning of the phrase 'and equipment especially designed or prepared' for the reprocessing of irradiated fuel elements include:

3.1. Irradiated fuel element chopping machines

INTRODUCTORY NOTE

This equipment breaches the cladding of the fuel to expose the irradiated nuclear material to dissolution. Especially designed metal cutting shears are the most commonly employed, although advanced equipment, such as lasers, may be used.

Remotely operated equipment especially designed or prepared for use in a reprocessing plant as identified above and intended to cut, chop or shear irradiated nuclear fuel assemblies, bundles or rods.

3.2. Dissolvers

INTRODUCTORY NOTE

Dissolvers normally receive the chopped-up spent fuel. In these critically safe vessels, the irradiated nuclear material is dissolved in nitric acid and the remaining hulls removed from the process stream.

Critically safe tanks (eg small diameter, annular or slab tanks) especially designed or prepared for use in a reprocessing plant as identified above, intended for dissolution of irradiated nuclear fuel and which are capable of withstanding hot, highly corrosive liquid, and which can be remotely loaded and maintained.

3.3. Solvent extractors and solvent extraction equipment

INTRODUCTORY NOTE

Solvent extractors both receive the solution of irradiated fuel from the dissolvers and the organic solution which separates the uranium, plutonium, and fission products. Solvent extraction equipment is normally designed to meet strict operating parameters, such as long operating lifetimes with no maintenance requirements or adaptability to easy replacement, simplicity of operation and control, and flexibility for variations in process conditions.

Especially designed or prepared solvent extractors such as packed or pulse columns, mixer settlers or centrifugal contactors for use in a plant for the reprocessing of irradiated fuel. Solvent extractors must be resistant to the corrosive effect of nitric acid. Solvent extractors are normally fabricated to extremely high standards (including special welding and inspection and quality assurance and quality control techniques) out of low carbon stainless steels, titanium, zirconium, or other high quality materials.

3.4. Chemical holding or storage vessels

INTRODUCTORY NOTE

Three main process liquor streams result from the solvent extraction step. Holding or storage vessels are used in the further processing of all three streams, as follows:

(*a*) The pure uranium nitrate solution is concentrated by evaporation and passed to a denitration process where it is converted to uranium oxide. This oxide is re-used in the nuclear fuel cycle.

(*b*) The intensely radioactive fission products solution is normally concentrated by evaporation and stored as a liquor concentrate. This concentrate may be subsequently evaporated and converted to a form suitable for storage or disposal.

(*c*) The pure plutonium nitrate solution is concentrated and stored pending its transfer to further process steps. In particular, holding or storage vessels for plutonium solutions are designed to avoid criticality problems resulting from changes in concentration and form of this stream.

Especially designed or prepared holding or storage vessels for use in a plant for the reprocessing of irradiated fuel. The holding or storage vessels must be resistant to the corrosive effect of nitric acid. The holding or storage vessels are normally fabricated of materials such as low carbon stainless steels, titanium or zirconium, or other high quality materials. Holding or storage vessels may be designed for remote operation and maintenance and may have the following features for control of nuclear criticality:

(1) walls or internal structures with a boron equivalent of at least two per cent, or

(2) a maximum diameter of 175 mm (7 in) for cylindrical vessels, or

(3) a maximum width of 75 mm (3 in) for either a slab or annular vessel.

3.5. Plutonium nitrate to oxide conversion system

INTRODUCTORY NOTE

In most reprocessing facilities, this final process involves the conversion of the plutonium nitrate solution to plutonium dioxide. The main functions involved in this process are: process feed storage and adjustment, precipitation and solid/liquor separation, calcination, product handling, ventilation, waste management, and process control.

Complete systems especially designed or prepared for the conversion of plutonium nitrate to plutonium oxide, in particular adapted so as to avoid criticality and radiation effects and to minimize toxicity hazards.

3.6. Plutonium oxide to metal production system

INTRODUCTORY NOTE

This process, which could be related to a reprocessing facility, involves the fluorination of plutonium dioxide, normally with highly corrosive hydrogen flouride, to produce plutonium flouride which is subsequently reduced using high purity calcium metal to produce metallic plutonium and a calcium flouride slag. The main functions involved in this process are: fluorination (eg involving equipment fabricated or lined with a precious metal), metal reduction (eg employing ceramic crucibles), slag recovery, product handling, ventilation, waste management and process control.

Complete systems especially designed or prepared for the production of plutonium metal, in particular adapted so as to avoid criticality and radiation effects and to minimize toxicity hazards.

4. Plants for the fabrication of fuel elements

A 'plant for the fabrication of fuel elements' includes the equipment:

(*a*) Which normally comes in direct contact with, or directly processes, or controls, the production flow of nuclear material, or

(*b*) Which seals the nuclear material within the cladding.

EXPORTS

The export of the whole set of items for the foregoing operations will take place only in accordance with the procedures of the Guidelines. The Government will also give consideration to application of the procedures of the Guidelines to individual items intended for any of the foregoing operations, as well as for other fuel fabrication operations such as checking the integrity of the cladding of the seal, and the finishing treatment of the sealed fuel.

5. Plants for the separation of isotopes of uranium and equipment, other than analytical instruments, especially designed or prepared therefor

Items of equipment that are considered to fall within the meaning of the phrase 'equipment other than analytical instruments, especially designed or prepared' for the separation of isotopes of uranium include:

5.1. Gas centrifuges and assemblies and components especially designed or prepared for use in gas centrifuges

INTRODUCTORY NOTE

The gas centrifuge normally consists of a thin-walled cylinder(s) of between 75 mm (3 in) and 400 mm (16 in) diameter contained in a vacuum environment and spun at high peripheral speed of the order of 300 m/s or more with its central axis vertical. In order to achieve high speed the materials of construction for the rotating components have to be of a high strength to density ratio and the rotor assembly, and hence its individual components, have to be manufactured to very close tolerances in order to minimize the unbalance. In contrast to other centrifuges, the gas centrifuge for uranium enrichment is characterized by having within the rotor chamber a rotating disc-shaped baffle(s) and a stationary tube arrangement for feeding and extracting the UF_6 gas and featuring at least 3 separate channels, of which 2 are connected to scoops extending from the rotor axis towards the periphery of the rotor chamber. Also contained within the vacuum environment are a number of critical items which do not rotate and which although they are especially designed are not difficult to fabricate nor are they fabricated out of unique materials. A centrifuge facility however requires a large number of these components, so that quantities can provide an important indication of end use.

5.1.1. Rotating components

(*a*) Complete rotor assemblies:

Thin-walled cylinders, or a number of interconnected thin-walled cylinders, manufactured from one or more of the high strength to density ratio materials described in the EXPLANATORY NOTE to this Section. If interconnected, the cylinders are joined together by flexible bellows or rings as described in section 5.1.1.(*c*) following. The rotor is fitted with an internal baffle(s) and end caps, as described in section 5.1.1.(*d*) and (*e*) following, if in final form. However the complete assembly may be delivered only partly assembled.

(*b*) Rotor tubes:

Especially designed or prepared thin-walled cylinders with thickness of 12 mm (0.5 in) or less, a diameter of between 75 mm (3 in) and 400 mm (16 in), and manufactured from one or more of the high strength to density ratio materials described in the EXPLANATORY NOTE to this Section.

(*c*) Rings or Bellows:

Components especially designed or prepared to give localized support to the rotor tube or to join together a number of rotor tubes. The bellows is a short cylinder of wall thickness 3 mm (0.12 in) or less, a diameter of between 75 mm (3 in) and 400 mm (16 in), having a convolute, and manufactured from one of the high strength to density ratio materials described in the EXPLANATORY NOTE to this Section.

(*d*) Baffles:

Disc-shaped components of between 75 mm (3 in) and 400 mm (16 in) diameter especially designed or prepared to be mounted inside the centrifuge rotor tube, in order to isolate the take-off chamber from the main separation chamber and, in some cases, to assist the UF_6 gas circulation within the main separation chamber of the rotor tube, and manufactured from one of the high strength to density ratio materials described in the EXPLANATORY NOTE to this Section.

(*e*) Top caps/Bottom caps:

Disc-shaped components of between 75 mm (3 in) and 400 mm (16 in) diameter especially designed or prepared to fit to the ends of the rotor tube, and so contain the UF_6 within the rotor tube, and in some cases to support, retain or contain as an integrated part an element of the upper bearing (top cap) or to carry the rotating elements of the motor and lower bearing (bottom cap), and manufactured from one of the high strength to density ratio materials described in the EXPLANATORY NOTE to this Section.

EXPLANATORY NOTE

The materials used for centrifuge rotating components are:

(*a*) Maraging steel capable of an ultimate tensile strength of $2.05 \cdot 10^9$ N/m^2 (300,000 psi) or more;

(*b*) Aluminium alloys capable of an ultimate tensile strength of $0.46 \cdot 10^9$ N/m^2 (67,000 psi) or more;

(*c*) Filamentary materials suitable for use in composite structures and having specific modulus of $12.3 \cdot 10^6$ m or greater and a specific ultimate tensile strength of $0.3 \cdot 10^6$ m or greater ('Specific Modulus' is the Young's Modulus in N/m^2 divided by the specific weight in N/m^3; 'Specific Ultimate Tensile Strength' is the ultimate tensile strength in N/m^2 divided by the specific weight in N/m^3).

5.1.2. Static components

(*a*) Magnetic suspension bearings:

Especially designed or prepared bearing assemblies consisting of an annular magnet suspended within a housing containing a damping medium. The housing will be manufactured from a UF_6-resistant material (see EXPLANATORY NOTE to Section 5.2.). The magnet couples with a pole piece or a second magnet fitted to the top cap described in Section 5.1.1.(*e*). The magnet may be ring-shaped with a relation between outer and inner diameter smaller or equal to 1.6:1. The magnet may be in a form having an initial permeability of 0.15 H/m (120,000 in CGS units) or more, or a remanence of 98.5% or more, or an energy product of greater than 80 kJ/m^3 (10^7 gauss-oersteds). In addition to the usual material properties, it is a prerequisite that the deviation of the magnetic axes from the geometrical axes is limited to very small tolerances (lower than 0.1 mm or 0.004 in) or that homogeneity of the material of the magnet is specially called for.

(*b*) Bearings/Dampers:

Especially designed or prepared bearings comprising a pivot/cup assembly mounted on a damper. The pivot is normally a hardened steel shaft with a hemisphere at one end with a means of attachment to the bottom cap described in section 5.1.1.(e) at the other. The shaft may however have a hydrodynamic bearing attached. The cup is pellet-shaped with a hemispherical indentation in one surface. These components are often supplied separately to the damper.

(*c*) Molecular pumps:

Especially designed or prepared cylinders having internally machined or extruded helical grooves and internally machined bores. Typical dimensions are as follows: 75 mm (3 in) to 400 mm (16 in) internal diameter, 10 mm (0.4 in) or more wall thickness, with the length equal to or greater than the diameter. The grooves are typically rectangular in cross-section and 2 mm (0.08 in) or more in depth.

(*d*) Motor stators:

Especially designed or prepared ring-shaped stators for high speed multiphase AC hysteresis (or reluctance) motors for synchronous operation within a vacuum in the frequency range of 600–2000 Hz and a power range of 50–1000 VA. The stators consist of multi-phase windings on a laminated low loss iron core comprised of thin layers typically 2.0 mm (0.08 in) thick or less.

(*e*) Centrifuge housing/recipients:

Components especially designed or prepared to contain the rotor tube assembly of a gas centrifuge. The housing consists of a rigid cylinder of wall thickness up to 30 mm (1.2 in) with precision machined ends to locate the bearings and with one or more flanges for mounting. The machined ends are parallel to each other and perpendicular to the cylinder's longitudinal axis to within 0.05 degrees or less. The housing may also be a honeycomb type structure to accommodate several rotor tubes. The housings are made of or protected by materials resistant to corrosion by UF_6.

(*f*) Scoops:

Especially designed or prepared tubes of up to 12 mm (0.5 in) internal diameter for the extraction of UF_6 gas from within the rotor tube by a Pitot tube action (that is, with an aperture facing into the circumferential gas flow within the rotor tube, for example by bending the end of a radially disposed tube) and capable of being fixed to the central gas extraction system. The tubes are made of or protected by materials resistant to corrosion by UF_6.

5.2. Especially designed or prepared auxiliary systems, equipment and components for gas centrifuge enrichment plants

INTRODUCTORY NOTE

The auxiliary systems, equipment and components for a gas centrifuge enrichment plant are the systems of plant needed to feed UF_6 to the centrifuges, to link the individual centrifuges to each other to form cascades (or stages) to allow for progressively higher enrichments and to extract the 'product' and 'tails' UF_6 from the centrifuges, together with the equipment required to drive the centrifuges or to control the plant.

Normally UF_6 is evaporated from the solid using heated autoclaves and is distributed in gaseous form to the centrifuges by way of cascade header pipework. The 'product' and 'tails' UF_6 gaseous streams flowing from the centrifuges are also passed by way of cascade header pipework to cold traps (operating at about 203 K (-70°C)) where they are condensed prior to onward transfer into suitable containers for transportation or storage. Because an enrichment plant consists of many thousands of centrifuges arranged in cascades there are many kilometers of cascade header pipework, incorporating thousands of welds with a substantial amount of repetition of layout. The equipment, components and piping systems are fabricated to very high vacuum and cleanliness standards.

5.2.1. Feed systems/product and tails withdrawal systems

Especially designed or prepared process systems including:

Feed autoclaves (or stations), used for passing UF_6 to the centrifuge cascades at up to 100 kPa (15 psi) and at a rate of 1 kg/h or more:

Desublimers (or cold traps) used to remove UF_6 from the cascades at up to 3 kPa (0.5 psi) pressure. The desublimers are capable of being chilled to 203 K (-70°C) and heated to 343 K (70°C);

'Product' and 'Tails' stations used for trapping UF_6 into containers.

This plant, equipment and pipework is wholly made of or lined with UF_6-resistant materials (see EXPLANATORY NOTE to this section) and is fabricated to very high vacuum and cleanliness standards.

5.2.2. Machine header piping systems

Especially designed or prepared piping systems and header systems for handling UF_6 within the centrifuge cascades. The piping network is normally of the 'triple' header system with each centrifuge connected to each of the headers. There is thus a substantial amount of repetition in its form. It is wholly made of UF_6-resistant materials (see EXPLANATORY NOTE to this section) and is fabricated to very high vacuum and cleanliness standards.

5.2.3. UF_6 mass spectrometers/ion sources

Especially designed or prepared magnetic or quadrupole mass spectrometers capable of taking 'on-line' samples of feed, product or tails, from UF_6 gas streams and having all of the following characteristics:

1. Unit resolution for atomic mass unit greater than 320;
2. Ion sources constructed of or lined with nichrome or monel or nickel plated;
3. Electron bombardment ionization sources;
4. Having a collector system suitable for isotopic analysis.

5.2.4. Frequency changers

Frequency changers (also known as converters or invertors) especially designed or prepared to supply motor stators as defined under 5.1.2.(d), or parts, components and sub-assemblies of such frequency changers having all of the following characteristics:

1. A multiphase output of 600 to 2000 Hz;
2. High stability (with frequency control better than 0.1%);
3. Low harmonic distortion (less than 2%); and
4. An efficiency of greater than 80%.

EXPLANATORY NOTE

The items listed above either come into direct contact with the UF_6 process gas or directly control the centrifuges and the passage of the gas from centrifuge to centrifuge and cascade to cascade.

Materials resistant to corrosion by UF_6 include stainless steel, aluminium, aluminium alloys, nickel or alloys containing 60% or more nickel.

5.3. Especially designed or prepared assemblies and components for use in gaseous diffusion enrichment

INTRODUCTORY NOTE

In the gaseous diffusion method of uranium isotope separation, the main technological assembly is a special porous gaseous diffusion barrier, heat exchanger for cooling the gas (which is heated by the process of compression), seal valves and control valves, and pipelines. Inasmuch as gaseous diffusion technology uses uranium hexafluoride (UF_6), all equipment, pipeline and instrumentation surfaces (that come in contact with the gas) must be made of materials that remain stable in contact with UF_6. A gaseous diffusion facility requires a number of these assemblies, so that quantities can provide an important indication of end use.

5.3.1. Gaseous diffusion barriers

(*a*) Especially designed or prepared thin, porous filters, with a pore size of 100–1,000 Å (angstroms), a thickness of 5 mm (0.2 in) or less, and for tubular forms, a diameter of 25 mm (1 in) or less, made of metallic, polymer or ceramic materials resistant to corrosion by UF_6, and

(*b*) especially prepared compounds or powders for the manufacture of such filters. Such compounds and powders include nickel or alloys containing 60 per cent or more nickel, aluminium oxide, or UF_6-resistant fully fluorinated hydrocarbon polymers having a purity of 99.9 per cent or more, a particle size less than 10 microns, and a high degree of particle size uniformity, which are especially prepared for the manufacture of gaseous diffusion barriers.

5.3.2. Diffuser housings

Especially designed or prepared hermetically sealed cylindrical vessels greater than 300 mm (12 in) in diameter and greater than 900 mm (35 in) in length, or rectangular vessels of comparable dimensions, which have an inlet connection and two outlet connections all of which are greater than 50 mm (2 in) in diameter, for containing the gaseous diffusion barrier, made of or lined with UF_6-resistant materials and designed for horizontal or vertical installation.

5.3.3. Compressors and gas blowers

Especially designed or prepared axial, centrifugal, or positive displacement compressors, or gas blowers with a suction volume capacity of 1 m^3/min or more of UF_6, and with a discharge pressure of up to several hundred kPa (100 psi), designed for long-term operation in the UF_6 environment with or without an electrical motor of appropriate power, as well as separate assemblies of such compressors and gas blowers. These compressors and gas blowers have a pressure ratio between 2:1 and 6:1 and are made of, or lined with, materials resistant to UF_6.

5.3.4. Rotary shaft seals

Especially designed or prepared vacuum seals, with seal feed and seal exhaust connections, for sealing the shaft connecting the compressor or the gas blower rotor with the driver motor so as to ensure a reliable seal against in-leaking of air into the inner chamber of the compressor or gas blower which is filled with UF_6. Such seals are normally designed for a buffer gas in-leakage rate of less than 1000 cm^3/min (60 in^3/min).

5.3.5. Heat exchangers for cooling UF_6

Especially designed or prepared heat exchangers made of or lined with UF_6-resistant materials (except stainless steel) or with copper or any combination of those metals, and intended for a leakage pressure change rate of less than 10 Pa (0.0015 psi) per hour under a pressure difference of 100 kPa (15 psi).

5.4. Especially designed or prepared auxiliary systems, equipment and components for use in gaseous diffusion enrichment

INTRODUCTORY NOTE

The auxiliary systems, equipment and components for gaseous diffusion enrichment plants are the systems of plant needed to feed UF_6 to the gaseous diffusion assembly, to link the individual assemblies to each other to form cascades (or stages) to allow for progressively higher enrichments and to extract the 'product' and 'tails' UF_6 from the diffusion cascades. Because of the high inertial properties of diffusion cascades, any interruption in their operation, and especially their shut-down, leads to serious consequences. Therefore, a strict and constant maintenance of vacuum in all technological systems, automatic protection from accidents, and precise automated regulation of the gas flow is of importance in a gaseous diffusion plant. All this leads to a need to equip the plant with a large number of special measuring, regulating and controlling systems.

Normally UF_6 is evaporated from cylinders placed within autoclaves and is distributed in gaseous form to the entry point by way of cascade header pipework. The 'product' and 'tails' UF_6 gaseous streams flowing from exit points are passed by way of cascade header pipework to either cold traps or to compression stations where the UF_6 gas is liquefied prior to onward transfer into suitable containers for transportation or storage. Because a gaseous diffusion enrichment plant consists of a large number of gaseous diffusion assemblies arranged in cascades, there are many kilometers of cascade header pipework, incorporating thousands of welds with substantial amounts of repetition of layout. The equipment, components and piping systems are fabricated to very high vacuum and cleanliness standards.

5.4.1. Feed systems/product and tails withdrawal systems

Especially designed or prepared process systems, capable of operating at pressures of 300 kPa (45 psi) or less, including:

Feed autoclaves (or systems), used for passing UF_6, to the gaseous diffusion cascades;

Desublimers (or cold traps) used to remove UF_6 from diffusion cascades;

Liquefaction stations where UF_6 gas from the cascade is compressed and cooled to form liquid UF_6;

'Product' or 'tails' stations used for transferring UF_6 into containers.

5.4.2. Header piping systems

Especially designed or prepared piping systems and header systems for handling UF_6 within the gaseous diffusion cascades. This piping network is normally of the 'double' header system with each cell connected to each of the headers.

5.4.3. Vacuum systems

(*a*) Especially designed or prepared large vacuum manifolds, vacuum headers and vacuum pumps having a suction capacity of 5 m^3/min (175 ft^3/min) or more.

(*b*) Vacuum pumps especially designed for service in UF_6-bearing atmospheres made of, or lined with, aluminium, nickel, or alloys bearing more than 60% nickel. These pumps may be either rotary or positive, may have displacement and fluorocarbon seals, and may have special working fluids present.

5.4.4. Special shut-off and control valves

Especially designed or prepared manual or automated shut-off and control bellows valves made of UF_6-resistant materials with a diameter of 40 to 1500 mm (1.5 to 59 in) for installation in main and auxiliary systems of gaseous diffusion enrichment plants.

5.4.5. UF_6 mass spectrometers/ion sources

Especially designed or prepared magnetic or quadrupole mass spectrometers capable of taking 'on-line' samples of feed, product or tails, from UF_6 gas streams and having all of the following characteristics:

1. Unit resolution for atomic mass unit greater than 320;

2. Ion sources constructed of or lined with nichrome or monel or nickel plated;

3. Electron bombardment ionization sources;

4. Collector system suitable for isotopic analysis.

EXPLANATORY NOTE

The items listed above either come into direct contact with the UF_6 process gas or directly control the flow within the cascade. All surfaces which come into contact with the process gas are wholly made of, or lined with, UF_6-resistant materials. For the purposes of the sections relating to gaseous diffusion items the materials resistant to corrosion by UF_6 include stainless steel, aluminium, aluminium alloys, aluminium oxide, nickel or alloys containing 60% or more nickel and UF_6-resistant fully fluorinated hydrocarbon polymers.

5.5. Especially designed or prepared systems, equipment and components for use in aerodynamic enrichment plants.

INTRODUCTORY NOTE

In aerodynamic enrichment processes, a mixture of gaseous UF_6 and light gas (hydrogen or helium) is compressed and then passed through separating elements wherein isotopic separation is accomplished by the generation of high centrifugal forces over a curved-wall geometry. Two processes of this type have been successfully developed: the separation nozzle process and the vortex tube process. For both processes the main components of a separation stage include cylindrical vessels housing the special separation elements (nozzles or vortex tubes), gas compressors and hear exchangers to remove the heat of compression. An aerodynamic plant requires a number of these stages, so that quantities can provide an important indication of end use. Since aerodynamic processes use UF_6, all equipment, pipeline and instrumentation surfaces (that come in contact with the gas) must be made of materials that remain stable in contact with UF_6.

EXPLANATORY NOTE

The items listed in this section either come into direct contact with the UF_6 process gas or directly control the flow within the cascade. All surfaces which come into contact with the process gas are wholly made of or protected by UF_6-resistant materials. For the purposes of the section relating to aerodynamic enrichment items, the materials resistant to corrosion by UF_6 include copper, stainless steel, aluminium, aluminium alloys, nickel or alloys containing 60% or more nickel and UF_6-resistant fully fluorinated hydrocarbon polymers.

5.5.1. Separation nozzles

Especially designed or prepared separation nozzles and assemblies thereof. The separation nozzles consist of slit-shaped, curved channels having a radius of curvature less than 1 mm (typically 0.1 to 0.05 mm), resistant to corrosion by UF_6 and having a knife-edge within the nozzle that separates the gas flowing through the nozzle into two fractions.

5.5.2. Vortex tubes

Especially designed or prepared vortex tubes and assemblies thereof. The vortex tubes are cylindrical or tapered, made of or protected by materials resistant to corrosion by UF_6, having a diameter of between 0.5 cm and 4 cm, a length to diameter ratio of 20:1 or less and with one or more tangential inlets. The tubes may be equipped with nozzle-type appendages at either or both ends.

EXPLANATORY NOTE

The feed gas enters the vortex tube tangentially at one end or through swirl vanes or at numerous tangential positions along the periphery of the tube.

5.5.3. Compressors and gas blowers

Especially designed or prepared axial, centrifugal or positive displacement compressors or gas blowers made of or protected by materials resistant to corrosion by UF_6 and with a suction volume capacity of 2 m^3/min or more of UF_6/carrier gas (hydrogen or helium) mixture.

EXPLANATORY NOTE

These compressors and gas blowers typically have a pressure ratio between 1.2:1 and 6:1.

5.5.4. Rotary shaft seals

Especially designed or prepared rotary shaft seals, with seal feed and seal exhaust connections, for sealing the shaft connecting the compressor rotor or the gas blower rotor with the driver motor so as to ensure a reliable seal against out-leakage of process gas or in-leakage of air or seal gas into the inner chamber of the compressor or gas blower which is filled with a UF_6/carrier gas mixture.

5.5.5. Heat exchangers for gas cooling

Especially designed or prepared heat exchangers made of or protected by materials resistant to corrosion by UF_6.

5.5.6. Separation element housings

Especially designed or prepared separation element housings, made of or protected by materials resistant to corrosion by UF_6, for containing vortex tubes or separation nozzles.

EXPLANATORY NOTE

These housings may be cylindrical vessels greater than 300 mm in diameter and greater than 900 mm in length, or may be rectangular vessels of comparable dimensions, and may be designed for horizontal or vertical installation.

5.5.7. Feed systems/product and tails withdrawal systems

Especially designed or prepared process systems or equipment for enrichment plants made of or protected by materials resistant to corrosion by UF_6, including:

(*a*) Feed autoclaves, ovens, or systems used for passing UF_6 to the enrichment process;

(*b*) Desublimers (or cold traps) used to remove UF_6 from the enrichment process for subsequent transfer upon heating;

(*c*) Solidification or liquefaction stations used to remove UF_6 from the enrichment process by compressing and converting UF_6 to a liquid or solid form;

(*d*) 'Product' or 'tails' stations used for transferring UF_6 into containers.

5.5.8. Header piping systems

Especially designed or prepared header piping systems, made of or protected by materials resistant to corrosion by UF_6, for handling UF_6 within the aerodynamic cascades. This piping network is normally of the 'double' header design with each stage or group of stages connected to each of the headers.

5.5.9. Vacuum systems and pumps

(*a*) Especially designed or prepared vacuum systems having a suction capacity of 5 m^3/min or more, consisting of vacuum manifolds, vacuum headers and vacuum pumps, and designed for service in UF_6-bearing atmospheres,

(*b*) Vacuum pumps especially designed or prepared for service in UF_6-bearing atmospheres and made of or protected by materials resistant to corrosion by UF_6. These pumps may use fluorocarbon seals and special working fluids.

5.5.10. Special shut-off and control valves

Especially designed or prepared manual or automated shut-off and control bellows valves made of or protected by materials resistant to corrosion by UF_6 with a diameter of 40 to 1500 mm for installation in main and auxiliary systems of aerodynamic enrichment plants.

5.5.11. UF_6 mass spectrometers/Ion sources

Especially designed or prepared magnetic or quadrupole mass spectrometers capable of taking 'on-line' samples of feed, 'product' or 'tails', from UF_6 gas streams and having all of the following characteristics:

1. Unit resolution for mass greater than 320;
2. Ion sources constructed of or lined with nichrome or monel or nickel plated;
3. Electron bombardment ionization sources;
4. Collector system suitable for isotopic analysis.

5.5.12. UF_6/carrier gas separation systems

Especially designed or prepared process systems for separating UF_6 from carrier gas (hydrogen or helium).

EXPLANATORY NOTE

These systems are designed to reduce the UF_6 content in the carrier gas to 1 ppm or less and may incorporate equipment such as:

(*a*) Cryogenic heat exchangers and cryoseparators capable of temperatures of -120°C or less, or

(*b*) Cryogenic refrigeration units capable of temperatures of -120°C or less, or

(*c*) Separation nozzle or vortex tube units for the separation of UF_6 from carrier gas, or

(*d*) UF_6 cold traps capable of temperatures of -20°C or less.

5.6. Especially designed or prepared systems, equipment and components for use in chemical exchange or ion exchange enrichment plants.

INTRODUCTORY NOTE

The slight difference in mass between the isotopes of uranium causes small changes in chemical reaction equilibria that can be used as a basis for separation of the isotopes. Two processes have been successfully developed: liquid-liquid chemical exchange and solid-liquid ion exchange.

In the liquid-liquid chemical exchange process, immiscible liquid phases (aqueous and organic) are countercurrently contacted to give the cascading effect of thousands of separation stages. The aqueous phase consists of uranium chloride in hydrochloric acid solution; the organic phase consists of an extractant containing uranium chloride in an organic solvent. The contactors employed in the separation cascade can be liquid-liquid exchange columns (such as pulsed columns with sieve plates) or liquid centrifugal contactors. Chemical conversions (oxidation and reduction) are required at both ends of the separation cascade in order to provide for the reflux requirements at each end. A major design concern is to avoid contamination of the process streams with certain metal ions. Plastic, plastic-lined (including use of fluorocarbon polymers) and/or glass-lined columns and piping are therefore used.

In the solid-liquid ion-exchange process, enrichment is accomplished by uranium adsorption/desorption on a special, very fast-acting, ion-exchange resin or adsorbent. A solution of uranium in hydrochloric acid and other chemical agents is passed through cylindrical enrichment columns containing packed beds of the adsorbent. For a continuous process, a reflux system is necessary to release the uranium from the adsorbent back into the liquid flow so that 'product' and 'tails' can be colected. This is accomplished with the use of suitable reduction/oxidation chemical agents that are fully regenerated in separate external circuits and that may be partially regenerated within the isotopic separation columns themselves. The presence of hot concentrated hydrochloric acid solutions in the process requires that the equipment be made of or protected by special corrosion-resistant materials.

5.6.1. Liquid-liquid exchange columns (Chemical exchange)

Countercurrent liquid-liquid exchange columns having mechanical power input (i.e., pulsed columns with sieve plates, reciprocating plate columns, and columns with internal turbine mixers), especially designed or prepared for uranium enrichment using the chemical exchange process. For corrosion resistance to concentrated hydrochloric acid solutions, these columns and their internals are made of or protected by suitable plastic materials (such as fluorocarbon polymers) or glass. The stage residence time of the columns is designed to be short (30 seconds or less).

5.6.2. Liquid-liquid centrifugal contactors (Chemical exchange)

Liquid-liquid centrifugal contactors especially designed or prepared for uranium enrichment using the chemical exchange process. Such contactors use rotation to achieve dispersion of the organic and aqueous streams and then centrifugal force to separate the phases. For corrosion resistance to concentrated hydrochloric acid solutions, the contactors are made of or are lined with suitable plastic materials (such as fluorocarbon polymers) or are lined with glass. The stage residence time of the centrifugal contactors is designed to be short (30 seconds or less).

5.6.3. Uranium reduction systems and equipment (Chemical exchange)

(*a*) Especially designed or prepared electrochemical reduction cells to reduce uranium from one valence state to another for uranium enrichment using the chemical exchange process. The cell materials in contact with process solutions must be corrosion resistant to concentrated hydrochloric acid solutions.

EXPLANATORY NOTE

The cell cathodic compartment must be designed to prevent re-oxidation of uranium to its higher valence state. To keep the uranium in the cathodic compartment, the cell may have an impervious diaphragm membrane constructed of special cation exchange material. The cathode consists of a suitable solid conductor such as graphite.

(*b*) Especially designed or prepared systems at the product end of the cascade for taking the U^{+4} out of the organic stream, adjusting the acid concentration and feeding to the electrochemical reduction cells.

EXPLANATORY NOTE

These systems consist of solvent extraction equipment for stripping the U^{+4} from the organic stream into an aqueous solution, evaporation and/or other equipment to accomplish solution pH adjustment and control, and pumps or other transfer devices for feeding to the electrochemical reduction cells. A major design concern is to avoid contamination of the aqueous steam with certain metal ions. Consequently, for those parts in contact with the process stream, the system is constructed of equipment made of or protected by suitable materials (such as glass, fluorocarbon polymers, polyphenyl sulfate, polyether sulfone, and resin-impregnated graphite).

5.6.4. Feed preparation systems (Chemical exchange)

Especially designed or prepared systems for producing high-purity uranium chloride feed solutions for chemical exchange uranium isotope separation plants.

EXPLANATORY NOTE

These systems consist of dissolution, solvent extraction and/or ion exchange equipment for purification and electrolytic cells for reducing the uranium U^{+6} or U^{+4} to U^{+3}. These systems produce uranium chloride solutions having only a few parts per million of metallic impurities such as chromium. iron, vanadium, molybdenum and other bivalent or higher multivalent cations. Materials of construction for portions of the system processing high-purity U^{+3} include glass, fluorocarbon polymers, polyphenyl sulfate or polyether sulfone plastic-lined and resin-impregnated graphite.

5.6.5. Uranium oxidation systems (Chemical exchange)

Especially designed or prepared systems for oxidation of U^{+3} to U^{+4} for return to the uranium isotope separation cascade in the chemical exchange enrichment process.

EXPLANATORY NOTE

These systems may incorporate equipment such as:

(*a*) Equipment for contacting chlorine and oxygen with the aqueous effluent from the isotope separation equipment and extracting the resultant U^{+4} into the stripped organic stream returning from the product end of the cascade.

(*b*) Equipment that separates water from hydrochloric acid so that the water and the concentrated hydrochloric acid may be reintroduced to the process at the proper locations.

5.6.6. Fast-reacting ion exchange resins/adsorbents (Ion exchange)

Fast-reacting ion-exchange resins or adsorbents especially designed or prepared for uranium enrichment using the ion exchange process, including porous macroreticular resins, and/or pellicular structures in which the active chemical exchange groups are limited to a coating on the surface of an inactive porous support structure, and other composite structures in any suitable form including particles or fibers. These ion exchange resins/adsorbents have diameters of 0.2 mm or less and must be chemically resistant to concentrated hydrochloric acid solutions as well as physically strong enough so as not to degrade in the exchange columns. The resins/adsorbents are especially designed to achieve very fast uranium isotope exchange kinetics (exchange rate half-time of less than 10 seconds) and are capable of operating at a temperature in the range of 100°C to 200°C.

5.6.7. Ion exchange columns (Ion exchange)

Cylindrical columns greater than 1000 mm in diameter for containing and supporting packed beds of ion exchange resin/adsorbent, especially designed or prepared for uranium enrichment using the ion exchange process. These columns are made of or protected by materials (such as titanium or fluorocarbon plastics) resistant to corrosion by concentrated hydrochloric acid solutions and are capable of operating at a temperature in the range of 100°C to 200°C and pressures above 0.7 MPa (102 psia).

5.6.8. Ion exchange reflux systems (Ion exchange)

(*a*) Especially designed or prepared chemical or electrochemical reduction systems for regeneration of the chemical reducing agent(s) used in ion exchange uranium enrichment cascades.

(*b*) Especially designed or prepared chemical or electrochemical oxidation systems for regeneration of the chemical oxidizing agent(s) used in ion exchange uranium enrichment cascades.

EXPLANATORY NOTE

The ion exchange enrichment process may use, for example, trivalent titanium (Ti^{+3}) as a reducing cation in which case the reduction system would regenerate Ti^{+3} by reducing Ti^{+4}.

The process may use, for example, trivalent iron (Fe^{+3}) as an oxidant in which case the oxidation system should regenerate Fe^{+3} by oxidizing Fe^{+2}.

5.7. Especially designed or prepared systems, equipment and components for use in laser-based enrichment plants.

INTRODUCTORY NOTE

Present systems for enrichment processes using lasers fall into two categories: those in which the process medium is atomic uranium vapor and those in which the process medium is the vapor of a uranium compound. Common nomenclature for such processes include: first category—atomic vapor laser isotope separation (AVLIS or SILVA); second category—molecular laser isotope separation (MLIS or MOLIS) and chemical reaction by isotope selective laser activation (CRISLA). The systems, equipment and components for laser enrichment plants embrace: (*a*) devices to feed uranium-metal vapor (for selective photo-ionization) or devices to feed the vapor of a uranium compound (for photodissociation or chemical activation); (*b*) devices to collect enriched and depleted uranium metal as 'product' and 'tails' in the first category, and devices to collect dissociated or reacted compounds as 'product' and unaffected material as 'tails' in the second category; (*c*) process laser systems to selectively excite the uranium-235 species; and (*d*) feed preparation and product conversion equipment. The complexity of the spectroscopy of uranium atoms and compounds may require incorporation of any of a number of available laser technologies.

EXPLANATORY NOTE

Many of the items listed in this section come into direct contact with uranium metal vapor or liquid or with process gas consisting of UF_6 or a mixture of UF_6 and other gases. All surfaces that come into contact with the uranium or UF_6 are wholly made of or protected by corrosion-resistant materials. For the purposes of the section relating to laser-based enrichment items, the materials resistant to corrosion by the vapor or liquid of uranium metal or uranium alloys include yttria-coated graphite and tantalum; and the materials resistant to corrosion by UF_6 include copper, stainless steel, aluminium, aluminium alloys, nickel or alloys containing 60% or more nickel and UF_6-resistant fully fluorinated hydrocarbon polymers.

5.7.1. Uranium vaporization systems (AVLIS)

Especially designed or prepared uranium vaporization systems which contain high-power strip or scanning electron beam guns with a delivered power on the target of more than 2.5 kW/cm.

5.7.2. Liquid uranium metal handling systems (AVLIS)

Especially designed or prepared liquid metal handling systems for molten uranium or uranium alloys, consisting of crucibles and cooling equipment for the crucibles.

EXPLANATORY NOTE

The crucibles and other parts of this system that come into contact with molten uranium or uranium alloys are made of or protected by materials of suitable corrosion and heat resistance. Suitable materials include tantalum, yttria-coated graphite, graphite coated with other rare earth oxides (see INFCIRC/254/Rev.1/Part 2, item 2.7) or mixtures thereof.

5.7.3. Uranium metal 'product' and 'tails' collector assemblies (AVLIS)

Especially designed or prepared 'product' and 'tails' collector assemblies for uranium metal in liquid or solid form.

EXPLANATORY NOTE

Components for these assemblies are made of or protected by materials resistant to the heat and corrosion of uranium metal vapor or liquid (such as yttria-coated graphite or tantalum) and may include pipes, valves, fittings, 'gutters', feed-throughs, heat exchangers and collector plates for magnetic, electrotatic or other separation methods.

5.7.4 Separator module housings (AVLIS)

Especially designed or prepared cylindrical or rectangular vessels for containing the uranium metal vapor source, the electron beam gun, and the 'product' and 'tails' collectors.

EXPLANATORY NOTE

These housings have multiplicity of ports for electrical and water feed-throughs, laser beam windows, vacuum pump connections and instrumentation diagnostics and monitoring. They have provisions for opening and closure to allow refurbishment of internal components.

5.7.5. Supersonic expansion nozzles (MLIS)

Especially designed or prepared supersonic expansion nozzles for cooling mixtures of UF_6 and carrier gas to 150 K or less and which are corrosion resistant to UF_6.

5.7.6. Uranium pentafluoride product collectors (MLIS)

Especially designed or prepared uranium pentafluoride (UF_5) solid product collectors consisting of filter, impact, or cyclone-type collectors, or combinations thereof, and which are corrosion resistant to the UF_5/UF_6 environment.

5.7.7. UF_6/carrier gas compressors (MLIS)

Especially designed or prepared compressors for UF_6/carrier gas mixtures, designed for long term operation in a UF_6 environment. The components of these compressors that come into contact with process gas are made of or protected by materials resistant to corrosion by UF_6.

5.7.8. Rotary shaft seals (MLIS)

Especially designed or prepared rotary shaft seals, with seal feed and seal exhaust connections, for sealing the shaft connecting the compressor rotor with the driver motor so as to ensure a reliable seal against out-leakage of process gas or in-leakage of air or seal gas into the inner chamber of the compressor which is filled with a UF_6/carrier gas mixture.

5.7.9. Fluorination systems (MLIS)

Especially designed or prepared systems for fluorinating UF_5 (solid) to UF_6 (gas).

EXPLANATORY NOTE

These systems are designed to fluorinate the collected UF_5 powder to UF_6 for subsequent collection in product containers or for transfer as feed to MLIS units for additional enrichment. In one approach, the fluorination reaction may be accomplished with the isotope separation system to react and recover directly off the product collectors. In another approach, the UF_5 powder may be removed/transferred from the 'product' collectors into a suitable reaction vessel (e.g., fluidized-bed reactor, screw reactor or flame tower) for fluorination. In both approaches, equipment for storage and transfer of fluorine (or other suitable fluorinating agents) and for collection and transfer of UF_6 are used.

5.7.10. UF_6 mass spectrometers/ion sources (MLIS)

Especially designed or prepared magnetic or quadruple mass spectrometers capable of taking 'on-line' samples of feed, 'product' or 'tails', from UF_6 gas streams and having all of the following characteristics:

1. Unit resolution for mass greater than 320;
2. Ion sources constructed of or lined with nichrome or monel or nickel plated;
3. Electron bombardment ionization sources;
4. Collector system suitable for isotopic analysis.

5.7.11. Feed systems/product and tails withdrawal systems (MLIS)

Especially designed or prepared process systems or equipment for enrichment plants made of or protected by materials resistant to corrosion by UF_6, including:

(*a*) Feed autoclaves, ovens, or systems used for passing UF_6 to the enrichment process;

(*b*) Desublimers (or cold traps) used to remove UF_6 from the enrichment process for subsequent transfer upon heating;

(*c*) Solidification or liquefaction stations used to remove UF_6 from the enrichment process by compressing and converting UF_6 to a liquid or solid form:

(*d*) 'Product' or 'tails' stations used for transferring UF_6 into containers.

5.7.12. UF_6/carrier gas separation systems (MLIS)

Especially designed or prepared process systems for separating UF_6 from carrier gas. The carrier gas may be nitrogen, argon, or other gas.

EXPLANATORY NOTE

These systems may incorporate equipment such as:

(*a*) Cryogenic heat exchangers or cryoseparators capable of temperatures of -120°C or less, or

(*b*) Cryogenic refrigeration units capable of temperatures of -120°C or less, or

(*c*) UF_6 cold traps capable of temperatures of -20°C or less.

5.7.13. Laser systems (AVLIS, MLIS and CRISLA)

Lasers or laser systems especially designed or prepared for the separation of uranium isotopes.

EXPLANATORY NOTE

The lasers and laser components of importance in laser-based enrichment processes include those identified in item 3.6 of INFCIRC/254/Rev. 1/ Part 2. The laser system for the AVLIS process usually consists of two lasers: a copper vapor laser and a dye laser. The laser system for MLIS usually consists of a CO_2 or excimer laser and a multi-pass optical cell with revolving mirrors at both ends. Lasers or laser systems for both processes require a spectrum frequency stabilizer for operation over extended periods of time.

5.8. Especially designed or prepared systems, equipment and components for use in plasma separation enrichment plants.

INTRODUCTORY NOTE

In the plasma separation process, a plasma of uranium ions passes through an electric field tuned to the ^{235}U ion resonance frequency so that they preferentially absorb energy and increase the diameter of their corkscrew-like orbits. Ions with a large-diameter path are trapped to produce a product enriched in ^{235}U. The plasma, which is made by ionizing uranium vapor, is contained in a vacuum chamber with a high-strength magnetic field produced by a superconducting magnet. The main technological systems of the process include the uranium plasma generation system, the separator module with superconducting magnet (see item 3.10 of INFCIRC/254/Rev. 1/Part 2), and metal removal systems for the collection of 'product' and 'tails'.

5.8.1. Microwave power sources and antennae

Especially designed or prepared microwave power sources and antennae for producing or accelerating ions and having the following characteristics: greater than 30 GHz frequency and greater than 50 kW mean power output for ion production.

5.8.2. Ion excitation coils

Especially designed or prepared radio frequency ion excitation coils for frequencies of more than 100 kHz and capable of handling more than 40 kW mean power.

5.8.3. Uranium plasma generation systems

Especially designed or prepared systems for the generation of uranium plasma, which may contain high-power strip or scanning electron beam guns with a delivered power on the target of more than 2.5 kW/cm.

5.8.4. Liquid uranium metal handling systems

Especially designed or prepared liquid metal handling systems for molten uranium or uranium alloys, consisting of crucibles and cooling equipment for the crucibles.

EXPLANATORY NOTE

The crucibles and other parts of this system that come into contact with molten uranium or uranium alloys are made of or protected by materials of suitable corrosion and heat resistance. Suitable materials include tantalum, yttria-coated graphite, graphite coated with other rare earth oxides (see INFCIRC/254/Rev. 1/Part 2, item 2.7) or mixtures thereof.

5.8.5. Uranium metal 'product' and 'tails' collector assemblies

Especially designed or prepared 'product' and 'tails' collector assemblies for uranium metal in solid form. These collector assemblies are made of or protected by materials resistant to the heat and corrosion of uranium metal vapor, such as yttria-coated graphite or tantalum.

5.8.6. Separator module housings

Cylindrical vessels especially designed or prepared for use in plasma separation enrichment plants for containing the uranium plasma source, radio-frequency drive coil and the 'product' and 'tails' collectors.

EXPLANATORY NOTE

These housings have a multiplicity of ports for electrical feed-throughs, diffusion pump connections and instrumentation diagnostics and monitoring. They have provisions for opening and closure to allow for refurbishment of internal components and are constructed of a suitable non-magnetic material such as stainless steel.

5.9. Especially designed or prepared systems, equipment and components for use in electromagnetic enrichment plants.

INTRODUCTORY NOTE

In the electromagnetic process, uranium metal ions produced by ionization of a salt feed material (typically UCl_4) are accelerated and passed through a magnetic field that has the effect of causing the ions of different isotopes to follow different paths. The major components of an electromagnetic isotope separator include: a magnetic field for ion-beam diversion/separation of the isotopes, an ion source with its acceleration system, and a collection system for the separated ions. Auxiliary systems for the process include the magnet power supply system, the ion source high-voltage power supply system, the vacuum system, and extensive chemical handling systems for recovery of product and cleaning/recycling of components.

5.9.1. Electromagnetic isotope separators

Electromagnetic isotope separators especially designed or prepared for the separation of uranium isotopes, and equipment and components therefor, including:

(*a*) Ion sources

Especially designed or prepared single or multiple uranium ion sources consisting of a vapor source, ionizer, and beam accelerator, constructed of suitable materials such as graphite, stainless steel, or copper, and capable of providing a total ion beam current of 50 mA or greater.

(*b*) Ion collectors

Collector plates consisting of two or more slits and pockets especially designed or prepared for collection of enriched and depleted uranium ion beams and constructed of suitable materials such as graphite or stainless steel.

(*c*) Vacuum housings

Especially designed or prepared vacuum housings for uranium electromagnetic separators, constructed of suitable non-magnetic materials such as stainless steel and designed for operation at pressures of 0.1 Pa or lower.

EXPLANATORY NOTE

The housings are specially designed to contain the ion sources, collector plates and water-cooled liners and have provision for diffusion pump connections and opening and closure for removal and reinstallation of these components.

(*d*) Magnet pole pieces

Especially designed or prepared magnet pole pieces having a diameter greater than 2 m used to maintain a constant magnetic field within an electromagnetic isotope separator and to transfer the magnetic field between adjoining separators.

5.9.2. High voltage power supplies

Especially designed or prepared high-voltage power supplies for ion sources, having all of the following characteristics: capable of continuous operation, output voltage of 20,000 V or greater, output current of 1 A or greater, and voltage regulation of better than 0.01% over a time period of 8 hours.

5.9.3. Magnet power supplies

Especially designed or prepared high-power, direct current magnet power supplies having all of the following characteristics: capable of continuously producing a current output of 500 A or greater at a voltage of 100 V or greater and with a current or voltage regulation better than 0.01% over a period of 8 hours.

6. Plants for the production of heavy water, deuterium and deuterium compounds and equipment especially designed or prepared therefor

INTRODUCTORY NOTE

Heavy water can be produced by a variety of processes. However, the two processes that have proven to be commercially viable are the water-hydrogen sulphide exchange process (GS process) and the ammonia-hydrogen exchange process.

The GS process is based upon the exchange of hydrogen and deuterium between water and hydrogen sulphide within a series of towers which are operated with the top section cold and the bottom section hot. Water flows down the towers while the hydrogen sulphide gas circulates from the bottom to the top of the towers. A series of perforated trays are used to promote mixing between the gas and the water. Deuterium migrates to the water at low temperatures and to the hydrogen sulphide at high temperatures. Gas or water, enriched in deuterium, is removed from the first stage towers at the junction of the hot and cold sections and the process is repeated in subsequent stage towers. the product of the last stage, water enriched up to 30% in deuterium, is sent to a distillation unit to produce reactor grade heavy water; i.e., 99.75% deuterium oxide.

The ammonia-hydrogen exchange process can extract deuterium from synthesis gas through contact with liquid ammonia in the presence of a catalyst. The synthesis gas is fed into exchange towers and to an ammonia converter. Inside the towers the gas flows from the bottom to the top while the liquid ammonia flows from the top to the bottom. The deuterium is stripped from the hydrogen in the synthesis gas and concentrated in the ammonia. The ammonia then flows into an ammonia cracker at the bottom of the tower while the gas flows into an ammonia converter at the top. Further enrichment takes place in subsequent stages and reactor grade heavy water is produced through final distillation. The synthesis gas feed can be provided by an ammonia plant that, in turn, can be constructed in association with a heavy water ammonia-hydrogen exchange plant. The ammonia-hydrogen exchange process can also use ordinary water as a feed source of deuterium.

Many of the key equipment items for heavy water production plants using GS or the ammonia-hydrogen exchange processes are common to several segments of the chemical and petroleum industries. This is particularly so for small plants using the GS process. However, few of the items are available 'off-the-shelf'. The GS and ammonia-hydrogen processes require the handling of large quantities of flammable, corrosive and toxic fluids at elevated pressures. Accordingly, in establishing the design and operating standards for plants and equipment using these processes, careful attention to the materials selection and specifications is required to ensure long service life with high safety and reliability factors. The choice of scale is primarily a function of economics and need. Thus, most of the equipment items would be prepared according to the requirements of the customer.

Finally, it should be noted that, in both the GS and the ammonia-hydrogen exchange processes, items of equipment which individually are not especially designed or prepared for heavy water production can be assembled into systems which are especially designed or prepared for producing heavy water. The catalyst production system used in the ammonia-hydrogen exchange process and water distillation systems used for the final concentration of heavy water to reactor-grade in either process are examples of such systems.

The items of equipment which are especially designed or prepared for the production of heavy water utilizing either the water-hydrogen sulphide exchange process or the ammonia-hydrogen exchange process include the following:

6.1. Water-Hydrogen Sulphide Exchange Towers

Exchange towers fabricated from fine carbon steel (such as ASTM A516) with diameters of 6 m (20 ft) to 9 m (30 ft), capable of operating at pressures greater than or equal to 2 MPa (300 psi) and with a corrosion allowance of 6 mm or greater, especially designed or prepared for heavy water production utilizing the water-hydrogen sulphide exchange process.

6.2. Blowers and Compressors

Single stage, low head (i.e., 0.2 MPa or 30 psi) centrifugal blowers or compressors for hydrogen-sulphide gas circulation (i.e., gas containing more than 70% H_2S) especially designed or prepared for heavy water production utilizing the water-hydrogen sulphide exchange process. These blowers or compressors have a throughput capacity greater than or equal to 56 m^3/second (120,000 SCFM) while operating at pressures greater than or equal to 1.8 MPa (260 psi) suction and have seals designed for wet H_2S service.

6.3. Ammonia-Hydrogen Exchange Towers

Ammonia-hydrogen exchange towers greater than or equal to 35 m (114.3 ft) in height with diameters of 1.5 m (4.9 ft) to 2.5 m (8.2 ft) capable of operating at pressures greater than 15 MPa (2225 psi) especially designed or prepared for heavy water production utilizing the ammonia-hydrogen exchange process. These towers also have at least one flanged, axial opening of the same diameter as the cylindrical part through which the tower internals can be inserted or withdrawn.

6.4. Tower Internals and Stage Pumps

Tower internals and stage pumps especially designed or prepared for towers for heavy water production utilizing the ammonia-hydrogen exchange process. Tower internals include especially designed stage contactors which promote intimate gas/liquid contact. Stage pumps include especially designed submersible pumps for circulation of liquid ammonia within a contacting stage internal to the stage towers.

6.5. Ammonia Crackers

Ammonia crackers with operating pressures greater than or equal to 3 MPa (450 psi) especially designed or prepared for heavy water production utilizing the ammonia-hydrogen exchange process.

6.6. Infrared Absorption Analyzers

Infrared absorption analyzers capable of 'on-line' hydrogen/deuterium ratio analysis where deuterium concentrations are equal to or greater than 90%.

6.7. Catalytic Burners

Catalytic burners for the conversion of enriched deuterium gas into heavy water especially designed or prepared for heavy water production utilizing the ammonia-hydrogen exchange process.

7. Plants for the conversion of uranium and equipment especially designed or prepared therefor

INTRODUCTORY NOTE

Uranium conversion plants and systems may perform one or more transformations from one uranium chemical species to another, including: conversion of uranium ore concentrates to UO_3, conversion of UO_3 to UO_2, conversion of uranium oxides to UF_4 or UF_6, conversion of UF_4 to UF_6, conversion of UF_6 to UF_4, conversion of UF_4 to uranium metal, and conversion of uranium fluorides to UO_2. Many of the key equipment items for uranium conversion plants are common to several segments of the chemical process industry. For example, the types of equipment employed in these processes may include: furnaces, rotary kilns, fluidized bed reactors, flame tower reactors, liquid centrifuges, distillation columns and liquid-liquid extraction columns. However, few of the items are available 'off-the-shelf'; most would be prepared according to the requirements and specifications of the customer. In some instances, special design and construction considerations are required to address the corrosive properties of some of the chemicals handled (HF, F_2, ClF_3, and uranium fluorides). Finally, it should be noted that, in all of the uranium conversion processes, items of equipment which individually are not especially designed or prepared for uranium conversion can be assembled into systems which are especially designed or prepared for use in uranium conversion.

7.1. Especially designed or prepared systems for the conversion of uranium ore concentrates to UO_3

EXPLANATORY NOTE

Conversion of uranium ore concentrates to UO_3 can be performed by first dissolving the ore in nitric acid and extracting purified uranyl nitrate using a solvent such as tributyl phosphate. Next, the uranyl nitrate is converted to UO_3 either by concentration and denitration or by neutralization with gaseous ammonia to produce ammonium diuranate with subsequent filtering, drying, and calcining.

7.2. Especially designed or prepared systems for the conversion of UO_3 to UF_6

EXPLANATORY NOTE

Conversion of UO_3 to UF_6 can be performed directly by fluorination. The process requires a source of fluorine gas or chlorine trifluoride.

7.3. Especially designed or prepared systems for the conversion of UO_3 to UO_2

EXPLANATORY NOTE

Conversion of UO_3 to UO_2 can be performed through reduction of UO_3 with cracked ammonia gas or hydrogen.

7.4. Especially designed or prepared systems for the conversion of UO_2 to UF_4

EXPLANATORY NOTE

Conversion of UO_2 to UF_4 can be performed by reacting UO_2 with hydrogen flouride gas (HF) at 300–500°C.

7.5. Especially designed or prepared systems for the conversion of UF_4 to UF_6

EXPLANATORY NOTE

Conversion of UF_4 to UF_6 is performed by exothermic reaction with fluorine in a tower reactor. UF_6 is condensed from the hot effluent gases by passing the effluent stream through a cold trap cooled to -10°C. The process requires a source of fluorine gas.

7.6. Especially designed or prepared systems for the conversion of UF_4 to U metal

EXPLANATORY NOTE

Conversion of UF_4 to U metal is performed by reduction with magnesium (large batches) or calcium (small batches). The reaction is carried out at temperatures above the melting point of uranium (1130°C).

7.7. Especially designed or prepared systems for the conversion of UF_5 to UO_2

EXPLANATORY NOTE

Conversion of UF_6 to UO_2 can be performed by one of three processes. In the first, UF_6 is reduced and hydrolyzed to UO_2 using hydrogen and steam. In the second, UF_6 is hydrolyzed by solution in water, ammonia is added to precipitate ammonium diuranate, and the diuranate is reduced to UO_2 with hydrogen at 820°C. In the third process, gaseous UF_6, CO_2, and NH_3 are combined in water, precipitating ammonium uranyl carbonate. The ammonium uranyl carbonate is combined with steam and hydrogen at 500–600°C to yield UO_2.

UF_6 to UO_2 conversion is often performed as the first stage of a fuel fabrication plant.

7.8. Especially designed or prepared systems for the conversion of UF_6 to UF_4

EXPLANATORY NOTE

Conversion of UF_6 to UF_4 is performed by reduction with hydrogen.

Source: IAEA document INFCIRC/254/Rev. 1/Part 1/Mod. 2, Annex (amended), IAEA, Vienna, Apr. 1994.

GUIDELINES FOR TRANSFERS OF NUCLEAR-RELATED DUAL-USE EQUIPMENT, MATERIAL AND RELATED TECHNOLOGY (WARSAW GUIDELINES)

Objective

1. With the objective of averting the proliferation of nuclear weapons, suppliers have had under consideration procedures in relation to the transfer of certain equipment, material, and related technology that could make a major contribution to a 'nuclear explosive activity' or an 'unsafeguarded nuclear fuel-cycle activity'. In this connection, suppliers have agreed on the following principles, common definitions, and an export control list of equipment, material, and related technology. The Guidelines are not designed to impede international cooperation as long as such cooperation will not contribute to a nuclear explosive activity or an unsafeguarded nuclear fuel-cycle activity'. Suppliers intend to implement the Guidelines in accordance with national legislation and international commitments.

Basic Principle

2. Suppliers should not authorize transfers of equipment, material, or related technology identified in the Annex:

– for use in a non-nuclear-weapon state in a nuclear explosive activity or an unsafeguarded nuclear fuel cycle activity, or

– in general, when there is an unacceptable risk of diversion to such an activity, or when the transfers are contrary to the objective of averting the proliferation of nuclear weapons.

Explanation of Terms

3. (*a*) 'Nuclear explosive activity' includes research on or development, design, manufacture, construction, testing or maintenance of any nuclear explosive device or components or subsystems of such a device.

(*b*) 'Unsafeguarded nuclear fuel-cycle activity' includes research on or development, design, manufacture, construction, operation or maintenance of any reactor, critical facility, conversion plant, fabrication plant, reprocessing plant, plant for the separation of isotopes of source or special fissionable material, or separate storage installation, where there is no obligation to accept International Atomic Energy Agency (IAEA) safeguards at the relevant facility or installation, existing or future, when it contains any source or special fissionable material; or of any heavy water production plant where there is no obligation to accept IAEA safeguards on any nuclear material produced by or used in connection with any heavy water produced therefrom; or where any such obligation is not met.

Establishment of Export Licensing Procedures

4. Suppliers should establish export licensing procedures for the transfer of equipment, material, and related technology identified in the Annex. These procedures should include enforcement measures for violations. In considering whether to authorize such transfers, suppliers should exercise prudence in order to carry out the Basic Principle and should take relevant factors into account, including:

(*a*) Whether the recipient state is a party to the Nuclear Non-Proliferation Treaty (NPT) or to the Treaty for the Prohibition of Nuclear Weapons in Latin America (Treaty of Tlatelolco), or to a similar international legally-binding nuclear non-proliferation agreement, and has an IAEA safeguards agreement in force applicable to all its peaceful nuclear activities;

(*b*) Whether any recipient state that is not party to the NPT, Treaty of Tlatelolco, or a similar international legally-binding nuclear non-proliferation agreement has any facilities or installations listed in paragraph 3(*b*) above that are operational or being designed or constructed that are not, or will not be, subject to IAEA safeguards;

(*c*) Whether the equipment, material, or related technology to be transferred is appropriate for the stated end-use and whether that stated end-use is appropriate for the end-user;

(*d*) Whether the equipment, material, or related technology to be transferred is to be used in research on or development, design, manufacture, construction, operation, or maintenance of any reprocessing or enrichment facility;

(*e*) Whether governmental actions, statements, and policies of the recipient state are supportive of nuclear non-proliferation and whether the recipient state is in compliance with its international obligations in the field of nonproliferation;

(*f*) Whether the recipients have been engaged in clandestine or illegal procurement activities; and

(*g*) Whether a transfer has not been authorized to the end-user or whether the end-user has diverted for purposes inconsistent with the Guidelines any transfer previously authorized.

Conditions for Transfers

5. In the process of determining that the transfer will not pose any unacceptable risk of diversion, in accordance with the Basic Principle and to meet the objectives of the Guidelines, the supplier should obtain, before authorizing the transfer and in a manner consistent with its national law and practices, the following:

(*a*) a statement from the end-user specifying the uses and end-use locations of the proposed transfers; and

(*b*) an assurance explicitly stating that the proposed transfer or any replica thereof will not be used in any nuclear explosive activity or unsafeguarded nuclear fuel-cycle activity.

Consent Rights over Retransfers

6. Before authorizing the transfer of equipment, material, or related technology identified in the Annex to a country not adhering to the Guidelines, suppliers should obtain assurances that their consent will be secured, in a manner consistent with their national law and practices, prior to any retransfer to a third country of the equipment, material, or related technology, or any replica thereof.

Concluding Provisions

7. The supplier reserves to itself discretion as to the application of the Guidelines to other items of significance in addition to those identified in the Annex, and as to the applica-

tion of other conditions for transfer that it may consider necessary in addition to those provided for in paragraph 5 of the Guidelines.

8. In furtherance of the effective implementation of the Guidelines, suppliers should, as necessary and appropriate, exchange relevant information and consult with other states adhering to the Guidelines.

9. In the interest of international peace and security, the adherence of all states to the Guidelines would be welcome.

ANNEX. LIST OF NUCLEAR-RELATED DUAL-USE EQUIPMENT AND MATERIALS AND RELATED TECHNOLOGY

Note: The International System of Units (SI) is used in this Annex. In many places, the approximately equivalent physical quantity in English units is given in parentheses () after the SI quantity. In all cases the physical quantity defined in SI units should be considered the official recommended control value. However, some machine tool parameters are given in their customary units, which are not SI.

Commonly used abbreviations (and their prefixes denoting size) in this Annex are as follows.

A—ampere(s)
°C—degree(s) Celsius
Ci—curie(s)
cm^3—cubic centimeter(s)
dB—decibel(s)
dBm—decibel referred to 1 milliwatt
g—gram(s); also, acceleration of gravity (9.81 m/second^2)
GBq—gigabecquerel(s)
GHz—gigahertz
Hz—hertz
J—joule(s)
K—kelvin
keV—thousand electron volts(s)
kg—kilogram(s)
kHz—kilohertz
kN—kilonewton(s)
kPa—kilopascal(s)
kW—kilowatt(s)
m—meter(s)
MeV—million electron volt(s)
MHz—megahertz
MPa—megapascal(s)
MW—megawatt(s)
µF—microfarad(s)
µm—micrometer(s)
µs—microsecond(s)
mm—millimeter(s)
N—newton(s)
nm—nanometer(s)
ns—nanosecond(s)
nH—nanohenry(ies)
ps—picosecond(s)
RMS—root mean square
TIR—total indicator reading
W—watt(s)

General Note

The following paragraphs are applied to the List of Nuclear-Related Dual-Use Equipment, Material, and Related Technology.

1. The description of any item on the List includes that item in either new or second-hand condition.

2. When the description of any item on the List contains no qualifications or specifications, it is regarded as including all varieties of that item. Category captions are only for convenience in reference and do not affect the interpretation of item definitions.

3. The object of these controls should not be defeated by the transfer of any non-controlled item (including plants) containing one or more controlled components when the controlled component or components are the principal element of the item and can feasibly be removed or used for other purposes.

Note:

In judging whether the controlled component or components are to be considered the principal element, governments should weigh the factors of quantity, value, and technological know-how involved and other special circumstances which might establish the controlled component or components as the principal element of the item being procured.

4. The object of these controls should not be defeated by the transfer of component parts. Each government will take such action as it can to achieve this aim and will continue to seek a workable definition for component parts, which could be used by all the suppliers.

Technology controls

The transfer of 'technology' directly associated with any items in the List will be subject to as great a degree of scrutiny and control as will the equipment itself, to the extent permitted by national legislation.

Controls on 'technology' transfer do not apply to information 'in the public domain' or to 'basic scientific research'.

Note:— The item on machine tools contains specific controls on technology.

Statement of understanding

The approval of any List item for export also authorizes the export to the same end user of the minimum technology required for the installation, operation, maintenance, and repair of the item.

Definitions

'Technology'—means specific information required for the 'development', 'production', or 'use' of any item contained in the List. This information may take the form of 'technical data' or 'technical assistance'.

'basic scientific research'—Experimental or theoretical work undertaken principally to acquire new knowledge of the fundamental principles of phenomena and observable facts, not primarily directed toward a specific practical aim or objective.

'development'—is related to all phases before 'production' such as:

- design
- design research
- design analysis
- design concepts
- assembly and testing of prototypes
- pilot production schemes
- design data
- process of transforming design data into a product
- configuration design
- integration design
- layouts

'in the public domain'—'In the public domain', as it applies herein, means technology that has been made available without restrictions upon its further dissemination. (Copyright restrictions do not remove technology from being in the public domain.)

'production'—means all production phases such as:

- construction
- production engineering
- manufacture
- integration
- assembly (mounting)
- inspection
- testing
- quality assurance

'Specially designed software'
The minimum 'operating systems', 'diagnostic systems', 'maintenance systems', and 'application software' necessary to be executed on particular equipment to perform the function for which it was designed. To make other, incompatible equipment perform the same function requires:

(*a*) modification of this 'software' or
(*b*) addition of 'programs'.

'technical assistance'—'Technical assistance' may take forms such as: instruction, skills, training, working knowledge, consulting services.

NOTE: 'Technical assistance' may involve transfer of 'technical data'.

'technical data'— 'Technical data' may take forms such as blueprints, plans, diagrams, models, formulae, engineering designs and specifications, manuals and instructions written or recorded on other media or devices such as disk, tape, read-only memories.

'use'—Operation, installation (including on-site installation), maintenance (checking), repair, overhaul, and refurbishing.

ANNEX CONTENTS

1. INDUSTRIAL EQUIPMENT
1.1. Spin-forming and flow-forming machines
1.2. 'Numerical control' units. . . machine tools
1.3. Dimensional inspection systems
1.4. Vacuum induction furnaces
1.5. Isostatic presses
1.6. Robots and end effectors
1.7. Vibration test equipment
1.8. Furnaces - arc remelt, electron beam, and plasma

2. MATERIALS
2.1. Aluminum, high-strength
2.2. Beryllium
2.3. Bismuth (high purity)
2.4. Boron (isotopically enriched in boron-10)
2.5. Calcium (high purity)
2.6. Chlorine trifluoride
2.7. Crucibles made of materials resistant to liquid actinide metals
2.8. Fibrous and filamentary materials
2.9. Hafnium
2.10. Lithium (isotopically enriched in lithium-6)
2.11. Magnesium (high purity)
2.12. Maraging steel, high-strength
2.13. Radium
2.14. Titanium alloys
2.15. Tungsten
2.16. Zirconium

3. URANIUM ISOTOPE SEPARATION EQUIPMENT AND COMPONENTS
3.1. Electrolytic cells for fluorine production
3.2. Rotor and bellows equipment
3.3. Centrifugal multiplane balancing machines
3.4. Filament winding machines
3.5. Frequency changers
3.6. Lasers, laser amplifiers, and oscillators
3.7. Mass spectrometers and mass spectrometer ion sources
3.8. Pressure measuring instruments, corrosion-resistant
3.9. Valves, corrosion-resistant
3.10. Superconducting solenoidal electromagnets
3.11. Vacuum pumps
3.12. Direct current high-power supplies (100 V or greater)
3.13. High-voltage direct current power supplies (20,000 V or greater)
3.14. Electromagnetic isotope separators

4. HEAVY WATER PRODUCTION PLANT RELATED EQUIPMENT
(Other Than Trigger List Items)
4.1. Specialized packings for water separation
4.2. Pumps for potassium amide/liquid ammonia
4.3. Water-hydrogen sulfide exchange tray columns
4.4. Hydrogen-cryogenic distillation columns
4.5. Ammonia converters or synthesis reactors

5. IMPLOSION SYSTEMS DEVELOPMENT EQUIPMENT
5.1. Flash x-ray equipment
5.2. Multistage light gas guns/high-velocity guns
5.3. Mechanical rotating mirror cameras
5.4. Electronic streak and framing cameras and tubes
5.5. Specialized instrumentation for hydrodynamic experiments

6. EXPLOSIVES AND RELATED EQUIPMENT
6.1. Detonators and multipoint initiation systems
6.2. Electronic components for firing sets
6.2.1. Switching devices
6.2.2. Capacitors
6.3. Firing sets and equivalent high-current pulsers (for controlled detonators)
6.4. High explosives relevant to nuclear weapons

7. NUCLEAR TESTING EQUIPMENT AND COMPONENTS
7.1. Oscilloscopes
7.2. Photomultiplier tubes
7.3. Pulse generators (high speed)

8. OTHER
8.1. Neutron generator systems
8.2. General nuclear related equipment
8.2.1. Remote manipulators
8.2.2. Radiation shielding windows
8.2.3. Radiation-hardened TV cameras
8.3. Tritium, tritium compounds, and mixtures
8.4. Tritium facilities or plants and components therefore
8.5. Platinized carbon catalysts
8.6. Helium
8.7. Alpha-emitting radionuclides

APPENDIX: DETAILED MACHINE TOOL SPECIFICATIONS

LIST OF OF NUCLEAR-RELATED DUAL-USE EQUIPMENT AND MATERIALS AND RELATED TECHNOLOGY

1. Industrial Equipment

1.1. Spin-forming and flow-forming machines which

a. according to the manufacturer's technical specification, can be equipped with 'numerical control' units or a computer control; and

b. with two or more axes that can be coordinated simultaneously for 'contouring control,'

and precision rotor-forming mandrels designed to form cylindrical rotors of inside diameter between 75 mm (3 in.) and 400 mm (16 in.) and specially designed software therefor.

Note: The only spin-forming machines controlled by this entry are those combining the function of spin-forming and flow-forming.

1.2. 'Numerical control' units, specially designed 'motion control boards' for 'numerical control' applications on machine tools, 'numerically controlled' machine tools, specially designed 'software,' and technology as follows.

Detailed specifications of the equipment are shown in the Appendix.

1.3. Dimensional inspection machines, devices, or systems, as follows, specially designed software therefor.

(*a*) Computer controlled or numerically controlled dimensional inspection machines having both of the following characteristics:

(1) two or more axes; *and*

(2) a one-dimensional length 'measurement uncertainty' equal to or less (better) than (1.25 + L/1000) μm tested with a probe of an 'accuracy' of less (better) than 0.2 μm (L is the measured length in millimeters)(Ref: VDI/VDE 2617 parts 1 and 2);

(*b*) Linear and angular displacement measuring devices, as follows:

(1) linear measuring instruments having any of the following characteristics:

(i) non-contact type measuring systems with a 'resolution' equal to or less (better) than 0.2 μm within a measuring range up to 0.2 mm;

(ii) linear variable differential transformer (LVDT) systems having both of the following characteristics:

(A) 'linearity' equal to or less (better) than 0.1% within a measuring range up to 5 mm; and

(B) drift equal to or less (better) than 0.1% per day at a standard ambient test room temperature ±1 K; or

(iii) measuring systems that have both of the following characteristics:

(A) contain a 'laser'; *and*

(B) maintain for at least 12 hours, over a temperature range of ±1 K around a standard temperature and a standard pressure:

(1) a 'resolution' over their full scale of 0.1 μm or better; *and*

(2) with a 'measurement uncertainty' equal to our less (better) than (0.2 + L/2000) μm (L is the measured length in millimeters); *except* measuring interferometer systems, without closed or open loop feedback, containing a 'laser' to measure slide movement errors of machine tools, dimensional inspection machines, or similar equipment;

(2) angular measuring instruments having an 'angular position deviation' equal to or less (better) than 0.00025°;

Note: The sub-item (*b*)(2) of this item does not control optical instruments, such as autocollimators, using collimated light to detect angular displacement of a mirror.

(*c*) Systems for simultaneously linear-angular inspection of hemishells, having both of the following characteristics:

(1) 'measurement uncertainty' along any linear axis equal to or less (better) than 3.5 μm per 5 mm; *and*

(2) 'angular position deviation' equal to or less than 0.02°.

Note: Specially designed software for the systems described in paragraph (*c*) of this item includes software for simultaneous measurements of wall thickness and contour.

Technical Note 1: Machine tools that can be used as measuring machines are controlled if they meet or exceed the criteria specified for the machine tool function or the measuring machine function.

Technical Note 2: A machine described in this section, 1.3., is controlled if it exceeds the control threshold anywhere within its operation range.

Technical Note 3: The probe used in determining the measurement uncertainty of a dimensional inspection system shall be as described in VDI/VDE 2617 parts 2, 3, and 4.

Technical Note 4: All parameters of measurement values in this item represent plus/minus, i.e., not total band.

'Measurement uncertainty'

The characteristic parameter which specifies in what range around the output value the correct value of the measurable variable lies with a confidence level of 95%. It includes the uncorrected systematic deviations, the uncorrected backlash, and the random deviations (Reference: VDI/DE 2617).

'Resolution'

The least increment of a measuring device; on digital instruments, the least significant bit (Reference: ANSI B-89.1.12).

'Linearity'

(Usually measured in terms of nonlinearity) is the maximum deviation of the actual characteristic (average of upscale and downscale readings), positive or negative, from a straight line so positioned as to equalize and minimize the maximum deviations.

'Angular position deviation'

The maximum difference between angular position and the actual, very accurately measured angular position after the workpiece mount of the table has been turned out of its initial position. (Reference: VDI/VDE 2617. Draft: 'Rotary table on coordinate measuring machines.')

1.4. Vacuum or controlled environment (inert gas) induction furnaces capable of operation above 850°C and having induction coils 600 mm (24 in.) or less in diameter, and power supplies specially designed for induction furnaces with a power supply of 5 kW or more.

Technical Note: This entry does not control furnaces designed for the processing of semiconductor wafers.

1.5. 'Isostatic presses' capable of achieving a maximum working pressure of 69 MPa (10,000 psi) or greater and having a chamber cavity with an inside diameter in excess of 152 mm (6 in.) and specially designed dies and molds, and controls and 'specially designed software' therefor.

Technical Notes:

(1) The inside chamber dimension is that of the chamber in which both the working temperature and the working pressure are achieved and does not include fixtures. That dimension will be the smaller of either the inside diameter of the pressure chamber or the inside diameter of the insulated furnace chamber, depending on which of the two chambers is located inside the other.

(2) 'Isostatic presses'

Equipment capable of pressurizing a closed cavity through various media (gas, liquid, solid particles, etc.) to create equal pressure in all directions within the cavity upon a workpiece or material.

1.6. 'Robots' and 'end-effectors' having either of the following characteristics:

(*a*) Specially designed to comply with national safety standards applicable to handling high explosives (for example, meeting electrical code ratings for high explosives); or

(*b*) Specially designed or rated as radiation hardened to withstand greater than 5×10^4 grays (Si) (5×10^6 rad (Si)) without operational degradation;

and specially designed controllers and 'specially designed software' therefor.

Technical Notes:

(1) 'Robot'

A manipulation mechanism, which may be of the continuous path or of the point-to-point variety, may use 'sensors,' and has all of the following characteristics:

(*a*) is multifunctional

(*b*) is capable of positioning or orienting material, parts, tools, or special devices through variable movements in three-dimensional space;

(*c*) incorporates three or more closed or open loop servo-devices which may include stepping motors; *and*

(*d*) has 'user-accessible programmability' by means of teach/playback method or by means of an electronic computer which may be a programmable logic controlled, i.e., without mechanical intervention.

N.B.: The above definition does not include the following devices:

(*a*) Manipulation mechanisms which are only manually/teleoperator controllable;

(*b*) Fixed sequence manipulation mechanisms which are automated moving devices operating according to mechanically fixed programmed motions. The program is mechanically limited by fixed stops, such as pins or cams. The sequence of motions and the election of paths or angles are not variable or changeable by mechanical, electronic, or electrical means;

(*c*) Mechanically controlled variable sequence manipulation mechanisms which are automated moving devices operating according to mechanically fixed programmed motions. The program is mechanically limited by fixed, but adjustable, stops such as pins or cams. The sequence of motions and the selection of paths or angles are variable within the fixed program pattern. Variations or modifications of the program pattern (e.g., changes of pins or exchanges of cams) in one or more motion axes are accomplished only through mechanical operations;

(*d*) Non-servo-controlled variable sequence manipulation mechanisms which are automated moving devices, operation according to mechanically fixed programmed motions. The program is variable but the sequence proceeds only by the binary signal from mechanically fixed electrical binary devices or adjustable stops;

(*e*) Stacker cranes defined as Cartesian coordinate manipulator systems manufactured as an integral part of a vertical array of storage bins and designed to access the contents of those bins for storage or retrieval.

(2) 'End-effectors'

'End-effectors' include grippers, 'active tooling units,' and any other tooling that is attached to the baseplate on the end of a 'robot' manipulator arm.

(3) The definition in (*a*) above is not designed to control robots specially designed for nonnuclear industrial applications such as automobile paint-spraying booths.

1.7. Vibration test equipment using digital control techniques and feedback or closed loop test equipment and software therefor capable of vibrating a system at 10 g RMS or more between 20 Hz and 2000 Hz, imparting forces of 50 kN (11 250 lbs) or greater.

1.8. Vacuum and controlled atmosphere metallurgical melting and casting furnaces as follows; and specially configured computer control and monitoring systems and 'specially designed software' therefore:

(*a*) Arc remelt and casting furnaces with consumable electrode capacities between 1000 cm^3 and 20,000 cm^3 and capable of operating with melting temperatures above 1700°C,

(*b*) Electron beam melting and plasma atomization and melting furnaces with a power of 50 kW or greater and capable of operating with melting temperatures above 1200°C.

2. Materials

2.1. Aluminum alloys capable of an ultimate tensile strength of 460 MPa (0.46×10^9 N/m^2) or more at 293 K (20°C), in the form of tubes or solid forms (including forgings) with an outside diameter of more than 75 mm (3 in.).
Technical Note: The phrase 'capable of' encompasses aluminum alloys before or after heat treatment.

2.2. Beryllium as follows: metal, alloys containing more than 50% of beryllium by weight, compounds containing beryllium, and manufactures thereof, *except*:

(a) Metal windows for X-ray machines;

(b) Oxide shapes in fabricated or semi-fabricated forms specially designed for electronic component parts or as substrates for electronic circuits.

Technical Note: This control applies to waste and scrap containing beryllium as defined here.

2.3. High-purity (99.99% or greater) bismuth with very low silver content (less than 10 parts per million).

2.4. Boron and boron compounds, mixtures, and loaded materials in which the boron-10 isotope is more than 20% by weight of the total boron content.

2.5. Calcium (high purity) containing both less than 1000 parts per million by weight of metallic impurities other than magnesium and less than 10 parts per million of boron.

2.6. Chlorine Trifluoride (ClF_3).

2.7. Crucibles made of materials resistant to liquid actinide metals, as follows:

(*a*) Crucibles with a volume of between 150 ml and 8 liters and made of or coated with any of the following materials having a purity of 98% or greater:

(i) Calcium fluoride (CaF_2),
(ii) Calcium zirconate (metazirconate) (Ca_2ZrO_3),
(iii) Cerium sulfide (Ce_2S_3),
(iv) Erbium oxide (erbia) (Er_2O_3),
(v) Hafnium oxide (hafnia) (HfO_2),
(vi) Magnesium oxide (MgO),
(vii) Nitrided niobium-titanium-tungsten alloy (approximately 50% Nb, 30% Ti, 20%W)
(viii) Yttrium oxide (yttria) (Y_2O_3)
(ix) Zirconium oxide (zirconia) (ZrO_2)

(*b*) Crucibles with a volume of between 50 ml and 2 liters and made of or lined with tantalum, having a purity of 99.9% or greater.

(*c*) Crucibles with a volume of between 50 ml and 2 liters and made of or lined with tantalum (having a purity of 98% or greater) coated with tantalum carbide, nitride, or boride (or any combination of these).

2.8. (*a*) Carbon or aramid 'fibrous and filamentary' materials having a 'specific modulus' of 12.7×10^6 m or greater or a 'specific tensile strength' of 23.5×10^4 m or greater; or

(*b*) Glass 'fibrous and filamentary' materials having a 'specific modulus' of 3.18×10^6 m or greater and a 'specific tensile strength' of 7.62×10^4 m or greater.

(*c*) Composite structures in the form of tubes with an inside diameter of between 75 mm (3 in.) and 400 mm (16 in.) made with 'fibrous and filamentary' materials controlled in (*a*) above.

Technical Note:

(*a*) The term 'fibrous and filamentary materials' includes continuous monofilaments, continuous yarns, and tapes.

(*b*) 'Specific modulus' is the Young's modulus in N/m^2 divided by the specific weight in N/m^3 when measured at a temperature of 23 ± 2° C and a relative humidity of 50 ± 5%;

(*c*) 'Specific tensile strength' is the ultimate tensile strength in N/m^2 divided by the specific weight in N/m^3 when measured at a temperature of 23 ± 2° C and a relative humidity of 50 ± 5%.

2.9. Hafnium of the following description: metal, alloys, and compounds of hafnium containing more than 60% hafnium by weight and manufactures thereof.

2.10. Lithium (isotopically enriched in lithium-6) as follows:

(*a*) Metal hydrides or alloys containing lithium enriched in the 6 isotope (^6Li) to a concentration higher than the one existing in nature (7.5% on an atom percentage basis);

(*b*) Any other materials containing lithium enriched in the 6 isotope (including compounds, mixtures, and concentrates), *except* ^6Li *incorporated in thermoluminescent dosimeters.*

2.11. Magnesium (high purity) containing both less than 200 parts per million by weight of metallic impurities other than calcium and less than 10 parts per million of boron.

2.12. Maraging steel capable of an ultimate tensile strength of 2050 MPa (2.050×10^9 N/m^2) (300 000 lb/in.^{2}) or more at 293 K (20°C) *except forms in which no linear dimension exceeds 75 mm.*

Technical Note: The phrase 'capable of' encompasses maraging steel before or after heat treatment.

2.13. Radium-226 *except radium contained in medical applicators.*

2.14. Titanium alloys capable of an ultimate tensile strength of 900 MPa (0.9×10^9 N/m^2) (130,500 lb/in.^{2}) or more at 293 K (20°C) in the form of tubes or solid forms (including forgings) with an outside diameter of more than 75 mm (3 in.).

Technical Note: The phrase 'capable of' encompasses titanium alloys before or after heat treatment.

2.15. Tungsten, as follows: parts made of tungsten, tungsten carbide, or tungsten alloys (greater than 90% tungsten) having a mass greater than 20 kg and a hollow cylindrical symmetry (including cylinder segments) with an inside diameter greater than 100 mm (4 in.) but less than 300 mm (12 in.), *except parts specifically designed for use as weights or gamma-ray collimators.*

2.16. Zirconium as follows: metal, alloys containing more than 50% zirconium by weight, and compounds in which the ratio of hafnium content to zirconium content is less than 1 part to 500 parts by weight, and manufactures wholly thereof; *except zirconium in the form of foil having a thickness not exceeding 0.10 mm (0.004 in.).*

Technical Note: This control applies to waste and scrap containing zirconium as defined here.

3. Uranium Isotope Separation Equipment and Components

3.1. Electrolytic cells for fluorine production with a production capacity greater than 250 g of fluorine per hour.

3.2. Rotor fabrication and assembly equipment and bellows-forming mandrels and dies, as follows:

(*a*) Rotor assembly equipment for assembly of gas centrifuge rotor tube sections, baffles, and end caps. Such equipment includes precision mandrels, clamps, and shrink fit machines.

(*b*) Rotor straightening equipment for alignment of gas centrifuge rotor tube sections to a common axis. (Note: Normally such equipment will consist of precision measuring probes linked to a computer that subsequently controls the action of, for example, pneumatic rams used for aligning the rotor tube sections.)

(*c*) Bellows-forming mandrels and dies for producing single-convolution bellows (bellows made of high-strength aluminum alloys, maraging steel, or high-strength filamentary materials). The bellows have all of the following dimensions:

(1) 75-mm to 400-mm (3-in. to 16-in.) inside diameter;

(2) 12.7 mm (0.5 in.) or more in length; and

(3) single convolution depth more than 2 mm (0.08 in.).

3.3. Centrifugal multiplane balancing machines, fixed or portable, horizontal or vertical, as follows:

(*a*) Centrifugal balancing machines designed for balancing flexible rotors having a length of 600 mm or more and having all of the following characteristics:

(1) a swing or journal diameter of 75 mm or more;

(2) mass capability of from 0.9 to 23 kg (2 to 50 lb.); and

(3) capable of balancing speed of revolution more than 5000 rpm;

(*b*) Centrifugal balancing machines designed for balancing hollow cylindrical rotor components and having all of the following characteristics:

(1) a journal diameter of 75 mm or more;

(2) mass capability of from 0.9 to 2 kg (2 to 50 lb.);

(3) capable of balancing to a residual imbalance of 0.010 kg mm/kg per plane or better; and

(4) belt drive type;

and 'specially designed software' therefor.

3.4. Filament winding machines in which the motions for positioning, wrapping, and winding fibers are coordinated and programmed in two or more axes, specially designed to fabricate composite structures or laminates from fibrous and filamentary materials and capable of winding cylindrical rotors of diameter between 75 mm (3 in.) and 400 mm (16 in.) and lengths of 600 mm (24 in.) or greater; coordinating and programming controls therefor; precision mandrels; and 'specially designed software' therefor.

3.5. Frequency changers (also known as converters or inverters) or generators having all of the following characteristics:

(*a*) A multiphase output capable of providing a power of 40 W or more;

(*b*) Capable of operating in the frequency range between 600 and 2000 Hz;

(*c*) Total harmonic distortion below 10%; and

(*d*) Frequency control better than 0.1%.

except such frequency changers specially designed or prepared to supply 'motor stators' (as defined below) and having the characteristics listed in (*b*) and (*d*) above, together with a total harmonic distortion of less than 2% and an efficiency of greater than 80%.

Definition:
'Motor stators': Specially designed or prepared ring-shaped stators for high-speed multiphase AC hysteresis (or reluctance) motors for synchronous operation within a vacuum in the frequency range of 600–2000 Hz and a power range of 50-1000 VA. The stators consist of multiphase windings on a laminated low-loss iron core comprising thin layers typically 2.0 mm (008 in.) thick or less.

3.6. Lasers, laser amplifiers, and oscillators as follows:

(*a*) Copper vapor lasers with 40 W or greater average output power operating at wavelengths between 500 nm and 600 nm;

(*b*) Argon ion lasers with greater than 40 W average output power operating at wavelengths between 400 nm and 515 nm;

(*c*) Neodymium-doped (other than glass) lasers as follows:

(1) having an output wavelength between 1000 nm and 1100 nm, being pulse-excited and Q-switched with a pulse duration equal to or greater than 1 ns, and having either of the following:

(*a*) A single-transverse mode output having an average output power exceeding 40 W;

(*b*) A multiple-transverse mode output having an average output power exceeding 50 W;

(2) operating at a wavelength between 1000 nm and 1100 nm and incorporating frequency doubling giving an output wavelength between 500 nm and 550 nm with an average power at the doubled frequency (new wavelength) of greater than 40 W;

(*d*) Tuneable pulsed single-mode dye oscillators capable of an average power output of greater than 1 W, a repetition rate greater than 1 kHz, a pulse less than 100 ns, and a wavelength between 300 nm and 800 nm;

(*e*) Tunable pulsed dye laser amplifiers and oscillators, *except single mode oscillators*, with an average power output of greater than 30 W, a repetition rate greater than 1 kHz, a pulse width less than 100 ns, and a wavelength between 300 nm and 800 nm;

(*f*) Alexandrite lasers with a bandwidth of 0.005 nm or less, a repetition rate of greater than 125 Hz, and an average power output greater than 30 W operating at wavelengths between 720 nm and 800 nm;

(*g*) Pulsed carbon dioxide lasers with a repetition rate greater than 250 Hz, an average power output of greater than 500 W, and a pulse of less than 200 ns operating at wavelengths between 9000 nm and 11 000 nm;

N.B. This specification is not intended to control the higher power (typically 1 to 5 kW) industrial CO_2 lasers used in applications such as cutting and welding, as these latter lasers are either continuous wave or are pulsed with a pulse width more than 200 ns.

(*h*) Pulsed excimer lasers (XeF, XeCl, KrF) with a repetition rate greater than 250 Hz and an average power output of greater than 500 W operating at wavelengths of between 240 and 360 nm;

(*i*) Para-hydrogen Raman shifters designed to operate at 16 μm output wavelength and at a repetition rate greater than 250 Hz.

Technical Note: Machine tools, measuring devices, and associated technology that have the potential for use in the nuclear industry are controlled under items 1.2 and 1.3 of this list.

3.7. Mass spectrometers capable of measuring ions of 230 atomic mass units or greater and having a resolution of better than 2 parts in 230, and ion sources therefor as follows:

(*a*) Inductively coupled plasma mass spectrometers (ICP/MS);

(*b*) Glow discharge mass spectrometers (GDMS);

(*c*) Thermal ionization mass spectrometers (TIMS);

(*d*) Electron bombardment mass spectrometers which have a source chamber constructed from or lined with or plated with materials resistant to UF_6;

(*e*) Molecular beam mass spectrometers as follows:

(1) which have a source chamber constructed from or lined with or plated with stain-

less steel or molybdenum and have a cold trap capable of cooling to 193 K (-80°C) or less; or

(2) which have a source chamber constructed from or lined with or plated with materials resistant to UF_6; or

(*f*) Mass spectrometers equipped with a microfluorination ion source designed for use with actinides or actinide fluorides;

except

specially designed or prepared magnetic or quadrupole mass spectrometers capable of taking 'on-line' samples of feed, product, or tails from UF_6 gas streams and having all of the following characteristics:

(1) Unit resolution for mass greater than 320;

(2) Ion sources constructed of or lined with nichrome or monel or nickel-plated;

(3) Electron bombardment ionization sources;

(4) Having a collector system suitable for isotopic analysis.

3.8. Instruments capable of measuring pressures up to 13 kPa (2 psi, 100 torr) to an accuracy of better than 1% (full-scale), with corrosion-resistant pressure-sensing elements constructed of nickel, nickel alloys, phosphor bronze, stainless steel, aluminum, or aluminum alloys.

3.9. Valves 5 mm (0.2 in.) or greater in diameter, with a bellows seal, wholly made of or lined with aluminum, aluminum alloy, nickel, or alloy containing 60% or more nickel, either manually or automatically operated.

3.10. Superconducting solenoidal electromagnets with all of the following characteristics:

(*a*) capable of creating magnetic fields of more than 2 teslas (20 kilogauss);

(*b*) with an L/D (length divided by inner diameter) greater than 2;

(*c*) with an inner diameter of more than 300 mm; and

(*d*) with a magnetic field uniform to better than 1% over the central 50% of the inner volume.

Note: The item does not cover magnets specially designed for and exported as parts of medical nuclear magnetic resonance (NMR) imaging systems. It is understood that the wording 'as part of' does not necessarily mean physical part in the same shipment. Separate shipments from different sources are allowed, provided the related export documents clearly specify the 'part of' relationship.

3.11. Vacuum pumps with an input throat size of 38 cm (15 in.) or greater with a pumping speed of 15 000 liters/second or greater and capable of producing an ultimate vacuum better than 10^{-4} Torr (0.76×10^{-4} mbar).

Technical Note: The ultimate vacuum is determined at the input of the pump with the input of the pump blocked off.

3.12. Direct current high-power supplies capable of continuously producing, over a time period of 8 hours, 100 V or greater with current output of 500 amps or greater and with current or voltage regulation better than 0.1%.

3.13. High-voltage direct current power supplies capable of continuously producing, over a time period of 8 hours, 20 000 V or greater with current output of 1 amp or greater and with current or voltage regulation better than 0.1%.

3.14. Electromagnetic isotope separators, designed for or equipped with, single or multiple ion sources capable of providing a total ion beam current of 50 mA or greater.

Notes:

1. This entry will control separators capable of enriching stable isotopes as well as those for uranium. A separator capable of separating the isotopes of lead with a one-mass unit difference is inherently capable of enriching the isotopes of uranium with a three-unit mass difference.

2. This entry includes separators with the ion sources and collectors both in the magnetic field and those configurations in which they are external to the field.

3. A single 50-mA ion source will produce less than 3 g of separated HEU per year from natural abundance feed.

4. Heavy Water Production Plant Related Equipment

(Other Than Trigger List Items)

4.1. Specialized packings for use in separating heavy water from ordinary water and made of phosphor bronze mesh or copper (both chemically treated to improve wettability) and designed for use in vacuum distillation towers.

4.2. Pumps circulating solutions of diluted or concentrated potassium amide catalyst in liquid ammonia (KNH_2/NH_3), with all of the following characteristics:

(*a*) airtight (i.e., hermetically sealed);

(*b*) for *concentrated* potassium amide solutions (1% or greater), operating pressure of

1.5–60 MPa [15–600 atmospheres (atm)]; for dilute potassium amide solutions (less than 1%), operating pressure of 20–60 MPa (200-600 atm); and

(*c*) a capacity greater than 8.5 m^3/h (5 cubic feet per minute).

4.3. Water-hydrogen sulfide exchange tray columns constructed from fine carbon steel (such as ASTM A516) with a diameter of 1.8 m (6 ft.) or greater to operate at a nominal pressure of 2 MPa (300 psi) or greater, except columns which are specially designed or prepared for the production of heavy water. Internal contactors of the columns are segmented trays with an effective assembled diameter of 1.8 m (6 ft.) or greater, such as sieve trays, valve trays, bubble cap trays, and turbogrid trays designed to facilitate countercurrent contacting and constructed of materials resistant to corrosion by hydrogen sulfide/water mixtures, such as 304L or 316 stainless steel.

4.4. Hydrogen-cryogenic distillation columns having all of the following applications:

(*a*) designed to operate with internal temperatures of -238°C (35 K) or less;

(*b*) designed to operate at internal pressure of 0.5 to 5 MPa (5 to 50 atmospheres);

(*c*) constructed of fine-grain stainless steels of the 300 series with low sulfur content or equivalent cryogenic and H_2-compatible materials; and

(*d*) with internal diameters of 1 m or greater and effective lengths of 5 m or greater.

4.5. Ammonia synthesis convertors, ammonia synthesis units in which the synthesis gas (nitrogen and hydrogen) is withdrawn from an ammonia/hydrogen high-pressure exchange column and the synthesized ammonia is returned to said column.

5. Implosion Systems Development Equipment

5.1. Flash x-ray generators of pulsed electron accelerators with peak energy of 500 keV or greater, as follows, *except accelerators that are component parts of devices designed for purposes other than electron beam or x-ray radiation (electron microscopy, for example) and those designed for medical purposes:*

(*a*) Having an accelerator peak electron energy of 500 keV or greater but less than 25 MeV and with a figure of merit (*K*) of 0.25 or greater, where *K* is defined as:

$K=1.7 \times 10^3 V^{265}Q$,

where V is the peak electron energy in million electron volts and Q is the total accelerated charge in coulombs if the accelerator beam pulse duration is less than or equal to 1 μs; if the accelerator beam pulse duration is greater than 1 μs, Q is the maximum accelerated charge in 1 μs [Q equals the integral of *i* with respect to *t*, over the lesser of 1 μs or the time duration of the beam pulse ($Q = \int idt$), where *i* is beam current in amperes and *t* is time in seconds] or,

(*b*) Having an accelerator peak electron energy of 25 MeV or greater and a peak power greater than 50 MW. [Peak power = (peak potential in volts) x (peak beam current in amperes).]

Technical Note:

Time duration of the beam pulse—In machines, based on microwave accelerating cavities, the time duration of the beam pulse is the lesser of 1 μs or the duration of the bunched beam packet resulting from one microwave modulator pulse.

Peak beam current—In machines based on microwave accelerating cavities, the peak beam current is the average current in the time duration of a bunched beam packet.

5.2. Multistage light gas guns or other high-velocity gun systems (coil, electromagnetic, electrothermal, or other advanced systems) capable of accelerating projectiles to 2 km per second or greater.

5.3. Mechanical rotating mirror cameras
Mechanical framing cameras with recording rates greater than 225,000 frames per second; streak cameras with writing speeds greater than 0.5 mm per microsecond; and parts, including specially designed synchronizing electronics and specially designed rotor assemblies (consisting of turbines, mirrors, and bearings).

5.4. Electronic streak and framing cameras and tubes as follows:

(*a*) Electronic streak cameras capable of 50 ns or less time resolution and streak tubes therefor;

(*b*) Electronic (or electronically shuttered) framing cameras capable of 50 ns or less frame exposure time;

(*c*) Framing tubes and solid-state imaging devices for use with cameras controlled in sub-item (*b*) above, as follows:

(1) proximity focused image intensifier tubes having the photocathode deposited on a transparent conductive coating to decrease photocathode sheet resistance;

(2) gate silicon intensifier target (SIT) vidicon tubes, where a fast system allows gating the photoelectrons from the photocathode before they impinge on the SIT plate;
(3) Kerr or pockel cell electro-optical shuttering; or
(4) Other framing tubes and solid-state imaging devices having a fast-image gating time of less than 50 ns specially designed for cameras controlled by sub-item (*b*) above.

5.5. Specialized instrumentation for hydrodynamic experiments as follows:

(*a*) Velocity interferometers for measuring velocities in excess of 1 km per second during time intervals less than 10 μs. (VISARs, Doppler laser interferometers, DLIs, etc.);

(*b*) manganin gauges for pressures greater than 100 kilobars; or

(*c*) quartz pressure transducers for pressures greater than 100 kilobars.

6. Explosives and related equipment

6.1. Detonators and multipoint initiation systems (exploding bridge wire, slapper, etc.)

(*a*) Electrically driven explosive detonators as follows:
(1) exploding bridge (EB);
(2) exploding bridge wire (EBW);
(3) slapper; and
(4) exploding foil initiators (EFI).

(*b*) Arrangements using single or multiple detonators designed to nearly simultaneously initiate an explosive surface (over greater than 5000 mm^2) from a single firing signal (with an initiation timing spread over the surface of less than 2.5 μs).

Description clarification: The detonators of concern all utilize a small electrical conductor (bridge, bridge wire, or foil) that explosively vaporizes when a fast, high current electrical pulse is passed through it. In nonslapper types, the exploding conductor starts a chemical detonation in a contacting high-explosive material such as PETN (pentaerythritoltetranitrate). In slapper detonators, the explosive vaporization of the electrical conductor drives a 'flyer' or 'slapper' across a gap, and the impact of the slapper on an explosive starts a chemical detonation. The slapper in some designs is driven by magnetic force. The term 'exploding foil' detonator may refer to either an EB or a slapper-type detonator. Also, the word 'initiator' is sometimes used in place of the word 'detonator.'

Detonators using only primary explosives, such as lead azide, are not subject to control.

6.2. Electronic components for firing sets (switching devices and pulse discharge capacitors)

6.2.1. Switching devices

(*a*) Cold-cathode tubes (including gas krytron tubes and vacuum sprytron tubes), whether gas filled or not, operating similarly to a spark gap, containing three or more electrodes, and having all of the following characteristics:
(1) Anode peak voltage rating of 2500 V or more,
(2) Anode peak current rating of 100 A or more,
(3) Anode delay time of 10 μs or less, and

(*b*) Triggered spark-gaps having an anode delay time of 15 μs or less and rated for peak current of 500 A or more;

(*c*) Modules or assemblies with a fast switching function having all of the following characteristics:
(1) Anode peak voltage rating greater than 2000 V;
(2) anode peak current rating of 500 A or more; and
(3) turn-on time of 1 μs or less.

6.2.2. Capacitors with the following characteristics:

(*a*) Voltage rating greater than 1.4 kV, energy storage greater than 10 J, capacitance greater than 0.5 μF, and series inductance less than 50 nH, *or*

(*b*) Voltage rating greater than 750 V, capacitance greater than 0.25 μF, and series inductance less than 10 nH.

6.3. Firing sets and equivalent high-current pulse generators (for controlled detonators), as follows:

(*a*) Explosive detonator firing sets designed to drive multiple controlled detonators covered under item 6.1. above;

(*b*) Modular electrical pulse generators (pulsers) designed for portable, mobile, or ruggedized use (including xenon flash-lamp drivers) having all the following characteristics:
(1) capable of delivering their energy in less than 15 μs;
(2) having an output greater than 100 A;
(3) having a rise time of less than 10 μs into loads of less than 40 ohms. (Rise time is defined as the time interval from 10% to 90% current amplitude when driving a resistive load);
(4) enclosed in a dust-tight enclosure;
(5) no dimension greater than 25.4 cm

(10 in.);

(6) weight less than 25 kg (55 lb.); and

(7) specified for use over an extended temperature range (-50°C to 100°C) or specified as suitable for aerospace use.

6.4. High explosives or substances or mixtures containing more than 2% of any of the following:

(*a*) Cyclotetramethylenetetranitramine (HMX);

(*b*) Cyclotrimethylenetrinitramine (RDX);

(*c*) Triaminotrinitrobenzene (TATB);

(*d*) Any explosive with a crystal density greater than 1.8 g/cm^3 and having a detonation velocity greater than 8000 m/s; or

(*e*) Hexanitrostilbene (HNS).

7. Nuclear testing equipment and components

7.1. Oscilloscopes and transient recorders and specially designed components as follows: plug-in units, external amplifiers, pre-amplifiers, sampling devices, and cathode ray tubes for analog oscilloscopes.

(*a*) Non-modular analog oscilloscopes having a 'bandwidth' of 1 GHz or greater;

(*b*) Modular analog oscilloscope systems having either of the following characteristics:

(i) a mainframe with a 'bandwidth' of 1 GHz or greater; or

(ii) Plug-in modules with an individual 'bandwidth' of 4 GHz or greater;

(*c*) Analog sampling oscilloscopes for the analysis of recurring phenomena with an effective 'bandwidth' greater than 4 GHz;

(*d*) Digital oscilloscopes and transient recorders, using analog-to-digital conversion techniques, capable of storing transients by sequentially sampling single-shot inputs at successive intervals of less than 1 ns (greater than 1 giga-sample per second), digitizing to 8 bits or greater resolution and storing 256 or more samples.

Technical Note: 'Bandwidth' is defined as the band of frequencies over which the deflection on the cathode ray tube does not fall below 70.7% of that at the maximum point measured with a constant input voltage to the oscilloscope amplifier.

7.2. Photomultiplier tubes with a photocathode area of greater than 20 cm^2 having an anode pulse rise time of less than 1 ns.

7.3. High-speed pulse generators with output voltages greater than 6 V into a less than 55-ohm resistive load, and with pulse transition times less than 500 ps (defined as the time interval between 10% and 90% voltage amplitude).

8. Other

8.1. Neutron generator systems, including tubes, designed for operation without an external vacuum system and utilizing electrostatic acceleration to induce a tritiumdeuterium nuclear reaction.

8.2. Equipment realted to nuclear material handling and processing and to nuclear reactors as follows:

8.2.1. Remote manipulators that provide mechanical translation of human operator actions by electrical, hydraulic, or mechanical means to an operating arm and terminal fixture that can be used to provide remote actions in radiochemical separation operations and 'hot cells.' The manipulators have a capability to penetrate 0.6 m or more (2 ft. or more) or cell wall or, alternatively, bridge over the top of a cell wall with a thickness of 0.6 m or more (2 ft. or more);

8.2.2. High-density (lead glass or other) radiation shielding windows greater than 0.3 m (1 ft.) on a side and with a density greater than 3 g/cm^3 and a thickness of 100 mm or greater; and specially designed frames therefor;

8.2.3. Radiation-hardened TV cameras specially designed or rated as radiation hardened to withstand greater than 5 x 10^4 grays (Si) (5 x 10^6 rad (Si)) without operational degradation and specially designed lenses used therein.

8.3. Tritium, tritium compounds, and mixtures containing tritium in which the ratio of tritium to hydrogen by atoms exceeds 1 part in 1000 *except a product or device containing not more than 40 Ci of tritium in any chemical or physical form.*

8.4. Facilities or plants for the production, recovery, extraction, concentration, or handling of tritium, and equipment as follows:

(*a*) Hydrogen or helium refrigeration units capable of cooling to -250°C (23 K) or less, with heat removal capacity greater than 150 watts or

(*b*) Hydrogen isotope storage and purification systems using metal hydrides as the storage, or purification medium.

8.5. Platinized catalysts specially designed or prepared for promoting the hydrogen isotope exchange reaction between hydrogen and water for the recovery of tritium from heavy water or for the production of heavy water.

8.6. Helium in any form isotopically enriched in the helium-3 isotope, whether or not mixed with other materials or contained in any equipment or device, *except products or devices containing less than 1 g of helium-3.*

8.7. Alpha-emitting radionuclides and equipment containing such radionuclides as follows:

All alpha-emitting radionuclides having an alpha half-life of 10 days or greater but less than 200 years, including compounds and mixtures containing these radionuclides with a total alpha activity of 1 curie per kilogram (37 GBq/kg) or greater *except for devices containing less than 100 millicuries (3.7 GBq) of alpha activity per device.*

ANNEX APPENDIX:

Detailed Specifications for Machine Tools (Item 1.2. in List of Nuclear Dual-Use Export Controls)

1.2. 'Numerical control' units, specially designed 'motion control boards' for 'numerical control' applications on machine tools, 'numerically controlled' machine tools, specially designed 'software', and technology as follows.

(*a*) **'Numerical control' units** for machine tools, as follows:

(1) Having more than four interpolating axes that can be coordinated simultaneously for 'contouring control' *or*

(2) Having two, three, or four interpolating axes that can be coordinated simultaneously for 'contouring control' and one or more of the following conditions are fulfilled:

(i) Capable of 'real-time processing' of data to modify the tool path during the machining operation by automatic calculation and modification of 'part program' data for machining in two or more axes by means of measuring cycles and access to source data;

(ii) Capable of receiving directly (on-line) and processing computer-aided design (CAD) data for internal preparation of machine instructions; or

(iii) Capable, without modification, according to the manufacturer's technical specifications, of accepting additional boards that would permit increasing the number of interpolating axes that can be coordinated simultaneously for 'contouring control', above the control levels, even if they do not contain these additional boards.

(*b*) **'Motion control boards'** specially designed for machine tools having one or more of the following characteristics:

(1) Providing interpolation in more than four axes;

(2) Capable or 'real-time processing' described in (*a*)(2)(i); *or*

(3) Capable of receiving and processing CAD data as described in (*a*)(2)(ii) above.

Note 1: Sub-items (*a*) and (*b*) do not control 'numerical control' units and 'motion control boards' if

(*a*) Modified for and incorporated in uncontrolled machines; *or*

(*b*) Specially designed for uncontrolled machines.

Note 2: 'Software' (including documentation) for 'numerical control' units that may be exported must be:

(*a*) In machine executable form only; and

(*b*) Limited to the minimum necessary for the use (i.e., installation, operation, and maintenance) of these units.

(*c*) **Machine tools,** as follows, for removing or cutting metals, ceramics, or composites, which, according to the manufacturer's technical specifications, can be equipped with electronic devices for simultaneous 'contouring control' in two or more axes:

Technical Note:

1. The c-axis on jig grinders used to maintain grinding wheels normal to the work surfaces is not considered a contouring rotary axis.

2. Not counted in the total number of contouring axes are secondary parallel contouring axes, e.g., a secondary rotary axis, the center line of which is parallel to the primary rotary axis.

3. Axis nomenclature shall be in accordance with International Standard ISO 841, 'Numerical Control Machines Axis and Motion Nomenclature'.

4. Rotary axes do not necessarily have to rotate over 360°. A rotary axis can be driven by a linear device, e.g., a screw or a rack-and-pinion.

(1) Machine tools for turning, grinding, milling, or any combination thereof that:

(i) Have two or more axes that can be

coordinated simultaneously for 'contouring control', *and*

(ii) Have any of the following characteristics:

(A) Two or more contouring rotary axes;

(B) One or more contouring 'tilting spindles';

Note: (*c*)(1)(ii)(B) applies to machine tools for grinding or milling only.

(C) 'Camming' (axial displacement) in one revolution of the spindle less (better) than 0.0006 mm total indicator reading (TIR);

Note: (*c*)(1)(ii)(C) applies to machine tools for turning only.

(D) 'Run out' (out-of-true running) in one revolution of the spindle less (better) than 0.0006 TIR.

(E) The 'positioning accuracies', with all compensations available, are less (better) than:

(1) 0.001° on any rotary axis

(2) (a) 0.004 mm along any linear axis (overall positioning) for grinding machines

(*b*) 0.006 mm along any linear axis (overall positioning) for milling or turning machines

Note: (*c*)(1)(ii)(E)(2)(*b*) does not control milling or turning machine tools with a positioning accuracy along one linear axis, with all compensations available, equal to or greater (worse) than 0.005 mm.

Notes:

(1) Sub-item (*c*) does not control cylindrical external, internal, and external-internal grinding machines having all of the following characteristics:

(*a*) Not centerless (shoe-type) grinding machines;

(*b*) Limited to cylindrical grinding;

(*c*) A maximum workpiece outside diameter or length of 150 mm;

(*d*) Only two axes that can be coordinated simultaneously for 'contouring control', *and*

(*e*) No contouring c axis.

(2) Sub-item (*c*) does not control machines designed specifically as jig grinders having both of the following characteristics:

(*a*) Axes limited to x, y, c, and a, where the c axis is used to maintain the grinding wheel normal to the work surface, and the a axis is configured to grind barrel cams *and*

(*b*) A spindle 'run-out' not less (not better) than 0.0006 mm.

(3) Sub-item (*c*) does not control tool or cutter grinding machines having all of the following characteristics:

(*a*) Shipped as a complete system with 'software' specially designed for the production of tools or cutters;

(*b*) No more than two rotary axes that can be coordinated simultaneously for 'contouring control',

(*c*) 'Run-out' (out-of-true running) in one revolution of the spindle not less (not better) than 0.0006 mm TIR; *and*

(*d*) The 'positioning accuracies', with all compensations available, are not less (not better) than:

(i) 0.004 mm along any linear axis for overall positioning; or

(ii) 0.001° for any rotary axis.

(2) Electrical discharge machines (EDM);

(i) Of the wire feed type that have five or more axes that can be coordinated simultaneously for 'contouring control',

(ii) Non-wire EDMs that have two or more contouring rotary axes and that can be coordinated simultaneously for 'contouring control'.

(3) Other machine tools for removing metals, ceramics, or composites:

(i) By means of:

(A) Water or other liquid jets, including those employing abrasive additives;

(B) Electron beam; *or*

(C) 'Laser' beam; *and*

(ii) Having two or more rotary axes that:

(A) Can be coordinated simultaneously for 'contouring control', *and*

(B) Have a 'positioning accuracy' of less (better) than 0.003°.

(*d*) 'Software'

(1) 'Software' specially designed or modified for the 'development', 'production', or 'use' of equipment controlled by sub-categories (a), (*b*), or (*c*) above;

(2) Specific 'software', as follows:

(i) 'Software' to provide 'adaptive control' and having both of the following characteristics:

(A) For 'flexible manufacturing units' (FMUs) that consist at least of equipment described in (*b*)(1) and (*b*)(2) of the definition of 'flexible manufacturing units'; *and*

(B) Capable of generating or modifying, in 'real time processing', 'part program' data by using the signals obtained simultaneously by means of at least two detection techniques, such as:

(1) Machine vision (optical ranging);

(2) Infrared imaging;

(3) Acoustical imaging (acoustical ranging);

(4) Tactile measurement;

(5) Inertial positioning;

(6) Force measurement;

(7) Torque measurement.

Note: This sub-item does not control 'software' that only provides rescheduling of functionally identical equipment within 'flexible manufacturing units' using prestored 'part programs' and a prestored strategy for the distribution of the 'part programs'.

(ii) 'Software' for electronic devices other than those described in sub-items (*a*) or (*b*) that provides the 'numerical control' capability of the equipment controlled in sub-item 1.2.

(*e*) Technology

(1) 'Technology' for the 'development' of equipment controlled by sub-items (*a*), (*b*), or (*c*) above, (*f*) or (*g*) below, and of the sub-item (*d*).

(2) 'Technology' for the 'production' of equipment controlled by sub-items (*a*), (*b*), or (*c*) above, (*f*) or (*g*) below;

(3) Other 'technology':

(i) For the 'development' of interactive graphics as an integrated part in 'numerical control' units for preparation or modification of 'part programs';

(ii) For the 'development' of integration 'software' for incorporation of expert systems for advanced decision support of shop floor operations into 'numerical control' units.

(*f*) Components and parts for machine tools controlled by sub-item (*c*) as follows:

(1) Spindle assemblies, consisting of spindles and bearings as a minimal assembly, with radial ('run-out') or axial ('camming') axis motion in one revolution of the spindle less (better) than 0.0006 mm TIR;

(2) Linear position feedback units (e.g., inductive-type devices, graduated scales, 'laser', or infrared systems) having, with compensation, an overall 'accuracy' better than 800 + (600 x L x 10^{-3}) nm, where *L* equals the effective length in millimeters of the linear measurement; *except* measuring interferometer systems, without closed or open loop feedback, containing a 'laser' to measure slide movement errors of machine tools, dimensional inspection machines, or similar equipment;

(3) Rotary position feedback units (e.g., inductive-type devices, graduated scales, 'laser', or infrared systems) having, with compensation, an 'accuracy' less (better) than 0.00025° of arc; *except* measuring interferometer systems, without closed or open loop feedback, containing a 'laser' to measure slide movement errors of machine tools, dimensional inspection machines, or similar equipment;

(4) Slide way assemblies consisting of a minimal assembly of ways, bed, and slide having all of the following characteristics:

(i) A yaw, pitch, or roll of less (better) than 2 seconds of arc TIR (Ref. ISO/DIS 230-1 over full travel);

(ii) A horizontal straightness of less (better) than 2 µm per 300 mm length; *and*

(iii) A vertical straightness of less (better) than 2 µm over full travel per 300 mm length;

(5) Single-point diamond-cutting tool inserts having all of the following characteristics:

(i) A flawless and chip-free cutting edge when magnified 400 times in any direction;

(ii) A cutting radius out-of-roundness less (better) than 0.002 mm TIR (also peak-to-peak); *and*

(iii) A cutting radius between 0.1 and 5.0 mm, inclusive.

(*g*) Specially designed components or sub-assemblies, as follows, capable of upgrading, according to the manufacturer's specifications, 'numerical control' units, motion control boards, machine tools, or feedback devices to or above the levels controlled in sub-items (*a*), (*b*), (*c*), (*f*)(2), or (*f*)(3):

(1) Printed circuit boards with mounted components and 'software' therefor;

(2) 'Compound rotary tables'.

Technical note: Definitions of terms:

'accuracy'—Usually measured in terms of inaccuracy, defined as the maximum deviation, positive or negative, of an indicated value from an accepted standard or true value.

'adaptive control'—a control system that adjusts the response from conditions detected during the operation (Ref. ISO 2806-1980).

'camming' (axial displacement)—Axial displacement in one revolution of the main spindle measured in a plane perpendicular to the spindle faceplate at a point next to the circumference of the spindle faceplate (Ref. ISO 230 Part 1-1986, paragraph 5.63).

'compound rotary table'—A table allowing the workpiece to rotate and tilt about two non-parallel axes, which can be coordinated simultaneously for 'contouring control'.

'contouring control'—Two or more 'numerically controlled' motions operating in accordance with instructions that specify the next required position and the required feed rates to

that position. These feed rates are varied in relation to each other so that a desired contour is generated (Ref. ISO/DIS 2806–1980).

'digital computer'—Equipment which can, in the form of one or more discrete variables:

a. Accept data;

b. Store data or instructions in fixed or alterable (writable) storage devices;

c. Process data by means of a stored sequence of instructions which is modifiable; and

d. Provide output of data.

N.B.: Modifications of a stored sequence of instructions include replacement of fixed storage devices, but not a physical change in wiring or interconnections.

'flexible manufacturing unit (FMU)' [sometimes also referred to as 'flexible manufacturing system' (FMS)' or 'flexible manufacturing cell (FMC)']

An entity which includes a combination of at least:

a. A 'digital computer' including its own 'main storage' and its own related equipment; and

b. Two or more of the following:

1. A machine tool described in Section 1.2.;

2. A dimensional inspection machine described in Section 1.3.;

3. A 'robot' controlled by Section 1.6.;

4. Digitally controlled equipment controlled by Section 3.4.

'laser'—An assembly of components which produce coherent light that is amplified by stimulated emission of radiation.

'main storage'—The primary storage for data or instructions for rapid access by a central processing unit. It consists of the internal storage of a 'digital computer' and any hierarchical extension thereto, such as cache storage or non-sequentially accessed extended storage.

'microprogram'—A sequence of elementary instructions, maintained in a special storage, the execution of which is initiated by the introduction of its reference instruction into an instruction register.

'motion control board'—An electronic assembly specially designed to provide a computer system with the capability to coordinate simultaneously the motion of axes of machine tools for 'contouring control'.

'numerical control'—The automatic control of a process performed by a device that makes use of numeric data usually introduced as the operation is in progress (Ref. ISO 2382).

'part program'—An ordered set of instructions in a language and in a format required to cause operations to be effected under automatic control, which is either written in the form of a machine program on an input medium or prepared as input data for processing in a computer to obtain a machine program (Ref. ISO 2806-1980).

'positioning accuracy'

Of 'numerically controlled' machine tools is to be determined and presented in accordance with paragraph 2.13, in conjunction with the requirements below:

(*a*) Test conditions (ISO/DIS/230/2, paragraph 3):

(1) For 12 hours before and during measurements, the machine tool and accuracy measuring equipment will be kept at the same ambient temperature. During the premeasurement time, the slides of the machine will be continuously cycled identically to the way they will be cycled during the accuracy measurements;

(2) The machine shall be equipped with any mechanical, electronic, or software compensation to be exported with the machine;

(3) Accuracy of measuring equipment for the measurements shall be at least four times more accurate than the expected machine tool accuracy;

(4) Power supply for slide drives shall be as follows:

(i) Line voltage variation shall not be greater than ± 10% of nominal rated voltage;

(ii) Frequency variation shall not be greater than ± 2 Hz of normal frequency;

(iii) Lineouts or interrupted service are not permitted.

(*b*) Test Program (paragraph 4):

(1) Feed rate (velocity of slides) during measurement shall be the rapid traverse rate;

N.B.: In the case of machine tools which generate optical quality surfaces, the feed rate shall be equal to or less than 50 mm per minute;

(2) Measurements shall be made in an incremental manner from one limit of the axis travel to the other without returning to the starting position for each move to the target position;

(3) Axes not being measured shall be retained at mid-travel during test of an axis.

(*c*) Presentation of test results (paragraph 2):

The results of the measurements must include:

(1) 'positioning accuracy' (A) *and*

(2) The mean reversal error (B).

'program'—A sequence of instructions to carry out a process in, or convertible into, a form executable by an electronic computer.

'real-time processing'—Processing of data by an electronic computer in response to an external event according to time requirements imposed by the external event.

'robot'—A manipulation mechanism, which may be of the continuous path or of the point-to-point variety, may use 'sensors' and has all the following characteristics:

a. Is multifunctional;

b. Is capable of positioning or orienting material, parts, tools or special devices through variable movements in three-dimensional space;

c. Incorporates three or more closed or open loop servo-devices which may include stepping motors; and

d. Has 'user-accessible programmability' by means of teach/playback method or by means of an electronic computer which may be a programmable logic controller, i.e., without mechanical intervention

N.B.: The above definition does not include the following devices:

a. Manipulation mechanisms which are only manually/teleoperator controllable;

b. Fixed sequence manipulation mechanisms which are automated moving devices, operating according to mechanically fixed programmed motions. The program is mechanically limited by fixed stops, such as pins or cams. The sequence of motions and the selection of paths or angles are not variable or changeable by mechanical, electronic or electrical means;

c. Mechanically controlled variable sequence manipulation mechanisms which are automated moving devices, operating according to mechanically fixed programmed motions. The program is mechanically limited by fixed, but adjustable, stops, such as pins or cams. The sequence of motions and the selection of paths or angles are variable within the fixed program pattern. Variations or modifications of the program pattern (e.g., changes of pins or exchanges of cams) in one or more motion axes are accomplished only through mechanical operations;

d. Non-servo-controlled variable sequence manipulation mechanisms which are automated moving devices, operating according to mechanically fixed programmed motions. The program is variable, but the sequence proceeds only by the binary signal from mechanically fixed electrical binary devices or adjustable stops;

e. Stacker cranes defined as Cartesian coordinate manipulator systems manufactured as an integral part of a vertical array of storage bins and designed to access the contents of those bins for storage or retrieval.

'run out' (out-of-true running)—Radial displacement in one revolution of the main spindle measured in a plane perpendicular to the spindle axis at a point on the external or internal revolving surface to be tested (Ref. ISO 230 Part 1-1986, paragraph 5.61).

'sensors'—Detectors of a physical phenomenon, the output of which (after conversion into a signal that can be interpreted by a controller) is able to generate 'programs' or modify programmed instructions or numerical program data. This includes 'sensors' with machine vision, infrared imaging, acoustical imaging, tactile feel, inertial position measuring, optical or acoustic ranging or force or torque measuring capabilities.

'software'—A collection of one or more 'programs' or 'microprograms' fixed in any tangible medium of expression.

'tilting spindle'—A tool-holding spindle that, during the machining process, alters the angular position of its center line with respect to any other axis.

'user-accessible programmability'

The facility allowing a user to insert, modify or replace 'programs' by means other than:

(*a*) A physical change in wiring or interconnections; or

(*b*) The setting of function controls including entry of parameters.

Source: IAEA document INFCIRC/254/Rev.1/ Part 2, July 1992

Appendix D. UN Security Council resolutions relating to Iraq

UN SECURITY COUNCIL RESOLUTION 687

3 April 1991

The Security Council,

Recalling its resolutions 660 (1990) of 2 August 1990, 661 (1990) of 6 August 1990, 662 (1990) of 9 August 1990, 664 (1990) of 18 August 1990, 665 (1990) of 25 August 1990, 666 (1990) of 13 September 1990, 667 (1990) of 16 September 1990, 669 (1990) of 24 September 1990, 670 (1990) of 25 September 1990, 674 (1990) of 29 October 1990, 677 (1990) of 28 November 1990, 678 (1990) of 29 November 1990 and 686 (1991) of 2 March 1991,

Welcoming the restoration to Kuwait of its sovereignty, independence and territorial integrity and the return of its legitimate Government,

Affirming the commitment of all Member States to the sovereignty, territorial integrity and political independence of Kuwait and Iraq, and noting the intention expressed by the Member States cooperating with Kuwait under paragraph 2 of resolution 678 (1990) to bring their military presence in Iraq to an end as soon as possible consistent with paragraph 8 of resolution 686 (1991),

Reaffirming the need to be assured of Iraq's peaceful intentions in the light of its unlawful invasion and occupation of Kuwait,

Taking note of the letter dated 27 February 1991 from the Deputy Prime Minister and Minister for Foreign Affairs of Iraq addressed to the President of the Security Council[1] and of his letters of the same date addressed to the President of the Council and to the Secretary-General,[2] and those letters dated 3 March [3] and 5 March[4] he addressed to them, pursuant to resolution 686 (1991),

Noting that Iraq and Kuwait, as independent sovereign States, signed at Baghdad on 4 October 1963 'Agreed Minutes between the State of Kuwait and the Republic of Iraq regarding the restoration of friendly relations, recognition and related matters',[5] thereby formally recognizing the boundary between Iraq and Kuwait and the allocation of islands, which Agreed Minutes were registered with the United Nations in accordance with Article 102 of the Charter of the United Nations and in which Iraq recognized the independence and complete sovereignty of the State of Kuwait with its boundaries as specified and accepted in the letter of the Prime Minister of Iraq dated 21 July 1932 and as accepted by the ruler of Kuwait in his letter dated 10 August 1932,

Conscious of the need for demarcation of the said boundary,

Conscious also of the statements by Iraq threatening to use weapons in violation of its obligations under the Protocol for the Prohibition of the Use in War of Asphyxiating, Poisonous or Other Gases, and of Bacteriological Methods of Warfare, signed at Geneva on 17 June 1925,[6] and of its prior use of chemical weapons, and affirming that grave consequences would follow any further use by Iraq of such weapons,

Recalling that Iraq has subscribed to the Final Declaration adopted by all States participating in the Conference of States Parties to the 1925 Geneva Protocol and Other Interested States, held in Paris from 7 to 11 January 1989,[7] establishing the objective of universal elimination of chemical and biological weapons,

Recalling also that Iraq has signed the Convention on the Prohibition of the Development, Production and Stockpiling of Bacteriological (Biological) and Toxin Weapons and

[1] *Official Records of the Security Council, Forty-sixth Year, Supplement for Jan., Feb. and Mar. 1991*, document S/22273.

[2] *Official Records* (note 1), documents S/22275 and S/22276.

[3] *Official Records* (note 1), documents S/22320 and S/22321.

[4] *Official Records* (note 1), document S/22330.

[5] United Nations, *Treaty Series,* vol. 485, No. 7063.

[6] League of Nations, *Treaty Series,* vol. XCIV (1929), No. 2138.

[7] A/44/88, annex.

on Their Destruction, of 10 April 1972,[8]

Noting the importance of Iraq ratifying the Convention,

Noting also the importance of all States adhering to this Convention and encouraging its forthcoming review conference to reinforce the authority, efficiency and universal scope of the Convention,

Stressing the importance of an early conclusion by the Conference on Disarmament of its work on a convention on the universal prohibition of chemical weapons and of universal adherence thereto,

Aware of the use by Iraq of ballistic missiles in unprovoked attacks and therefore of the need to take specific measures in regard to such missiles located in Iraq,

Concerned by the reports in the hands of Member States that Iraq has attempted to acquire materials for a nuclear-weapons programme contrary to its obligations under the Treaty on the Non-Proliferation of Nuclear Weapons of 1 July 1968,[9]

Recalling the objective of the establishment of a nuclear-weapons-free zone in the region of the Middle East,

Conscious of the threat that all weapons of mass destruction pose to peace and security in the area and of the need to work towards the establishment in the Middle East of a zone free of such weapons,

Conscious also of the objective of achieving balanced and comprehensive control of armaments in the region,

Conscious further of the importance of achieving the objectives noted above using all available means, including a dialogue among the States of the region,

Noting that resolution 686 (1991) marked the lifting of the measures imposed by resolution 661 (1990) in so far as they applied to Kuwait,

Noting also that despite the progress being made in fulfilling the obligations of resolution 686 (1991), many Kuwaiti and third-State nationals are still not accounted for and property remains unreturned,

Recalling the International Convention against the Taking of Hostages,[10] opened for signature in New York on 18 December 1979, which categorizes all acts of taking hostages as manifestations of international terrorism,

Deploring threats made by Iraq during the recent conflict to make use of terrorism against targets outside Iraq and the taking of hostages by Iraq,

Taking note with grave concern of the reports transmitted by the Secretary-General on 20 March[11] and 28 March 1991,[12] and conscious of the necessity to meet urgently the humanitarian needs in Kuwait and Iraq,

Bearing in mind its objective of restoring international peace and security in the area as set out in recent resolutions,

Conscious of the need to take the following measures acting under Chapter VII of the Charter,

1. *Affirms* all thirteen resolutions noted above, except as expressly changed below to achieve the goals of this resolution, including a formal cease-fire;

A

2. *Demands* that Iraq and Kuwait respect the inviolability of the international boundary and the allocation of islands set out in the 'Agreed Minutes between the State of Kuwait and the Republic of Iraq regarding the restoration of friendly relations, recognition and related matters',[13] signed by them in the exercise of their sovereignty at Baghdad on 4 October 1963 and registered with the United Nations and published by the United Nations;

3. *Calls upon* the Secretary-General to lend his assistance to make arrangements with Iraq and Kuwait to demarcate the boundary between Iraq and Kuwait, drawing on appropriate material including the maps transmitted with the letter dated 28 March 1991 addressed to him by the Permanent Representative of the United Kingdom of Great Britain and Northern Ireland to the United Nations,[14] and to report back to the Council within one month;

4. *Decides* to guarantee the inviolability of the above-mentioned international boundary and to take, as appropriate, all necessary measures to that end in accordance with the Charter of the United Nations;

---

[8] General Assembly resolution 2826 (XXVI), annex.

[9] United Nations, *Treaty Series,* vol. 729, No. 10485.

[10] General Assembly resolution 34/146, annex.

[11] *Official Records of the Security Council, Forty-sixth Year, Supplement for Apr., May and June 1991*, document S/22366, annex.

[12] *Official Records* (note 1), document S/22409, annex.

[13] United Nations (note 5).

[14] *Official Records* (note 1), document S/22412.

B

5. *Requests* the Secretary-General, after consulting with Iraq and Kuwait, to submit within three days to the Council for its approval a plan for the immediate deployment of a United Nations observer unit to monitor the Khawr 'Abd Allah and a demilitarized zone, which is hereby established, extending ten kilometres into Iraq and five kilometres into Kuwait from the boundary referred to in the 'Agreed Minutes Between the State of Kuwait and the Republic of Iraq regarding the restoration of friendly relations, recognition and related matters'; to deter violations of the boundary through its presence in and surveillance of the demilitarized zone and to observe any hostile or potentially hostile action mounted from the territory of one State against the other; and also requests the Secretary-General to report regularly to the Council on the operations of the unit and to do so immediately if there are serious violations of the zone or potential threats to peace;

6. *Notes* that as soon as the Secretary-General notifies the Council of the completion of the deployment of the United Nations observer unit, the conditions will be established for the Member States cooperating with Kuwait in accordance with resolution 678 (1990) to bring their military presence in Iraq to an end consistent with resolution 686 (1991);

C

7. *Invites* Iraq to reaffirm unconditionally its obligations under the Protocol for the Prohibition of the Use in War of Asphyxiating, Poisonous or Other Gases, and of Bacteriological Methods of Warfare, signed at Geneva on 17 June 1925,[15] and to ratify the Convention on the Prohibition of the Development, Production and Stockpiling of Bacteriological (Biological) and Toxin Weapons and on Their Destruction, of 10 April 1972;[16]

8. *Decides* that Iraq shall unconditionally accept the destruction, removal, or rendering harmless, under international supervision, of:

(*a*) All chemical and biological weapons and all stocks of agents and all related subsystems and components and all research, development, support and manufacturing facilities related thereto;

(*b*) All ballistic missiles with a range greater than one hundred and fifty kilometres, and related major parts and repair and production facilities;

9. *Decides also*, for the implementation of paragraph 8, the following:

(*a*) Iraq shall submit to the Secretary-General, within fifteen days of the adoption of the present resolution, a declaration on the locations, amounts and types of all items specified in paragraph 8 and agree to urgent, on-site inspection as specified below;

(*b*) The Secretary-General, in consultation with the appropriate Governments and, where appropriate, with the Director-General of the World Health Organization, within forty-five days of the adoption of the present resolution shall develop and submit to the Council for approval a plan calling for the completion of the following acts within forty-five days of such approval:

(i) The forming of a special commission, which shall carry out immediate on-site inspection of Iraq's biological, chemical and missile capabilities, based on Iraq's declarations and the designation of any additional locations by the Special Commission itself;

(ii) The yielding by Iraq of possession to the Special Commission for destruction, removal or rendering harmless, taking into account the requirements of public safety, of all items specified under paragraph 8(*a*), including items at the additional locations designated by the Special Commission under paragraph (i) and the destruction by Iraq, under the supervision of the Special Commission, of all its missile capabilities, including launchers, as specified under paragraph 8(*b*);

(iii) The provision by the Special Commission to the Director General of the International Atomic Energy Agency of the assistance and cooperation required in paragraphs 12 and 13;

10. *Decides further* that Iraq shall unconditionally undertake not to use, develop, construct or acquire any of the items specified in paragraphs 8 and 9, and requests the Secretary-General, in consultation with the Special Commission, to develop a plan for the future ongoing monitoring and verification of Iraq's compliance with the present paragraph, to be submitted to the Council for approval within one hundred and twenty days of the passage of the present resolution;

11. *Invites* Iraq to reaffirm unconditionally its obligations under the Treaty on the Non-Proliferation of Nuclear Weapons of 1 July

[15] League of Nations (note 6), No. 2138.

[16] General Assembly (note 8).

1968;[17]

12. *Decides* that Iraq shall unconditionally agree not to acquire or develop nuclear weapons or nuclear-weapon-usable material or any subsystems or components or any research, development, support or manufacturing facilities related to the above; to submit to the Secretary-General and the Director General of the International Atomic Energy Agency within fifteen days of the adoption of the present resolution a declaration of the locations, amounts, and types of all items specified above; to place all of its nuclear-weapon-usable materials under the exclusive control, for custody and removal, of the Agency, with the assistance and cooperation of the Special Commission as provided for in the plan of the Secretary-General discussed in paragraph 9(*b*); to accept, in accordance with the arrangements provided for in paragraph 13, urgent on-site inspection and the destruction, removal or rendering harmless as appropriate of all items specified above; and to accept the plan discussed in paragraph 13 for the future ongoing monitoring and verification of its compliance with these undertakings;

13. *Requests* the Director General of the International Atomic Energy Agency, through the Secretary-General, with the assistance and cooperation of the Special Commission as provided for in the plan of the Secretary-General referred to in paragraph 9(*b*), to carry out immediate on-site inspection of Iraq's nuclear capabilities based on Iraq's declarations and the designation of any additional locations by the Special Commission; to develop a plan for submission to the Council within forty-five days calling for the destruction, removal or rendering harmless as appropriate of all items listed in paragraph 12; to carry out the plan within forty-five days following approval by the Council and to develop a plan, taking into account the rights and obligations of Iraq under the Treaty on the Non-Proliferation of Nuclear Weapons, for the future ongoing monitoring and verification of Iraq's compliance with paragraph 12, including an inventory of all nuclear material in Iraq subject to the Agency's verification and inspections to confirm that Agency safeguards cover all relevant nuclear activities in Iraq, to be submitted to the Council for approval within one hundred and twenty days of the adoption of the present resolution;

[17] United Nations (note 9).

14. *Notes* that the actions to be taken by Iraq in paragraphs 8 to 13 represent steps towards the goal of establishing in the Middle East a zone free from weapons of mass destruction and all missiles for their delivery and the objective of a global ban on chemical weapons;

D

15. *Requests* the Secretary-General to report to the Council on the steps taken to facilitate the return of all Kuwaiti property seized by Iraq, including a list of any property that Kuwait claims has not been returned or which has not been returned intact;

E

16. *Reaffirms* that Iraq, without prejudice to its debts and obligations arising prior to 2 August 1990, which will be addressed through the normal mechanisms, is liable under international law for any direct loss, damage—including environmental damage and the depletion of natural resources—or injury to foreign Governments, nationals and corporations as a result of its unlawful invasion and occupation of Kuwait;

17. *Decides* that all Iraqi statements made since 2 August 1990 repudiating its foreign debt are null and void, and demands that Iraq adhere scrupulously to all of its obligations concerning servicing and repayment of its foreign debt;

18. *Decides also* to create a fund to pay compensation for claims that fall within paragraph 16 and to establish a commission that will administer the fund;

19. *Directs* the Secretary-General to develop and present to the Council for decision, no later than thirty days following the adoption of the present resolution, recommendations for the Fund to be established in accordance with paragraph 18 and for a programme to implement the decisions in paragraphs 16 to 18, including the following: administration of the Fund; mechanisms for determining the appropriate level of Iraq's contribution to the Fund, based on a percentage of the value of its exports of petroleum and petroleum products, not to exceed a figure to be suggested to the Council by the Secretary-General, taking into account the requirements of the people of Iraq, Iraq's payment capacity as assessed in conjunction with the international financial institutions taking into consideration external debt service, and the needs of the Iraqi economy; arrange-

ments for ensuring that payments are made to the Fund; the process by which funds will be allocated and claims paid; appropriate procedures for evaluating losses, listing claims and verifying their validity, and resolving disputed claims in respect of Iraq's liability as specified in paragraph 16; and the composition of the Commission designated above;

F

20. *Decides*, effective immediately, that the prohibitions against the sale or supply to Iraq of commodities or products, other than medicine and health supplies, and prohibitions against financial transactions related thereto contained in resolution 661 (1990), shall not apply to foodstuffs notified to the Security Council Committee established by resolution 661 (1990) concerning the situation between Iraq and Kuwait or, with the approval of that Committee, under the simplified and accelerated 'no-objection' procedure, to materials and supplies for essential civilian needs as identified in the report to the Secretary-General dated 20 March 1991,[18] and in any further findings of humanitarian need by the Committee;

21. *Decides* to review the provisions of paragraph 20 every sixty days in the light of the policies and practices of the Government of Iraq, including the implementation of all relevant resolutions of the Council, for the purpose of determining whether to reduce or lift the prohibitions referred to therein;

22. *Decides also* that upon the approval by the Council of the programme called for in paragraph 19 above and upon Council agreement that Iraq has completed all actions contemplated in paragraphs 8 to 13, the prohibitions against the import of commodities and products originating in Iraq and the prohibitions against financial transactions related thereto contained in resolution 661 (1990) shall have no further force or effect;

23. *Decides further* that, pending action by the Council under paragraph 22, the Security Council Committee established by resolution 661 (1990) concerning the situation between Iraq and Kuwait shall be empowered to approve, when required to assure adequate financial resources on the part of Iraq to carry out the activities under paragraph 20, exceptions to the prohibition against the import of commodities and products originating in Iraq;

24. *Decides* that, in accordance with resolution 661 (1990) and subsequent related resolutions and until it takes a further decision, all States shall continue to prevent the sale or supply to Iraq, or the promotion or facilitation of such sale or supply, by their nationals or from their territories or using their flag vessels or aircraft, of:

(*a*) Arms and related *matériel* of all types, specifically including the sale or transfer through other means of all forms of conventional military equipment, including for paramilitary forces, and spare parts and components and their means of production for such equipment;

(*b*) Items specified and defined in paragraphs 8 and 12 not otherwise covered above;

(*c*) Technology under licensing or other transfer arrangements used in the production, utilization or stockpiling of items specified in subparagraphs (*a*) and (*b*);

(*d*) Personnel or materials for training or technical support services relating to the design, development, manufacture, use, maintenance or support of items specified in subparagraphs (*a*) and (*b*);

25. *Calls upon* all States and international organizations to act strictly in accordance with paragraph 24, notwithstanding the existence of any contracts, agreements, licences or any other arrangements;

26. *Requests* the Secretary-General, in consultation with appropriate Governments, to develop within sixty days, for the approval of the Council, guidelines to facilitate full international implementation of paragraphs 24, 25 and 27, and to make them available to all States and to establish a procedure for updating these guidelines periodically;

27. *Calls upon* all States to maintain such national controls and procedures and to take such other actions consistent with the guidelines to be established by the Council under paragraph 26 as may be necessary to ensure compliance with the terms of paragraph 24, and calls upon international organizations to take all appropriate steps to assist in ensuring such full compliance;

28. *Agrees* to review its decisions in paragraphs 22 to 25, except for the items specified and defined in paragraphs 8 and 12, on a regular basis and in any case one hundred and twenty days following the adoption of the present resolution, taking into account Iraq's compliance with the resolution and general progress towards the control of armaments in the region;

---

[18] *Official Records* (note 1), document S/22366, annex.

29. *Decides* that all States, including Iraq, shall take the necessary measures to ensure that no claim shall lie at the instance of the Government of Iraq, or of any person or body in Iraq, or of any person claiming through or for the benefit of any such person or body, in connection with any contract or other transaction where its performance was affected by reason of the measures taken by the Council in resolution 661 (1990) and related resolutions;

G

30. *Decides* that, in furtherance of its commitment to facilitate the repatriation of all Kuwaiti and third-State nationals, Iraq shall extend all necessary cooperation to the International Committee of the Red Cross by providing lists of such persons, facilitating the access of the International Committee to all such persons wherever located or detained and facilitating the search by the International Committee for those Kuwaiti and third-State nationals still unaccounted for;

31. *Invites* the International Committee of the Red Cross to keep the Secretary-General apprised, as appropriate, of all activities undertaken in connection with facilitating the repatriation or return of all Kuwaiti and third-State nationals or their remains present in Iraq on or after 2 August 1990;

H

32. *Requires* Iraq to inform the Council that it will not commit or support any act of international terrorism or allow any organization directed towards commission of such acts to operate within its territory and to condemn unequivocally and renounce all acts, methods and practices of terrorism;

I

33. *Declares* that, upon official notification by Iraq to the Secretary-General and to the Security Council of its acceptance of the above provisions, a formal cease-fire is effective between Iraq and Kuwait and the Member States cooperating with Kuwait in accordance with resolution 678 (1990);

34. *Decides* to remain seized of the matter and to take such further steps as may be required for the implementation of the present resolution and to secure peace and security in the region.

Adopted at the 2981st meeting by 12 votes to 1 (Cuba) with 2 abstentions (Equador, Yemen).

Decision

At its 2983rd meeting, on 9 April 1991, the Council decided to invite the representatives of Iraq and Kuwait to participate, without vote, in the discussion of the item entitled 'The situation between Iraq and Kuwait: report of the Secretary-General on the implementation of paragraph 5 of Security Council resolution 687 (1991) (S/22454 and Add.1–3)'[19]

Source: UN, *Resolutions and Decisions of the Security Council 1991*, Security Council Official Records: Forth-Sixth Year (United Nations, New York, 1993), pp. 11–15.

UN SECURITY COUNCIL RESOLUTION 707

15 August 1991

The Security Council,

Recalling its resolution 687 (1991) of 3 April 1991 and its other resolutions on this matter,

Recalling also the letter of 11 April 1991 from the President of the Security Council to the Permanent Representative of Iraq to the United Nations,[20] in which he noted that on the basis of Iraq's written agreement[21] to implement fully resolution 687 (1991), the preconditions for a cease-fire established in paragraph 33 of that resolution for a cease-fire had been met,

Taking note with grave concern of the letters dated 26 and 28 June and 4 July 1991 from the Secretary-General to the President of the Security Council, conveying information received from the Executive Chairman of the Special Commission[22] and from the high-level mission to Iraq[23] which establishes Iraq's failure to comply with its obligations under resolution 687 (1991),

---

[19] See *Official Records* (note 11).

[20] S/22485.

[21] *Official Records* (note 11), document S/22456.

[22] *Official Records* (note 11), documents S/22739 and S/22743.

[23] *Official Records* (note 11), document S/22761.

Recalling further the statement issued by the President of the Security Council on 28 June 1991[24] requesting that a high-level mission consisting of the Executive Chairman of the Special Commission, the Director General of the International Atomic Energy Agency and the Under-Secretary-General for Disarmament Affairs be dispatched to meet with officials at the highest levels of the Government of Iraq at the earliest opportunity to obtain written assurance that Iraq will fully and immediately cooperate in the inspection of the locations identified by the Special Commission and present for immediate inspection any of those items that may have been transported from those locations,

Having taking note with dismay of the report of the high-level mission to the Secretary-General on the results of its meetings with the highest levels of the Iraqi Government,[25]

Gravely concerned by the information provided to the Council by the International Atomic Energy Agency on 15[26] July 1991 and 25 July 1991[27] regarding the actions of the Government of Iraq in flagrant violation of resolution 687 (1991),

Gravely concerned also by the letter of 7 July 1991 from the Minister of Foreign Affairs of Iraq addressed to the Secretary-General and subsequent statements and findings that Iraq's notifications of 18 and 28 April were incomplete and that certain related activities had been concealed, facts both of which constitute material breaches of its obligations under resolution 687 (1991),

Noting , having been informed by the letters dated 26 and 28 June and 4 July 1991 from the Secretary-General, that Iraq has not fully complied with all of its undertakings relating to the privileges, immunities and facilities to be accorded to the Special Commission and the Agency inspection teams mandated under resolution 687 (1991),

Affirming that in order for the Special Commission to carry out its mandate under paragraph 9 (*b*) (iii) of resolution 687 (1991) to inspect Iraq's chemical and biological weapons and ballistic missile capabilities and to take possession of the elements referred to in that resolution for destruction, removal or rendering harmless, full disclosure on the part of Iraq as required in paragraph 9 (*a*) of resolution 687 (1991) is essential,

Affirming also that in order for the International Atomic Energy Agency, with the assistance and cooperation of the Special Commission, to determine what nuclear-weapon-usable material or any subsystems or components or any research, development, support or manufacturing facilities related to them need, in accordance with paragraph 13 of resolution 687 (1991), to be destroyed, removed or rendered harmless, Iraq is required to make a declaration of all its nuclear programmes, including any which it claims are for purposes not related to nuclear-weapon-usable material,

Affirming further that the aforementioned failures of Iraq to act in strict conformity with its obligations under resolution 687 (1991) constitute a material breach of its acceptance of the relevant provisions of that resolution which established a cease-fire and provided the conditions essential to the restoration of peace and security in the region,

*Affirming, moreover, th*at Iraq's failure to comply with its safeguards agreement it concluded with the International Atomic Energy Agency concluded pursuant to the Treaty on the Non-Proliferation of Nuclear Weapons of 1 July 1968,[28] as established by the Board of Governors of the Agency in its resolution of 18 July 1991,[29] constitutes a breach of its international obligations,

Determined to ensure full compliance with resolution 687 (1991) and in particular its section C,

Acting under Chapter VII of the Charter of the United Nations,

1. *Condemns* Iraq's serious violation of a number of its obligations under section C of resolution 687 (1991) and of its undertakings to cooperate with the Special Commission and the International Atomic Energy Agency, which constitutes a material breach of the relevant provisions of that resolution which established a cease-fire and provided the conditions essential to the restoration of peace and security in the region;

2. *Also condemns* non-compliance by the Government of Iraq with its obligations under

[24] S/22746.

[25] *Official Records of the Security Council, Forty-sixth Year, Supplement for July, Aug. and Sep. 1991*, document S/22761, annex.

[26] *Official Records* (note 25), document S/22788.

[27] *Official Records* (note 25), document S/22837.

[28] United Nations (note 9), No. 10485.

[29] *Official Records* (note 25), document S/22812, annex, appendix.

its safeguards agreement with the International Atomic Energy Agency, as established by the Board of Governors in its resolution of 18 July 1991,[30] which constitutes a violation of its commitments as a party to the Treaty on the Non-Proliferation of Nuclear Weapons of 1 July 1968;[31]

3. *Demands* that Iraq:

(*a*) Provide without further delay full, final and complete disclosure, as required by resolution 687 (1991), of all aspects of its programmes to develop weapons of mass destruction and ballistic missiles with a range greater than one hundred and fifty kilometres and of all holdings of such weapons, their components and production facilities and locations, as well as all other nuclear programmes, including any which it claims are for purposes not related to nuclear-weapon-usable material;

(*b*) Allow the Special Commission, the International Atomic Energy Agency and their inspection teams immediate, unconditional and unrestricted access to any and all areas, facilities, equipment, records and means of transportation which they wish to inspect;

(*c*) Cease immediately any attempt to conceal, move or destroy any material or equipment relating to its nuclear, chemical or biological weapons or ballistic missile programmes, or material or equipment relating to its other nuclear activities, without notification to and prior consent of the Special Commission;

(*d*) Make available immediately to the Special Commission, the Agency and their inspection teams any items to which they were previously denied access;

(*e*) Allow the Special Commission, the Agency and their inspection teams to conduct both fixed-wing and helicopter flights throughout Iraq for all relevant purposes, including inspection, surveillance, aerial surveys, transportation and logistics, without interference of any kind and upon such terms and conditions as may be determined by the Special Commission, and to make full use of their own aircraft and such airfields in Iraq as they may determine are most appropriate for the work of the Commission;

(*f*) Halt all nuclear activities of any kind, except for use of isotopes for medical, agricultural or industrial purposes, until the Council determines that Iraq is in full compliance with the present resolution and with paragraphs 12 and 13 of resolution 687 (1991) and the Agency determines that Iraq is in full compliance with its safeguards agreement with the Agency;

(*g*) Ensure the complete enjoyment in accordance with its previous undertakings, of the privileges, immunities and facilities accorded to the representatives of the Special Commission and the Agency and guarantee their complete safety and freedom of movement;

(*h*) Immediately provide or facilitate the provision of any transportation and medical or logistical support requested by the Special Commission, the Agency and their inspection teams;

(*i*) Respond fully, completely and promptly to any questions or requests from the Special Commission, the Agency and their inspection teams;

4. *Determines* that Iraq retains no ownership interest in items to be destroyed, removed or rendered harmless pursuant to paragraph 12 of resolution 687 (1991);

5. *Requires* that the Government of Iraq forthwith to comply fully and without delay with all its international obligations, including those set out in the present resolution, in resolution 687 (1991), in the Treaty on the Non-Proliferation of Nuclear Weapons of 1 July 1968 and its safeguards agreement with the International Atomic Energy Agency;

6. *Decides* to remain seized of this matter.

Adopted unanimously at the 3004th meeting.

Decision

At its 3008th meeting, on 19 September 1991, the Council invited the representative of Iraq to participate, without vote, in the discussion of the item entitled "The situation between Iraq and Kuwait: report of the Secretary-General pursuant to paragraph 5 of Security Council resolution 706 (1991) (S/23006 and Corr.2)".[32]

Source: UN, *Resolutions and Decisions of the Security Council 1991*, Security Council Official Records: Forth-Sixth Year (United Nations, New York, 1993), pp. 22–24.

[30] *Official Records* (note 25), document S/22812, annex, appendix.

[31] United Nations, *Treaty Series*, vol. 729, No. 10485.

[32] *Official Records* (note 25).

UN SECURITY COUNCIL RESOLUTION 715

11 October 1991

The Security Council,

Recalling its resolutions 687 (1991) of 3 April 1991 and 707 (1991) of 15 August 1991 and its other resolutions on this matter,

Recalling in particular that under resolution 687 (1991) the Secretary-General and the Director General of the International Atomic Energy Agency (IAEA) were requested to develop plans for future ongoing monitoring and verification and to submit them to the Security Council for approval,

Taking note of the report[33] and note[34] of the Secretary-General, transmitting the plans submitted by the Secretary-General and the Director General of the Agency,

Acting under Chapter VII of the Charter of the United Nations,

1. *Approves*, in accordance with the provisions of resolutions 687 (1991), 707 (1991) and the present resolution, the plans submitted by the Secretary-General[35] and the Director General of the International Atomic Energy Agency;[36]

2. *Decides* that the Special Commission shall carry out the plan submitted by the Secretary-General, as well as continuing to discharge its other responsibilities under resolutions 687 (1991), 699 (1991) of 17 June 1991 and 707 (1991) and performing such other functions as are conferred upon it under the present resolution;

3. *Requests* the Director General of the Agency to carry out, with the assistance and cooperation of the Special Commission, the plan submitted by him and to continue to discharge his other responsibilities under resolutions 687 (1991), 699 (1991) and 707 (1991);

4. *Decides* that the Special Commission, in the exercise of its responsibilities as a subsidiary organ of the Security Council, shall:

(*a*) Continue to have the responsibility for designating additional locations for inspection and overflights;

(*b*) Continue to render assistance and cooperation to the Director General of the Agency by providing him by mutual agreement, with the necessary special expertise and logistical, informational and other operational support for the carrying out of the plan submitted by him;

(*c*) Perform such other functions, in cooperation in the nuclear field with the Director General of the Agency, as may be necessary to coordinate activities under the plans approved by the present resolution, including making use of commonly available services and information to the fullest extent possible, in order to achieve maximum efficiency and optimum use of resources;

5. *Demands* that Iraq meet unconditionally all its obligations under the plans approved by the present resolution and cooperate fully with the Special Commission and the Director General of the Agency in carrying out the plans;

6. *Decides* to encourage the maximum assistance, in cash and in kind, from all Member States to support the Special Commission and the Director General of the Agency in carrying out their activities under the plans approved by the present resolution, without prejudice to Iraq's liability for the full costs of such activities;

7. *Requests* the Security Council Committee established under resolution 661 (1990), concerning the situation between Iraq and Kuwait, the Special Commission and the Director General of the Agency to develop in cooperation a mechanism for monitoring any future sales or supplies by other countries to Iraq of items relevant to the implementation of section C of resolution 687 (1991) and other relevant resolutions, including the present resolution and the plans approved hereunder;

8. *Requests* the Secretary-General and the Director General of the Agency to submit to the Security Council reports on the implementation of the plans approved by the present resolution, when requested by the Security Council and in any event at least every six months after the adoption of this resolution;

9. *Decides* to remain seized of the matter.

Adopted unanimously at the 3012th meeting.

Decision

After the consultations held on 20 December 1991, the President of the Security Council made the following statement to the media on

---

[33] *Official Records of the Security Council, Forty-sixth Year, Supplement for Oct., Nov. and Dec. 1991,* document S/2871/Rev.1.

[34] *Official Records* (note 33), document S/22872/Rev.1 and Corr.1.

[35] *Official Records* (note 33), document S/23106 and Add.1.

[36] *Official Records* (note 33), document S/22872/Rev.1 and Corr.1.

behalf of the members of the Council:[37]

'The members of the Security Council held informal consultations on 6 December 1991 pursuant to paragraph 28 of resolution 687 (1991) of 3 April 1991, paragraph 6 of resolution 700 (1991) of 17 June 1991 and paragraph 21 of resolution 687 (1991). After hearing all the opinions expressed in the course of the consultations, the President of the Council concluded that there was no agreement that the necessary conditions existed for a modification of the regimes established in paragraphs 22 to 25, as referred to in paragraph 28 of resolution 687 (1991), in paragraph 6 of resolution 700 (1991), and in paragraph 20, as referred to in paragraph 21 of resolution 687 (1991).

'However, with a view to alleviating the humanitarian conditions for the civilian population in Iraq and in order to facilitate the utilization of paragraph 20 of resolution 687 (1991), the Security Council Committee established under resolution 661 (1990) concerning the situation between Iraq and Kuwait is requested to study immediately those materials and supplies for essential civilian and humanitarian needs as identified in the Ahtisaari report[38] with the purpose of drawing up a list of items which may, with the Council's approval, be transferred from the "no-objection" procedure to a simple notification procedure. Members of the Council may submit proposals of items for this purpose.

'With regard to imports of items subject to prior approval under the "no-objection" procedure by the Committee (i.e. items other than food and medicine), any member of the Committee putting forward an objection to such an import will offer a specific explanation at a meeting of the Committee.

'The members of the Council are aware of reports received concerning the approximately 2,000 Kuwaitis believed to be still detained in Iraq, access by the International Committee of the Red Cross to all detainees and places of detention, the return of Kuwaiti property, and particularly the return of Kuwaiti military equipment and their bearing upon the present state of Iraqi compliance with resolution 687 (1991).

'In light of the above, the Council will request the Secretary-General to prepare a factual report on Iraq's compliance with all the obligations placed upon it by resolution 697 (1991) and subsequent relevant resolutions. This report will be made available to the Council in good time before it undertakes its next review under paragraph 21 of resolution 687 (1991).

'In the course of consultations it was noted that resolutions 706 (1991) of 15 August 1991 and 712 (1991) of 19 September 1991 gave to Iraq the possibility for oil sales to finance the purchase of foodstuffs, medicines and materials and supplies for essential civilian needs for the purpose of providing humanitarian relief. However, this possibility has not yet been used.'

Source: UN, *Resolutions and Decisions of the Security Council 1991*, Security Council Official Records: Forth-Sixth Year (United Nations, New York, 1993), pp. 26–27.

[37] S/23305.

[38] *Official Records* (note 1), document S/22409, annex.

Index